# Global Perspectives on Change Management and Leadership in the Post-COVID-19 Era

Ebtihaj Al-Aali
*University of Bahrain, Bahrain*

Meryem Masmoudi
*University of Bahrain, Bahrain*

IGI Global
PUBLISHER of TIMELY KNOWLEDGE

A volume in the Advances in Logistics, Operations, and Management Science (ALOMS) Book Series

Published in the United States of America by
IGI Global
Business Science Reference (an imprint of IGI Global)
701 E. Chocolate Avenue
Hershey PA, USA 17033
Tel: 717-533-8845
Fax: 717-533-8661
E-mail: cust@igi-global.com
Web site: http://www.igi-global.com



Library of Congress Cataloging-in-Publication Data

Names: Al-A'Ali, Ebtihaj Ahmad, 1957- editor. | Masmoudi, Meryem, 1979- editor.
Title: Global perspectives on change management and leadership in the post-COVID-19 era / Ebtihaj Al-Aali, and Meryem Masmoudi, editors.
Description: Hershey, PA : Business Science Reference, [2021] | Includes bibliographical references and index. | Summary: "The book highlights the global perspectives of COVID-19 crisis on change management and leadership for practitioners who want to be successful change leaders in the post-COVID-19 era and for researchers who need to understand new trend in change management and leadership"-- Provided by publisher.
Identifiers: LCCN 2020050618 (print) | LCCN 2020050619 (ebook) | ISBN 9781799869481 (hardcover) | ISBN 9781799869498 (paperback) | ISBN 9781799869504 (ebook)
Subjects: LCSH: Organizational change--Management. | Strategic planning. | Crisis management. | Leadership. | COVID-19 (Disease)--Economic aspects.
Classification: LCC HD58.8 .G5857 2021 (print) | LCC HD58.8 (ebook) | DDC 658.4/06--dc23
LC record available at https://lccn.loc.gov/2020050618
LC ebook record available at https://lccn.loc.gov/2020050619

This book is published in the IGI Global book series Advances in Logistics, Operations, and Management Science (ALOMS) (ISSN: 2327-350X; eISSN: 2327-3518)

British Cataloguing in Publication Data
A Cataloguing in Publication record for this book is available from the British Library.



For electronic access to this publication, please contact: eresources@igi-global.com.

# Advances in Logistics, Operations, and Management Science (ALOMS) Book Series

John Wang
Montclair State University, USA

ISSN:2327-350X
EISSN:2327-3518

## Mission

Operations research and management science continue to influence business processes, administration, and management information systems, particularly in covering the application methods for decision-making processes. New case studies and applications on management science, operations management, social sciences, and other behavioral sciences have been incorporated into business and organizations real-world objectives.

The **Advances in Logistics, Operations, and Management Science** (ALOMS) Book Series provides a collection of reference publications on the current trends, applications, theories, and practices in the management science field. Providing relevant and current research, this series and its individual publications would be useful for academics, researchers, scholars, and practitioners interested in improving decision making models and business functions.

## Coverage

- Operations Management
- Information Management
- Organizational Behavior
- Finance
- Marketing engineering
- Services management
- Risk Management
- Networks
- Political Science
- Production Management

IGI Global is currently accepting manuscripts for publication within this series. To submit a proposal for a volume in this series, please contact our Acquisition Editors at Acquisitions@igi-global.com or visit: http://www.igi-global.com/publish/.

The Advances in Logistics, Operations, and Management Science (ALOMS) Book Series (ISSN 2327-350X) is published by IGI Global, 701 E. Chocolate Avenue, Hershey, PA 17033-1240, USA, www.igi-global.com. This series is composed of titles available for purchase individually; each title is edited to be contextually exclusive from any other title within the series. For pricing and ordering information please visit http://www.igi-global.com/book-series/advances-logistics-operations-management-science/37170. Postmaster: Send all address changes to above address. 

## Titles in this Series

*For a list of additional titles in this series, please visit: http://www.igi-global.com/book-series/advances-logistics-operations-management-science/37170*

***Handbook of Research on Innate Leadership Characteristics and Examinations of Successful First-Time Leaders***
Matthew Waritay Guah (South Carolina State University, USA)
Business Science Reference • © 2021 • 500pp • H/C (ISBN: 9781799875925) • US $285.00

***Handbook of Research on Recent Perspectives on Management, International Trade, and Logistics***
Güner Koç Aytekin (Ufuk University, Turkey) and Çağlar Doğru (Ufuk University, Turkey)
Business Science Reference • © 2021 • 490pp • H/C (ISBN: 9781799858867) • US $345.00

***Handbook of Research on Multidisciplinary Perspectives on Managerial and Leadership Psychology***
Rick D. Johnson (Johnson Professionals, Inc., USA)
Business Science Reference • © 2021 • 742pp • H/C (ISBN: 9781799838111) • US $285.00

***Transforming Corporate Governance and Developing Models for Board Effectiveness***
Qaiser Rafique Yasser (Centre for Rural Economy, Pakistan) and Abdullah Al-Mamun (University of Wollongong, Australia)
Business Science Reference • © 2021 • 345pp • H/C (ISBN: 9781799866695) • US $195.00

***Encyclopedia of Organizational Knowledge, Administration, and Technology***
Mehdi Khosrow-Pour D.B.A. (Information Resources Management Association, USA)
Business Science Reference • © 2021 • 2734pp • H/C (ISBN: 9781799834731) • US $3,950.00

***Corporate Leadership and Its Role in Shaping Organizational Culture and Performance***
Azza Bejaoui (High Institute of Management of Tunis, Tunisia)
Business Science Reference • © 2021 • 350pp • H/C (ISBN: 9781522582663) • US $195.00

***Demand Forecasting and Order Planning in Supply Chains and Humanitarian Logistics***
Atour Taghipour (Normandy University, France)
Business Science Reference • © 2021 • 313pp • H/C (ISBN: 9781799838050) • US $195.00

***Interdisciplinary Perspectives on Operations Management and Service Evaluation***
Panagiotis Manolitzas (Ionian University, Greece) Constantin Zopounidis (School of Production Engineering and Management, Technical University of Crete, Greece & Audencia Business School, France) Michael Talias (Open University of Cyprus, Cyprus) Evangelos Grigoroudis (Technical University of Crete, Greece) and Nikolaos Matsatsinis (Technical University of Crete, Greece)
Business Science Reference • © 2021 • 401pp • H/C (ISBN: 9781799854425) • US $195.00

IGI Global
PUBLISHER of TIMELY KNOWLEDGE

701 East Chocolate Avenue, Hershey, PA 17033, USA
Tel: 717-533-8845 x100 • Fax: 717-533-8661
E-Mail: cust@igi-global.com • www.igi-global.com

*To the government of the Kingdom of Bahrain, and all governments worldwide. To all pharmaceutical companies. To frontline workers.*

# Table of Contents

**Preface** ........ xvi

**Chapter 1**
Necessary Changes in Healthcare of German-Speaking Countries ........ 1
*Stephanie Krebs, Ostfalia University of Applied Sciences, Germany*
*Anna Larina Lietz, Ostfalia University of Applied Sciences, Germany*
*Martina Hasseler, Ostfalia University of Applied Sciences, Germany*

**Chapter 2**
Psychiatry in the Midst of the Pandemic: A Narrative Perspective ........ 24
*Gardenia AlSaffar, Royal Hospital of Bahrain, Bahrain*
*Ebtihaj Al-Aali, University of Bahrain, Bahrain*

**Chapter 3**
Whole-of-Nation Approach in COVID-19 Management: The Case of Brunei Darussalam ........ 35
*Abdul Malik Omar, University Brunei Darussalam, Brunei*
*Amanina Halim, Independent Researcher, Brunei*

**Chapter 4**
COVID-19 Being Positive Strategically in the Context of SDG and NDC ........ 56
*Nikhil Kant, School of Management Studies, Indira Gandhi National Open University (IGNOU), India*
*Kumari Anjali, School of Sciences, Indira Gandhi National Open University (IGNOU), India*

**Chapter 5**
Adaptive Performance: A Review of Managerial Interventions ........ 71
*Timothy C. Bednall, Swinburne University of Technology, Australia*
*Matthew D. Henricks, The University of New South Wales, Australia*

**Chapter 6**
Change Management Strategies as the Nexus of Performance Improvement in African Universities Post-COVID-19 Pandemic ........ 90
*Bethuel Sibongiseni Ngcamu, Nelson Mandela University, South Africa*

**Chapter 7**
Success Factors of Future-Viable Organizations in the Post-COVID-19 Era .................................... 106
*Peter Behrendt, Freiburg Institut, Germany*
*Alexander Holicki, Freiburg Institut, Germany*
*Veronika Matzner, Freiburg Institut, Germany*

**Chapter 8**
The Impact of COVID-19 on the Corporations and Management Change ....................................... 125
*Adel Ismail Al-Alawi, University of Bahrain, Bahrain*
*Arpita A. Mehrotra, Royal University for Women, Bahrain*
*Sohayla Khidir Sanosi, University of Bahrain, Bahrain*

**Chapter 9**
Shock Leadership: Leading Amidst Pandemics and Other Chaotic Change .................................... 136
*Anton Shufutinsky, Cabrini University, USA*
*Bena Long, Institute of Interdisciplinary Leadership Education and Development, USA*
*James R. Sibel, Institute of Interdisciplinary Leadership Education and Development, USA*
*Darrell Norman Burrell, The Florida Institute of Technology, USA*

**Chapter 10**
COVID-19 and Leadership: Impacts and Responses ........................................................................ 160
*Asma Ayari, University of Bahrain, Bahrain*

**Chapter 11**
New Challenges for Leading the Change for the Psychological Consequences of Pandemics: Workplace Loneliness, Work Alienation, and Spiritual Well-Being in the Post-COVID-19 Era....... 169
*Mehmet Çetin, Istanbul Sabahattin Zaim University, Turkey*

**Chapter 12**
Responding to the Challenge of Employee Engagement During Uncertain Times: Adaptive Leadership is the Answer ............................................................................................................ 188
*Mohammad Faraz Naim, Department of Management, Birla Institute of Technology and Science, Pilani, India*

**Chapter 13**
Leadership in the Post-COVID-19 Era: New Leaders of the New Normal ....................................... 199
*Yeşim Kurt, Kırklareli University, Turkey*
*Dilek Erdoğan, Gaziantep University, Turkey*

**Chapter 14**
COVID-19 and the Call for Elder Change Leadership ..................................................................... 218
*Stan Amaladas, Baker College, USA*

**Chapter 15**
Task Forces as Silver Bullets for Crisis Management: A Case Study of an SME During COVID-19240
*Laura Schärrer, University of Lucerne, Switzerland*
*Reto M. Wegmann, University of Lucerne, Switzerland*

**Chapter 16**
Leadership as a Change Trigger in Unsettling Conditions: The Case of Werenbach Watches........... 254
*Vasilios Stouraitis, Glasgow Caledonian University, UK*
*Andres J. Arenas F., Universidad Antonio de Nebrija, Spain*
*Kostantinos Tsanis, Hult International Business School, USA*
*Jessica Bayón Pérez, Universidad Antonio de Nebrija, Spain*

**Chapter 17**
The Banking Sector During COVID-19: The Case of Bahrain Islamic Bank.................................. 274
*Yomna Abdulla, University of Bahrain, Bahrain*

**Chapter 18**
The Role of Leadership and Related Work Factors Caused by COVID-19: The Impact on
Employee Effectiveness ........................................................................................................ 285
*Adel Ismail Al-Alawi, University of Bahrain, Bahrain*
*Arpita Anshu Mehrotra, Royal University for Women, Bahrain*
*Samah Sabri Ali, University of Bahrain, Bahrain*
*Fatima Ali Al-Ammar, University of Bahrain, Bahrain*

**Chapter 19**
Impact of COVID-19 on an Educational Institution of India: Perceptions of Teachers Towards
Online Classes.......................................................................................................................... 300
*Elizabeth Madathilathu Samuel, Royal University for Women, Bahrain*

**Compilation of References** .................................................................................................. 312

**About the Contributors** ........................................................................................................ 365

**Index**...................................................................................................................................... 372

# Detailed Table of Contents

**Preface**............................................................................................................................................xvi

**Chapter 1**
Necessary Changes in Healthcare of German-Speaking Countries......................................................1
*Stephanie Krebs, Ostfalia University of Applied Sciences, Germany*
*Anna Larina Lietz, Ostfalia University of Applied Sciences, Germany*
*Martina Hasseler, Ostfalia University of Applied Sciences, Germany*

The COVID-19 pandemic has suddenly gained urgency in Germany for implementation of new structures in healthcare sector to take care of seriously ill COVID-19 patients. The shortage of skilled healthcare workers, which has already been discussed before the pandemic situation, has become more tangible than ever. Society relies on a properly working healthcare system, especially in a pandemic like the one we now witness. After the comparatively mild course of the first COVID-19 wave in Germany, the interest in long overdue changes decreased. The second wave of the pandemic occurred in Germany as well. Also, in the meantime of the first and the second wave, numerous findings were collected and presented, where changes could have an effect. To motivate going forward, the text describes John P. Kotter's model of change management, eight steps to describe necessary changes in organizations and leadership in the German healthcare system.

**Chapter 2**
Psychiatry in the Midst of the Pandemic: A Narrative Perspective.....................................................24
*Gardenia AlSaffar, Royal Hospital of Bahrain, Bahrain*
*Ebtihaj Al-Aali, University of Bahrain, Bahrain*

The era of COVID-19 has initiated dramatic and unexpected changes related to all aspects of life. The impact of these changes is unforeseeable. Health services have encountered many challenges, which one country cannot deal with alone. The contagion of the disease requires changes in all walks of life, specifically health services. Psychiatric services have seen an increased demand from mental health patients and many people alike. This is due to unrest, anxiety, stressful, and the ambiguous characteristics of the present situation. This chapter presents reflections of the first author, the psychiatrist, on the major stakeholders for health systems at the present situation. These stakeholders are regulations, patients, pharmacies, society and community, and psychiatrists themselves. Despite all efforts to deal with the impacts of COVID-19, the need for transforming health systems in general and psychiatry in specific still persists. One of the major conclusions is to develop programs enabling psychiatrists and physicians to deal with their own distress.

**Chapter 3**
Whole-of-Nation Approach in COVID-19 Management: The Case of Brunei Darussalam ................ 35
*Abdul Malik Omar, University Brunei Darussalam, Brunei*
*Amanina Halim, Independent Researcher, Brunei*

The emergence of COVID-19 has swept the globe by storm, taking the lives of hundreds of thousands of people and infecting millions worldwide. As the virus continues to spread, governments have pursued strategies and action plans, with some achieving notable successes, while others fail miserably. This research focuses on how the Brunei government has become an outlier in tackling the COVID-19 pandemic. As such, this chapter provides substantive content useful for policymakers and experts to learn from the Brunei experience in pandemic management through a whole-of-nation framework, effectively contributing to both theory and practice in public policy and governance. The research on Brunei further gives credence on the need for governments to administer participation among the private sector and society to tackle grand challenges of the 21st century, particularly in preparation for the 'Great Reset' amid post-COVID-19. Policy recommendations have been presented.

**Chapter 4**
COVID-19 Being Positive Strategically in the Context of SDG and NDC ........................................ 56
*Nikhil Kant, School of Management Studies, Indira Gandhi National Open University (IGNOU), India*
*Kumari Anjali, School of Sciences, Indira Gandhi National Open University (IGNOU), India*

Sustainable Development Goals (SDG) and nationally determined contributions (NDC), normally operated in silos at national level in developing countries despite their greater interrelation, require an aligned implementation. The chapter probes into the opportunities visible in the actions of different actors to tackle COVID-19 that can be continued or replicated for combating the menace of climate crisis and achieving sustainable development in post-COVID times. This chapter discusses the challenges that the contemporary issue of sustainability has faced due to the occurrence of this pandemic. The chapter concludes that at a time when no one wishes to be tested positive for COVID-19, there is a need to be positive strategically so that the potential opportunities of achieving goals and commitments under SDG and NDC could be sensed and seized by re-configuring resources and capabilities according to the actual needs for a sustainable future.

**Chapter 5**
Adaptive Performance: A Review of Managerial Interventions ........................................................ 71
*Timothy C. Bednall, Swinburne University of Technology, Australia*
*Matthew D. Henricks, The University of New South Wales, Australia*

COVID-19 has prompted an urgent need for organisations to adapt to continuously changing circumstances. Given the unpredictable challenges, a traditional, tightly planned approach to managing episodic change is likely to be suboptimal. Based on the need to manage continuous change and ensure workplaces are prepared for further unexpected events, it is argued that developing employees' adaptive performance is a better approach. Drawing on the literature identified in Park and Park's recent review of adaptive performance and its antecedents, the authors conduct a parallel review of the managerial implications of these findings. Findings are organised into sections related to employee selection, training, work design, leader behaviour, and organisational climate. Each practical recommendation is reviewed in terms of its feasibility of implementation and likely effectiveness.

**Chapter 6**
Change Management Strategies as the Nexus of Performance Improvement in African Universities Post-COVID-19 Pandemic ........ 90
*Bethuel Sibongiseni Ngcamu, Nelson Mandela University, South Africa*

The COVID-19 pandemic, which started in China in late 2019, came as the perfect storm at a time when leadership in African universities is leaving much to be desired. This status quo is what has triggered the current chapter, which sets out to explore responsive leadership development and the change management interventions that are required after the pandemic and which can make universities' operations agile. The chapter aims to investigate the nature of change management interventions, including agile talent management. This can help to ensure that African universities are effective and efficient in Africa post-COVID-19. The chapter employs different research methods; for instance, a literature review is synthesised on previously published studies that relate to the relevant applications and impacts of agile transformation in universities as a way of guiding leaders in their response to the challenges of a post-coronavirus world. Furthermore, the document analysis followed examines a number of documents related to leadership, development, and change post the pandemic.

**Chapter 7**
Success Factors of Future-Viable Organizations in the Post-COVID-19 Era ........ 106
*Peter Behrendt, Freiburg Institut, Germany*
*Alexander Holicki, Freiburg Institut, Germany*
*Veronika Matzner, Freiburg Institut, Germany*

The COVID-19 crisis has disrupted societies and will be succeeded by economic and social dynamics. Therefore, organizations need to adapt and seize new opportunities quickly. To learn from the early part of the COVID-19 crisis, 24 leader interviews were conducted and categorized based on the integrative model of leadership behavior. In consequence, eight success factors were derived that foster the future-viability of organizations in times of crisis: the three success factors, (1) providing iterative leadership within uncertainty, (2) promoting absolute customer-loyalty, and (3) providing sustainable public value, foster coordination with internal and external actors and provide meaning. Two factors, (4) promoting a culture of trust and (5) establishing collaborative ecosystems of organizations, promote cooperation and sustain trust. The final three success factors, (6) creating an agile culture, (7) driving digital processes, and (8) ensuring economic agility, enhance agility by activating internal and external resources.

**Chapter 8**
The Impact of COVID-19 on the Corporations and Management Change ........ 125
*Adel Ismail Al-Alawi, University of Bahrain, Bahrain*
*Arpita A. Mehrotra, Royal University for Women, Bahrain*
*Sohayla Khidir Sanosi, University of Bahrain, Bahrain*

The purpose of this study is to analyze the impact of COVID-19 on different identities such as corporations, leadership, employees, human resources teams, customers, government bodies, and management change. Desk research based on secondary data analysis methodology was used for this study. Better crisis management plans can enable corporate to control and hybrid working environment to guide businesses to prepare and make strategies that can persist sustainably in a future crisis. It can be concluded that different corporations have faced the additional impact of the pandemic on their businesses. COVID-19 has changed the way businesses perform. Consequently, it can be inferred that leadership and leadership transition can lead to victory if leaders take the time to discover what works and what does not. This will allow the enterprise to change the next steps accordingly and save it from failure to pursue the outcomes.

**Chapter 9**
Shock Leadership: Leading Amidst Pandemics and Other Chaotic Change ..................................... 136
*Anton Shufutinsky, Cabrini University, USA*
*Bena Long, Institute of Interdisciplinary Leadership Education and Development, USA*
*James R. Sibel, Institute of Interdisciplinary Leadership Education and Development, USA*
*Darrell Norman Burrell, The Florida Institute of Technology, USA*

Global crises that jolt entire systems, such as the COVID-19 pandemic, can place groups, organizations, and communities in volatile, uncertain, complex, and ambiguous (VUCA) environments that affect all sectors of society, having potentially disastrous effects including high morbidity and mortality rates, political upheaval, and extensive disruption of entire economic systems, causing damage that can last for months or even years. Effective leadership is a pivotal organizational commodity in times of normalcy, and it becomes increasingly critical during crises and the subsequent environments of discontinuous change. There has been a consistent level of international criticism regarding national, state, local, and corporate leadership during the COVID-19 crisis. This chapter explores the leadership challenges associated with highly chaotic environments and introduces an advanced model of leadership—shock leadership—and leadership development framework necessary for higher leader reliability and effectiveness in disasters and other crises.

**Chapter 10**
COVID-19 and Leadership: Impacts and Responses ........................................................................ 160
*Asma Ayari, University of Bahrain, Bahrain*

The main aim of this chapter is to investigate and report the specific personality traits, attitudes, styles of individual leaders, and learning experience of Bahraini leaders during COVID-19. A qualitative study technique used in order to purse the objectives of this research. Semi-directive interviews were conducted with 15 Bahraini leaders from different companies and sectors. The data was analysed and discussed based on themes related to the crisis management and effective leadership style. The results revealed that an exceptional leadership style has emerged in the Bahraini organizational environment to instill confidence and resilience to staff, customers, and external stakeholders during crisis. The findings of the current study will offer a comprehensive framework for effective leadership performance in times of crisis. In addition, the results of this study will be beneficial for the field of gender and culture studies, for instance culture diversification and its relationship with leadership styles.

**Chapter 11**
New Challenges for Leading the Change for the Psychological Consequences of Pandemics: Workplace Loneliness, Work Alienation, and Spiritual Well-Being in the Post-COVID-19 Era....... 169
*Mehmet Çetin, Istanbul Sabahattin Zaim University, Turkey*

With the needs for change and adaptation brought by the COVID-19 pandemic, management of the concerns regarding workplace loneliness, work alienation, and spiritual well-being stands as a critical challenge for the organizations. Although these concepts are not new and have increasingly been a focus of attention in recent decades, contemporary radical changes in work methods and work concept such as increased use of technology, digitalization, social distancing at work, and virtual working make them much more crucial for the success of organizations. The purpose of this chapter is to address adverse psychological work-related outcomes of the pandemic and provide practical implications and recommendations for leaders for effective management of the processes regarding these outcomes during and after the pandemic.

**Chapter 12**
Responding to the Challenge of Employee Engagement During Uncertain Times: Adaptive Leadership is the Answer.......... 188
*Mohammad Faraz Naim, Department of Management, Birla Institute of Technology and Science, Pilani, India*

This chapter aims to combat the challenge of employee engagement faced by organizations across the globe during this uncertain world. This theoretical study suggests a conceptual model that explores adaptive leadership to evoke employee engagement in this pandemic context. Based on the theoretical lens of social exchange theory (SET), the conceptual model of the study illustrates the role of adaptive leaders in facilitating employee development, formation of social capital, and articulation of organizational vision. This, in turn, boosts employee engagement levels, in particular affective, cognitive, and physical engagement. The rationale of the conceptual model is provided with testable propositions. This chapter extends the human resource management scholarship on how to deal with employee engagement challenge. Simultaneously, it takes aim to expand the adaptive leadership theory research by exploring its possible effect on employee engagement outcomes.

**Chapter 13**
Leadership in the Post-COVID-19 Era: New Leaders of the New Normal.......... 199
*Yeşim Kurt, Kırklareli University, Turkey*
*Dilek Erdoğan, Gaziantep University, Turkey*

The purpose of this study is to explain the relationship between the COVID-19 crisis and leadership and to demonstrate the leadership skills necessary in the post-COVID-19 era. This study is based on literature research. In the study, firstly, the effects of COVID-19 on human life are explained. Then, the relationship between crisis management and leadership is discussed. Later, the features of the new era after COVID-19 and the concept of the digital age are explained. The role of leaders in this new era is emphasized. In the last part of this study, three leadership types that attract attention during the pandemic process are briefly explained. These are ethical, digital, and pandemic leadership. In the last section, the skills and abilities required for leaders who are to succeed after COVID-19 also add value to the research.

**Chapter 14**
COVID-19 and the Call for Elder Change Leadership.......... 218
*Stan Amaladas, Baker College, USA*

The author argues that post-COVID-19 change leadership is neither a matter of technically improving what change leaders are already doing or refining existing systems and regulation. Within the context of abrupt, sudden, and unexpected change, two questions are raised. First, if it is not a matter of technically improving what change leaders are already doing, or refining existing systems, what more do post-COVID-19 change leaders need to do? Second, what new qualities would change leaders need to embrace (theory) so that they can meaningfully fulfill their change leadership practices in a post-COVID-19 era? Approaching various paradigms of change leadership as stories, the author addresses (1) the seduction of pre-COVID-19 story of change leadership, (2) offers a post-COVID-19 elder change leadership model, (3) offers a post-COVID-19 elder change leadership framework centered around four dimensions: humility, generating meaning amid chaos, compassion and empathy, and affirming hope through story telling.

**Chapter 15**
Task Forces as Silver Bullets for Crisis Management: A Case Study of an SME During COVID-19240
*Laura Schärrer, University of Lucerne, Switzerland*
*Reto M. Wegmann, University of Lucerne, Switzerland*

In 2020, the corona virus disease 2019 (COVID-19) triggered a global health crisis, disrupting economies, societies, and private companies. Organizations faced urgent challenges, and most of them installed so called "task forces" to respond. Small or medium enterprises (SMEs), which play a major role in most economies, however, often encounter problems of limited resources to do so. The purpose of this chapter is to derive theoretical and practical implications on how such crises can be handled. A literature review identifies the characteristics of successful task forces and then validates them with a case study of a Swiss transport company during COVID-19, which is based on multiple interviews with the CEO between Spring 2020 and in Fall 2020. The findings include that task forces are crucial for SMEs despite their limited resources. A critical success factor is the quality of human resources, which demands careful selection. Concepts used in crisis management can also be applied in day-to-day operations to increase the organization's resilience and also general profitability.

**Chapter 16**
Leadership as a Change Trigger in Unsettling Conditions: The Case of Werenbach Watches........... 254
*Vasilios Stouraitis, Glasgow Caledonian University, UK*
*Andres J. Arenas F., Universidad Antonio de Nebrija, Spain*
*Kostantinos Tsanis, Hult International Business School, USA*
*Jessica Bayón Pérez, Universidad Antonio de Nebrija, Spain*

The case focuses on Werenbach watches, a micro SME based in Switzerland which managed to survive the current crisis of COVID-19 in an innovative way. The focus is on the behavioural aspects of leadership present in the case and which have led to tangible innovations. The innovations examined have led to the ability to source extensively and access funding to create a stronger global presence. The reasons for choosing servant leadership as an example are presented and the moderating links between attitude and implementation are listed and examined. Suggestions for managers and further research are presented. The chapter aims to be a toolkit for micro SMEs' CEOs willing to understand the fundamental behaviours behind access of funds and sources for a small firm.

**Chapter 17**
The Banking Sector During COVID-19: The Case of Bahrain Islamic Bank.................................... 274
*Yomna Abdulla, University of Bahrain, Bahrain*

In this chapter, the authors explore the banking sector during coronavirus era by using Bahrain Islamic Bank as a case. Overall, the pandemic has speeded several decisions and actions in the digital transformation journey of the banking sector. Prior literature has identified four main strategies, namely retrenchment, preserving, innovating, and exit in response to a crisis. The findings show that the decisions taken by Bahrain Islamic Bank support the preserving and innovating strategies, which are mostly related to the continuation of its operations and preservation of its market share and customers as well as digitalization of their services and reliance on technological solutions to cope with the precautionary measures imposed by the pandemic.

**Chapter 18**
The Role of Leadership and Related Work Factors Caused by COVID-19: The Impact on Employee Effectiveness ............ 285
*Adel Ismail Al-Alawi, University of Bahrain, Bahrain*
*Arpita Anshu Mehrotra, Royal University for Women, Bahrain*
*Samah Sabri Ali, University of Bahrain, Bahrain*
*Fatima Ali Al-Ammar, University of Bahrain, Bahrain*

This chapter aims to analyze the role of leadership and related work factors caused by COVID-19, the impact on employee effectiveness, and workforce performance in the workplace. Several studies have examined the effect of such crises in different sectors and countries that shed an interesting comparison and distinction. Still, there is limited research published on the workplace's impact due to COVID-19 concerning employee productivity. However, most studies highlight different independent variables on employees and the organization's work effectiveness. A limited number of systemic research studies have led to various studies conducted based on new theoretical frameworks. The literature on change management's effectiveness during such a pandemic is not widely available. Future research should cover various factors such as motivation, remuneration, global environment, employee stress, health and safety, and HRM policies. Moreover, demographic variables should be taken into account as studies have briefly found that some age groups are affected differently than others.

**Chapter 19**
Impact of COVID-19 on an Educational Institution of India: Perceptions of Teachers Towards Online Classes ............ 300
*Elizabeth Madathilathu Samuel, Royal University for Women, Bahrain*

The year 2020 has made a mark in the history of mankind. India, too, was affected by the pandemic. To ensure a curb on the spread of the disease, India adopted a sequence emergency mechanism. It announced the closure of all educational institutions along with all the other establishments as a part of strict social distancing measures. The traditional mode of teaching and learning transitioned into online teaching. Online learning and virtual classrooms became the 'new normal'. The analysis was carried out using the data collected through structured questionnaire from 35 teachers in Kottayam District, Kerala a southern state of India. Data collected was analyzed using descriptive statistics. It is evident from the study that the teachers lack in the use of various teaching methods for motivating and encouraging students. Further on, since the teachers were caught off guard, they had not received any formal or professional training to conduct online classes or use the advanced modes of technology.

**Compilation of References** ............ 312

**About the Contributors** ............ 365

**Index** ............ 372

# Preface

Covid-19 has changed the globe drastically. Individuals and their organizations encounter serious challenges to deal with. Challenges can be personal, economic, and political. Consequences resulting from the challenges are long lasting if not permanent. This entails states, individuals, groups, non-governmental and business organizations to collaborate for addressing the issue of consequences of Covid-19. Consequences are related to changes of leadership styles, nation and business strategies, stakeholder's analysis, job design, internet business, online education, and most important health systems.

The book presents 19 selected chapters from 27 papers. Contributors are from Africa, Asia, Europe, North America, Australia. The book can be utilised by practitioners and researchers in states, non-governmental, and business organizations.

The Chapters revolve around the following topics:

- Changes inf health systems
- Stakeholders of health systems and health strategies
- Nations wide strategies
- Revolving leadership styles
- Job design, employee's engagement, and motivation
- Internet business and education
- Approaches for managerial Interventions
- Business sustainability and growth in crisis era
- Business strategies for post Covid-19 era

In Chapter 1 authors state that health systems in German speaking language require changes. Health systems cannot be maintained by only medical services and economical resources. All other stakeholders are important to consider. This enables health systems to deliver the needed health services. Nurses are important stakeholders to involve in developing new perspective for health services. The paper illustrates that the eight steps of Kotter's model of change can help to organize health services in a more proactive style rather than being reactive.

Chapter 2 then examines stakeholders for health systems. This examination aims to develop resilient strategies. The paper exhibits the impacts of COVID-19 on stakeholders of health systems. It argues that stakeholders must be studied continuously to decide their demands and concerns based on different situations. It provides contributions to practitioners and researchers to develop better understandings of health services

Chapter 3 describes Whole-a-nation strategies. The paper analyses nations strategies and governance policies employed by Government of Brunei to deal with COVID-19. The paper mentions 5 policy recommendations to handle the present and future pandemics. The first is to establish a controlling system for monitoring a pandemic. The system should be supported by international organizations. The second is to build policies on scientific evidence not in speculations. The third is to engage private sector and people to dealing with the pandemic. The fourth is to move toward digitalisation era. The fifth and last is to utilise technology to spread awareness and interacts with people.

In Chapter 4 authors examine the impacts of pandemic on sustainable development goals (SDG) and Nationally Determined Contribution (NDC). It shows that COVID-19 can be viewed as an opportunity and not a source of threats. The importance of ethical consumption, green production and clean energy are highlighted because of the present pandemic. National policies must be re designed to deal with the post era requirements of this present pandemic

Chapter 5 examines interventions strategies to enhance employee's adaptive performance during a crisis. It provides contributions to practitioners and researchers in relation to how implement and promote new perspectives for performance strategies.

Chapter 6 ponders on change management as the nexus of performance improvements. The paper explains that universities in Africa must revisit their policies, systems, strategic plans, and implementations. It concludes that universities are urged to follow innovative intervention strategies and change plans. It adds as well that a new leadership styles enable to deal with unexpected consequences of COVID-19.

Chapter 7 outlines success factors of future viable organizations. The paper elaborates on success factors for future organizations. These are leadership capacity to deal with uncertainty, promoting customers loyalty, adding value recognized by the public, developing a culture based on trust, evolving collaborative environments, maintaining a culture of agility, moving toward digitalization, and finally sustaining economic agility.

Chapter 8 illustrates that businesses encounter many challenges because of COVID-19. Business corporations are suggested to launch programs to improve well-being, skills, and rewards of employees. Human resource departments must employ innovative ways to move businesses and employees toward digitalisation. This can help leadership to play a major role during the present pandemic.

Chapter 9 contemplates on shock leadership. The paper argues that there is a need to develop a new model of leadership. The new model reflects all attributes, behavioural and situational characteristics of earlier leadership styles discussed by literature. The model can go beyond for having unique attributes enabling leaders to deal with crisis like the present pandemic. Training programs for the new model i.e., shock leadership relies on Real-time Scenario. Besides developing shock leadership in civilian establishments requires mindfulness training programs.

Chapter 10 states that COVID-19 is an opportunity for leaders to exhibit their personal qualities. Strategies to deal with emotions and decisions based on simplicity and creativity are the most qualities for leadership to deal with the present pandemic.

Chapter 11 elaborates on new challenges for leading the changes in the era of Covid-19. The chapter argues that organisational leadership should realise and act according to the concerns and demands of the COVID-19 era. Consequences such as work alienation, loneliness at workplace, and spiritual well-being are examined. Redesigning jobs, informal communication and relationships, employees' training and attention paid to work-family interventions are methods to deal with consequences of COVID-19.

Chapter 12 expounds on the challenges of employee engagement during uncertain times, such as the present pandemic. The author argus that adaptive leadership can lead to enhance engagement. The present pandemic of COVID-19 has declined motivation and engagement of employees. Engagement and motivation are the trigger for competitive advantage. Adaptive leadership develops the vision leading to improve social capital and employees 'development.

Chapter 13 exhibits feature of leadership in the post COVID-19 era. Leadership roles have changed because of COVID-19. Such roles have been transformed by the present digital age. The success of leadership in this era is based on many factors. These factors are emotional intelligence, skills related to communication, decision-making abilities, digital skills, scientific knowledge updating and awareness of self.

Chapter 14 focuses on COVID-19 and call for elderly change leadership. The paper develops "a new post COVID-19 Elder change leadership model". It presents 11 recommendations. These to change leaders' perceptions of themselves, employees and then organisations and their cultures in a total perspective.

Chapter 15 the chapter identifies the main characteristics of task forces in small and medium organisations enabling them to deal with the present pandemic. Changes of processes and structure, qualities and talents of task force members, training programs, time pressures and task force leaders as team members and mentors. are the major characteristics.

Chapter 16 presents a case of leadership dealing with present pandemic. It argues that leadership be a change trigger in unsettling conditions. The presentation revolves around the case of Werenbach watches. The paper discusses a case of company that has managed to grow during this pandemic era. CEO of the company follows the servant leadership style; the servant leadership employs innovative approaches to achieve turnaround. These approaches are concerned with the leadership cognitive, moral and self-determination, interpersonal and employee's reciprocity, a large customer base due to widening products types in term of pricing and utilising social media and internet business.

Chapter 17 evaluates strategies followed by one bank in Bahrain to deal with the prevailing pandemic. The paper examines strategies employed by Bahrain Islamic bank during COVID-19. The strategies being focused on are retrenchment, innovating, preserving, and exiting. It is found that the bank being scanned is following the preserving and innovating strategies at the present.

Authors in Chapter 18 investigate impacts of leadership on employees' effectiveness. They state that research on leadership roles, work-life balance, work design, motivation and remuneration are a few in crisis situations. The paper recommends conducting extensive research on leadership impacts on work environment and human resources.

Chapter 19 looks at impacts of COVID-19 on education institution of India. The paper scans opinions of teachers in a South Indian region in relation to their views of online classes. The author states that the sudden changes to online teaching have positive and negative consequences. Students can have access to teaching resources at any time. Teachers however lack the proper training and support to use online technologies in relation motivation and encouragement of students. This is due to the changes of students' roles in online teachings. A learner- centred approach substitutes the spoon-fed methods traditionally implemented.

*Ebtihaj Al-Aali*
*University of Bahrain, Bahrain*

*Meryem Masmoudi*
*University of Bahrain, Bahrain*

# Chapter 1
# Necessary Changes in Healthcare of German-Speaking Countries

**Stephanie Krebs**
*Ostfalia University of Applied Sciences, Germany*

**Anna Larina Lietz**
*Ostfalia University of Applied Sciences, Germany*

**Martina Hasseler**
*Ostfalia University of Applied Sciences, Germany*

## ABSTRACT

*The COVID-19 pandemic has suddenly gained urgency in Germany for implementation of new structures in healthcare sector to take care of seriously ill COVID-19 patients. The shortage of skilled healthcare workers, which has already been discussed before the pandemic situation, has become more tangible than ever. Society relies on a properly working healthcare system, especially in a pandemic like the one we now witness. After the comparatively mild course of the first COVID-19 wave in Germany, the interest in long overdue changes decreased. The second wave of the pandemic occurred in Germany as well. Also, in the meantime of the first and the second wave, numerous findings were collected and presented, where changes could have an effect. To motivate going forward, the text describes John P. Kotter's model of change management, eight steps to describe necessary changes in organizations and leadership in the German healthcare system.*

## INTRODUCTION

During a pandemic, a country's health system is a crucial factor in preventing the disease from spreading. It is also responsible for helping sick people and alleviating symptoms. In the first wave of Covid-19 pandemic in Germany, employees of the health care system were identified as "systemically relevant".

DOI: 10.4018/978-1-7998-6948-1.ch001

In contrast to 61% of German employees, who were accompanied to work at home (ifo Institut, 2020b) and 5.6 million people, who were put on short time working (ifo Institut, 2020a), employees of the health care system were asked to work overtime at the source of the event (Arndt, 2020).

This approaches are justified by the nature of SARS-CoV-2 (Severe Acute Respiratory Syndrome Coronavirus Type 2). The virus can be transmitted between humans mainly through droplets and aerosols generated by breathing, coughing, talking, singing and sneezing (Haslbeck et al., 2010; Ji et al., 2018; Robert-Koch-Institut [RKI], 2020a). Within a radius of 1 to 2 meter around an infected person the probability of exposure to infectious particles of any size is increased (Liu et al., 2017). The probability for an exposure also exists in small, poorly ventilated or unventilated rooms (Robert-Koch-Institut [RKI], 2020a). The course of the disease varies in symptoms and severity, from asymptomatic infections to severe pneumonia with respiratory failure and death (Robert-Koch-Institut [RKI], 2020a).

The SARS-CoV-2 virus has only recently crossed over to humans from animal reservoirs (Cui et al., 2019). For this reason, little scientific knowledge was available at the outset. However, it quickly became clear that the risk of infection had to be minimized in order to protect human lives and subsequently, the economy. The so-called exponential growth of the infection numbers, which is to be expected usually in a pandemic, leads to a high amount of the number in a very short time. It was also warned that the existing resources of the health care system would not be sufficient to counter the number of infections in Germany (RWI - Leibniz-Institut für Wirtschaftsforschung e.V., 2020). The conditions described required rapid decision-making and action. The resulting measures, which are summarized under the term "hard lockdown," involved reducing public life in private and working environments.

Due to a shortage of skilled health care workers, medical students, reassigned nurses, retired doctors or care assistants have been requested to help in the German health care. Furthermore Covid-19 wards and makeshift hospitals were recommended (RKI, 2020b). Also, hospitals and the government had to buy a lot of new equipment for protection against Covid-19 and for patient care: masks, protective gowns and safety goggles, e.g. But this equipment only becomes useful, if it comes hand in hand with special staff training in proper hygiene, artificial respiration and other Covid-19 related care-skills (Kluge et al., 2020b). In case of this, rapid knowledge management became necessary.

Moreover, the pandemic causes changes in the German-speaking health care sector in operational business as well as in leadership. Some of them, (e.g. lower personnel limits, documentation obligations, sufficient protective equipment and correct handling as well as targeted use, increase of intensive care bed capacities and care by qualified intensive care personnel were already tied into the discussion of the "COVID-19-Krankenhausentlastungsgesetz", which was passed at short notice in April 2020 (Millich, 2020). But, with the (temporary) flattening of the first wave, the (perceived) urgency or even necessity of changes regarding Covid-19 has decreased in Germany. Within the public discussion, it seemed that the German population and responsible executives were striving for a return to the previously existing processes and structures. This becomes visible in the demonstrations against the Covid-19-measures. The demonstrations were no longer visited only by conspiracy theorists, but crowded by people of the middle of society as well (Breyton & Naber, 2020).

Nevertheless, this was an unfavorable endeavor. The second wave of Covid-19 has reached Germany as well as other states worldwide. On 13rd November 2020 the RKI-Dashboard showed a total amount of 751.095 Covid-19 infected and an increase of +23.542 infected in Germany in comparison to the day before (RKI, 2020). The rates continued to increase in December 2020 and January 2021. Within this context, various studies discuss an additional enormous number of unreported cases of infected persons.

For example in case of various use of PCR-tests (Dorn et al., 2020). Nevertheless, chains of infection cannot be traced, because contact details are not available or counterfeit (tagesschau.de, 2020).

Until the second wave could have taken place, different knowledge about the impacts and consequences of the Covid-19 pandemic was build up. In addition, further knowledge is generated during the second wave. This knowledge shows that changes in the German health care sector are necessary in the time of this pandemic and beyond. These changes must be implemented and accepted by decision-makers, realized by the various professional groups in the healthcare system, and accepted and supported by society. This requires a good crisis management based on evidence and various skills at different hierarchical levels and population sectors.

To achieve this goal, the following text describes along John P. Kotter's model of Change Management eight steps to describe necessary changes in organizations and leadership. Kotter developed this model based on generalized observations of well-positioned companies that made changes to remain competitive. The companies applied various levers (total quality management, reengineering, right sizing, restructuring, cultural change and turnaround) and were able to achieve different goals. However, the different approaches also revealed similar mistakes and lessons learned. On this basis, Kotter derived eight phases that must be passed through during a change process. He emphasizes that this process takes time and that mistakes in one of these phases can limit or destroy both the overall goal and therefore successes achieved up to this point (Kotter, 1995).

The first phase includes to establish a sense of urgency. It aims to ensure that everyone involved recognizes that a change is necessary. In the second and third phases, responsible persons and managers should create a guiding coalition to build up an overview, develop und discuss ideas and necessary measures. Within the following phase, the vision of change has to be communicated for buy-in. In the best case, everyone understands the new way of thinking as well as acting and goes along with it, so challenges can be reduced (phase five). Because of this, short-term wins occur in phase six. At this moment it is crucial to go on (phase seven) until the necessary changes are integrated into the culture and daily-business (Phase eight) (Kotter, 1995; Kotter, 2015).

The model of change management can be used fundamentally to lead necessary changes in the German healthcare system. In order to do so, the model has to be applied to the German healthcare systems as a whole. (Individual hospitals (chains) or specific institutions of the health care are not considered). Figure 1 represents the "big picture" of this work. It shows Kotter's 8 phases, which already reflect the necessary changes of the German health care system in a bullet point manner. It is essential to consider all phases in context and not to be discouraged by setbacks. To motivate this process across the hierarchy, in the following, every phase of figure 1 will be described in detail and discussed based on a German-speaking countries-related research status by November 2020. Also necessary factors of crisis management as well as competencies in leadership will be explained.

*Figure 1. Necessary Changes in the Health Care Sector in German-speaking Countries along Kotter`s Model of Change Management*
*Source: own research*

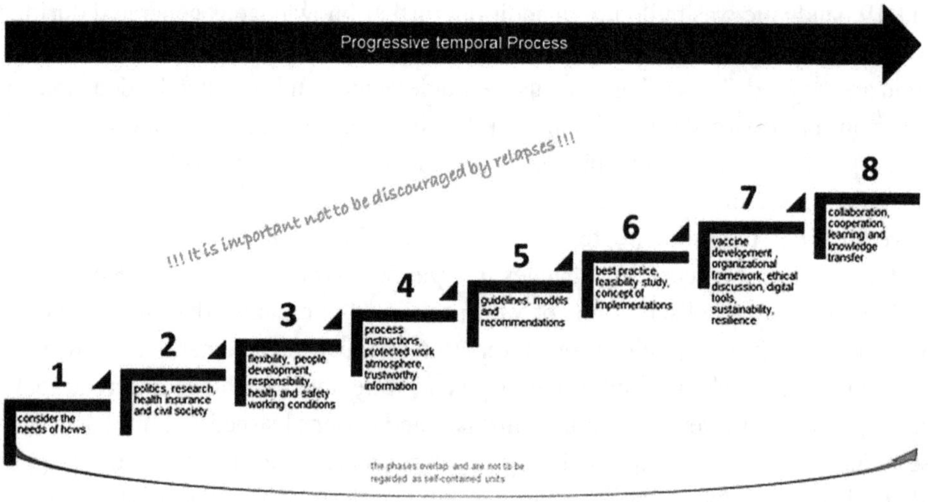


## Phase One: Establish a Sense of Urgency

According to Kotter, 50% of companies fail in the first step. As seen, so did the German health care system after the first wave of the Covid-19 pandemic. It is crucial to be recognized by a large number that "business as usual" is unacceptable. This goes hand in hand with leaving the so-called "comfort zone", i.e. where everyone knows their way around and feels comfortable. Kotter stresses, the so called "aggressive cooperation" of different stakeholders in order of beginning a change (Kotter, 1995).

This "aggressive cooperation" was shown very well during the first wave. But, after some time the health care workers (hcws) were an underestimated factor in the discussions about change management and leadership. Among others, an narrative overview of Mulfinger discusses mental stress due to epidemics among German health care workers (Mulfinger et al., 2020). Therefore, Hower et al. conduct a scientific study on challenges and pressures from the perspective of executives of nursing homes. They name concerns about Covid-19 infections of those in need of care and employees as one of the main factor of psychological stress. Another fear includes uncertainty about measures when Covid-19 cases occur. Due to educational work and a lack of support from relatives to create understanding for the situation by nursing home residents, the workload increase as well. Therefore, the procurement and the consumption of protective equipment, the adherence to hygiene regulations, the contradictoriness, intransparency of work-critical information and guidelines as well as losses of income are the challenges faced within this sector (Hower et al., 2020).

Wolf-Ostermann et al. describe the same challenges after performing an online survey about the (partially) inpatient and outpatient long-term care. Based on the results of this study employees in long-term care are on high risk of infection. At the same time half of all nursing services and nursing homes during the pandemic had problems in obtaining enough protective equipment for employees. More than two thirds of all nursing homes report a Covid-19-induced loss of up to 10% of their staff (Wolf-Ostermann et al., 2020).

Hasseler and Hartleb discuss psychological stress factors which burden nursing staff in long-term care as well as nursing home residents on international level. Furthermore, increased psychological stress in the hospital setting is pointed out. Among other things, the question of guilt is quoted to carry the virus on the one hand into the private surrounding field, on the other hand, from the private surrounding field into the stationary mechanism (Hasseler & Hartleb, in press).

Moreover, Dr. Gerald Gaß, President of the German Hospital Association (DKG) points out in a press release on 17th September 2020 that the pandemic was extremely challenging for hospital staff as well. Among other things hcws have to include delivery problems of personal protective equipment in their daily work with infected patients (German Hospital Association, 2020b). It promotes fear for their own health. Even so, long services, but also the decisions about intensive treatment affects the work force (Simhofer, 2020). "The Covid-19 pandemic placed an extreme burden on healthcare workers. Patient safety is only possible, if the safety of employees and good working conditions are also guaranteed", Gaß pointed out, too (German Hospital Association, 2020b).

But, due to a shortage of skilled workers, for hcws quarantine rules have been loosened so they were forced to work with FFP2 mask (Online-Portal für professionell Pflegende, 2020). On October 15, 2020 it was also published that cases of infected nursing staff took care for infected residents in long-term care. This was conducted in the voluntary nature of those affected and only when certain conditions applied: freedom from symptoms, wearing a FFP2 mask, exclusive treatment of residents who have also been tested positive, special access routes as well as travel to work with one's own car or bicycle (vom Lehn, 2020). Nevertheless, care associations reject this as disproportionate (Online-Portal für professionell Pflegende, 2020). Either way, it shows that the lack of skilled workers leads to solutions that are subject to strong reservations.

The described insights should be understood as a warning sign: Everything must be done to reduce the shortage of skilled workers. So the urgency is there: The human resource is strongly connected to sufficient intensive care beds and the care of the Covid-19 patients (Wirtz & Stöckle, 2020). To encourage the professional hcws to maintain in their daily business it is very clear that shown respect and gratitude in the form of applause is not enough (Schäfer, 2020). Further steps of appreciation and recognition as well as structural changes of the basic conditions for the execution and different activities in the nursing and medical care are absolutely necessary.

### To Take in Mind 1

A shortage of skilled workers in the health care sector was discussed in Germany before the Covid-19 pandemic already (Jacobs et al., 2020; Watzka, 2018). Therefore, an increasing decimation of nursing and medical staff must be avoided at all costs, especially in a crisis. A consideration of the additional mental and physical strain of hcws must be taken into account. Improvements and the working condition is essential to maintain an "aggressive cooperation" regarding upcoming changes.

## Phase Two: Create a Guiding Coalition

In phase two Kotter is focusing on a guiding coalition outside of existing structural and hierarchical systems. Every important stakeholder, even if they may have a different opinion or only contribute a small part in the course of the process, should be involved at an early stage and a common goal should be agreed on (Kotter, 1995).

The Covid-19 crisis came with many new challenges that could not be solved in ad hoc manner by means of ready-made action plans. In case of this, new ideas had to be developed, tested, evaluated and, if necessary, adapted. During the crisis, different Covid-19 measures were developed by federal state politics. In a second step these were discussed among themselves and coordinated with the state government. The federalist system in Germany has often been disparaged: The difference in the rules of the various states were often considered as inconsistent leadership before. Various Covid-19 measures led to confusion, lack of understanding, insecurities and perceived disadvantage and were strongly criticized (tagesschau, 2020). In other cases, it became obvious, making distinctions between different regions and to reflect these in political decisions is reasonable. It can be recorded: Efficient communication and coordination are two factors in a decentralized pandemic response (Münch, 2020).

Therefore, a great guiding coalition between politics and science is built-up in Germany during the crisis. Several scientists are involved in providing advice to politicians and the public. Federal and state governments are open to scientific advice. The RKI presents daily updated information and further information are published in podcast series. The German interdisciplinary association for intensive and emergency medicine (DIVI) publishes current recommendations for treatment, care, physiotherapy and clinical-ethical on Covis-19 (DIVI, 2020b).

At the beginning, representatives of medicine and virologists stood in the medial focus. Later, specialists from other professions were also included (Arnold, 2020). Dinges (2020) points out that more weight should be given to the nursing science perspective. Some of the now discussed effects of e.g. isolation as well as missing contacts and visits to old people are already well investigated on the part of the care science - and nevertheless these study results were hardly considered in the decisions and recommendations for the (stationary) old person assistance. Nevertheless, ethics consultancy achieves a supporting effect as well and should be discussed (Dinges, 2020). Furthermore, the German Society for Internal Intensive Care and Emergency Medicine (DGIIN) calls for intensive care to be more involved in the development of pandemic plans, guidelines, operational plans and preventive measures, as well as in public health (DGIIN, 2020). Additionally, conditions for ethical debate should also be developed for clinical care decisions. Moreover, autonomy and responsibility for intensive care nurses should be introduced (Begerow et al., 2020).

Coordination between politics, employer and employee of the health care sector as well as the civic society are also important. Roth (2020) summarizes different ways to implement democracy and participation in political decision-making during and after the Covid-19 crisis (Roth, 2020).The DKG shows that hospitals depend on the support of health insurance companies and politicians (German Hospital Association, 2020a). To create a guiding coalition, all stakeholders have to be involved. This is also shown by the discussion on "forced labor": On the part of the North Rhine-Westphalian state government, a commitment to take up activities during the Covid-19 pandemic was initiated. A fine of up to 500,000 € was also provided for those who would not comply with the demand. Nurses and doctors saw this as forced labor of "massive interference with basic rights" (Biermann & Gutensohn, 2020). There was obviously a lack of cooperation between politicians and Employers association on how to mobilize human resources in the short term. Politicians tried to enforce solutions with regulations and penalties. This led to resistance from the hcws.

## To Take in Mind 2

It becomes clear at all levels that a strong leadership coalition should strive to a balance between medical, nursing and economic goals (Wirtz & Stöckle, 2020) in accordance with scientific recommendations and political decisions. Decisions must be made jointly and transparently.

## Phase Three: Develop a Change

Kotter points out that it is necessary in phase 3 to create a vision which is easy to understand for everyone. Communicated regulations as well as visualizations can help to make the overall goal more tangible for different stakeholders. This enables stakeholders to align their actions with these targets (Kotter, 1995).

The development of a change in the health sector is inevitably linked to action sequences of hcws. In case of this, public recognition of the nursing profession must extend to all health care institutions: Hospitals as well as nursing homes and general practitioners' practices and outpatient care services (Dinges, 2020). The Hans Böckler Foundation is compiling an overview of various perspectives on better working conditions for nursing staff. The researcher stresses that physical and mental stress of these are far above average, but the average pay, including bonuses, is only slightly higher than the average wage of all employees (Hans Böckler Foundation, 2020).

In addition to wage raises, working conditions must comply with the labor laws. As described before hcws have to work overtime during the pandemic. Therefore, it is important that a balancing act between the protection of the employees and the adequate care of the patients takes place. Eufinger suggests a "virus-friendly" - and thus pragmatic - procedure. He explains that this goes in accordance with the very strict German labor laws. It limits the daily shifts to eight hours, but an exceptional shift can go for as long as ten hours (§3 Abs. 1 Arbeitszeitgesetz (ArbZG)). Eufinger points to the exception in certain cases, and claims that this exception, that allows for 12 hour shifts, often applies here (§ 14 Abs. 1 ArbZG, § 15 Abs. 2 ArbZG). He explains that could justify the change from usual shifts with eight or ten hours according to § 3 ArbZG to 12-hour shifts for Covid-19 patient care. But it has to include that special conditions must be met. For example, the special hospital must be located in a Covid-19 hotspot or the supervisory authority grants an exemption in the public interest (Eufinger, 2020).

To provide another part of a possible vision and way for relief of nursing staffs, Hasseler et al. (2020) have developed a delegation model that allows intensive care experts to delegate tasks to supporting staff, which was discussed in the introduction of this chapter. The delegation model is based on a fast and targeted self-assessment and external assessment of a supporting staff member along a four-field matrix, which classifies individuals according to their specific requirements (Hasseler, Lietz et al., 2020). The delegation model requires trust, team atmosphere and cooperation so changes at the organizational level are indispensable. For this, it calls for building-up special competences to delegate more tasks. These have to be supported by trainings, practical experience and people development (Hasseler, Krebs et al., 2020).

An example of possible training is developed by the training center of the university hospital Muenster called"crash-course Covid-19". It divides human resources in seven levels. The levels 1, 2 and 3 are defined as staff for intensive care, Level 4 and 5 for regular wards and level 6 and 7 independent of location. A personnel planning is made according to the classification, trainings and infrastructure (Gräuler, 2020). In contrast, a very simple partition of supporting forces is the division of the Berliner Bildungscampus für Gesundheitsberufe gGmbH (2020) into three groups: Group 1: very unskilled / experience in nursing service without training, group 2: Returnees from the care/health professions and group 3: Active nurses in preparation for Covid-19 patients requiring intensive care. On this basis a training concept for care in a crisis was developed. It is divided into 17 training modules as followed: 1. Basics about Covid-19, disaster control and organization, 2. Basics of hygiene (Hygiene in an emergency), 3. Basics of body care, 4. Mobilization support, 5. Recognition of dangerous situations / vital signs, 6. Support within the scope of nutrition, 7. Communication in care and in crisis, 8. Support in the context of eliminations, 9. Fever and dealing with (high) feverish people, 10. Breath-supporting measures, 11. Data protection, confidentiality, documentation, 12. Working in the intensive care unit -Admission, transport and transfer of a patient, 13. Basics Monitoring, 14. Handling of continuous intravenous medication, 15. Handling of non-invasive and invasive ventilation, 16. Basic-Life-Support, 17. Basic care in the intensive care unit (Berliner Bildungscampus für Gesundheitsberufe gGmbH, 2020)

Nevertheless, it must be taken into account that training does not equate the supporting staff with trained intensive hcws. Various experiences with the employment of returning hcws during the first wave of the crisis are gathered. 72% of those surveyed cited problems with the induction and training of former nursing staff, 71% complained of outdated expertise, lack of current qualifications and lack of routine, 32% see patient care exposed to increased risk (Hollaus, 2020).

In the light of these experiences, it is all the more important that intensive care workers learn to delegate and take responsibility. The DGIIN Maintenance Section expressly declares its willingness to cooperate in future changes and has already developed a proposal that includes the following five points: 1. Monitoring of intensive care capacities, including a qualified care key (skills-grade mix also of auxiliary staff), 2. development of training programs, 3. integration of relatives and psychosocial care, 4. development of hygiene and pandemic plans and 5. revision of personnel calculation (Hermes & Ochmann, 2020).

### To Take in Mind 3

To create a vision for the necessary changes flexibility, people development and managers take responsibility for a team with different qualifications are indispensable. Therefore, occupational health and safety as well changes at the organizational level must be considered. The care of a seriously ill covid-19 patient requires professional care. Supporting staff may be helpful with specific tasks, but they cannot replace the expertise of certified and academic nurses. Decision makers have to make sure that working conditions are supportive and comply with the labor laws.

## Phase Four: Communicate the Vision for Buy-in

Kotter´s defined phases are not to be regarded as self-contained units; they overlap. The congruence of what key players say to their actions and the role model function is indispensable in order to constantly remind people of the necessary changes (Kotter, 1995). A good example can be seen in the description of preparation of process instruction at the Robert Bosch Hospital. Roigk and Becker show the way the recommendations for contact person tracking of the RKI were specified for one hospital by translating them into a procedural instruction. It helps to align processes precisely, to make decisions and to communicate who is responsible for it. The process instruction consists of four columns: 1. Recommendation of the RKI, 2. Individually adaptable structures and process steps in a process instruction, 3. Responsibilities, 4. Further procedural instructions and documents to be created and used. The authors point out, it is crucial that the persons involved, work together to develop the necessary process changes, communicate and act along to this (Roigk & Becker, 2020) A targeted communication and information ensure the coordination of resources and control of all processes (Silies et al., 2020).

It is important to create an atmosphere for questions in the case of an uncertainty. Furthermore, the communication during a crisis need trustworthy information and significantly increase interest in expert knowledge. This could be reached, by considering the following communication style:

- Truthful and cautious (factual, transparent, and without speculation)
- Understandable (short, simple, and catchy messages)
- Fast (active and early)
- Consistent (uniform, coordinated, and continuous)
- Explanatory (committed to gaining knowledge)
- Addressing different target groups via appropriate channels (Bodenheimer & Leidenberger, 2020).

Procedural instructions should be distributed through different channels. An information overload that creates the necessity to filter for important ones should be avoided (Lesch & Schütt, 2017). Nevertheless, it must be considered that small time contingents in practice to take information lead to a delayed implementation. Additionally, uncertainties and fears that circulate in the media and politics due to different information should be reflected (Kienast, 2020).

### To Take in Mind 4

Communication is the central instrument in a change as well as in and after a crisis. It is crucial that all stakeholders involved are informed, understand and implement the benefits of new actions. Furthermore, key player, executives and leaders should ensure that content matches and actions align with communicated content.

## Phase Five: Empower Broad-Based Action

In the fifth phase, it must be taken into account that the change may be associated with challenges and resistance (Kotter, 1995). The Covid-19 pandemic has several challenges. Since the beginning of the crisis, various stakeholder developed approaches for different recommendations and guidelines to get an orientation to meet the challenges. (none insists on completeness):

- AWMF published an S1 guideline in September about: SARS-CoV-2 infection in healthcare workers - the importance of RT-PCR testing (Janssens et al., 2020).
- The existing challenge is to estimate the needed number of beds and protective material. On the one hand, there are storage costs, on the other hand, a shortage of beds and material may make treatment and protection impossible. To avoid having to make costs based on uncertain forecasts, a tool for stockpiling PPE materials has been developed. (possibly not fully developed)) (Pfenninger & Kaisers, 2020)
- Halek et. al set out six points on what can be done in residential care facilities/nursing homes to meet the challenges:
    - Early contact with health authorities, communities and treating physicians
    - Discussion with relatives, caregivers and home advisory boards

    - A reduction in the size of the organizational units. Employees should not be deployed in different living areas.
    - The situation for protected areas remains unclear (accommodation decision). The teams have to develop individual solutions.
    - In cooperation with the competent authorities, the institutions have to consider opening up the facilities to families and develop concepts. It must be examined whether relatives may accompany their loved ones with protective equipment e.g. outside.
    - Residents with a risk of social deprivation must be identified and individual measures must be taken. Creative thinking is necessary and individual solutions are needed (Halek et al., 2020).
- Even so scientific societies relevant societies give clinical and ethical recommendations in "Decisions on the allocation of intensive care resources in the context of the COVID-19 pandemic" (Marckmann et al., 2020).
- Additionally a "Position Paper for the State of the Art Application of Respiratory Support in Patients with COVID-19" is published by German Respiratory Society (Glöckl et al., 2020; Pfeifer et al., 2020).
- Furthermore, a S1 guideline: Neurological manifestations in COVID-19, was developed (Berlit, 2020).

### To Take in Mind 5

Various challenges are to be expected during a change process, but these do not have to be addressed individually. Recommendations and guidelines of various professional associations bundle existing knowledge to support actions. Nevertheless, these are not regarded as comprehensive and final. It is crucial to discuss the challenges so that common and better solutions can be found in the future.

## Phase Six: Generate Short-Term Wins

Compared to challenges, already existing short-term successes, perhaps not yet fully developed but fundamentally applicable, are essential to sustain the benefits and the urgency of the desired change over time (Kotter, 1995). Short-term successes also occurred with regard to various instruments and measures according Covid-19. Some of these are listed here (none insists on completeness as well):

- **Coordinating emergency rooms:** First description of helpful processes in Handling of COVID-19 in the emergency department and targeted further treatment are published (Dodt & Schneider, 2020; Wennmann et al., 2020).
- **Short-term training:** A digital strategy was used to supplement nursing staff in the short term (Hahnen et al., 2020).
- **Caution instead of indulgence:** It is important to ensure occupational health and safety for hospital employees. In case of this patients with an unclear infection status or urgent suspicion of infection should be classified as infectious until proven otherwise (Schnitzbauer et al., 2020).
- **Implementation of a cohort ward:** Rabes et al. report on a special unit for Covid-19 patients that included structural and technical planning, infection control measures, the establishment of interprofessional structures and internal communication. This resulted in experience of optimal

care, with well-functioning processes, sufficient material, sufficient personnel and a very good interprofessional cooperation. High infection rates as well as psychological and physical stress did not occur (Rabes et al., 2020).

- **Care and diagnostics:** First studies also deal with recommendations in diagnostics and therapy for patients with COVID-19 in intensive care (Bein et al., 2020; Kluge et al., 2020a). Therefore, special treatment and technical ventilation in geriatric patients are discussed (Zeeh et al., 2020).
- **Dying Patients:** Münch et al. describe recommendations for dealing with dying patients, which have to be treated separately with regard to contact restrictions and visiting prohibitions to reduce the psychological stress of patients, their relatives and the hospital staff (Münch et al., 2020).
- **Covid-19 ambulances:** In order to relieve hospitals and general practitioners, Covid-19 ambulances were installed. A few descriptions of their construction and treatment are published, too (Bleckwenn, 2020).
- **Psychosocial support:** Reinhardt et al. develop a concept for psychosocial support during the COVID 19 pandemic. It consists of five components:
    - Patient hotline # WirsindfürSieda (translation: #We are there for you),
    - psychosocial support of inpatients of COVID-19 using Tablet #Zusammengegendiekrise (translation: #Together against the crisis),
    - psychiatric conciliar service,
    - psychosocial support for relatives,
    - Staff hotline #HelpTheHelper. (Reinhard et al., 2020)
- **Use of video consultations**: A German feasibility study and clinical application during the COVID 19 pandemic indicates the good practicability and acceptance of video consultations by psychotherapists and patients (Haun et al., 2020).

### To Take in Mind 6

Different short-term wins occur. It is important to show these in order to motivate a change process. Nonetheless, the listed studies point out that the results are based on initial observations and must be further developed and evaluated. In addition, there are certainly other smaller successes that are not listed here. Therefore, ethical discussion about limited resources, advance planning of care, weighing up infection prevention against the disadvantages of long-term social isolation receive more and more consideration (Sieber, 2020).

## Phase Seven: Never Let Up

Subsequently to phase six and the restrictions named there, also according to Kotter, in many cases the final goal achievement is announced too early and all related efforts are neglected. There is a danger that old processes will creep back in, as regulations that have been introduced are relaxed. By that, critics, as well as skeptics who could not be convinced of the necessity of change up to this point are given access to undermine what has been newly introduced (Kotter, 1995).

With regard to phase six, which clearly indicates that the initial successes should be pursued and expanded, the observed decrease in the urgency for change after the first wave is all the more regrettable. Also, a large part of the population has recognized the vulnerability of the system. Therefore, hardly any undertakings were made to construct a solution to organize a future social coexistence with the virus.

Everywhere, the adjustment processes concentrate on a return to 'pre-crisis normality' as quickly as possible (Kropp, 2020). This idea also ran through the health care system. Most health care institutions were switched back to "business as usual". It seems to be forgotten that Covid-19 cases still occur in hospitals, even though they are not always treated in the intensive care unit (Lambrecht & Baars, 2020).

Moreover, very often the vaccine development and positive forecasts for rapid approvals are communicated. But it is fully pushed into the background that a vaccine development against a new pathogen takes long. Even the vaccination against the H1N1 Influenza virus needed six months in the development, although in this only from a triple flu vaccine to a single vaccine had to happen. To develop a vaccine against SARS-CoV-2 virus there are new problems, with a virus that has only just appeared and cannot simply be adapted to existing vaccines. (Amanat & Krammer, 2020). Thanks to strong research activity, it is possible to use an approved vaccine in Germany since December 2020. Therefore, a great deal of skepticism about vaccination among the population has to take in consideration. Survey results indicate that willingness to be vaccinated shows a significant relationship with trust in government institutions, academia, and traditional media, as well as satisfaction with past Corona policies, refusal is associated with increased conspiracy mentality (Universität Heidelberg, 2020).

Besides research in vaccine there should be more knowledge building in treatment and care models for Covid-19 patients as well as necessary organizational framework conditions. To achieve these framework conditions, regional care and research networks must be established, controlled by university medicine. This also must provide additional laboratory capacity and technical facilities. The inpatient and outpatient sectors must be networked, the public health service must be strengthened, digitization must be expanded, basic research must be expanded both nationally and internationally, and the existing per-case flat rate system in Germany must be expanded (Leopoldina - Nationale Akademie der Wissenschaften, 2020).

Talevi et al. demand a new psychological crisis intervention model (Talevi et al., 2020). Vindegaard and Benros also stress that neuropsychiatric consequences and the indirect effects on mental health is highly needed to improve treatment, mental health care planning and for preventive measures during potential subsequent pandemics (Vindegaard & Benros, 2020). Therefore, the expansion of digitization in Germany is of great importance for diagnosis, therapy as well as prevention (Klös, 2020) in situations where personal contacts and patient visits as well as patient transportation are limited.

In addition to focal developments within the health care system, changes in the civic must be taken into account. Social sciences are making proposals for "multi resilience" based on "basic robustness". It follows the idea of making societies more capable of reacting and solving problems in completely different crisis contexts (Fathi, 2020). In close connection, social changes of mutuality and understanding of social roles play a major role (Kortmann & Schulze, 2020). In nursing, but also in medicine, many positions are occupied by women. Part-time work has also increased, in hospital medical service from 8% in 2009 to 36% in 2019 (Augurzky & Schmidt, 2020). The Covid-19 pandemic has shown that flexible working time models and a good work-life balance are more important than ever (Kortmann & Schulze, 2020).

The Technical University of Munich has provided a variety of ideas for sustainable action according to Covid-19, which includes various focal points. It becomes clear that a sustainable change has to take place in cooperation between science, economy, media and politics. Basic research, digitization, medicine and health in the broader sense, education and change in the world of work as well. In addition to national opportunities for improvement, international cooperation is considered important. The German government will continue to pursue this after the pandemic (afp/aerzteblatt.de, 2020).

## To Take in Mind 7

It is crucial not to give too much weight to small successes in order to distract from bigger challenges ahead. The change in the German healthcare system must be tackled in a sustainable manner. The Covid-19 crisis not only requires the development of a suitable vaccine. It calls for comprehensive and sustainable developments in supply and organizational/institutional structures, political cooperation and decision-making, psychological strengthening of the civilian population and digitization.

## Phase Eight: Incorporate Changes Into Culture

According to Kotter, it can only be assumed that a change is implemented in a corporate culture if the next generation of top management really does personify the new approach. Otherwise decisions are made against the change (Kotter, 1995).Considering that Covid-19 requires multiple changes, it must be kept in mind that this comprehensive change takes time. So, necessary changes can only be expected in small steps and along various political terms. That in mind, it is gratifying to see that some changes have already been incorporated into various corporate cultures in the healthcare sector, which are also listed here. There is no claim to completeness. But it should be emphasized that cultural change is possible.

1. **OWM- networks:** With the concept of so-called "One Minute Wonder", learning content is to be conveyed via learning boards with short waiting times. In 2016 these were tested in a German intensive care unit and found to be effective. This concept was adopted for all intensive care units in the hospital and is supervised by authorized persons. Such learning boards were also created for the treatment and care of patients with Covid-19. These are used, constantly updated and also made available to other hospitals via an online platform. (*OMW-Netzwerk* I, 2020)
2. **Distance Learning:** Distance learning was introduced during the first lockdown in the training of paramedics. It was recognized that this can serve not only as a secondary replacement for face-to-face training, but that a combination of face-to-face and distance learning can help to create transparency and improve the quality of training. (Regener et al., 2020)
3. **New links within German hospital networks:** A hospital network is dependent on environmental input factors. The Covid-19 pandemic has led to new linkages in bureaucratically shaped hospital structures. This helps to establish so-called economized structures and further organizational development. (Wolf & Molzberger, 2021)
4. **Interprofessional task forces**: To translate the generally applicable political decisions to the various health care institutions cross-department and interprofessional task forces in individual crisis staff have to be set up (Silies et al., 2020). Schmitz et al. report about professional crisis management group of hospitals in Germany and Switzerland three positive aspects: 1. The willingness to cooperate under crisis conditions, 2. The possibility of (unexpected) rapid changes and 3. The opportunity for agile action. They explain these by the open-minded adjustment of the various parties. And the absence of the suspicion of merely wanting to protect their own interests. (Schmitz et al., 2020)
5. **Mandatory report of intensive care beds:** The government has introduced a mandatory report for hospitals on the number of intensive care beds available. This continues to exist and is being developed further. For example, it is now possible to view time series. (DIVI, 2020a)

6. **National and Global Health Think Tanks:** National Global Health Think Tanks are not yet as well developed in Germany as in other countries. The Institute for Global Health Berlin (IGGB) was founded in 2017 as an academic think tank and knowledge platform in Berlin. Here, transnational health problems, determinants and solutions at the interfaces between politics, science and society are dealt with against the background of promoting interdisciplinary cooperation (Bonk et al., 2020). The Covid-19 pandemic has shown that this form of science is important to address global health problems. Therefore, more work like this should be done in Germany as well.

### To Take in Mind 8

It becomes clear that new forms of collaboration, cooperation, learning and knowledge transfer found their way to different institutions already. Moreover, it is essential that necessary changes within the German healthcare system are focused, supported and pursued across all parties.

## CONCLUSION

Along Kotter`s model of change it becomes obvious that a country's health system and structures of social coexistence are closely interrelated. Due to nationalization, management issues in the German health care system are always linked to political decisions. It must be taken into account that these decisions should be taken evidence-based. Furthermore, it has to be possible to implement these decisions in a simple and targeted manner in everyday practice across professional groups, which are understood and accepted by those affected, i.e. the civilian population. It should also be borne in mind that hcws are also part of the civilian population cause, there is a lack of understanding, where there are rules for the civilian population that are softened for hcws. Health protection measures and human working conditions are indisputable to achieve and maintain. Where support through digitization and technical aids is possible, this should be used. It is crucial that adapted learning formats lead to a safe handling of these aids by employees.

An overall understanding that Covid-19 causes irreversible changes is necessary. Efforts should therefore be invested early on in solutions that embrace these changes rather than in solutions that convulsively try to restore the pre-pandemic state. Communication and cooperation is necessary across professional groups, sectors and hierarchies. In addition to that, every change needs time and experience. Experience was simply not available at the beginning of the pandemic. This led to trial-and-error scheme. It is crucial to evaluate these experiences, and, if they had shown or promise some advantages, adapt them. This requires acceptance that an idea may not develop as positively as it seemed at the beginning. In addition, developments, which have often been ignored in the past must be regarded. This means that a health care system is based on more factors than the medical and economical aspects. The crisis clearly shows that nursing care is relevant to the system, too. Nursing science and professional associations in the field of nursing science must assert their claims for change and strengthen nursing science (Stemmer et al., 2020). Wirth and Hülsken-Giesler call for new forms of management in nursing that not only react to market-changing innovations, but also understand the pandemic as a learning opportunity, rethink structural support and further development of nursing care (Wirth & Hülsken-Giesler, 2020).

In this context the Federal Center for Health Education is a specialized authority in the portfolio of the Federal Ministry of Health and points out the following:

"Public Health includes all organized, multidisciplinary and multiprofessional approaches in disease prevention, health promotion, disease control, disease management, rehabilitation and care. Special emphasis is placed on the management and evaluation of collective health problems and the design of care with the aim of developing and controlling a health care system that offers the entire population (or larger subpopulations) the best possible health care that meets their needs - using culturally and medically appropriate, effective and ethically and economically justifiable means." (Franzkowiak, 2015)

In case of this, it can be summarized that Kotter's model offers a good opportunity to implement changes in a structured and systematic way even in times of a pandemic. Concerning the health care system in German-speaking countries, it is fundamental that change decisions are made within the system. This requires an overarching perspective of needs-based patient care and the involvement and participation of all stakeholders. It applies to both the overall management and the management of the various health care institutions. Medical, nursing and other service providers must work together on an (inter-)professional, (inter-)setting and (inter-)sectoral basis to create a functioning system. This must be supported by direct and targeted communication, technology and other innovations. A sensible balance between ethical and economic aspects must be struck, so that efficiency and effectiveness can be achieved not only on the basis of economic indicators but above all in positive emotions, quality of life and health. Every political term should focus on the health of the German population. In order for evidence-based decisions to be made, this is also a call for science to provide tractable research results. To support this change in the long term, research with regard to varying focal points as well as interdisciplinary research approaches are necessary. A necessary personnel development and a suitable skill grade can be observed and analyzed from the perspective of nursing science, medicine, human resources and organizational science. An exchange and accumulation of different perspectives create even greater benefits under systems theory teachings. Necessary communication patterns are to be developed in cooperation with psychologists, linguists and experts from the professional groups concerned. Further research should be focusing the civil population and transparent exchanges of political decisions as well as their effect on the general sentiment of the civil population.

## REFERENCES

(2020, May 27). *Coronavirus-Pandemie: medizinische Versorgung und patientennahe Forschung in einem adaptiven gesundheitssystem: 4. Ad-hoc Stellungnahme.* Leopoldina - Nationale Akademie der Wissenschaften. https://www.leopoldina.org/uploads/tx_leopublication/2020_05_27_Stellungnahme_Corona_Gesundheitssystem.pdf

afp/aerzteblatt.de. (2020, October 7). *Bundesregierung will internationale Zusammenarbeit in Gesundheitsfragen stärken* [Press release]. https://www.aerzteblatt.de/nachrichten/117189/Bundesregierung-will-internationale-Zusammenarbeit-in-Gesundheitsfragen-staerken

Amanat, F., & Krammer, F. (2020). Sars-CoV-2 Vaccines: Status Report. *Immunity, 52*(4), 583–589. https://doi.org/10.1016/j.immuni.2020.03.007

Arndt, M. (2020). *Ärzteschaft und Pflege „dürfen" jetzt länger arbeiten.* https://ku-gesundheitsmanagement.de/2020/06/12/aerzteschaft-und-pflege-duerfen-jetzt-laenger-arbeiten/

Arnold, N. (2020). *Wissenschaftliche Politikberatung zur gesundheitlichen Bewältigung der Corona-Pandemie. Analysen & Argumente* (Vol. 394). Konrad-Adenauer-Stiftung.

Augurzky, B., & Schmidt, C. M. (2020). *Nach Corona: Jetzt stabile Krankenhausstrukturenschaffen* (RWI Positionen No. 79). https://www.econstor.eu/bitstream/10419/225077/1/1735634603.pdf

Begerow, A., Michaelis, U., & Gaidys, U. (2020). Wahrnehmungen von Pflegenden im Bereich der Intensivpflege während der COVID-19-Pandemie. *Pflege, 33*(4), 229–236. https://doi.org/10.1024/1012-5302/a000744

Bein, B., Bachmann, M., Huggett, S., & Wegermann, P. (2020). SARS-CoV-2/COVID-19: Empfehlungen zu Diagnostik und Therapie [SARS CoV-2/COVID-19: Evidence-Based Recommendation on Diagnosis and Therapy]. *Anästhesiologie, Intensivmedizin, Notfallmedizin, Schmerztherapie, 55*(4), 257–265. https://doi.org/10.1055/a-1146-8674

Berliner Bildungscampus für Gesundheitsberufe gGmbH. (2020, March 29). *CORONA -Schulungskonzepte für die pflege in der krisensituation.* Berlin. https://www.bildungscampus-berlin.de/fileadmin/content/news/downloads/Schulungskonzept_Corona_BBG.pdf

Berlit, P. (2020). S1-Leitlinie: Neurologische Manifestationen bei COVID-19. *DGNeurologie, 3*(6), 495–519. doi:10.100742451-020-00254-x

Biermann, K., & Gutensohn, D. (2020, April 1). Ärzte und Pfleger warnen vor Zwangsarbeit. *ZEIT ONLINE GmbH.* https://www.zeit.de/arbeit/2020-04/corona-krise-aerzte-pflegekraefte-arbeit-verpflichtung-armin-laschet

Bleckwenn, M. (2020). Behandlung von Patienten in Corona-Ambulanzen: COVID-19-Pandemie [Treatment of patients in a corona ambulance]. *MMW Fortschritte der Medizin, 162*(9), 54–56. https://doi.org/10.1007/s15006-020-0479-7

Bodenheimer, M., & Leidenberger, J. (2020). COVID-19 as a window of opportunity for sustainability transitions? Narratives and communication strategies beyond the pandemic. *Sustainability: Science, Practice and Policy, 16*(1), 61–66. doi:10.1080/15487733.2020.1766318

Bonk, M., Döring, O., & Ulrichs, T. (2020). Global Health Think Tanks – Think Tanks im Bereich der Globalen Gesundheit. In D. Matusiewicz (Ed.), FOM-Edition. Think tanks im gesundheitswesen: Deutsche denkfabriken und ihre (pp. 307–324). Gabler. https://doi.org/10.1007/978-3-658-29728-2_25

Breyton, R., & Naber, I. (2020, November 3). Berliner Polizeipräsidentin: „Auf Corona-Demos auch Menschen, die mit Messern bewaffnet sind". *WELT.* https://www.welt.de/politik/deutschland/plus219211512/Berliner-Polizeipraesidentin-Auf-Corona-Demos-auch-Menschen-die-mit-Messern-bewaffnet-sind.html?cid=onsite.onsitesearch#Comments

Cui, J., Li, F., & Shi, Z. L. (2019). *Origin and evolution of pathogenic coronaviruses.* doi:10.103841579-018-0118-9

DGIIN. (2020, May 25). *Intensivpflege als tragende Säule bei der Pandemie-Bewältigung Arbeitsbedingungen in der Intensivpflege prekärer denn je – DGIIN veröffentlicht Stellungnahme* [Press release]. https://dgiin.de/allgemeines/pressemitteilungen/pm-leser/intensivpflege-als-tragende-saeule-bei-der-pandemie-bewaeltigung-arbeitsbedingungen-in-der-intensivpflege-prekaerer-denn-je.html

Dinges, S. (2020). Corona und die Alten – um wen sorgen wir uns wirklich? In W. Kröll, J. Platzer, H.-W. Ruckenbauer, & W. Schaupp (Eds.), *Die Corona-Pandemie* (pp. 69–84). Nomos Verlagsgesellschaft mbH & Co. KG. doi:10.5771/9783748910589-69

DIVI. (2020a). *DIVI Intensivregister*. https://www.intensivregister.de/#/index

DIVI. (2020b). *Handlungsempfehlungen der DIVI zu COVID-19*. https://www.divi.de/register/aktuelle-informationen

Dodt, C., & Schneider, N. (2020). Notfallmedizinische und intensivmedizinische Aspekte von COVID-19-Infektionen [Emergency and intensive care medicine aspects of COVID-19 infections]. *Der Radiologe*, *60*(10), 899–907. https://doi.org/10.1007/s00117-020-00742-x

Dorn, F., Fuest, C., Gstrein, D., Peichl, A., & Stöckli, M. (2020, October 12). *Corona-Infektionen und die Dunkelziffer: Vergleichen wir Äpfel mit Birnen?* ifo Institut – Leibniz-Institut für Wirtschaftsforschung an der Universität München e.V. https://www.nordthueringen.de/_daten/mm_objekte/2020/10/607552_1012_97493801.pdf

Eufinger, A. (2020). Die COVID-19-Pandemie: Arbeitsrecht im Krankenhaus in bewegten Zeiten. *Medizinrecht: MedR*, 1–8. doi:10.100700350-020-5559-2

Fathi, K. (2020). Die multi-resiliente Gesellschaft: Orientierungspunkte für die Corona-Krise und darüber hinaus. *Forschungsjournal Soziale Bewegungen*, *33*(1), 22–36. https://doi.org/10.1515/fjsb-2020-0004

Franzkowiak, P. (2015). *Gesundheitswissenschaften / Public Health*. https://www.leitbegriffe.bzga.de/alphabetisches-verzeichnis/gesundheitswissenschaften-public-health/ https://doi.org/10.17623/BZGA:224-I061-1.0

German Hospital Association. (2020a, September 17). *DKG zum Welttag der Patientensicherheit: Ohne engagierte kompetente Mitarbeiterinnen und Mitarbeiter ist Versorgung nicht möglich* [Press release]. https://www.dkgev.de/dkg/presse/details/ohne-engagierte-kompetente-mitarbeiterinnen-und-mitarbeiter-ist-versorgung-nicht-moeglich/

German Hospital Association. (2020b, October 15). *DKG zu steigenden Infektionszahlen: Krankenhäuser blicken mit Sorge auf die steigende Zahl an Neuinfektionen* [Press release]. https://www.dkgev.de/dkg/presse/details/krankenhaeuser-blicken-mit-sorge-auf-die-steigende-zahl-an-neuinfektionen/

Glöckl, R., Buhr-Schinner, H., Koczulla, A. R., Schipmann, R., Schultz, K., Spielmanns, M., Stenzel, N., & Dewey, S. (2020). Recommendations from the German Respiratory Society for Pulmonary Rehabilitation in Patients with COVID-19. *Pneumologie (Stuttgart, Germany)*, *74*(8). https://doi.org/10.1055/a-1193-9315

Gräuler, V. (2020). *Organisation einer strukturierten Personalführung im Pandemiefall: Crashkurs Covid-19*. WWU Münster; UKM Trainingszentrum. https://www.divi.de/joomlatools-files/docman-files/publikationen/covid-19-dokumente/Organisation%20Personalnachf%C3%BChrung_final.pdf

Hahnen, D., Reichartz, P., Heßling, C., & Markus, S. (2020). Schulentwicklung in Zeiten der Pandemie: Wie eine Berufsfachschule für den Rettungsdienst die Krise als Chance zur Weiterentwicklung nutzt. *Pflegewissenschaft, Sonderausgabe: Die Corona-Pandemie,* (April), 165–169.

Halek, M., Reuther, S., & Schmidt, J. (2020). Herausforderungen für die pflegerische Versorgung in der stationären Altenhilfe. *MMW Fortschr Med, 162*(9), 51–53.

Hans Böckler Foundation. (2020). *Arbeitsbedingungen in der Pflege.* https://www.boeckler.de/de/auf-einen-blick-17945-zahlen-und-studien-zum-pflegenotstand-und-wege-hinaus-17962.htm

Haslbeck, K., Schwarz, K., Hohlfeld, J. M., Seume, J. R., & Koch, W. (2010). Submicron droplet formation in the human lung. *Journal of Aerosol Science, 41*(5), 429–438. https://doi.org/10.1016/j.jaerosci.2010.02.010

Hasseler, M., & Hartleb, B. (n.d.). Stationäre Langzeitpflege unter Covid-19 Bedingungen –: ein reflektiert-kritischer Blick auf die derzeitige Situation und zukünftige Entwicklungen. Pflege in Zeiten der Pandemie.

Hasseler, M., Krebs, S., & Lietz, A. L. (2020). Vertrauens- und kompetenzbasiertes Delegationsmodell in Zeiten von Corona. *Pflegewissenschaft (Sonderausgabe: Die Corona-Pandemie),* 109-111.

Hasseler, M., Lietz, A. L., & Krebs, S. (2020). Delegation im Krisenfall: Entscheidungen erleichtern. *Pflege Zeitschrift*, 6.

Haun, M. W., Hoffmann, M., Tönnies, J., Dinger, U., Hartmann, M., & Friederich, H.-C. (2020). Videokonsultationen durch Psychotherapeuten in Zeiten der COVID-19-Pandemie: Wirksamkeit, Gestaltung des Settings und erste Erfahrungen aus einer Machbarkeitsstudie sowie mit dem Routineangebot im Krankenhaus [Realtime video consultations by psychotherapists in times of the COVID-19 pandemic]. *Psychotherapeut*, 1–6. doi:10.100700278-020-00438-6

Hermes, C., & Ochmann, T. (2020). Nursing Division on the current intensive care situation in Germany: Working group of the Nursing Division of the German Society of Medical Intensive Care and Emergency Medicine (DGIIN). *Medizinische Klinik, Intensivmedizin und Notfallmedizin, 115*(6). https://doi.org/10.1007/s00063-020-00705-z

Hollaus, S. (2020). *Pflege-Berufsaussteiger kommen in der Corona-Krise zurück – und nun? - Marktforschung.* https://newsroom.psyma.com/de/themen/pflegemarktforschung/pflege-berufsaussteiger-kommen-in-der-corona-krise-zurueck-und-nun/

Hower, K. I., Pförtner, T.-K., & Pfaff, H. (2020). *Pflegerische Versorgung in Zeiten von Corona -Drohender Systemkollaps oder normaler Wahnsinn? Wissenschaftliche Studie zu Herausforderungen und Belastungen aus der Sichtweise von Leitungskräften.* https://kups.ub.uni-koeln.de/11201/1/Pflegerische%20Versorgung%20in%20Zeiten%20von%20Corona_Ergebnisbericht.pdf

ifo Institut. (2020a). *Corona-Krise: Anzahl der Kurzarbeiter in Deutschland nach Sektoren im Juli 2020* [Press release]. https://www.ifo.de/node/57307

ifo Institut. (2020b). *Sonderfragen im 2. Quartal 2020: Homeoffice und Digitalisierung unter Corona.* https://www.ifo.de/personalleiterbefragung/202008-q2

Jacobs, K., Kuhlmey, A., Greß, S., Klauber, J., & Schwinger, A. (2020). *Pflege-Report 2019*. Springer Berlin Heidelberg. doi:10.1007/978-3-662-58935-9

Janssens, U., Schlitt, A., Hein, A., Salzberger, B., Grill, E., Kaduszkiewicz, H., Platz, T., Rossaint, R., Böttiger, B. W., Dietz, A., Borucki, K., Fickenscher, H., Al-Nawas, B., Marini, A., Kersten, A., & Stemmer, R. (2020). *SARS-CoV-2 Infektion bei Mitarbeiterinnen und Mitarbeitern im Gesundheitswesen – Bedeutung der RT-PCR Testung*. https://www.awmf.org/uploads/tx_szleitlinien/040-015l_S1_SARS-CoV-2-Infektion-im-Gesundheitswesen%E2%80%93RT-PCR_2020-09_2.pdf

Ji, Y., Qian, H., Ye, J., & Zheng, X. (2018). The impact of ambient humidity on the evaporation and dispersion of exhaled breathing droplets: A numerical investigation. *Journal of Aerosol Science, 115*, 164–172. https://doi.org/10.1016/j.jaerosci.2017.10.009

Kienast, V. (2020). Zweifel & Angst. *Procare: das forbildungsmagazin fur pflegeberufe, 25*(4), 1. doi:10.100700735-020-1183-7

Klös, H.-P. (2020). *Nach dem Corona-Schock: Digitalisierungspotenziale für Deutschland* (IW-Policy Paper 14/2020). https://www.econstor.eu/handle/10419/219033

Kluge, S., Janssens, U., Welte, T., Weber-Carstens, S., Marx, G., & Karagiannidis, C. (2020a). Empfehlungen zur intensivmedizinischen Therapie von Patienten mit COVID-19 [Recommendations for critically ill patients with COVID-19]. *Medizinische Klinik, Intensivmedizin und Notfallmedizin, 115*(3), 175–177. https://doi.org/10.1007/s00063-020-00674-3

Kluge, S., Janssens, U., Welte, T., Weber-Carstens, S., Marx, G., & Karagiannidis, C. (2020b). Empfehlungen zur intensivmedizinischen Therapie von Patienten mit COVID-19 [Recommendations for critically ill patients with COVID-19]. *Medizinische Klinik, Intensivmedizin und Notfallmedizin.* Advance online publication. doi:10.100700063-020-00674-3

Kortmann, B., & Schulze, G. G. (2020). *Jenseits von Corona: Unsere Welt nach der Pandemie - Perspektiven aus der Wissenschaft. X-Texte zu Kultur und Gesellschaft.* Transcipt Verlag.

Kotter, J. P. (1995). Leading Change: Why Tranformation Efforts Fail. *Harvard Business Review, 73*(2), 59–67.

Kotter, J. P. (2015). *Leading change: Wie Sie Ihr Unternehmen in acht Schritten erfolgreich verändern* (W. Seidenschwarz, Trans.). Vahlen.

Kropp, C. (2020). *Pandemien, globaler Umweltwandel und 'smarte' Risikopolitik: Chancen für Wandel?* Advance online publication. doi:10.17879/SUN-2020-2943

Lambrecht, O., & Baars, C. (2020, October 14). Corona-Pandemie: Mehr Covid-19-Patienten in Kliniken. *Tagesschau.De*. https://www.tagesschau.de/inland/corona-kliniken-107.html

Lesch, W., & Schütt, A. (2017). *Gesundheitsforschung kommunizieren, Stakeholder Engagement gestalten.* Medizinisch Wissenschaftliche Verlagsgesellschaft. doi:10.32745/9783954663637

Liu, L., Li, Y., Nielsen, P. V., Wei, J., & Jensen, R. L. (2017). Short-range airborne transmission of expiratory droplets between two people. *Indoor Air, 27*(2). https://doi.org/10.1111/ina.12314

Marckmann, G., Neitzke, G., Schildmann, J., Michalsen, A., Dutzmann, J., Hartog, C., Jöbges, S., Knochel, K., Michels, G., Pin, M., Riessen, R., Rogge, A., Taupitz, J., & Janssens, U. (2020). Decisions on the allocation of intensive care resources in the context of the COVID-19 pandemic: Clinical and ethical recommendations of DIVI, DGINA, DGAI, DGIIN, DGNI, DGP, DGP and AEM. German version. *Medizinische Klinik, Intensivmedizin und Notfallmedizin, 115*(6). https://doi.org/10.1007/s00063-020-00708-w

Millich, N. (2020, April 6). *Wie das Coronavirus die Pflege beeinflusst.* https://www.bibliomed-pflege.de/news/40233-wie-das-coronavirus-die-pflege-beeinflusst

Mulfinger, N., Lampl, J., Dinkel, A., Weidner, K., Beutel, M. E., Jarczok, M. N., Hildenbrand, G., Kruse, J., Seifried-Dübon, T., Junne, F., Beschoner, P., & Gündel, H. (2020). Psychische Belastungen durch Epidemien bei Beschäftigten im Gesundheitswesen und Implikationen für die Bewältigung der Corona-Krise: Eine Literaturübersicht [Psychological stress caused by epidemics among health care workers and implications for coping with the corona crisis: a literature review]. *Zeitschrift für Psychosomatische Medizin und Psychotherapie, 66*(3), 220–242. https://doi.org/10.13109/zptm.2020.66.3.220

Münch, U. (2020). Wenn dem Bundesstaat die Stunde der Exekutive schlägt: der deutsche (Exekutiv-) Föderalismus in Zeiten der Coronakrise. In *Jahrbuch des Föderalismus 2020* (pp. 207–226). Nomos Verlagsgesellschaft mbH & Co. KG. doi:10.5771/9783748910817-207

Münch, U., Müller, H., Deffner, T., von, S. A., Kern, M., Kiepke-Ziemes, S., & Radbruch, L. (2020). Recommendations for the support of suffering, severely ill, dying or grieving persons in the corona pandemic from a palliative care perspective: Recommendations of the German Society for Palliative Medicine (DGP), the German Interdisciplinary Association for Intensive and Emergency Medicine (DIVI), the Federal Association for Grief Counseling (BVT), the Working Group for Psycho-oncology in the German Cancer Society, the German Association for Social Work in the Healthcare System (DVSG) and the German Association for Systemic Therapy, Counseling and Family Therapy (DGSF). *Schmerz (Berlin, Germany), 34*(4). doi:10.100700482-020-00483-9

OMW-Netzwerk. (2020, October 20). https://omw.hdz-nrw.de/omw-netzwerk.html

Online-Portal für professionell Pflegende. (2020, October 29). *Arbeiten trotz Corona-Infektion - DBfK lehnt RKI-Empfehlung grundsätzlich ab.* https://www.bibliomed-pflege.de/news/dbfk-lehnt-rki-empfehlung-grundsaetzlich-ab

Pfeifer, M., Ewig, S., Voshaar, T., Randerath, W., Bauer, T., Geiseler, J., Dellweg, D., Westhoff, M., Windisch, W., Schönhofer, B., Kluge, S., & Lepper, P. M. (2020). Positionspapier zur praktischen Umsetzung der apparativen Differenzialtherapie der akuten respiratorischen Insuffizienz bei COVID-19 [Position Paper for the State of the Art Application of Respiratory Support in Patients with COVID-19 - German Respiratory Society]. *Pneumologie (Stuttgart, Germany), 74*(6), 337–357. https://doi.org/10.1055/a-1157-9976

Pfenninger, E. G., & Kaisers, U. X. (2020). Bevorratung persönlicher Schutzausrüstung in Kliniken zur Vorbereitung auf eine Pandemie [Provisioning of personal protective equipment in hospitals in preparation for a pandemic]. *Der Anaesthesist.* Advance online publication. doi:10.100700101-020-00843-1

Rabes, C., Bläuer, C., Büche, V., Gisler Ries, I., Knüppel Lauener, S., Kuehl, R., Osthoff, M., Pfeiffer, M., Probst, S., Todorov, V., & Panfil, E.-M. (2020). Zwischen Traum und Trauma - Aufbau und Betrieb einer Kohortenstation für Patient_innen mit COVID-19 in einem Akutspital. *Pflege, 33*(4), 247–255. https://doi.org/10.1024/1012-5302/a000746

Regener, H., Cranshaw, A., & Hofmann, K. (2020). Corona-Pandemie:Wie hat sich die rettungsdienstliche Bildung verändert? *Rettungsdienst, 43*(6), 534–539. https://backend.paraplegie.ch/sites/default/files/2020-07/distance_learning_waehrend_corona._rettungsdienst_sk_06_2020.pdf

Reinhard, M. A., Burkhardt, G., Grosse-Wentrup, F., Eser-Valerie, D., Mumm, F. H. A., & Barniko, B.-O. (2020). Psychosoziale Unterstützung während der COVID-19-Pandemie: interdisziplinäres Versorgungskonzept an einem Universitätsklinikum. *Der Nervenarzt,* 1–7. doi:10.100700115-020-01014-8

RKI. (2020, November 13). *Täglicher Lagebericht des RKI zur Coronavirus-Krankheit-2019 (Covid-19).* https://www.rki.de/DE/Content/InfAZ/N/Neuartiges_Coronavirus/Situationsberichte/Nov_2020/2020-11-13-de.pdf?__blob=publicationFile

Robert-Koch-Institut. (2020a). *Epidemiologischer Steckbrief zu SARS-CoV-2 und COVID-19.* https://www.rki.de/DE/Content/InfAZ/N/Neuartiges_Coronavirus/Steckbrief.html

Robert-Koch-Institut. (2020b, May 13). *Optionen zur getrennten Versorgung von COVID-19-Fällen, Verdachtsfällen und anderen Patienten im stationären Bereich* [Press release]. https://www.rki.de/DE/Content/InfAZ/N/Neuartiges_Coronavirus/Getrennte_Patientenversorg_stationaer.html

Roigk, P., & Becker, C. (2020). Umsetzung einer Empfehlung des Robert-Koch-Institutes im Kontext der Corona-Pandemie in die Strukturen und Prozesse eines Krankenhauses - Ein Praxisbericht. *Pflegewissenschaft,* 47–48.

Roth, R. (2020). *Demokratie und Bürgerbeteiligung in Zeiten von COVID-19* (Opuscula, 141). https://nbn-resolving.org/urn:nbn:de:0168-ssoar-68889-1

RWI - Leibniz-Institut für Wirtschaftsforschung e. V. (2020, March 25). *Unstatistik - Corona-Pandemie: Statistische Konzepte und ihre Grenzen* [Press release]. https://www.rwi-essen.de/unstatistik/101/

Schäfer, C. (2020). Wenn nicht jetzt, wann dann? *Dialyse Aktuell, 24*(4), 145. doi:10.1055/a-1076-4335

Schmitz, C., Zwahlen, M., & Berchtold, P. (2020). Management und Medizin post-Corona. *Bulletin Des Médecins Suisses.* Advance online publication. doi:10.4414/bms.2020.19137

Schnitzbauer, A. A., Kempf, V. A. J., Hack, D., Ciesek, S., Meier, S., Vehreschild, M. J. G. T., Wicker, S., Kippke, U., Graf, J., & Marzi, I. (2020). SARS-CoV-2/COVID-19: Systematischer Review zu Anforderungen an die persönliche Schutzausrüstung bei primärem Patientenkontakt und Strukturierung des Operationsbereiches [SARS-CoV-2/COVID-19: systematic review of requirements for personal protective equipment in primary patient contact and organization of the operating area]. *Der Chirurg; Zeitschrift fur alle Gebiete der operativen Medizen, 91*(7), 576–585. doi:10.100700104-020-01229-0

Sieber, C. (2020). COVID-19 aus Sicht der Geriatrie [COVID-19: a geriatric point-of-view]. *Deutsche medizinische Wochenschrift, 145*(15), 1039–1043. doi:10.1055/a-1164-4261

Silies, K., Schley, A., Sill, J., Fleischer, S., Müller, M., & Balzer, K. (2020). Die COVID-19-Pandemie im akutstationären Setting aus Sicht von Führungspersonen und Hygienefachkräften in der Pflege. *Pflege, 33*(5), 289–298. https://doi.org/10.1024/1012-5302/a000756

Simhofer, D. (2020). Arbeiten am Limit. *Psychopraxis. Neuropraxis, 23*(3), 107–109. doi:10.100700739-020-00645-5

Stemmer, R., Sirsch, E., Büker, C., Holle, B., & Köpke, S. (2020). COVID-19 und die Rolle der Pflege(wissenschaft). *Pflegewissenschaft, Sonderausgabe: Die Corona-Pandemie,* (April), 116–117.

tagesschau. (2020, May 6). Bund überlässt Ländern die Verantwortung bei Corona-Lockerungen. *Tagesschau.De*. https://www.tagesschau.de/inland/merkel-ministerpraesidenten-lockerungen-107.html

tagesschau.de. (2020). *Corona-Gästelisten: Lokale wollen nicht selbst kontrollieren.* tagesschau.de. https://www.tagesschau.de/inland/kontrollen-restaurants-corona-101.html

Talevi, D., Socci, V., Carai, M., Carnaghi, G., Faleri, S., Trebbi, E., Di Bernardo, A., Capelli, F., & Pacitti, F. (2020). Mental health outcomes of the CoViD-19 pandemic. *Rivista di Psichiatria, 55*(3), 137–144. https://doi.org/10.1708/3382.33569

Universität Heidelberg. (2020, December 21). *Angst vor Corona und Impfskepsis: Nr. 115/2020* [Press release]. https://www.uni-heidelberg.de/de/newsroom/angst-vor-corona-und-impfskepsis

Vindegaard, N., & Benros, M. E. (2020). COVID-19 pandemic and mental health consequences: Systematic review of the current evidence. *Brain, Behavior, and Immunity, 89*. doi:10.1016/j.bbi.2020.05.048

vom Lehn, B. (2020, October 15). *Erstmals arbeiten Pflegekräfte mit Corona-Infektion*. pflege-online.de. https://www.pflegen-online.de/erstmals-arbeiten-pflegekraefte-mit-corona-infektion

Watzka, K. (2018). *Fachkräftemangel in der Pflege: Kritische Situationsbewertung und Skizzierung einer Handlungsalternative*. Jena contributions to economic research: Jahrgang 2018, Heft 2. Ernst-Abbe-Hochschule Fachbereich Betriebswirtschaft. http://hdl.handle.net/10419/181866

Wennmann, D. O., Dlugos, C. P., Hofschröer, A., Hennies, M., Kühn, J., Hafezi, W., Kampmeier, S., Mellmann, A., Triphaus, S., Sackarnd, J., Tepasse, P., Keller, M., van Aken, H., Pavenstädt, H., & Kümpers, P. (2020). Umgang mit COVID-19 in der Notaufnahme: Erfahrungsbericht der interdisziplinären Notaufnahme des Universitätsklinikums Münster [Handling of COVID-19 in the emergency department: Field report of the emergency ward of the University Hospital Münster]. *Medizinische Klinik, Intensivmedizin und Notfallmedizin, 115*(5), 380–387. https://doi.org/10.1007/s00063-020-00693-0

Wirth, L. M., & Hülsken-Giesler, M. (2020). Wenn nicht jetzt, wann dann? *Pflegewissenschaft, Sonderausgabe: Die Corona-Pandemie,* (April), 118–120.

Wirtz, D. C., & Stöckle, U. (2020). Künftige Versorgungsstrukturen in Deutschland: Gibt es Lehren aus der Corona-Pandemie? *Zeitschrift fur Orthopadie und Unfallchirurgie, 158*(2), 163–164. https://doi.org/10.1055/a-0876-4652

Wolf, J., & Molzberger, K. (2021). Das Krankenhaus als anpassungsfähiges Netzwerkarrangement? In C. Stegbauer & I. Clemens (Eds.), Corona-netzwerke - Gesellschaft im zeichen des virus (pp. 139–150). VS Verlag fur Sozialwisse., https://doi.org/10.1007/978-3-658-31394-4_14.

Wolf-Ostermann, K., Rothgang, H., Domhoff, D., Friedrich, A.-C., Heinze, F., Preuß, B., Schmidt, A., Seibert, K., & Stolle, C. (2020). *Zur Situation der Langzeitpflege in Deutschland während der Corona-Pandemie. Ergebnisse einer Online-Befragung in Einrichtungen der (teil)stationären und ambulanten Langzeitpflege.* doi:10.26092/ELIB/116

Zeeh, J., Memm, K., Heppner, H.-J., & Kwetkat, A. (2020). Beatmung geriatrischer Patienten— Ein ethisches Dilemma? Corona-Pandemie 2020. *MMW Fortschritte der Medizin*, *162*(9), 40–45. https://doi.org/10.1007/s15006-020-0475-y

# Chapter 2
# Psychiatry in the Midst of the Pandemic: A Narrative Perspective

**Gardenia AlSaffar**
*Royal Hospital of Bahrain, Bahrain*

**Ebtihaj Al-Aali**
*University of Bahrain, Bahrain*

## ABSTRACT

*The era of COVID-19 has initiated dramatic and unexpected changes related to all aspects of life. The impact of these changes is unforeseeable. Health services have encountered many challenges, which one country cannot deal with alone. The contagion of the disease requires changes in all walks of life, specifically health services. Psychiatric services have seen an increased demand from mental health patients and many people alike. This is due to unrest, anxiety, stressful, and the ambiguous characteristics of the present situation. This chapter presents reflections of the first author, the psychiatrist, on the major stakeholders for health systems at the present situation. These stakeholders are regulations, patients, pharmacies, society and community, and psychiatrists themselves. Despite all efforts to deal with the impacts of COVID-19, the need for transforming health systems in general and psychiatry in specific still persists. One of the major conclusions is to develop programs enabling psychiatrists and physicians to deal with their own distress.*

## 1. INTRODUCTION

COVID-19 pandemic is leading to uncertainty in all walks of life. This pandemic, since its declaration by World Health Organisation in March 2020, has been accompanied with the unpredictability of health concerns globally. For psychiatry, these health concerns were exacerbated due to the unique nature of mental health diseases. The unforeseen and unanticipated consequences of COVID-19 on mental health patients aggravate their sufferings. This is primarily due to physical distancing and lockdown. Healthy

DOI: 10.4018/978-1-7998-6948-1.ch002

individuals are also vulnerable to mental health issues. The fear of contracting the disease on the one hand, and the possibility of job loss and poverty due to economic problems on the other hand, are making many individuals susceptible to mental health problems. COVID-19 is transforming relationships between stakeholders for health care systems. Health practitioners, psychiatrists, and health service workers are not exempt from the impacts of COVID-19. They are in contact with this pandemic on a daily basis, doing their best to avoid being infected . This paper examines stakeholders for health systems . The most important stakeholders are reflected on from a narrative perspective. These stakeholders are regulations, patients, pharmacies, society and community and psychiatrists. This paper consists of six sections. Section two examines the methodology employed. Section three elaborates on the stakeholders for health systems. Section four then narrates reflections on the main stakeholders for health systems during the COVID-19. Section five presents implications and conclusion. The last section next states limitations and future researches. The paper argues that regulations have to change on a continuous basis to cope up with requirements for every era differently. Regulations concerning psychiatrists and physicians in Bahrain still lag behind in comparison to other countries.

## 2. METHODOLOGY

The COVID-19 pandemic is a new phenomenon. Such a phenomenon is still under research.

Al A'Ali and Al-Sarraf (2016) state that qualitative research is most suitable for relatively contemporary phenomena. The qualitative methodology allows for advancing and developing comprehensive understandings of the phenomena being examined.

Qualitative research scrutinizes the contents of information collected employing different methods. Reflection and narration methods are heavily used in papers reviewed (Moreno et al.(2020); Goldman et al. (2020) ; Vieta, pe'erez and Arango (2920) ; Rajkumar (2020); and Negam (2020). However, most quantitative research reviewed was to study the impacts of COVID-19 rather than developing a holistic understanding (Al-Hanawi et al. (2020) ; Alsalman et al.(2020) ; Bojdani et al. (2020)).

This paper is a qualitative work for two reasons. First, the phenomenon is still being researched and more investigations are required. Second, reflections based on a narrative perspective used can complement the majority of quantitative researches administrated in Bahrain. Literature is analyzed through narrations. Reflections then attempt to relate literature narrated to the context in Bahrain.

## 3. STAKEHOLDERS FOR HEALTH SYSTEMS

In this section the definition of stakeholders is discussed. The process of evaluating stakeholders and advantages of such evaluation is elaborated on. Then lastly stakeholders for health systems are examined.

### 3-1. Definition of Stakeholders

Ali, Ramly and Chai (2014). and Crane and Matten (2016) state that stakeholders are defined differently by various researchers. They then explain that stakeholders are affected by businesses which in turn are affected by stakeholders. This is to say that it is a two sided relationship between businesses and stakeholders. Therefore businesses' decisions are influenced by interests of stakeholders.

There are two types of stakeholders (Al- A'ali, (2020)). These are primary and secondary. Primary stakeholders are necessary for businesses to succeed. Consumers, employees, suppliers, shareholders and investors, communities, and governments are primary stakeholders. Groups that have no direct stake in businesses are called secondary stakeholders. These are pressure groups, non profit organizations, trade associations and media. However, failure to meet the concerns of these secondary stakeholders might lead to a negative reflection on the image of businesses. (Ferrell, Fraedrich and Ferrell (2015)).

Addressing stakeholders demands and concerns is completed through a stakeholders orientation. This consists of three steps. The first is for businesses to collect information about their stakeholders. The second then is to distribute to and to assess information collected by all organisational levels. The last is to respond to information collected about stakeholders (Ferrell, Fraedrich and Ferrell (2015)). The stakeholders analysis according to Ali, Ramly and Chai (2014) can explore the relative importance of each stakeholder. This can achieve two main advantages. Business organisations firstly learn about the stakeholders having the greatest influence on their success at a given point of time. Secondly, business organisations then will address the demands and concerns of the most influential stakeholders at that moment of time. The analysis of stakeholders enables business organisations to measure their performance in an efficient and effective manner through designing successful business strategies. These strategies reflect key success factors related to stakeholders (Henry (2008)).

## 3-2. Stakeholders for Health Care Systems

The perspective of stakeholders for health care systems illustrated by Stanwick and Stanwick (2009) consists of seven groups. These are health care provider including hospitals, pharmaceutical businesses, patients' families, Union of Doctors, health insurance companies, government medicaid and health services, and "managed care". These seven groups are characterized by two things. First, each of these groups has different relationships with a doctor and a patient. Second, in a given situation one group's needs might be satisfied while other groups might not be served. There is another accountability perspective, according to Stanwick and Stanwick (2009), leading physicians to experience different demands and concerns from nine types of stakeholders. These accountability stakeholders are hospitals, patients, employees, lawyers, professional association, investors, government, private patients and "managed care plans".

### 3-2-1. NHRA and Stakeholders in Bahrain

The National Health Regulatory Authority NHRA in Bahrain was established in 2009 by Law Decree No 38. NHRA is managed by a body consisting of members of both public and private sectors, headed by a representative from the Bahrain Defence Force. Regulations, laws, and procedures in relation to all stakeholders of health systems in Bahrain are enacted by NHRA. Figure 1 below illustrates all stakeholders which NHRA considers important to enhance health services. (Al- saffar, (2020).

*Figure 1. NHRA 's stakeholders for health systems in Bahrain*

In 2017, NHRA outlined Code of Conduct for professionals providing health care in Bahrain . Based on this Code of Conduct, Figure 2 exhibits accountability stakeholders for physicians. Physicians are in ongoing reciprocal interactions with their own stakeholders. These interactions lead to have mutual influence on both physicians and stakeholders. The Code of Conduct of professionals is assumed to relate to all health professions. AlSaffar (2020) explains that psychiatry, due to its unique nature, might require a different code of conduct. Such a code of conduct is currently lacked. Therefore this paper employs accountability stakeholders of physicians according to NHRA. These stakeholders are shown in Figure-2.

*Figure 2. The Accountability Stakeholders for Physicians based on Code of Conduct developed by NHRA (2017)*

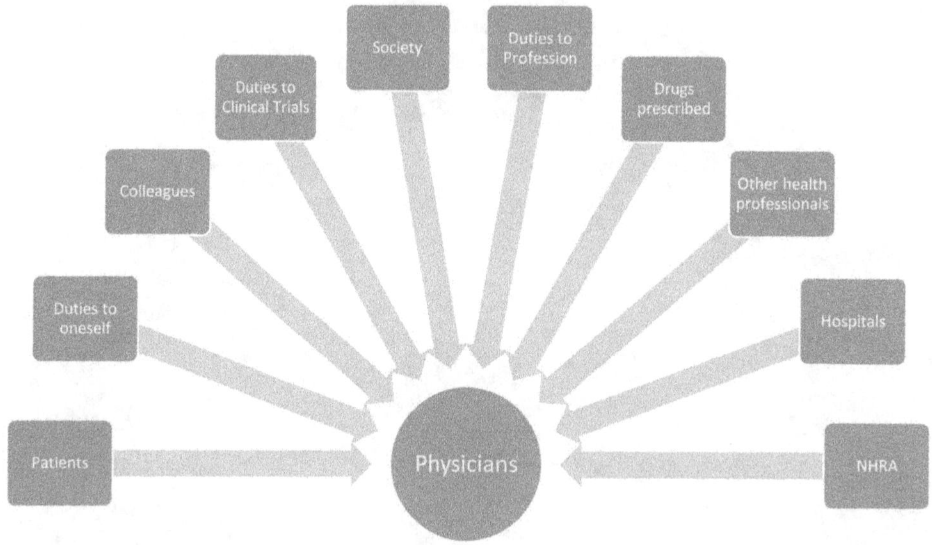


The paper examines reflections of the first author, the psychiatrist, on the most important accountability stakeholders shown in figure 2. The importance is decided based on the ongoing interactions between the stakeholders and the impacts of the present situation. Impacts of the situation refer to concerns and demands require to deal with as consequences of Covid-19. Stakeholders reflected on are as follows:

1. Regulations of NHRA to meet concerns of this present time
2. Demands and concerns of patients and their families
3. Pharmacies and drugs prescribed
4. Society and community
5. Physicians/psychiatrists 'wellbeing.

## 4. REFLECTIONS ON STAKEHOLDER OF HEALTH CARE SYSTEMS: A NARRATIVE PERSPECTIVE

In this section, reflections on Accountability Stakeholders of Physicians and Psychiatrists are discussed. Legislations, patients, pharmacies, society and community, and psychiatrists' wellbeing are the main, frequently elucidated stakeholders (Moreno, et al. (2020); Vieta, P'evez and Arango (2020) ; Bojdani et al. (2020)). Reflections are presented based on literature narrated . Stakeholders are examined according to their relative importance at the present time .

### 4-1. Regulations

Authorities and institutions regulating health services are the first stakeholder to study. These authorities and institutions specify the contexts in which other stakeholders operate. In a situation of crisis such as the COVID-19 pandemic, regulations can facilitate practices of the stakeholders. This explains the reasons for discussing them first.

Telehealth is approved by health authorities to cope with the unique situation created by the swift spread of COVID-19. Many studies illustrate the benefits of such treatment approach.

Karim et al. (2020) state that mental health services are mainly state-funded in Qatar. They add that telehealth in psychiatry is assisting to meet the increasing demands on such services during the COVID-19 time. They also explain that telehealth can be a complementary treatment approach after the present pandemic. This is for two reasons. First, telehealth assures privacy for patients avoiding to be stigmatized. This is congruent to the findings of AlAtteq et al. (2018). They explain that stigma is a fear that mental health patients try to avoid. The stigma is directed against individuals suffering from mental health diseases . This is also compatible to the findings of the psychiatrist, the first author of this paper. The author argues that patients prefer appointments and treatments on WhatsApp rather than the official site specified by the hospital. The reason according to patients, is to assure privacy. The first author of this paper, as well agrees with Karim et al. (2020) that telehealth can still be employed in the future for the purposes of convenience. The second reason, according to Karim et al. (2020) for using telehealth in the post COVID-19 era is the paucity of human resources. This seems to be the case in the United States. In March 2020, the government of the United States has relinquished many regulations restricting telehealth temporarily. Moreover, guidance for practicing has been issued by the American Psychiatric association (Bojdani et al. (2020)).

## 4-2. Patients

Patients represent the second type of stakeholders to probe. The entire purpose of the health care system is to serve patients. COVID-19 does not only affect mental health patients. Many people are vulnerable to mental health diseases as a consequence of Covid-19. Alsalman et al. (2020) conclude that around one-third of the Bahraini population suffer from varying degrees of psychological impacts as consequences of Covid-19. These psychological impacts are illustrated in stress, anxiety and depression. Karim et al. (2020) notice that the demand on telepsychiatry has increased by 36.5% during four months of the study in Qatar. Similar findings are reported in the U.K. Reuters, on 20 November 2020, states that health services should be prepared to meet the increasing demands on mental health services (reuters.com, 2020). It also states that 20% of Covid-19 recovered patients suffer from mental illness. Naqvi (2020) argues that life threats caused by COVID-19 lead people to undergo depression, stress and anxiety in Pakistan. Moreno et al. (2020) assert that during COVID-19 mental health patients report overeating and drug misuse. They (2020) affirm that suicidal behaviour can be a consequence of social distancing. Reuters on 20 November2020 affirms that 65% of mental health patients are more susceptible to contract Covid-19.

Bojdani et al. (2020) contend that psychiatric services have changed in the United States as a result of the COVID-19 pandemic. They add that COVID-19 has transformed methods for the psychiatric treatment for inpatients, emergency rooms, the Consultation Liaison overseeing inpatients and emergency rooms 'patients. They expound as well that psychiatric services have to adjust according to the needs of the patients' population in any given community. They (2020) assure that telehealth is an alternative treatment approach employed by psychiatrists at this time. This is congruent to the argument stated in regulation.

World Health Organisation (WHO, (2006)) elaborates on mental health services in Bahrain. WHO expounds that primary care physicians and family practitioners are trained by the psychiatry department to deal with mental health disorders. There are 23 primary care centres which have psychiatric drugs available to prescribe. Community care is also provided for mental health patients. Home visits at which family members attend are planned. Treatment procedures are provided and are explained to out-patients and their families. There are mental health programs for the elderly and children as well. Psychiatric services in Bahrain serve a broad spectrum. All these services are based on face-to-face treatment. This face-to-face treatment is avoided by the majority of patients and psychiatrists as a result of the contagious nature of COVID-19. However, psychiatrists at The Psychiatric Hospital in Bahrain still engage in face-to face treatment with three groups of patients. These groups are new patients, patients with severe psychiatric disorders, and patients requiring direct treatment from psychiatrists, e.g. injections given. In addition, The Psychiatric Hospital still arranges for home visits to patients and their families.

The first author of this paper observes that COVID-19 recovered patients in Bahrain require mental health treatment as well for two reasons. The first reason is related to pain, depression, stress, anxiety, and fear of the loss of life, and insomnia that are still experienced by COVID-19 recovered patients. The second reason is a stigma associated with Covid-19 recovered patients. This leads relatives and friends to avoid socializing with them. The avoidance is underpinned by a fear of contracting Covid-19. The second reason highlights the importance of psychiatrists' educational roles to patients recovered and to the society alike .

## 4-3. Pharmacies and Drugs Prescribed

Although there is no real separation between patients and drugs prescribed but for the purpose of analysis, pharmacies are listed as number three accountability stakeholder. Medicines for mental health patients should be monitored and controlled by psychiatrists in cooperation with pharmacies. The latter are ruled by health regulations.

Goldman et al. (2020) state that the Food and Drug Administration in the United Stated has loosened the regulations to dispense of some medications. Cozapine, an anti-psychotic for example, can be dispensed by pharmacies without meeting neutrophil count reporting.

Medicines for mental health patients in Bahrain can be dispensed through two avenues. The first is for the Psychiatric Hospital to arrange for home delivery. The second is for private hospitals and clinics to dispense medicines through pharmacies. Both avenues can contribute to reduce the possibility of contracting COVID-19.

## 4-4 Society and Community

The COVID-19 diagnostic test is administered free of charge by the Ministry of Health in Bahrain. Bahrain is one of the pioneer countries in the Middle East to launch a national education campaign for the COVID-19 pandemic. The campaign is to outline symptoms and prevention methods. Social distancing, lockdown and curfews were some of the measures put in place to control the spread of COVID-19. Home-quarantine is employed as well. Masks-wearing in public has been mandatory since April 2020 (Maher Negm, 2020). Measures to contain the pandemic have compounded problems of mental health patients. Healthy individuals also suffer because of the implemented measures. Stress, anxiety and depression are experienced by these people. Such experiences lead them to seek mental health treatment. This highlights the different roles of psychiatrists. These roles are first as health professionals via the treatment of patients, second as informative through their educational roles to train and to teach people how to deal with their distress, and the lastly the role to maintain their own wellbeing and broadening professional practices.

Different businesses these days in cooperation with psychiatrists, such as the first author of this paper, organise seminars about COVID-19 pandemic. These seminars aim at discussing the impact of the pandemic. Elaboration on methods of dealing with such impacts are illustrated as well. Seminars are provided online.

In addition, The Psychiatric Hospital still serves the society through arranging the regular visits to mental health patients and their families.

## 4-5. Psychiatrists' (Physicians) Well Being

According to the World Health Organisation, 10% of those infected by COVID-19 globally are health workers (DW- breaking world news(2020)).

Mental health services mainly revolve around patients and psychiatrists. However, the latter lack many supporting regulations and methods. AlSaffar (2020) states that psychiatry as a medical speciality requires its own codes of conduct. The lack of such codes represents one of the reasons for the absence of support methods. Health practitioners, as a result of their contact with patients, suffer from mild to severe distress. This suffering is exacerbated as the number of COVID-19 patients increases in health facilities (Al-Hanawi et al. (2020)).

Rajkumar (2020) states that there is few research about the impact of COVID-19 on health workers. The papers reviewed by Rajkumar (2020) are mainly conducted in China. He elaborates that based on experiments, it is found that some methods can help health workers to deal with distress caused by COVID-19 . These methods focus attention on physicians' physical needs such as food, psychological needs such as rest areas visited periodically by a counsellor, and training programs in relation to caring for COVID-19 patients and measures to protect themselves i.e health workers. Such programs are still being developed. He (2020) adds that telephone helplines addressing mental health problems of health workers seem to have positive impacts . Such programs discussed by Rajkumar (2020) are not available for psychiatrists in Bahrain. No support methods and systems are designed to assist in dealing with negative impacts of COVID-19 on psychiatrists/physicians.

# 5. IMPLICATIONS AND CONCLUSION

The above literature reviewed and reflections illustrate the need to examine stakeholders' requirements on a regular basis. However, in a situation of unexpected crisis such as COVID-19, dealing with stakeholders is a must. The Kingdom of Bahrain has reacted swiftly to the spread of COVID-19. Many measures have been implemented to monitor COVID-19 patients. Other methods are implemented to control the transmission of the pandemic. However, this is a global disease which one country cannot deal with alone. There is still place for improvements. Based on the above reflections, the improvements suggested can be as follows:

1. NHRA has to develop different codes of conduct for every medical speciality based on its uniqueness. The pandemic demonstrates the need to have codes of conduct for psychiatrists as a matter of

urgency. This is suggested by AlSaffar (2020). The suggested code can help to improve practices based on urgencies of situations.

2. Regulations have to be loosened to leave room for future situations. The literature review mentioned above states that telehealth can still be used as a regular treatment approach even when the present pandemic is over.
3. Medicine prescribed is dispensed either directly through pharmacies or home delivery. There an obvious need for a centralize agency. This would prevent patients from collecting the same drugs from different psychiatrists as happens in substance abuse and prevent the hoarding of medications due to fears of unavailability The misuse of drugs makes them in short supply for the patients who need them the most.
4. Non-Governmental Organisations should play active roles in dealing with the present pandemic. Researches on charity organisations, professional societies, and religious bodies can shed light on the desired contribution of non-government organizations to contain the spread of a pandemic. This can complement the official efforts launched by the government .
5. Psychiatrists and physicians and other health workers are the front lines. Health authorities and health facilities should introduce methods and techniques to assist psychiatrists and physicians to deal with distress experienced. The least of which is the introduction of help lines as stated above and found by Rajkumar(2020).

## 6. LIMITATIONS AND FUTURE RESEARCH

This paper examines the impacts of Covid-19 on stakeholders of health systems. Such an examination has not been studied in the context of Bahrain. Besides, the paper is based on narration and reflection methods of qualitative methodology. These methods add broader descriptions of the issue being scanned. However, quantitative methodology can shed different understandings for the pandemic being scrutinised .

It is suggested that future researches should focus on the following areas:

- Investigating stakeholders of health systems and their interactions on a regular basis
- Studying methods and programs to help psychiatrists \ physicians and health workers to deal with their own distress
- Researching processes of the phenomenon of stigma against both mental health patients and Covid-19 recovered patients.
- Probing regulations enacted by health authority.
- Assessing roles of non-governmental organizations to deal with such societal crisis
- Exploring new approaches for treatment of health illness .

## REFERENCES

Abdul Karim, M., & Wadoo, O. (2020). In the Arabian Gulf region - Implications beyond the Covid-19 pandemic. *Asian Journal of Psychiatry*, *54*, 102397. Advance online publication. doi:10.1016/j.ajp.2020.102397 PMID:33271697

Al-A'Ali, E. (2020). *The role of Auditing Firms in promoting Ethical Consumerism: Ethical programs for business companies in Ethical Consumerism and comparative studies Across Different Cultures*. IGI Global. doi:10.4018/978-1-7998-0272-3.ch004

Al A'ali, E. A., & Al-Sarraf, A. R. (2016). Ethical Consumerism: Contextual Issues of Ethical Decision-Making processes: An Exploratory Study. In Ethical and Social Perspectives on Global Business interaction in Emerging Markets (pp.133-149). IGI Global.

Al-Hanawi, M.K., Mwale, M.L., & Alsharqi, O. (2020). *Psychological Distress Among Health Workers and the General Public During the COVID-19 Pandemic in Saudi Arabia*. Dove Press. DOI doi:10.2147/RMHP.S264037.volume2020:13

AlAteeq, D., AlDaoud, A., AlHadi, A., AlKhalaf, H., & Milev, R. (2018). The experience and impacts of stigma in Saudi people with mood disorder. *Annals of General Psychiatry*, *17*(1), 51. doi:10.118612991-018-0221-3 PMID:30498517

Ali, K. K., Ramly, Z., & Chai, L. T. (2014). *Business Ethics*. Oxford Fajar Sdn.

AlSaffar, G. (2020). *Ethical Programs for Patients in Bahrain in Ethical Consumerism and Comparative studies Across Cultures*. IGI Global.

Alsalman, A., Mubarak, H., Aljabal, M., Abdulnabi, M., Ishaq, A., Yusuf, A., . . . Jahrami, H. (2020). *The Psychological Impact of COVID-19 Pandemic on the Population of Bahrain*. Available at SSRN: https://ssrn.com/abstract=3660648

Crane, A., & Matten, D. (2016). *Business ethics: Managing corporate citizenship and sustainability in the age of globalization*. Oxford, UK: University Press.

Ferrell, O. C., Fraedrich, J., & Ferrell, L. (2015). *Business ethics: Ethical decision making and cases*. Cengage Learning.

Goldman, Benjamin, & Dixon. (2020). Mental Health Policy in the Era of COVID-19. *Psychiatry On Line*. doi:10.1176/appi.ps.202000219

Henry, A. (2008). *Understanding Strategic Management*. Oxford University Press.

-Maher Negm, H. (2020). Could COVID-19 improve psychiatric awareness at the heart of the Middle East?- A personal reflection on Bahrain' response. *Irish Journal of Psychological Medicine*, 1-8. doi:10.1017/IOMC.2020.74

Moreno, C., Wykes, T., Galderisi, S., Nordentoft, M., Crossley, N., Jones, N., Cannon, M., Correll, C. U., Byrne, L., Carr, S., Chen, E. Y. H., Gorwood, P., Johnson, S., Kärkkäinen, H., Krystal, J. H., Lee, J., Lieberman, J., López-Jaramillo, C., Männikkö, M., ... Arango, C. (2020, September 1). How mental health care should change as a consequence of the COVID-19 pandemic, THE. *The Lancet. Psychiatry*, *7*(9), 813–824. doi:10.1016/S2215-0366(20)30307-2 PMID:32682460

Naqvi, H. A. (n.d.). Mental health in the aftermath of COVID-19: A new normal. *Journal of Pakistan Medical Association, 70*(Sppl 3). doi:10.5455/JPMA.30

National Health Regulatory Authority. (2017). *Annual report of 2017*. Retrieved from www.nhra.bh

Rajkumar, R. V. (2020). COVID-19 and mental health: A review of the existing literature. *Asian Journal of Psychiatry, 52*. DOI:.2020.102066 doi:10.1016/j.ajp

Stanwick, P. S., & Stanwick, S. D. (2009). *Understanding Business Ethics*. Pearson Education, Inc.

Vieta, E., Pe'rez, V., & Arango, C. (2020). Psychiatry in the aftermath of COVID-19. *Journal of Psychiatry and Mental Health, 13*(2). Advance online publication. doi:10.1026/j.rpsm.2020.04.004

World Health Organization. (2006). Mental health in the Eastern Mediterranean Region. Reaching the unreached. *WHO Regional Publications. Eastern Mediterranean Series*, 29.

# Chapter 3
# Whole-of-Nation Approach in COVID-19 Management:
## The Case of Brunei Darussalam

**Abdul Malik Omar**
https://orcid.org/0000-0002-7623-8969
*University Brunei Darussalam, Brunei*

**Amanina Halim**
*Independent Researcher, Brunei*

## ABSTRACT

*The emergence of COVID-19 has swept the globe by storm, taking the lives of hundreds of thousands of people and infecting millions worldwide. As the virus continues to spread, governments have pursued strategies and action plans, with some achieving notable successes, while others fail miserably. This research focuses on how the Brunei government has become an outlier in tackling the COVID-19 pandemic. As such, this chapter provides substantive content useful for policymakers and experts to learn from the Brunei experience in pandemic management through a whole-of-nation framework, effectively contributing to both theory and practice in public policy and governance. The research on Brunei further gives credence on the need for governments to administer participation among the private sector and society to tackle grand challenges of the 21st century, particularly in preparation for the 'Great Reset' amid post-COVID-19. Policy recommendations have been presented.*

## INTRODUCTION

COVID-19 is a highly transmittable and pathogenic viral infection caused by severe acute respiratory syndrome (Sheeren et al., 2020) with an estimated fatality rate of 2%, as reported on the 29th January 2020 (WHO, 2020). The virus emerged from Wuhan and spread to Chinese cities and abroad around 6th October and 11th December 2019 (van Dorp et al., 2020). On 30th January 2020, the WHO (World Health Organization) declared the virus as a Public Health Emergency of International Concern. As of

DOI: 10.4018/978-1-7998-6948-1.ch003

4 January 2021, there have been 83,322,449 confirmed cases of COVID-19 including 1,831,412 deaths, reported to WHO (Covid19.who.int), affecting over 200 countries and territories. The global economy contracted in the second quarter of 2020 as COVID-19 containment measures disrupted production and labor movement (CSPS, 2020b). In May 2020, the Asian Development Bank estimated that COVID-19 could cost the global economy up to USD$8.8 trillion (ADB, 2020). As the virus wreak havoc, other countries have attained notable successes in containing COVID-19. One example is New Zealand, which took rapid, science-based risk assessment and early action at various levels (border-control measures, community-transmission control measures and case-based control measures); plus a strong leadership to confront the Pandemic as a "united team of 5 million" (Baker et al., 2020). However, one country that has been overlooked by the global media and academia is Brunei Darussalam. Since the first case was detected on 5th March 2020, the Government of Brunei (henceforth GoB) has taken drastic and immediate action to manage the virus spread, resulting in the successful containment of the disease. In this book chapter, a case study is be done on how the country's strict approach in nipping the issue in the bud has enabled the country to ride the COVID-19 storm, utilizing the Whole-of-Nation approach (Omar, 2020) as a governance framework to analyze the Government's response.

The research contributes to the growing scholarship relating to how Brunei Darussalam has dealt with the COVID-19 crisis from a pandemic management and public policy perspective. Various studies have emerged relating to the GoB's policy responses (Chaw et. al, 2020; Wong et al. 2020a, Wong et al. 2020b; Wong et al. 2020c; Koh et al, 2020); its effect in leadership and crisis communication (Pang, 2020); creative expressions in Social Media (Mohamad, 2020); and the virus' impact on Islamic and Social Finance (Hidayat, 2020; Basir, 2020) and the economy (CSPS, 2020a, 2020b). This chapter adds to the growing contribution in scholarship, in hopes that it can be useful for policy-makers, experts and students of public policy and governance on how Brunei controlled COVID-19. The Whole-of-Nation approach is also an increasingly prominent field in governance that needs further substantiation, which this chapter aims to do. The analysis of policies by the Government relating to having strong top-down governance, continual engagement of the private sector and society, and the continued urgency placed upon every member of society in tackling COVID-19 would further contribute to the conceptual and practical insights needed for readers of this chapter to further understand how Whole-of-Nation can be understood and operationalized, especially in adjusting towards the Great Reset in a post-COVID-19 global society (Schwab and Malleret, 2020). For the concept of Whole-of-Nation governance centers in taking care for and working with the people, and doing so would help to strengthen trust and dynamic capabilities in tackling the grand challenges of the 21st century (Mazzucato and Kattel, 2020).

## BACKGROUND

### 1. Brunei Darussalam

Brunei's political system is characterized as a resilient monarchy (Talib, 2002), with a long history stretching over 600 years (De Vienne, 2015). The GoB is highly centralized and its economy is fueled by hydrocarbon resources (Cheung, 2017). Close to 33.8% of the national workforce are in the public sector (DEPD, 2020), which makes public sector employment in the country higher than the regional standard of 15% (OECD, 2019). The country also has universal healthcare coverage, with citizens only paying a single Brunei dollar for every consultation to the hospital and is free for anyone under 12 years old (Brunei

Year Book, 2015). The strong healthcare system is in line with His Majesty the Sultan of Brunei's *Titah* (or Speech) to strengthen efforts towards improving the welfare of the people and stability of the nation (Borneo Bulletin, 2011), along the lines of its own socio-political and cultural background (Rahman et al., 2019). As of 2020, the two most significant issues identified and faced by the nation is the depletion of Oil and Gas Resources (Baskaran, 2010), increasing unemployment levels, and job mismatch (Musa and Idris, 2020). In response to overcoming these issues, Wawasan 2035 was envisioned (Hashim, 2010; Hamdan and Hoon, 2019), one that entails turning Brunei into a nation known for its high standard of living and highly educated and skilled populace. There is also the need to rethink job futures and to adopt Brunei for the Fourth Industrial Revolution (Cheong, 2019), with the latter spearheaded by the Digital Economy Council (The Scoop, 2020a). As such, major decisions are normally made through a Whole-of-Nation approach (Omar, 2020b), later to be useful in responding to crisis such as COVID-19.

## 2. Factor Endowment of Brunei

Factor endowments have contributed to Brunei's status as an outlier in tackling COVID-19. It is imperative to take into account the unique strengths of each country to avoid making grand generalizations of this study. First, Brunei is a pro-family Malay Muslim majority country (Ahmad, 2018) with a small population of 469,400, meaning that it is relatively much easier to conduct contact tracing, testing and isolation policies (Wong et al., 2020a), compared to other countries with tens of millions of population. Secondly, the GoB has a robust healthcare system with universal health coverage and a high human development index, sustained by its robust welfare policy (Ibid). It also has BND15 million allocated for outbreaks and public health emergencies (Ibid). Third, its Oil and Gas resources were able to sustain the economy despite border closures. The abundance of resources were also prudently channelled in strategic areas of interest, such as the setting up of a BND$569,348 virology lab (The Bruneian, 2020a; The Scoop; 2020b) to increase the COVID-19 testing capacity by tenfold (The Star; 2020a) and to build the BND$11 million hospital wing in National Isolation Centre in Tutong (The Scoop, 2020c) to double the capacity of beds. Investments were made without overloading the national budget. Finally, Brunei has a strong central government headed by the Sultan of Brunei, enabling for fast and drastic strategic decisions to be made by a GoB populated with a competent and highly educated and skilled bureaucratic elite. All the above endowments have contributed to the success of Brunei's experience.

## 3. Status of Covid-19 in Brunei (as of 4th January 2021)

The first detected case of COVID-19 in Brunei was of a male aged 53 on the 5th of March 2020. He was part of a group of 19 people who attended a religious gathering (Tabligh) at Jamek Sri Petaling Mosque, KL. The group quickly devolved into becoming Brunei's first cluster of SARS-CoV-2, transmitting the disease to 52 others (Chaw et al., 2020). The origins of the first cluster was traced back to the Tabligh event, which was attended by 19,000 people (Mat et al., 2020; NST, 2020). It became a SSE (Super Spreader Event), triggering governments around Southeast Asia to contain the virus mass outbreak. The Brunei Government is credited for having identified and informed regional governments on the issue. Following the outbreak, outbound travel was restricted for all Brunei residents on the 15th of March, and a ban on all foreign citizens entering the country enacted on the 23rd of March. From 20th of March, all individuals entering Brunei underwent RT-PCR testing on arrival and 14-day quarantine at a designated facility. Three Bruneians (males aged 64, 56, and 67) succumbed to the virus; while 149 others recovered. The last locally recorded COVID-19 case was in the 6th of May 2020, or 242 days as of the 4th January 2021 (Borneo Bulletin, 2021). There were a total of 172 cases, with 20 imported active cases receiving treatment at the NIC with another being admitted to the Intensive Care Unit (ICU). Since March 2020, 10,519 individuals have completed mandatory self-isolation, with 572 undergoing the process at government monitoring centres after arriving from overseas (Ibid). The total number of lab test since January 2020 is 83,775.

## LITERATURE REVIEW

### 1. Whole of Nation

Governance is a perennial field that requires a continual update in scholarship to tackle ongoing challenges facing nation-states and society. Central to these studies are the role of the State or Government. The State is the primary unit upon which a society is governed by. Max Weber arguably pioneered the study of the State through his work Bureaucracy (Weber, 2015). The main idea he proposed was the need to rationalize policies to tackle issues confronting society. In the mid-19th century, Woodrow Wilson wrote 'The Study of Public Administration' (Wilson, 1886), which laid out the aim of the study of administration so as to straighten "the paths of government, to make its business less unbusinesslike, to strengthen and purify its organization, and to crown its duties with dutifulness…" (Ibid). The journal legitimized the study as science in academia. Ever since then, theories come and go. Among these include New Public Management (Lane, 2000), Joined-up-Governance (Keast, 2011), Whole-of-Government (Christensen and Laegreid, 2007), and Digital Era Governance (Dunleavy et al., 2006). They emerged to answer Woodrow Wilson's challenge almost 134 years ago. Each idea has had its meaningful impact in the way how governments – mainly Western governments – operate, ranging from being primarily business-like (NPM), to decentralized (JUG), to centralized (WOG), and of being digitized (DEG). The study of Public Administration has gone a long way since its inception and will continue to evolve, but even then there have been calls to add non-State organizations into the governance process.

Enter Whole-of-Nation into the equation. The approach works to incorporate non-State actors into the governance process. These non-state actors include those from the private sector and general society. WHO (2012) even affirmed the important role played by "relevant stakeholders, including individuals, families and communities, intergovernmental organizations and religious institutions, civil society, academia, the media, voluntary associations and, where and as appropriate, the private sector and industry, in support of national efforts for non- communicable disease prevention and control, and recognize the need to further support the strengthening of coordination among these stakeholders in order to improve the effectiveness of these efforts" This "comprehensive" governance approach (Doyle, 2019) must not be mistaken with decentralization, but rather to utilize a pragmatic approach in which the State can galvanize non-State actors to administer all sectors of society in tackling emerging issues or existing crisis. Doing so would result in economic dividends (Pike, et al, 2012). In turn, the people are also involved enabling them to secure critical experiences and other benefits, enabling them to be empowered (Gruber and Trickett, 1987) as well as to achieve self-government (Rasmussen, 2011). This form of inclusive governance also has the chances to strengthen the State's legitimacy and capacity in governing, allowing for the State to focus on key areas that matter the most to get the best results possible for the society. Whole-of-Nation also aims to administering public participation (Eckerd and Heidelberg, 2020) among non-State actors. The best way to do so is to invite non-State actors to play their part in nation-building. Participation is a central part of public administration, and public administration is defined as how leaders translate politics into the a reality citizens can see every day (Kettl, 2016). Indeed, it is from the local or bottom-level that has roots and experience to dealing with themselves, further increasing the efficiency and effectiveness of the state and society to govern themselves forward in tackling the grand challenges of the 21st century with innovative and dynamic policies.

## 2. Pandemic Management

Academia has an important field in global health titled Pandemic Management. A sub-field of Crisis Management, Pandemic Management aims to mitigate and contain risks, impacts, and to fill in knowledge gaps to tackling pandemic outbreaks (Madhav et al., 2017). Whilst the pandemic like Covid-19 is unprecedented, it is not the first of its kind. Indeed, the pandemics of the past have resulted in significant implications for global history. For example, history would change had the plague did not ravage Athens during the Peloponnesian War (Warner, 1962). The same case can be made to Europe's Black Death that killed an estimated 25 million people, almost a third of the continent's population (Gottfried, 2010). There is also the 1918 Spanish Flu, killing between 20 to 50 million people worldwide (Trilla et al., 2008). Significant advancements in global healthcare, studies in health policies, cooperation at the international level supported by institutions like the WHO, and other pandemic management innovations (WHO, 2018) and technologies since the 21st century are making a concerted effort to control crisis like these. This includes epidemics such as SARS, H1NI, Ebola, MERS, Ebola, Zika, as well as other known epidemic diseases that still ravage today's societies, such as cholera, HIV infection, influenza, meningitis, malaria, tuberculosis and yellow fever (Ibid, 2018). With COVID-19's emergence, the scholarly work on pandemic management has only gained prominence as a core part in global governance. On this particular note, it is no longer enough for countries to be the only agency to tackle pandemics. Preferably, it has to be a concerted global and local effort in the process of Pandemic Management (Verbeke, 2020), hence the need to incorporate a Whole-of-Nation approach to the entire process.

Evidence-based policies (EBP) pertaining to pandemic management is also vital to effectively tackle, manage, and mitigate a global pandemic (Murray and Lopez, 1996; Cairney, 2020) as well as to tackle misinformation (Harley and Vu, 2020) or Infodemic (Zarocostas, 2020). Working based on science and rationality as an extension of public policy would also result in better decisions being made, resulting in people to trust the government. Policies have necessarily been polished over the years, as evidenced by healthcare experts and doctors prescribing policies for a society that involves the need to practice social distancing (Brzezinski, e al, 2020; Wilasang et al., 2020), to maintain their hygiene (such as by using sanitizers), the need to close off public venues to mitigate any incidence of mass outbreaks of the virus. A good process of Epidemic or Pandemic management has been outlined by the WHO (2018), in which countries have to anticipate new and re-emerging diseases "to facilitate faster detection and response; followed by their early detection of emergence in animal and human populations; the third stage is the containment of the disease at the early stages of transmission; followed by the control and mitigation of the epidemic during its amplification; and fifth, the elimination of the risk of outbreak or eradication of the infectious disease. Crisis communication directed to "flatten the curve", involving the need to avoid overloading healthcare capacities, are also emphasized and socialized to society (Malecki et al, 2020) as with the need to combat Fake News. At the foundational level, all these policies have to be backed by science and evidence for a better and informed decision-making and policy result.

## 3. Whole-of-Nation in Pandemic Management

The research gaps within the literature have identified the deficiency of matrimony between Whole-of-Nation and Pandemic Management amid COVID-19. Most of the theories and practice have only confined themselves having the State to do most of the heavy load in Pandemic Management. While the State is crucial and central to pandemic management, non-state actors or groups, primarily the private sector and general society, must not be treated as a mere periphery to the governance equation. It is a mistake to preclude non-governmental entities, especially when the dividends that can arise from a united front by all members of society in tackling a pandemic or, any other challenge for that matter, could bring about positive significance, such as greater efficiency and the potential increase in state capacity and legitimacy, as well as societal empowerment. The added benefits would prepare general society for future challenges, in turn. Moreover, it would bring about great advantage for state leaders, healthcare professionals, and non-state leaders to take this opportunity to learn and embed the Whole-of-Nation framework in the path to transform how global or local governance operates in the 21st century. This approach would also allow potentially for the Whole-of-Nation governance to become Whole-of-Global governance to effectively embrace the 'Great Reset' (Swab and Mallerett, 2020). That would, of course, be an area that requires deep pondering and serious scholarship for another day. For now, this book chapter integrates the theories of Whole-of-Nation and Pandemic Management during the COVID-19 crisis focusing Brunei as a case study.

## RESEARCH METHODS

This book chapter has deployed Case Study as a research method (Yin, 2017; Stake, 2005). Qualitative case study refers to the substantiation of academic work through the extraction of theories and meanings from the 'thick description' based on primary and secondary sources (Cousin, 2005). In this research, sources have included government press releases, press conference speeches, news articles, literature review, observation of researcher, and more. First, this work will utilize the press releases published by the Ministry of Health since the COVID-19 crisis began in January 2020 to November 2020 to examine the evolution of how the Brunei Government has reacted towards the management of COVID-19. Key speeches delivered by the government ministers of Brunei in its Press Conferences will also be analyzed to see the patterns of policy development and governance process. Next, this work has reviewed critical articles by news articles by the national media organizations, such as Borneo Bulletin, RTB, The Scoop, and many others. A secondary literature review on the COVID-19 situation and the Whole-of-Nation concept have also been done. The Case Study has also incorporated this researcher's observation on COVID-19. The first-hand observation would provide depth and richness to the meaning extracted (Morgan et al., 2017) from the Brunei experience in overcoming the COVID-19 crisis. Overall, the Case Study method is suitable in analyzing how the Brunei Government emerged as a high performer in the COVID-19 crisis.

## FINDINGS AND DISCUSSION

### 1. The State of Brunei

The role of the State or Government is crucial and central to the Whole-of-Nation approach, as in the case of Brunei in tackling Covid-19. For one, the GoB took tentative steps to coordinate with international health organizations such as the WHO to keep abreast of the issues happening in China. Since the 6th January 2020, or two months before the virus spread to Brunei, the Government is already monitoring the COVID-19 cases (MoH, 2020a). The GoB has also taken tentative steps to inform the public health-related advice, to inform the public from going to certain parts of China at that time whilst stepping up its vigilance and preparedness to control the entry of the virus into Brunei Darussalam. Measures include introducing body temperature screening for passengers arriving in the country via the Brunei International Airport, especially from cities in China starting in 21st January 2020, strengthening the implementation of SOP in government clinics and hospitals, as well as the continuous risk monitoring and assessment of the infection worldwide (MoH, 2020b) The existence of the early monitoring capacity continued throughout the months. The virus eventually spread in Brunei with aggressive ferocity from 5th March 2020 (MoH, 2020c), resulting in over 148 people infected by the virus by 20th November 2020. The GoB's robust monitoring and surveillance system and bold decision to intervene early, buttressed by an aggressive test, isolate, and tracing system were crucial in flattening the curve.

The other key areas that are attributed to the GoB's success was its open communication and transparency in dealing with the virus. When the virus was discovered and was linked to the religious gathering (Tabligh) participants, the GoB organized daily press conference, with the Minister of Health himself as spokesperson (MoH, 2020c). The Tabligh gathering in KL devolved into an SSE, resulting in thousands of regional participants from Southeast Asia getting infected by the virus. The immediacy of the message was echoed to other Governments, causing countries to prepare for the spread of the pandemic. Sure enough, other countries also took steps to test, isolate, and trace the pandemic outbreak. The level of transparency exhibited by the Government of Brunei has helped Southeast Asian countries to tackle the virus spread. At home, the level of transparency demonstrated by the GoB has further been strengthened by continuous press conferences and information spread through Old and New Media, such as Social Media (Omar, 2020a). The concerted action further enhanced public confidence as well as to tackle fake news or Infodemics, both of which "could cause more anxiety or panic in the local community" (Borneo Bulletin, 2020c). In turn, the Brunei population was continually fed key information on how to play their part in becoming a solution to the problem. For this, the GoB advised the people to maintain social distancing, to wear masks, and to take other safety and hygienic precautions.

It was not just a ministerial effort that went to tackle the disease but the entire government executive ranches – all 13 ministries of the GoB – were galvanized to pursue policies to take care of the people's welfare amid the Covid-19 crisis. With the Sultan of Brunei leading the Government, all the ministries got directly or indirectly involved in waging war against Covid-19. It was a grand exercise, arguably rarely if never observed before, when ministers from the Ministry of Health, Ministry of Culture, Youth and Sports, Ministry of Religious Affairs, Ministry of Finance and Economy, Ministry of Transport and Info-Communications, Ministry of Industry and Primary Resources and the other key elites of the country got involved in the daily press conference to inform to the public of the key developments of policies and efforts carried out by their respective ministries. The concerted and collaborative Whole-of-Nation effort exemplified by GoB increased people's confidence in the Government and may have most likely allayed people's worries and anxieties, particularly on the uncertainties that engulfed Brunei Darussalam during those difficult times. Information was communicated to the public, and the ministries socialized policies transparently and openly. The ministers have also communicated openly and answered questions on what the GoB is going to do whenever they were asked by the media press and bloggers during the press conference.

The GoB has also enforced the amended Infectious Diseases Act 2020 (Borneo Bulletin, 2020d), which came into effect on 30th January 2020. Lawbreakers would be fined up to BND$10,000 or jailed up to 6 months through the law. When the policies to shut down selected businesses were enacted, a well-known gym business was fined BND$5,500 for flaunting the policy (Borneo Bulletin, 2020e). The GoB has also taken strong measures to tackle fake news or misinformation being spread in its Fifth Domain. Social media outlets were most likely heavily monitored by the GoB to nip misinformation. The GoB fined on a 21-year old for causing a breach of peace (Borneo Bulletin, 2020f). Following the punishment, the public was "strongly advised to refrain from publishing, forwarding or creating fake news and misinformation about COVID-19 as these may be regarded as offences under the legislation including Section 34 of the Public Order Act, Chapter 148 which carries a penalty of a fine of BND3,000 and imprisonment for three years" (Ibid) . Further enforcement was carried, with business premises fined when they fail to follow regulations, such its ongoing 'Operasi Merati' operations (Borneo Bulletin, 2020g). In other matters, twelve irresponsible partygoers were jailed after flouting COVID-19 restrictions. The Sultan himself referred the hotel incident in a special Titah on the 21st March 2020 to highlight the need to follow the law to ensure regulations are adequately enforced by the Government and for people in Brunei society to abide by them in order to beat Covid-19 (Borneo Bulletin, 2020h; The Scoop, 2020d).

Finally, the GoB further facilitated regulations and policies based on scientific evidence and best practices from other countries. GoB have taken cues from other countries' and international organization's experience and expertise in pandemic management, whereby tackling the issue early on would reduce the spread and hence save lives. It even took the initiative to implement innovative policies. For example, the Government was also an early adopter of "RT-PCR testing in the absence of symptoms, making it mandatory under the Infectious Disease Act for all individuals with (i) travel or close-contact history (regardless of symptoms); (ii) pneumonia; or (ii) present a second time at a health care facility for an influenza-like illness within a 14-day period…random sampling is also conducted in community health centers, and among the large foreign worker population" (Wong et al., 2020a). The Government actively advised the public to follow health advices and instructions, including the need to maintain social distancing, to wear a mask, to use hand sanitizers, to report themselves if they are not feeling well to the hospital, and even to cancel wedding events to contain the COVID-19 spread. All these advice and policies were all backed by scientific information and socialized for the public to understand and follow. This 'mass education programme' was communicated through Old and New media continuously, to the point it may have become borderline repetitive. Nevertheless, the process arguably worked, and it is from the education given to the people that they comply willingly with the regulations implemented, for people are confident that the regulations and policies were reasonable.

## 2. Role of the Private Sector

The private sector in Brunei employs 66.2% of the workforce (DEPD, 2020), employing 74,400 persons in 2019. The main generators of GDP are the Oil and Gas industry. Brunei Shell Petroleum (BSP) is by far the largest private sector in the country, employing an estimated 4,000 employees and more than

20,000 contractors (BSP, N/A). As for non-Oil and Gas sector, they make up the rest, employing the remaining private-sector workforce. Amid Covid-19, the private sector in the country was badly hit and had to undergo a difficult adjustment period. In this matter, the GoB outlined measures requiring businesses to adhere to regulations and policies, which the private sector has to follow. Among the policies required were having the private sector to install the contact-tracing software PremiseScan App (The Bruneian, 2020b). With over 10,709 downloads as of June 26, 2020 (The Scoop, 2020e), the App is used for the Government's contact tracing efforts, where workers, customers or visitors of a business premise has to scan every time stakeholders visit the business or attend work. Following the App, businesses were also told to follow strict guidelines, such as having them to do temperature checks by the entrances, to scan the QR code or otherwise write their details in a logbook, to have their workers wear masks, to have customers abide by social distancing measures, and to ensure cleanliness and hygiene in the premise should not be compromised. Businesses across Brunei has to, therefore, adjust to the 'new normal' (Yang, 2020).

In light of Covid-19, the IT private sector took the initiative to jointly-produce self-screening mobile application integrated with artificial intelligence and data analytic capabilities with the Government. The PremiseScan and the BruHealth App were materialized and enhanced with the support of Ministry of Home Affairs (MoHA), MoH and Ministry of Transport and Infocommunications as well as IT Protective Security Services Sdn Bhd (ITPSS), Dynamik Technologies Sdn Bhd, Unified National Networks Sdn Bhd (UNN) and EVYD Technology (Borneo Bulletin, 2020i). The BruHealth app became a notable success, with over 436,047 downloads being made since May 14 (Ibid). This meant that the App has a significant penetration rate of 92.7% among the populace. The App was later modified and further polished by a China-based company. New advances were made since enabling people to get real-time updated data on the Covid-19 statistics and to access their personal healthcare information, which is a leap forward in the digitization drive in the national healthcare system. Aside from the contact-tracing software, telecommunication companies such as UNN Sdn Bhd complemented the digitization drive by providing quality and affordable internet connection services, particularly to those who are not privileged, such as students with no internet to facilitate online learning (Borneo Bulletin, 2020j). On the whole, the IT and telecommunication sectors played their role to digitize Brunei during the Covid-19 pandemic and moving the nation one step closer to the 4th Industrial Revolution.

When it comes to the private sector adjustability amid Covid-19, there were bumps and hurdles along the way faced by companies in transitioning to a 'Work from Home' model (ILO Monitor, 2020) or remote working. The entire process was particularly novel for Brunei. However, the guidance and encouragement to pursue the 'Work from Home' policy led primarily by large private sector companies and government-linked organizations have most likely helped the transition process for non-state organizations. The measure was implemented to mitigate community spread (The Asean Post, 2020). Hence, it became an imperative for the companies mentioned to adapt to the model to their workforce, where possible, especially when their business was affected by Government's temporary closures of businesses. For example, private school and tuition centres that saw classes done online, such as through Zoom (Borneo Bulletin, 2020k). Restaurants, however, have no choice other than to provide service delivery during the shutdown period. Delivery apps, such as GoMamam, grew in popularity in those period (Biz Brunei, 2020), although the trend may have been slowing down since. Other businesses may find 'Work from Home' model to be unsuitable, however. These businesses include cinemas, gyms, golf courses, and bowling alleys – they have been opened since. In any case, the 'Work from Home' model has most likely increased the digitization drive in the country, whereas those companies that could not carry the model out due to the nature of their business had to endure difficult times, sometimes shutting their business for good. Nevertheless, Covid-19 accelerated digitization.

The adverse effects on businesses by policy restrictions amid Covid-19 have particularly hit companies hard. During the period, it became increasingly difficult for employers to bring their foreign workers into the country because of the travel restrictions imposed by the GoB (Moh, 2020d). As part of the virus containment policy, the GoB suspended foreign workers still outside the country from coming to Brunei. The business uncertainty and potential losses faced by businesses may have resulted in Brunei companies to hire locals. As such, the GoB expanded the "i-Ready" programme to help business in Brunei to hire and train locals in the process (MOFE, 2020). Business, sensing the uncertainty caused by Covid-19, took on the chance by enrolling into the programme and hiring locals to further adjust with the times. The resulting effect had three consequences, namely 1) it reduced the unemployment rate in Brunei; 2) provide a breathing space for the private sector to hire locals and hence to help them to stabilize operations in the absence of foreign workers; 3) and to train locals in the process in various industries and sectors so they can become skilled. Other than that, businesses have taken initiative to hire locals in light of foreign supply restrictions. Hua Ho, Brunei's biggest retail shop chain, has opened up 300 job openings between October and November 2020 (Facebook, 2020a). The job opportunities would afford people jobs. The 'Bruneinization'' drive would most likely continue in the near future.

The Whole-of-Nation approach would not have been complete without taking into account the role of mass media in the country. Media in Brunei include Borneo Bulletin, Media Permata, and Sin Chew Daily all played vital roles in the dissemination of information to the mass public. Their continuous reporting of the press conference briefings, publications of government health information and advice, and many others have contributed to the socialization and awareness of people towards the Covid-19 situation. The media has also deployed Social Media to reach out to the public. Bruneians are heavy users of internet (Anshari et al. 2017) and has the third-largest user per capita of Social Media in the planet in 2018, with the Government having the most active Instagram account worldwide (Omar, 2020a; Kemp, 2019; Borneo Bulletin, 2020l). As such, people get their news on Social Media and the content related to COVID-19 in Brunei were mostly generated and shared by the media outlet. Thus, private media companies become influential in influencing the mass public. The role of State media must also not be underestimated as they primàrily set the public agenda, in which other media has to get their information from. The influence and the partnership between state and private media resulted in strong control of information throughout the process, allowing for people hence to get news, advice, and information on Covid-19, as well as to fight Fake News and Infodemics.

## 3. Society

General society including those from the NGO sector were galvanized to support the GoB. The Youth Volunteer Ad-Hoc Committee was set up by the Ministry of Culture, Youth and Sports to recruit volunteers who wish to assist in handling the outbreak as well as coordinate the distribution of volunteers to assist the MoH (MOFE, 2020). The committee is comprised of NGOs, such as Brunei Youth Council, Malam Minggu Pusat Belia (MMPB), Belia Cinta Tanah Air Alumni Programme (PBCTA), Youth Transformation Community Club (KKBT), All Life Emergency Response Team (ALERT), National Service Programme (PAPKBN) Alumni, Brunei Darussalam Scout Association (PPNBD), Darussalam Motorcycle Association (PEMODA). Students and government and company officials were also involved (Borneo Bulletin, 2020m). Their responsibilities involve in low-risk tasks such as checking body temperature; assisting in secretarial work in monitoring or isolation facilities; to facilitate and distribute food donations to front-liners; receive returning Bruneians at the Brunei International Airport; provide aid in the discharge process of those who completed their 14-day isolation; and so on. The purpose of which is to reduce costs and leverage on volunteers' energies, thereby reducing the workload stress put on the Government, resulting in the State to channel its resources towards strategic areas of healthcare management. The effort was also lauded by His Majesty the Sultan of Brunei as it is in reflective of the Whole-of-Nation approach to involve society in tackling the Covid-19 challenge (The Scoop, 2020f).

The COVID-19 Relief Fund was also set up the GoB on 21st March 2020 (BIBD, 2020). The Covid-19 relief fund was a fund where the public can donate towards helping the Government reduce the financial burden to help tackle the spread of COVID-19. The fund got an overwhelmingly positive response where, as of 13th June 2020, the fund has raised more than BND$14.35 million dollars within three months (The Scoop, 2020g). The donation came in from the public, third sector organizations and the private sectors. The flow of funds has also helped the GoB in meeting unexpected expenses. Public donations on funds would necessarily require a level of transparency and how the ministers manage the fund. In response to this, the GoB informed the public the funds are to be managed co-jointly by the Ministry of Health and the Ministry of Finance and Economy. These organizations will have the final say where the funds will go too. Moreover, the continued successes and visible projects developed (such as the establishment of the new virology lab) resulting from the Covid-19 pandemic management response has most probably increased people's confidence towards the Government, hence leading to people to contribute more into the fund. Various organizations joined in the effort to pool money in. Even the government ministers have also contributed BND$100,000 from their savings into the effort (The Star, 2020b). The Whole-of-Nation spirit was exhibited brilliantly through the success of the COVID-19 Relief Fund.

There was also the non-monetary contribution by the people. Donations took in the form of canned foods and drinks, rice bags, cooked meals, dried food, and other essential healthcare-related items such as sanitizers, gloves, bleach, masks, and more were received by the health officials and frontline workers. Teachers from JIS, a well-known international school in Brunei, took the initiative to 3D print 100 face shields, subsequently donating them to the MoH (Borneo Bulletin, 2020n). What emerged from the whole moment was the generosity demonstrated by the people in helping the nurses and healthcare workers. There is no dispute the frontline health workers face difficulties in being confined in the healthcare centres for long weeks and sometimes for months to treat patients. In the process, they had to sacrifice their family time, as well as to expose themselves to the risk of danger. The viral video of a sad nurse who shared her challenging experience (Facebook, 2020b) may have resulted in more people to pour in donations in Brunei Darussalam. Her message has also pressed home the need for people to be socially responsible and do their part in helping the frontlines, as the Government can only do so much. As the Minister of Health warned individuals to play their part to avoid a second wave of COVID-19, which may undermine the frontline workers' efforts so far. The support given by the people showed an impressive feat of Whole-of-Nation unity.

The public tip-off or intelligence sharing were crucial for government monitoring purposes. Through Social Media and the healthcare 148 Health Advice Hotline, a 24-hour hotline for public inquiries expressly set up for COVID-19 purposes worked tremendously well in giving essential information to help the GoB in enforcing the laws. A viral video showing a mass gathering queuing for the opening up of a new shopping centre was shared in Brunei's Social Media on the 8th November 2020, notably Reddit (2020). The GoB caught wind of the information, resulting in the authorities to swiftly arrive on the scene to break up the mass gathering. As a consequence, the business was fined a compound of

BND$5,000 for holding a "promotional sales event and encouraged large gatherings of more than 350 people without implementing any appropriate regulatory measures." (MoH, 2020e). There was also the unfortunate incident of the youth who was fined by the Government for spreading misinformation (Borneo Bulletin, 2020f). People who saw it has probably forwarded it to the GoB to take action, and take action they did. The examples mentioned above further demonstrate that the public can be an asset for the Government for monitoring purposes and to tackle misinformation.

The involvement by influential non-state actors as an online socializing agent needs attention. In Brunei where Social Media is influential as a medium of information, bloggers and online news media outlets came to help to socialize the public to best practises in taking care of their health. These also include giving the public health-related advice and warnings, resulting in the increased awareness of people to follow the law and the guidelines set out by the Government. Some information is mundane, such as telling people not to forget to wear their masks, maintain social distancing, and to use hand sanitizers. Nevertheless, these non-state actors have effectively become an appendage to the Government, allowing these 'influencers' or influential personalities to engage with the public. Nationally-renowned bloggers, such as RanoAdidas, and independent news sites, such as The Scoop, The Bruneian, and BizBrunei.com possess media power that can easily reach out to the mass populace. Hence, it is from their influence that would be key in disseminating government information. Apart from that, the bloggers and non-state journalists also get the chance to channel people's questions to the ministers in the daily press conferences (Whatsneue.com, 2020). Questions regarding the future of the airline workforce, Work from Home model, Covid-19 fund, motherly care, and other pertinent issues were raised, allowing the public to get further engaged in the story and, in the process, receive vital information in these Press Conferences.

## CONCLUSION

During the COVID-19 pandemic crisis, the GoB has demonstrated its ability to administer participation through a Whole-of-Nation approach, one that gelled together state and non-state actors to collectively contribute to tackling the COVID-19 pandemic. While the COVID-19 crisis is still a present danger worldwide, as of 4th January 2021, the GoB has shown it is sensible in its policy-making decisions and executions. By far, it spared no expense when it comes to taking care of the people, as demonstrated by the massive investments in the upgrade of healthcare capacity and strict regulations put in place as containment and deterrence to the spread of COVID-19. The private sector also played their part in working to help the GoB in its own unique ways by adapting to the changes such as the 'Work from Home' model, contributing to the digitization drive, and being considerate in weathering the crisis together, with some businesses taking positive action steps by hiring and training locals. Finally, the Brunei society has also shown in this whole process as being in unison with the GoB, with volunteers and NGOS willing to help the state in the form of monetary and non-monetary assistance. Although there are no official polls carried out, judging from the mood of the public and from the evidence so far, this researcher can confidently say trust towards the Government is at an all-time high. Indeed, the crisis has strengthened the country's unity, knowing they all share the same destiny in overcoming COVID-19. While the economy was hit by the low oil prices and a sharp decline in the travel and tourism industry (CSPS, 2020; Chan and King, 2020), it never daunted the GoB to utilize its financial war chest to realize His Majesty the Sultan of Brunei's ongoing mission, that is to take care of the people's welfare and to maintain national stability. Whole-of-Nation offered this solution, and this researcher hopes the Brunei lesson can give salient lessons for other policy-makers a thing or two in dealing emerging crisis so their societies can eventually emerge and be poised for the Fourth Industrial Revolution and the 'Great Reset'.

## LIMITATIONS OF STUDY & THE WAY FORWARD

The book chapter is not the first, nor will it be the final study to be made on the experience of Brunei facing Covid-19. Indeed, in the coming years, the scholarly work in this unique field will only multiply and evolve. While this chapter has aimed is to document the Brunei experience and its application of Whole-of-Nation concept in tackling the crisis, there are notable areas that require highlighting for the informed researchers concerning this research, namely after having utilized the Case Study, there may be elements of biasness (being a Bruneian himself) and subjectivity that would naturally be accompanied in the qualitative process. These are well-known limitations of qualitative research of this nature, but the limitations are overcome by the hard evidence, using secondary data to substantiate this chapter's storyline. Moreover, this work will not say Brunei is totally free from COVID-19, as things can change in the coming years or even months, but the country has done well thus far and for these lessons can be extracted and learned. Overall, the Whole-of-Nation in the field of Public Policy and Pandemic Management are still in need of review, given the notable absence of engagement being placed as a priority in development that takes into account all actors in society, be they State or non-state actors. However, this work challenges future researchers to identify areas to build on, especially concerning the theoretical and practical application of Whole-of-Nation in their own experiences and national contexts, as a means to develop innovative policy toolkits further to make the global society and economy more resilient in the face of future crisis.

## POLICY RECOMMENDATIONS IN MANAGING PANDEMICS

The policy recommendations arising from this study are five-fold:

### 1. Robust Monitoring and Surveillance System in Place

A robust monitoring and Surveillance System must be in place for governments, supported by international organizations to help prepare for incoming or current global pandemics. The system would allow governments to make adequate preparations based on emerging issues and to nip them in the bud when it does emerge. The GoB is credited for taking early steps to get updated with WHO. This was as early in January 2020. What was then known as 'acute cases of hypothermia' went on into becoming the full-blown deadly COVID-19. By then, Brunei was already preparing for the virus, and when the virus did hit national shores, the government was able to take decisive action despite its limited experience in managing a nation-wide pandemic.

### 2. Evidenced-backed Policies (EBP)

Evidenced-based Pandemic Management policies are needed to successfully tackle any incoming virus, or at least manage its spread. The advice socialized by the GoB to the society, as well as the policies imposed, were backed by Scientific studies and evidence, resulting in the successful tackling of Covid-19. It would not bode well, particularly for people, let alone government leaders, to ignore their scientists and experts. One can sadly observe this tragedy elsewhere when one global leader flaunt Covid-19 as a 'political conspiracy' (Dyer, 2020). With technologies today, even a tweet can spawn a damaging conspiracy theory (Gruzd and Mai, 2020) that may jeopardize the war against COVID-19. The unnecessary tragic loss of hundreds of thousands of lives around the globe is a testament to the fundamental mistake in people ignoring science.

## 3. Whole-of-Nation Governance

Governments must not only look at their selves as the leading player in dealing with a pandemic. It has to take into account the private sector and society in the entire process, termed as the Whole-of-Nation approach. Doing so would necessitate the colossal and strategic effort to socialize non-state actors to play their part, pressing them on the vital need to help the Government to tackle the crisis. The State must necessarily still lead, but it must actively treat non-state actors as partners too. This crisis can also be a good opportunity to re-articulate and re-arrange the social contract between the state and people in the 'Great Reset' in a Post-COVID-19 era.

## 4. Drive Digitisation Forward

Amid the Covid-19 pandemic, where millions of workers around the globe are affected to the point their working model has shifted online, it is probably best for countries to take this opportunity to push for digitization. Digitization must encompass the Government and ICT sectors as well as people in all demographics, not just the young but the elderly too. Doing so would is needed to reduce the 'digital divide' (Seifert et al., 2020) and to prime the global cities and economies for the 4th Industrial Revolution.

## 5. Utilize Digital Technology (Social Media and Big Data)

Countries need to utilize digital technology like Social Media and Big Data to help the effort to contain the virus. Social Media can be used to spread government-sanction advice and tips to the mass public. They can also engage with them to increase e-participation. Big Data is now being used as a primary by-product of the PremiseScan and BruHealth apps in Brunei's healthcare setting, thus accelerating its E-Government drive (Anshari and Lim, 2017). Thus, with Social Media and Big Data, governments can further develop their monitoring and dynamic capabilities whilst at the same time providing healthcare services to their societies. Other countries and cities (Zaini, 2020) can follow Brunei's suit.

## REFERENCES

ADB. (2020). *COVID-19 Economic Impact Could Reach $8.8 Trillion Globally*. New ADB Report.

Ahmad, N. (2018). Attitudes Towards Family Formation Among Young Adults in Brunei Darussalam. *Pakistan Journal of Women's Studies*, *25*(1).

Anshari, M., Almunawar, M. N., Shahrill, M., Wicaksono, D. K., & Huda, M. (2017). Smartphones usage in the classrooms: Learning aid or interference? *Education and Information Technologies*, *22*(6), 3063–3079. doi:10.100710639-017-9572-7

Anshari, M., & Lim, S. A. (2017). E-government with big data enabled through smartphone for public services: Possibilities and challenges. *International Journal of Public Administration*, *40*(13), 1143–1158. doi:10.1080/01900692.2016.1242619

Baker, M. G., Wilson, N., & Anglemyer, A. (2020). Successful elimination of Covid-19 transmission in New Zealand. *The New England Journal of Medicine*, *383*(8), e56. doi:10.1056/NEJMc2025203 PMID:32767891

Basir, K. H. (2021). COVID-19 and Islamic Social Finance. Unlocking Islamic Social Finance to Assist Micro Small Medium Enterprises (Msmes). In *Brunei Darussalam*. Routledge.

Bhaskaran, M. (2010). Economic diversification in Brunei Darussalam. *CSPS Strategy and Policy Journal*, *1*(1), 1–12.

BIBD. (2020). *Easing the Nation's Support of the Covid-19 Relief Fund*. http://www.bibd.com.bn/assets/pdf/media-centre/media-releases/2020/PR018_BIBD_QUICKPAY_COVID_19.pdf

Biz Brunei. (2020). *Live tracking, tiered delivery rates see GoMamam reach 200 daily orders*. https://www.bizbrunei.com/2020/04/live-tracking-tiered-delivery-rates-see-gomamam-reach-200-daily-orders/

Borneo Bulletin. (2011). *Monetary authority to ensure nation's stability*. Author.

Borneo Bulletin. (2020a). *Solidarity strong in fighting COVID-19*. https://borneobulletin.com.bn/2020/04/solidarity-strong-in-fighting-covid-19/

Borneo Bulletin. (2020b). *DCCA warns against hiking medical mask, hand sanitiser prices*. https://borneobulletin.com.bn/2020/02/dcca-warns-hiking-medical-mask-hand-sanitiser-prices

Borneo Bulletin. (2020c). *Preparedness, cooperation are key*. https://borneobulletin.com.bn/2020/09/preparedness-cooperation-are-key/

Borneo Bulletin. (2020d). *Stiff penalty for Infectious Disease Act violations*. https://borneobulletin.com.bn/2020/06/stiff-penalty-for-infectious-disease-act-violations/

Borneo Bulletin. (2020e). *Gym owner in the soup for breaking MoH rules*. https://borneobulletin.com.bn/2020/04/gym-owner-in-the-soup-for-breaking-moh-rules-2/

Borneo Bulletin. (2020f). *Youth charged for posting video breaching peace*. https://borneobulletin.com.bn/2020/03/youth-charged-for-posting-video-breaching-peace/

Borneo Bulletin. (2020g). *'Operasi Merati' At Business Premises*. https://www.brudirect.com/news.php?id=106329

Borneo Bulletin. (2020h). *'Party-goers' to learn fate on Saturday*. https://borneobulletin.com.bn/2020/06/party-goers-to-learn-fate-on-saturday-2/

Borneo Bulletin. (2020i). *BruHealth app to get new features.* https://www.mofe.gov.bn/Lists/News/NewDispForm.aspx?ID=164

Borneo Bulletin. (2020j). *UNN working with ministries to facilitate online learning.* https://borneobulletin.com.bn/2020/03/unn-working-with-ministries-to-facilitate-online-learning/

Borneo Bulletin. (2020k). *Tutors go online with classes.* https://borneobulletin.com.bn/2020/04/tutors-go-online-with-classes/

Borneo Bulletin. (2020l). *Brunei Info Department the most active Instagram government account in the world.* https://borneobulletin.com.bn/ig-posts-info-dept-is-top-of-the-world/

Borneo Bulletin. (2020m). *COVID-19 Brunei: Youth volunteers heed nation's call.* https://borneobulletin.com.bn/2020/04/youth-volunteers-heed-nations-call/

Borneo Bulletin. (2020n). *JIS teachers produce 100 face shields for frontliners.* https://borneobulletin.com.bn/2020/04/jis-teachers-produce-100-face-shields-for-frontliners/

Borneo Bulletin. (2021). *15 new imported cases found.* Accessed https://borneobulletin.com.bn/2021/01/15-new-imported-cases-found-2/

Brunei Year Book. (2015). *Brunei Year Book.* Brunei Press Sdn Bhd.

Brzezinski, A., Kecht, V., Van Dijcke, D., & Wright, A. L. (2020). *Belief in science influences physical distancing in response to covid-19 lockdown policies.* University of Chicago, Becker Friedman Institute for Economics Working Paper, (2020-56).

BSP. (n.d.). *Overview of our Business.* https://www.bsp.com.bn/main/about-bsp/overview-of-our-business

Cairney, P. (2020). The UK government's COVID-19 policy: Assessing evidence-informed policy analysis in real time. *British Politics*, 1–27.

Chan, J. K. L., & King, V. T. (2019). Covid-19 and Tourism in Southeast Asia. *Network (Bristol, England).*

Chaw, L., Koh, W. C., Jamaludin, S. A., Naing, L., Alikhan, M. F., & Wong, J. (2020). Analysis of SARS-CoV-2 transmission in different settings, Brunei. *Emerging Infectious Diseases*, *26*(11), 2598–2606. doi:10.3201/eid2611.202263 PMID:33035448

Cheong, D. (2019). *The Fourth Industrial Revolution, Job Futures and Policy Implications for Reducing Youth Unemployment in Brunei Darussalam.* CSPS.

Cheung, J. C. S. (2017). Rentier welfare states in hydrocarbon-based economies: Brunei Darussalam and Islamic Republic of Iran in comparative context. *Journal of Asian Public Policy*, *10*(3), 287–301. doi:10.1080/17516234.2015.1130468

Christensen, T., & Lægreid, P. (2007). The whole-of-government approach to public sector reform. *Public Administration Review*, *67*(6), 1059–1066. doi:10.1111/j.1540-6210.2007.00797.x

Cousin, G. (2005). Case study research. *Journal of Geography in Higher Education*, *29*(3), 421–427. doi:10.1080/03098260500290967

CSPS. (2020a). *Brunei Economic Update, July 2020.* CSPS.

CSPS. (2020b). *Brunei Economic Update, October 2020*. CSPS.

De Vienne, M. S. (2015). Brunei: From the age of commerce to the 21st century. NUS Press.

DEPD. (2020). *Labor Force Survey 2019*. http://www.deps.gov.bn/DEPD%20Documents%20Library/DOS/Labour%20force%20survey_KTK/2019/KTK_2019.pdf

Doyle, B. (2019). *The Whole-of-Nation and Whole-of-Government Approaches in Action*. Academic Press.

Dunleavy, P., Margetts, H., Bastow, S., & Tinkler, J. (2006). New public management is dead—Long live digital-era governance. *Journal of Public Administration: Research and Theory*, *16*(3), 467–494. doi:10.1093/jopart/mui057

Dyer, O. (2020). Trump claims public health warnings on covid-19 are a conspiracy against him. *BMJ*, *368*, m941.

Eckerd, A., & Heidelberg, R. L. (2020). Administering Public Participation. *American Review of Public Administration*, *50*(2), 133–147. doi:10.1177/0275074019871368

Facebook. (2020a). *Hua Ho Job Ad for 300 Positions*. https://www.facebook.com/HuaHoSymbOFFICIAL/photos/pb.123990884417648.-2207520000./1813899762093410/?type=3&theater

Facebook. (2020b). *MOH COVID-19 Awareness Video*. https://www.facebook.com/692035914258111/videos/203051744287275

Gottfried, R. S. (2010). *Black death*. Simon and Schuster.

Gruber, J., & Trickett, E. J. (1987). Can we empower others? The paradox of empowerment in the governing of an alternative public school. *American Journal of Community Psychology*, *15*(3), 353–371. doi:10.1007/BF00922703

Gruzd, A., & Mai, P. (2020). Going viral: How a single tweet spawned a COVID-19 conspiracy theory on Twitter. *Big Data & Society*, *7*(2). doi:10.1177/2053951720938405

Hamdan, M., & Hoon, C. Y. (2019). Brunei Darussalam: Making strides with a renewed focus on the future. *Southeast Asian Affairs*, *2019*(1), 84–102.

Hartley, K., & Vu, M. K. (2020). Fighting fake news in the COVID-19 era: Policy insights from an equilibrium model. *Policy Sciences*, *53*(4), 735–758. doi:10.100711077-020-09405-z PMID:32921821

Hashim, A. A. H. (2010). Challenges in achieving wawasan 2035 goals: Economic diversification in perspective. *CSPS Strategy and Policy Journal*, *1*(1), 29–54.

Hidayat, S. E. (2020). *Islamic Economy in ASEAN Countries During the Covid-19 Era*. Academic Press.

Keast, R. (2011). Joined-up governance in Australia: How the past can inform the future. *International Journal of Public Administration*, *34*(4), 221–231. doi:10.1080/01900692.2010.549799

Kemp, S. (2019). *Global Digital Report 2019-We Are Social*. We Are Social.

Kettl, D. F. (2016). *Politics of the administrative process*. Cq Press.

Koh, W. C., Naing, L., & Wong, J. (2020). Estimating the impact of physical distancing measures in containing COVID-19: An empirical analysis. *International Journal of Infectious Diseases*, *100*, 42–49. doi:10.1016/j.ijid.2020.08.026 PMID:32800859

Lane, J. E. (2000). *New public management*. Taylor & Francis US.

Madhav, N., Oppenheim, B., Gallivan, M., Mulembakani, P., Rubin, E., & Wolfe, N. (2017). *Pandemics: risks, impacts, and mitigation*. Academic Press.

Malecki, K., Keating, J. A., & Safdar, N. (2020). Crisis communication and public perception of COVID-19 risk in the era of social media. *Clinical Infectious Diseases*, ciaa758. doi:10.1093/cid/ciaa758 PMID:32544242

Mat, N. F. C., Edinur, H. A., Razab, M. K. A. A., & Safuan, S. (2020). A single mass gathering resulted in massive transmission of COVID-19 infections in Malaysia with further international spread. *Journal of Travel Medicine*. PMID:32307549

Mazzucato, M., & Kattel, R. (2020). COVID-19 and Public-sector Capacity. *Oxford Review of Economic Policy*, *36*(Supplement_1), S256–S269. doi:10.1093/oxrep/graa031

MOFE. (2020). *Measures Undertaken by the Government in Addressing the Impact of Covid-19 in Brunei Darussalam*. https://www.mofe.gov.bn/Shared%20Documents/MEASURES%20UNDERTAKEN%20BY%20THE%20GOVERNMENT%20IN%20HANDLING%20THE%20IMPACT%20OF%20COVID-19%20%20issued%2027.04.2020%20v7.pdf

MoH. (2020a). *PR: Health Information Regarding Severe Pneumonia Cases in Wuhan, China*. http://www.moh.gov.bn/Shared%20Documents/2019%20ncov/FINAL%20Wuhan_Pneumonia_6-1-2020_PR.pdf

MoH. (2020b). *PR: 24th January 2020*. http://www.moh.gov.bn/Shared%20Documents/2019%20ncov/FINAL%20Press%20Release%20(eng)%20-%20SOP%20MOH%20terhadap%20Influenza%20dan%20Mesej%20Tular%20mengenai%20Influenza%2024%20Jan%202020.pdf

MoH. (2020c). *PR: Detection of the First Case of Covid-19 Infection in Brunei Darussalam*. Accessed http://www.moh.gov.bn/Shared%20Documents/2019%20ncov/press%20releases/FINAL%20Press%20Release%20(eng)%20-%20First%20Case%20COVID-19%20in%20Brunei%20Darussalam%20(2).pdf

MoH. (2020d). *PR: Travel Restrictions During COPVID-19 Pandemic Brunei Darussalam*. http://www.moh.gov.bn/Shared%20Documents/2019%20ncov/Travel_English%20version.pdf

MoH. (2020e). *PR: 9th November 2020*. http://www.moh.gov.bn/Shared%20Documents/2019%20ncov/press%20releases/Press%20Release%20on%20the%20current%20situation%20of%20COVID-19%20in%20Brunei%20Darussalam%20(09.11.2020).pdf

Mohamad, S. M. (n.d.). *Creative Production of 'COVID-19 Social Distancing' Narratives on Social Media*. Tijdschrift voor economische en sociale geografie.

Monitor, I. L. O. (2020). *COVID-19 and the world of work. Updated estimates and analysis*. Author.

Morgan, S. J., Pullon, S. R., Macdonald, L. M., McKinlay, E. M., & Gray, B. V. (2017). Case study observational research: A framework for conducting case study research where observation data are the focus. *Qualitative Health Research*, *27*(7), 1060–1068. doi:10.1177/1049732316649160 PMID:27217290

Murray, C. J., & Lopez, A. D. (1996). Evidence-based health policy—Lessons from the Global Burden of Disease Study. *Science*, *274*(5288), 740–743. doi:10.1126cience.274.5288.740 PMID:8966556

Musa, S. F. P. D., & Idris, D. S. R. P. H. (2020). Addressing Issues of Unemployment in Brunei: The Mismatch Between Employers Expectations and Employees Aspirations. *International Journal of Asian Business and Information Management*, *11*(2), 88–101. doi:10.4018/IJABIM.2020040106

NST. (2020). *How Sri Petaling tabligh became Southeast Asia's Covid-19 hotspot*. https://www.nst.com.my/news/nation/2020/03/575560/how-sri-petaling-tabligh-became-southeast-asias-covid-19-hotspot

OECD. (2019). *Government at a Glance Southeast Asia 2019 Country Fact Sheet. Brunei Darussalam*. https://www.oecd.org/gov/gov-at-a-glance-sea-country-factsheet-brunei-darussalam.pdf

Omar, A. M. (2020a). Digital Era Governance and Social Media: The Case of Information Department Brunei. In Employing Recent Technologies for Improved Digital Governance (pp. 19-35). IGI Global.

Omar, A. M. (2020b). The Whole-of-Nation Approach: The Case of Brunei Darussalam, Wawasan 2035, and the 4th Industrial Revolution. In Handbook of Research on Global Challenges for Improving Public Services and Government Operations (pp. 291-309). IGI Global.

Pang, L. L. (2020). Leadership and Crisis Communication During Covid-19: The Case of Brunei Darussalam. *Indonesian Association of Public Administration (IAPA) Virtual Conference 2020*.

Pike, A., Rodríguez-Pose, A., Tomaney, J., Torrisi, G., & Tselios, V. (2012). In search of the 'economic dividend' of devolution: Spatial disparities, spatial economic policy, and decentralisation in the UK. *Environment and Planning. C, Government & Policy*, *30*(1), 10–28. doi:10.1068/c10214r

Rahman, H. A., Aziz, A. A., Ibrahim, M. A., Suhaili, N. A., Daud, A. Z., & Naing, L. (2019). Development and validation of Islamic Governance Examination tool in healthcare settings. *International Journal of Health Governance*.

Rasmussen, C. E. (2011). *The autonomous animal: Self-governance and the modern subject*. U of Minnesota Press. doi:10.5749/minnesota/9780816669561.001.0001

Reddit. (2020). *Circulated Via whatsapp SKH Sg. Hanching grand opening. Where are the MOH guidelines & social distancing measures?* https://www.reddit.com/r/Brunei/comments/jq9yt7/circulated_via_whatsapp_skh_sg_hanching_grand/

Schwab, K., & Malleret, T. (2020). *Covid-19: The Great Reset*. Forum Publishing. World Economic Forum.

Seifert, A., Batsis, J. A., & Smith, A. C. (2020). Telemedicine in Long-Term Care Facilities During and Beyond COVID-19: Challenges Caused by the Digital Divide. *Frontiers in Public Health*, *8*, 690. doi:10.3389/fpubh.2020.601595 PMID:33194999

Shereen, M. A., Khan, S., Kazmi, A., Bashir, N., & Siddique, R. (2020). COVID-19 infection: Origin, transmission, and characteristics of human coronaviruses. *Journal of Advanced Research*, *24*, 91–98. doi:10.1016/j.jare.2020.03.005 PMID:32257431

Stake, R. E. (2005). *Qualitative case studies*. Academic Press.

Talib, N. S. (2002). A resilient monarchy: The Sultanate of Brunei and regime legitimacy in an era of democratic nation-states. *New Zealand Journal of Asian Studies*, *4*(2), 134–147.

The ASEAN Post. (2020). *Brunei's Response To COVID-19*. https://theaseanpost.com/article/bruneis-response-covid-19

The Bruneian. (2020a) *Health Minister Officiates New Virology Laboratory*. Author.

The Bruneian. (2020b). *Government Introduces Premises Scan App*. https://www.thebruneian.news/government-introduces-premisescan-app/

The Scoop. (2020a). *Gov't releases first digital economy masterplan*. https://thescoop.co/2020/06/05/govt-releases-first-digital-economy-masterplan/

The Scoop. (2020b). *COVID-19 live updates: March archive*. https://thescoop.co/2020/03/13/covid-19-live-updates/

The Scoop. (2020c). *New isolation centre building set to more than double number of beds*. https://thescoop.co/2020/04/24/new-isolation-centre-building-set-to-more-than-double-number-of-beds/

The Scoop. (2020d). *Aman Hills partygoers jailed for flouting COVID-19 restrictions*. https://thescoop.co/2020/06/14/aman-hills-party-goers-jailed-for-flouting-covid-19-restrictions/

The Scoop. (2020e). *COVID-19 live updates: June archive*. https://thescoop.co/2020/06/01/covid-19-live-updates-4/

The Scoop. (2020f). *HM announces special $400 monthly allowance for healthcare workers*. https://thescoop.co/2020/04/14/hm-announces-special-400-monthly-allowance-for-healthcare-workers/

The Scoop. (2020g). *COVID-19 live updates: June archive*. https://thescoop.co/2020/06/01/covid-19-live-updates-4/

The Star. (2020a). *Sultan: Brunei to expand virus testing capacity with new virology lab*. Author.

The Star. (2020b). *Brunei Cabinet donates BN$100,000 to fight Covid-19*. https://www.thestar.com.my/news/regional/2020/04/23/brunei-cabinet-donates-bn100000-to-fight-covid-19

Trilla, A., Trilla, G., & Daer, C. (2008). The 1918 "Spanish flu" in Spain. *Clinical Infectious Diseases*, *47*(5), 668–673. doi:10.1086/590567 PMID:18652556

van Dorp, L., Acman, M., Richard, D., Shaw, L. P., Ford, C. E., Ormond, L., ... Ortiz, A. T. (2020). Emergence of genomic diversity and recurrent mutations in SARS-CoV-2. *Infection, Genetics and Evolution*, *83*, 104351. doi:10.1016/j.meegid.2020.104351 PMID:32387564

Verbeke, A. (2020). Will the COVID-19 pandemic really change the governance of global value chains? *British Journal of Management*, *31*(3), 444–446. doi:10.1111/1467-8551.12422

Warner, R. (1962). *The Peloponnesian War*. Cassell.

Weber, M. (2015). Bureaucracy. In Working in America (pp. 29-34). Routledge.

Whatsneue.online. (2020). *9 To 5: What's Neue With Rano Adidas*. https://www.whatsneue.online/2020/05/25/9-to-5-rano-adidas/

WHO. (2012). *Resolution adopted by the General Assembly*. https://www.who.int/nmh/events/un_ncd_summit2011/political_declaration_en.pdf

WHO. (2020). *Live from Geneva on the new #coronavirus outbreak*. WHO.

WHO. (n.d.). *Coronavirus Disease (COVID-19) Dashboard*. https://covid19.who.int/

Wilasang, C., Sararat, C., Jitsuk, N. C., Yolai, N., Thammawijaya, P., Auewarakul, P., & Modchang, C. (2020). Reduction in effective reproduction number of COVID-19 is higher in countries employing active case detection with prompt isolation. *Journal of Travel Medicine*, *27*(5), taaa095. doi:10.1093/jtm/taaa095 PMID:32519743

Wilson, W. (1886). *The study of public administration*. Academic Press.

Wong, J., Abdul Aziz, A. B., Chaw, L., Mahamud, A., Griffith, M. M., Ying-Ru, L. O., & Naing, L. (2020b). High proportion of asymptomatic and presymptomatic COVID-19 infections in travelers and returning residents to Brunei. *Journal of Travel Medicine*.

Wong, J., Chaw, L., Koh, W. C., Alikhan, M. F., Jamaludin, S. A., Poh, W. W. P., & Naing, L. (2020c). Epidemiological investigation of the first 135 COVID-19 cases in Brunei: Implications for surveillance, control, and travel restrictions. *The American Journal of Tropical Medicine and Hygiene*, *103*(4), 1608–1613. doi:10.4269/ajtmh.20-0771 PMID:32815514

Wong, J., Koh, W. C., Alikhan, M. F., Aziz, A. B. A., & Naing, L. (2020a). Responding to COVID-19 in Brunei Darussalam: Lessons for small countries. *Journal of Global Health*, *10*(1), 010363. doi:10.7189/jogh.10.010363 PMID:32566154

Yang, K. (2020). Unprecedented Challenges, Familiar Paradoxes: COVID-19 and Governance in a New Normal State of Risks. *Public Administration Review*, *80*(4), 657–664. doi:10.1111/puar.13248 PMID:32836451

Yin, R. K. (2017). *Case study research and applications: Design and methods*. Sage publications.

Zaini, K. H. (2020). *Cities and Pandemics: a look into urban preparedness in COVID19 era*. University Putera Malaysia.

Zarocostas, J. (2020). How to fight an infodemic. *Lancet*, *395*(10225), 676. doi:10.1016/S0140-6736(20)30461-X PMID:32113495

# Chapter 4

# COVID-19 Being Positive Strategically in the Context of SDG and NDC

**Nikhil Kant**

https://orcid.org/0000-0002-0157-2866

*School of Management Studies, Indira Gandhi National Open University (IGNOU), India*

**Kumari Anjali**

*School of Sciences, Indira Gandhi National Open University (IGNOU), India*

## ABSTRACT

*Sustainable Development Goals (SDG) and nationally determined contributions (NDC), normally operated in silos at national level in developing countries despite their greater interrelation, require an aligned implementation. The chapter probes into the opportunities visible in the actions of different actors to tackle COVID-19 that can be continued or replicated for combating the menace of climate crisis and achieving sustainable development in post-COVID times. This chapter discusses the challenges that the contemporary issue of sustainability has faced due to the occurrence of this pandemic. The chapter concludes that at a time when no one wishes to be tested positive for COVID-19, there is a need to be positive strategically so that the potential opportunities of achieving goals and commitments under SDG and NDC could be sensed and seized by re-configuring resources and capabilities according to the actual needs for a sustainable future.*

## INTRODUCTION

The ruthless assault of a widespread infectious epidemic which crosses international boundaries and kills substantial population is referred to as a pandemic by the World Health Organization (WHO), and the COVID-19 (SARS-CoV-2) currently spread by a novel coronavirus infecting considerable population across the planet presents itself as such a pandemic. WHO informs that there is plethora of ongoing clinical trials which are underway in different countries to make available specific vaccines for this viral

DOI: 10.4018/978-1-7998-6948-1.ch004

disease which does not have any viable treatments as on date. Patients who are of old age and have co-morbid ailments are more likely to develop serious health problems which might lead them to demise. The COVID-19 pandemic taking entire world by storm and catching it unprepared stalled the world economy compelling countries to close their international as well as domestic borders for curbing its spread pushing them to go under lockdown immediately (Zakeri et al., 2020). UN ECLAC (2020) calls it an unprecedented humanitarian and health crisis which could damage an already weakened global economy and therefore require pursuance of suitable and sustainable courses of actions. This unprecedented assault can cause slipping back of the countries onto the sustainability pathways. While this pandemic has caused huge global upheaval impacting each country, it has increased uncertainties and challenges with respect to economy and environment. International Monetary Fund (IMF) has estimated that its impacts could be as huge as the historical 9/11 or the 2008 financial crises on the economy but stand incomparable as regards the capability of reshaping society.

Nonetheless, Dente & Hashimoto (2020) underscore the idiosyncratic opportunities, provided by the COVID-19 pandemic, in capturing the positive impact of the efforts made to handle it which can contribute to achieving sustainability in post COVID-19 times. The plethora of initiatives in the fight against COVID-19 at the technology, governance and other levels, if continued in post COVID-19 times, could have greater positive implications for achieving SDG and NDC for a sustainable future. Despite the fact that COVID-19 has posed huge challenges derailing the achievement of ambitious SDG and NDC, being optimistic, considering it as an opportunity of using the learning gained from the COVID-19 crisis times in combating climate crisis, can offer huge potentialities in achieving goals and commitments under SDG and NDC for a sustainable future. The chapter discusses how the learning during the pandemic COVID-19 times can be strategically utilized as an opportunity in achieving Sustainable Development Goals (SDG) and Nationally Determined Contributions (NDC) so that it could be helpful for policy-makers, researchers, practitioners, and many others continuously looking out for the impacts of the COVID-19 on the sustainable development and climate change issues. With the limitlessness of the research potential as regards the impact of COVID-19, the research studies to understand its impacts on the achievement of SDG and NDC are still not available sufficiently. The main hindrance might be the incompleteness of the relevant data related to COVID-19 and inadequacy of relevant peer-reviewed published literature because of passage of a very short period. Nonetheless, as the time rolls by, this chapter would become more helpful with the increasing availability of relevant data attracting more researchers to undertake research on these issues. This chapter highlights the challenges thrown by COVID-19 against the achievements of SDG and NDC which have normally operated in silos at national level in developing countries despite their greater interrelations requiring an aligned implementation of the two processes for meeting international sustainable development goals and climate commitments. It further probes into the opportunities visible in the actions of different actors tackling this pandemic that can be continued or replicated for combating the menace of climate crisis and achieving sustainable development in post COVID-19 times. The scholarly value of the chapter is that as an exploratory study it discusses the challenges that the contemporary issues of sustainability and climate crisis have faced due to sudden assault of this pandemic COVID-19, and therefore the chapter would enable researchers in different regions to work on similar projects by encouraging them to fill the research gaps with the help of learning from the COVID-19 crisis which will be helpful to different stakeholders interested in management of change during and post COVID-19 times, evaluating its impacts on SDG and NDC, and formulating suitable policies, more particularly in the developing countries.

## KNOWING ABOUT COVID-19

A widespread infectious epidemic crossing international boundaries and killing substantial number of people is defined as a pandemic by the World Health Organization (WHO). COVID-19 (SARS-CoV-2) currently spread by a newly discovered coronavirus having infected millions of people in different countries across the globe is a perfect example of such a pandemic. Normally majority of infected people with COVID-19 experience mild to moderate respiratory problems before recovering without any special medical treatment. However, persons and also older persons with underlying co-morbid ailments such as cardiovascular disease, diabetes, chronic respiratory disease, cancer etc. can develop serious health problems leading to their death. Though no specific vaccines or treatments are available for this viral disease as on date, many ongoing clinical trials are underway, informs WHO which keeps monitoring and providing updated information as an apex intergovernmental agency.

In general terms, this pandemic COVID-19 as a disease has been spreading with the support of close human contacts taking place in the routine social interactions through a novel coronavirus which, without any conclusive authentic evidence so far, is said to have been developed by humans, and there are people who believe it to have been developed as a biological weapon. The impact, nonetheless, has been severe across the globe directly affecting considerably the elderly people or people having co-morbidity leading them untimely to their demise, with varying percentage in different countries. The COVID-19 pandemic which was first reported in China in December 2019, the last month of the last year of the decade, took the entire planet by storm in the very initial months of the new decade so fast that it did not give ample time to be anticipated as a major risk which could bring the world economy to a stalling halt within only 3-4 weeks as it did. The countries, one after another, closed not only their international but also domestic borders to curb its transmission, invariably followed by nearly half the world which went under lockdown within merely 3 months (Zakeri et al., 2020).

UN ECLAC (2020) refers it as an unprecedented humanitarian and health crisis responsible for damaging an already weakened global economy, and cautions against its devastating impacts at the present time when there is an uncertainty about its likely intensity and duration which requires appropriate responses accompanied by reflection and actions to pursue sustainable courses of action. Although the restrictive measures have been relaxed with the passage of time, huge long term impact is certain in different countries across the globe with uncertainty in terms of scale. The unprecedented assault of this pandemic is also feared to cause slipping back of the countries onto the pathways leading to a situation in which its effects could be devastating in the short term and could hinder the process of recovery and development in the long term.

It is believed that the pandemic COVID-19, which has caused much upheaval across the globe leaving no country unaffected in the world, has raised the level of uncertainties and numerous challenges in assessing its impact on the economy. As per the estimates of the international intergovernmental agencies such as International Monetary Fund (IMF), the impacts of the pandemic COVID-19, the largest global health crisis faced by the mankind since World War II, could be comparable to the historical 9/11 or the 2008 financial crises, not only on the economy but also in terms of the capability of reshaping society for longer terms including but not limited to the impacts on the models, lifestyles and mindsets related to purchasing, travelling, getting education, and seeking healthcare. The pandemic has thrown huge challenges to the individuals and the institutions to establish clarity in their vision to adapt to the fast changes in an understandable and motivating manner making decisions strategically for management of climate and sustainable development issues in the post COVID-19 revival times (Prasad & Kant, 2020).

## KNOWING ABOUT THE SDG AND NDC

The father of the nation of India Mahatma Gandhi had shared his enlightening expressions "Earth provides enough to satisfy every man's needs, but not every man's greed"[1], and later the Brundtland Commission constituted by the United Nations (UN) in the year 1983 publishing its landmark report 'Our Common Future' in 1987 brought out, on the similar lines, the official and also most widely accepted definition of sustainable development (SD). This Commission referred SD as the "...development that meets the needs of the present without compromising the ability of future generations to meet their own needs" (WCED, 1987). The commonly known Brundtland Commission was originally constituted by the UN as the World Commission on Environment and Development (WCED) which remained functional for the period of 1983-87. It highlighted SD as a "…process of change in which the exploitation of resources, the direction of investments, the orientation of technological development, and institutional change are all in harmony and enhance both current and future potential to meet human needs and aspirations" (WCED, 1987).

These contributions of the commission and the UN were not the outcome of the efforts of a few for a short period but were actually the culmination of the grave concerns and varied contributions of many representing different regions, disciplines, sectors, groups, communities etc. starting from the 16th century emphasizing the need for sustainable use of resources including natural resources as human overpopulation and their increasing interventions were getting apparently visible. It is notable that the concept of sustainability had existed in the ancient philosophy and evolved globally since then. However, since the decade of 1970 the sustainability issues have become more prominent than ever amidst the increased attention on climate change and sustainable issues. The subsequent decades have witnessed the emergence of the sustainability issues attracting truly global attention under the leadership of the UN which could garner active support of plethora of Intergovernmental and Nongovernmental agencies in addition to the governments themselves (Kant & Anjali, 2020).

While the decade of 1970 is known to be significant as the starting point of seriously taking up the sustainability issues, the decade is also significant for drawing attention for the first time towards the realization with respect to the widening of the gap between developed and developing countries. These gaps were increasing not only in terms of growth but also in terms of the impact of natural hazards and frequency and severity of human induced disasters. These gaps hinted at an urgent need to adopt significantly different approach as regards developmental issues across the globe. This decade of 1970 thus witnessed the emergence of the Stockholm Declaration which made major public and private parties realize that human developmental activities in the present unsustainable form cannot be continued on earth indefinitely. The highly significant UN Conference on the Human Environment (UNCHE) also happened in this decade which was held in Stockholm to present to the global community the SD visions in the year of 1972. This was the same year which witnessed the publishing of the seminal book 'Limits to Growth' by the 'Club of Rome' which highlighted the requirement of a model output encompassing a system of a sustainable world which could satisfy the basic material needs of every resident without facing any abrupt and uncontrollable collapse (Kant, 2020).

Subsequent decade of 1980 brought the baton ahead with the publication of the landmark report of the Brundtland Commission (1983-87) with the name 'Our Common Future' in the year 1987 which underscored the strength of the three pillars of People-Planet-Profit which encompassed social equity, environmental protection, and economic growth respectively as three significant dimensions of SD. The decade also witnessed the foundation of the Intergovernmental Panel on Climate Change (IPCC) in the year of 1988 by the World Meteorological Organization (WMO) getting support of the UN Environment Programme (UNEP). This intergovernmental agency IPCC came into existence to collate and assess scientific evidences on climate change (Kant & Anjali, 2020).

The last decade of the previous century i.e. 1990 witnessed the happening of a highly significant Earth Summit held in Rio in the year 1992 and the birth of the UN Framework Convention on Climate Change (UNFCCC) in the year 1994, and also the seminal Kyoto Protocol in the year 1997. The first decade of the new century starting from 2000 witnessed the birth of ambitious 8 Millennium Development Goals (MDGs) as an outcome of the UN Millennium Summit held in 2000, and also the acceptance of Kyoto Protocol in 2005 as an international law. The next decade starting from 2010 is considered to be the most significant decade which has also been referred to as the decade with the 'Turbulent Teens' also, for the occurrence of plethora of anthropogenic contributions which forced the rechristening of climate change as climate crisis (WBCSD, n.d.). this decade was dotted with the significant event of the UN Conference on Sustainable Development held in Rio in 2012, 20 years later than the significant earth summit event of 1992 and hence commonly known as Rio+20; the Sustainable Development Summit held in New York in the year 2015; and also the Paris Climate Agreement emerged in COP21 (Conference of Parties 21) in the same year 2015. An abridged timeframe is presented in *Table 1* for reference.

*Table 1. Timeframe of Major Events related to Sustainability*

| Year | Major Events |
|---|---|
| Till 1972-73 | Publication of "Silent Spring" (Carson, 1962); "The Population Bomb: Population Control or Race to Oblivion" (Ehrlich, 1968); "The Closing Circle" (Commoner, 1971); "The Limits to Growth: A Report for the Club of Rome's Project on the Predicament of Mankind" (Meadows, 1972); "Only One Earth: The Care and Maintenance of a Small Planet" (Ward and Dubos, 1972); "Under siege: man, men and earth" (Wagner, Bailey & Campbell, 1973). |
| 1972 | UN Conference on the Human Environment in Stockholm |
| 1983 | UN World Commission on Environment and Development (UNWCED) |
| 1992 | UN Conference on Environment and Development (Earth Summit 1992) at Rio |
| 2000 | UN Millennium Summit giving birth to the MDG |
| 2002 | UN World Summit on Sustainable Development (RIO+10) at Johannesburg |
| 2012 | UN Conference on Sustainable Development (Earth Summit 2012; RIO+20) at Rio |
| 2015 | UN General Assembly giving birth to the SDG; and<br>UN FCCC COP21 giving birth to the NDC |

Climate change is a harsh demonstration of the inequality prevailing across the globe where the richest countries/people having higher incomes have contributed to climate change much more than poor countries/people having lower incomes historically; and poorer countries/people in terms of income, and more particularly small island developing states (SIDS), are much less resilient and hence more vulnerable to the socioeconomic costs related to climate change (UN ECLAC, 2020). It is notable that during these decades, the UN has been effectively instrumental in providing the member countries with an important multilateral dialogue platform to engage in developing purposeful global agenda of national and global developmental paths after discussions. These UN efforts culminated into what came in 2015 i.e. the Sustainable Development Goals (SDG) and the 2030 Agenda coming into existence in the UN Sustainable Development Summit; and Nationally Determined Contributions (NDC) and the Paris Climate Agreement as an actionable agreement coming into existence in the UNFCCC COP21 intending to strengthen global efforts of restricting the rise in global mean temperature under 2°C above pre-industrial level by 2100 with the consistent efforts of limiting it to 1.5°C. SDG and NDC both are known to nourish the intent to handle the social-environmental-economic challenges collectively with the concerted efforts of all the countries to for a sustainable future (Kant & Anjali, 2020). Both collectively call for ensuring peace with the help of partnership of the member countries of the UN to tackle the climate crisis harnessing accelerated actions and enhanced investments. The journey from SD to SDG has included several new dimensions i.e. 2 more Ps -Peace and Partnership- to the existing 3Ps i.e. People, Planet, and Profit. The inclusion of these dimensions strengthens the efforts of combating climate crisis helping in garner support of more dimensions i.e. Rs –Recover, Redesign, Remanufacture, Rethink, Refuse, Replace, Repurpose to the existing 3Rs i.e. Reduce, Reuse, and Recycle. Indian Prime Minister, Narendra Modi, has emphasized that this may also lead to attain another R i.e. Rejoice (complete blissfulness) to encourage citizens for implementing them in routine lives so that they could lessen problems, enhance suitability of solutions, and achieve sustainable development. This indicates that the menace of climate change can be combated with the help of appropriate climate action at the appropriate time.

According to the Paris Climate Agreement, the NDC represents climate plans at the national level which are submitted to the UNFCCC by member countries outlining their mitigation and adaptation actions to address climate change. Nonetheless, the issues of climate change significantly relate directly or indirectly to SDGs, for e.g. 'SDG 13: Climate Action' recognizes its importance directly while different SDGs recognize it indirectly as a cross-cutting issue and a major threat to SD with increased severity in future which needs be resolved for successful achievement of all 17 SDGs (UNSD, 2019). The major threat are, to name a few, undermining of the development gains, hindering further progress, lowering incomes and opportunities of vulnerable people, changing rainfall and droughts patterns, acidifying oceans, increasing frequency as well as intensity of natural hazards, rising sea levels, lessening water availability and access, reducing food security, increasing migration, reducing livelihoods, deteriorating health, and damaging infrastructure etc. It is notable that for the first time in the last 10 years, the 'Global Risks Report'-An annual publication by World Economic Forum - published in the year 2020 has found that all of the 'top five global risks in terms of likelihood' are environmental while there was none which were related to environment in the year 2010. This reports also hints that global mean temperatures are set to exceed 3°C by the end of century, double of what is prescribed by UNFCCC and IPCC to avoid the maximum impact severity of the social-environmental-economic consequences (WEF, 2020). SDG and NDC represent two of the most significant universal and holistic international development result frameworks. They should not be implemented in silos, and be evaluated collectively based on the vision, principles, implementation and follow-up mechanisms encompassing the above mentioned 5Ps and 6Rs, though both of them are voluntary and not legally binding. Actions determined for meeting SDG and NDC must have the potential to contribute towards both of them at the national level keeping in view that operation and implementation in an aligned manner for achieving both of them can offer huge opportunities at a time when the global mean temperature stands exceeded 1.1°C above the benchmark level. Here, it is pertinent to realize that any further delay cannot be afforded as it can cost much higher in future if not tackled today by enhancing the understanding and harnessing the synergy of NDC and SDG for longer term.

UNSD (2019) encourages the adoption of an integrated approach using the underlying synergy in its Global Sustainable Development Report-2019 which also underscores the need for a systemic approach for not deviating from the right path. SDG and NDC both are the most ambitious plans of actions, and the most comprehensive blueprints for the sustainability of the planet motivating different member countries and other actors in the UN system to adopt transformative and proactive actions for leading the world on to a sustainable path. SDG and NDC both are built on the premise that enjoyment of fulfilling lives by all human beings can be ensured by developments achieved in harmony with nature which can increase opportunities and decrease disruptions, emphasizing thereby the Ps and Rs explained above, if harnessed optimally to attain universal SD with the support of co-creation and collaboration along with innovations, can represent a holistic approach to manage developmental challenges.

At a time when majority of the countries lag far behind the level of achievement desired by SDG and NDC, achieving them will require wide-ranging economic and social transformations (Brandi, Dzebo, & Janetschek, 2017). Climate change recognized as a cross-cutting issue in the UN 2030 Agenda because of its impact on the 5Ps can set back the developmental gains of the past, present and future if not tackled properly using suitable mitigation and adaptation actions. While mitigation denotes reducing Greenhouse gases (GHGs) emissions through, for e.g., conservation of forests-ocean ecosystems and using renewable energy sources, adaptation denotes protection of human population and their livelihoods and settlements from the negative consequences of climate change. The Executive Secretary of the UNFCCC, Patricia Espinosa, considers climate change as the biggest threat facing humanity over the long term today, and the UN Secretary-General, António Guterres, considers that climate change has assumed the top position, far and away, in the list of global mega trends putting countries and communities under immense pressure. The WMO Secretary General, Petteri Taalas, informs also that following the current emissions path, the world is moving to see a global mean temperature increase between 3ºC-5ºC by the end of century. It is notable that addressing climate change by limiting global temperature to 1.5ºC instead of 2ºC above levels can decrease exposure of people to climate risks and vulnerability to poverty by 62 to 457 million. Nonetheless, the Global Sustainable Development Report 2019 (UNSD, 2019) hints at the silver lining in the possible solution pathways and huge opportunities which can emerge from tackling climate crisis using suitable adaptation and mitigation actions which offer huge potentialities for positive SD outcomes broadly including health benefits, sustainable livelihoods, employment opportunities, improved energy access, resilient economies, and reduced poverty through mitigation measures and investments in renewable energy, conservation of forests and oceans ecosystems, and through other adaptation measures.

## COVID-19: BEING POSITIVE STRATEGICALLY

UN ECLAC (2020) highlights the essentiality of this pandemic COVID-19 crisis culminating into new forms of globalization and geopolitics, underscoring also the need to consider it an opportunity for harnessing the advantages associated with multilateralism to strengthen action to achieve sustainable development. Kedia et al. (2020) underscore that the pandemic COVID-19 has laid greater emphasis on the significance of reducing environmental risks while undertaking developmental activities in future, and also on the need to look at more holistically on the planetary health comprising not only health of the humans but also of the ecology. Gutteres (2020) emphasizes that Covid-19 crisis, despite having caused extensive sufferings for the mankind, has opened up at the same time new opportunities for better revival with the help of building more resilient, inclusive, and sustainable societies. Zakeri et al. (2020) highlight that majority of consumers have started using the convenience of online shopping removing the entry barriers while coming across during lockdown period at individual level while at the industry level, new industry in terms of scale and efficiency has emerged riding on unprecedented innovations and offering new job opportunities, which provide the direction of the need to align economy recovery packages to put the industries on a clean path. Dente & Hashimoto (2020) underscore the idiosyncratic opportunity provided by the COVID-19 pandemic in capturing the positive impact of the efforts in handling it which can contribute to the sustainability in post COVID-19 times while concluding that multitude of uncertainties remain on its positive and negative impacts which might be clearer by virtue of our ability to collect and analyze unconventional data evolving with the passage of time.

The current situations warrant revisiting of what the President & CEO of the World Business Council for Sustainable Development (WBCSD) Peter White had articulated, a few years back, underscoring the willingness of big corporations as major parties in extending support to the acceleration of the transition to a sustainable future with the science-based targets, making good on global initiatives of the UN. He had articulated that the decade of 2010 had the 'Turbulent Teens', further hinting that the aims of the business community were to move from the 'Turbulent Teens' to the 'Transformation Times' when the new decade would start in 2020 (WBCSD, n.d.). This nomenclature of 'Turbulent Teens' coined by him proved its appropriateness since this period was fraught with multitude environmental risks and challenges and had the warmest five-years (2015-19) and ten-years (2010-19) periods, the highest recorded temperatures for oceans, several warmest years on record, most acidic sea water, lowest Arctic sea ice and Antarctica ice, and most importantly the announcement of the president of the USA exiting the Paris Climate Agreement. As if these were not enough, at this crucial time when the majority of the UN member countries individually and collectively were already lagging behind the scale and speed to meet SDG and NDC (UNSD, 2019), the opening year of new decade of 2020 witnessed the assault of an unprecedented COVID-19 pandemic crisis which has been responsible for huge loss of human lives, and incomparable collapse in economy leading it to an unforeseen conundrum witnessing huge investment outflow from emerging economy in first few months of the year compelling the IMF to project fall of global growth to -3% underlining it as the all-times worst recession.

The Asia-Pacific region, more particularly, with the most of the vulnerable population of the world, is feared to be impacted by the huge drop in global demands and GDP weakening their fiscal position and exacerbating new debt crisis which will be in addition to already less tax revenues and private investments. While they were at a the crossroad to make all possible efforts to maintain a sustainable planet, the pandemic COVID-19 has pushed us in the 'Turbulent Times' catching us unprepared, rather than making an entry into 'Transformation Times' after exiting the 'Turbulent Teens'. COVID-19, having emerged as a global pandemic and threatened the entire world, requires massive investments in the healthcare system in different countries. It is notable that rejuvenating economies in the post COVID times would also require greater investments compulsively diverting from the potential investments in climate mitigation and adaptation actions, further pushing forward the deadlines delaying these mitigation and adaptation projects.

Risks and challenges related to sustainable development and climate change appearing similar to COVID-19 on a variety of counts are unevenly distributed globally, and have greater impacts on vulnerable disadvantaged population. However, the significant motivations from what Winston Churchill once said after World War II while contributing to the formation of the United Nations that "Never let a good crisis go to waste", can be used during these 'Turbulent Times' by taking COVID-19 as a test case in the context of SDG and NDC. In these situations affected by the COVID-19 when the investments are bound to be diverted to healthcare and economic recovery, they need to be directed towards low-carbon opportunities in various sectors. It has been observed that the conventional energy sector has suffered more damage than the renewable energy sector during the COVID-19 period implying thereby the lesser market disruptions proneness of the renewable energy industry. The learning can be a boon if it could be utilized properly in post COVID-19 times (Kedia et al., 2020). Further, as the more efficient SDG and NDC than the MDGs and Kyoto Protocol respectively are founded on the learning received from their failures and successes, similar learning from COVID-19 can also show the right pathways and directions for tackling the challenges in the way of achieving SDG and NDC.

Karunathilake (2020), while warning that the COVID-19 pandemic might directly impact achievements of sustainability immensely due to less allocation of finances, emphasize categorically that this pandemic has demonstrated more positive effect than negative ones underscoring the need for the appropriate governments actions and attitudinal change. The actions of SAARC countries of getting reunited during these testing times for extending financial support to poorer nations, and enhancing regional cooperation in their fight against the pandemic have innumerable positive outcomes, which might be positively affected by the new world order, giving rise to discoveries and innovations at different levels and in different sectors boosting demand and production for domestic products and services strengthening the local supply chains, micro-small-medium local handicraft productions, and responsible consumptions of resources taking commensurate support of low-cost efficient productions with appropriate technological use.

No doubt, these health emergency situations sparked by COVID-19 forecast worst economic scenario of the century, but the key lies in the right policy responses which can obviate any risk arising from the deepening of climate crisis any further. Moreover, these situations have provided us with the much needed time to redefine and rediscover our relations with the Nature. This is high time that the incentives for adopting more climate friendly practices were encouraged by the governments. Corporations which have shown their responsibilities towards society during COVID-19 can continue and so must be encouraged to continue for optimum utilization of the approaches such as Corporate Social Responsibility (CSR), Life Cycle Assessment (LCA), Climate Strategy Proactivity (CSP), Circular Economy, to name a few in the post COVID-19 by adequately incentivizing them. NDC already has incorporated provisions to adequately incentivize private sectors for securing their support for meeting the climate action commitment. Kedia et al. (2020) underscore the need of greening the development process in anticipation of seeking help to reduce future risks while considering the COVID-19 linked disruptions and kick-starting of the economy could be an opportunity not only for economic but for environmental revival also. Prasad & Kant (2020) posit that future plans need to be aligned with the SDG and NDC both simultaneously.

Temporary reduction in expenditure in defence sector resulting into reduced fear of war, optimum use of resources and sustainable approaches, reduction in the use of plastic and polythene, reduction in the use vehicles and industries resulting into lesser emissions offer huge potentialities of the reduction in environmental degradations (Karunathilake, 2020) which can contribute immensely to the efforts of achieving SDG and NDC if these trends could be continued post COVID-19 pandemic times. During COVID-19 times, the emissions levels across the globe have reduced significantly marking the largest annual emissions reduction since World War II. It would not be out of place to mention that at a time when 'Work from Home'(WFH) and 'Online Conference and Meetings' have gained traction (Corlett et al., 2020) emerging significantly as viable models of new normal reducing emissions from different transportation modes including heavily polluting airplanes, and if harnessed strategically in future, they can be significantly helpful in achieving SDG and NDC. With the global lockdown having reduced activities related to construction, industries, tourism, material demand, and mobility has impacted different sectors of the economy globally witnessing movements towards and away from sustainability, key trends observed include welcome reductions in emissions and air pollution showcasing enormous opportunities for new, digitalized and responsible business models and lifestyle choices, and efforts need to be accelerated to restrict backward movement towards business as usual (Zakeri et al., 2020). Corporations globally too have reassessed the viability of the short and simple supply-chains for avoiding the impact of shortages during imposed lockdown periods and is continuance of such strategic approach could have positive impact on the emissions and operational risks in future. The government revenue freed by the pandemic induced world oil price crash need to be used to incentivize sustainability and support climate resilient measures while continuing with the aggressive taxing regime on fossil fuels and luxury goods affecting climate negatively (Kedia et al., 2020). With the pray that the global pandemic of this scale does not emerge again, these positive actions responsible for the emissions reductions could be replicated in the new normal situations strategically with the support of enough scientific evidences that would be available to support such emissions reducing initiatives which otherwise would not have been available.

The onset of COVID-19 postponing the COP26 for one additional year - originally to be held in Glasgow in November, 2020 to November, 2021- has further delayed the process of finalizing the much-awaited rulebook of Paris Climate Agreement (Corlett et al., 2020). However, this delay needs to be seen as an opportunity for the UNFCCC and member countries to revisit their different priorities and the processes and models of COP, as in the past since inauguration of COP25 years ago, its hectic annual schedules have never given them such extra time. The other priorities might include, for e.g., according priorities to take suitable steps to bring relevant educational initiatives to a meaningful end in the Article 12 (of Paris Climate Agreement) and Article 6 (of the UNFCCC) which enshrines the agenda of education - training - awareness (Action on Climate Empowerment – ACE) for member countries. With the huge transformation brought about by the pandemic COVID-19 in the teaching-learning process shifting focus on the Open & Distance Learning (ODL), ODL offers huge potentialities for this specific purpose of providing education - training - awareness as it can strategically align the OERs, MOOC, Podcasting, e-libraries and Social Media contents to strategically harness the future online teaching-learning opportunities. Engaging premier ODL institutions, for e.g. IGNOU with the proven capacity of serving the learning needs of millions of learners, which have been successful in their attempts emphasizing the effective and efficient combination of these features can help governments harness ODL to achieve the desired speed and scale (Nayak, Kant, & Anjali, 2020).

The onset of COVID-19 pandemic providing the extra time can also be used as an opportunity by the UN and member countries to revisit and rethink, and critically evaluate, for e.g., the usage of the words "…exploitation of resources…" in the definition of SD given by the Brundtland Commission which indicate the mindset of taking resources for granted, and substitute it with more suitable words such as "…judicious utilization of resources…". It is notable that the concept of sustainability which is remarkably associated with the concept of 'Tragedy of the Commons' highlights that good for all is good for each of us, and therefore warns against a myopic vision. Further, there is a need to have a suitable mechanisms to fix the accountability and obviate the risk of 'responsibility of everybody is responsibility of nobody' for making an effective use of the term "…common but differentiated responsibilities.." in the Paris Climate Agreement intended to facilitate effective partnerships amongst different actors.

Kedia et al. (2020) argue that the post COVID-19 pandemic times also offers opportunity to initiate projects through bilateral cooperation to fund SDG and NDC activities if the international cooperation opportunities for a circular economy could be effectively explored in addition to delving into the environmental domain by using SDG/NDC-aligned budgeting aligning government spending with environmental and sustainable development goals with an intent to move towards integration of these concerns and concepts into developmental planning. The UN has encouraged to adopt measures to address these challenges which mainly include calling for display of immediate and coordinated responses by policy makers, governments and monetary authorities for negating the effect of COVID-19; and ensuring channelization of adequate finance to SDG and NDC with the strategic use of the coordinated stimulus package to permit immediate suspension of debt payments, to reassess debt sustainability, to partner with financial institutions to roll over debts, to stabilize financial markets with the injection of adequate liquidity, to facilitate public and private investment in SD, to strengthen social protection systems, to invest additionally in crisis prevention/risk reduction/planning, and to remove trade barriers affecting supply chains amongst others.

It is notable that the vision of the current Indian Prime Minister, displayed while promulgating the adoption of model of 'Atma-nirbhar' (originally in Hindi- the national language of India which means 'Self-reliance') and calling for being 'Vocal for Local' during and post COVID-19 pandemic times, emphasizes the need of appropriate interventions with the participation of various actors at the local levels. These interventions can present suitable climate solutions also with the help of a bottom-up approach integrating the participation, engagement, leadership, innovation, co-creation and collaboration aligned with the need of the local people. Such local and participative approach offers huge potentialities for the emergence of the climate actions not compromising the economic development which, long time ago, had also been emphasized by Mahatma Gandhi's 'Sarvodaya' (originally in Hindi- the national language of India which means 'development of all') underscoring the need for local sustainable agricultural and small-cottage industry methods challenging the need for unsustainable rapid industrialization methods. His emphasis highlights his favor for providing support to the production and consumption at local level with local resources finding them as most sustainable which he focused in his landmark book the 'Hind Swaraj' which is considered informally as a Manifesto of Sustainable Development (Prasad & Kant, 2020). These approaches have inherent potentialities for achieving NDC and SDG if used strategically during and post- COVID pandemic times, for e.g. by decreasing carbon footprints resulting from lesser 'food miles' and transportation of non-local products. Nonetheless, these 'Turbulent Times' call all the major parties for making the right choices of policies and decisions to ensure better healthcare system for one and all, without ignoring the goals and commitments under SDG and NDC for a sustainable future.

A basic framework of the chapter is presented in *Figure 1* for an enhanced understanding.

*Figure 1. Basic Framework of the Chapter*

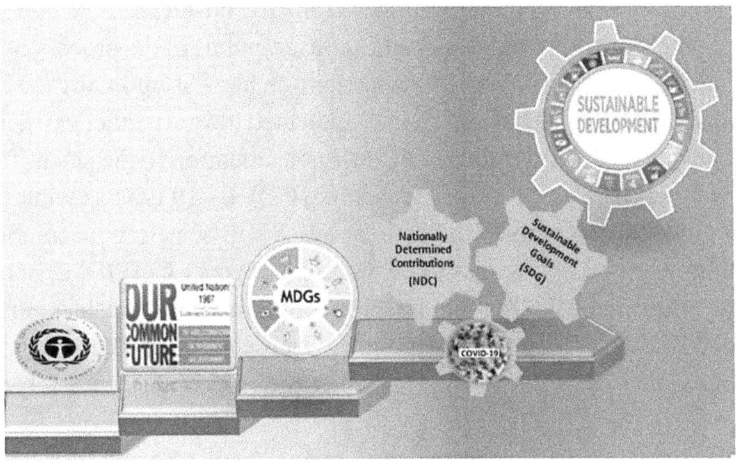


## LIMITATIONS OF THE CHAPTER

Given that the purpose of the chapter is broad, the intention of the author was never to focus on investigating the health or healthcare related aspects of the pandemic COVID-19. The chapter limits itself to cover only those aspects which relate to achievements of SDG and NDC. In addition, it is notable that the chapter aims to touch upon the different important but not all aspects of the sustainability issues affected by COVID-19.

## CONCLUDING COMMENTS

While the world has entered the 20s of the century and has exited its 'Turbulent Teens' aspiring to enter 'Transformation Times' without caring for the adverse effects of the anthropogenic actions undertaken in its 'Turbulent Teens' which could unfold multiple unprecedented consequences. Nonetheless, the national level reports warn that despite progress being made in some or the other indicators of these result frameworks of SDG and NDC, the overall actions are not as per the desired scale and speed to achieve these ambitious goals and commitments.

In the meantime, since the onset of the pandemic COVID-19 welcoming the new decade, each passing day has been a day of great learning in more than one ways pointing towards unavoidable temporary as well as permanent transformations. The transformations include new models and mindsets at the individual and institutional levels such as working from home or anywhere without compromising with the quality and productivity, resorting to videoconferencing instead of travelling through air, seeking education through ODL, to name a few, harnessing the information and communication technological advancements. All these initiatives at the technology, governance and other levels must be continued which have greater positive implications for achieving SDG and NDC for a sustainable future, though they were resorted to as the responses to the troubled times. Here, the role of the government would be of great importance for incentivizing industry working in the right directions to achieve sustainable pathways.

It is notable that COVID-19 has posed huge challenges derailing the achievement of ambitious SDG and NDC, Nonetheless, there is a need to be optimistic and to consider it as an opportunity for boosting clean technology, green productions and responsible consumptions in the process of economic recovery using the learning gained from the COVID-19 crisis times to harness optimally the benefits of cooperation and multilateralism. COVID-19 has sufficiently indicated towards either existence or emergence of the political leaderships at different levels paying desirable attention to the scientific suggestions to be replicated in combating climate change too. Meanwhile, COVID-19 era has witnessed the remarkable facilitation of collaborations with global implications which will be helpful in combating climate crisis. Conclusively, at a time when no one wishes to be tested positive for COVID-19 pandemic test, there is a need to be positive strategically so that the potential opportunities for achieving goals and commitments under SDG and NDC could be sensed and seized by reconfiguring according to the actual needs for a sustainable future.

## REFERENCES

Brandi, C., Dzebo, A., & Janetschek, H. (2017). *The Case for Connecting the Implementation of the Paris Climate Agreement and the 2030 Agenda for Sustainable Development*. Briefing Paper 21/2017.

Corlett, R. T., Primack, R. B., Devictor, V., Maas, B., Goswami, V. R., Bates, A. E., ... Pakeman, R. J. (2020). Impacts of the coronavirus pandemic on biodiversity conservation. *Biological Conservation, 246*, 108571. Advance online publication. doi:10.1016/j.biocon.2020.108571 PMID:32292203

Dente, S. M. R., & Hashimoto, S. (2020). COVID-19: A pandemic with positive and negative outcomes on resource and waste flows and stocks. *Resources, Conservation & Recycling Journal*, (161), 104979. doi:10.1016/j.resconrec.2020.104979

Gutteres, A. (2020). *Climate Change and COVID-19: UN urges nations to 'recover better'*. UN Department of Global Communications. Retrieved August 22, 2020, from https://www.un.org/en/un-coronavirus-communications-team/un-urges-countries-'build-back-better'

Kant, N. (2020). Climate Strategy Proactivity (CSP) and its Theoretical Underpinnings. In W. L. Filho, A. M. Azul, L. Brandli, A. L. Salvia, & T. Wall (Eds.), *Industry, Innovation and Infrastructure, Encyclopedia of the UN Sustainable Development Goals (Living Reference). Switzerland AG: Springer Nature.*

Kant, N., & Anjali, K. (2020). Climate Strategy Proactivity (CSP): A Stakeholders-Centric Concept. In W. L. Filho, A. M. Azul, L. Brandli, A. L. Salvia, & T. Wall (Eds.), *Partnerships for the Goals, Encyclopedia of the UN Sustainable Development Goals (Living Reference). Switzerland AG: Springer Nature.* doi:10.1007/978-3-319-71067-9_121-1

Karunathilake, K. (2020). Positive and negative impacts of COVID - 19, an analysis with special reference to challenges on the supply chain in South Asian countries. *Journal of Social and Economic Development*. Advance online publication. doi:10.100740847-020-00107-z

Kedia, S., Sinha, R., Pandey, R., Bhattacharjya, S., Syiemlieh, J. D., Chaudhury, S., . . . Bajpai, N. (2020). Greening Post COVID-19 Economic Recovery in India: A Case for Green Fiscal Stimulus. Academic Press.

Nayak, S. R., Kant, N., & Anjali, K. (2020). *Strategy of Using ICT in ODL to Disseminate Higher Education in Tribal Communities: A Case of MP*. *Asian Association of Open Universities Journal.*

Prasad, K. D., & Kant, N. (2020, Nov.). Achieving SDGs & NDCs. *Yojana, A Development Monthly*, 70–76.

UN ECLAC. (2020). The 2030 Agenda for Sustainable Development in the new global and regional context: Scenarios and projections in the current crisis. Author.

UNSD. (2019). *The Sustainable Development Goals Report 2019*. UNSD.

WBCSD. (n.d.). *Moving beyond the "turbulent teens."* Author.

WCED. (1987). *Our Common Future*. World Commission on Environment and Development. doi:10.1080/07488008808408783

WEF. (2020). The Global Risks Report 2020. Geneva, Switzerland: WEF.

Zakeri, B., Barreto, L., Boza-kiss, B., Echeverri, L. G., Fritz, S., Ghoneim, R., … Srivastava, L. (2020). Bouncing Forward Sustainably : Pathways to a post-COVID World. *Sustainable Energy, 43*(June), 1–13.

## ADDITIONAL READING

Dagnet, Y., Cogswell, N., & Mendoza, J. M. (2020). 4 Ways to Strengthen Climate Action in the Wake of COVID-19, 6th May 2020. Retrieved August 22, 2020, from https://www.wri.org/blog/2020/05/coronavirus-strengthen-climate-action

UNFCCC. (2020). UN CLIMATE STATEMENT, Call to Action for a Climate-Resilient Recovery from COVID- 19, 09 JUL, 2020 Retrieved August 22, 2020, from https://unfccc.int/news/call-to-action-for-a-climate-resilient-recovery-from-covid-19

## KEY TERMS AND DEFINITIONS

**COVID-19:** An infectious disease spread as pandemic across the globe in almost all the countries caused by a newly discovered coronavirus where normally the infected persons experience mild to moderate respiratory illness and recover without requiring special treatment while the persons including older persons with co-morbid ailments such as cardiovascular disease, diabetes, chronic respiratory disease, and cancer can develop more serious illness.

**Nationally Determined Contributions (NDC):** Considered to be at the heart of the Paris Climate Agreement of the UNFCCC embodying efforts of each country for reducing national emissions and adapting to the impacts of climate change. The Article 4, paragraph 2 of the agreement requires each Party to prepare, communicate and maintain their post-2020 climate actions, known as their NDC, what it intends to achieve.

**Pandemic:** A pandemic is a form of an epidemic with a scale crossing international boundaries to affect persons across the globe killing substantial number of people being widespread and infectious, and currently spread COVID-19 (SARS-CoV-2) is a perfect example of pandemic.

**Sustainable Development Goals (SDG):** Adopted by all the member states of the United Nations in 2015 as a universal call to action to end poverty, protect the planet, and ensure peace and prosperity for all by 2030. All the 17 SDGs are integrated in such a way that action in one area will affect outcomes in others to achieve sustainable development balanced in terms of social, economic and environmental, intending to leave no one behind.

## ENDNOTE

1 Mahatma Gandhi, quoted by E. F. Schumacher in Small Is Beautiful: A Study of Economics as if People Mattered (Blond and Briggs, 1973).

# Chapter 5
# Adaptive Performance:
## A Review of Managerial Interventions

**Timothy C. Bednall**
https://orcid.org/0000-0001-7385-8751
*Swinburne University of Technology, Australia*

**Matthew D. Henricks**
https://orcid.org/0000-0001-8736-0225
*The University of New South Wales, Australia*

## ABSTRACT

*COVID-19 has prompted an urgent need for organisations to adapt to continuously changing circumstances. Given the unpredictable challenges, a traditional, tightly planned approach to managing episodic change is likely to be suboptimal. Based on the need to manage continuous change and ensure workplaces are prepared for further unexpected events, it is argued that developing employees' adaptive performance is a better approach. Drawing on the literature identified in Park and Park's recent review of adaptive performance and its antecedents, the authors conduct a parallel review of the managerial implications of these findings. Findings are organised into sections related to employee selection, training, work design, leader behaviour, and organisational climate. Each practical recommendation is reviewed in terms of its feasibility of implementation and likely effectiveness.*

## INTRODUCTION

COVID-19 has created an urgent need for organisations to adapt to rapidly changing circumstances under conditions of great uncertainty. These disruptions have affected organisations' long-term plans, their business models, the size and composition of their workforce, and employees' everyday working conditions. The ability to lead and implement change in such circumstances has never been more important. However, due to the ongoing unpredictable challenges posed by the disruptions, a tightly planned approach is less feasible. Based on the need to make continuous change, we conduct a review of proposed managerial interventions for supporting employee *adaptive performance*.

DOI: 10.4018/978-1-7998-6948-1.ch005

Adaptive performance refers to employees' capabilities to adapt to rapidly changing work situations (Neal & Hesketh, 1999), and it is thought to include dimensions of problem solving, dealing with uncertainty, learning new tasks and procedures, and interpersonal, cultural and physical adaptability (Pulakos et al., 2000). Adaptive performance has been distinguished from task proficiency and proactivity (Griffin et al., 2007), with the former describing behaviours that are not formalised nor embedded within a social context, and the latter with anticipatory, self-directed behaviours intended to achieve desired outcomes.

We argue that a focus on encouraging employee adaptive performance is likely to complement and enhance managerial change efforts. While prominent change management theories have provided important insights into how to lead change effectively (Beer & Nohria, 2000; Bridges, 2009; Goldratt, 1999; Kotter, 1996), they have traditionally emphasised a planned approach in which change is characterised as episodic, with a clear beginning, middle and end (Bouckenooghe, 2010). Such approaches have arguably been well-suited to dealing with the initial COVID-19 outbreak. The outbreak presents a clearly defined problem with profound negative consequences (a "burning platform") if the organization fails to act quickly and decisively. However, the COVID-19 situation does not offer a clearly defined endpoint, making these models less suitable for managing an uncertain future. Even with the development of several promising vaccines, it is unlikely that the economic climate and workplace culture will snap back to "normal". Alternatively, if treatments turn out to lack long-term effectiveness or a new vaccine-resistant strain of coronavirus emerges, organisations will need to make significant changes to adapt to this new, permanent situation. Hence, the COVID situation requires both leadership capable of managing ongoing changes, and employees prepared to embrace a state of continuous organisational change.

Managing ongoing change requires a different approach to episodic change. For episodic change, Weick and Quinn (1999) theorise a leader's role is to initiate and drive changes with employees who are often resistant to that change. In contrast, when managing continuous change, a leader's role may be described as that of a "sense maker" (Weick & Quinn, 1999, p. 366), where leaders help reframe opinions that employees may already hold, rather than imposing their own planned agenda on their team. If the COVID situation continues to evolve as a continuous, relatively unpredictable series of changes, such a perspective suggests that it may be incumbent on leaders to take on a notably different role in managing change than that propagated by prominent traditional theorists (Beer & Nohria, 2000; Bridges, 2009; Goldratt, 1999; Kotter, 1996).

From an employee perspective, embracing continuous organisational change may require adaptation to a variety of new stressors, along with a concurrent need to abandon established methods. A context of continuous change may require adoption of new roles or responsibilities, abandonment of important past accountabilities, major changes to an employee's day-to-day working schedule, and layoffs of colleagues. In such an environment, an employee's general attitude toward change may be more relevant than any specific attitude held towards any one component they are required to adapt to.

Not all employees are willing or able to accept change, and some researchers have theorised that employee resistance to change is a trait-like construct possessed in greater measure by some employees (e.g., Oreg, 2003; Saksvik & Hetland, 2009). As well as resistance to change, the preparedness of employees to adapt to changes has also been investigated through the lens of change readiness (e.g., Rafferty et al., 2012), which is assumed to be more state-like. Studies investigating both trait resistance and state readiness have tended to be cross-sectional with few studies investigating either construct over time. However, a recent study by Henricks et al. (2020) suggested that neither construct is completely trait-like or state-like. Although both constructs are relatively stable over time (as indicated by test-retest correlations of .50 for change readiness and .62 for resistance to change), they are nonetheless malleable to the potential influence of leaders and other contextual factors. Michel et al.(2013) have also pointed towards the absence of a consistent moderation effect across workplace contexts, in questioning the trait-like status of resistance to change. Context may play a larger role in shaping general attitudes toward change than historically presumed (Caldwell, 2013; Michel et al., 2013).

For these reasons, rather than attempting to deal with the many unpredictable challenges posed by the COVID situation through a tightly planned process, we argue that a more fruitful approach is to explore how *adaptive performance* may be supported and developed in employees. Park and Park (2019) conducted a recent review of the literature on adaptive performance, which included 34 empirical studies that had studied its antecedents. Among these antecedents, the review identified individual characteristics (e.g., personality, self-efficacy, self-regulation), job characteristics (e.g., decision-making autonomy and job resources), group characteristics (e.g., supervisor support), and organizational characteristics (e.g., leader vision).

In this chapter, we conduct a parallel review of the *managerial implications* of these findings, which we source from the recommendations of the body of studies collected by Park and Park (2019). While none of these studies were conducted during the COVID era, we extrapolate relevant managerial implications from this research and explain how it may be applied to support employee adaptability during organisational disruptions. We include both explicit recommendations for interventions made in these studies, as well as implicit implications of their main findings. Based on the major outcomes described in this collection of studies, we organise these findings into sections related to employee selection, training and performance management, work design and job resources, leader behaviour, and organisational climate and culture. This structure also provides a framework for leaders to consider the different types of interventions that are available. We evaluate each recommendation in terms of its feasibility of implementation and likely effectiveness.

## EMPLOYEE SELECTION

Several studies reviewed in Park and Park (2019) focused on employee characteristics as antecedents of adaptive performance. These included cognitive flexibility (Good, 2014), Big Five personality factors or more specific dispositional facets (Griffin & Hesketh, 2003; Griffin & Hesketh, 2005; Huang et al., 2014), as well as additional individual differences not covered by extant models of personality (Bartone et al., 2013; Hauschildt & Konradt, 2012; Zhang et al., 2016). Many such factors are considered either difficult or impossible to shift. Thus, these studies imply that during times of disruption—such as the COVID-19 pandemic—employee selection processes should place greater emphasis on these individual differences to bolster a workplace's adaptive performance.

### Personality Measures

Huang et al. (2014) conducted a meta-analysis of 71 independent samples (total $N = 7{,}535$) all collected using the Hogan Personality Inventory (Hogan & Hogan, 2007). They found that emotional stability and ambition were both significantly associated with adaptive performance. In relation to emotional stability, Huang et al. (2014) theorised that employees who were highly emotionally stable were more likely to tolerate and attempt potentially stressful workplace changes, whereas less emotionally stable employees were more likely to avoid such stressors by procrastinating or clinging to old policies and processes. In relation to ambition, Huang et al. (2014) theorised that highly ambitious employees were more likely to seize opportunities that presented themselves during periods of change, whereas less ambitious employees may be less motivated by such opportunities. Despite the limitations of their cross-sectional design, Huang et al. (2014) asserted that these personality traits were the two primary personality-related predictors of adaptive performance within the workplace and implied that measurement of both traits should be used for pre-employment screening purposes.

Over a century of research has consistently found that conscientiousness is a significant predictor of employee task performance across a wide range of occupations (Schmidt & Hunter, 1998; Wilmot & Ones, 2019). Zhang et al. (2012) investigated whether conscientiousness may have a similar association with adaptive performance. Specifically, Zhang et al. (2012) conducted two studies among full-time employees based in Beijing and their supervisors. They found that while the relationship between conscientiousness and job performance is best described as curvilinear (i.e., reaches a plateau), the positive association between conscientiousness and adaptive performance was best described as linear with a small effect size ($r = .17, p < .05$). Given the relatively pervasive use of conscientiousness in existing employee selection practices, Zhang et al.'s (2012) findings imply that maintaining this status quo is appropriate. However, Zhang et al. (2012) also cautioned that despite the potential utility of conscientiousness as a predictor of adaptive performance, empirical research to date has typically observed only small effect sizes. There are clearly other factors which shape an employee's adaptive performance in the workplace.

Studies which examine the relationship between conscientiousness and adaptive performance have not always found a consistent association. In one early study, Griffin and Hesketh (2003) noted that conscientiousness was not a significant predictor of adaptive performance in either of the two organisations that they surveyed ($r$s = .06, -.04, $p$s >.05). However, in a follow-up study with a different sample, Griffin and Hesketh (2005) investigated personality correlates of adaptive performance at a facet level. Griffin and Hesketh (2005) observed that two sub-facets of conscientiousness were both significantly associated with adaptive performance, namely achievement-orientation and dependability. Specifically, employees who scored highly on the achievement scale were more likely to be adaptable, whereas those with high scores on the dependability facets were less likely to be adaptable. Such findings suggest a more subtle and nuanced association between conscientiousness and adaptive performance similar to that observed by Stewart and Nandkeolyar (2006). Stewart and Nandkeolyar (2006) observed that the association between conscientiousness and adaptive performance may differ by role. Specifically, they suggested that conscientiousness would only predict adaptive performance within positions which require employees to seize sales opportunities. In contrast, Stewart and Nandkeolyar (2006) suggested that openness to experience may be a better predictor of adaptive performance within other roles.

Considering the various recommendations reviewed, the case for pre-employment screening based on existing personality measures is mixed. There exists a degree of consensus that facet-level personality traits may be more useful in predicting adaptive performance than Big Five personality factors (Griffin & Hesketh, 2005; Huang et al., 2014). However, each of the studies which examined facet-level correlates of adaptive performance have identified slightly different facets. Furthermore, research also suggests the personality traits which predict adaptive performance may differ by role (Stewart & Nandkeolyar, 2006). Given the mixed evidence reviewed combined with a lack of replication studies across different contexts, it would be unwise to reweight the interpretation of pre-employment personality assessments away from a century of evidence predicting conventional / task performance (Schmidt & Hunter, 1998; Wilmot & Ones, 2019) toward the relatively scant and contradictory literature available on adaptive performance. As such, given the research available at the time of writing this chapter, both the feasibility and likelihood of success for personality-related pre-employment screening to boost adaptive performance must both be judged low.

## Other Individual Differences

Given the success of employment screening based on personality is far from guaranteed, several studies have examined a range of other individual differences that may predict adaptive performance during employee selection processes. Bartone et al. (2013) conducted a longitudinal study in which they administered a survey to military cadets at Westpoint during the beginning of their training then again seven years later following their graduation. They found that two specific forms of psychological hardiness, as measured by the Dispositional Resilience Scale (Bartone, 1995), significantly predicted adaptability seven years later. Specifically, the Commitment subscale which purports to measure active engagement in life significantly predicted self-assessed adaptability ($r = .24$, $p<.01$), but not supervisor ratings of adaptability ($p >.05$). The Control subscale which purports to measure the belief that an individual can personally influence events predicted both self-assessments of adaptability ($r = .25$, $p <.01$) and supervisor ratings of adaptability ($r = .36$, $p < .01$) seven years later. Using hierarchical regression, Bartone et al. (2013) controlled for both scholastic aptitude and the composite candidate rating scales prior to admission into Westpoint, and found via hierarchical regression analysis that 9% of variance in self-assessed adaptability seven years later could be predicted using a model that included Commitment and Control sub-scales of the resilience measure ($F(5,628) = 13.23$, $p <.01$). In contrast, 18% of variance in later supervisor adaptability assessments could be predicted using a model that included only the Control sub-scale of the resilience measure ($F(5,118) = 5.23$, $p <.01$). Given the theorised temporal stability of dispositional resilience (Bartone, 1995), and its predictive association with adaptive performance, Bartone et al. (2013) implied that such a characteristic may be used as an effective pre-employment screening tool.

Cognitive flexibility has also been suggested as a useful predictor of adaptive performance. Good (2014) found that pre-task cognitive flexibility as measured by performance on a Stroop task (Stroop, 1935) predicted 11% of variance in adaptive performance within a computer simulated environment where participants play the role of a fire chief. Good (2014) cautioned that a self-reported measure of cognitive flexibility showed an inverse association with adaptive performance on the same task. Such a finding illustrates the importance of performance-based assessment versus self-report inventories. On the basis of Good's (2014) findings, although pre-screening of cognitive flexibility may be a useful predictor of adaptive performance, any screening must be directly assessed using objective measures, rather than self-reports.

Hauschildt and Konradt (2012) explored employee self-regulation when engaged in work that is not naturally motivating. They labelled this form of self-regulation as self-leadership and theorised that it may be an antecedent of adaptive performance. Hauschildt and Konradt (2012) found a positive association between self-leadership and employee adaptive performance in a single cross-sectional study. However, they did not test the stability over time of self-leadership and instead asserted that these behaviours may be shaped via combination of leadership behaviour and training. As such, employee screening based on self-leadership would appear premature.

## Personal and Organisational Goal Congruence

In contrast to the examination of individual differences, other researchers have advocated for selection based on individual attitudes that may be more dynamic. Zhang et al. (2016) found that motivation was higher among employees whose goals were congruent with their employer's objectives. Building on this finding, they theorised that selecting employees whose personal goals and values aligned with that of their company would likely prompt higher adaptive performance during times of change. Zhang et al. (2016) did not examine the extent to which personal and workplace goal alignment may converge or diverge over time. As such, the predictive validity of using such an approach is difficult to assess, given that both personal and workplace goals are potentially dynamic constructs.

## Age

It is a common assumption among HR professionals that older employees may become more set in their ways (Gostautaite & Buciuniene, 2015). Only one of the papers reviewed by Park and Park (2019) focused on testing the association between age and adaptive performance, but failed to detect a significant association ($r = -.09, p > .05$) among employees of a retail bank in Lithuania. Gostautaite and Buciuniene (2015) further observed that under certain circumstances, specifically a high degree of work scheduling autonomy and low degree of decision-making autonomy, older workers are likely to present with higher adaptive performance. Another study by Ghitulescu (2013) among 621 special education teachers observed similar findings. Ghitulescu (2013) observed that those with more experience in their job tended to demonstrate higher levels of both adaptive and proactive behaviours. Both findings (Ghitulescu, 2013; Gostautaite & Buciuniene, 2015) contrast with the common assumption that older employees might be less flexible during times of change. In fact, Ghitulescu's (2013) finding suggests quite the opposite possibility; as an employee gains more experience over time, they become equipped with a wider array of skills and knowledge to apply in solving novel problems. In many parts of the world, discriminating against employees based on their age is unlawful. These results suggest that in addition to being unlawful, selecting employees based on age does not make business sense, especially during the COVID period where adaptive performance is likely to become more important.

## Selection Based on Adaptive Performance, Not Its Antecedents

Rather than selecting employees based on hypothesised antecedents of adaptive performance, others have suggested that pre-employment screening should consider direct measures of adaptive performance. Charbonnier-Voirin et al. (2012) developed a self-report adaptive performance scale to measure five distinct aspects of this employee characteristics. The resultant scale possessed a hierarchical structure including one overall adaptive performance scale, together with five sub-scales which were labelled as creativity, reactivity in the face of emergencies or unexpected circumstances, interpersonal adaptability, training and learning effort, and managing work stress. Charbonnier-Voirin et al. (2012) presented some preliminary evidence of the convergent validity of the scale by demonstrating modest to large correlations between their overall adaptive performance scale and both a measure of transformational leadership ($r = .41, p < .01$) a measure of contextual performance ($r = .60, p < .01$). Despite the absence of any predictive validity studies, Charbonnier-Voirin et al. (2012) asserted that the scale may be used for employee selection purposes.

## TRAINING AND PERFORMANCE MANAGEMENT

Most of the articles reviewed in Park and Park (2019) imply that it is difficult to train adaptive performance directly. Instead, these studies imply that a more fruitful approach is to help employees develop relevant domain knowledge, improve the self-regulatory capabilities of individuals and teams, incorporating adaptive performance into performance appraisal systems, and retaining experienced employees. We argue that these strategies are likely to be particularly effective in preparing organisations for the impact of disruptions related to COVID-19.

Studies of adaptive performance have indicated that adaptivity tends to emerge from a person's expertise within a knowledge domain; in other words, that it represents a higher level of functioning than basic task proficiency. For instance, Chen et al. (2005) found that individual knowledge and skill within a flight simulator task was associated with adaptive performance. In a study of international military personnel, Sahin and Gurbuz (2014) found that expertise in cultural intelligence was associated with greater adaptive performance in cross-cultural situations. Thus, these researchers suggest that adaptive performance can be enhanced through extensive training and/or experience in a domain, thereby allowing employees to acquire flexible knowledge schemas that can be applied in unfamiliar situations.

In addition to domain content knowledge, studies have focused on both individual and team regulatory processes as antecedents of adaptive performance. Hauschildt and Konradt's (2012) study revealed a positive relationship between self-leadership and employee adaptive performance. Their measure of self-leadership encompassed a range of self-regulatory processes, including goal setting, self-reward and punishment, observation, self-cueing, and constructive self-talk. In a similar vein, Chen et al.'s (2005) study additionally focused on team coordination process (i.e., monitoring goal progress, systems monitoring, team monitoring and backup behaviour). Their findings revealed that these coordination processes were stronger antecedents of team performance than individual expertise. Thus, both studies imply that training, managerial support and encouragement for individual and team regulatory processes is likely to enhance adaptive performance.

Other researchers have recommended incorporating adaptive performance into HR systems, including applicant selection criteria, performance appraisal and position descriptions. In a study of sales representatives, Stewart and Nandkeolyar (2006) found that employees' overall performance fluctuated according to situational opportunity (i.e., the number of sales referrals received); yet adaptive employees were better able to take advantage of such opportunities. For performance appraisals, they recommended accounting for variability in situational opportunity, as well as employees' capabilities in seizing opportunities. In a similar vein, Charbonnier-Voirin and Roussel (2012) recommended including a measure of adaptive performance into formal performance appraisal, and suggested it could also be used as an employee selection tool. Moreover, Griffin et al. (2007; 2010) distinguish between *task proficiency* (i.e., performance on core job tasks), *proactivity* (i.e., self-directed action), and *adaptivity* (i.e., adapting to changes in a work system and work roles), and they argue that these categories should be incorporated into performance evaluation systems. Griffin et al. (2007) further suggested that job descriptions should not be regarded as static; rather, managers should recognise roles as flexible and emergent, and they should provide opportunities for employees to self-initiate new tasks and customise their roles.

Finally, at least two studies have reported a positive relationship between employees' length of tenure in a role and adaptive performance (Ghitulescu, 2013; Sahin & Gurbuz, 2014). These findings imply that more experienced employees are likely to develop a broader repertoire of knowledge, thereby facilitating their adaptive performance. Alternatively, this relationship may signify a survivorship bias: that already adaptable employees are more likely to have successfully navigated previous changes and remain employed. To build adaptivity within a workforce, these findings suggest that organisations should engage in employee retention strategies for longstanding workers, particularly those who have already successfully adapted to change. Pulakos et al. (2002) also argued for measuring past experience in adapting as an indicator of future adaptive performance. In order to enrich employee knowledge and maximise the benefits of experience, both Ghitulescu (2013) and Sahin and Gurbuz (2014) recommended exposing employees to diverse work experiences, such as job rotations, novel work environments, information about the larger organisational context, and greater interactions with colleagues. Although such intervention will impose a steeper learning curve, such diverse experiences should prepare a workforce for significant changes to everyday work tasks and roles brought about by major disruptions.

## WORK DESIGN AND JOB RESOURCES

Research has also investigated how a range of work design aspects influence employees' level of adaptive performance. These initiatives include providing greater autonomy to employees, supporting greater social connectedness among colleagues, providing workplace challenges to enhance employees' self-efficacy, and improving self-regulation by supporting employees' participation in goal setting.

With regard to autonomy, researchers have argued that it benefits employees in multiple ways (Gostautaite & Buciuniene, 2015), including providing greater work knowledge, providing greater flexibility to approach tasks in a different way when circumstances change, and instilling greater motivation through being trusted with additional responsibilities. These studies have drawn a distinction between *decision-making autonomy* (referring to discretion given to employees to make important decisions related to their job) and *work-scheduling autonomy* (referring to employee control over the sequence and timing of work tasks) (Morgeson & Humphrey, 2006).

Although the benefits of autonomy appear obvious, results regarding its effects on adaptive performance have been mixed. Among a study of manufacturing employees, Sherehiy and Karwowski (2014) found that general job autonomy was not associated with adaptive performance. However, both Ghitulescu (2013) and Gostautaite and Buciuniene (2015) observed that employees with high decision-making autonomy generally demonstrated greater adaptive performance. Gostautaite and Buciuniene (2015) found that older workers benefitted from work-scheduling autonomy but not decision-making autonomy. In general, these authors recommend providing greater autonomy to workers to support adaptive performance, but doing so with consideration to employees' circumstances, capabilities and goals. For instance, while some employees may perform capably while working at home during office shutdowns, other employees may need greater levels of direction and support from their manager and colleagues.

Research has also examined how interactions with other workers affect employees' adaptive performance, including their task interdependence and social support. Task interdependence refers to the extent to which employees need to coordinate with colleagues and other stakeholders to perform their job. In a study of teachers, Ghitulescu (2013) reported a negative relationship between task interdependence and adaptive performance. She argued that interdependence reduces autonomy and increases reliance on others for information and resources. Thus, this finding implies that adaptive performance suffers if interdependences imposes excessive work demands and constraints on employees. In contrast, Ghitulescu (2013) found that an employee's number of social ties increases adaptive performance. She interpreted this result as suggesting that social ties provide additional social support, information, and advice. Thus, she recommended facilitating interactions among colleagues, but not designing work that required co-workers to rely on each other excessively. This recommendation is likely to be especially relevant for employees who are required to socially distance themselves from their colleagues and those who work from home.

As a further motivational process, many of the studies reviewed by Park and Park (2019) have also investigated *self-efficacy* as a possible antecedent of adaptive performance. Self-efficacy refers to a person's judgement that they possess the necessary capabilities to perform a task or obtain a desired outcome successfully (Bandura, 1986). Self-efficacy represents a source of motivation; highly efficacious employees are more likely to put more effort into a task, initiate actions to help them cope with a new situation and persist when faced with challenging and/or uncertain situations. This view has been supported by the study of Chen et al. (2005), who found that employees' individual self-efficacy increases goal striving (allocating and sustaining effort), which itself is positively related to adaptive performance. Other findings regarding the relationship between self-efficacy and adaptive performance have been mixed. Although most of the reviewed studies reported a positive correlation between self-efficacy and adaptive performance (e.g., Griffin & Hesketh, 2003; Griffin et al., 2010; Pulakos, Schmitt, Dorsey, Arad, Borman, et al., 2002), this relationship often disappeared when additional predictors were investigated in more complex models. For instance, Griffin et al. (2010) found that self-efficacy no longer predicted adaptive performance when conscientiousness was entered into the model.

Nonetheless, several authors have recommended interventions for improving employees' self-efficacy. For instance, both Chen et al. (2005) and Sahin and Gurbuz (2014) suggest that motivational interventions directed at increasing both individual and team self-efficacy is likely to increase adaptive performance, although these authors do not elaborate on what such interventions would entail. Traditionally, interventions for self-efficacy have included providing "mastery" experiences (i.e., facilitating success on a relevant task), vicarious experiences (i.e., observing the behaviour of role models similar to oneself), social persuasion (i.e., expressing a belief in an employee's ability to succeed), and to reduce negative emotional states such as stress (Gallagher, 2012). Similar to the "mastery" intervention, both Bartone et al. (2013) and Griffin and Hesketh (2003) recommended providing challenging tasks and experiences to help employees develop a strong sense of self-efficacy, thereby preparing them for the need to demonstrate adaptive performance in the face of change. Most other authors, however, do not offer specific recommendations for increasing self-efficacy.

Studies by Hauschildt and Konradt (2012) and Zhang et al. (2016) also suggest ways in which goal setting techniques can be used to improve employees' ability to self-regulate their behaviour and improve their adaptive performance. As previously described, Hauschildt and Kondradt (2012) found that self-leadership was positively associated with adaptive performance. They therefore argued that self-leadership should be encouraged through supporting employee-directed goal setting, as well as by providing constructive feedback and emphasising shared purpose, vision and values. In the study of Zhang et al. (2016), the authors examined different forms of regulation, including external regulation (i.e., participating because of external demands or rewards), introjected (i.e., participating to maintain self-worth), identified (i.e., participating because a goal is valued), and intrinsic (i.e., participating because a task is interesting / enjoyable) regulation. They found that only identified regulation was associated with adaptive performance, and the other forms of self-regulation (even intrinsic regulation) did not influence performance. Thus, they recommended interventions for increasing identified regulation by encouraging employees to internalise the value and importance of the goals they set out to achieve.

In the COVID era, leaders should make efforts to keep physically distant employees informed about the direction of the organisation and how their efforts contribute to its long-term success.

## LEADER BEHAVIOUR AND LEADER DEVELOPMENT

Although leaders play a central role in selecting employees, training them, evaluating their performance, and designing their work, several studies reviewed by Park and Park (2019) suggested the importance of specific behaviours among leaders that were independent of their designated role within such processes. Such recommendations included behavioural role-modelling, specific training that may be advantageous for leaders, and social processes that leaders may instigate or encourage within their teams. These actions are likely to be especially important for virtual teams operating within a COVID environment, as physical disconnectedness makes it more difficult for teams to implement shared goals and build trust (Hertel et al., 2005).

### Transformational Leadership

Two studies reviewed by Park and Park (2019) observed the apparent association between transformational leadership behaviour and adaptive performance among employees. In a survey among employees of a French aeronautical company, Charbonnier-Voirin et al. (2010) observed a significant medium association between transformational leadership and adaptive performance ($r = .44, p < .01$). As employee assessments regarding their leaders' behaviours become more positive, so did self-assessed adaptive performance. Using hierarchical linear modelling, Charbonnier-Voirin et al. (2010) further showed that an innovative organisational climate as assessed by leaders moderated the association between transformational leadership and adaptive performance. The moderating influence of organisational climate significantly dampened the association between transformational leadership and adaptive performance such that highly innovative teams demonstrated a stronger positive association between leadership assessments and adaptive performance, whereas this association, while still positive, was relatively weaker among relatively less innovative teams. Despite the cross-sectional nature of their study, Charbonnier-Voirin et al. (2010) nevertheless concluded that leadership behaviour was likely to have a causal influence on employee adaptive performance. Accordingly, they recommended leaders may shape adaptive behaviour among employees at both an individual and team-level. When working one-on-one with individuals, Charbonnier-Voirin et al. (2010) suggested that leaders should provide tailored support and development based on unique individual employee needs. Still at any individual-level, they further suggested that leaders may enable employees to achieve their individual potential by adjusting task assignment and performance feedback based on each individual's reasoning ability and job-related skills. When working at a team-level, Charbonnier-Voirin et al. (2010) recommended that leaders articulate a clear and challenging vision, whilst encouraging a positive attitude regarding the team's ability to achieve challenging goals.

Griffin et al. (2010) conducted a longitudinal study in which they tested the predictive association between transformational leadership vision and adaptive performance using two repeated survey administrations among public sector employees separated by one year. Griffin et al. (2010) failed to detect a correlation between the clear and compelling presentation of a vision by leaders at Time 1 and either self-assessed adaptivity among employees at Time 1 ($r = -.09, p > .05$) or twelve months later at Time 2, ($r = -.02, p > .05$). However, they did observe that leader vision interacted with employee openness to role changes to predict adaptivity. Specifically, those who observed leaders with a clear vision at Time 1 but were not open to a role change at Time 1 reported the lowest adaptivity at Time 2. In contrast, those who both assessed leaders with a clear vision at Time 1 and were open to a role change at Time 1 reported the highest level of adaptivity. Griffin et al. (2010) concluded that transformational visions presented by leaders may not be sufficient in isolation to prompt adaptive performance among employees. However, where employees are already predisposed to embrace the changes being suggested, a clear and compelling vision presented by leaders can act as a catalyst to disrupt the status quo accelerate an employee's adaptive performance.

### Leadership Training and Social Processes

Other researchers have suggested that leaders may improve the adaptive performance of their teams by supporting effective team processes. Chen et al. (2005) demonstrated the importance of post-training regulation processes in shaping later adaptive performance among 156 individuals on a computerised flight simulator. They found that leaders may play a critical role, particularly in complex environments, in encouraging post-training regulation within their teams by providing transparent tools to measure performance and prompting reflective discussion among employees about those results. In a similar vein, Chiaburu et al. (2013) suggested the importance of supportive leadership to bring out the best in teams, particularly during times of change. Chiaburu et al. (2013) asserted that leadership training during organisational change should focus in equal measure on both change-oriented supportive leadership behaviours, such as being open to suggestions about the change, and involving employees in key-decisions during the change.

Schraub et al. (2011) examined a different process labelled as expressive suppression which they suggested leaders may use to prompt adaptive performance during organisational changes. Schraub et al. (2011) found that those employees who were more likely to supress spontaneous emotions regarding proposed organisational changes, tended to report less tension associated with proposed changes, and ultimately higher adaptive performance. Schraub et al. (2011) theorised that negative emotions about proposed changes may prolong an employee's cognitive focus on the unfavourable aspects of a proposed change, which in turn may prolong the emotional detachment that is necessary for adaptive performance. As such, Schraub et al. (2011) asserted that leaders should closely attend to their employee's subjective experience of change and try where possible to encourage employees to talk in a constructive way about proposed changes. Such an approach would be consistent with promoting employee participation throughout large-scale changes, without allowing that participation to become an opportunity for employees to emotionally vent their frustration. In addition to reducing an individual's personal adaptive performance, Schraub et al. (2011) suggested that expressing negative emotions regarding a change can also become contagious within work-teams. They suggested that leaders should therefore dissuade employees from reflecting openly on their negative feelings about a change lest they influence others, instead they suggested leaders promote constructive approaches to such conversations.

## ORGANISATIONAL CLIMATE AND CULTURE

With many teams forced to work remotely due to COVID restrictions, a major challenge for leaders is to maintain a positive working culture that promotes adaptability. A small number of studies reviewed by

Park and Park (2019) make recommendations regarding the optimal organisational context for employee adaptive performance to occur. Recommendations from these studies include promoting a team culture of learning, promoting an organisational climate for innovation and learning, and adopting an organic organisational structure.

Team norms appear to influence how individual team members engage in adaptive performance. In a study of service employees, Han and Williams (2008) investigated how their team's learning climate influenced both individual and team performance. They characterized learning climate as norms relating to openness to change and new ideas, tolerance of mistakes, and high-performance expectations and accountability. They found that strong team norms were associated with individual (but not team) adaptive performance. Based on these results, they suggested selecting and developing employees who were likely to succeed in such an environment, and they also recommended fostering a learning climate within teams.

In a similar vein, Charbonnier-Voirin et al. (2010) discussed how a climate for innovation influenced adaptive performance. Similar to learning climate, they depicted a climate for innovation as one that comprised norms and practices that encouraged flexibility, the free expression of creative ideas, ongoing learning, and independence and empowerment to achieve the team's goals. Although they failed to observe a direct benefit of innovation climate on adaptive performance, their findings revealed that transformational leaders were even more effective in facilitating adaptive performance amongst their employees when they worked in such a climate. They similarly recommended supporting a climate for innovation within organizations, although this study (nor the previous one) provided clear guidance about how such a climate might be achieved.

Other researchers have elaborated on this issue and made more specific recommendations. After observing a robust relationship between a learning climate and employee adaptive performance, Eldor and Harpaz (2016) outlined several recommendations. They suggested that leaders should encourage employees to learn, facilitate knowledge exchanges and collaborations, involve employees in crafting an organisational vision, and empower employees within their roles. These authors also observed that employee engagement mediated the relationship between learning climate and adaptivity. They therefore made recommendations for enhancing engagement, including leaders playing a role in facilitating (as opposed to managing) performance, and helping employees to re-craft their roles to accommodate externally driven changes.

Research has also examined how organizational structure influences an organization's learning culture. Kanten et al. (2015) described learning culture as a type of organisation that encourages employees to engage in ongoing learning activities, and one that proactively develops strategies to encourage learning. They compared employees who reported working for organisations with a mechanistic structure (i.e., one that is highly formalised, standardised, hierarchical, and centralised, with inflexible job roles, policies, practices and procedures) versus those with an organic structure (i.e., one that is flat, flexible, adaptable and informal). They found that *both* types of structure had a positive influence on an organisation's learning culture, which in turn facilitated employees' adaptive performance. Thus, these authors recommended developing a structure (either mechanistic or organic) that best suited the relevant internal and external conditions faced by the organization, as well as taking steps to facilitate a learning culture.

## DISCUSSION AND CONCLUSION

In the context of COVID-19, there is no single intervention that will ensure the adaptability of a workforce. Instead, the collection of studies reviewed in Park and Park (2019) suggest that a multifaceted approach is needed, and that leaders should consider a range of interventions, including improvements to organisational systems, work design, leader behaviour, and organisational culture. We present a summary of these interventions in Table 1.

While the evidence from the studies reviewed in this chapter suggests that many of the interventions will increase adaptive performance, we urge practitioners to observe several cautions when considering each for implementation. First, none of the studies reviewed in this chapter were conducted in the context of COVID-19. Thus, it is unclear how contextual differences in each of the studies will influence the applicability of the managerial interventions in the context of COVID-related changes.

Second, contextual differences in the studies – particularly concerning the nature and scope of changes employees were required to adapt to – may limit generalisations about the effectiveness of each intervention. The studies covered a wide range of settings, as well as challenges that employees needed to adapt to. Some of the studies were experimental (e.g., Chen et al., 2005; LePine et al., 2000), requiring a short-term adaptation to changing circumstances. Other studies required employees to seize momentary opportunities (Stewart & Nandkeolyar, 2006). Some studies assessed adaptive performance in a much more general workplace context (e.g., Griffin & Hesketh, 2003), assessing employees' ability to adapt to the daily changing requirements of their role. Thus, it is unclear precisely which aspects of adaptive performance are most important for managing these situations effectively.

As described by Pulakos et al. (2002), the construct of adaptive performance is quite broad, comprising aspects such as creative problem solving, dealing with uncertain situations, learning new procedures, interpersonal adaptability, handling work stress, and dealing with emergencies. In line with later conceptualisations of adaptive performance (e.g., Griffin et al., 2007), the studies we reviewed mainly focused on the more general, overarching adaptive performance construct. In reality, there may be specific facets of adaptive performance that are more important in some situations. For instance, opportunity seizing among new customers may require adaptability in interpersonal skills. Handling work stress is likely to be important when faced with multiple responsibilities. Thus, interventions to improve general adaptivity may be less useful when more specific characteristics are required to manage different types of disruptions.

Moreover, the body of studies on the antecedents of adaptive performance is relatively small compared to other forms of performance, such as task performance. There is a lack of consistent replication studies on the antecedents of adaptive performance, which means that it is difficult to assess how universally effective specific managerial interventions are likely to be, as well as determine any relevant boundary conditions that may limit their effectiveness.

The majority of studies were non-experimental, and as such, the levels of adaptive performance and antecedent factors were not randomly assigned. These study designs cast some doubt about the direction of causality in some of the findings. For instance, some of the studies reviewed described decision-making and task-scheduling autonomy as antecedents of adaptive performance (e.g., Gostautaite & Buciuniene, 2015). However, it is possible that already high-performing employees will be trusted with greater autonomy by their supervisors *because* of their adaptivity. Thus, we recommend that practitioners observe caution in applying interventions based on non-experimental research, such as conducting small-scale trials before implementing interventions more broadly.

*Table 1. Summary of Managerial Interventions for Supporting Adaptive Performance*

| Intervention | Our Recommendation | Supporting References |
|---|---|---|
| Employee Selection | | |
| Select employees based on facets of Conscientiousness (achievement orientation, dependability) | Consider these facets as secondary selection criteria after screening for more well-established measures (e.g., cognitive ability, personality) for specific roles. | Griffin and Hesketh (2005) |
| Select employees for facets of psychological hardiness, including commitment and (locus of) control | As above | Bartone et al. (2013) |
| Select employees for cognitive flexibility | As above; use objective measures of cognitive flexibility. | Good (2014) |
| Select employees based on goal congruence with organisational goals | Consider person-organisation fit as a secondary criterion; encourage employees to internalise the importance of organisational goals. | Hauschildt and Konradt (2012) |
| Select employees based on past adaptive performance | Include as a criterion, but assess using validated instruments and/or relevant real-life instances | Charbonnier-Voirin (2012) |
| Training and Performance Management | | |
| Develop expertise and in-role performance | Provide a mix of formal and informal learning; provide ongoing employee development | Chen et al. (2005); Sahin and Gurbuz (2014) |
| Support the development of individual and team self-regulatory processes | Provide formal training and/or support to help individuals and teams improve self-management | Chen et al., (2005); Hauschildt and Konradt (2012) |
| Modify performance appraisal to consider adaptive performance | Adopt long-term measures of performance; account for variability and situational opportunities / barriers | Charbonnier-Voirin (2012); Griffin et al. (2007; 2010) |
| Retain experienced employees, especially those that have already successfully adapted to change | Retain experienced employees, and enrich employees' knowledge through diverse work experiences (e.g., job rotations) | Ghitulescu (2013); Sahin and Gurbuz (2014) |
| Work Design | | |
| Provide employees with greater autonomy | Provide decision-making and work-scheduling autonomy with appropriate oversight, and when employees are capable of working independently | Ghitulescu (2013); Gostautaite and Buciuniene (2015) |
| Encourage worker interactions | Encourage and facilitate employee collaboration and social support, but reduce task interdependence | Ghitulescu (2013) |
| Help employees to develop greater self-efficacy | Increase employee capabilities through developmental challenges; develop self-efficacy as a by-product | Bartone et al. (2013); Griffin and Hesketh (2003) |
| Implement interventions for encouraging employees to internalise organisational goals | Collaborate with employees to help them set appropriate work goals in line with their own values, long-term ambitions and capabilities | Hauschildt and Konradt (2012); Zhang, Zhang, Song and Gong (2016) |
| Leader Behaviour and Leader Development | | |
| Adopt transformational leadership behaviours, including a vision and positive attitude towards team's ability | Support the change readiness of teams, and then present a compelling vision | Charbonnier-Voirin et al. (2010); Griffin et al. (2010) |
| Support team processes and interactions | Encourage post-task reflections, demonstrate support for team members, involve employees in key decisions | Chiaburu et al. (2013) |
| Discourage negative expressions of emotions in response to changes | Encourage constructive discussions about change processes and promote employee participation in such discussions | Schraub et al. (2011) |
| Organisational Climate and Culture | | |
| Promote a positive team climate for learning | Establish team norms related to openness to change and new ideas, tolerance of mistakes, and high-performance expectations | Han and Williams (2008) |
| Promote a climate for innovation | Encourage employees to learn, facilitate knowledge exchanges and collaborations, empower employees within their role, permit employees to re-craft their roles to accommodate change | Charbonnier-Voirin et al. (2010); Eldor and Harpaz (2016) |
| Adopt a mechanistic or organic organisational structure to develop a learning culture | Choose the organizational structure that best suits the strategic needs of the organization; work within the structure to develop a learning culture | Kanten, Kanten and Gurlek (2015) |

In summary, our chapter points to a range of interventions that leaders may implement to support employees' adaptive performance during the COVID era. This chapter makes at least three useful contributions to both research and practice. First, as one of the intended audiences of this chapter is practitioners, the chapter should provide a useful overview of interventions for enhancing employee adaptive performance that can be adopted by organisational leaders. Second, our critical review of the managerial implications is likely to provide an impetus for future intervention studies designed to enhance adaptive performance. Finally, while managerial implications are often provided in research articles, they have seldom received critical attention. Our review should help researchers propose more considered interventions that are more likely to be effective.

## REFERENCES

Bandura, A. (1986). *Social foundations of thought and action: A social cognitive theory*. Prentice-Hall.

Bartone, P. T. (1995). A short hardiness scale *American Psychological Society Annual Convention*, New York, NY.

Bartone, P. T., Kelly, D. R., & Matthews, M. D. (2013). Psychological Hardiness Predicts Adaptability in Military Leaders: A prospective study. *International Journal of Selection and Assessment, 21*(2), 200–210. doi:10.1111/ijsa.12029

Beer, M., & Nohria, N. (2000). Cracking the code of change. *Harvard Business Review, 78*(3), 133–141. PMID:11183975

Bouckenooghe, D. (2010). Positioning change recipients' attitudes toward change in the organizational change literature. *The Journal of Applied Behavioral Science, 46*(4), 500–531. doi:10.1177/0021886310367944

Bridges, W. (2009). *Managing transitions: Making the most of change*. Addison Wesley.

Caldwell, S. D. (2013). Are Change Readiness Strategies Overrated? A Commentary on Boundary Conditions. *Journal of Change Management, 13*(1), 19–35. doi:10.1080/14697017.2013.768428

Charbonnier-Voirin, A., El Akremi, A., & Vandenberghe, C. (2010). A multilevel model of transformational leadership and adaptive performance and the moderating role of climate for innovation. *Group & Organization Management, 35*(6), 699–726. doi:10.1177/1059601110390833

Charbonnier-Voirin, A., & Roussel, P. (2012). Adaptive Performance: A New Scale to Measure Individual Performance in Organizations. *Canadian Journal of Administrative Sciences-Revue Canadienne Des Sciences De L Administration, 29*(3), 280-293. doi:10.1002/cjas.232

Chen, G., Thomas, B., & Wallace, J. C. (2005). A multilevel examination of the relationships among training outcomes, mediating regulatory processes, and adaptive performance. *The Journal of Applied Psychology, 90*(5), 827–841. doi:10.1037/0021-9010.90.5.827 PMID:16162057

Chiaburu, D. S., Lorinkova, N. M., & Van Dyne, L. (2013). Employees' Social Context and Change-Oriented Citizenship: A Meta-Analysis of Leader, Coworker, and Organizational Influences. *Group & Organization Management, 38*(3), 291–333. doi:10.1177/1059601113476736

Eldor, L., & Harpaz, I. (2016). A process model of employee engagement: The learning climate and its relationship with extra-role performance behaviors. *Journal of Organizational Behavior, 37*(2), 213–235. doi:10.1002/job.2037

Gallagher, M. W. (2012). Self-Efficacy. In V. S. Ramachandran (Ed.), *Encyclopedia of Human Behavior* (2nd ed., pp. 314–320). Academic Press., doi:10.1016/B978-0-12-375000-6.00312-8

Ghitulescu, B. E. (2013). Making Change Happen: The Impact of Work Context on Adaptive and Proactive Behaviors. *The Journal of Applied Behavioral Science, 49*(2), 206–245. doi:10.1177/0021886312469254

Goldratt, E. (1999). *Theory of constraints.* North River Press.

Good, D. (2014). Predicting real-time adaptive performance in a dynamic decision-making context. *Journal of Management & Organization, 20*(6), 715–732. doi:10.1017/jmo.2014.54

Gostautaite, B., & Buciuniene, I. (2015). The role of work characteristics in enhancing older employees' performance: Evidence from a post-Soviet country. *International Journal of Human Resource Management, 26*(6), 757–782. doi:10.1080/09585192.2014.949820

Griffin, B., & Hesketh, B. (2003). Adaptable behaviours for successful work and career adjustment. *Australian Journal of Psychology, 55*(2), 65–73. doi:10.1080/00049530412331312914

Griffin, B., & Hesketh, B. (2005). Are Conscientious Workers Adaptable? *Australian Journal of Management, 30*(2), 245–259. doi:10.1177/031289620503000204

Griffin, M. A., Neal, A., & Parker, S. K. (2007). A new model of work role performance: Positive behavior in uncertain and interdependent contexts. *Academy of Management Journal, 50*(2), 327–347. doi:10.5465/amj.2007.24634438

Griffin, M. A., Parker, S. K., & Mason, C. M. (2010). Leader Vision and the Development of Adaptive and Proactive Performance: A Longitudinal Study. *The Journal of Applied Psychology, 95*(1), 174–182. doi:10.1037/a0017263 PMID:20085414

Han, T. Y., & Williams, K. J. (2008). Multilevel Investigation of Adaptive Performance Individual- and Team-Level Relationships. *Group & Organization Management, 33*(6), 657–684. doi:10.1177/1059601108326799

Hauschildt, K., & Konradt, U. (2012). Self-leadership and team members' work role performance. *Journal of Managerial Psychology, 27*(5-6), 497–517. doi:10.1108/02683941211235409

Henricks, M. D., Young, M., & Kehoe, E. J. (2020). Attitudes toward Change and Transformational Leadership: A Longitudinal Study. *Journal of Change Management, 20*(3), 1–18. doi:10.1080/14697017.2020.1758529

Hertel, G., Geister, S., & Konradt, U. (2005). Managing virtual teams: A review of current empirical research. *Human Resource Management Review, 15*(1), 69–95. doi:10.1016/j.hrmr.2005.01.002

Hogan, R., & Hogan, J. (2007). *Hogan Personality Inventory Manual* (3rd ed.). Hogan Assessment Systems.

Huang, J. L., Ryan, A. M., Zabel, K. L., & Palmer, A. (2014). Personality and Adaptive Performance at Work: A Meta-Analytic Investigation. *The Journal of Applied Psychology, 99*(1), 162–179. doi:10.1037/a0034285 PMID:24016205

Kanten, P., Kanten, S., & Gurlek, M. (2015). The effects of organizational structures and learning organization on job embeddedness and individual adaptive performance. In A. I. Iacob (Ed.), *2nd Global Conference on Business, Economics, Management and Tourism* (Vol. 23, pp. 1358-1366). 10.1016/S2212-5671(15)00523-7

Kotter, J. P. (1996). *Leading change*. Harvard Business School Press.

LePine, J. A., Colquitt, J. A., & Erez, A. (2000). Adaptability to changing task contexts: Effects of general cognitive ability conscientiousness, and openness to experience. *Personnel Psychology*, *53*(3), 563–593. doi:10.1111/j.1744-6570.2000.tb00214.x

Michel, A., By, R. T., & Burnes, B. (2013). The limitations of dispositional resistance in relation to organizational change. *Management Decision*, *51*(4), 761–780. doi:10.1108/00251741311326554

Morgeson, F. P., & Humphrey, S. E. (2006). The Work Design Questionnaire (WDQ): Developing and validating a comprehensive measure for assessing job design and the nature of work. *The Journal of Applied Psychology*, *91*(6), 1321–1339. doi:10.1037/0021-9010.91.6.1321 PMID:17100487

Neal, A. F., & Hesketh, B. (1999). Technology and performance. In D. Ilgen & D. Pulakos (Eds.), *The Changing Nature of performance: Implications for Staffing, Motivation and Development* (pp. 21–55). Jossey-Bass.

Oreg, S. (2003). Resistance to change: Developing an individual differences measure. *The Journal of Applied Psychology*, *88*(4), 680–693. doi:10.1037/0021-9010.88.4.680 PMID:12940408

Park, S., & Park, S. (2019). Employee Adaptive Performance and Its Antecedents: Review and Synthesis. *Human Resource Development Review*, *18*(3), 294–324. doi:10.1177/1534484319836315

Pulakos, E. D., Arad, S., Donovan, M. A., & Plamondon, K. E. (2000). Adaptability in the workplace: Development of a taxonomy of adaptive performance. *The Journal of Applied Psychology*, *85*(4), 612–624. doi:10.1037/0021-9010.85.4.612 PMID:10948805

Pulakos, E. D., Schmitt, N., Dorsey, D. W., Arad, S., Borman, W. C., & Hedge, J. W. (2002). Predicting adaptive performance: Further tests of a model of adaptability. *Human Performance*, *15*(4), 299–323. doi:10.1207/S15327043HUP1504_01

Pulakos, E. D., Schmitt, N., Dorsey, D. W., Arad, S., Hedge, J. W., & Borman, W. C. (2002). Predicting adaptive performance: Further tests of a model of adaptability. *Human Performance*, *15*(4), 299–323. doi:10.1207/S15327043HUP1504_01

Rafferty, A. E., Jimmieson, N. L., & Armenakis, A. A. (2012). Change Readiness. *Journal of Management*, *39*(1), 110–135. doi:10.1177/0149206312457417

Sahin, F., & Gurbuz, S. (2014). Cultural intelligence as a predictor of individuals' adaptive performance: A study in a multicultural environment. *International Area Studies Review*, *17*(4), 394–413. doi:10.1177/2233865914550727

Saksvik, I. B., & Hetland, H. (2009). Exploring dispositional resistance to change. *Journal of Leadership & Organizational Studies*, *16*(2), 175–183. doi:10.1177/1548051809335357

Schmidt, F. L., & Hunter, J. E. (1998). The Validity and Utility of Selection Methods in Personnel Psychology: Practical and Theoretical Implications of 85 Years of Research Findings. *Psychological Bulletin, 124*(2), 262–274. doi:10.1037/0033-2909.124.2.262

Schraub, E. M., Stegmaier, R., & Sonntag, K. (2011). The Effect of Change On Adaptive Performance: Does Expressive Suppression Moderate the Indirect Effect of Strain? *Journal of Change Management, 11*(1), 21–44. doi:10.1080/14697017.2010.514002

Sherehiy, B., & Karwowski, W. (2014). The relationship between work organization and workforce agility in small manufacturing enterprises. *International Journal of Industrial Ergonomics, 44*(3), 466–473. doi:10.1016/j.ergon.2014.01.002

Stewart, G. L., & Nandkeolyar, A. K. (2006). Adaptation and intraindividual variation in sales outcomes: Exploring the interactive effects of personality and environmental opportunity. *Personnel Psychology, 59*(2), 307–332. doi:10.1111/j.1744-6570.2006.00016.x

Stroop, J. R. (1935). Studies of interference in serial verbal reactions. *Journal of Experimental Psychology, 18*(6), 643–662. doi:10.1037/h0054651

Weick, K. E., & Quinn, R. E. (1999). Organizational change and development. *Annual Review of Psychology, 50*(1), 361–386. doi:10.1146/annurev.psych.50.1.361 PMID:15012461

Wilmot, M. P., & Ones, D. S. (2019). A century of research on conscientiousness at work. *Proceedings of the National Academy of Sciences of the United States of America, 116*(46), 23004–23010. doi:10.1073/pnas.1908430116 PMID:31666330

Zhang, J., Zhang, Y., Song, Y. H., & Gong, Z. X. (2016). The different relations of extrinsic, introjected, identified regulation and intrinsic motivation on employees' performance Empirical studies following self-determination theory. *Management Decision, 54*(10), 2393–2412. doi:10.1108/MD-01-2016-0007

Zhang, S. S., Zhou, M. J., Zhang, J. X., & Chen, S. (2012). The nonlinear effects of conscientiousness on overall job performance and performance dimensions in the Chinese context. *Asian Journal of Social Psychology, 15*(4), 231–237. doi:10.1111/j.1467-839X.2012.01375.x

## KEY TERMS AND DEFINITIONS

**Adaptive Performance:** Employees' capabilities to adapt to rapidly changing work situations, which includes elements of problem solving, coping with uncertainty, learning new tasks and procedures, and interpersonal, cultural, and physical adaptability.

**Employee Selection:** The set of procedures and criteria used by employers to choose the optimal person (or people) for a role from a larger pool of candidates.

**Goal Congruence:** The extent to which an individual's personal goals are consistent with the organization's goals.

**Job Resources:** Physical, psychological, social, or organizational aspects of a job that support work goals, reduce job demands, or support personal and/or professional development.

**Organizational Climate:** Shared perceptions regarding the meaning attached to policies, practices, and procedures employees experience.

**Organizational Culture:** The shared basic assumptions, values, and beliefs that characterize a workplace.

**Work Design:** The content and organisation of an employee's work tasks, activities, relationships, and responsibilities.

# Chapter 6
# Change Management Strategies as the Nexus of Performance Improvement in African Universities Post-COVID-19 Pandemic

**Bethuel Sibongiseni Ngcamu**
*Nelson Mandela University, South Africa*

## ABSTRACT

*The COVID-19 pandemic, which started in China in late 2019, came as the perfect storm at a time when leadership in African universities is leaving much to be desired. This status quo is what has triggered the current chapter, which sets out to explore responsive leadership development and the change management interventions that are required after the pandemic and which can make universities' operations agile. The chapter aims to investigate the nature of change management interventions, including agile talent management. This can help to ensure that African universities are effective and efficient in Africa post-COVID-19. The chapter employs different research methods; for instance, a literature review is synthesised on previously published studies that relate to the relevant applications and impacts of agile transformation in universities as a way of guiding leaders in their response to the challenges of a post-coronavirus world. Furthermore, the document analysis followed examines a number of documents related to leadership, development, and change post the pandemic.*

## INTRODUCTION

The infamous "Chinese curse" has given rise to both risks and opportunities for African universities. Managing such a crisis with imperfect leadership during and after the disruptive months of such a disaster requires leaders who possess in-depth change management knowledge, competencies and skills, which are mostly inconspicuous among university leaders. This has influenced them to embark on unprecedented,

DOI: 10.4018/978-1-7998-6948-1.ch006

radical re-engineering of their business processes, systems, practices and structures. Furthermore, the novel coronavirus has changed the mindset of university leaders in Africa at different levels, encouraging them to become adaptive, flexible, nimble and resilient to the unusual, unfavourable, complex and uncertain leadership conditions. Numerous researchers (Atchyutimi & Narasareddy, 2018; Harris & Jones, 2020; Yawson & Greiman, 2016) observed that flexibility and nimbleness are required in organisations if they are to respond to dynamic environments and the new leadership structure brought about by the coronavirus. Recently published research on agile, flexible and nimble leadership has offered an explanation for the private sector, but limited empirical studies have been conducted in universities.

Agile and nimble strategies and other suggested leadership development and change management interventions will play a vital role in policy direction and alignment, which seeks to promote regular performance feedback, agile performance management, employee engagement and team-based structures. The agile leadership framework is guided by a plethora of principles which include leaders to have an ability to deal with change, organisations being viewed as fluid, with adaptive systems dominated by intelligent employees (Parker, Holesgrove and Pathak, 2014). In addition, a recognition of the limits of external control in establishing order as opposed to the intelligent control, humanistic problem-solving approach by recognising employees' skills and valuable stakeholders, independent teams as having a collective ability to solve a problem as some of the principles. Lastly, this framework relies on pre-planning, reacts to the emergent outcomes from the self-organised team, and removes the outcomes that prevent the team in realising their set goals (Parker, Holesgrove and Pathak, 2014).

This book chapter sheds light on this issue by investigating the application of change management interventions in universities, including agile transformation methodology, which will assist HR managers in reviewing HR policies, processes, systems and practices. The required change management interventions that are applicable and relevant in post-COVID-19 universities are investigated in order to provide solutions to human resources (HR) practitioners and decision-makers to ensure that sound systems, practices, structures and policies contribute to the universities' goals. The policies and procedures of universities would have to change from the short- to the long-term for them to be effective, efficient and productive, and to change the organisational culture. The short-term changes that are cost-effective to organisations would include meetings and workshops being conducted virtually by using various digital tools and channels. Long-term changes would include a blended means of operating such as the application of flexible working arrangements, which would mostly favour women in the workplace. However, the quality and work output of employees should be measured pre-COVID-19, during the pandemic and in the aftermath in order to apply innovative strategies where there are gaps.

The leadership approaches appropriate after the coronavirus crisis are dissected in this book chapter, which will drive the transformation agenda of these universities post-COVID-19. One of the prominent leadership approach which was mentioned by Ngcamu (2019) is digital leadership. The author posits that such approach of leadership influences and enhance the university leaders and subordinates to transform systems, practices, business processes, and change the culture through the application of the digital tools. Ngcamu (2019) further cites a myriad of leadership approaches which are relevant during this era of the Forth Industrial Revultion. These include: the transformational (which motives and coerce employees to exceed the standards), adaptive (all employees working towards a solution), and transactional leadership approach (which promotes efficiency and effectiveness by providing employees with both financial and non-financial rewards). A selective of the abovementioned leadership approaches such as the transformational leadership have been positively associated to the lecturers' increased performance and satisfaction in the Islamic University as compared to the transactional approach (Azizah et al. 2020). Meanwhile, a new situational leadership called New Normal Leadership (NNL) approach has emerged during the Covid-19 pandemic in the Phillippine (Francisco et al. 2020). This leadership approach emerged from a qualitative research that was gleaned from the school administrators who were selected and interviewed. Francisco et al. (2020) found a myriad traits of the NNL as including: adaptaive leaders while staying strong with one's commitment, effective instructional decision-making, and a leaders who is a good planner, vigilant, and a initiator. The nature of the leadership competencies needed after the pandemic are investigated and clearly articulated to ensure that decisions are made more promptly and are more accurate, multi-dimensional, efficient and effective.

Furthermore, the strategic plans of universities and HR departments are analysed to determine the application of change management interventions (including agile management) to HR functions in African universities. In addition, the purpose of this chapter is to examine the signs of the application of agile transformation techniques in responding to HR challenges in the Fourth Industrial Revolution (and after the coronavirus).

The technological advances and radical changes in the private sector, which took place during the COVID-19 pandemic, have usurped business processes, systems and practices, while agile transformation at universities in Africa have been slow-moving or static. Meanwhile, African universities have been under the stress of an incomparable magnitude due to the coronavirus, which hit their leadership teams unprepared. During the pandemic, an interest in leadership and the momentum of change emerged, which might create unexpected opportunities in the aftermath of the pandemic. This latter analogy has been supported by a plethora of authors (Barr et al., 2020; Georgiades, 2019; Halawi et al., 2020), who observed an emerging theory, issues of leadership, and change momentum, which might create unexpected opportunities in different sectors.

## MATERIALS AND METHODS

In the search for relevant literature on leadership development and change management strategies that are relevant post-COVID-19 in universities in Africa, secondary sources of data were retrieved from search engines and academic databases such as Google Scholar. Media articles, reports and book chapters were retrieved, searched, classified and thematically mapped to generate patterns and trends concerning the strategies universities would implement after the COVID-19 era. To develop a search strategy, a librarian who specialises in higher education was enlisted. "Leadership development" and "change management interventions post-COVID-19" were used as keywords in the study. There were a limited number of journal articles and reports that were relevant to the objectives of the present study and which have been used. This has necessitated the researcher to apply ethnographic methods in writing this book chapter. The researcher also acted as a participant observer due to extensive experience as an organisational development specialist, a consultant, and a researcher in universities in different countries in Africa. A hermeneutic framework and grounded theory are used to categorise, codify and develop themes, patterns and trends that emerged from the analysed data.

## LEADERSHIP APPROACHES IN THE POST-COVID-19 ERA

University leadership post the pandemic should be visible to the workforce in different employment categories as well as to the trade unions, ensuring their needs are prioritised. Bolden (2020) postulates that unique leadership qualities are essential in this epoch of the pandemic, requiring leaders with a shared purpose and who unite the workforce. Collective leadership rather than widely anticipated traits and behaviours are associated with good leadership. The author suggests that leaders as a collective should lead individuals and teams that achieve the leadership outcomes. Leaders should clarify and direct during such uncertain time, be visible, and display active fellowship. While Ngwenya et al. (2020: 431) cite that collective leadership could generate appropriate and context-specific solutions in organisations, they conceptualise collective leadership as "a systems-based approach to identify and tackle root causes of critical problems through inclusive interdisciplinary thought, decision-making and action across sectors."

In addition, Wolff et al. (2016) opine that collective leadership is crucial as it overcomes socio-economic injustices and biases that are rooted in racism and which create barriers to addressing environmental crises. Bolden (2020) further alludes to the fact that systems leadership should be applied during the pandemic to influence both the internal and external stakeholders to initiate new patterns of behaviour. This scholar asserts that the application of systems leadership should involve re-engineering the building systems, structures and business processes (both physical and psychological). Sense-making and place-based leadership have also been considered by Bolden (2020) as pivotal during disastrous and catastrophic periods in universities to enable different stakeholders to make sense of the situation and respond to the crisis by harnessing multiple perspectives and expertise. Meanwhile, Ahlsson (2020) coins some pertinent principles to transform universities, which include the common sense of urgency; the return of professionalism; and competency first. The continuation of the digitalisation of the ever-changing workforce in this sector has necessitated employees to change their mindset, behaviour and attitude towards their activities. However, university leaders, in the aftermath of the pandemic, should decentralise the decision-making powers and lead together with all the employees and other stakeholders. This is done in order to achieve the set objectives and standards of the specific university, increasing the performance and productivity of the institution.

## LEADERSHIP SKILLS, KNOWLEDGE AND COMPETENCIES TO IMPROVE PERFORMANCE POST-COVID-19

The new normal that will be experienced post the pandemic will change HR departments in universities. Human resources practitioners need to transform the new normal into an opportunity to radically change operations and to be led by digital tools. This can be realised if continuous, on-the-job training of leaders and their subordinates becomes the norm, which should scientifically driven by a talented HR development (HRD) unit. Accordingly, HRD can play a pivotal role in the ramifications of the pandemic by providing relevant and appropriate skills development, which can change the university landscape after the coronavirus. According to Dirani et al. (2020: 383), HRD is of the utmost importance during a crisis to accentuate the significance of the human capital's well-being. The authors further highlight the importance of such departments; for instance, in the promotion of health and values, and the organisational need to take care of its valuable assets: human capital (Dirani et al., 2020). The HRD is considered as key in developing the human expertise to adapt to new challenges that are brought by the COVID-19 pandemic (Byrd, 2020). In addition, these authors indicate that HRD acts as an umbilical cord between leaders and employees, influencing leaders to listen, providing psychological empowerment and keeping employees updated (Dirani et al., 2020).

The leaders who will successfully manage universities in Africa post the COVID-19 pandemic should possess certain skills and competences which should be constantly audited and improved through leadership development programmes. Yawson (2020) has proposed the application of the Strategic Flexibility Framework (SFF) to explore the possibilities of HRD after the coronavirus and coined four relevant scenarios: leadership, the meaning of work, contactless commerce, and education and volunteerism.

Flexibility and nimbleness are pivotal to agile transformation in universities. Atchyutimi and Narasareddy (2018) suggest that the agile methodology or technique ensures HR departments improve flexibility and nimbleness to proactively respond to challenges, both internal and external, thus improving productivity. The authors posit that agility as a technique – termed agile talent management – can be applied to a plethora of disciplines including HR management (HRM) (Atchyutimi & Narasareddy, 2018). Agile talent management is focused on improvements to HR policies and systems, thereby increasing performance and productivity. Parker, Holesgrove and Patha (2015) opine that leaders who follow flexible and agile practices become adaptive leaders, set the direction, simplify the processes and generative rules of the system, and promote regular feedback, adaptability and collaboration. Yawson and Greiman (2016) consider strategic flexibility as playing a crucial role in organisations, considered as a capability of responding to a dynamic environment through continuous changes and systematic actions. Strategic flexibility in organisations is ensuring strategic options that are developed through the combined effects of an institution's coordination flexibility in terms of acquiring and using flexible resources (Sanchez, 1997). Numerous researchers (Brozovic, 2018; Stieglitz, Knudsen & Becker, 2016) suggest that the single best plan during such uncertain environments and dynamism is an unrealistic objective, while effective strategic flexibility has been emphasised.

Line managers would be well advised to harness the existing workforce's core competences and skills in order to achieve the organisational continuity goals and objectives. These include micro skills such as empathy, goal-setting, charisma, listening, problem-solving, emotional intelligence, trust relationships, change management and difficult conversations. In addition, leaders in African universities are supposed to have the following qualities: empathy, being able to stabilise the organisation during a crisis, finding opportunities, being decisive and being transparent. Yawson (2020) believes that significant transformations are needed due to the anticipated disruptions that could be brought about by the effects of COVID-19 and shift action as well as avoiding the social exclusion of key stakeholders. This author indicates that employees can be apart physically, but not socially and emotionally. Yawson (2020) cautions authors about the adverse implications of misjudging the impacts of COVID-19, advising readers of the unattended consequences of overacting and recognising the problems associated with it. The HRD practitioners should equip leaders to develop and increase their emotional quotient and emotional intelligence (Farnia & Nafukho, 2016). Some of researchers echo this latter assertion that, during a crisis, leaders need to be virtual in order to determine organisational outcomes (Antonakis & Day, 2017); provide reassurance through a balanced mix of optimism and realism (Antonakis et al., 2016); foster participatory relationships (Antonakis & Atwater, 2002); communicate an ambitious vision; and boost confidence to achieve the strategic objectives (Antonakis & Atwater, 2002). Furthermore, training and development practitioners should also follow Bar-On's (1997) model of emotional-social intelligence to guide development programmes for leaders. This researcher suggests that leadership development programmes should focus on the incumbent's intrapersonal skills, interpersonal skills, stress management, adaptability and general mood. The "social awareness", originally from Goleman's EI competency model (1998), can also be included in the previous model.

Skills development practitioners are considered to play a leading role post-pandemic in universities, conducting skills audits for the workforce and working collaboratively with line managers in different departments. The skills audit should determine whether the skills and knowledge of the current workforce do fit the current reality. These practitioners should then devise a training schedule for employees in different employment categories, which should be informed by the gaps in training in terms of short-, medium- and long-term training needs. Once the training gaps have been identified, skills development practitioners, in consultation with line managers, should set up a (preferably virtual) training programme, develop tools to monitor skills and knowledge, and improve performance. Furthermore, the personalised learning, bespoke learning and development design, which should be applied by organisations, will increase employees' engagement, performance and productivity. In addition, employees should have a learning mindset and agile functioning so that universities can thrive in their core business. The rapid upskilling and reskilling is of paramount importance to the current workforce in universities in order to adapt to the abruptly changing environment in the sector and to suit the "new normal" working conditions post-coronavirus.

## HUMAN RESOURCES DEPARTMENTS

Prior to COVID-19, universities in Africa were embroiled in ongoing conflicts, influenced mostly by states' failure to transform university systems and processes even while a host of key stakeholders' lofty goals remain unrealised. The majority of African universities are still trapped in traditional business operations, which are reactive and lacking the adaptations required to respond to the radical changes needed due to the coronavirus – which demands leaders to change rapidly. This is exemplified by HR departments, which are instrumental in adopting agile techniques for their workforces: processes to develop their leaders, and initiatives to implement change management interventions that are outdated. Where this is lacking, it has led to the paralysis of the entire organisation as the HR department is the engine of any successful organisation, ensuring that both internal stakeholders and external partners are nimble and flexible.

The HR departments in universities have been directly affected by the dramatic changes brought about by the coronavirus, with some concerns from other departments – for instance, internal and external key stakeholders accusing HR departments of being technologically obsolescent and delinquent; fragmented and untransformed business processes and practices; and inflexible and minimal agility and nimbleness. This has resulted in the exodus of talented human capital. A dissection of leadership development and change management interventions is essential in a post-COVID-19 world to develop leaders who are able to respond to the challenges brought about by the virus. Furthermore, HR departments have failed to acquire and retain flexible and innovative, talented employees in the turbulent culture (the COVID-19 period seen in universities). In addition, organisational structures are seen as hierarchical, with seamless communication channels and interpersonal relational goals becoming clogged and cumbersome. Borders and performance goals are rigid; and employee engagement, succession planning and leadership development is absent, even during the slow-killing virus.

In the period after the pandemic, talent acquisition should not be reactional and transactional in universities, as is the norm. Existing skills gaps need to be filled by attracting talented workers who have digitally orientated skills and competencies. In addition, the recruitment and selection policies and practices should be revisited to determine which roles need to be redefined and mainstreamed according to the new job demands.

## BUSINESS UNUSUAL POST-PANDEMIC IN UNIVERSITIES

Post-COVID-19, universities in Africa are facing a myriad of structural-, process- and systems-based challenges and changes which require agile strategies to manage them. These short- and long-term challenges and changes can be reversed by redesigning work teams, managing the work–home balance, reviewing and amending policies, revising working schedules, and evaluating and monitoring workplace health protocols. However, the preparedness for the "new normal" would vary from nation to nation as well from university to university. These radical changes also include reconfiguring workstations, the application of digital tools and digitalising day-to-day activities. In addition, university leaders in Africa need to hone digital skills and invest in IT infrastructure in order to realise the goals of the institution. The blended use of communication channels to respond to the diverse needs of different key stakeholders in universities in South Africa is also needed.

## BUSINESS PROCESS REENGINEERING (BPR) INTERVENTIONS IN AFRICAN UNIVERSITIES

The HRM departments in universities should devise a post-COVID-19 strategy in conjunction with both academic and non-academic leaders. The HRM's operations as it relates to the Fourth Industrial Revolution and COVID-19 in African universities is manual. Such critical departments should map their AS-IS business processes and design the TO-BE in order to improve their productivity in the post-pandemic world. Purnamasari, Heriyanto and Oliver (2020) opine that organisations have required immediate changes in the Fourth Industrial Revolution and demanded an accelerated BPR. These authors believe that BPR radically changes business processes to creatively keep the business wheel running HR systems and processes. This should be automated, providing them with the opportunity to perform better. Such universities should be evaluated holistically and should harness the good practices that were explored during the pandemic. Tertiary institutions should introduce the Total Reward Strategy or create a culture conducive to a healthy work–life balance, flexible working hours, and schedules and activities that allow employees to work from home.

There are serious change ramifications for the university sector in Africa as employees' activities must adapt to the new normal. A myriad of interventions on radically re-engineering business processes in both the administrative and academic sections should be the norm in the sector. In addition, the culture surveys on change would be conducted in order to determine the existing state of employees and customers (students) and a culture that is conductive to managing change efficiently and delivering benefits post-COVID-19. However, a change management plan is required for every university as any change has a myriad of good and bad consequences. Post-pandemic, each university must assess, plan and map all the impacts of radical changes throughout the institutional operations. The customised change journeys should be developed for individual employees or teams to capacitate and equip the workforce with skills, knowledge and confidence to achieve the set goals and objectives during the new normal brought about by the pandemic. Furthermore, change agents should dissect the causes and effects concerning the business operations, stakeholders' and employees' interactions and business processes. The change management interventions should take into cognisance the effects of unprecedented change on the university's business processes, employees and customer well-being, digital tools and information. Furthermore, the psychological well-being of the workforce and its effects on people working from home (or teleworking) should be taken into consideration.

The migration of work from workstations at the university to remote environments would be the new normal and mandatory post the pandemic, due to a myriad of constraints in universities. This has been confirmed by a survey conducted by Gartner (2020) in 222 HR departments in various organisations. The study depicted the disproportionately high percentage of 80% of the departments having employees working remotely, and projected a long-term increase of employees working in virtual environments after the pandemic. Meanwhile, remote working is considered to be complex as an employee who can work anywhere is beneficial to other specialists who need less interaction with peers (Allen, Cho & Meier, 2014). However, there are challenges to remote working, including insufficient space in the home to effectively and efficiently perform duties with those staying or staying with people having unique challenges (Kniffin et al., 2020). Nevertheless, working from home can bring unknown challenges to the university sector, including a lack of control over employees, employees' resistance to modes of surveillance, perceived stress due to continuous monitoring and the invasion of privacy, and an increase in centralisation. According to Bhave, Teo and Dalal (2020), some sectors and organisations have introduced sociometric sensors to monitor their employees' whereabouts. In the aftermath of COVID-19, employee assistance programme (EAP) practitioners will play a pivotal role in promoting the well-being of the workforce. This will encourage employees to be effective and efficient, and to perform their duties appropriately.

## PERFORMANCE AND PRODUCTIVITY IMPROVEMENT POST THE COVID-19 ERA

The COVID-19 pandemic is considered as a catalyst for radically changing how employees should be managed and led in universities in Africa. The rapid transformation of campuses, driven by technology, is changing the roles and responsibilities of both the academic and non-academic workforce in the higher education sector. Universities in Africa should assess and determine the elements of behaviour change that need to be permanent and ensure the unwanted aspects are eliminated. The core values and principles which can improve performance and productivity post-pandemic include improving trust relationships among employees in different employment categories, and displaying transparency and openness.

Progressive leadership strategies are essential in universities post-COVID-19, helping institutions to proactively adapt to the new culture of uncertainty and preparing employees to exceed performance expectations. Leaders should ensure they devise transparent and innovative communication channels through digital tools. They also need to promote teamwork and collaboration; introduce adaptive strategies among employees; and ensure resilience and smooth systems that promote innovation and higher performance. Nandy, Lodh and Tang (2020) are of the understanding that resilience is essential in the university sector in order to continuously build emotional and mental fitness. These authors associate resilience with sustainability, which can increase productivity in the sector and increase the marketability and employability of students.

## LEADERSHIP DEVELOPMENT PROGRAMMES AND STRATEGIES THAT CAN BE IMPLEMENTED POST-COVID-19

The coronavirus struck leaderless universities in Africa that were unprepared, those that had outdated and inconsistent leadership development curricula which were not directed towards achieving the approved organisational strategies. It is urgent that, in the wake of the pandemic, a consistent and integrated approach to leadership development should be developed in universities and ingrained in daily operations at different levels. Such intertwined programmes with the inflow of daily activities will achieve the goals and objectives of universities. Universities should avoid relying on external consultants who have minimal leadership acumen and experience in tertiary education, and rather develop internal leadership development programmes and "lead by doing". On-the-job leadership development programmes which are supplemented with mentoring and coaching interventions should be promoted. Such strategies would equip leaders to respond to institutional challenges as the universities pursue general teaching objectives and individual goals that are aligned with the overall strategy of the institution. The university leaders need to develop the leadership skills that would be applied to ready situations in the organisation while executing and adjusting the strategy of the university as time passes after the pandemic. The universities in Africa should also explore an overlooked practice by scholars and practitioners in the leadership development sub-discipline – which is leadership analytics. Leaders in African universities are mostly leading through hearsay and gut feelings, and thumb sucking their strategies, which have had an adverse impact and resulted in failure to achieve the set goals and standards. These universities are not data-driven and mostly do not value facts. They lack leadership analytics strategies which have the potential to influence their leadership development and evaluation efforts in terms of the impacts, effects and outcomes of the recipients of such programmes. Universities need to conduct (quantitative) barometer surveys to ascertain the behaviour changes for their leaders and measure their performance levels during different phases after the coronavirus. The strong and reliable data collected from employees should guide and provide direction to university leaders in implementing the intervention changes that would yield positive results.

The period after the coronavirus requires multiplicity and a diversity of leadership development programmes that are conducted for a particular situation. For instance, academic leaders cannot enrol in a programme that is similar to non-academic leaders, as the needs, demands and peculiarities are dissimilar. In hindsight, leaders (both academic and non-academic) at different leadership levels (operational, tactical and strategic/executive) cannot be capacitated on a particular programmed set of leadership skills as their contexts and levels of operation vary. In addition, in the university sector during this period, there is no "one size fits all" propositions in terms of leadership as it is always evolving and is largely informed by context. Leaders post-COVID-19 therefore need to embrace and resolve complex challenges rather than complicating problems as such challenges would emanate from the home and have adverse effects in the workplace.

In the period after the coronavirus, universities are likely to be psychologically stressed by the adverse conditions that resulted from the pandemic. For instance, a host of researchers (Charoensukmongkol & Phungsoonthorn, 2020; DePietro, 2020; Hamouche, 2020; Sahu, 2020) mention that the crisis brought about by the coronavirus has not only had a negative impact on organisations, but also on the psychological well-being of employees and their work in the education sector. In a study by Nandy et al. (2020), extreme challenges are expected in universities post-COVID-19. These authors suggest that such institutions need to address the socio-psychological damage to stakeholders in order to continue to perform their activities efficiently. Further, the authors recommend an all-inclusive resilience model to deal with the aftershock among employees and that universities implement an antifragile model for the advancement and betterment of individuals' experiences. However, leaders should understand each and every employee's challenges and counsel them to overcome the problems (Dirani et al., 2020). University leaders must create an environment that allows members of staff to grieve and to express their feelings (Rocco & Shuck, 2019). During and after leadership development programmes, leaders would be informed by collective intelligence and collaboration, which will positively influence individual employees and team members. This will assist in achieving the goals and objectives of their respective universities. The common leadership language, which promotes good leadership practices, should be incorporated into leadership development and used across institutions in order to secure the long-term success of programmes and set a culture of leadership excellence. Both macro and micro skills are essential for leaders to have in the aftermath of the pandemic; however, the toolbox of influential soft skills is also critical, which promotes the networking of leaders and team-based operations.

## ARE CHANGE MANAGEMENT INTERVENTIONS REQUIRED POST THE PANDEMIC?

A holistic change management strategy with innovative best practices borrowed from a myriad of sectors is needed in universities once the pandemic has passed. This can lead to employees being empowered if the existing leaders are resilient; if they genuinely collaborate and partner with both internal and external key stakeholders; and if they have open, honest and vibrant debates with similar thinking and strive towards achieving their respective goals and objectives. Ergonomics exercises should be conducted in universities in order for them to consider redesigning and rearranging the workforce in existing workplaces that have limited office space, which could help to limit high overhead costs. Implementing these interventions will help universities to become agile, nimble and innovative, with improved performance and productivity. This would potentially improve the quality of work life of a talented workforce. Further, the chapter adds new insights into how agile transformation and other sustainable leadership development and change management interventions can alter the organisational culture, performance, productivity, efficiencies and effectiveness in a post-COVID-19 era in the university sector. It further fills the gap in the existing but scant literature on the nature and competencies required from leaders in poorly resourced African universities in the aftermath of COVID-19.

Universities in Africa will continue to have their staff work remotely in order to promote physical distancing of employees and students as well as to promote the well-being and health of key stakeholders. The impacts of the pandemic will remain with the university sector for the foreseeable future. In the aftermath of the pandemic, specialists who deal with the planning of offices (office planners), architects and technologists will be heavily occupied with designing sustainable environments. The shortage of office space in African universities encourages individual universities to promote flexible working arrangements and remote ways of working in the wake of the pandemic. This can be achieved if individual universities invest in collaborative technology which can connect their members of staff in different settings and inaccessible locations. The innovations and transformations that would be brought about by technology in universities and workplaces will become employee-centric and autonomous. University leaders would need to change their centralised and hierarchal decision-making processes and embrace more staff-focused technology to pursue a radical change of the institutional culture. Dirani et al. (2020:

387) argue that "technology can aid in easing the stress of the managers and workers by making the process more flexible. Technology has helped in making it possible for working from alternate locations".

Meanwhile, cloud environment servers should be introduced in universities in order to improve the system in terms of data privacy and security. Face-to-face meetings should be restricted to certain activities that can be performed remotely, although performance needs to be effectively measured. Nonetheless, universities should embark on a project to identify those employees who are able to work from home and those who can resume their duties at the workplace. The culture of high performance associated with mentoring and coaching in a virtual setting is encouraged, supported by redesigned structures and the implementation of a performance management system. A mutually constructive conversation between team members and line managers should focus on what should be done and which activities can be performed from the home.

## ENSURING UNIVERSITY OPERATIONS ARE AGILE, EFFECTIVE AND EFFICIENT AFTER THE PANDEMIC

It is of paramount importance to adopt working agile principles in universities after the pandemic in order to promote campuses working virtually and remotely. The agile approach cannot be considered as a wish list in this period; it is increasingly essential post-COVID-19. Universities in Africa need to be agile as this approach is inextricably associated with digital transformation. Crucial departments (such as the Human Resources) in universities can drive radical changes which can yield favourable results. This can be achieved through the application of digital transformation strategies which can encourage employees to continue working remotely, while managing talent and setting goals. In addition, African universities should harness agile leadership education to move with speed and be adaptive and flexible. This is necessary in the aftermath of the coronavirus so that universities can withstand any crisis that might surface. Marinoni, Van't Land and Jensen (2020) contend that the COVID-19 crisis has provided universities with innumerable opportunities to effectively deal with such crises in the future and to learn more efficiently about the application of crisis management principles. The authors further assert that this will enable universities to increase their resilience and agility when responding to unforeseen circumstances in the future (Marinoni et al., 2020). It is inevitable that, once the pandemic has passed, a myriad of programmes will be offered virtually, with remote working promoted among the workforce.

The agile concept was coined in the 1930s and focused on the process of improvement (Bell Labs & Deming). The agile leadership style has four traits in its model, which includes technical, cooperative, collaborative and generative leadership. African universities need to be agile, proactive and resilient in the immediate future after the pandemic. These sentiments have been echoed by Verma (2020), that university managers and leaders should be agile by being innovative and inspiring team members to proactively respond to a crisis, overcoming the predicament collectively. However, the model of leadership style that is suitable to universities (considered to be diverse, challenging and dealing with lifelong learnings post the coronavirus) has not been explored from a scholarly perspective. Agile principles include setting up expectations post-pandemic; establishing a cross-sectional system to drive collaboration; having regular check-ins in different employment categories; acknowledging risk due to the change in performance culture; and increasing compliance and governance systems. There are other leadership approaches that are associated with the former approach and which can be applied by leaders in the aftermath of the pandemic, such as the inclusive leadership style.

Leaders during the post-COVID-19 phase should exhibit the ethos of inclusive leadership principles by honestly appreciating employees' contributions, irrespective of their hierarchical level. Leaders need to share information and be visible, available and accessible to their subordinates (Carmeli, Reiter-Palmon & Ziv, 2010; Hassan & Jiang, 2019). Stoker, Garretsen and Soudis (2019) posit that a crisis such as the coronavirus can bring changes in leadership styles in organisations, although it is difficult for leaders to emulate and adopt certain leadership approaches and standards during such a disruptive and chaotic period. Leading during such a troublesome time requires leaders to navigate an unstable and periodic trajectory to learn distinct approaches that can achieve an organisation's goals and objectives. This has been echoed by Harris and Jones (2020), that in the education sector, a new leadership order has emerged which has been characterised by a lack of leadership standards, and limited leadership development programmes, benchmarks and KPIs. The authors further opine that the pandemic did not prepare leaders with the precedents and blueprints to assist them in the maelstrom of the COVID-19 pandemic. This has been echoed by Ngwenya et al. (2020), who state that a leader can be any member of society and can introduce radical change by building capacity, listening, and enabling and empowering others.

However, Schwella's (2020) contribution in universities post-COVID-19 suggests that learning leadership is a relevant one where good leaders facilitate prototype solutions to complex societal challenges. The author opines that learning leadership skills relies on evidence-based influences and inputs such as evidence, information, knowledge and informed partnerships. According to Schwella (2020), leaders who follow learning leadership rely on learning experimentation, and facilitate individual competencies and institutional capacity towards resilient, agile and sustainable prototype solutions. The author further posits that learning leadership is instrumental in finding answers to pertinent learning leadership questions.

The first pertinent learning leadership question that should be posed by leaders in universities post the pandemic is: *What happened?* This question has an impact in terms of providing systematic and descriptive qualitative and quantitative assessments of performance trends that are informed by the empirical findings. The second question is: *Why did this happen?* This can be answered by using a diagnostic analytical tool to unearth the provisional explanations of actions and impacts on the reduction in performance. The third question is: *What can I or we learn from this?* This learning leadership question espouses lessons that can be learned to improve individual-based competencies that contribute to personal mastery, team learning and systems thinking (which challenges current mental modes through individual empowerment and team learning). The last question is: *How can the learning be used and built back into the system to improve the quality and performance of the system?* This focuses the institutional capacity on continuous improvements.

## UNIVERSITY POLICIES AND STRUCTURES TO BE CHANGED POST-COVID-19

It is quite clear that, post the pandemic, university campuses in Africa will continue working remotely due to the shortage of adequate office space and lecture venues that are safe and ensure physical distancing. Consequently, universities should support this "new normal" by developing health policies and procedures, and amending existing ones to support universities' remote working arrangements. For instance, the wellness policies need to be aligned, even though university leaders do not readily admit that; whilst; the COVID-19 is causing psychological havoc. Also, managers need to be skilled and trained on how to regularly check in with employees, without being intrusive. In addition, policy changes are essential post this era, working from home, brings about new challenges, which need to be covered in

HR policies. Moreover, performance management takes on a whole new challenge of managing outputs. For instance, if employees did not understand the standards of performance before the pandemic while they were present at workplace, how much more important now that they work from home. There are a host of soft skills that will become all the more important. What are these skills? How do we assess for these in recruitment and selection process? The training and development policies would need to be reviewed as the academic leadership and leadership in general would take new challenges and these challenges are not yet known, how to identify and develop such skills. The career pathing and the integrated development policies would have to be reviewed to respond to the post COVID-19 era. This will minimise the risk of misalignment and poorer collaboration that can result from staff working remotely.

## CONCLUSION

The post-coronavirus era does not necessarily require leaders to apply anticipated leadership styles or approaches in universities. New leadership approaches have been unearthed, which can yield good results and improve performance and productivity in universities. These pertinent approaches include inclusive leadership, collective leadership and systems leadership, which are relevant in the post-COVID-19 era in African universities. Leaders are advised to include all employees, and promote collectivism and a systems approach in order to deal with both internal and external stakeholders. This will assist team members in the university sector in achieving the goals and objectives of the university. Furthermore, it is suggested that for leaders to be sustainable and productive post the pandemic, HR development practitioners should invest in continuous training, and develop their workforce in both macro and micro skills. In addition, such practitioners should ensure that employees have scientific tools in place to determine the skills gap of employees and equip them with the relevant macro and micro skills. Visibility management and crisis management come very strongly to the fore in this chapter as the current pandemic has taught university leaders to be prepared for future crises and to be visible in their respective institutions.

Nevertheless, the post-COVID-19 era is considered to be the most challenging period as universities in Africa still subscribe to outdated change management interventions. It is recommended that the university sector conduct radical interventions of change, including BPR, to redesign business processes and improve productivity. This can be achieved through change management plans that promote digitalisation, teamwork and collaboration. There should be clear objectives to influence behavioural changes, thus achieving the goals and objectives of the university. The reconfiguration of workstations or ergonomics exercises is essential in universities to ensure that the health and safety of employees takes priority and that workstations are customer-focused. What is noteworthy in this chapter is that universities have not yet reviewed their policies, systems, strategic plans and practices, many of which are counter to the demands of the new normal post-COVID-19.

There is limited scholarly work that has been published on African universities' preparedness after the COVID-19 era and this is a serious limitation of the study. The paucity of published studies on change management and leadership development in different sectors, limited the researcher to support his work that has been observed in the past two decades. Another limitation is methodological as the book chapter has relied on desktop analysis, without collecting empirical data. Against this backdrop, future researchers are advised to apply a myriad of research methodologies to investigate leadership development and change management strategies that can be used in universities post the pandemic and which can improve employees' performance, productivity and mental well-being.

## REFERENCES

Ahlsson, A. (2020). *Why change? Lessons in leadership from the COVID-19 pandemic*. Academic Press.

Allen, T. D., Cho, E., & Meier, L. L. (2014). Work–family boundary dynamics. *Annual Review of Organizational Psychology and Organizational Behavior, 1*(1), 99–121. doi:10.1146/annurev-orgpsych-031413-091330

Antonakis, J., & Atwater, L. (2002). Leader distance: A review and a proposed theory. *The Leadership Quarterly, 13*(6), 673–704. doi:10.1016/S1048-9843(02)00155-8

Antonakis, J., Bastardoz, N., Jacquart, P., & Shamir, B. (2016). Charisma: An ill-defined and ill-measured gift. *Annual Review of Organizational Psychology and Organizational Behavior, 3*(1), 293–319. doi:10.1146/annurev-orgpsych-041015-062305

Antonakis, J., & Day, D. V. (2017). Leadership: Past, present, and future. In J. Antonakis & D. Day (Eds.), *The nature of leadership* (3rd ed., pp. 56–81). SAGE Publications.

Azizaha, Y. N., Rijalb, M. K., Rumainurc, U. N. R., Pranajayae, S. A., Ngiuf, Z., Mufidg, A., ... Maui, D. H. (2020). Transformational or Transactional Leadership Style: Which Affects Work Satisfaction and Performance of Islamic University Lecturers During COVID-19 Pandemic. *Systematic Reviews in Pharmacy, 11*(7), 577–588.

Bar-On, R. (1997). EQ-i Bar-On emotional quotient inventory: A measure of emotional intelligence. Toronto: Technical Manual, Multi Health Systems.

Barr, J., Hwang, E. S., & Shortell, C. K. (2020). *Surgeons, plague, and leadership: A historical mantle to carry forward*. Academic Press.

Bhave, D. P., Teo, L. H., & Dalal, R. S. (2020). Privacy at work: A review and a research agenda for a contested terrain. *Journal of Management, 46*(1), 127–164. doi:10.1177/0149206319878254

Bolden, R. (2020). *Leadership, complexity and change: Learning from the Covid-19 pandemic*. Research, Business and Innovation.

Brozovic, D. (2018). Strategic flexibility: A review of the literature. *International Journal of Management Reviews, 20*(1), 3–31. doi:10.1111/ijmr.12111

Byrd, M. Y. (2020). *A New Normal: The Changed Landscape of Human Resource Development in the Wake of COVID-19*. Academic Press.

Carmeli, A., Reiter-Palmon, R., & Ziv, E. (2010). Inclusive leadership and employee involvement in creative tasks in the workplace: The mediating role of psychological safety. *Creativity Research Journal, 22*(3), 250–260. doi:10.1080/10400419.2010.504654

Charoensukmongkol, P., & Phungsoonthorn, T. (2020). The effectiveness of supervisor support in lessening perceived uncertainties and emotional exhaustion of university employees during the COVID-19 crisis: The constraining role of organizational intransigence. *The Journal of General Psychology*, 1–20. PMID:32691689

DePietro, A. (2020). *Here's a look at the impact of coronavirus (COVID-19) on colleges and universities in the U.S.* Retrieved from https://www.forbes.com/sites/andrewdepietro/2020/04/30/impact-coronavirus-covid-19-colleges-universities/#44fea1bf61a6

Dirani, K. M., Abadi, M., Alizadeh, A., Barhate, B., Garza, R. C., Gunasekara, N., Ibrahim, G., & Majzun, Z. (2020). Leadership competencies and the essential role of human resource development in times of crisis: A response to Covid-19 pandemic. *Human Resource Development International, 23*(4), 380–394. doi:10.1080/13678868.2020.1780078

Farnia, F., & Nafukho, F. M. (2016). Emotional intelligence research within human resource development scholarship. *European Journal of Training and Development, 40*(2), 90–110. doi:10.1108/EJTD-11-2014-0073

Francisco, C., & Nuqui, A. (2020). *Emergence of a situational leadership during COVID-19 pandemic called New Normal Leadership*. Academic Press.

Gartner. (2020, Apr. 14). Gartner HR survey reveals 41% of employees likely to work remotely at least some of the time post coronavirus pandemic. *News Release*.

Goleman, D. (1998). *Working with emotional intelligence*. Bantam Books.

Hamouche, S. (2020). COVID-19 and employees' mental health: Stressors, moderators and agenda for organizational actions. *Emerald Open Research, 2*, 15. doi:10.35241/emeraldopenres.13550.1

Harris, A., & Jones, M. (2020). *COVID 19: School leadership in disruptive times*. Academic Press.

Hassan, S., & Jiang, Z. N. (2019). Facilitating learning to improve performance of law enforcement workgroups: The role of inclusive leadership behavior. *International Public Management Journal, 25*, 1–25. Advance online publication. doi:10.1080/10967494.2019.1680465

Kniffin, K. M., Narayanan, J., Anseel, F., Antonakis, J., Ashford, S. J., Bakker, A. B., ... Creary, S. J. (2020). *COVID-19 and the workplace: Implications, issues, and insights for future research and action*. Academic Press.

Marinoni, G., Van't Land, H., & Jensen, T. (2020). *The impact of Covid-19 on higher education around the world.* IAU Global Survey Report.

Nandy, M., Lodh, S., & Tang, A. (2020). Lessons from COVID-19 and a resilience model for higher education. *Industry and Higher Education*.

Ngcamu, B. S. (2019). Digitalizing South African Universities: Exploring Benefits, Barriers and Risks. In Digital Leadership-A New Leadership Style for the 21st Century. IntechOpen.

Ngwenya, N., Helfand, R., McNamara, A., Cooper, M., Espinosa, P. A. O. L. A., Flenley, D., Steiner, N., Awoyemi, S., Dicke, I., Musasa, M., & Sandbrook, C. (2020). A call for collective crisis leadership. *Oryx, 54*(4), 431–432. doi:10.1017/S0030605320000496

Parker, D. W., Holesgrove, M., & Pathak, R. (2015). Improving productivity with self-organised teams and agile leadership. *International Journal of Productivity and Performance Management*.

Parker, D. W., Holesgrove, M., & Pathak, R. (2015). Improving productivity with self-organised teams and agile leadership. *International Journal of Productivity and Performance Management.*

Purnamasari, D. I., Heriyanto, H., & Oliver, S. S. (2020). *Similarity factors affecting the use of online applications for business process reengineering (BPR) acceleration in micro, small and medium enterprises (MSMEs) as a consequence of Covid-19 pandemic*. Academic Press.

Rocco, T. S., & Shuck, B. (2019). Death and dying: Grief, compassion and workplace responses. *New Horizons in Adult Education and Human Resource Development*, *32*(1), 1–4. doi:10.1002/nha3.20268

Sahu, P. (2020). Closure of universities due to coronavirus disease 2019 (COVID-19): Impact on education and mental health of students and academic staff. *Cureus*, *12*(4), e7541. doi:10.7759/cureus.7541 PMID:32377489

Sanchez, R. (1997). Preparing for an uncertain future: Managing organizations for strategic flexibility. *International Studies of Management & Organization*, *27*(2), 71–94. doi:10.1080/00208825.1997.11656708

Schwella, E. (2020). *Post-COVID academic pointers: On social innovation, engaged scholarship, and learning leadership*. School of Social Innovation, Hugenote College.

Stieglitz, N. T., Knudsen, T., & Becker, M. C. (2016). Adaptation and inertia in dynamic environments. *Strategic Management Journal*, *37*(9), 1854–1864. doi:10.1002mj.2433

Stoker, J. I., Garretsen, H., & Soudis, D. (2019). Tightening the leash after a threat: A multi-level event study on leadership behavior following the financial crisis. *The Leadership Quarterly*, *30*(2), 199–214. doi:10.1016/j.leaqua.2018.08.004

Verma, B. (2020). *Agile leadership for higher education: Post COVID-19 response*. Mediawire.

Wolff, T., Minkler, M., Wolfe, S. M., Berkowitz, B., Bowen, L., Butterfoss, F. D., & … . (2016). Collaborating for equity and justice: Moving beyond collective impact. *The Nonprofit Quarterly*, *24*, 42–52.

Yawson, R. (2020). Strategic flexibility analysis of HRD research and practice post COVID-19 pandemic. *Human Resource Development International*, *23*(4), 406–417. doi:10.1080/13678868.2020.1779169

Yawson, R. M., & Greiman, B. C. (2017). Strategic flexibility analysis of agrifood nanotechnology skill needs identification. *Technological Forecasting and Social Change*, *118*(C), 184–194. doi:10.1016/j.techfore.2017.02.019

# Chapter 7
# Success Factors of Future-Viable Organizations in the Post-COVID-19 Era

**Peter Behrendt**
*Freiburg Institut, Germany*

**Alexander Holicki**
*Freiburg Institut, Germany*

**Veronika Matzner**
*Freiburg Institut, Germany*

## ABSTRACT

*The COVID-19 crisis has disrupted societies and will be succeeded by economic and social dynamics. Therefore, organizations need to adapt and seize new opportunities quickly. To learn from the early part of the COVID-19 crisis, 24 leader interviews were conducted and categorized based on the integrative model of leadership behavior. In consequence, eight success factors were derived that foster the future-viability of organizations in times of crisis: the three success factors, (1) providing iterative leadership within uncertainty, (2) promoting absolute customer-loyalty, and (3) providing sustainable public value, foster coordination with internal and external actors and provide meaning. Two factors, (4) promoting a culture of trust and (5) establishing collaborative ecosystems of organizations, promote cooperation and sustain trust. The final three success factors, (6) creating an agile culture, (7) driving digital processes, and (8) ensuring economic agility, enhance agility by activating internal and external resources.*

## INTRODUCTION

The COVID-19 crisis has disrupted global economies and societies. Besides the pandemic crisis, many other social dynamics can be expected: significant changes are very likely due to the expected climate crisis, further digital change, global migration dynamics, and higher instabilities in the political systems

DOI: 10.4018/978-1-7998-6948-1.ch007

of many countries. Therefore, the post-COVID-19 era will be characterized by increased social and economic dynamics. To successfully get through the next decades, organizations need to effectively cope with the upcoming challenges and seize resulting opportunities. Organizational leaders should prepare their organizations for this endeavor and steer them through these challenges. Unfortunately, the detailed dynamics of those changes are unpredictable. Therefore, it is essential for organizations and their leaders to continually learn within and from the crises, to successfully manage their present and future.

To learn from the COVID-19 crisis quickly and anticipate success factors for future crises, the authors have interviewed 24 social and organizational leaders and consulted well-grounded leadership theory. Based on the overarching question regarding success factors of future-viable organizations, the leaders were asked to externalize their learnings from the COVID-19 crisis and predict success factors for future-viability and crisis survival. The results of these interviews were categorized based on existing leadership theory: the integrative model of leadership behavior (IMoLB; Behrendt, Matz & Göritz, 2017). This model integrates the results of decades of leadership behavior research (e.g., Burke et al., 2006; DeRue, Nahrgang, Wellman & Humphrey, 2011; Yukl, 2012) in a parsimonious model and is based on well-established fundamental psychological theory: the theory of planned behavior (Ajzen, 1991), the Rubicon model (Achtziger & Gollwitzer, 2008), the Ringelmann effect (Ingham, Levinger, Graves & Peckham, 1974), the model of social loafing (Karau & Williams, 1993), the job demands-resources model (Bakker & Demerouti, 2007), the group identity perspective (Ellemers, De Gilder & Haslam, 2004), and several others (Behrendt et al., 2017).

From the expert interviews and the theoretically derived leadership behaviors, success factors can be delineated that contribute to the future-viability of organizations in times of crisis. As a result, this chapter demarcates essential success factors for future-viable organizations and exemplifies those success factors based on expert experiences within the COVID-19 crisis. The resulting model of success factors of a future-viable organization in the post-COVID-19 era is provided to the scientific and practice community for further development. The model could be challenged in further theoretic refinements, used for the development of theory-based measurements, and tested in corresponding future research.

## Integrative Model of Leadership Behavior

IMoLB builds on extensive previous leadership research (Fleishman, 1953; Halpin & Winer, 1957; House, 1971; Likert, 1961; Misumi & Peterson, 1985; Yukl, 2012). IMoLB integrates previous findings within a theory-based model that is grounded in well-established theories from fundamental psychology. Studies on leadership behavior so far have used primarily expert interviews or questionnaires in favor of practical relevance. This, however, compromised the validity of the studies and associated leadership behavior models (see van Knippenberg & Sitkin, 2013). Consequently, the conceptualizations of leadership behavior were based on behaviors attributed to successful leaders. Criticism emerged that the perception of behavior differs from the behavior itself, due to observational errors (e.g., Dinh et al., 2014). Lay observers are, for example, prone to the halo effect (Thorndike, 1920), confirmation biases based on implicit leadership theories (Phillips & Lord, 1986), and the need to answer consistently (Podsakoff & Organ, 1986). These errors appear to be systematic, leading many studies to establish high correlations between theoretically different constructs. These methodological flaws, as well as conceptual overlaps, in return hindered the establishment of precise causal models (van Knippenberg & Sitkin, 2013). Yukl (2012) suggested a comprehensive taxonomy of effective leadership behavior perceptions to integrate existing findings and to provide a structured overview. Yukl's four behavioral meta-categories included

15 component behaviors and thereby reduced many overlaps. Since this taxonomy was based on the available empirical research, though, it failed to respond to criticism that derived from systematic observation errors. Departing from Yukl's integrative taxonomy (2012), IMoLB tackles this criticism by consulting psychological theories outside of the core leadership literature.

Leadership is defined as "influencing and facilitating individual and collective efforts to accomplish shared objectives" (Yukl, 2012, p. 66). Based on this definition of leadership, IMoLB delineates two meta-categories of leadership behaviors: task-oriented and relations-oriented leadership behavior. Both meta-categories include three leadership behavior categories, each of which is further specified by several distinct leadership behaviors. Figure 1 exhibits the three task-oriented behavior categories—*enhancing understanding*, *strengthening motivation*, and *facilitating implementation*—and the three relations-oriented leadership behavior categories—*fostering coordination*, *promoting cooperation*, and *activating resources*.

*Figure 1. Integrative Model of Leadership Behavior (IMoLB)*

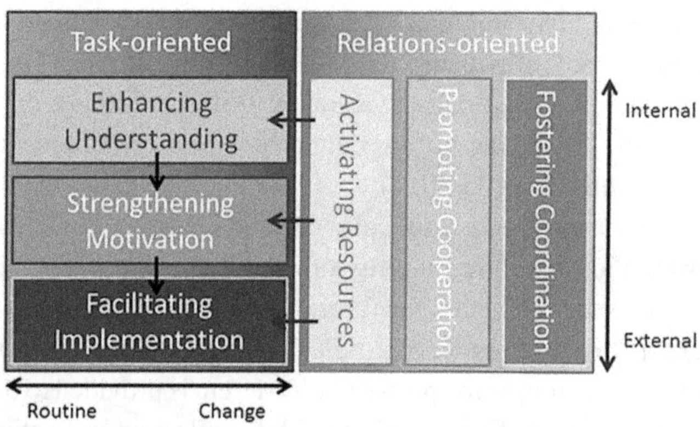


## Task-Oriented Leadership Behaviors

Task-oriented leadership behaviors support the process of accomplishing objectives substantiated by fundamental psychological motivation and action theories. The Rubicon model derived from expectancy-value theories (Fishbein & Ajzen, 1975; Heckhausen & Gollwitzer, 1987) proposes four phases in a course of action: (1) evaluation, (2) deliberation, (3) planning, and (4) action (Achtziger & Gollwitzer, 2008). Leaders are typically present in Phases 1 to 3. Consequently, IMoLB delineates three task-oriented leadership behavior categories that support the process of accomplishing objectives.

The first task-oriented leadership behavior, *enhancing understanding*, is relevant in the evaluation phase. This phase concerns the evaluation of prior actions and their results (Achtziger & Gollwitzer, 2008). Leadership behaviors are supposed to provide relevant information, facilitate accurate assessment, and thereby enhance well-adjusted future behavior.

The second task-oriented leadership behavior category, *strengthening motivation*, is relevant in the deliberation phase. This phase concerns deliberating alternative objectives and deciding on one (Achtziger & Gollwitzer, 2008). Leadership behaviors are supposed to foster appropriate decisions by deliberating the consequences and the value of possible objectives and by strengthening the motivation to pursue those objectives that are in the shared interest.

The third task-oriented leadership behavior category, *facilitating implementation*, supports the planning phase. This phase concerns the transformation of objectives into concrete implementation plans, which are finally executed in the action phase. Leadership behaviors are supposed to form appropriate plans, identify opportunities for execution, and thereby promote successful intention realization.

## Relations-Oriented Leadership Behaviors

Relations-oriented leadership behaviors influence individuals so they invest their efforts in the process of accomplishing objectives. According to the Ringelmann effect, groups do not exploit the full potential of their combined effort (Ingham et al., 1974) due to insufficient coordination and suboptimal engagement (Ingham et al., 1974; Karau & Williams, 1993). Accordingly, IMoLB postulates appropriate leader behavior to counter this effect by increasing collective coordination and individual engagement (Behrendt et al., 2017). Substantiated by group and engagement research, IMoLB postulates three relations-oriented behavior categories leading to effective follower engagement in the process of accomplishing objectives.

The first relations-oriented behavior category, *fostering coordination*, addresses the loss of coordination in group activities. Leadership behaviors are supposed to synchronize collective efforts and embrace well-adjusted individual contributions. This includes the establishment of explicit procedures and structures of communication, ensuring decisions, and in that aim conveying the leader's competence and certainty in the process.

The second relations-oriented behavior category, *promoting cooperation*, addresses the loss of effort in group activities. Leadership behaviors are supposed to allow every member of the group to contribute their unique competence and to motivate every single member to invest maximum effort. Leadership behaviors focus on encouraging individual contributions, underline their uniqueness and indispensability, encouraging social support, and permitting autonomy in tasks.

The third relations-oriented behavior category, *activating resources*, also address the engagement in groups—in this case, by creating positivity regarding engaged behaviors and ensuing outcomes. These leadership behaviors strengthen a positive group identity and reward valuable contributions. This includes prompting self-efficacy and a positive mindset regarding the group's experiences, accomplishments, and expectations.

## IMoLB's Theoretic Value

Overall, IMoLB's contributions represent the integration of previous leadership behavior taxonomies within a more parsimonious framework, the reduction of conceptual redundancies, and the delineation of theory-based relationships between those concepts. Furthermore, it calls for the exact discrimination of actual behavior from perceived behavior by considering lay observers' cognitive biases and by providing a set of concrete observable behaviors in each category. Finally, the integration of established psychological theories accesses a wealth of research results and sparks further theoretic proliferation and hypothesis building rooted in research insights outside of the core leadership literature.

## PRESENT INTERVIEW STUDY

The present study investigates the question of how IMoLB can help understand and categorize organizational success factors of future-viability in the post-COVID-19 era.

### 24 Expert Interviews With Organizational and Social Leaders

To investigate success factors for future-viability in an explorative approach, the authors decided to interview a variety of organizational and social leaders. The leaders were asked to explicate their learnings from early in the COVID-19 crisis and how organizations were able to successfully adapt within the present crisis and what can be derived from the current situation to predict success factors of future crisis-viability and survival.

### The Research Sample of Interviewers and Interviewees

The interview team consists of five professional psychologists and pedagogues: Dr. Peter Behrendt, Annette Bohland, Frank Domonell, Veronika Matzner, and Elke Mowat. They professionally accompany organizations in change and development processes and possess altogether over 80 years of professional experience. The interview team selects five interviewees each from their professional network, deliberately selecting representatives from a diverse set of organizations predominantly in southwest Germany, ranging from a youth leader in a social movement to clerical leaders, governmental representatives, organizational entrepreneurs, industrial managers, and research professors. A total of 24 leaders were interviewed. As organizational and social leaders, they possess practical, procedural, and interpretative knowledge in their field. In addition to their functional expertise, they have practical insights into their organizations, gain access to strategic decisions, and bear high levels of responsibility.

### Interview Methodology

The interviews examined the research topic in an explorative, open-minded way to explicate the expert's practical learnings from adaptation early in the COVID-19 crisis and their predictions for the future-viability of organizations in times of crisis. The one-to-one interviews were conducted in July 2020 in person, by telephone, or by virtual videocalls. They lasted 30 to 60 minutes. The interviews were semi-standardized with a set of ten predefined questions, which served as the starting point. Exemplary questions were:

- "What have you learned within the COVID-19 crisis, and maybe also in previous crises, regarding future-viability of organizations?"
- "If you were to mandate a study to measure the future-viability of a company, which verification criteria would you mandate?"
- "If you were minister of economy and could spend €10 billion, according to which criteria would you determine which companies to secure?"
- "How will society determine ten years from now which organizations or economies to hold, promote, or preserve?"

- "What do you see as glaring examples of a lack of future-viability and why? Where is future-viability being faked—what criteria are being overlooked or overplayed?"
- "If you were to set up a new company, what would it look like? What criteria would you focus on to make it future-viable?"

Interviewers were asked to actively listen and ask deepening questions to elicit explanations and concretizations of the initial interviewees' statements. To not influence the answers, the interviewers were prohibited from sharing their own ideas, opinions, and views. Interviewee statements were directly protocolled by the interviewers.

### Methodology of Analysis and Categorization

As the first step of analysis and based upon the 24 interview protocols, every expert statement regarding potential success factors was extracted and noted with key words on cards. As a second step, these cards were sorted according to their content and categorized based on IMoLB's theoretic categories by the main author. As a second step, the whole interview team reviewed the extracted content for completeness and the created structure for consistency and comprehensibility. In this step, the interviewers ensured that no interview statements regarding success factors were overlooked. Finally, the created model was presented to another group of eight organizational and social leaders as well as to a group of a dozen organizational consultants, discussed, and again reviewed for completeness, consistency, and comprehensibility. These consecutive reviews did result in slight adaptations especially in wording, balancing, and precision of the created categories.

## SUCCESS FACTORS OF FUTURE-VIABLE ORGANIZATIONS IN THE POST-COVID-19 ERA

### Behaviors 1-3: Task-Oriented Leadership

Based on IMoLB, the tasks of the members of crisis-hit organizations are threefold (Behrendt et al., 2017):

1. quickly enhance understanding of the changing environment and the resulting effects on the organization,
2. strengthen the motivation in the organization to quickly adapt to these changes,
3. facilitate bold implementation of first adaptation ideas,

and assure that the organization swiftly learns from these implementation experiments in iterative cycles by repeating Steps 1 to 3. Organizations can adapt their understanding, motivational aspiration, and implementation activities to the crisis-driven change, step-by-step. By these iterative cycles, the organization will develop new routines that are adapted to the changed situation.

According to the IMoLB, the task-oriented behaviors directly contribute to the accomplishment of objectives, whereas the relations-oriented leadership behaviors indirectly support this process by providing followers' engagement. In that aim, relations-oriented leadership behaviors focus more on the interaction style, rather than the content.

## Behaviors 4–6: Relations-Oriented Leadership

Based on IMoLB, three relations-oriented leadership behavior categories ensure that individuals invest their efforts in this process of shared goal accomplishment and organizational crisis adaptation (see Figure 2).

*Figure 2. Relations-oriented leadership behavior and resulting success factors of future-viability*

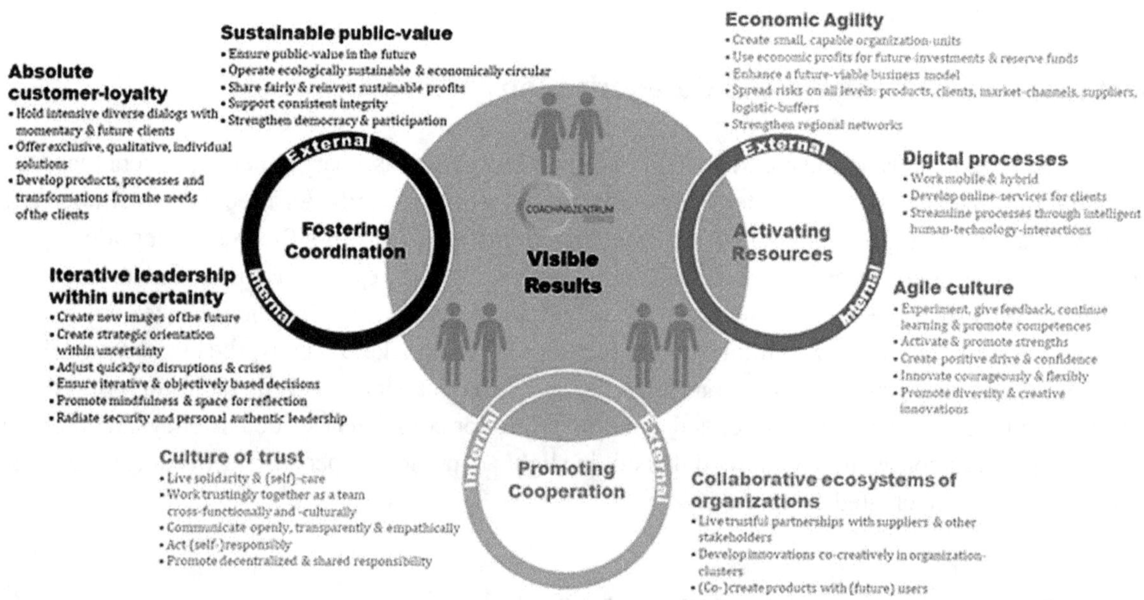


### Behavior 4: Fostering Coordination …

#### *(I) … of Internal Actors by "Providing Iterative Leadership Within Uncertainty"*

Especially in times of crisis and uncertainty, it is important to sustain the coordination of internal actors by providing the organization with a sense of meaning and general direction while adjusting quickly to the changed situation. The quick adjustments need organizational decision competence as well as crisis teams that allow fast, sound, and objectively based decisions to ensure effective coordination. These decisions should be adjustable within quick iteration cycles whenever new situations or learnings emerge. These iterative feedback-cycles are particularly important in times of uncertainty regarding the current situation, future, and possible outcomes of actions taken (Theodoridis & Priporas, 2013). Especially in emotionally straining situations, leaders should guide with a role model of serenity to limit the stress level and protect the organization's ability to act and reflect themselves objectively. Promoting mindfulness and creating space for deep reflection supports that aim. Leadership strategies can foster effective coordination by creating clarity of roles and simplifying the complexity of the critical changes (Pulakos, Kantrowitz & Schneider, 2019). As the interviewed experts confirm, reducing complexity helps to maintain orientation, especially in times of change and uncertainty: in the current COVID-19 crisis, informing employees at an early stage and to keep them informed was one of the most central reported tasks of management—even if the management was yet not fully aware of all objectives and next steps to be taken. To provide sound general direction in fast-changing situations, leaders will need the ability to anticipate futures significantly deviant to conventional extrapolation: This capability to understand and apply anticipations of completely changed futures is called *futures literacy* (Miller, 2018).

Summing up, the success factor *providing iterative leadership within uncertainty* includes the following organizational capabilities: (a) creating new images of the future, (b) creating strategic orientation within uncertainty, (c) adjusting quickly to disruptions and crisis, (d) ensuring iterative and objectively based decisions, (e) promoting mindfulness and space for reflection, and (f) radiating security and personal authentic leadership.

### *(II) ... With External Proximal Actors by "Promoting Absolute Customer-Loyalty"*

Good coordination with external actors is especially threatened in times of crisis. Crises often reduce available resources, complicate access to services, and quickly change the critical needs of customers. This is especially true for the national shutdowns during the COVID-19 crisis. In these times of reduced budgets, customers check which products and services are disposable and which providers are to be kept despite hindrances. During the COVID-19 crisis, many customers even continued payments while they were not able to receive services to support their preferred organizations and suppliers or deliberately spent money at their preferred restaurants and shops to ensure their survival. Accordingly, Well-established customer loyalty has been shown to be crucial for business profitability and competitiveness (Buchanan & Gillies, 1990). Furthermore, the loyalty is of particular importance in times of crisis, because it increases the commitment and investment in the relationship (see Salo, Tähtinen & Ulkuniemi, 2009). Almost every expert interviewee working in organizations with customer contact has validated this argument. Therefore, organizations are more crisis-viable who have bonded best with their customers by providing individual services or exclusive products with a quality the customers value most. To achieve strong customer loyalty, products, services, processes, and their continued transformation should be developed consequently from the customer-perspective and really address their needs (Kim, Beckman & Agogino, 2018; Coelho & Henseler, 2012; Salomo, Steinhoff & Trommsdorff, 2003). In that aim, regular, intense dialogs with momentary and potential future customers are critical to observe, identify, and understand shifting or emerging needs—not only but especially in times of crisis and social dynamics. The close communication and appropriate adaptations ensure good coordination with customer needs—representing one of the most important external actors for most organizations.

Summing up, the success factor *promoting absolute customer-loyalty* includes the following organizational capabilities: (a) holding intensive diverse dialogs with momentary and future clients; (b) developing products, processes, and transformations from the needs of the clients; and (c) offering according exclusive, qualitative, and individual solutions.

### *(III) ... With External Actors by "Providing Sustainable Public Value"*

In the post-COVID-19 era, another external actor becomes more important to coordinate with: During the financial crisis and the COVID-19 crisis, as well as in the expected climate crisis, the public state becomes a more powerful and important actor. Although, this contradicts the so far predominating neo-liberal economic principle of non-intervening states. It became the state's role to decide which crisis-hit organizations to save financially and which organizations to support, allow, or impair for sustainable changes in our economies. In the financial crisis, state support was not combined with any other expectations than the economic survival of the organizations that were too big to fail. But lately, stronger demands emerged, calling out for a transition to an economic system that serves the "common good," and that motivates organizations to act more sustainably and socially (Felber, 2019). Now, several state governments consider integrating principles of the "Economy for the Common Good" in order to develop new laws (Felber, 2019), and the European Union, for example, adopted a "Circular Economy Action Plan" (European Commission, 2018) to make production more sustainable and less wasteful. The goal of combining economic growth with sustainability secured the open support by various political and economic actors (e.g., OECD, World Economic Forum, advocacy associations, and leading corporations; Corvellec, Böhm, Stowell & Valenzuela, 2020). Accordingly, during the tax evasion scandal "CumEx affair", a public citizens movement was the main force pushing forward the persecution of criminal organizational leaders, calling for more democratic participation (CumEx Haltet die Steuerdiebe, 2020). Also early in the COVID-19 crisis, public opinion and media questioned the financial support of organizations that were scandal-hit, have just dumped massive bonus payments to managers and dividends to shareholders, or those that undermined states' functioning by shifting revenues to offshore tax shelters. Consequently, some states like France and Germany already combined the significant financial support with concrete expectations towards the organizations or tailored the support to organizations of "systemic relevance." The climate crisis will likely strengthen that tendency because it enforces the need for systemic economic changes. In consequence, the crisis-viability of organizations increases by adding measurable and sustainable public value (Kaufman, 2010). This public value needs to be adapted to and coordinated with shifting social priorities in times of crisis. Furthermore, in times of increasing sensitivity to organizational scandals of well-marketed organization, this public value should also be validated by neutral ethical reviews or consistent certification processes. Overall, this factor was the one most often referenced by the interviewed leaders as a new emerging success factor for future-viability.

Summing up, the success factor *providing sustainable public value* includes the following organizational capabilities: (a) ensuring public-value in the future, (b) operating ecologically sustainable and economically circular, (c) sharing fairly and reinvest sustainable profits, (d) supporting consistent integrity, (e) strengthening democracy and participation.

## Behavior 5: Promoting Cooperation ...

### *(IV) ... of Internal Actors by "Promoting a Culture of Trust"*

Sustaining internal cooperation provides specific challenges in times of crisis, as they generate significant change and diverse personal threats. To swiftly learn and adapt, it is important to disseminate new information within the organization quickly. Trust in this information, as well as trust among employees, is an essential condition for organizational learning (Hoe, 2007). At the same time, it is important that individuals trust new adapted guidelines and implement them quickly while providing open, constructive feedback. Furthermore, organizations need to rely on the cooperation of all members in the best interest of all and the provision of solidarity where needed to cope with threats and change. Accordingly, perceived supervisor–subordinate solidarity leads to higher motivation and job satisfaction among employees (MacDonald, Kelly & Christen, 2014). Open and empathetic communication promotes that solidarity (Kelly & MacDonald, 2014). In critical times, missing trust cannot be replaced by the same level of control as it is possible in established routine processes, due to higher transaction costs of control (Jäckel, 2018). The interviewed leaders reported this experience early in the COVID-19 crisis, when many employees suddenly had to be working in the home office—far away from potential control of their peers and supervisors. Within those conditions, individuals at all levels need to be trusted to concertedly develop the needed adaptations, create and share knowledge (Jäckel, 2018) without waiting for long bureaucratic decisions in distant headquarters. Trust needs to be so high that, where necessary, individuals are even empowered to deviate from pre-crisis guidelines that no longer apply and to experiment without fear (Pulakos et al., 2019; Boes, Kämpf, Lühr & Ziegler, 2018). To adapt quickly to the changing situations and customer concerns early in the COVID-19 crisis, employees needed decision-making freedom, which furthermore promoted the willingness to learn and change, according to the interviewed leaders. New, more decentralized, and less hierarchic organization structures are currently promoted to increase organizational agility (see Robertson, 2015, "Holacracy"; Laloux, 2014, "Teal Organization"; and Romme, 1995, "Sociocracy"). Therein, the decentralization principals and the shared responsibility address the delineated needs for individual freedom, responsibility, and mutual ownership.

Summing up, the success factor *promoting a culture of trust* includes the following organizational capabilities: (a) living solidarity and (self)-care; (b) working trustingly together as a team cross-functionally and cross-culturally; (c) communicating openly, transparently, and empathically; (d) acting (self-) responsibly; and (e) promoting decentralized and shared responsibility.

### *(V) ... of External Actors by "Establishing Collaborative Ecosystems of Organizations"*

The disruptions in times of crisis also threaten external cooperation, as many partner organizations need to reduce their spending, readjust their focus, and therefore rearrange their external relationships. Rearranging external relationships can change dysfunctional ecosystems in a both corrective and preventive fashion (Bernardez & Mead, 2009) to overcome past or future crises. The stronger the bond with important cooperation partners, such as suppliers and customer organizations, the more likely these partners keep their loyalty to the organization throughout disruptions. *Boundary spanning* described the establishment and sustainment of cooperation with team-external partners and was established as one of the most successful leadership behaviors (Burke et al., 2006). Accordingly, the interviewed leaders stated that organizations should promote network thinking instead of competitive thinking to increase their future-viability. Accordingly, business ecosystems prove to be more resilient to economic downturns (Bernandez & Mead, 2009). These ecosystems are often the result of common goals, such as shared individual, organizational, or public benefits (Bernardez & Mead, 2009). Hence, high personal trust to the deciders in the partner organizations facilitates the development of strong partnerships by means of successful co-creation and cooperation (Alrubaiee & Al-Nazer, 2010; Schumacher, 2006). In that vein, shared experience in solving previous crises can strengthen the partnership bond (Nätti, Rahkolin & Saraniemi, 2014). Many successful organizations like Google, Facebook, and Amazon include not only suppliers in the process of product and service creation but also the users themselves.

Summing up, the success factor *establishing collaborative ecosystems of organizations* includes the following organizational capabilities: (a) living trustful partnerships with suppliers and other stakeholders, (b) developing innovations co-creatively in organization-clusters, and (c) (co-)creating products with (future) users.

## Behavior 6: Activating Resources …

### *(VI) … of Internal Actors by "Creating an Agile Culture"*

Organizations should activate all available resources to react quickly and flexibly to crises (Grewal & Tansuhaj, 2001). Especially in threatening situations, quick reactions need courage from organizational members and leaders. Besides quick reactions, organizations need to gradually adjust to the new circumstances, risks, and opportunities (Fowler & Highsmith, 2001). As reported by one interviewed leader, at the beginning of the COVID-19 crisis, the entire company revenue collapsed because personal events were no longer allowed or desired by customers. Despite that disruption, the flexibility and creativity of the team helped them to create new offerings within a very short timeframe and to keep the business running. In that aim of innovative exploration, it is important that organizations foster quick experimentation, feedback, and ensuing learning (Fowler & Highsmith, 2001; O'Reilly & Tushman, 2008). To allow for quick parallel adaptation at many locations within the organization, a high decision leeway for individuals and teams as well as a creative innovation spirit are essential (Kramer & Amabile, 2011). Relentlessly managing organizational performance in real-time is essential to ensure high performance in rapidly changing business environments (Mueller-Hanson & Pulakos, 2018). To keep the experimentation-learning-cycles ongoing despite natural setbacks, organization members need to sustain positive drive and confidence (Bandura, 1977). A leader's talent and strengths focus on activating a "productive organization energy" for that manner (Bruch & Ghoshal, 2013). To preserve the organization from one-sided decisions, a diversity of perspectives, experiences, and competencies is valuable. To integrate those diverse perspectives into better solutions, high competence in conflict resolution and facilitation of controversial decisions is beneficial (Council of Industry and Higher Education, 2011).

Summing up, the success factor *creating an agile culture* includes the following organizational capabilities: (a) experimenting, giving feedback, continuing learning and promoting competences, (b) acting courageously, flexibly and quickly, (c) creating positive drive and confidence, (d) activating and promoting strengths, (e) promoting diversity and conflict resolution skills, (f) creating leeway for decisions, (g) promoting creative innovations.

### *(VII) … of Internal and External Actors by "Driving Digital Processes"*

It is critical for organizations to sustain their access to activated internal and external resources in times of disruptive crises. Today, digital processes are key to ensure internal and external actors easy access to the processes and offerings of an organization (Gergs, 2019; Kauffeld, 2019). Digital offerings and change communication can multiplicate the accessibility, especially when markets completely shift into the Internet. As reported by the interviewed leaders, digital processes were critical to sustaining operation during times of the COVID-19 shutdowns and quarantine, accelerating the growth in e-commerce and digitalization (Pantelimon, Georgescu & Podesaru, 2020). Furthermore, virtual collaboration also creates new opportunities for employee work–life balance and organizational efficiencies (Kauffeld & Maier, 2020). Several interviewed leaders predicted that private life and work would be further integrated when employees no longer appear at the office at a certain time but schedule their working hours and locations completely freely around the world. Finally, the digitalization of processes should create intelligent human–machine interfaces that create efficiencies by automating laborious subprocesses.

Summing up, the success factor *driving digital processes* includes the following organizational capabilities: (a) working mobile and hybrid, (b) developing online services for clients, and (c) streamlining processes through intelligent human–technology interactions.

### *(VIII) … of External Resources by "Ensuring Economic Agility"*

Organizations need to secure their access to financial and other external resources in times of crisis. In today's competitive business environment, even more in times of crisis, organizations need latitude to flexibly react to unpredicted disruptions (Pulakos et al., 2019). Therefore, interviewed leaders reported that organizations were more vulnerable if they did not possess any savings and leeway in their margins to digest unexpected missing inflows or invest in critical changes early in the COVID-19 crisis. As disruptions accelerate change, it is vital for organizations to also adjust their business models to the changing conditions and markets (Wadin & Ode, 2019). Organizations are more vulnerable if their business model was already becoming outdated before the crisis and also if their opportunity and risk are completely bound to one product, one customer, one supplier, or one supply path (Rumelt, 1982; Mak & Shen, 2012). According to the interviewed leaders, risk diversification through different business segments should be systematically established. In times of crisis, single-supplier, just-in-time-production is directly hit, even by small disruptions in the plan execution. In consequence, organizations should disperse their risk and include buffers. The COVID-19 crisis has shown that complex, global supply networks are more vulnerable than local networks with direct supply on the spot. Therefore, interviewed leaders have suggested that organizations should strengthen their regional networks. To conclude, huge, centralized organizations are less capable of reacting to changes flexibly, as they need to find solutions that fit for many diverse players. On the contrary, decentralized organizations were suggested to increase the organization's capability to quickly adjust to emerging and diverging local needs (see Treiblmaier, 2018).

Summing up, the success factor *ensuring economic agility* includes the following organizational capabilities: (a) creating small, capable organization units; (b) using economic profits for future-investments and reserve funds; (c) enhancing a future-viable business model; (d) spreading risks on all levels, including products, clients, market channels, suppliers, and logistic buffers; and (e) strengthening regional networks.

## DISCUSSION

The proposed eight success factors are inspired by the learnings from 24 interviewed leaders and were categorized and sophisticated based upon the integrative model of leadership behavior (IMoLB). The theoretic model IMoLB conveys sound theoretic validity as it delivers the delineated model with a high generality, external consistency with empiric findings, internal consistency, testability, and parsimony (Behrendt et al., 2017). This is underlined by the broad literature cited that supports the suggested success factors.

At the same time, the resulting success factor structure is of exploratory nature. The researchers have interviewed 24 practical experts of the professional networks of five interviewers. The selection could not claim generality for all other potentially interviewed experts. The qualitative analyses are built on the subjective interpretation of the analyzers. The review and refinement of the first model draft by all five interviewers and two groups of practical expert controls for that individual subjectivity. Nevertheless, the derived success factors include these experts' and the analyzers' subjectivity. Therefore, the high variability of the experts' backgrounds is of particular importance, ranging from science, economics, religion, politics, and state organizations to youth movements. Merging these backgrounds, the findings should be applicable to many branches.

Furthermore, the reported learnings from early in the COVID-19 crisis are provisional. Empirical tests might uncover neglected additions or even contradict these experts' perceptions. Additionally, nobody can provide certainty that these learnings from early in the COVID-19 crisis really sustain later in the COVID-19 crisis and even transmit to future crises.

These concerns are alleviated by the high validity of IMoLB as an underlying theoretic basis. Nevertheless, these limitations should be thoroughly addressed in future research and considered in practical application. Summing up, the provided model of success factors summarizes early learnings from a wide variety of South-German practical experts within a sound theoretic structure.

## SCIENTIFIC IMPLICATIONS

The proposed success factor model of organizational future-viability provides the first theory draft a scientific basis for future studies. The first draft will need further theoretic refinement and scientific testing. It should be examined in additional qualitative interview studies as well as in empirical tests.

First, the scientific community needs to develop valid measurements to allow rigorous empirical studies. These measures should validly determine internal and external actor coordination, cooperation, and activation. Consequently, the measurements should comprise multi-perspective survey scales, including the perspective of internal leaders and employees as well as external customers, suppliers, and other relevant stakeholders. Additionally, scientific video-based observation measures using scientifically trained observers could complement subjective survey scales of internal and external coordination, cooperation, and activation. The ensuing measure validation should include content validation by experts as well as item validation and factor structure examination. Thereby, the model's theoretic validity will be further enhanced.

As a second step, the developed measures should be used to study the success factors' criterion validity. As a first indicator, studies should examine how success factors can explain the varying organizational success early in the COVID-19 crisis, post hoc. Furthermore, studies should test how success factors predict organizational success and survival in the future, during the COVID-19 crisis and thereafter. These studies should include the assessment of potential moderator and mediator variables to better understand the factors' effect and mode of value creation.

Finally, experimental field studies should scrutinize the causal effects of the most promising factors based on a systematic practical variation of single success factors in different organizations (see the next section).

## PRACTICAL IMPLICATIONS

If scientific tests confirm the proposed model of success factors of future-viability, then their implementation in daily organizational life should be further concretized. In that aim, practical researchers should identify best practice case studies for diverse industries. Therefore, the developed measurements could identify and confirm organizational excellence accordingly.

Based on these practical implementation examples, organizational leaders could improve the future-viability of their organization. In that aim, IMoLB suggests the following iterative adaptation cycle.

1. **Diagnoses for enhanced understanding:** Leaders should use the developed scientific measurements to find a solid diagnosis of their organizational strengths and potential for improvements. If available, leaders should use leader, employee, customer, and other stakeholder perspectives to receive broad feedback. A thorough analysis of this feedback should provide a clear picture of the general future-viability and the organizational preparedness for expected crises in each of the success factors.
2. **Strategic deliberation to clarify strategy and strengthen motivation:** Based on the strengths and improvement potential discovered in Step 1, leaders should deliberate on the most critical success factor for their own organization's success. The importance of single success factors probably depends on industrial, social, and other moderating factors. Additionally, leaders should weigh the convertibility of each success factor in their organization. As organizational change is complicated and strenuous, leaders should focus the organization on the improvement of a single critical and leverageable factor. The results from Steps 1 and 2 should be communicated to and validated with the organization to strengthen the motivation.
3. **Implementation:** Based on the deliberation in Phase 2, leaders should implement improvements of the chosen success factor to increase adaptation and improve the organization's preparedness for future crises. As outlined, the success factors can be implemented according to leadership behavior. Leadership behavior is embedded in and influenced by the organization's behavioral culture as well as the organizational processes, structures, and material resources. To enhance behavior, culture, processes, structures, and resources, leaders should leverage the identified best practice case studies as leading examples (see above). In that aim, comprehensive organizational change programs, accompanied by systematic training and development programs, are most promising to initiate sustainable organizational change. To close the iterative cycle, the diagnostic measurements could provide leaders with sound feedback on progress and steer iterative program adaptation. If successfully implemented, the improvements can provide organization members with a shared sense of meaning and thereby strengthen organizational identity.

## CONCLUSION

Summing up, the proposed chapter provides organizational leaders and consultants with a theory-based framework for preparing their organizations for the expected crises of the post-COVID-19 era. A sound crisis-viability, quick adaptations, and seizure of opportunities will be critical for the successful survival of organizations. Because of the associated unpredictability of these dynamics, leaders need to prepare their organizations, so they can quickly react and learn in the face of future crises. The framework demarcates eight concrete success factors for crisis-viable organizations based on learnings in the COVID-19 crisis: (I) "providing iterative leadership within uncertainty," (II) "promoting absolute customer-loyalty," (III) "providing sustainable public value," (IV) promoting a culture of trust," (V) "establishing collaborative ecosystems of organizations," (VI) "creating an agile culture," (VII) driving digital processes," and (VIII) "ensuring economic agility." These success factors are provided to the practical and scientific community as a first draft for practical adaptation and learning, as well as for further theoretic refinement, development, and scientific testing. If these success factors could explain organizational success early in the COVID-19 crisis and eventually predict future success in the upcoming decades, the model would provide essential value to organizations and their societies.

## REFERENCES

Achtziger, A., & Gollwitzer, R. M. (2008). Motivation and volition in the course of action. In J. Heckhausen & H. Heckhausen (Eds.), *Motivation and action* (2nd ed., pp. 272–295). Cambridge University Press. doi:10.1017/CBO9780511499821.012

Ajzen, I. (1991). The theory of planned behavior. *Organizational Behavior and Human Decision Processes*, *50*(2), 179–211. doi:10.1016/0749-5978(91)90020-T

Alrubaiee, L., & Al-Nazer, N. (2010). Investigate the impact of relationship marketing orientation on customer loyalty: The customer's perspective. *International Journal of Marketing Studies*, *2*(1), 155–174. doi:10.5539/ijms.v2n1p155

Bakker, A. B., & Demerouti, E. (2007). The job demands-resources model: State of the art. *Journal of Managerial Psychology*, *22*(3), 309–328. doi:10.1108/02683940710733115

Bandura, A. (1977). Self-efficacy: Toward a unifying theory of behavioral change. *Psychological Review*, *84*(2), 191–215. doi:10.1037/0033-295X.84.2.191 PMID:847061

Behrendt, P., Matz, S., & Göritz, A. S. (2017). An integrative model of leadership behavior. *The Leadership Quarterly*, *28*(1), 229–244. doi:10.1016/j.leaqua.2016.08.002

Bernardez, M., & Mead, M. (2009). The power of entrepreneurial ecosystems: Extracting boom from bust. *PII Review*, *2*(2), 12–45.

Boes, A., Kämpf, T., Lühr, T., & Ziegler, A. (2018). Is agility an opportunity for a new attempt towards a democratic company? *Berliner Journal fur Soziologie*, *28*(1–2), 181–208. doi:10.100711609-018-0367-5

Bruch, H., & Ghoshal, S. (2003). Unleashing organizational energy. *MIT Sloan Management Review*, *45*(1), 45–52.

Buchanan, R. W., & Gillies, C. S. (1990). Value managed relationships: The key to customer retention and profitability. *European Management Journal*, *8*(4), 523–526. doi:10.1016/0263-2373(90)90115-M

Burke, C. S., Stagl, K. C., Klein, C., Goodwin, G. F., Salas, E., & Halpin, S. M. (2006). What type of leadership behaviors are functional in teams? A meta-analysis. *The Leadership Quarterly*, *17*(3), 288–307. doi:10.1016/j.leaqua.2006.02.007

Coelho, P. S., & Henseler, J. (2012). Creating customer loyalty through service customization. *European Journal of Marketing*, *46*(3–4), 331–356. doi:10.1108/03090561211202503

Corvellec, H., Böhm, S., Stowell, A., & Valenzuela, F. (2020). Introduction to the special issue on the contested realities of the circular economy. *Culture and Organization*, *26*(2), 97–102. doi:10.1080/14759551.2020.1717733

Council for Industry and Higher Education. (2011). *Global graduates into global leaders*. http://www.cihe.co.uk/category/knowledge/publications/

CumEx Haltet die Steuerdiebe. (2020, September 7). Retrieved from https://www.finanzwende.de/themen/cumex/?L=0

DeRue, D. S., Nahrgang, J. D., Wellman, N. E. D., & Humphrey, S. E. (2011). Trait and behavioral theories of leadership: An integration and meta-analytic test of their relative validity. *Personnel Psychology*, *64*(1), 7–52. doi:10.1111/j.1744-6570.2010.01201.x

Dinh, J. E., Lord, R. G., Gardner, W. L., Meuser, J. D., Liden, R. C., & Hu, J. (2014). Leadership theory and research in the new millennium: Current theoretical trends and changing perspectives. *The Leadership Quarterly*, *25*(1), 36–62. doi:10.1016/j.leaqua.2013.11.005

Ellemers, N., De Gilder, D., & Haslam, S. A. (2004). Motivating individuals and groups at work: A social identity perspective on leadership and group performance. *Academy of Management Review*, *29*(3), 459–478. doi:10.5465/amr.2004.13670967

European Commission. (2018). *Circular economy: Implementation of the Circular Economy Action Plan*. https://ec.europa.eu/environment/circular-economy/index_en.htm

Felber, C. (2019). *Change everything: Creating an economy for the common good*. Zed Books.

Fishbein, M., & Ajzen, I. (1975). *Belief, attitude, intention and behavior: An introduction to theory and research*. Addison–Wesley.

Fleishman, E. A. (1953). The description of supervisory behavior. *The Journal of Applied Psychology*, *37*(1), 1–6. doi:10.1037/h0056314 PMID:6038475

Fowler, M., & Highsmith, J. (2001). The agile manifesto. *Software Development*, *9*(8), 28–35.

Gergs, H. J. (2019). Agilität und Organisationsentwicklung – Ziemlich beste Freunde? *Gruppe. Interaktion. Organisation Zeitschrift für Angewandte Organisationspsychologie*, *50*(2), 101–110.

Grewal, R., & Tansuhaj, P. (2001). Building organizational capabilities for managing economic crisis: The role of market orientation and strategic flexibility. *Journal of Marketing*, *65*(2), 67–80. doi:10.1509/jmkg.65.2.67.18259

Halpin, A. W., & Winer, B. J. (1957). A factorial study of the leader behavior descriptions. In R. M. Stogdill & A. E. Coons (Eds.), Leader behavior: Its description and measurement (pp. 39–51). Columbus, OH: Bureau of Business Research, Ohio State University.

Heckhausen, H., & Gollwitzer, P. (1987). Thought contents and cognitive functioning in motivational versus volitional states of mind. *Motivation and Emotion*, *11*(2), 101–120. doi:10.1007/BF00992338

Hoe, S. L. (2007). Is interpersonal trust a necessary condition for organisational learning? *Journal of Organisational Transformation & Social Change*, *4*(2), 149–156. doi:10.1386/jots.4.2.149_1

House, R. (1971). A Path Goal Theory of Leader Effectiveness. *Administrative Science Quarterly*, *16*(3), 321–339. doi:10.2307/2391905

Ingham, A. G., Levinger, G., Graves, J., & Peckham, V. (1974). The Ringelmann effect: Studies of group size and group performance. *Journal of Experimental Social Psychology*, *10*(4), 371–384. doi:10.1016/0022-1031(74)90033-X

Jäckel, A. (2018). *Gesundes Vertrauen in Organisationen*. Springer Fachmedien Wiesbaden. doi:10.1007/978-3-658-19253-2

Karau, S. J., & Williams, K. D. (1993). Social loafing: A meta-analytic review and theoretical integration. *Journal of Personality and Social Psychology*, *65*(4), 681–706. doi:10.1037/0022-3514.65.4.681

Kauffeld, S. (2019). Einführung in die Arbeits-, Organisations- und Personalpsychologie. In S. Kauffeld (Ed.), *Arbeits-, Organisations- und Personalpsychologie für Bachelor* (2nd ed., pp. 1–20). Springer. doi:10.1007/978-3-662-56013-6_1

Kauffeld, S., & Maier, G. W. (2020). Schöne digitale Arbeitswelt: Chancen, Risiken und Herausforderungen. *Gr Interakt Org*, *51*(3), 255–258. doi:10.100711612-020-00532-y

Kaufman, R. (2010). From myths to creating a new future: A crisis is a terrible thing to waste. *Performance Improvement*, *49*(2), 37–44. doi:10.1002/pfi.20125

Kelly, S., & MacDonald, P. (2019). A look at leadership styles and workplace solidarity communication. *International Journal of Business Communication*, *56*(3), 432–448. doi:10.1177/2329488416664176

Kim, E., Beckman, S. L., & Agogino, A. (2018). Design roadmapping in an uncertain world: Implementing a customer-experience-focused strategy. *California Management Review*, *61*(1), 43–70. doi:10.1177/0008125618796489

Kramer, S. J., & Amabile, T. M. (2011). The Progress Principle: Using Small Wins to Ignite Joy, Engagement, and Creativity at Work. Harvard Business School Press Books.

Laloux, F. (2014). *Reinventing organizations: A guide to creating organizations inspired by the next stage in human consciousness*. Nelson Parker.

Likert, R. (1961). *New patterns of management*. McGraw-Hill.

MacDonald, P., Kelly, S., & Christen, S. (2014). A path model of workplace solidarity, satisfaction, burnout, and motivation. *International Journal of Business Communication*, *52*, 1–19. doi:10.1177/2329488414525467

Mak, H.-Y., & Shen, Z.-J. (2012). Risk diversification and risk pooling in supply chain design. *IIE Transactions*, *44*(8), 603–621. doi:10.1080/0740817X.2011.635178

Miller, R. (2018). *Transforming the future: anticipation in the 21st century*. Taylor & Francis.

Misumi, J., & Peterson, M. (1985). The Performance-Maintenance (PM) Theory of Leadership: Review of a Japanese Research Program. *Administrative Science Quarterly*, *30*(2), 198–223. doi:10.2307/2393105

Mueller-Hanson, R. A., & Pulakos, E. D. (2018). *Transforming performance management to drive performance: An evidence-based roadmap*. Routledge. doi:10.4324/9781315168128

Nätti, S., Rahkolin, S., & Saraniemi, S. (2014). Crisis communication in key account relationships. *Corporate Communications*, *19*(3), 234–246. doi:10.1108/CCIJ-08-2012-0056

O'Reilly, C. A. III, & Tushman, M. L. (2008). Ambidexterity as a dynamic capability: Resolving the innovator's dilemma. *Research in Organizational Behavior*, *28*, 185–206. doi:10.1016/j.riob.2008.06.002

Pantelimon, F. V., Georgescu, T. M., & Posedaru, B. Ş. (2020). The impact of mobile e-commerce on GDP: A comparative analysis between Romania and Germany and how COVID-19 influences the e-commerce activity worldwide. *Informações Econômicas*, *24*(2), 27–41. doi:10.24818/issn14531305/24.2.2020.03

Phillips, J. S., & Lord, R. G. (1986). Notes on the practical and theoretical consequences of implicit leadership theories for the future of leadership measurement. *Journal of Management*, *12*(1), 31–41. doi:10.1177/014920638601200104

Podsakoff, P. M., & Organ, D. W. (1986). Self-reports in organizational research: Problems and prospects. *Journal of Management*, *12*(4), 531–544. doi:10.1177/014920638601200408

Pulakos, E. D., Kantrowitz, T., & Schneider, B. (2019). What leads to organizational agility: It's not what you think. *Consulting Psychology Journal*, *71*(4), 305–320. doi:10.1037/cpb0000150

Robertson, B. J. (2015). *Holacracy: The new management system for a rapidly changing world*. Henry Holt and Company.

Romme, A. G. L. (1995). The sociocratic model of organizing. *Journal of Strategic Change*, *4*(4), 209–215. doi:10.1002/jsc.4240040404

Rumelt, R. (1982). Diversification Strategy and Profitability. *Strategic Management Journal*, *3*(4), 359–369. doi:10.1002mj.4250030407

Salo, A., Tähtinen, J., & Ulkuniemi, P. (2009). Twists and turns of triadic business relationship recovery. *Industrial Marketing Management*, *38*(6), 618–632. doi:10.1016/j.indmarman.2009.05.009

Salomo, S., Steinhoff, F., & Trommsdorff, V. (2003). Customer orientation in innovation projects and new product development success-the moderating effect of product innovativeness. *International Journal of Technology Management*, *26*(5–6), 442–463. doi:10.1504/IJTM.2003.003417

Schumacher, C. (2006). Trust: A source of success in strategic alliances? *Schmalenbach Business Review*, *58*(3), 259–278. doi:10.1007/BF03396734

Steil, J. J., & Maier, G. W. (2017). Robots in the digitalized workplace. In G. Hertel, D. Stone, R. Johnson, & J. Passmore (Eds.), *Wiley Blackwell handbook of the psychology of the Internet at work* (pp. 403–422). Wiley–Blackwell. doi:10.1002/9781119256151.ch18

Theodoridis, C., & Priporas, C. V. (2013). Strategic decision-making during uncertainty: Implications for SMEs. In D. Vrontis & A. Thrassou (Eds.), *Innovative business practices: Prevailing a turbulent era* (pp. 87–111). Scholars Publishing.

Thorndike, E. L. (1920). A constant error in psychological ratings. *The Journal of Applied Psychology*, *4*(1), 25–29. doi:10.1037/h0071663

Treiblmaier, H. (2018). Optimal levels of (de)centralization for resilient supply chains. *International Journal of Logistics Management*, *29*(1), 435–455. doi:10.1108/IJLM-01-2017-0013

van Knippenberg, D., & Sitkin, S. B. (2013). A critical assessment of charismatic–transformational leadership research: Back to the drawing board? *The Academy of Management Annals*, *7*(1), 1–60. doi:10.5465/19416520.2013.759433

Wadin, J. L., & Ode, K. A. (2019). Business Models for Sustainability-Change in Dynamic Environments. *Journal of Business Models*, *7*(1), 13–38.

Yukl, G. (2012). Effective leadership behavior: What we know and what questions need more attention. *The Academy of Management Perspectives*, *26*(4), 66–85. doi:10.5465/amp.2012.0088

## KEY TERMS AND DEFINITIONS

**Crisis:** Disruptive social situations that completely change the boundary conditions of organizational functioning and success creation and therefore threaten organizational survival and consequently force organizations to adapt quickly.

**Future-Viability:** The capability of an organization to create sustainable success and survive in the future, despite increasing economic and social challenges. As the post-COVID-19 era is expected to be characterized by further crises, future-viability in this era includes an organization's capability to adapt to resulting disruptions quickly.

**Leadership:** Leadership is defined as "influencing and facilitating individual and collective efforts to accomplish shared objectives" (Yukl, 2012).

**Success Factor:** Organizational factors that enhance an organization's success and accordingly predict organizational survival and adaptation in the times of crisis of the post-COVID-19 era.

# Chapter 8
# The Impact of COVID-19 on the Corporations and Management Change

**Adel Ismail Al-Alawi**
https://orcid.org/0000-0003-0775-4406
*University of Bahrain, Bahrain*

**Arpita A. Mehrotra**
*Royal University for Women, Bahrain*

**Sohayla Khidir Sanosi**
*University of Bahrain, Bahrain*

## ABSTRACT

*The purpose of this study is to analyze the impact of COVID-19 on different identities such as corporations, leadership, employees, human resources teams, customers, government bodies, and management change. Desk research based on secondary data analysis methodology was used for this study. Better crisis management plans can enable corporate to control and hybrid working environment to guide businesses to prepare and make strategies that can persist sustainably in a future crisis. It can be concluded that different corporations have faced the additional impact of the pandemic on their businesses. COVID-19 has changed the way businesses perform. Consequently, it can be inferred that leadership and leadership transition can lead to victory if leaders take the time to discover what works and what does not. This will allow the enterprise to change the next steps accordingly and save it from failure to pursue the outcomes.*

DOI: 10.4018/978-1-7998-6948-1.ch008

## INTRODUCTION

One of the significant economic effects linked to global pandemic has included an accelerated digitization rate. Many companies are now required to use various digital platforms to provide efficient access to their respective employees' different job opportunities. Human resource management (HRM) has been highlighted as one of the most vital roles to play in helping organizations navigate various conditions adequately. This might be linked to dramatic changes that are likely to emerge due to the pandemic, currently affecting almost every country across the entire world (Gigauri, 2020a). Furthermore, they suggest possible activities and considerations that businesses should be involved in to ensure such crises are appropriately managed in the future.

The global arena has been impacted due to Covid19, categorically in the organizational agenda. Firms have also tried to remain high-end effective, and sustainable in the long run through CSR practices. This can help the firm maintain its brand loyalty and consumer retention power by reflecting upon the organizational Human resource operations in their training and development agenda. As a multinational firm, Apple has consistently operated over the years, and even during the pandemic scenario.

Therefore, the purpose of the chapter is to analyze the impact of COVID-19 upon their key operations. It will provide a complete comprehension of their strategic rubric to adapt to the change management procedure in the long run with long-term effectiveness and efficiency.

## SITUATIONAL ANALYSIS AND EFFECTS OF COVID-19 ON COMPANIES

COVID-19 emerged as one of the worst pandemics in this period due to its ability to affect almost every country across the world negatively. Corporations were not left behind, and many were negatively influenced by their operational modes. As a result of this, it has been quite difficult for most companies to take appropriate steps in addressing the nature of their respective targeted goals within their respective markets of operation (Gigauri, 2020b). Various conditions attached to COVID-19 have adequately influenced some companies' practices due to the change in multiple modes of operations that align with the COVID-19 measures to curb the virus's contagious spread. As a result, the pandemic has negatively influenced various HRM practices across various companies in several ways. According to the listed surveys above, many companies face significant challenges (Clift & Court, 2020). The considerable difficulties include a reduced number of workers following the World Health Organization's new policies to curb the disease's spread and reduced operations following fewer employees. This exercise affected the global economy and reduced sales, as the business-customers interaction facilitated organizations that have not put up profitable online businesses and lowered revenue collections (WHO, 2020).

The COVID-19 pandemic has brought with it the fast-moving and unpredictable market. Some harmed the economy, and companies were not prepared for those. It's undeniable that COVID-19 harms most offline businesses that did not have an online presence, and businesses online were negatively impacted. However, they could still recover faster in comparison to those offline. Commonly, every country worldwide had a lockdown from March and could not conduct their business and regular daily activities. People had to stay in and maintain distance from others (Clift & Court, 2020). The corporate faced many issues as they could not earn profits and sell products; even online business sites such as Amazon could not sell because of restrictions on transportation and lack of personnel to deliver the products. The COVID-19 pandemic has reduced operations conducted by businesses, which consequently led to curtailing manpower in order to lower the risk of the disease escalation. Sourcing of materials has become an issue as movements both internally and abroad have been minimized, leading to a longer time spent acquiring raw materials and getting finished products to the market (Akkermans, Richardson &Kraimer, 2020). On the other hand, market interaction has been moved swiftly from the traditional interaction to digital interaction hence hindering small organizations that are not well organized in digital marketing and selling (Gigauri, 2020a). Businesses understood that the need of the hour is to move online and use a digital payment method to avoid human contact.

People were caught unaware with harsh situations, while adopting measures to avoid going out and maintain social distancing. The government restricted people from buying groceries, and lack of groceries was another problem that occurred because of COVID-19. Farmers and those in the agricultural business could not earn their wages because no one was buying the products they were selling. The corporate did not engage in production and messed up with the people who provided raw materials (WHO, 2020). People in the manufacturing business faced issues because they could not clear their stocks and could not produce more in need. Even if they wanted to, such companies could not go online and conduct their business because they were not selling finished products; they were selling raw materials for some other firm.

Transportation facility got restricted, airplanes were not flying, people were not traveling, and all of this impacted the economy and the way business used to operate. After 5-6 months of lockdown, almost every country started reopening the activities. Preparation will play a vital role in a post-corona virus world, and businesses are seen taking steps to be ready for that time. It is expected that as soon as everything goes back to normal again, businesses and consumers will both return to normal (Bartik et al., 2020).

## RESPONSES BY COMPANIES TO THE COVID-19 PANDEMIC

Companies are embracing unique strategies to keep their businesses alive and operational. Harsh situations do not deter them in functionality. The post coronavirus world will be a positive threshold of opportunities for those who survive these challenges, since a number of corporations in the concerned field will be scaled down. This research has shown that many companies have turned their attention to virtual operations putting up remote business operations in departments that can be handled remotely to reduce the number of employees within the workplaces. Businesses have been pushed to the wall to retrench some of their employees to meet the WHO's standards regarding the COVID-19 pandemic. The better part of the situation is that organizations have realized the importance of proper contingency plans against possible pandemics in the future (WHO, 2020).

More than 1000 cases are diagnosed daily; the SAR and its communities in Hong Kong need support. Hong Kong Exchanges and Clearing Limited (HKEx) has contributed to the development of the financial market and has helped the business build sustainability and help the underprivileged populations. Katherine Ng said, "The social and economic challenges posed by COVID-19 have emphasized the true value of identifying business strengths and weaknesses, as well as recognizing and mitigating material risks". The company has also supported Hong Kong businesses to learn how to fight the COVID-19 and overcome the situations (HKEx, 2020).

Swiss Company, the Adecco Group, has released a paper comparing the government responses related to COVID-19; they tried to determine which policies and decisions have led to the best economic outcomes. They are using macro-economic indicators in 12 countries to compare with the company and consider those companies' policies to form the best support measures for their workers and employees to keep their jobs and welfare possible (Adeccogroup, 2020).

As countries are starting to recover from the worst effects of the pandemic, countries that have successfully mitigated the labor market and those who responded more quickly with economic support and helped employees stay in the work process as much as possible are performing better. In response to the COVID-19, most companies created crisis management teams or committees to make proper decisions and keep the business working. They formed immediate plans that focused on covering the issues related to senior executives' succession plans, rules, and guidelines, including protocols for remote working, transferring significant operations to less-affected geographies and reducing business operations to critical functions only (Whiteside, 2020). Another committee was set to monitor the business impact and efforts to protect or sustain business functions. The HR team focused on analyzing and forecasting the pandemic's impact and while keeping an eye on supply chains and providers for potential challenges arising from their side. Employees should also learn new technologies to be able to conduct their daily activities productively. Technologies used daily in this environment are Google excel, Google word, zoom, Skype, and other Microsoft tools (Donthu & Gustafsson, 2020).

## THE HUMAN RESOURCE MANAGEMENT OPERATION

The pandemic has thrown the whole world into chaos, and everybody is uncertain what people will face now or when everything will go back like the world without COVID-19. The need for remote working would grow for sure after the COVID-19. People have become comfortable at home, spending time with their families and looking for remote opportunities without working in an office (Seetharaman, 2020). From the researches above, it is pointed out that many organizations are involving themselves in employment activities, training of employees, where some companies have been pointed out to conduct training so that their employees are ready for the new world. Still, it has been seen that employees are not prepared enough for that world, and they are taking minimal steps because the future is uncertain, and will they have a job after a week is uncertain (Gigauri, 2020a). It has been seen that some firms are rarely considering the employee's welfare during these circumstances. Such operations negatively impact the company's working; all of this is done by the COVID-19 pandemic. The interactions of the employees with the company HR have been minimized. Companies do minimal employments with minimal or no physical training because the future is uncertain. If given a better opportunity, they will leave the organization as there is no emotional bond with the company. They want a better opportunity in this time of chaos (Akkermans, Richardson &Kraimer, 2020). This has reduced many businesses' performance, as training is used to properly engage employees and enable them to learn various operations through demonstrations successfully. Many corporations started working and conducting online platforms to sell products and services; more and more people began to learn how to operate technology.

The other challenge pointed out by these researches is the welfare of employees. The HRM used to hold various team building programs and events to help employees bond well for proper collaboration reflected in their overall outcome. This has not been able to carry on as gatherings are limited, allowing HRM's minimal chances to identify challenges within their workplaces. The advantage of having to work from home is that they will face zero employee's politics and bad behavior from their colleagues. A more comfortable workplace will also elevate the performance of the company (Gigauri, 2020b). But the disadvantage is that the employees cannot take help from their friends. They will not be able to enjoy social interactions with their colleagues. They will not work if the company has strict working hours as a comfortable environment can even distract some employees. Some houses may be calm at home, but some are very noisy, negatively impacting the employees' performance. Companies are not seen helping employees. They are very hesitant as the times are very challenging, and employees may or may not stick with the company for a long time (Gigauri, 2020b).

## LEADERSHIP CHANGE DURING COVID-19

In times like these, there is instability, confusion, complexity, and ambiguity in a limited knowledge environment that requires fast, high-impact decisions. Members need to handle these aspects, learn new lessons along the way, and help create several innovative problem-solving techniques to keep their company operational and safe. Early estimation of a crisis's cumulative clinical practice effect, such as COVID-19, is an important and nuanced activity. Initial decisions are focused on the commitment of therapeutic urgency and the appreciation of true potential. Although multi-society recommendations on this issue have been proposed, it is a challenging exercise to triage the sequencing of patient treatment with potentially important health, ethical, and medico-legal as well as financial consequences. The complexities of subspecialty GI (gastrointestinal) activities need to be integrated into these decisions, better made with the provider teams' guidance and administrative leadership (Chhaya, 2020).

On the organizational front, the capability depends on the extent of the workforce, PPE, COVID-19 screening, the level of redeployment of vendors and personnel to other therapeutic fields, and the supply of equipment and inventory of consumables. It is prudent to set up an operations team that solves these challenges in real-time and moves nimbly to resolve concerns that occur both in the hospital, clinic, and endoscopy unit (Vaziri et al., 2020).

The significant adverse financial effect is felt in the system. Division administrators (and medical practitioners) and chiefs/chairs (and private managed services partners) need to live with this situation and work together at the organizational level with senior management, factoring in updated sales forecasts and loss reduction plans. Good collaboration, managing employee and supplier distress, and ensuring accountability are essential resources to help bring the team united and focused on their primary missions. The solutions vary by position and period and include the last resort, redeployment, shift of execution, and straightforward proportional decreases in pay (Bhargava et al. 2020).

During the COVID-19 crisis, teaching and schooling, which are vital missions for academic programs, have been interrupted. Core curriculum leadership needs to identify goals for education and instruction that need to be met and execute a plan to accomplish that goal. Fortunately, there are well-established tools available to provide remote learning remotely, and they must be used now and into the future to support curricular needs. In order to optimize trainee protection, primary clinical rotations need to be established, and trainees rotated through those in a restricted manner. During this time, endoscopy simulation models may be a good training platform to consider. These periods can provide trainees with opportunities to catch up on study or academic assignments or training for examinations. Downtime attributable to COVID-19, with re-imagined educational frameworks to test after the recession, is also a chance to hold further conversations on policy and transformative reform going forward (Rangachari et al., 2020).

Covid19 has been potentially detrimental in terms of maintaining the DNA of the workplace ecosystem. The organizations tend to follow a visible change in the leadership ways to help the organization maintain its market positioning and increased collaborative and team working schedule to reflect upon their profitability quotient to a great extent. The upheaval of anxiety and cynicism within the workplace has been the reason for an inverse reflection upon the firm's overall outcomes. The leaders need to focus more on optimizing this organizational risk through their remote working facilities and lowered practicing of employee layoffs or pay-cuts. Secondly, communication effectiveness and efficiency during this pandemic scenario can impact employee reliance on the firms with the transparent work culture and climate in the long run. It can motivate employees by understanding the entire situation and providing them with a long-term sufficient opportunity to give their employees a sensible workplace. Fourthly, the management of hybrid teams of diverse cultures has been a critical challenge to the employees that have also reflected the firm's operational efficiency to a great extent. Finally, the active listening power from the employee's ends can also potentially define organizational success in the long run.

The COVID19 crisis gives a core insight into the under-preparedness of humans as a discipline and as a nation while coping with such a crisis. A few examples involve establishing good relationships with key stakeholders, providing a clear view of each leader's role in a potential crisis, and creating reliable supply chains and other processes. It is crucial to provide these arrangements at the divisional, administrative, operational, and national and regional level (Bolton, 2020).

## MANAGEMENT CHANGE DURING COVID-19

While change management faces a particular set of challenges at each point and is often different for each sector, leaders face a few typical challenges during the COVID-19 pandemic. Several occupations involve individuals or organizations repeatedly performing particular activities, which most individuals grow familiar with overtime over the period of time. Although many individuals see their worth as a successful operations manager, technical architect, or security professional, they can resist when asked to take on a different position. This also affects individuals who often fail when asked to take on a new task, often with outstanding technological expertise, so they now have to learn new skills or work for others and are no longer praised for the skills that make them successful (RussellReynolds, 2020).

HR's role in the crisis management for the organization has been high end crucial as they are the ones who help the business to sustain in the long run through effective and efficient transparent practices and mitigation of the organizational short and long term goals. Possible care for the individuals and the concern of empathy empathetic concern have been a connecting factor towards creating leaders and the subordinates' interdependence to ensure right and high end effective cultural panorama by the navigation of the individual needs and the organizational requirement of strategic alignment. The need assessment and the risk mitigation part also need to be channelized through the HR personnel's operational excellence, helping the employees remain proactive in providing their crucial response. In a crisis situation like the pandemic scenario, the HR department of Apple needs to stay specifically concerned about their employee engagement criteria and lead them through a change management approach over the years of their operations. With the training and development programs organized by them in terms of their e-commerce operation and the adaptability to the technological advancements, they have maintained their performance throughout and have effectively managed the crisis situation cohesively and collaboratively.

Execution is vital for every project as organizations should not get involved at the grass-root stage in carrying out a project. If the appointed person in position is not courageous enough to face the obstacles and defend the preferred solution and why the alternatives were dismissed, then it is a catastrophe formula. This also adds to a negative effect on the workers who are impacted by the transition, as they will not be able to empathize with the people who hate the new way of working without getting all the information in hand. It is a recognized reality that, initially, citizens and organizations oppose reform to some extent. It is also difficult for professional change managing executives to embrace the company's emotional vitality and adapt it to new technologies (Charoensukmongkol et al., 2020).

Therefore, individuals must be able to examine new knowledge and incorporate new attitudes and techniques, much as cultural willingness (Al-Alawi et al., 2007). It is also noted that most individuals only consider improvements that make sense and strengthen their work material or work environment. If strategic leadership does not pay attention to this, it will result in a lost opportunity to reinforce a new development that can benefit the organization. The idea that midlevel and frontline workers will make or break a significant initiative is something leaders sometimes miss out on. These departments appreciate the existing procedures' organizational specifics and predict future concerns and possible consumer reactions (He et al., 2020).

Although it is preferable to have less staff early in the process, it will effectively build a more dedicated workforce to recognize people in every team who are not responsive to disruptions that cause dramatic change. Also, their recommendations are more likely to be adopted to help the eventual results of doing so. The primary project team is frequently consumed by business process improvements for some significant alterations, such as COVID-19. Suppose successful change implementation is not introduced into the picture, along with the majority of the new systems. In that case, there could be a risk of end-users, both staff and consumers, facing opposition (Cortez et al., 2020).

When workers are offered a range of ways to connect, the likelihood of change management success improves. This can be achieved, during or after the COVID-19 pandemic, by providing a consistent vision of corporate priorities, identifying how the improvements can help accomplish those goals and how they will impact workers at an individual level.

Help forms the foundation of successful transformation programs, marked by the leader's eliminating challenges to an employee's progress. This entails professional challenges, such as the time and money taken to carry out a reform strategy. When leaders rely solely on performance, their workers do not have the help needed for transition. It also helps to map out the essential agents of evolution by recognizing critical partners, including board members, C-suite leaders, consumers, and others presenting to them the idea of significant change. In addition, it is crucial never to presume that they have all the answers to be a good leader of transformation (Suprapti et al., 2020).

Table-1 and Table-2 below analyze various literature on HRM and the Effects of COVID-19 from digitalization and work-life balance.

*Table 1. Influence of COVID-19 Crisis on HRM*

| **Author's name** | Gigauri (2020b) |
|---|---|
| **Purpose** | This research investigates various challenges facing HRM in Georgia concerning the COVID-19 crisis and finds solutions to tackle the challenges. |
| **Research methodology** | This research is based on a qualitative research method that employs expert interviews to collect the required data. |
| **Research questions/ hypothesis** | i. Why and how were companies and employees affected by COVID-19 in Georgia?<br>ii. How was the HRM operation in Georgian companies affected by COVID-19?<br>iii. What were the responses by HRM, and how effective were the responses? |
| **Independent variable** | Human resource management<br>Crisis and contingency plans |
| **Dependent variable** | Employees recruitment<br>Employees training<br>Employees welfare and workplace relationship |
| **Key findings** | This study finds that many organizations in Georgia have not put up better crisis management plans to enable remote business controls and hybrid working systems. |
| **Research gap and limitations/ future research** | The findings of this research should guide businesses within and outside Georgia to prepare and make policies and strategies that can enable them to remain viable in a future crisis. This research focuses on the independent variable, the business environment affected by calamities; hence, businesses should consider such unavoidable conditions when putting up business plans. |
| **Remarks** | This research involved key individuals who are knowledgeable and can give relevant and accurate information for the research. This makes the findings of the research to be more reliable. |

## CONCLUSION AND RECOMMENDATIONS FOR ANY FUTURE RESEARCH

Based on the above discussion, it can be concluded that different companies have faced the additional impact of the pandemic on their businesses. COVID-19 has changed the way businesses operate and the unpredictable aspects of business which leaves the future uncertain. The current business environment presents challenges that make human resource management strategic and quick to enable proper operations to remain relevant. HRM's role is still as vital as it was earlier; employee's motivation and the formation of a personal bond with the company is always important (Al-Alawi, Al-Azri& Mohammad, 2016). The research discussed above is essential as they investigate business challenges during this particular time of COVID-19, especially by the human resource department.

As per the data above, it can be seen that, to some extent, companies can take a few measures to fight against COVID-19. Those are encouraging the well-being of the employees and providing them with the training required in this time, and proper rewards and salary should be formed, as they can leave the company whenever they want to. Another measure is HRM should be up-to-date and use innovative methods to help the company and employees. New technologies should be taught to employees so that they can perform functions and daily activities productively. Technologies used daily in this environment are Google excel, Google word, zoom, Skype, and other Microsoft tools. Having the latest technology and methods will help the company to perform better and stay in the market.

*Table 2. Effects of COVID-19 on HRM from the perspective of digitalization and work-life-balance*

| Author's name | Gigauri (2020a) |
|---|---|
| **Purpose** | This research aims to study and understand various HRM operations that have been affected by the COVID-19. It looks into the plans that business within Georgia has put in management, to curb COVID-19 effects and possible future outcomes. |
| **Research methodology** | A qualitative method has been applied as video interviews were conducted for data collection. |
| **Research questions/ hypothesis** | i. What effects did the COVID-19 pandemic bring to businesses in Georgia?<br>ii. What makes remote working the best alternative for HRM during this pandemic period?<br>iii. How did the businesses in Georgia respond to the pandemic, and how did businesses create conditions to enable employees' adaptability? |
| **Independent variable** | Human resource management<br>Crisis and contingency plans |
| **Dependent variable** | Employees recruitment<br>Employees training<br>Employees welfare and workplace relationship |
| **Key findings** | This research finds out that shared workspace increases stress among employees, and digitization is the future of businesses. |
| **Research gap and limitations/ future research** | Many businesses have not put up any future business strategies as the COVID-19 pandemic has set the pace. This research points out the business trend and the projected direction that the businesses are taking. This, therefore, presents an environment for other researchers to conduct more studies on digitization and remote working in the future. |
| **Remarks** | The research was designed to determine the impact of the COVID-19 crisis on HRM. Including the digitalization and the work-life balance issues of the employees or workers. It also shows that HRM plays a significant role in organizations, mainly in times of crisis. |

Hence, it can be inferred that leadership and leadership transition can lead to victory if leaders take the time to discover what works and what does not. This will allow the enterprise to change its course and tread cautiously, to pursue conflicting outcomes that rob the organization of the information needed. It is essential for any significant transition to conventionally center the emphasis on devising the right strategic and operational strategies. However, to excel, an organization must still have an intuitive knowledge of change management's human side, i.e., aligning its philosophy, beliefs, employees, and attitudes.

## REFERENCES

Adeccogroup. (2020). *Comparing Government economic responses to COVID-19: Short-time work and size of stimulus package matter most*. Retrieved October 5, 2020, from https://press.adeccogroup.com/news/comparing-government-economic-responses-to-covid-19-short-time-work-and-size-of-stimulus-package-matter-most-3cb2-2cb12.html

Akkermans, J., Richardson, J., & Kraimer, M. (2020). The Covid-19 crisis as a career shock: Implications for careers and vocational behavior. *Journal of Vocational Behavior*, *119*(June), 103434. Advance online publication. doi:10.1016/j.jvb.2020.103434 PMID:32390655

Al-Alawi, A. I., Al-Azri, A. S., & Mohammad, H. N. (2016). Investigating the factors affecting job satisfaction and turnover: Case of Sultan Qaboos University. *Journal of Human Resources Management Research, 2016*, c1–c15. doi:10.5171/2016.301731

Al-Alawi, A. I., Al-Marzooqi, N. Y., & Mohammed, Y. F. (2007). Organizational culture and knowledge sharing: Critical success factors. *Journal of Knowledge Management, 2*(11), 22–42. doi:10.1108/13673270710738898

Al-Youbi, A. O., Al-Hayani, A., Rizwan, A., & Choudhry, H. (2020). Implications of COVID-19 on the Labor Market of Saudi Arabia: The Role of Universities for a Sustainable Workforce. *Sustainability, 12*(17), 7090. doi:10.3390u12177090

Bartik, A. W., Bertrand, M., Cullen, Z., Glaeser, E. L., Luca, M., & Stanton, C. (2020). The impact of COVID-19 on small business outcomes and expectations. *Proceedings of the National Academy of Sciences of the United States of America, 117*(30), 17656–17666. doi:10.1073/pnas.2006991117 PMID:32651281

Bartsch, S., Weber, E., Büttgen, M., & Huber, A. (2020). Leadership matters in crisis-induced digital transformation: How to lead service employees effectively during the COVID-19 pandemic. *Journal of Service Management, 32*(1), 71–85. Advance online publication. doi:10.1108/JOSM-05-2020-0160

Bhargava, S., Sarkar, R., & Kroumpouzos, G. (2020). Mental distress in dermatologists during COVID-19 pandemic: Assessment and risk factors in a global, cross-sectional study. *Dermatologic Therapy, e14161*(6). doi:10.1111/dth.14161 PMID:32770716

Bolton, A. (2020). *H-E-B continues to evolve procedures during COVID-19 emergency*. Retrieved November 4, 2020, from http://a.msn.com/05/en-us/BB11ZzaZ?ocid=se

Charoensukmongkol, P., & Phungsoonthorn, T. (2020). The effectiveness of supervisor support in lessening perceived uncertainties and emotional exhaustion of university employees during the COVID-19 crisis: The constraining role of organizational intransigence. *The Journal of General Psychology*, 1–20. doi:10.1080/00221309.2020.1795613 PMID:32691689

Chhaya, N. (2020). *Here Are The Top Five Leadership Challenges During The Coronavirus Pandemic*. Retrieved November 1, 2020, from https://www.forbes.com/sites/niharchhaya/2020/03/23/here-are-the-top-five-leadership-challenges-during-the-coronavirus-pandemic/

Clift, K., & Court, A. (2020). *COVID-19: How companies are responding to the coronavirus crisis?* Retrieved October 1, 2020, from https://www.weforum.org/agenda/2020/03/how-are-companies-responding-to-the-coronavirus-crisis-d15bed6137/

Cortez, R. M., & Johnston, W. J. (2020). The Coronavirus crisis in B2B settings: Crisis uniqueness and managerial implications based on social exchange theory. *Industrial Marketing Management, 88*, 125–135. doi:10.1016/j.indmarman.2020.05.004

Donthu, N., & Gustafsson, A. (2020). Effects of COVID-19 on business and research. *Journal of Business Research, 117*, 284–289. doi:10.1016/j.jbusres.2020.06.008 PMID:32536736

Gigauri, I. (2020a). Effects of covid-19 on human resource management from the perspective of digitalization and work-life-balance. *International Journal of Innovative Technologies in Economy*, *4*(31). Advance online publication. doi:10.31435/rsglobal_ijite/30092020/7148

Gigauri, I. (2020b). Influence of Covid-19 Crisis on Human Resource Management and Companies' Response: The Expert Study. *International Journal of Management Science and Business Administration*, 15-24. doi:10.18775/ijmsba.1849-5664-5419.2014.66.1002

He, H., & Harris, L. (2020). The Impact of Covid-19 Pandemic on Corporate Social Responsibility and Marketing Philosophy. *Journal of Business Research*, *116*, 176–182. Advance online publication. doi:10.1016/j.jbusres.2020.05.030 PMID:32457556

HKEx. (2020). *News Centre*. Retrieved November 14, 2020, from https://www.hkex.com.hk/News/News-Centre?sc_lang=en

Rangachari, P., & Woods, L, J. (2020). Preserving organizational resilience, patient safety, and staff retention during COVID-19 requires a holistic consideration of the psychological safety of healthcare workers. *International Journal of Environmental Research and Public Health*, *17*(12), 4267. doi:10.3390/ijerph17124267 PMID:32549273

RussellReynolds. (2020). *Leadership through Uncertainty 10 Enduring lessons for turbulent times*. Retrieved November 5, 2020, from www.russellreynolds.com/insights/thought-leadership/leadership-through-uncertainty

Seetharaman, P. (2020). Business models shifts: Impact of Covid-19. *International Journal of Information Management*, *54*, 102173. doi:10.1016/j.ijinfomgt.2020.102173 PMID:32834338

Suprapti, S., Asbari, M., Cahyono, Y., & Mufid, A. (2020). Leadership Style, Organizational Culture And Innovative Behavior On Public Health Center Performance During Pandemic COVID-19. *Journal of Industrial Engineering & Management Research*, *1*(2), 76–88. doi:10.7777/jiemar.v1i2

Vaziri, H., Casper, W. J., Wayne, J. H., & Matthews, R. A. (2020). Changes to the work-family interface during the COVID-19 pandemic: Examining predictors and implications using latent transition analysis. *The Journal of Applied Psychology*, *105*(10), 1073–1087. Advance online publication. doi:10.1037/apl0000819 PMID:32866024

Whiteside, S. (2020). *How major companies are responding to COVID-19*. Retrieved October 25, 2020, from https://www.warc.com/newsandopinion/opinion/how-major-companies-are-responding-to-covid-19/3473

WHO. (2020). *Coronavirus disease (COVID-19)*. Retrieved October20, 2020, from https://www.who.int/emergencies/diseases/novel-coronavirus-2019

# Chapter 9
# Shock Leadership: Leading Amidst Pandemics and Other Chaotic Change

**Anton Shufutinsky**
https://orcid.org/0000-0003-3819-0623
*Cabrini University, USA*

**Bena Long**
*Institute of Interdisciplinary Leadership Education and Development, USA*

**James R. Sibel**
*Institute of Interdisciplinary Leadership Education and Development, USA*

**Darrell Norman Burrell**
https://orcid.org/0000-0002-4675-9544
*The Florida Institute of Technology, USA*

## ABSTRACT

*Global crises that jolt entire systems, such as the COVID-19 pandemic, can place groups, organizations, and communities in volatile, uncertain, complex, and ambiguous (VUCA) environments that affect all sectors of society, having potentially disastrous effects including high morbidity and mortality rates, political upheaval, and extensive disruption of entire economic systems, causing damage that can last for months or even years. Effective leadership is a pivotal organizational commodity in times of normalcy, and it becomes increasingly critical during crises and the subsequent environments of discontinuous change. There has been a consistent level of international criticism regarding national, state, local, and corporate leadership during the COVID-19 crisis. This chapter explores the leadership challenges associated with highly chaotic environments and introduces an advanced model of leadership—shock leadership—and leadership development framework necessary for higher leader reliability and effectiveness in disasters and other crises.*

DOI: 10.4018/978-1-7998-6948-1.ch009

## INTRODUCTION

Over the past two decades, amid the continually disruptive environment of the fourth industrial revolution (Industry 4.0), the world has become accustomed to the continuous technological change and the related effects that the rapid technological advancements and roll-outs have on businesses, including positive and negative outcomes. The world has grown used to the need for fast and repeated change, and businesses and other organizations have changed the way that they deal with market competitiveness that comes with Industry 4.0, often predicting the shifts and building change into their strategies (Shufutinsky et al., 2020a; 2020b). Despite this acclimation to rapid and continuous change, the level of adaptation and response to massive and highly disruptive events is different and requires a different response. Situations, events, or scenarios that have a strong disruptive effect and jolt entire systems are often classified as crises or disasters, and they are not endemic only to government agencies and nations, but can and do have serious implications for all sectors, including communities, non-profits, small businesses, learning institutions, and corporations, among others. These scenarios can range in type from natural disasters, to man-made disasters, to political and economic collapses, and can last for any span of time, ranging from days to months or even years (Dayton, 2015; Shufutinsky et al., 2020a). In 2020, the world was turned upside down by a series of highly disruptive events, creating an environment of increasing complexity relative to national security, personal safety, public health, employment, global transportation, and economics (Burrell, 2020; Shufutinsky et al., 2020; Triggs & Kharas, 2020), and with this complexity comes uncertainty, volatility, and ambiguity (VUCA) regarding the current and future state of organizations, communities, and nations (Shufutinsky et al., 2020).

Warren Bennis (2007), one of the most respected minds regarding business, management, and leadership, wrote that, among the threats to this world, two of the main threats to stability are leadership during increased globalization, and pandemics. Pandemics, already known to be highly problematic to stability from a public health perspective, have significant potential for driving organizations, communities, nations, and entire populations into a jolted environment, bringing whole systems to increased levels of VUCA. The world has witnessed this in 2020, exemplified by the global spread of the novel coronavirus (COVID-19), and simultaneous, compounding international crises occurring, including agricultural plagues, political conflict in different parts of the world, continued racism and race-related violence, terrorism, rioting, massive wildfires, disastrous weather events, and the varying effectiveness of responses to these scenarios. It has become apparent that Warren Bennis' hypotheses pertaining to these two threats of inadequate leadership and pandemics are not mutually exclusive, and that the overlap of leadership in the context of increased globalization, during the coronavirus pandemic, has destabilized many systems in this interconnected global society (Shufutinsky et al., 2020a). International criticism continues to mount regarding management of the pandemic by national, state, & local government as well as corporate and medical leaders, as they scramble to respond (Shear et al., 2020; Walker, 2020) to the discontinuously changing scenario. Presented here is an overview of the context in which this discontinuous change is evident, internationally. Also presented is an exploration of the leadership challenges that are associated with the VUCA-rich and chaotic COVID-19 environment. Amidst this unstable and complex environment of increased non-linear circumstances of crises, a particular kind of advanced leadership is needed—a leadership style that can display increased awareness, flexibility, adaptability, sense-making, and decision-making for comprehensively effective responses to whole system shock. This leadership style is termed *Shock Leadership* (Shufutinsky et al., 2020a).

## PANDEMICS, PREPAREDNESS, AND LEADERSHIP NEEDS IN DISCONTINUOUS CHANGE

Organizations, communities, and nations potentially face a plethora of different types of crises, but among them, pandemics, such as COVID-19, have exhibited the capability of creating extremely complex disruption (Shufutinsky et al., 2020a). The current mass-scale pandemic has disturbed people's collective lives more than any other seen over the past century, and the damage has arguably been more widespread than most crises. Although pandemics that result in overwhelming counts of critically ill people are not a new phenomenon, and governments, institutions of higher learning, and militaries have deliberated and argued for preparedness for the potentiality of having to respond to this type of global threat should one occur, (Gomersall et al., 2007), pandemic preparedness has continued to be overlooked, addressed in policy only, or even ignored, often being placed on the back-burner as something to develop in the future. Even more traditional emergency response and disaster preparedness programs have only rarely been allocated with sufficient resources (Bowers et al., 2017). In the United States, it is not yet a distant memory when the nation was struck with a national catastrophe. The research exhibits that, despite the terrorist attacks that created the 9/11 disaster, nearly half of all U.S. organizations failed to develop or revise their emergency response or disaster preparedness plans within five years of the crisis (Lockwood, 2005). Additionally, among leaders of some corporate and non-governmental organizations, a pervasive attitude has existed that dismissed preparedness work as not being a corporate responsibility, thus avoiding the work. Such attitudes, and overall failures to accept the corporate social responsibilities of crisis response, can have significant consequences, including increased losses of life and property (Ha, 2019; McMenamin, 2009; Shrivastava, 1995). Also, on those occasions when pandemic preparedness plans are present, the programs often ignore critical community and local-level operational challenges (Burkle, 2010).

The COVID-19 global crisis has proven to differ from other disasters. Many other types of nature-driven or man-made crises, such as those caused by weather or geological shifts, or terrorism, among others, cause disruption to business operations, leading to problems that are generally facility- or equipment-related. The COVID-19 pandemic has shown disruption that considerably contrasts what has been seen in other crises. The 2020 global environment exhibited that pandemics can severely impact human resources in organizations, potentially driving mass-absenteeism and business closures resulting from employees' infections, family morbidity, and mandated isolation and quarantine. During the coronavirus pandemic, communities around the world experienced closures of educational facilities, shopping centers, childcare centers, dining establishments, public transportation, and many other organizations. For many enterprises, this resulted in shuttering entire company sites (Shufutinsky et al., 2019). Additionally, pandemics are not only disruptors of social dynamics, affecting cultural needs and interrupting social cues (Mariner et al., 2009), but they shift organizational leaders' routine foci from fostering innovation, concentrating on corporate revenues, sustaining budgets, and gaining market shares to dealing with supply chain issues, employee shortages, operational setbacks, and maintenance of liquidity, exemplifying the diversity of leadership challenges that can accompany pandemic crises (Nichols et al., 2020; Shufutinsky et al., 2020a).

As explained above, societies have experienced in 2020, and will likely in the future experience paradigmatic, unpredictable, non-linear states, characterized as discontinuous change. Discontinuous change accompanies mass scale disruptions, creating disequilibrium in environments (Nadler & Tushman, 1995), impacting an organizational system's fundamental components and imploring accelerated responses to changing conditions, often for the single purpose of organizational survival. In environments of large-scale discontinuous change, even those organizations that have previously been successful, adaptive, and resilient often fail to effectively respond to this level of disruption (Birkenshaw et al., 2016), and their leaders find themselves overwhelmed and their organizations beset with complex challenges (Lant and Mezias, 1990). The failure to effectively respond can be at least partly explained by the fact that organizations dealing with discontinuous disruption do not have the luxury of making incremental modifications and adjustments. Alternatively, these organizational leaders must pursue broader, more comprehensive redevelopment of many facets of their organizations, including work processes, systems, and strategy, among others (Nadler and Shaw, 1994; Lant and Mezias, 1990), beginning with a reconceptualization of formerly held fundamental assumptions (Birkenshaw et al., 2016; Shufutinsky et al., 2020a).

During crises, it is no secret that different organizations tend to respond differently, with reactions ranging from panic and mayhem to more controlled, effective resolutions. This varies by organization and by leader, and this vast range of potential responses, and where any organization lands in it depends significantly on the characteristics, abilities, and capacities of its leaders (Bowers et al., 2017). Thus, during these chaotic environments of discontinuous change, organizations need a framework of re-creation, and this re-creation mindset needs organizational leaders who are mindful, aware, able to anticipate rapid disruption and precipitously lead their organizations into re-creation, even in absence of the benefits of time or resources to pore over ideas, tactics, strategies, nor the luxury of time for experimentation and evaluation (Nadler and Tushman, 1995; Shufutinsky et al., 2020a).

## LEADERSHIP NEEDS IN TIMES OF TURBULENCE

As aforementioned, leaders are a critical resource in turbulent times, such as the COVID-19 crisis, among many others. Leadership is one of the most comprehensively researched and written-about topics in the behavioral sciences because all economic, political, and organizational systems depend to a high degree on effective leader direction and guidance (Barrow 1977; Parris & Peachey, 2013), and thus the ability to predict and understand the critical factors needed for organizations to succeed in any particular scenario is undertaken through the study of the organization's leaders (Parris & Peachey, 2013).

Leader effectiveness is considered one of the most vital components for organizations in times of normalcy as well as times of crisis (Shufutinsky et al., 2020a). Although global epidemics are no new phenomenon, the population finds itself in the heart of a changed world—one in which they, as a population, have started to recognize the havoc and uncertainty wrought from the global spread of a highly infectious virus, along with a surplus of leaders across the globe who are unprepared to handle these disruptive, chaotic events and their resultant rapidly and unpredictably shifting conditions (Shufutinsky et al., 2020a). The media has been littered with stories addressing leadership failures in politics, emergency response organizations, corporations, medical establishments, law enforcement, and local agencies, including corporations that have refused or found themselves unable to fund employee time off. Reports of leader failures to implement precautionary public health protections, including those based on expert advice, and engagine in authoritarian, dishonest, greedy, non-empathetic, and unhumanitarian behaviors in a time of a global disease crisis and economic and social turmoil are not an anomaly (Amante, 2020; Rasheed, 2020; Shear et al., 2020; Treverton & Jahn, 2020; Walker, 2020). There have been historical accounts of similar leadership problems during other disasters, with acts of unjust and race-based implementation of quarantine, inequitable medical treatment, unwarranted forcible vaccination, and other dark leadership disgraces during plague, smallpox, and other outbreaks, resulting in mistrust and setting the stage for protest, uprising, and violence (Kapucu & Van Wart, 2008; Mariner et al., 2009). Those who lead organizations during times of normalcy may not be appropriate to lead their organizations through times of disaster, and may provide inadequate and problematic leadership that yields further damage. Many organizations normally operate in reactive mode, which is problematic in crises, where at least some form of proactive approach can make considerable strides towards the effective management of disruption (Girboveanu & Pavel, 2010). Being unprepared, untrained, and inexperienced environments of crises, these leaders may inappropriately concentrate and apply resources on mitigation strategies that focus on appearances, media cylces, and other distractions when prioritization should should focus actions on actual crisis response and relevant organizational needs (Bowers et al., 2017; Shufutinsky et al., 2020a). Thus, the typical definition of leadership effectiveness being measured by attainment of goals and objectives (Northouse, 2016), or meeting leadership practice inventory (Kouzes & Posner, 1995) statistics do not sufficiently apply in times like the 2020 pandemic, because leadership requirements change in emergency, mass-system disruption, and crisis situations.

Although leadership is a key component of organization design and is pivotal to organization effectiveness, an agreed-upon definition or conceptualization of leadership is lacking, as evidenced by the surplus of leadership literature displaying innumerous definitions (Bennis, 2007). This is not only unsurprising, but is aligned with the reality that there are many leadership styles and numerous leadership attributes needed at different times and exhibited differently depending on environment and context (McConnell & Drennan, 2006). Leadership plays a vital role in most organizational environments, and the need for and importance of effective leadership is present in disaster planning, management, and response. In fact, it can be argued that it is in fact even more evident and often takes center-stage (Shufutinsky et al., 2020a) in disaster preparedness and response. However, it is first necessary to understand what effective leadership may look like in crises, such as COVID-19.

Leading in crises demands bold adaptation, rapid and precise decision-making, and effective situational assessment and sense-making (Bowers et al., 2017; Nichols et al., 2020; Shufutinsky et al., 2020a). This capacity of leadership is rare and is not easily found in routine business acumen but, instead, requires a different type of capability, practice, and experience. In such environments, organizations cannot rely on leaders who are ignorant to the needs and appropriations of resources. A capacity to effectively respond and lead groups, teams, organizations, or communities through disasters is complex, and requires an adaptive and situational leadership perspective (Burrell et al., 2010) with a highly advanced level of flexibility, agility, decision-making, and actionability—leadership capacity that this misappropriation of resources or ignorance of needs prevents (Shufutinsky et al., 2020a).

One fundamental challenge to effective functionality of leaders, particularly with these capacities and capabilities, is being prone to becoming myopic, insular, and disconnected in the VUCA environment of crisis situations. This can occur in such environments when leaders are not trained, experienced, and lack the ability of functional mindfulness, causing the thinking processes to become problematic and incoherent when left unchecked without sufficient awareness and mindfulness in day-to-day operations (Bohm, 1992). However, even seasoned leaders can feel threatened during chaotic times, and all leaders can acquire patterns of stress. The internalization of stress can affect judgment and decision-making, and can result in withdrawal and the inability to move through discomfort into the reality of the chaotic environment, also resulting in the potential loss of an ability to engage varying leadership behaviors or varying leadership styles.

Without this presence of awareness, the unconscious mental processes take over and enter a defensive state, filtering or manipulating experiences of reality to conform to them and their desires rather than reality. The need to re-recreate must include a thorough understanding of preconceived notions of who one is along with what one knows, to overcome the inherent self-deception defended in the desired images of self and the social world it creates (Arbinger Institute, 2010).

In order for organizations to emerge intact from crisis environments (Birkenshaw et al., 2016), they must be prepared to respond to non-linear, discontinuous change such as the COVID-19 pandemic, through leaders that are able to accept and embrace unlearning, discomfort, conflict, continual inquiry, and to lead constant knowledge development in uncertain, complex, and volatile scenarios through mindful processes (Malhotra, 1997; Miller & Katz, 2013; Nadler & Shaw, 1995), hence supporting continuity across organizational culture, strategy, structure, and systems (Sutton, 1999). This includes the unavoidable need to advance and accelerate leaders' capacities and capabilities (Shufutinsky et al., 2020a).

## PANDEMIC LEADERSHIP DEVELOPMENT

People's general tendency is to be resistant to change (Dent & Goldberg, 1999; Worley et al., 1996), and to respond to unconventional and ambiguous challenges conventionally, thus addressing scenarios they are unfamiliar with through methods they are accustomed to using. Because of this unfamiliarity and discomfort, leaders have to grapple with the challenges associated with crisis situations. However, although often unexpected and unpredictable, crises are an indispensable part of the workplace and in society (Celik, 2016). Even when faced with disruption, leaders can adapt and alter their leadership styles and responsive actions from prior experience, in order to push the disruption back towards what they perceive as a state of normalcy or stasis (Celik et al., 2016; Hunt et al., 2009; Shufutinsky et al., 2020a).

In pandemics and similar crises, companies, agencies, communities, and society-at-large require honesty, transparency, authenticity, and impactful care from their leaders (Campbell, 2015; Cavanaugh, 2006; Doe & Pumplampu, 2018; Mariner et al., 2009). A global epidemic, such as COVID-19, however, is the archetype of complexity and a prime atmosphere for complex systems, thus requiring much more from organizational leaders. It is therefore vital that organizational leaders understand the value of specific leadership styles, and how to employ them during the VUCA environment of pandemics in order to ensure significant positive impact on organizational function, effectiveness, survival, and organizations' members. Unfortunately, leadership problems, such as executives and managers displaying the dark side of leadership in organizations and teams, potentially compound the threat of viral pandemics (Shufutinsky et al., 2020a). Although dark leadership behaviors can be problematic to organizations at all times, large-scale epidemics that affect organizations and their people are a particularly poor time for ineffective, laissez-faire, toxic, abusive, detached, dishonest, coercive, narcissistic and destructive leadership styles that result in declining performance, increased workplace deviance, increased stress, and lower levels of job satisfaction, engagement, and employee commitment (Kurtulmus, 2019; Mathieu et al., 2014; Milosevic et al., 2019). Thus, it is apparent that, during pandemic crises, organizations of all types require effective employment of numerous leadership styles and characteristics (Cavanaugh, 2006; Doe & Pumplampu, 2018; Mariner et al., 2009).

A pandemic leadership style must be (a) highly responsive, (b) highly flexible and adaptive to changing situations and environments, (c) reflective and confident, (d) honest and transparent, (e) stable and engaged, (f) compassionate and empathetic, (g) collaborative and culturally sensitive, (h) globally-minded and ethical, (i) reasonably utilitarian, (j) systems-thinking and sense-making, (k) intuitive and open to learning, and (l) simultaneously calm and able to accept and be resilient in discomfort and discontinuous or non-linear change (Shufutinsky et al., 2020a). These vital attributes are present in numerous highly important leadership styles, including (a) authentic leadership, (b) transparent leadership, (c) situational leadership, (d) adaptive leadership, (e) communicative leadership, (f) mindful leadership, (g) transformational leadership, (h) systems leadership, (i) strategic leadership, (j) servant leadership, and (k) edge of chaos leadership (Bennis, 2007; Hunt et al., 2009; Johannson et al., 2014; Maitlis & Sonenshein, 2010; Weick, 1993; Wise, 2006), among others. Leadership, in a mass crisis such as the coronavirus pandemic, must be comprehensive and able to employ and combine these different attributes and styles of leadership for proper response and situation management.

To some, this may appear as an impossible task—a task that can only be accomplished by a superhuman being. However, in reality, effectively trained, developed, experienced leaders can potentiate a comprehensive ability to agilely shift and use a combination of the needed attributes of numerous leadership styles when necessary, including attributes from the critical leadership styles discussed below. Development of leaders with such comprehensive abilities will be further addressed in the following text.

**Authentic Leadership.** One of the leadership styles associated and oft defined as an ethical one is authentic leadership. This leadership theory is based on positive psychology, self-regulation, self-awareness, and self-actualization, including a high level of awareness of own emotions, self-identities, abilities, and capacity, with an equal focus on honesty, trust, altruism, accountability, and openness to learning from feedback and mistakes (Avolio et al., 2004; Gardner et al., 2005; George, 2003; Northouse, 2016). In this unstable, VUCA environment of the coronavirus pandemic, trust, honesty, accountability, optimism, altruism, and emphasis on follower welfare are very important to organizations and to the general public (Yukl, 2013).

**Transparent Leadership.** Also important to followers, organizations, and the public during this critical time is the ability for leaders to be transparent. Although not generally cited as a competitive tool in business, honesty, integrity, and clarity are vital values to effective organizational management and leadership. These values are espoused in transparent leadership. Without transparency, leadership behaviors and leaders' decision-making eventually affected, often not resulting in right, just, or beneficial actions (Houser et al., 2014). Similar to and overlapping with authentic leadership, transparent leadership is focused on openness, honesty, and trust. Leaders of organizations must observe their responsibility to be truthful, honest, and open about operations, successes, and failures (Baum, 2005). If they are not, then there is a high likelihood of a decline in trust, and subsequently engagement and loyalty, potentially creating, driving, or exacerbating toxic cultures and possible organizational failures. The COVID-19 pandemic has demonstrated the need for these values to be espoused in the short-term as well, especially in highly chaotic global, national, community, and organizational environments, because transparent leadership enhances cooperation and collaboration and reduces variation in responsive action, as followers and the public are more inclined to follow leaders' suggestions and advice if they are known to be transparent and straight-forward (Houser et al., 2014; Salvatico, 2006).

**Adaptive and Situational Leadership.** These two leadership theories are similar, and often used interchangeably, although they do differ. Situational leadership derives from a contingency theory that explains that situations directly influence or moderate leader behavior and that leaders need to be able to adapt leadership style and behaviors to the situation at hand (Yukl, 2013). Using this situation-based approach to leadership hypothesized that different situations demand different leadership behaviors, and thus leaders need to be adept at identifying the situation and the necessary leadership style and attributes to use based on the current situation (Blanchard et al., 1993; Hersey & Blanchard, 1977; Northouse, 2016). This requires flexibility, reflexivity, and self-awareness not only to be able to learn how to use a variety of leadership attributes and leadership styles, but to be aware of the leadership behaviors one is espousing in any given situation (Yukl, 2013).

With situational leadership being focused on adapting leadership styles to suit the need of the situation, adaptive leadership emphasizes how leaders behave and act to influence and encourage others to adapt to challenging situations and change (Northouse, 2016), including non-linear change in complex environments. Adaptive leadership stresses the leader's activities relative to the work, challenges, and well-being of others, focusing on how leaders mobilize, stimulate, orient, and focus others' attentions to help them accomplish their mission in the face of change and complexity (Heifetz, et al., 2009; Northouse, 2016). These leadership styles can be vital in disaster scenarios, and it has been determined that the inability to lead effectively in rapid, non-linear change, and the lack of adaptive capability during disasters can be catastrophic. This was exhibited during Hurricane Katrina, showing poor planning, lack of systems integration, and inadequate and inappropriate response measures that exacerbated the challenges, the disaster, and the threat to health, safety, and homeland security (Burrell et al., 2010; Wise, 2006).

**Mindful Leadership.** Conceptual and cognitive ways of doing things can easily be lost in the strain of the brain's shift into primitive emotional reactivity during the threat and complexity of turbulent and chaotic environments. This new environment of disruptive change may feel like metaphorically drinking from a firehose, and this uncomfortable experience can cause a shift into survival mode. During mental panic, the most primitive part of the brain makes the decisions, and these decisions often result in rushing to inadequate solutions—solutions that are designed for routine operations and organizational normalcy, thus potentially only creating additional problems. Effective leadership during crises must be bold, and be willing to lean headfirst into discomfort, moving into the unknown by accessing learning not just from the past, but also mindfully from the yet to be embodied future (Sharmer, 2009). Mindful leadership is, in most simple terms, the purposeful use of attention and awareness in leadership processes. The ability to assess and make meaning of situations and respond appropriately, making analytical in-the-moment decisions is critical in crisis management. Leaders who are experienced in the practice of mindfulness have focused and acclimated their attentions and are better able to carry out real-time evaluation, sense-making, and decision-making. This practice of mindfulness has demonstrated a positive impact on the human domains of physiology, as well as cognition, emotion, and behavior, that synergize to foster better relationships, enhanced well-being, and ultimately improved performance (Good et al., 2016). The literature on contingency theory shows that the mindfulness-driven attentional breadth, and subsequent control on stability of attention of relevant tasks, results in overall performance improvement (Brewer et al., 2011; Dane, 2011; Reb et al., 2014). In situations of urgency and continual change, such as the one the world faces with COVID-19, the ability to stay consistent with minimal mind-wandering and increased stability of attention on in-the-moment presence is pivotal, and this is improved through mindfulness (Long, 2020a; 2020b; Lykins & Baer, 2009; MacLean et al., 2010; Smallwood & Schooler, 2015).

**Communicative Leadership.** Leadership has a significant basis on the ability of leaders to communicate. This ability is largely influenced by the context in which the individual finds oneself (Hamrefors, 2010). Like many other factors of behavior, communication is contextually situational, with effectiveness differing drastically dependent on location, time, space, or social circumstances (Burrell, 2020). A communicative leadership is achieved by a leader "...who engages employees in dialogue, actively shares and seeks feedback, practices participative decision making, and is perceived as open and involved" (Johansson et al., 2014). Communicative leadership highlights that communication is more than just charismatic messaging, as sometimes described in transformational leadership communication—particularly incomplete or pseudo transformational leadership. Rather, leaders' communication behaviors, such as attentive listening, two-way communication, and upward influence through co-worker involvement can be vital to achieving organizational objectives (Johansson et al., 2014; Shufutinsky et al., 2020a; Tyssen et al., 2014).

An incapacity to practice leadership from this communicative style can trigger problems with the audience, and communications may become further complicated by preconceptions about the topic or the communicator (Nijkrake et al., 2015; Parsons et al., 2017). These complicated preconceptions can result from numerous communications flaws by inexperienced, unprepared, inauthentic communicators, sometimes because they are overwhelmed with the disaster situation, such as a pandemic. As with other organizational disruption, communication with the workforce in an organization or members of a community should begin immediately upon recognizing that there is a threat to operations, the workforce, the organization, the community, or the nation. These communications from voices of authority must be crafted carefully because, honesty, transparency, accuracy, specificity, and evidence of collaboration, provided consistently, can calm the public and cultivate trust in chaotic times (Parsons et al., 2017). The SARS epidemic, for example, demonstrated the value of effective, accurate, and honest information to the public and to health care providers—communications that were particularly beneficial to the health-care system in Canada during the outbreak (Mariner et al., 2009). This type of effective communication methodology can help prevent panic, anger, disorganization, and unnecessary concern in organizations and in surrounding communities (Mariner et al., 2009; Parsons et al., 2017; Shufutinsky et al., 2020a).

Research exhibits that leaders who participate in dialogue and responsive communication behaviors are more effective in co-worker and follower engagement, empowerment, and that they drive better organizational learning and decision-making (Johansson, 2015). Using a communicative leadership approach that embraces these attributes and exhibits a listening, two-way communication method, can increase trust, participation, and action even in a highly VUCA environment.

**Systems Leadership.** Many organizations are complex adaptive systems, and no research, analysis, or response to one element of a complex system will provide an understanding of or effective change in the whole system (Uhl-Bien et al., 2007). Complexity science exhibits that leadership is a product of the interaction dynamics of of all of the people and the system, and meaning and pespective emerge from those interactions (Lichtenstein & Ploman, 2009). Thus, organizational change materializes from the inter-related facets and interactions within the entire system in the organization or in self-organizing networks in society (Onyx & Leonard, 2011; Shufutinsky et al., 2020). Systems leadership is based on these interacting system dynamics, addressing the emergence that arises out of the complexity of system-wide interactions. Systems leaders are able to function through a systems-thinking lens, assessing the entire system and the interactions of the people in the system with the components of the system (Northouse, 2015; Uhl-Bien et al., 2007; Yukl, 2013). This requires the use of holistic frameworks of organizational design, including components such as environment, strategy, mission, vision, cultures, structures, systems, and behaviors (Jamieson, 2016) consistently. The way in which these components are inter-related and impact each other as the situation evolves continuously is key to organizational effectiveness and survival (Shufutinsky et al., 2020; 2020b).

**Transformational Leadership.** Transformational leadership, giving considerable attention to charismatic and effective leadership elements, is one of the most studied and debated leadership theories in the past two decades (Díaz-Sáenz, 2011). This leadership style gives emphasis to intrinsic motivation and follower development, designed to provide inspiration and empowerment to today's workforce in uncertain times (Bass & Riggio, 2006; Northouse, 2016). The premise of this leadership style is that it is supposed to transform people via an exceptional mode of influence. It is intended to tap into the motives of followers and encourage them to complete goals and objectives and surpass expectations (Northouse, 2016). The leader, paying attention to the needs of the followers, takes action to try to help them achieve their fullest potential. Transformational leadership, concerned with the improvement of follower performance, consists of four factors. These include charismatic influence, inspirational motivation, intellectual stimulation, and individualized consideration, and the combination of all four are supposed to improve organizational members' performance. Transformational leaders have sound internal values and pay close attention to follower needs, ideas, thoughts, and abilities (Northouse, 2016). This leadership theory asserts that leaders ensure organization performance by transforming followers through displaying charisma and painting captivating and persuasive visions of the future (Shufutinsky et al., 2020; Tyssen, Wald, & Heidenreich, 2014). The charisma and idealistic influence and inspiration components of transformational leadership can be critical to leading in turbulent times, especially in times of fear and uncertainty like the COVID-19 pandemic. Pandemic leaders can benefit greatly from understanding how to use these attributes effectively. However, charisma in leadership, without the other necessary theory elements of intellectual stimulation and personalized consideration, spawns pseudo-transformational leadership (Northouse, 2016), which can create numerous ramifications in chaotic environments. Charisma alone is not enough to sustain an organization (Nadler & Tushman, 1990), community, government, or nation during chaotic discontinuous change, such the 2019-2020 coronavirus pandemic (Shufutinsky et al., 2020a).

**Servant Leadership.** Similar to transformational leadership, servant leadership is focused on ensuring that stakeholders, including followers, are provided with their due needs and necessities. This leadership style is engaged in service, with serving being the most important building block not only in the leadership behaviors, but to the organization. As such, servant leadership emphasizes service to others and espouses that the most important building block of an organization is the organization's people, and thus the leader ensures the followers—the vital building block—are a main focus (Barrow, 1977; Schneider, 1987). Because servant leadership is focused on the good of the followers over the leader, which emphasizes (a) valuing and developing people, (b) practicing authenticity, (c) building community, (d) leading for the good of followers, and (e) sharing status and power (Laub, 1999; Washington et al., 2014), this leadership style contains many of the leadership attributes necessary to lead in crisis environments, such as COVID-19, where people need guidance, need honesty and transparency, and need care and empathy for their struggles.

**Edge of Chaos Leadership.** Many organizations operate in an imbalanced state between order and disorder. This space of disequilibrium is termed the edge of chaos (Hunt et al., 2007; McDaniel, 1997) and this boundary is a transition zone that approaches an imbalanced, disorderly condition of ambiguity and volatility, positioned at the boundary of order, yet necessitating constant adjustments to rapidly changing systems. This dynamic exists in numerous organizations and has been readily visible in the high tech industry but has moved into other historically more conventional industries as well (Hunt et al., 2007).

Edge of chaos scenarios, however, usually affect only a portion of an organization's units undergoing a chaotic state, while the other major units sustain stability (Hunt et al., 2007). Thus, although some may suggest that the entire system, or multiple inter-related components of the system are simultaneously undergoing dramatic, disruptive change, this has historically not been the case. Although these relatively unstable scenarios still necessitate constant adaptive and situational leadership in order to be agile and responsive to the change that is occurring, the unpredictability is not generally so much that the organization could not survive (Osborn et al., 2002) because the vast and majority portions of the organization are stable (Hunt et al., 2007). Thus, a situational and adaptive leadership style—edge of chaos leadership—is necessary in order to adapt to the change that occurs in the complex transition zone of stable equilibrium and randomness (Hunt et al., 2007; Hunt & Ropo, 2003; Shufutinsky et al., 2020a). Edge of chaos leadership, therefore, continues the adaptive leadership progression from measuring leadership by performance into the realm of exploring the evolutionary dynamics among the organization's environment, leadership, and viability at multiple levels (Hunt et al., 2007), including a level of constant instability.

Amidst chaotic situations, leadership needs to transcend the edge of chaos. In such environments, these adaptive and situational leadership needs must be taken to a different, more complex level, potentially entangled in a continual state of non-linear, chaotic, discontinuous change with the necessity to adapt in order to carry the organization back into the boundary of order and some state of stable equilibrium. This type of leadership requires, at a minimum, the potential use of all of the aforementioned attributes, and the ability to move between or to combine these different leadership styles for the purposes of dealing with the jolt that has shocked, dislodged, and disrupted systems to increasingly high complexity levels. This comprehensive leadership style is called *Shock Leadership.*

## SHOCK LEADERSHIP: LEADING THE WAY FORWARD IN CHAOTIC CHANGE ENVIRONMENTS

Understanding the aforementioned leadership styles is essential to leaders in routine organizational processes and conditions, and is even more important in states of disruption, such as crises. However, just studying and understanding these leadership styles and practices, while important, is not enough. For leaders to excel and be successful in leading their organizations in times of great need, in periods of discontinuous change and chaos, and in moments of crisis, leaders must be able to reach within and employ these different leadership attributes, styles, and behaviors as they adapt to a chaotic and shifting environment. Leaders that are able to adapt to highly chaotic and changing situations, and surge forward to do this effectively, are *shock leaders.*

A *shock leader* needs to be able to assess the situation, lean into discomfort and preserve a high level of resilience with it, listen attentively as an ally to the affected and to advisors, communicate accurately, honestly, and transparently the situational status and intent, and observe, evaluate, and analyze from multiple lenses and points of view in order to have a broader situational awareness and understanding so that the best sense-making can occur and the greatest decisions can be made (Katz & Miller, 2013; Miller & Katz, 2013). This is part of the essential adaptation to the continual, non-linear, rapidly changing events that occur in situations like the COVID-19 pandemic, and requires fluency with and the ability to integrate transparent leadership, authentic leadership, situational leadership, adaptive leadership, mindful leadership, communicative leadership, systems leadership, transformational leadership, and edge of chaos leadership, among others. Using these leadership styles and their aforementioned attributes, and agilely amending them to situational changes, a *Shock Leader* is able to react effectively to disruptive, threatening, and destabilizing conditions that shock systems, whether they are corporate divisions, non-profit organizations, school systems, universities, governmental agencies, or local, state, or provincial communities. To some, this capability may sound too good to be true, as leaders across corporate, government, non-profit, and other organizations have considerable difficulty learning even how to lead in routine operations and conditions of relative normalcy. However, just as some leaders excel in those environments, and do so rapidly, so can some leaders in crises, particularly when they have the knowledge, aptitude, experience, and capacity to respond effectively through the employment of this combination of leadership tenets. It may not be simple, but shock leadership capability is possible, and it is necessary.

*Shock Leadership* capability and experience can offer increased levels of situational awareness, improve collaboration, group cohesion, and teamwork, reduce response times, enhance decision-making, boost surge capacity, generate improved inter-organizational interoperability, and heighten leader elasticity and tractability, all of which are crucial for managing through extreme, vastly complex environments with fluctuating unknowns and variable VUCA exacerbation. *Shock Leadership* is the comprehensive, although complex, leadership model for emergencies and catastrophes that shock entire systems, such as the COVID-19 pandemic. However, just as aforementioned, *Shock Leadership* cannot be simply embrace by any leader in order to succeed in tumultuous times. It requires knowledge, experience, and a certain level of leadership development. Organizational preparedness for these crisis conditions is critical and developing shock leaders is a pivotal element in it (Shufutinsky et al., 2020a).

## DEVELOPING SHOCK LEADERS

In crises, the needs and requirements of organizations are different. Crisis response yearns for non-traditional capabilities with the aptitude for ad hoc reactions, sense-making, and decision-making, and because crisis management is concerned with the entire timeline, focused on the before, now, and after, suggests the necessity for components of emergent leadership and committed emergency and crisis preparedness in organizations and communities (James et al., 2011; Shufutinsky et al., 2020a). Working from a place of constant reaction is inadequate if there is any expectation of leading effectively through crises and coming out in a sustainable or thriving state (Girboveanu & Pavel, 2010). Leaders need to be able to take action before crises occur, and it is those actions that can have considerable influence on the enablement of effective navigation through organizational crises when they do happen (James & Wooten, 2010; Shufutinsky et al., 2020a; Williams et al., 2017). Therefore, it is evident that continued and persistent leadership development and preparedness are critical for leaders who potentially encounter disasters, and in situations such as the global COVID-19 disaster, that would include most leaders of most organizations and communities.

Too often, leadership development is defined in terms of mentoring, coaching, and consultation regarding leadership practices, and organizations often undertake leadership development in the context of succession planning. However, leadership learning and development should be addressed from a much broader scope of organizational purpose, including the ability to drive organizational success, as well as the ability to lead organizational resilience in adverse conditions. Thus, leadership development is critical for a learning and development tool for leaders at all stages, and from the context of crisis preparedness.

Leadership development is implemented in different ways by different organizations, and no single leader can be developed in the same exact way as any other leader. Furthermore, leadership development will differ between organizations. There is no *"magic box"* of instruments and methods for developing effective leaders, especially with the different needs of organizations during routine operations, let alone crises. Nevertheless, it is possible to combine a variety of leadership development instruments and methods to ensure development of particular skills, capabilities, and levels of capacity that may prove valuable for leaders amid scenarios that jolt whole organizational systems (Shufutinsky et al., 2020a). Despite the highly complex and uncertain nature of leadership, particularly in volatile and chaotic environments rich in rapidly shifting needs and situations and, as with COVID-19, unprecedented for many organizational leaders, it is possible to empower leaders to be ready for and even proactive toward effectual reactivity (Shufutinsky et al., 2020a).

Our recently performed research exhibits that leaders can be readied for effective leading and managing effectively in crisis situations. These shock leaders can be developed via a course of three continual methods of leadership development as detailed by *Shock Leadership Development* (Shufutinsky et al., 2020). These continual leadership development methods include the creation and deployment of ongoing real-time, live action, scenario-based critical training in and practice with a diversity of leadership styles for agile adaptation when the situational needs arise in crisis, as well as mindfulness training and practice (Shufutinsky, 2020a).

## REAL-TIME SCENARIO-BASED TRAINING

One of the interesting leadership phenomena regarding military leadership that is rarely expressed, and is generally not described in peer-reviewed leadership literature is the leadership style that is often used, without a whole lot of purposeful notoriety, in ascetic, resource-poor, complex and rapidly changing environments, that focuses on quick sense-making, decision-making, and surge capacity. Although it has historically lacked a single definable term, from a literary perspective, this leadership style has been unofficially called *Surge Leadership.* Constant and repetitive, yet variable real-time simulation training and continual operational posture, ready to deploy at any given time, affords military leaders the ability to respond to these austere and chaotic conditions with rapid, amply analytical decisiveness, often affording effective inter-unit communication, joint interoperability, and effectual use of strategic and collaborative command structures while flexible with room for scaling and cooperation (Shufutinsky et al., 2020a). Although this leadership style is not officially defined, it is certainly not accidental. This phenomenon is arguably a normal and necessary way of life for military organizations, even when they are not deployed (Shufutinsky et al., 2020a).

Live training drills are a consistent reality to ensure combat readiness, whether it is for wartime deployment, anti-terrorism actions, coastal enforcement, or humanitarian missions. Military commands undergo an exorbitant variety of real-time drills, including live-fire exercises in fabricated villages with staged housing structures and enemies, as well as exercises through virtual reality/augmented reality (VR/AR) technologies (Hsu et al., 2013; Shufutinsky, 2018; 2020a). U.S. Naval forces undertake live-fire combatant training at-sea, missile launch tests, continuous aircraft launch-and-recovery, and weekly, or even daily firefighting, collision, flooding, combat, mass-casualty medical, and other disaster scenario drills when out to sea and when ported. These training scenarios and drills are performed in land-based domestic training sites as well as in deployed environments, such as their ships, camps, field hospitals, or other live locations (Shufutinsky et al., 2020a). These drills are performed in as realistic conditions as possible, including full-dress, fully-equipped, and fully-armed scenarios. Through these methods, including regular deployment, military organizations achieve levels of constant and consistent readiness for an array of scenarios, including potential crises. Such modalities of training heighten organizational readiness by increasing organization response time, individual situational awareness, inter-organizational communication, technical knowledge, teamwork, surge capacity, multi-commnad interoperability, leadership capacity, and followership effectiveness (Shufutinsky et al., 2020a). For the military services, this type of real-time training results in continual, advanced disaster preparedness. This practice exemplifies that leadership preparedness is indispensable for crisis preparedness, and that it works in a variety of scenarios, including critical decision-making and continuity of operations during pandemics.

Another benefit of the employment of real-time drills and simulations is the ability for military leaders across different stages of leadership to employ and test their leadership skills, including those competencies and attributes necessary in different leadership styles. Some important aspects of leadership effectiveness in the military are the training, mentorship, and knowledge that leaders develop through leadership courses, experience, and diverse training. This aids in readiness with regard to sense- and decision-making. For this to happen, these *surge leaders* need to be able to evaluate situations, step into discomfort, maintain elevated levels of resilience, listen diligently and authentically (Katz & Miller, 2013; Miller & Katz, 2013) to followers and advisors, communicate intentionally, accurately, and transparently, and observe, evaluate, assess, and analyze their situations from multiple perspectives in order to have a more robust understanding (Shufutinsky et al., 2020a). This means understanding of, fluency with, and ability to adapt and integrate numerous leadership styles for the best use of their traits, in order to lead effectively at or above the boundary of chaos (Hunt et al., 2007; Shufutinsky et al., 2020a; Stringham, 2012). Therefore, learning and training with numerous leadership styles, and being able to integrate and agilely adjust them with the shifting environment, gives *surge leaders* an advantage to react more effectively to disruptive, and destabilizing conditions that jolt systems (Shufutinsky et al., 2020a). This type of knowledge, aptitude, and capacity derives from practice, training, and development.

Although simulations, real-time drills, and training differ between commands, the continuity of real-time, scenario-based training affords opportunities for leaders to utilize different leadership styles, as needed, in diverse disaster and crisis situations, including real scenarios during operational periods, giving them plentiful and repeated chances to try, test, adapt, and adjust leadership styles and attributes, preparing leaders for increased agility in future actual crises (Shufutinsky et al., 2020a). Through live simulations and real-time drills, leaders can receive the necessary on-the-job training and experience, even if sometimes unplanned, in authentic, transparent, communicative, transformational, adaptive, situational, authoritative, and systems leadership styles, among others aforementioned. There is ample opportunity, often called for by the situation, to employ and practice attributes such as self-regulation, self- and situational awareness, honesty, trust, clarity, transparency, accountability, strength, guidance, inspiration, and systems thinking, all of which can be necessary in different situations and during different times in crisis scenarios (Avolio et al., 2004; Boin et al., 2013; George, 2003; Shufutinsky et al., 2020a; Yukl, 2013). The combination of real-time exercises and drills with leadership knowledge-building and experiential employment, and mindfulness training, can drive surge leadership to a new capacity to dealing with whole system shocks.

*Figure 1. The Shock Leadership Framework*

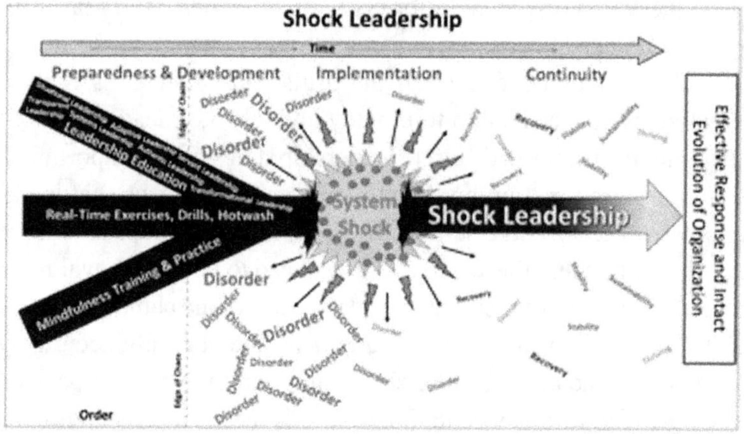


## MINDFULNESS TRAINING

The third critical component of *Shock Leadership Development* is mindfulness training. Mindfulness practice has been found to be effective for leaders in numerous ways, across industries and around the globe. Essentially, leaders well-versed and practiced in mindfulness have trained attentions and are generally better able to perform real-time assessment as well as sense- and decision-making in most situations (Good et al., 2016; Long, 2019; 2020a; 2020b). For leaders, mindfulness has had significantly positive effects with regards to cognition, emotions, physiology, and behavior, driving improved breathing and more effective control and maintenance of attention on the task-at-hand, reducing focus on distractions. Further, mindfulness positively impacts relationships, well-being, and performance for individuals and for organizations (Dane,

2011; Good et al., 2016, Long, 2019; Reb et al., 2014). In environments of discontinuous change and chaos, the abilities to stay on task, avoid irrelevant distractions, maintain well-being, and work effectively through relationships is critical, and mindfulness has the ability to foster these abilities, allowing leaders to show up, remain present and consistent in-the-moment, and to minimize mind-wandering and emotional reactivity (Brewer et al., 2011; Brown et al., 2012; Cahn et al., 2012; Desbordes et al., 2012; Kozasa et al., 2012; Long, 2019; Lutz et al., 2008; Lykins & Baer, 2009; MacLead et al., 2010; Tang et al., 2007; Taylor et al., 2011). With expanded cognitive capacity, mindful leaders are better able to effectively use cognitive resources in disruptive environments and distracting situations, such as many experienced during crises (Shufutinsky et al., 2020a).

## DEVELOPING SHOCK LEADERS IN CIVILIAN ORGANIZATIONS

Non-military organizations can learn from military commands regarding leadership and leadership development for VUCA and chaotic environs. As displayed in the Shock Leadership Model (Figure 1), developing preparedness plans, designing and participating in simulations, response drills, as well as receiving education and training regarding numerous leadership styles and competencies, and implementing lessons learned "*hotwash*" sessions from drills and training, can increase the likelihood of organizational survival, stability, resilience, and thriving as a result of shock leadership (Shufutinsky et al., 2020a). Addition of mindfulness training and practice creates an aptitude for increased attention, focus, and decreased distraction, only supplementing potential for leadership effectiveness in shock environments. Organizational leaders can prepare for and obtain competency in *Shock Leadership*, providing them the skills necessary for employing numerous leadership styles and attributes to lead organizations, whether non-profit, corporate, educational, governmental, or community, toward intact sustainment during future crisis events (Shufutinsky et al., 2020a).

Thus, for events that shock entire systems, creating environments of chaos and discontinuous change, an advanced type of situational, agile, flexible, and adaptive leadership style is necessary, and this type of leadership is not a simple phenomenon learned through previous leadership experience in routine or even crisis scenarios. Leading effectively in such environments requires continuity of education, preparedness, and experience. By employing an aggregate of long-term design, development, and implementation of similar real-time, scenario-based simulation training programs, mindfulness development, and the integration of various leadership styles in these training scenarios, organizations can prepare and enable their leaders to improve flexibility, adaptability, and surge capacity to handle rapidly wavering, non-linear, discontinuous change in tragic and destabilizing situations, and to respond more effectively, as *Shock Leaders,* to whole system jolts in their organizations.

## CONCLUSION

Many organizations continue to learn lessons from the COVID-19 pandemic and the related systemic effects. Not only has this global disaster taken nations, governments, corporations, and other organizations by surprise, it has shocked the global system, creating mass casualties, overwhelming medical and public health infrastructures, shuttering schools and businesses, driving product shortages, pushing innumerable amounts of work, workers, and students onto virtual platforms, reducing global travel and trade, decreasing trust in news media and governmental communications, and in countless cases, increasing the potential to exacerbate conditions of poverty, malnutrition, and poor sanitation, among many other disruptions. The likelihood exists that the effects will linger for years in the aftermath of the pandemic. In the wake of this global crisis, societal change will continue rapidly, and further disruptions to system are not only possible, they are expected. Despite some economic predictions, it is not known what the lasting effects of quarantines and closed economies will lead to, or the potential lasting changes they may have on the manner in which people interact, work, shop, dine, socialize, engage in entertainment, and get around. Leaders at every level, throughout industries, in governmental, non-profit, or corporate organizations of all sizes, have been experiencing increases in VUCA, and this is likely to persist during stages of recovery. Numerous research studies are already ongoing regarding many areas of interest, including international and inter-regional infection rates, differences in response measures to deal with the crisis between countries, and an examination of what worked and what did not. Research will focus not only on medicine and public health infrastructure, but also on healthcare systems, government systems, communications systems, and many others. Urban development, city planning, media responses, political conflict, and the benefits, drawbacks, and side-effects of virtual work and learning will undoubtedly be examined. One of the major areas in which exploration will almost definitely continue is the study of crisis leadership, and the disparities in effectiveness that leaders have had and will continue to have in this unprecedented crises in which situational leadership needs have been pushed to extremes, and leaders must respond to conditions in environments for which nobody has clear and absolute answers on appropriate and adequate leadership and management, even when they have been working tirelessly to respond as effectively as possible to the ongoing, rapidly-altering, discontinuous change.

What has surfaced, and what the research by Shufutinsky et al. (2020c) have discovered, is the need for a special type of comprehensive and malleable leadership model for organizations and communities of all scales to effectively respond in crises such as the one the world has undergone in 2020, and during potential subsequent waves of outbreaks, as well as during recovery periods in the aftermath. This comprehensive leadership style itself demands a great degree of skill, knowledge, critical thinking, flexibility, and agility to rapidly adapt to environments that are equally rapid in change and disruption. Therefore, there is an inherent need to be able to use numerous leadership attributes, and leadership styles, often simultaneously, in order to react and respond to the environmental conditions and to lead effectively. Additionally, even though responses in such rapidly shifting environments that shock entire systems are highly reactive, the current research indicates that leaders can respond more decisively and effectively, and that this generally occurs in organizations with proactive and preparedness-based processes and means—those that prepare the organizations and the organizational leadership for the potential of crises. This culture of preparedness can make leaders and organizations more capable of success in leading through troublesome and turbulent times. These *Surge Leaders* cannot become effective leaders simply because they routinely lead organizations, have tacit knowledge and technical or professional skills, or have undergone disaster management or crisis leadership classes. This kind of leadership requires constant preparedness through continual training, using authentic or actual real-time and disruptive live scenarios to provide experiential knowledge for response, leadership, and management in crises, developing *Shock Leaders* that can lead through system shock and disorder towards transitioning organizations back into conditions of recovery, stability, sustainability, and thriving. This necessary level of preparedness can be approached through the *Shock Leadership Development* framework, and is needed not just for the anticipated lengthy recovery from COVID-19, but for ensuring that organizations are not caught unprepared, unaware, or incapacitated in the event of similar crises in the future.

## REFERENCES

Amante, A. (2020). Help Us Like You Were Helped After War, Italy's Virus Hit Cities Tell Germany. *Reuters*. Retrieved from https://www.reuters.com/article us-health-coronavirus-italy-germany/help-us-like-you-were-helped-after-war-italys-virus-hit-cities-tell-german-idUSKBNZ1I1HT

Arbinger Institute. (2010). *Leadership and self-deception* (2nd ed.). San Francisco: Berrett-Koehler.

Avolio, B. J., Gardner, W. L., Walumbwa, F. O., Luthans, F., & May, D. R. (2004). Unlocking the mask: A look at the process by which authentic leaders impact follower attitudes and behaviors. *The Leadership Quarterly*, *15*(6), 801–823. doi:10.1016/j.leaqua.2004.09.003

Barrow, J. C. (1977). The variables of leadership: A review and conceptual framework. *Academy of Management Review*, *2*(2), 233–251. doi:10.5465/amr.1977.4409046

Baum, H. (2005). Transparent leadership. *Leader to Leader*, *2005*(37), 41–47. doi:10.1002/ltl.139

Bennett, N., & Lemoine, G. J. (2014). What a difference a word makes: Understanding threats to performance in a VUCA world. *Business Horizons*, *57*(3), 311–317. doi:10.1016/j.bushor.2014.01.001

Bennis, W. (2007). The challenges of leadership in the modern world: Introduction to the special issue. *The American Psychologist*, *62*(1), 2–5. doi:10.1037/0003-066X.62.1.2 PMID:17209674

Birkenshaw, J., Zimmermann, A., & Raisch, S. (2016). How do firms adapt to discontinuous change? Bridging the dynamic capabilities and ambidexterity perspectives. University of California, Berkeley.

Bohm, D. (1992). *Thought as a system*. Routledge.

Boin, A., Kuipers, S., & Overdijk, W. (2013). Leadership in times of crisis: A framework for assessment. *International Review of Public Administration*, *18*(1), 79–91. doi:10.1080/12294659.2013.10805241

Bowers, M. R., Hall, J. R., & Srinivasan, M. M. (2017). Organizational culture and leadership style: The missing combination for selecting the right leader for effective crisis management. *Business Horizons*, *60*(4), 551–563. doi:10.1016/j.bushor.2017.04.001

Brewer, J. A., Worhunsky, P. D., Gray, J. R., Tang, Y. Y., & Weber, J., & kober, H. (2011). Meditation experience is associated with differences in default mode network activity and connectivity. *Proceedings of the National Academy of Sciences*, *108*(50), 20254-20259. 10.1073/pnas.1112029108

Brown, K. W., Ryan, R. M., Loverich, T. M., Biegel, G. M., & West, A. M. (2011). Out of the armchair and into the streets: Measuring mindfulness advances knowledge and improves interventions: Reply to Grossman. *Psychological Assessment*, *23*(4), 1041–1046. doi:10.1037/a0025781

Burkle, F. M. Jr. (2010). Do Pandemic Preparedness Planning Systems Ignore Critical Community and Local-Level Operational Challenges? *Disaster Medicine and Public Health Preparedness*, *4*(1), 24–29. doi:10.1097/DMP.0b013e3181cb4193 PMID:20389192

Burrell, D. N. (2020). Understanding the Talent Management Intricacies of Remote Cybersecurity Teams in Covid-19 Induced Telework Organizational Ecosystems. *Land Forces Academy Review*, *25*(3), 232–244. doi:10.2478/raft-2020-0028

Burrell, D. N., Abdul-Malik, O., Rahim, E., Huff, A., & Finklea, K. (2010). An analysis of the application of situational leadership in the post 9/11 evolving public health managerial environments. *Leadership Journal*, *5*(1), 49-59.

Cahn, B. R., Delorme, A., & Polich, J. (2012). Event-related delta, theta, alpha and gamma correlates to auditory oddball processing during Vipassana meditation. *Social Cognitive and Affective Neuroscience*, *8*(1), 100–111. doi:10.1093can/nss060 PMID:22648958

Campbell, K. A. (2015). Can effective risk management signal virtue-based leadership? *Journal of Business Ethics*, *129*(1), 115–130. doi:10.100710551-014-2129-4

Cavanaugh, J. C. (2006). Effectively managing major disasters. *The Psychologist Manager Journal*, *9*(1), 3–11. doi:10.120715503461tpmj0901_2

Celik, A., Akgemci, T., & Akyazi, T. E. (2016). A comparison between the styles of transformational leaders and authentic leaders in crisis management. *International Journal of Academic Research in Business & Social Sciences*, *6*(2), 183–196. doi:10.6007/IJARBSS/v6-i2/2023

Dane, E. (2011). Paying attention to mindfulness and its effects on task performance in the workplace. *Journal of Management*, *37*(4), 997–1018. doi:10.1177/0149206310367948

Dayton, B. W., & Bernhardsdottir, A. (2015). *Crisis management*. International Encyclopedia of Peace.

Dennis, R. S., Kinzler-Norheim, L., & Bocarnea, M. (2010). Servant leadership theory. In *Servant leadership* (pp. 169–179). Palgrave Macmillan. doi:10.1057/9780230299184_14

Dent, E. B., & Goldberg, S. G. (1999). Challenging "resistance to change". *The Journal of Applied Behavioral Science*, *35*(1), 25–41. doi:10.1177/0021886399351003

Desbordes, G., Negi, L. T., Pace, T. W., Wallace, B. A., Raison, C. L., & Schwartz, E. L. (2012). Effects of mindful-attention and compassion meditation training on amygdala response to emotional stimuli in an ordinary, non-meditative state. *Frontiers in Human Neuroscience*, *6*, 292. doi:10.3389/fnhum.2012.00292 PMID:23125828

Doe, F., & Puplampu, B. B. (2019). Coercive management behaviour causes scale: Validation and reliability. *The International Journal of Organizational Analysis*, *27*(3), 729–744. doi:10.1108/IJOA-08-2018-1508

Doshi, P. (2011). The elusive definition of pandemic influenza. *Bulletin of the World Health Organization*, *89*(7), 532–538. doi:10.2471/BLT.11.086173 PMID:21734768

Drabek, T. E., & McEntire, D. A. (2003). Emergent phenomena and the sociology of disaster: Lessons, trends and opportunities from the research literature. *Disaster Prevention and Management*, *12*(2), 97–112. doi:10.1108/09653560310474214

Fineberg, H. V. (2014). Pandemic preparedness and response—Lessons from the H1N1 influenza of 2009. *The New England Journal of Medicine*, *370*(14), 1335–1342. doi:10.1056/NEJMra1208802 PMID:24693893

Gardner, W. L., Avolio, B. J., Luthans, F., May, D. R., & Walumbwa, F. (2005). "Can you see the real me?" A self-based model of authentic leader and follower development. *The Leadership Quarterly*, *16*(3), 343–372. doi:10.1016/j.leaqua.2005.03.003

George, B. (2003). *Authentic leadership: Rediscovering the secrets to creating lasting value*. John Wiley & Sons.

Girboveanu, S., & Pavel, S. (2010). How to manage a public relations crisis. *Annals of University of Craiova — Economic Sciences Series, 3*(38). Available at http://feaa.ucv.ro/ annals/v3_2010/0038v3-038.pdf

Gomersall, C. D., Loo, S., Joynt, G. M., & Taylor, B. L. (2007). Pandemic preparedness. *Current Opinion in Critical Care, 13*(6), 742–747. doi:10.1097/MCC.0b013e3282f1bafd PMID:17975401

Good, D. J., Lyddy, C. J., Glomb, T. M., Bono, J. E., Brown, K. W., Duffy, M. K., & Lazar, S. W. (2016). Contemplating mindfulness at work: An integrative review. *Journal of Management*, *42*(1), 114–142. doi:10.1177/0149206315617003

Ha, K. M. (2019). Learning or Ignoring Lessons from Natural Disasters. *Journal of Professional Issues in Engineering Education and Practice*, *145*(4), 02519001. doi:10.1061/(ASCE)EI.1943-5541.0000428

Haddon, A., Loughlin, C., & McNally, C. (2015). Leadership in a time of financial crisis: What do we want from our leaders? *Leadership and Organization Development Journal*, *36*(5), 612–637. doi:10.1108/LODJ-12-2013-0166

Hamrefors, S. (2010). Communicative leadership. *Journal of Communication Management (London)*, *14*(2), 141–152. doi:10.1108/13632541011034592

Hayashi, C., & Soo, A. (2012). Adaptive leadership in times of crisis. *Prism*, *4*(1), 78–86.

Heifetz, R. A., Grashow, A., & Linsky, M. (2009). *The practice of adaptive leadership: Tools and tactics for changing your organization and the world.* Harvard Business Press.

Heifetz, R. A., & Heifetz, R. (1994). *Leadership without easy answers.* Harvard University Press.

Herbane, B. (2013). Exploring crisis management in UK small-and medium-sized enterprises. *Journal of Contingencies and Crisis Management*, *21*(2), 82–95. doi:10.1111/1468-5973.12006

Houser, D., Levy, D. M., Padgitt, K., Peart, S. J., & Xiao, E. (2014). Raising the price of talk: An experimental analysis of transparent leadership. *Journal of Economic Behavior & Organization*, *105*, 208–218. doi:10.1016/j.jebo.2014.05.003

Hsu, E. B., Li, Y., Bayram, J. D., Levinson, D., Yang, S., & Monahan, C. (2013). State of virtual reality based disaster preparedness and response training. *PLoS Currents*, **•••**, 5. doi:10.1371/currents.dis.1ea2b2e71237d5337fa53982a38b2aff PMID:23653102

Hunt, J. G. J., Osborn, R. N., & Boal, K. B. (2009). The architecture of managerial leadership: Stimulation and channeling of organizational emergence. *The Leadership Quarterly*, *20*(4), 503–516. doi:10.1016/j.leaqua.2009.04.010

James, E. H., & Wooten, L. P. (2010). *Leading under pressure: From surviving to thriving before, during, and after a crisis.* Routledge Academic.

James, E. H., Wooten, L. P., & Dushek, K. (2011). Crisis management: Informing a new leadership research agenda. *The Academy of Management Annals*, *5*(1), 455–493. doi:10.5465/19416520.2011.589594

Johansson, C., Miller, V. D., & Hamrin, S. (2014). Conceptualizing Communicative Leadership. *Corporate Communications*, *2*(2), 147–165. doi:10.1108/CCIJ-02-2013-0007

Kapucu, N., & Van Wart, M. (2008). Making Matters Worse: An Anatomy of Leadership Failures in Managing Catastrophic Events. *Administration & Society*, *40*(7), 711–740. doi:10.1177/0095399708323143

Katz, J. H., & Miller, F. A. (2013). *Opening doors to teamwork and collaboration: 4 keys that change everything.* Berrett-Koehler Publishers.

Kouzes, O., & Posner, B. (1995). *The leadership challenge.* Jossey-Bass.

Kozasa, E. H., Sato, J. R., Lacerda, S. S., Barreiros, M. A., Radvany, J., Russell, T. A., & Amaro, E. Jr. (2012). Meditation training increases brain efficiency in an attention task. *NeuroImage*, *59*(1), 745–749. doi:10.1016/j.neuroimage.2011.06.088 PMID:21763432

Lant, T. K., & Mezias, S. J. (1990). Managing discontinuous change: A simulation study of organizational learning and entrepreneurship. *Strategic Management Journal*, 147–179.

Laub, J. A. (1999). *Assessing the servant organization: Development of the servant organizational leadership assessment (SOLA) instrument* (Doctoral Dissertation). Florida Atlantic University.

Lerbinger, O. (2012). *The crisis manager: Facing disasters, conflicts, and failures*. Routledge. doi:10.4324/9780203222133

Lichtenstein, B. B., & Plowman, D. A. (2009). The leadership of emergence: A complex systems leadership theory of emergence at successive organizational levels. *The Leadership Quarterly*, *20*(4), 617–630. doi:10.1016/j.leaqua.2009.04.006

Lockwood, N. R. (2005). Crisis management in today's business environment: HR's strategic role. *HR Magazine, 50*(12), 1-10.

Long, B. (2019). *Mindfulness and Leadership: The Lived Experience of Long-term Mindfulness Practitioners*. Proquest Dissertations.

Long, B. (2020a). The Universe's Doorway: Long-Term Mindfulness as a Way to Leadership. In D. Satinder (Ed.), *The Routledge Companion to Mindfulness at Work*. Routledge.

Long, B. (2020b). Mindfulness and Use of Self Better Together. *Organization Development Review, 52*(1).

Lutz, A., Slagter, H. A., Dunne, J. D., & Davidson, R. J. (2008). Attention regulation and monitoring in meditation. *Trends in Cognitive Sciences*, *12*(4), 163–169. doi:10.1016/j.tics.2008.01.005 PMID:18329323

Lvina, E. (2015). The Role of Cross-Cultural Communication Competence: Effective Transformational Leadership Across Cultures. *Jurnal Ilmiah Peuradeun*, *3*(1), 1–18.

Lykins, E. L., & Baer, R. A. (2009). Psychological functioning in a sample of long-term practitioners of mindfulness meditation. *Journal of Cognitive Psychotherapy*, *23*(3), 226–241. doi:10.1891/0889-8391.23.3.226

MacLean, E. L., & Baer, R. A. (2009). Psychological functioning in a sample long-term practitioners of mindfulness meditation. *Journal of Cognitive Psychotherapy*, *23*(3), 226–241. doi:10.1891/0889-8391.23.3.226

Malhotra, Y. (1997). Knowledge management in inquiring organizations. *Proceedings of 3rd Americas Conference on Information Systems, August*, 293-295.

Mariner, W. K., Annas, G. J., & Parmet, W. E. (2009). Pandemic preparedness: A return to the rule of law. *Drexel L. Rev.*, *1*, 341.

McConnell, A., & Drennan, L. (2006). Mission Impossible? Planning and Preparing for Crisis. *Journal of Contingencies and Crisis Management*, *14*(2), 59–70. doi:10.1111/j.1468-5973.2006.00482.x

McDaniel, R. R. Jr. (1997). Strategic leadership: A view from quantum and chaos theories. *Health Care Management Review*, *22*(1), 21–37. doi:10.1097/00004010-199724000-00003 PMID:9058085

McMenamin, J. P. (2009). Pandemic Influenza: Is There a Corporate Duty to Prepare. *Food and Drug Law Journal*, *64*, 69. PMID:19998573

Men, L. R. (2014a). Why leadership matters to internal communication: Linking transformational leadership, symmetrical communication, and employee outcomes. *Journal of Public Relations Research*, *26*(3), 256–279. doi:10.1080/1062726X.2014.908719

Men, L. R. (2014b). Strategic internal communication: Transformational leadership, communication channels, and employee satisfaction. *Management Communication Quarterly*, *28*(2), 264–284. doi:10.1177/0893318914524536

Miller, F. A., & Katz, J. H. (2013). 4 Keys to Accelerating Collaboration. *Core Practices*, *46*(1), 6.

Nadler, D. A., & Shaw, R. B. (1995). Change leadership: Core competency for the twenty-first century. In Discontinuous change: Leading organizational transformation. San Francisco: Jossey-Bass.

Nadler, D. A., & Tushman, M. L. (1990). Beyond the charismatic leader: Leadership and organizational change. *California Management Review*, *32*(2), 77–97. doi:10.2307/41166606

Nadler, D. A., & Tushman, M. L. (1995). Types of organizational change: From incremental improvement to discontinuous transformation. In Discontinuous change: Leading organizational transformation. San Francisco: Jossey-Bass.

Nichols, C., Chatterjee-Hayden, S., & Trendler, C. (2020). Four Behaviors That Help Leaders Manage Crisis. *Harvard Business Review.* Retrieved from https://hbr.org/2020/04/4_behaviorsthat_help_leaders_manage_crisis

Nijkrake, J., Gosselt, J. F., & Gutteling, J. M. (2015). Competing frames and tone in corporate communication versus media coverage during a crisis. *Public Relations Review*, *41*(1), 80–88. doi:10.1016/j.pubrev.2014.10.010

Northouse, P. G. (2016). *Leadership: Theory and Practice* (7th ed.). Sage Publications.

Onyx, J., & Leonard, R. J. (2011). Complex systems leadership in emergent community projects. *Community Development Journal: An International Forum*, *46*(4), 493–510. doi:10.1093/cdj/bsq041

Osborn, R. N., Hunt, J. G., & Jauch, L. R. (2002). Toward a contextual theory of leadership. *The Leadership Quarterly Yearly Review of Leadership*, *13*(6), 797–837. doi:10.1016/S1048-9843(02)00154-6

Parris, D. L., & Peachey, J. W. (2013). A systematic literature review of servant leadership theory in organizational contexts. *Journal of Business Ethics*, *113*(3), 377–393. doi:10.100710551-012-1322-6

Parson, K., Allen, M. P., Alvarado-Little, W., & Rudd, R. (2017). *Health literacy insights for health crises. NAM Perspectives*. Discussion Paper, National Academy of Medicine. doi:10.31478/201707f

Rasheed, Z. (2020). COVID-19 Pandemic is Testing Worlds Leaders. Who's Stepping Up? *Aljazeera.* Retrieved from https://aljazeera.com/news/2020/04/covid-10-pandemic-is-testing-leaders-whos-stepping-up-200402201221844

Reb, J., Narayanan, J., & Chaturvedi, S. (2014). Leading mindfully: Two studies on the influence of supervisor trait mindfulness on employee well-being and performance. *Mindfulness, 5*(1), 36–45. doi:10.100712671-012-0144-z

Reynolds, B., & Quinn, S. C. (2008). Effective communication during an influenza pandemic: The value of using a crisis and emergency risk communication framework. *Health Promotion Practice, 9*(4, suppl), 13S–17S. doi:10.1177/1524839908325267 PMID:18936255

Rochlin, G. I., La Porte, T. R., & Roberts, K. H. (1987). The self-designing high-reliability organization: Aircraft carrier flight operations at sea. *Naval War College Review, 40*(4), 76–92.

Roux-Dufort, C., & Lalonde, C. (2013). Editorial: Exploring the theoretical foundations of crisis management. *Journal of Contingencies and Crisis Management, 21*(1), 1–3. doi:10.1111/1468-5973.12014

Salvatico, R. (2006). Enabling transparent leadership: A small business manager's perspective. *Journal of Management Development, 25*(10), 1018–1020. doi:10.1108/02621710610708658

Scharmer, C. O. (2009). *Theory U: Learning from the future as it emerges.* Berrett-Koehler Publishers
Schneider, B. (1987). The people make the place. *Personnel Psychology, 40*, 437–453.

Shadraconis, S. (2013). Organizational Leadership in Times of Uncertainty: Is Transformational Leadership the Answer? *LUX: A Journal of Transdisciplinary Writing and Research from Claremont Graduate University, 2*(1), 28.

Shear, M. D., Goodnough, A., Kaplan, S., Fink, S., Thomas, K., & Weiland, N. (2020, March 29). The lost month: How the failure to test blinded the U.S. to covid-19. *New York Times*. https://www.nytimes.com/2020/03/28/us/testing-coronavirus-pandemic.html

Shrivastava, P. (1995). Industrial/ environmental crises and corporate social responsibility. *Journal of Socio-Economics, 24*(1), 211–227. doi:10.1016/1053-5357(95)90036-5

Shufutinsky, A. (2019). Tribalism and Clone Theory in New Leaders and the Resulting Degradation of Organizational Culture. *Psychology and Behavioral Science International Journal, 10*(2).

Shufutinsky, A., DePorres, D., Long, B., & Sibel, J. (2020). Shock Leadership Development for the Modern Era of Pandemic Management and Preparedness. *International Journal of Organizational Innovation, 13*(1), 1–23.

Shufutinsky, A., Sibel, J., Murray Hayden, P., Shufutinsky, D., & Cox, R. (2018). Holoportation: The Disruptive Technology that Will Change the Practice of Conflict Analysis and Resolution. *OD Practitioner, 50*(3).

Shufutinsky, A., Sibel, J.R., Beach, A. A., Saraceno, A. J. (2020b). OD for Robots? Industry 4.0, Emerging Technologies, and the Implications on Organizational Talent Acquisition and Development Practices. *Organization Development Journal, 38*(3).

Shufutinsky, A., Sibel, J. R., Long, B., & Kravitz, C. (2020c). *Comparison of Leadership in Large Enterprises During the Whole System Shock of the 2019-2020 Coronavirus Pandemic*. Unpublished Research.

Skolnik, R. L. (2008). *Essentials of global health.* Jones & Bartlett Publishers.

Smallwood, J., & Schooler, J. W. (2015). The science of mind wandering: Empirically navigating the stream of consciousness. *Annual Review of Psychology*, *66*(1), 487–518. doi:10.1146/annurev-psych-010814-015331 PMID:25293689

Stringham, S. (2012). *Strategic leadership and strategic management: Leading and managing change on the edge of chaos*. iUniverse.

Sutton, S. A. (1999). The panda syndrome II: Innovation, discontinuous change and LIS education. *Journal of Education for Library and Information Science*, *40*(4), 247–262. doi:10.2307/40324096

Tang, Y., Ma, Y., Wang, J., Fan, Y., Feng, S., Lu, Q., & Posner, M. I. (2007). Short-term meditation training improves attention and self-regulation. *Proceedings of the National Academy of Sciences of the United States of America*, *104*(43), 17152–17156. doi:10.1073/pnas.0707678104 PMID:17940025

Taylor, V. A., Grant, J., Daneault, V., Scavone, G., Breton, E., Roffe-Vidal, S., & Beauregard, M. (2011). Impact of mindfulness on the neural responses to emotional pictures in experienced and beginner meditators. *NeuroImage*, *57*(4), 1524–1533. doi:10.1016/j.neuroimage.2011.06.001 PMID:21679770

Treverton, G. F., & Jahn, M. (2020). COVID-19: We Had The Warning But We Lacked The Leadership. *The Hill.* Retrieved from https://www.thehill.com/opinion/

Triggs, A., & Kharas, H. (2020). *The Triple Economic Shock of COVID-19 and Priorities for an Emergency G-20 Leaders Meeting*. Brookings Institution.

Tyssen, A. K., Wald, A., & Heidenreich, S. (2014). Leadership in the Context of Temporary Organizations: A Study on the Effects of Transactional and Transformational Leadership on Followers' Commitment in Projects. *Journal of Leadership & Organizational Studies*, *21*(4), 376–393. doi:10.1177/1548051813502086

Uhl-Bien, M., Marion, R., & McKelvey, B. (2007). Complexity leadership theory: Shifting leadership from the industrial age to the knowledge era. *The Leadership Quarterly*, *18*(4), 298–318.

Van Wart, M., & Kapucu, N. (2011). Crisis management competencies: The case of emergency managers in the USA. *Public Management Review*, *13*(4), 489–511.

Walker, S. (2020). Covid-19 Was a Leadership Test. It Came Back Negative. *Wall Street Journal.* Retrieved from https://www.wsj.com/article/great-leaders-are-killjoys-nags-or-neurotics-until-theres-a-pandemic-11584144175

Williams, T. A., Gruber, D. A., Sutcliffe, K. M., Shepherd, D. A., & Zhao, E. Y. (2017). Organizational response to adversity: Fusing crisis management and resilience research streams. *The Academy of Management Annals*, *11*(2), 733–769.

Worley, C. G. (1996). *Integrated strategic change: How OD builds competitive advantage*. Ft Press.

Yukl, G. (2013). *Leadership in organizations* (8th ed.). Upper Saddle River.

Zhang, Z., Jia, M., & Gu, L. (2012). Transformational leadership in crisis situations: Evidence from the People's Republic of China. *International Journal of Human Resource Management*, *23*(19), 4085–4109.

# Chapter 10
# COVID-19 and Leadership:
## Impacts and Responses

**Asma Ayari**
https://orcid.org/0000-0002-2134-0624
*University of Bahrain, Bahrain*

## ABSTRACT

*The main aim of this chapter is to investigate and report the specific personality traits, attitudes, styles of individual leaders, and learning experience of Bahraini leaders during COVID-19. A qualitative study technique used in order to purse the objectives of this research. Semi-directive interviews were conducted with 15 Bahraini leaders from different companies and sectors. The data was analysed and discussed based on themes related to the crisis management and effective leadership style. The results revealed that an exceptional leadership style has emerged in the Bahraini organizational environment to instill confidence and resilience to staff, customers, and external stakeholders during crisis. The findings of the current study will offer a comprehensive framework for effective leadership performance in times of crisis. In addition, the results of this study will be beneficial for the field of gender and culture studies, for instance culture diversification and its relationship with leadership styles.*

## 1. INTRODUCTION

The coronavirus COVID-19 pandemic is the defining global health crisis of our time and the greatest challenge we have faced since the Second World War. Since its emergence in Asia at the end of last year, the virus has spread to all continents, with cases increasing daily in Africa, the Americas and Europe. Countries are struggling to slow the spread of the disease by testing and treating patients, conducting contact searches, restricting travel, quarantining citizens and cancelling large gatherings such as sporting events, concerts and schools. The cases in the world appeared to increase day by day, kingdom of Bahrain was not saved, the virus was confirmed to have reached Bahrain on 21 February 2020. As of 17 September, there have been a total of 62,484 confirmed cases, of which 55,444 have recovered and 217 have died. As of 9 October 2020, Bahrain has the highest number of cases per head of population of any country or territory in the world. A total of 1,288,374 tests were conducted[12]. The pandemic is moving

DOI: 10.4018/978-1-7998-6948-1.ch010

like a wave—one that may yet crash on those least able to cope. But COVID-19 is much more than a health crisis. By stressing every one of the countries it touches, it has the potential to create devastating social, economic and political crises that will leave deep scars[3].

In response to this crisis, Bahrain has set up a committed National Taskforce "Team Bahrain" to handle the spread of the Covid-19 virus and took measures to guarantee that testing and isolated facilities were set up immediately. Bahrain has one of the highest testing rates per capita, obtaining the acknowledgment of the World Health Organization (WHO) for its professional reaction. The Kingdom stands prepared to initiate further actions to avoid the spreading of the virus. Furthermore, the government of Bahrain is supporting individuals and companies through a comprehensive US$11.4 bn economic stimulus package[4].

During crisis and extremis situation, management must continue to provide essential services to society and preserve the jobs of tomorrow (Kolditz & Brazil, 2005). This exceptional situation requires managers a great ability to lead, motivate and manage dispersed teams, whose members can work in extremely heterogeneous and stressful conditions (Kolditz, 2005). *So how do we meet these challenges?*

Different are the researches in which authors identified a consistent pattern of traits, attitudes and behaviours that characterises successful leadership such as staying calm, communication, collaboration, coordination and providing support (Kolditz, 2005). Recently, there is a surging interest for in *extremis* leaders. Defined as situation in which leaders' and followers lives are at high risk (Dixon & Weeks, 2017). Leading in risky and uncertain environments contrasts sharply with doing so under stable and predictable situation. This uncertainty make it difficult for leaders to navigate through event, in order to make timely and effective decisions (Bolman & Deal, 2013). During Covid-19 pandemic, leaders everywhere were forced to face a crisis and preparing all aspects of the crisis scenarios. This also include the challenge of making real-time decisions about their companies and employees and handling the potential of more threats with incomplete information.

This chapter, will focus on the different challenges and managerial responses of Bahraini leaders who have faced Covid-19 crises and have a lived experience worth exploring. This study does not seek to create a framework for administrators, but rather, to offer insight into how Bahraini leaders respond to crisis times, in order to help others to be prepared for the future. In fact, the essence of the human experience offers values to those seeking to be prepared for potential trauma, and how best to approach a high risk situation in the future (Moore, 2018). The study will try to answer the following research questions to better understand the context:

- *What are the impacts of the crisis on the leaders?*
- *and How do the leaders make decisions during Covid-19 crisis?*

## 2. LEADERSHIP IN TIMES OF CRISIS

According to Kargas, & Varoutas (2015), "leadership refers to capabilities of a person that could influence the rest of the group of people to achieve an goal or set of goals". Therefore, "the abilities and competences that a leadership demonstrates to affect a group of people to obtain a vision or a created set of objectives, additionally, leadership is concerning duplicating with transform and vision creation for inspiring individuals" (Cruz-Milán et al., 2016). It is factual to explain that, leadership effectiveness within an organization relies on how individuals perform and act concerning of objectives accomplishment fruitfully, and for this aim, a successful leaders those who are able to provide value, by determining the best suit to the situation (Jong, et al., 2016). Meanwhile, a successful style of leadership targets to determine what the organization's future looks like to be and assist in bringing together individual with leader's vision and affect each individual to achieve organizational vision regardless of the all barriers (Jordan, et al., 2016). Furthermore, the functional method involves that, leadership happens according on four significant actions: ability to adapt the change, being committed to the organization and organizational vision, setting the direction, establishing organizational mission (Lai, et al., 2016). ***But, what about leadership during crisis? How the crisis can impact the leadership style?***

In fact, "crisis is an unpredictable state that disrupts normal operations of the organization and that requires immediate action taking. Crisis cannot be predicted beforehand and they deactivate normal processes, it is required to plan an efficient crisis management" (Fener & Cevik, 2015) and to adopt exceptional style of leadership. So, when the organization encounter a danger or unpredictable event, this requires from the leader a great mental effort to implant confidence and resilience to staff, customers and external stakeholders (Kolditz & Brazil, 2005). During crisis, the organisation encounter chaos and disturbance accompanied with demotivated and confused staff, dissatisfied customers, and negative publicity (AlKnawy, 2018). Leaders make frequently crucial decisions and expect good results in achieving the objective that they have in mind. These decisions are taking to give an order, to solve a problem to manage a crisis or to deal with many ineffective situations. Mostly important is to take the good right decision which is generally linked to leadership in order to deal or to solve any problem or any crisis (Hasan & Rjoub, 2017).

Many researchers recognized that leaders during crisis emphasises specific personality traits, attitudes and styles of individual leadership. In his article "*COVID-19, when leadership calls*", Shingler-Nace (2020) identifies five elements to successful leadership during the crisis such as, firstly *Staying calm.* The leader is considered as a model behaviour and his actions will guide the behaviour, attitudes and the reactions of the followers. Then the communication which can help the employees to perform their jobs and responsibilities. The communication should be pertinent especially during crisis. Leaders must inform managers and employees which can help them to remain confident in their message and decision making. The collaboration is another important trait during crisis. In fact, the members of the organization should participate and work in a committed team. During challenging time coordinating the work efforts is imperative for the success and efficiency of the leader during crisis time. Finally, Shingler-Nace (2020) added the support and mentioned that leaders can use the moment of crisis to hear the customers and support employees which can provide ideas and success.

Moreover, Kolditz (2005) identified also, another consistent pattern of traits, attitudes and behaviours that characterises successful leadership in hazardous situations. The successful leaders in extremis display the following characteristics: they are inherently motivated; they embrace continuous learning; they share risk with their followers; they are not elitist and adopt a lifestyle in common with their followers; and they are highly competent, inspiring trust and loyalty (Kolditz & Brazil, 2005).

Cener (2007) identify different qualifications of leader and managers during crisis management and are stated as below:

- "The ability to catch the signals of crisis.
- Preparation and protection against crisis.
- Efficient decision taking throughout the crisis management process.
- The ability to use power throughout the crisis management process.
- The ability to plan the crisis management process.

- The ability to organize the crisis management process.
- The ability to ensure communication throughout the crisis management process.
- The ability to ensure coordination throughout the crisis management process.
- The ability to supervise the crisis management process.
- The ability to shift to normal state.
- The ability to learn and assess throughout the crisis management process.
- The ability to ensure coordination throughout the crisis management process.
- The ability to supervise the crisis management process.
- The ability to shift to normal state.
- The ability to learn and assess throughout the crisis management process" (Fener & Cevik, 2015, pp. 698-669).

Covid-19 has a negative outcomes on the organizations so the response of the leaders matters.

This chapter has the potential to reflect and view Covid-19 crisis through the lens of 15 Bahrainis managers and leaders and include their decisions, actions and outcomes.

## 3. RESEARCH DESIGN METHODOLOGY

Our inquiry focuses on organizational leadership behaviours exhibited in situation of crisis, such as covid-19. A number of studies addressed how leaders make sense of in extremis environments (Weick & Obstfeld, 2005). The majority of the empirical studies are made and appeared in military journals. These studies focus on how leaders make sense of in extremis situation. What has not been studied in depth, however, is how leaders lead and influence subordinates during extremis conditions. To address this gap in the literature, a qualitative research study was conducted based on semi-structured interview that seek to obtain the knowledge and data that will help to answer the research questions posed. The use of semi-structured, was selected to help guide a naturally emerge in the conversation and allow for deeper thoughts to answer pre-set questions selected to align with the research questions and data being probed (Kvale, 1996; McLeod, 2014). The data was collected and analysed in which, the Bahraini leaders were talking and describing a rich and thick lived experiences during Covid-19 pandemic.

The sample of 15 leaders has been contacted for the purpose of gathering data to target our research objectives and answer our research questions. The criteria were the following: leaders or managers responsible of at least 10 to 15 employees and who have had recent leadership role during the covid-19 pandemic in Bahrain. The leaders were chosen from different industries such as higher education, retail sector, Banks, telecommunication, restaurant and international organizations. When reporting data, and for confidentiality purposes, the names and identity of the interviewees will be changed to a pseudonym that will be used trough the analysis. The demographics are presented in Table 1.

*Table 1. Leaders Demographics*

| Pseudonym | Gender | Age | Marital Status | Educational Level | Position | Sector/Industry | Seniority |
|---|---|---|---|---|---|---|---|
| Hala | Female | 30-39 | Single | Ph.D. | Director of quality assurance | Higher Education | 1-5 years |
| Adam | Male | 40-49 | Married | B.Sc. | Business Owner | Insurance | 6-10 years |
| Karim | Male | 40-49 | Married | Ph.D. | Head of Department | Higher Education | More than 10 years |
| Nawaf | Male | 30-39 | Married | B.Sc. | Business owner | Services | More than 10 years |
| Ahmed | Male | 30-39 | Divorced | B.Sc. | Sales manager | Telecommunication | 6-10 years |
| Mohamed | Male | 40-49 | Married | Ph.D. | director of quality assurance | Higher Education | More than 10 years |
| Mounir | Male | 30-39 | Single | B.Sc. | Business development manager | Gas and Oil | 6-10 years |
| Malek | Male | 30-39 | Married | M.Sc. | Department manager | Bank | 6-10 years |
| Adel | Male | 30-39 | Married | Still earnings M.Sc. | Department manager | Bank | 6-10 years |
| Mohamed | Male | 30-39 | Married | Ph.D. | Head of Department | Higher Education | 1-5 years |
| Khaled | Male | 40-49 | Married | M.Sc. | Business owner | Restaurant | 1-5 years |
| Amal | Female | 30-39 | Single | Ph.D. | Director of quality assurance | Higher Education | More than 10 years |
| Amir | Male | 30-39 | Divorced | M.Sc. | Department manager | Bank | More than 10 years |
| Salman | Male | 30-39 | Married | M.Sc. | Business development manager | Airline company | More than 10 years |
| Huda | Female | 30-39 | Single | Ph.D. | Head of Department | Higher Education | 1-5 years |

All interviews had been conducted with Ms-Teams and Zoom, during the date and time of their convenience within the kingdom of Bahrain and findings of the research will be presented upon request once the study is completed. Interviews were recoded (with the respondents' consent) and then transcribed the verbatim. The transcribed data was then read and re-read again to ensure accuracy. The interviews resulted in extensive textual data, which was analysed using thematic analysis in order to identify similar activities among leaders of different companies and thus understand the overall picture. Template analysis is an effective qualitative research method for an experiential approach. It is a style of thematic analysis that allows a researcher to maintain structure in the method of analysing textual data while adapting it to the need of the study (King, 2012). Meaningful themes related to propositions and objectives were identified which in turn helped in answering our research questions.

## 4. ANALYSIS AND FINDINGS

By analysing the narratives of the 15 Bahraini leaders different categories and themes emerged. Those categories and themes then were compared back to the initial research questions to help explain the phenomena. The themes were combined in three categories: (1) ***the Leader perception of the crisis,*** (2) ***Leaders skills to manage the crisis***, (3) ***Creative and simple decisions***

### 4.1. The Leader Perception of the Crisis

The majority of the leaders (14/15) perceive COVID-19 as a "*problem*", "*crisis*", "*threat*" and "*in extremis situation*", "*an alert*", "*was not expected at all*", "*threat for my company and the economy of Bahrain*".

Leaders faced a complex, risky and unpredictable environment, that is why they should be aware to the context of the organization and detect every change. The Bahraini leaders mentioned that the crisis awareness is '*vital*' and '*a must*'. Moreover, the majority (13/15) of the interviewees consider that taking decision in risky and uncertain environment can be difficult: "*I felt very scared about the decisions I took*", "*I was very worried if my decisions were effective enough or not*". The totality of the Bahraini leaders confirm that leader must be decisive in difficult times: "*the need for taking a decision was the most important activity of the leader*". The speed of the decision was a great concern during the crisis: "*the most difficult part is time to take a decision for a major change or shift in the organization*". Swift action is essential to contain any crisis and its consequences, and a leader must have the confidence to make a calculated decision, keeping in mind that it might not be the 'best' decision as seen by various constituents (AlKnawy, 2018). Making critical decisions during a crisis can feel an almost impossible task: "*my challenge was to make critical decision after the first case of infection detected in the company*"; "*we judged that closure of the company were a must to protect the employees and our customers*". One of the 15 leaders was an owner of a restaurant mentioned that "*closing the restaurant was a radical measure and required high risk because of the impact on our customers and the employees, but it was deemed necessary to contain the outbreak*"; "*at the same time, the importance of managing the impact of the restaurant closure was made clear to our staff*".

One leader consider COVID-19 as an opportunity: "*we have an opportunity due COVID-19 to stop, to review what we are doing and think how to do things better*".

### 4.2. Leaders Skills to Manage the Crisis

The majority (14/15) of the Bahraini leaders identified different skills related to the leadership during covid-19 when answering the question related to the needed skills: *Based on your experience what are the most important skills a leader need it to manage people during Crisis/COVID-19?*

#### 4.2.1. Effective Communication

Communication was recognized by the majority (12/15) of the leaders interviewed as one of the most important skills and tool used to manage crisis. In fact during COVID-19 pandemic the Bahraini government has set up a clear, concise and effective communication program related to the pandemic. All the interviewees declared that Bahraini government communication program was effective compare to other countries and some of them they added that: "*the powerful tool to fight corona virus is a clear communication message*", "*from the first day, the government message was clear and transparent about what happen*". The majority (11/15) of the leaders consider communication is a main tool to "*inform employees*", "*explain what the company is doing*", "*enable feedback*", and "*promote wide-scale consultation and involvement*". Some of the interviewees (4/15) mentioned that an effective communication is a "*powerful way to present complex information during crisis*" and " *a tool to instil confidence and to show that the situation is under control*".

### 4.2.2. Coordination and Support

One of the most important challenges that encounter the leader during the pandemic was coordinate and motivate the employees: "*my most difficult leadership challenge was to motivate the staff to serve the customers well. Indeed, my waiters were too scared to assist any customer considering the fact how the virus can spread* ". Some leaders (6/15) the heads of departments and directors working in higher education institution mentioned when the government and the university started sending students and professors home due to COVID-19 and they start the online classes: "*the real challenge was about how the leader can keep the employees productive while working from home*", " *the swift to remote education was so rapid. I wasn't sure about the effectiveness of the teacher to move from face to face to remote classes*", "*I was wondering about the effectiveness of such an option, are they (students and teachers) ready for the remote education?*". Also, some (7/15) leaders mentioned the support as an important means needed during the pandemic: "*my biggest concern as a leader was to provide support to my employees as their salary is being decreased until the end of the year*", "*I was in a position if giving support to my colleagues and even to the students... Explain to them what worked and what went wrong during the pandemic, to help restore trust in the organisation at the same time making difficult decisions and communicate day to day crisis resolution* ".

### 4.2.3. Emotional Effectiveness

During covid-19 the majority (10/15) of the leaders faced additional stressors: "*during times of crisis, emotions take a more prominent and powerful role; they are harder to ignore*". They also advanced that: " *we have a choice between putting their heads down and ignoring*" or "*dealing with the bad feeling during the pandemic*". They added that: "*an emotionally intelligent leader can completely handle a crisis*". One of the interviewees, a manager in an airlines company, highlighted that: "*these aren't normal circumstances, but as a leader, I have to effectively manage my teams, deal with the work changes.... Social and emotional competencies are well to manage during this pandemic* ".

However, a minority (4/15) of leaders mentioned that is harder to ignore bad emotions and stress during times of crisis: "*I have to understand, face and recognize* ". They added that an effective leader should support the subordinates to cope effectively with bad emotions during crisis and enable them to achieve high performance: "*leaders are putting under test during crisis situation that arise without warming* ".

One of the leaders mentioned that time was an important factor to react and take decision and not to manage the bad feelings related to the pandemic: " *I don't have time to feel bad or miserable*", "*these bad feelings was not effective at a time when we need to be on top of the game, resourceful, supportive, and innovative*".

### 4.3. Creative and Simple Decisions

The majority of the leaders (14/15) advanced that during crisis: "*it is natural that people get stuck in detail and complexity when debating solutions*", "*the managers try to make the best and the most creative decision and to understand the critical details from various aspects*". However, they mentioned that: "is not a must to be interested to get sank in small details". There is widespread agreement among the majority (13/15) of the leaders should instead of getting engaged with operational decision making should have only "*think about the bigger picture*" and only concern themselves with "*strategic issues*".

They advanced that the decisions must be: "*pragmatic, simple and effective solution*". One of the interviewees describe how his decision regarding closing his restaurant and starting home delivery food was simple decision: ""*as the decision for companies closure was taken, there was much debate among my employees about how best to serve our customers; many suggestions were put forward, increasing in complexity. However, a simple, effective solution that had not been considered in the midst of the detail was to simply move to home delivery*" .

Creativity was also mentioned by some (6/15) of the leaders. They advanced that during crisis they "*overcome the disruptive noise of a crisis with creative thinking*". They also add that Covid-19 pandemic boost their creativity and help them to break old rules and focus better on the problem: "*we're all facing a collective crisis like COVID-19....old rules are obsolete...we should think outside the book... the problem to be solved is very well-defined... new creative decisions are made under these pressures*". A female leader remarqued that: "*all the unpleasantly emotions such as anxiety and depression should be used to fight.... with your brain, technical skills, and emotional skills, not your fists..... then the crisis-related fear you feel is experienced as less unpleasant*".

## 5. CONCLUSION: EXCEPTIONAL LEADERSHIP IN TIMES OF CRISIS

Our work has implications for both scholarship and practice, it also have implications for both future research and practice regarding leadership during crisis. This chapter offered a number of future research directions and a comprehensive research agenda for scholars interested in crisis and crisis management (Bundy, et al., 2017). Actually, while the COVID-19 pandemic has had a negative impact, it also represents an opportunity which provide day after day Bahraini leaders with an opportunity to redeem themselves by demonstrating their leadership qualities. An exceptional leadership arise during Covid-19. During the covid-19 leaders use core of competencies to manage crisis in a relevant and adequate way. The majority of the leaders agree about a group of skills related to exceptional leadership managing the crisis such as effective communication, emotions coping strategies and taking simple and creative decisions. Communicating effectively in risk circumstances like the coronavirus epidemic requires from leaders to pay attention to objective indicators and is not enough to consider only objective information, leaders should give a lot of attention to perceptions (Fener & Cevik, 2015). Speed of the decision making is also important because time can erode into the organisation's desire to make changes (Bolman & Deal, 2013). Then the majority of leaders advanced that during the pandemic is important to understand that risks brings fears, and fear is a very strong emotion, leaders should take an approach of addressing the crisis and to be really empathetic, be a good listener, be aware to implement a best communication channels (Wang, 2008). Finally, leader should learn from the crisis by optimally addressing challenges and opportunities during crisis.

## REFERENCES

AlKnawy, B. (2018). Leadership in times of crisis. *BMJ Leader, 3*(1), 1–5. doi:10.1136/leader-2018-000100

Bolman, L., & Deal, T. (2013). Reframing organizations: Artistry, choice, and leadership (5th ed.). Hoboken, NJ: John Wiley & Sons.

Bundy, J., Pfarrer, M. D., & Coombs, W. T. (2017). Crises and Crisis Management: Integration, Interpretation, and Research Development. *Journal of Management, 43*(6), 1661–1692. doi:10.1177/0149206316680030

Cener, P. (2007). *Crisis management*. Academic Press.

Dixon, D. P., & Weeks, M. R. (2017). Leading in Extremis Situations: how can leaders improve? In Leadership in Extreme Situations. doi:10.1007/978-3-319-55059-6_14

Fener, T., & Cevik, T. (2015). Leadership in crisis management: Separation of leadership executive concepts. *Procedia Economics and Finance, 26*, 695–701. doi:10.1016/S2212-5671(15)00817-5

Hasan, A., & Rjoub, H. (2017). The role of effective leadership styles in crisis. *International Journal of Economics, Commerce and Management, 5*(4), 107-121.

King, N. (2012). *Doing template analysis. Qualitative organizational research: Core*. Academic Press.

Kolditz, T. A. (2005). The in Extremis Leader. In *Leader to leader* (pp. 6–18). John Wiley.

Kolditz, T. A., & Brazil, D. M. (2005). Authentic Leadership in In Extremis Settings: A Concept for Extraordinary Leaders in Exceptional Situations. In Monographs in Leadership and Management. Authentic Leadership Theory and Practice: Origins, Effects and Development. Elsevier.

Moore, M. (2018). *Leadership under fire: A Phenomenological Study of Senior Administrator's Perceived Leadership Identity and Crisis Response at Higher Education Institutions in the United States*. Fisher Digital Publications.

Shingler-Nace, A. (2020). COVID-19 when leadership calls. *Nurse Leader, 18*(3), 202–203.

Wang, J. (2008). Developing Organizational Learning Capacity in Crisis Management. *Advances in Developing Human Resources, 10*, 425–445.

Weick, k. & Obstfeld, D., 2005. Organization and the process of sensemaking. *Organ Sci, 16*(4), 409-421.

## ENDNOTES

1 *Johns Hopkins CSSE. "Coronavirus COVID19 (2019-nCoV)" (ArcGIS). Coronavirus COVID-19 Global Cases. Retrieved 18 September 2020.*

2 *"Coronavirus COVID-19 - Summary of cases"* Ministry of Health. *Retrieved 10 September 2020.*

3 https://www.asia-pacific.undp.org/content/rbap/en/home/coronavirus.html

4 https://home.kpmg/xx/en/home/insights/2020/04/bahrain-government-and-institution-measures-in-response-to-covid.html

# Chapter 11
# New Challenges for Leading the Change for the Psychological Consequences of Pandemics:
## Workplace Loneliness, Work Alienation, and Spiritual Well-Being in the Post-COVID-19 Era

**Mehmet Çetin**
*Istanbul Sabahattin Zaim University, Turkey*

## ABSTRACT

*With the needs for change and adaptation brought by the COVID-19 pandemic, management of the concerns regarding workplace loneliness, work alienation, and spiritual well-being stands as a critical challenge for the organizations. Although these concepts are not new and have increasingly been a focus of attention in recent decades, contemporary radical changes in work methods and work concept such as increased use of technology, digitalization, social distancing at work, and virtual working make them much more crucial for the success of organizations. The purpose of this chapter is to address adverse psychological work-related outcomes of the pandemic and provide practical implications and recommendations for leaders for effective management of the processes regarding these outcomes during and after the pandemic.*

## INTRODUCTION

In addition to the economic, social, psychological and health related adverse effects of the pandemic that spillover to work life; individuals also directly face various changes regarding the work itself. Pandemic has been affecting every aspect of life, as well, it reshapes the work domain. Compulsory changes in the methods and conditions of work formed by the Covid-19 Pandemic, such as distance working, increased use of technology and social distancing bring new challenges for leaders regarding the human side of the

DOI: 10.4018/978-1-7998-6948-1.ch011

organization. Psychological consequences of the drastic changes brought by the pandemic necessitate special concern and leadership effort addressing employee well-being. With the new normal and new order of work, employees are more prone to loneliness, alienation and spiritual wellbeing related problems and the need for effective management of such concerns is crucial during and after the pandemic.

To cope with the fast spread of the virus and increasing numbers of cases, policymakers all around the world had to implement strict psychical distancing interventions. Although social distancing policies such as stay at home orders are one of the most popular and effective ways for combating the fast spread of the virus, they have adverse effects on psychological wellbeing as they significantly boost worries, anxiety and loneliness (Tull et al., 2020). Even when the lockdown is not coercive (mild lockdown) it causes high levels of loneliness, poor interpersonal relationships, psychological distress and depression (Morin & Carrier, 2020; Yamamoto et al., 2020). Some professionals suggest that the pandemic is creating a 'parallel pandemic' of psychological disorders regarding stress, sleep, depression and even suicide (Mucci, Mucci & Diolaiuti, 2020, p.63).

New conditions brought by the pandemic threatens the spiritual wellbeing of employees and elevate their alienation levels which in turn cause psychological adversities and negative performance outcomes at individual and organizational levels. This chapter aims to analyze the antecedents and consequences of contemporary organizational behavior concepts related to the possible consequences of the Covid-19 Pandemic. Specifically, concerns regarding workplace loneliness, work alienation and spiritual well-being are addressed. Although these concepts are relatively new and the contemporary conditions paving the way for them are unique, they have been a central concern for leaders to sustain healthy organizations. Another purpose of the study is to provide practical recommendations and insights for leaders for effective management of the change and necessary processes regarding these variables during and after the pandemic.

## BACKGROUND

Although there are numerous studies addressing the psychological effects of the pandemic (e.g. Akat & Karataş, 2020; Cullen, Gulati & Kelly, 2020; Sood, 2020; Zheng, Miao & Gan, 2020) few specifically address the reflections of them in the workplace (e.g. Kaushik & Guleria, 2020). In addition, the scopes of most of these studies are more specific such as health care professionals (as they are in the frontline in the combat with the pandemic). Understanding the effects of the pandemic on the work domain is very crucial. Work has always been a central theme in human's life. Most of the quality time in daily life is spent in the workplace or while doing work related activities. What we do, what we know, what we become are mostly linked with and grounded on work. Changes in work spillover to other life domains and radical changes in other life domains affect work related variables (Kirchmeyer, 1992; Leiter & Durup, 1996; Sirgy et al., 2001).

Work stands as a major resource to attain and answer human needs. It serves as a source for basic survival needs in the Maslow's Hierarchy of Needs (Maslow, 1954) as well as higher order needs such as affiliation, esteem and self-actualization. For food, for health, for rent, we earn through work. Work provides safety and security not only through providing money for accommodation, but also through the sense of having a role and place in society; identifying with a group, organization or institution and having a sustainable order in life. Workplace also serves as a foundation where employees socialize with their colleagues. For many individuals, after a certain age and as the career pressure and workload increase, their colleagues remain as one of the most important sources of companionship and social affiliation that they can spend sufficient time to know and socialize with.

Work experience is an essential source of meaning. Changes in the work concept affect the perceptions and attitudes regarding the meaning of life. Rosso, Dekas, & Wrzesniewski (2010) emphasize the increasing importance of 'meaning of work' as it is an antecedent of various organizational outcomes. With the conditions of the pandemic, radical changes in the underlying factors that form the meaning of work should be revisited. Employee's interpersonal relations and experiences with others (coworkers, groups, leaders) in the workplace are significant sources of meaning in work (Rosso, Dekas, & Wrzesniewski, 2010) which are highly affected by the pandemic.

Considering the aforementioned links regarding human motivation, meaning and work, the new normal may not be 'normal' for human phyco-social needs. Distance working will change the cohesiveness, organizational climate and frequency of face-to-face interaction, which will obstruct the actualization of such needs and in turn boost the loneliness and alienation levels of employees and threaten their spiritual wellbeing.

## PSYCHOLOGICAL OUTCOMES OF PANDEMIC

### Loneliness and Workplace Loneliness

Loneliness stands as one of the most significant problems regarding the effects of the pandemic especially for older adults (Berg-Weger & Morley, 2020). Most of the activities people frequently attend for fun and socializing such as sports games, theaters, concerts, festivals or events for big family gatherings such as weddings, traditional ceremonies etc. are canceled due to pandemic. People isolating themselves and canceling social companionship reluctantly decrease the social support that they could get from others and increase their levels of loneliness. Some scholars refer to Covid-19 as the "loneliness virus" (Odekerken-Schröder et al., 2020). A comprehensive study conducted in the UK revealed that the level of loneliness during the pandemic is critically high that necessitates considering loneliness as a significant public health problem (Groarke et al., 2020). Considering the possible outcomes of loneliness, this stands as a serious threat for individuals and organizations. Loneliness and social isolation can cause serious problems regarding physical and psychological health, it can even increase mortality (Holt-Lunstad et al., 2015).

Workplace loneliness can be defined as the "perceived lack of quality relationships" employees have in the workplace (Wright, Burt & Strongman, 2006, p.60). Employees not eating together, not celebrating special occasions together, not visiting each other's offices for small talks or not using the same transportation to work will have less informal interaction. It will certainly serve as a new challenge for leaders to sustain quality interpersonal relationships among employees given the decreased level of social interaction and face to face communication.

### Spiritual Well-Being

Individuals also seek meaning and calling through work. Spirituality in the workplace has been a focus of attention for the last two decades. Religions or belief systems attribute large importance to work (Çetin, 2019). Spiritual well-being can be defined as a positive state where individuals experience "a sense of identity, wholeness, satisfaction, joy, contentment, beauty, love, respect, positive attitudes, inner peace and harmony, and purpose and direction in life" through the integration of positive cognitions regarding the self, others and the environment (Gomez & Fisher, 2003, p.1976). Where people seek for, achieve and feel most of the concepts in the given definition is the workplace. Individuals identify with their teams, colleagues or organizations and experience belongingness to larger groups in the workplace. Work serves a significant role in the self-concept. For many individuals, work serves as the central course where they can reflect their potentials, skills and effort and get recognition for them. What people often praise themselves about is mostly something directly or indirectly linked with their jobs; their salary, their position, promotion, achievement etc. Work satisfaction is directly and significantly linked with life satisfaction (Rice, Near & Hunt, 1980). The conditions imposed by the pandemic create significant changes in the concept and methods of work and threaten the aforementioned components of spiritual wellbeing. Employees experience lower levels of job satisfaction (Said & El-Shafei, 2020; Zhang et al., 2020); and occupational status, calling, and meaning in jobs are being reshaped with the pandemic (Kramer & Kramer 2020). Meaning in life and life satisfaction are negatively associated with Covid-19 related stress (Trzebiński, Cabański & Czarnecka, 2020).

Numerous studies address the dichotomy or conceptual links of spirituality and religion (e.g. Benefiel, Fry & Geigle, 2014; Lazenby, 2010 and Pesut et al., 2008). Although they are conceptually different, the concepts are also often used interchangeably (Tanyi, 2002). Religion differs from spirituality with its systematic, more precise principles and rituals and practices (Hill et al., 2000). Work serves as an important source and nest for spirituality. Spirituality at work has been a focus of attention among scholars in the last decades (Dan, 1999; Joelle & Coelho, 2019; Sachdeva, 2019). Ashmos and Duchon (2000) define workplace spirituality with three components: A sense of community that people feel connected with others, meaningful and purposeful work that creates a calling and inner life that employees can express and reflect their being to work. Studies addressing the consequences of spirituality at work emphasize its importance for employee wellbeing and organizational performance (Chawla & Guda, 2010; Garg, 2017; Jurkiewicz & Giacalone, 2004; Karakas, 2010; Walia, 2018). Workplace spirituality also associates with other variables that are the focus of this chapter. Lack of workplace spirituality can yield to workplace loneliness which in turn increases turnover intention (Ghadi, 2017).

Working from distance results in less time spent with colleagues and lower levels of experience of the workplace. Employee gatherings, work rituals, ceremonies and friendships in the workplace as well as the daily routine experienced together are critical sources for the belongingness and identification with the organization and its psychological components. The absence of belongingness to a larger group (Perlman and Peplau, 1981) or lack of experience of emotional closeness (Weiss, 1973) are the fundamental pillars of loneliness. Measures taken for the prevention of the virus transmission canceled or decreased these kinds of social events and resources of cohesion. Higher levels of feedback from the work itself and the interested parties such as customers and superiors are available in face to face workplace interactions where people can engage in relationships without concerns for virus transmission. When the work and all communication regarding the work are carried to digital platforms, the level of interaction with the organization and the people in it decreases to a minimum. Thus, significant sources and components of spiritual wellbeing regarding human interaction are reduced. Today, even when the work relationship is not virtual, keeping the social distance or planning meetings as short as possible with fewer people is crucial. Working with reduced numbers of people in the offices in the rotation is also common which again reduces quality human interaction.

The transportation between workplace and home is another important experience that can have significant effects on individuals' psychological states regarding the work and personal life. In big cities where that experience can take more than hours a day, it becomes a critical life event that its effects on wellbeing cannot be ignored. Employees using work shuttles spend a significant amount of time together in a less formal setting, which is an opportunity for further socializing. Employees walking from home to public transportation points experience the same neighborhood every day which can create an identity and belongingness to the close neighborhood and the people in it. Individuals come across various kinds of people from every segment of the society in public transportation vehicles. Although spending time in traffic can be stressful, individuals develop daily routines like listening to their favorite radio show or chatting with friends. Decreased levels of work home transportation experience due to pandemic can save time and effort for employees but on the other hand it can be another source of increased loneliness and alienation. Lack of healthy and satisfying social companionship can directly and indirectly affect the work outcomes. Being away from the coworkers can bring psychological adversities at the individual level which in turn can result in organizational outcomes. Empirical evidence demonstrates that colleague isolation can even significantly decrease employee performance (Chen & Kao, 2012).

### Work Alienation

A parallel negative psychological outcome of the pandemic is alienation. With extreme uncertainties and disrupted comfort zones, individuals feel more powerless and less in control of what is happening in their lives in difficult times such as pandemics. They are more prone to hopelessness and apathy and lack of social direction (Menon, Padhy & Pattnaik, 2020). This general psychological state reflects work behaviors and attitudes and elevates the levels of work alienation. Work alienation refers to a state where employees are disengaged from work due to decreased levels of meaning and increased levels of isolation (Hirschfeld & Feild, 2000). When people introduce themselves to others one of the first things that usually come up is their jobs and positions. Work is an essential source of meaning, connection with the world and self-identification. Pandemic, by bringing major concerns regarding the health of individuals and their loved ones, affects the centrality of work and its meaning. It also increases the level of isolation which has been already high in our modern world (Hwang et al., 2020). Uncertainties regarding the work and the compulsory changes in working methods affect the feelings of control and sense of direction in life.

Work alienation can be conceptualized as psychologically distancing one's self from the work (Kanungo, 1979. p.131). Spending less time in the workplace with colleagues and all environmental factors can keep them distant from the work concept also psychologically. The concept of work does not only consist of the tasks and duties individuals perform daily, but it also includes the experience employees have with their coworkers, superiors and customers. Even the physical interior (the garden, restaurant, office, etc.) stands as a factor that creates the picture of work concept when individuals think about their job. Being away from the workplace significantly alters the psychological experiences of individuals.

## ADVANTAGES AND DISADVANTAGES OF DISTANCE WORKING

Remote work, distance working, or virtual work have been the focus of attention as flexible and outside the workplace working styles became increasingly more popular in the last two decades. Studies addressing the consequences of such working systems, before the Covid-19 pandemic, can enlighten the way how organizations can benefit from the advantages and avoid the disadvantages of new working conditions shaped by the pandemic.

There are potential advantages of distance working that leaders can use for higher productivity and employee wellbeing. Findings of Diab-Bahman & Al-Enzi (2000) demonstrate that majority (68% to 86%) of the employees enjoy the flexibility of work hours, more quality time with their families, and feels more productive with the remote working style that is formed with the pandemic. More to that, they expect changes regarding the old work conditions after the pandemic. Leaders will be required to reshape the conventional ways of working in a hybrid new method where employees will continue to enjoy the autonomy and work-life balance and also benefit from the sources that being in the workplace provides.

Although there are possible advantages of teleworking such as higher flexibility and autonomy, it also brings disadvantages such as the conflict between work-family roles, social isolation and lack of social support (Tavares, 2017). Given the psychical distance and isolation from the workplace and colleagues organizational identification is more difficult to achieve and sustain status for employees and leaders working remotely. Although enabling working from home increases employee morale in general, its commonly neglected psychological side (increased isolation and loneliness) necessitates leaders to take important precautions (Kaushik & Guleria, 2020).

One disadvantage of distance working is increased levels of technology usage and online time. Wrong conceptualization and understanding of the technology can bring alienation (Heidegger, 1954). Thus, we should develop the right ways and approaches to utilize technology for benefiting its advantages for positive consequences. Changing the nature of the work due to increased digitalization creates critical outcomes regarding the wellbeing of employees in the organizations. We already experience various psychological, individual and organizational consequences of high technology usage at work (Öge, Çetin & Top; 2018).

## SOLUTIONS AND RECOMMENDATIONS

Returning to the workplace after the pandemic is a complex and multifaceted matter that entails careful management of many aspects of human life such as social, psychological and organizational domains (Shaw et al., 2020). Organizations are responsible for the health and wellbeing of their employees. During this demanding process, they need to both adapt policies for protecting their employees from the virus and also save them from the negative externalities of these policies (Bouziri et al., 2020).

Although pandemic drastically increased the level of distance working, research on the consequences of such working style was already a center of attention before the pandemic as growing numbers of organizations were utilizing forms of remote working. Extant studies addressing the psychological wellbeing of employees who are working remotely can illuminate the way to cope with the possible disadvantages of distance working. A study conducted on information technology employees revealed that organizational policies, communication and organizational climate are critical determinants of the psychological wellbeing of employees that are working remotely (Prasad et al., 2020). Habits and daily normal activities change during the pandemic and this change yields to wellbeing related problems. More time spent in front of the screen, decreased physical activity and unhealthy eating boost psychological problems such as depression anxiety and loneliness (Mata et al., 2020).

Although online substitutions for the daily activities that people used to have before the pandemic can serve as a solution to mitigate the adverse effects of social isolation (Galea, Merchant & Lurie, 2020) longer times online, or in front of the screen and prolonged sitting can also yield to negative outcomes (Cooley, Pedersen & Mainsbridge, 2014; Foerster et al., 2019; Laconi, Tricard & Chabrol, 2015). Exercise and increased physical activity are recommended as key solutions for rebalancing mental wellbeing during the pandemic (Matias, Dominski & Marks, 2020). Organizations can encourage physical activity and provide online support for staging opportunities that are enabling regular collective exercise with colleagues. This way, employees may both benefit from physical activity and socializing with their coworkers.

The levels of social support and quality human interaction are affected by the pandemic. Friendship in the workplace is a significant source of social support (Berman, West & Richter, 2002). Workplace loneliness forms as a state of emotion characterized by negative feelings sourcing from isolation, lack of social support and quality relationships with others in the organization (Wright, Burt, & Strongman, 2006). Although employees maintain their friendships, inevitably the level of interaction and social companionship decrease due to distancing and isolation. Telecommunication cannot entirely substitute the role of face to face interactions in the workplace. Employees who were able to decrease their stress levels by talking about their daily problems to their colleagues now need to be supported by other channels and sources. One possible solution to decreased levels of social support can be teleconsultation that organizations facilitate their employees for listening to their problems and concerns (Bouziri et al., 2020). Employees' need for affiliation and their perceptions regarding social support are the antecedents of organizational identification in virtual work settings (Wiesenfeld, Raghuram & Garud, 2001). Leaders should give a special effort to ensure that employees get sufficient social support during the pandemic. This can be achieved through quality leader-member exchange and sustained informal relationships among employees.

Informal relationships in the workplace are important for organizational attitudes such as organizational commitment, job satisfaction and intention to leave (Akila & Priyadarshini, 2018; Lopes Morrison, 2005). Organizations should develop methods and policies to support informal interpersonal relationships in the organization to decrease the adverse effects of a decreased level of social interaction between employees on organizational attitudes. For this, organizations should benefit from the positive impact of support from colleagues as well as leadership support. Peer support is very crucial for mitigating loneliness during the pandemic (Joensen et al., 2020). Kaushik & Guleria (2020) recommend some organizational practices to combat the loneliness and isolation brought by the conditions of the pandemic. Platforms that employees can use for socializing, such as weekly social meetings, online celebrations for special days of employees and gamification of the work that would enhance sharing and friendly competition among employees are listed among these practices (p.12).

New conditions shaped by the pandemic require employees to be more creative and proactive. Unique problems in this unique process require unique solutions. Customer contact and expectations necessitate more flexibility and responsiveness. Extra role behaviors become more critical as the roles and job definitions are fuzzy due to the radical changes brought by the pandemic. Thus, employees need more resources and leadership support to cope with these new demands. On the other hand, pandemic also threatens the psychological resources of employees and the quality of the leader-member interaction that they can experience. Leader-member exchange (LMX), which can be defined as the nature of the expectations and experiences of a leader and a follower regarding each other's roles (Dansereau, Graen and Haga, 1975) is a significant determinant on organizational variables that is also being reshaped by the pandemic. Workplace loneliness is an antecedent for the quality of the leader-member relationship and extra-role behaviors (Lam & Lau, 2012). It is significantly and negatively associated with LMX and creativity (Peng et al., 2017). Although the general stream of findings demonstrates a negative relationship between LMX and loneliness; Anand, & Mishra (2019) provided evidence for a positive association between the concepts indicating that so much of LMX can be detrimental for employee loneliness and the link between the two concepts is complex. This emphasizes the importance of the management of leader-member exchange in this unique process.

Another important component of healthy and effective management of the transition processes during the pandemic is effective communication of the right information. Misinformation in the media and social media can have a significant adverse effect on individuals' psychological responses to the pandemic. Organizations should acknowledge the contemporary popular media and make necessary declarations and corrections of information regarding the work that would decrease the concerns and fears of employees. Farooq, Laato & Islam (2020)'s findings demonstrate that frequent use of social media, Cyberchondria and information overload shape individuals' perceptions and behaviors regarding self-isolation. Since pandemic decreased the frequency of human interaction, informal channels of communication in the workplace, which have been serving as a reliable source of information for many employees are now closed or depleted. Organizations need to substitute this channel and source of information to provide employees with the feeling that they are included and aware of the processes of the organization. Lack of information or gaps in the communication can easily be replaced with misinformation that can lead to increased uncertainty and anxiety. Thus, the management of information and effective communication is very important in this process.

Work home interference and work–life balance are other important variables that organizations should manage effectively during and after the pandemic. Work to family conflict and family to work conflict as well as work to family enrichment and family to work enrichment will be more critical determinants for organizational and individual outcomes with the new order of working conditions as employees spend much more time at home compared to pre-pandemic life. Evidence shows that work schedule, dependency on supervisor and workload are antecedents for work-home interference, which is an antecedent for significant work and general health outcomes (Geurts, Rutte & Peeters, 1999). Although distance working seems more enabling for creating own work time schedule, it also blurs the boundaries between work and private time. The concept of working hours is evolving to a much fuzzy term for many employees who had certain work hours before the pandemic. The working hours might have been much clear for employees that had already been working distance (before the pandemic) but for most of the employees and managers, who compulsorily started to work from distance, the concept of working hours and non-working hours remain unclear after the pandemic. As employees are not always online during the normal work hours it is somehow more expected for the employees to answer for work related issues outside the regular work hours. In most of the countries around the world, schools and kindergartens were closed or decreased their working days or even they were still serving some parents did not want to send their children because of the pandemic. Parents needed to take care of their children during the day and satisfy all their social and educational needs. Thus, if there were no others to help in the house, which was also not convenient because of the social distancing measures, parents had to multifunction simultaneously with work and their children. Especially, parents with little children and small houses experienced difficulties engaging in online meetings with their microphones and cameras on because it is was not quite possible to be sure about interruptions. More effort and time were expected from women regarding taking care of the children and dealing with the housework which yielded to a gender gap in perceived productivity and satisfaction levels during the pandemic (Feng & Savani, 2020).

Leaders should acknowledge the possible increase in work-home interaction and the gender gap regarding this interference and take the necessary precautions. Groarke et al., (2020) emphasize the need for interventions especially addressing young adults. Demographic variables such as gender, marital status and age become more important for considering the possible effects of the pandemic on employees. For instance, the psychological effects of isolation are more severe on single individuals as it is less convenient for them to find familial social support (Gao & Sai, 2020). Considering the fact that an increasing number of people today live in large cities away from their families and more people chose to remain single; this information becomes prominent.

Empirical evidence demonstrates that work alienation is significantly related with job characteristics (autonomy, feedback, skill variety) and leadership (Banai, Reisel, & Probst, 2004). Transformed work conditions due to pandemic can have significant effects on perceived job characteristics. Leadership efforts are determinative on how these characteristics will be shaped during and after the pandemic. For instance, distance working can increase the levels of autonomy that employees experience as they are on their own without being physically close to their managers. On the other hand, managers can use these conditions as an excuse for their micromanagement. Keeping track of the work processes without causing employees to feel that they are closely and constantly under control is more complex and difficult with digitalized working methods. One condition that employees frequently complain about the changing work conditions during the pandemic is being under closer control and having less autonomy. Wiesenfeld, Raghuram & Garud (2001) emphasize the need for training employees for the difficulties of virtual work and frequent communication through weekly meetings where employees can freely exchange their experiences and concerns. Other important matters they underline are the pressure that employees feel about being forced to appear at the office more frequently and micromanagement.

Employees address the increasing demands in their lives with their resources (Demerouti et al., 2001). Individual resources, along with the social support, are essential to cope with increased demands and challenges brought by the pandemic. Enhancing and supporting psychological capacities and resources of the employees during and after this demanding period can augment the efficacy and mitigate the adverse effects of the pandemic. Emotional intelligence serves as a moderator for the effects of pandemic on employee wellbeing and training and interventions addressing the enhancement of emotional intelligence can support employees in coping more effectively with the possible burden of the pandemic (Issa & Jaleel, 2020). Investing in the psychological capital of employees can also serve as a useful policy to carry the organizations out from this pandemic safe and successful with their members. By its nature, psychological capital is manageable and malleable (Luthans, Luthans & Luthans, 2004) it can serve as an effective resource for combating the stress levels of employees (Avey, Luthans & Jensen, 2009). Individual differences such as the need for affiliation become less effectual on employees' organizational identification if they perceive high levels of organizational social support (Wiesenfeld, Raghuram & Garud, 2001).

Effects of the pandemic on some employees can be more serious in accordance with the severity of their experiences during this challenging process. Employees that faced serious health problems themselves or in their family members, have major economic problems or lost their loved ones can be more prone the enduring negative effects. Posttraumatic stress disorder (PTSD), a psychological condition that source from severe stressful experiences, has long-lasting effects on employee wellbeing as well as on their work behaviors, performance and interpersonal dynamics (Williams & Williams, 2020). Given the radical changes and major stressors brought by the pandemic number of employees suffering from PTSD will be a significant challenge for the organizations and leaders in the post-pandemic era. Williams & Williams (2020) list some prevention and coping approaches and practices that organizations can adopt to mitigate the adverse effects of PTSD on employee wellbeing and performance. Disaster planning, empathetic leadership, mental health literacy initiatives, and employee assistance programs can be used for preventing the antecedents and coping with the consequences of PTSD (p.24).

## CONCLUSION

The covid-19 pandemic has been crucially affecting every aspect of our lives. Directly and indirectly, pandemic reshapes the work life, as well as it transforms other life domains. Social, economic and psychological changes that every individual faces in daily life spillover to the work domain (Champoux, 1978; Crouter,1984). Employees naturally reflect their negative experiences and psychological states to workplace. New methods of working and all changes that the pandemic brought to the work life also directly reform the work concept. Especially, psychological outcomes of the pandemic have long-lasting effects on individuals that require change and special leadership concern. This chapter focuses on the change and possible managerial practices regarding workplace loneliness, work alienation and spiritual well-being, which will be significant determinants for organizational effectiveness in the post-Covid-19 era. *Figure 1* provides a model depicting a summary of the antecedents and moderators for the work related psychological outcomes of the pandemic. The model indicates that the reshaped work conditions due to the pandemic are potential antecedents for psychological outcomes and leadership and managerial practices can serve as moderators forming this association. Effective leadership and right practices can mitigate potentially adverse effects of a new working style and even can benefit from its advantages.

Organizations need to manage organizational processes with the awareness of their responsibility for the wellbeing of employees. As the demands arising from the conditions of this difficult period increase, possible supplies that employees have, continuously deplete. How work answers to our needs change in these challenging times. Considering the relationship between employee needs and work through the perspective of McClelland's Social Needs Theory (McClelland, 1987) can depict a picture that enables us to see the effects of pandemic from a different perspective. Where individuals gather and use most of the power is the workplace. One of the most important places where people affiliate with others and larger entities is work. Work also serves as a source of achievement and recognition as where individuals compete and achieve is mostly the work. Most of the quality time in our lives is spent in the workplace. A major source of the experiences of autonomy is work. Analyzing the changes brought by pandemic through the ways it changed how employees obtain their social needs can further enlighten the understanding of the adverse outcomes and possible ways to combat with them. New ways and conditions of working can be more challenging for satisfying the need for affiliation. Conditions of the pandemic significantly decreased human companionship and the quality time experienced in the workplace with the members of the organization which make feeling identification and affiliation much more difficult. New working methods may be more enabling for the need for autonomy as increasing numbers of employees are working from distance. New conditions may give employees more freedom for reflecting their preferences and choices on their methods of working as they are usually alone at home or with decreased numbers of people at work with more distance. Still, this can also give managers an excuse to exercise higher supervision or micromanagement. For the needs for power, feeling less in control of what is happening regarding the work can cause higher levels of powerlessness which is a dimension for alienation. For this, leaders should implement new ways of keeping employees informed and included in work processes. The need for achievement in this challenging period requires leaders to establish well-designed feedback mechanisms that will ensure feelings of recognition.

*Figure 1. The model for the antecedents and moderators of the work-related psychological outcomes of the pandemic*

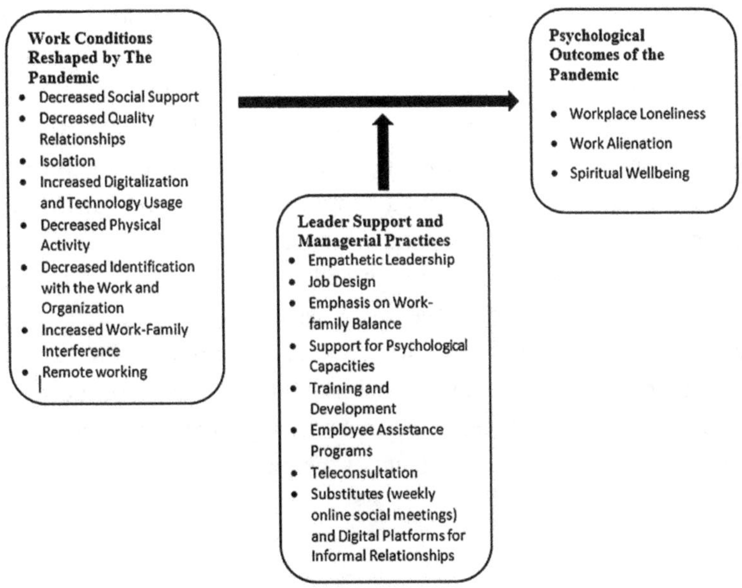


The change regarding increased levels of distance working promises a critical impact on personal and interpersonal variables. The time spent with colleagues and the frequency of rich human interaction are decreasing with the conditions of the pandemic. Social distancing and isolation, which are common effective methods for coping with the spread of the virus, increase the loneliness levels of employees. Emotional loneliness stands as the most prevailing psychological problem regarding the outcomes of the pandemic for older adults (van Tilburg et al., 2020). Loneliness is also associated with important individual and organizational outcomes (Chen & Kao, 2012). Leaders should provide employees assistance and support and the necessary platforms for socializing with colleagues. One possible way to assure this can be organizing leisure activities and discretionary informal meetings online for employees. Online social activities, gamification and online training can also serve as platforms for cohesion.

With the conditions of pandemic, the time spent in the workplace is decreasing and numerous employees work from distance. Distancing from workplace physically means being away from all these familiar experiences and psychological sources which in turn impair workplace spirituality. Workplace spirituality has been considered as a significant antecedent for creating a fulfilling and healthy work environment (Ghadi, 2017). Leaders should implement policies for fostering spirituality which is also significantly associated with other concepts that this chapter addresses (Ghadi, 2017). Supporting feelings of inclusion and cohesion (Ashmos & Duchon, 2000) can enhance the spiritual wellbeing of employees.

The long-lasting effects of pandemic will continue to critically change the circumstances for leaders to manage employees' psychological needs in the post pandemic era. This chapter addresses adverse psychological work related outcomes of the pandemic that require special managerial concern and attention. Although workplace loneliness, work alienation and spiritual well-being have been increasingly a focus of attention in the literature; unique conditions of the pandemic necessitate further investigation and reanalysis of the concept for the management of the change in the Post-COVID-19 Era. The chapter examines the transformation of work related circumstances regarding the variables and provides recommendations for effective management of the human side of adverse outcomes of the pandemic.

Redesigning the works in a way that they will provide for basic employee needs and in accordance with Job Characteristics Theory that they would create intrinsic motivation is crucial for managing the change compelled by the pandemic. Sustaining high quality leader-member exchange and organizational support, managing the information including the informal channels and effective communication and providing platforms for informal relationships are important pillars for combating adverse psychological effects of the pandemic. Realizing individual and demographic differences regarding the experience and effects of the pandemic is crucial. Awareness for the increased family-work interference and managing the processes for benefiting work-family enrichment and avoiding from work family conflict can serve substantially for the effective management of the transmission processes during and after the pandemic. Finding effective ways to monitor employees without engaging in micromanagement and creating feelings of exclusion also stands as a serious concern with the digitalization of the work. Supporting individual psychological capacities of employees with consultancy and trainings will help them to be more psychologically resilient against the adverse effects of the pandemic.

## REFERENCES

Akat, M., & Karataş, K. (2020). Psychological Effects of COVID-19 Pandemic on Society and Its Reflections on Education. *Electronic Turkish Studies, 15*(4).

Akila, A., & Priyadarshini, R. G. (2018). The impact of workplace friendships on organizational commitment and intention to leave. *IOP Conference Series. Materials Science and Engineering*, *390*(1), 012064. doi:10.1088/1757-899X/390/1/012064

Anand, P., & Mishra, S. K. (2019). Linking core self-evaluation and emotional exhaustion with workplace loneliness: Does high LMX make the consequence worse? *International Journal of Human Resource Management*, 1–26. doi:10.1080/09585192.2019.1570308

Ashmos, D. P., & Duchon, D. (2000). Spirituality at work: A conceptualization and measure. *Journal of Management Inquiry*, *9*(2), 134–144. doi:10.1177/105649260092008

Avey, J. B., Luthans, F., & Jensen, S. M. (2009). Psychological capital: A positive resource for combating employee stress and turnover. *Human Resource Management*, *48*(5), 677–693. doi:10.1002/hrm.20294

Banai, M., Reisel, W. D., & Probst, T. M. (2004). A managerial and personal control model: Predictions of work alienation and organizational commitment in Hungary. *Journal of International Management*, *10*(3), 375–392. doi:10.1016/j.intman.2004.05.002

Benefiel, M., Fry, L. W., & Geigle, D. (2014). Spirituality and religion in the workplace: History, theory, and research. *Psychology of Religion and Spirituality*, *6*(3), 175–187. doi:10.1037/a0036597

Berg-Weger, M., & Morley, J. E. (2020). Loneliness and Social Isolation in Older Adults During the Covid-19 Pandemic: Implications for Gerontological Social Work. *The Journal of Nutrition, Health & Aging*, *24*(5), 1–3. doi:10.100712603-020-1366-8 PMID:32346678

Berman, E. M., West, J. P., & Richter, M. N. Jr. (2002). Workplace relations: Friendship patterns and consequences (according to managers). *Public Administration Review*, *62*(2), 217–230. doi:10.1111/0033-3352.00172

Bouziri, H., Smith, D. R., Descatha, A., Dab, W., & Jean, K. (2020). Working from home in the time of covid-19: How to best preserve occupational health? *Occupational and Environmental Medicine*, *77*(7), 509–510. doi:10.1136/oemed-2020-106599 PMID:32354748

Çetin, M. (2019). Effects of Religious Participation on Social Inclusion and Existential Well-Being Levels of Muslim Refugees and Immigrants in Turkey. *The International Journal for the Psychology of Religion*, *29*(2), 64–76. doi:10.1080/10508619.2019.1580092

Champoux, J. E. (1978). Perceptions of work and nonwork: A reexamination of the compensatory and spillover models. *Sociology of Work and Occupations*, *5*(4), 402–422. doi:10.1177/073088847800500402

Chawla, V., & Guda, S. (2010). Individual spirituality at work and its relationship with job satisfaction, propensity to leave and job commitment: An exploratory study among sales professionals. *Journal of Human Values*, *16*(2), 157–167. doi:10.1177/097168581001600203

Chen, C. F., & Kao, Y. L. (2012). Investigating the antecedents and consequences of burnout and isolation among flight attendants. *Tourism Management*, *33*(4), 868–874. doi:10.1016/j.tourman.2011.09.008

Cooley, D., Pedersen, S., & Mainsbridge, C. (2014). Assessment of the impact of a workplace intervention to reduce prolonged occupational sitting time. *Qualitative Health Research*, *24*(1), 90–101. doi:10.1177/1049732313513503 PMID:24231074

Crouter, A. C. (1984). Spillover from family to work: The neglected side of the work-family interface. *Human Relations*, *37*(6), 425–441. doi:10.1177/001872678403700601

Cullen, W., Gulati, G., & Kelly, B. D. (2020). Mental health in the Covid-19 pandemic. *QJM: An International Journal of Medicine*, *113*(5), 311–312. doi:10.1093/qjmed/hcaa110 PMID:32227218

Dan, B. (1999). Spirituality at work: An overview. *Journal of Organizational Change Management*, *12*(4), 328–332. doi:10.1108/09534819910282162

Dansereau, F. Jr, Graen, G., & Haga, W. J. (1975). A vertical dyad linkage approach to leadership within formal organizations: A longitudinal investigation of the role making process. *Organizational Behavior and Human Performance, Vol*, *13*(1), 46–78. doi:10.1016/0030-5073(75)90005-7

Demerouti, E., Bakker, A. B., Nachreiner, F., & Schaufeli, W. B. (2001). The job demands-resources model of burnout. *The Journal of Applied Psychology*, *86*(3), 499–512. doi:10.1037/0021-9010.86.3.499 PMID:11419809

Diab-Bahman, R., & Al-Enzi, A. (2020). The impact of COVID-19 pandemic on conventional work settings. *The International Journal of Sociology and Social Policy*, *40*(9/10), 909–927. doi:10.1108/IJSSP-07-2020-0262

Farooq, A., Laato, S., & Islam, A. N. (2020). Impact of online information on self-isolation intention during the COVID-19 pandemic: Cross-sectional study. *Journal of Medical Internet Research*, *22*(5), e19128. doi:10.2196/19128 PMID:32330115

Feng, Z., & Savani, K. (2020). Covid-19 created a gender gap in perceived work productivity and job satisfaction: Implications for dual-career parents working from home. *Gender in Management*, *35*(7/8), 719–736. doi:10.1108/GM-07-2020-0202

Foerster, M., Henneke, A., Chetty-Mhlanga, S., & Röösli, M. (2019). Impact of adolescents' screen time and nocturnal mobile phone-related awakenings on sleep and general health symptoms: A prospective cohort study. *International Journal of Environmental Research and Public Health*, *16*(3), 518. doi:10.3390/ijerph16030518 PMID:30759792

Galea, S., Merchant, R. M., & Lurie, N. (2020). The mental health consequences of COVID-19 and physical distancing: The need for prevention and early intervention. *JAMA Internal Medicine*, *180*(6), 817–818. doi:10.1001/jamainternmed.2020.1562 PMID:32275292

Gao, G., & Sai, L. (2020). Towards a 'virtual'world: Social isolation and struggles during the COVID-19 pandemic as single women living alone. *Gender, Work and Organization*, *27*(5), 754–762. doi:10.1111/gwao.12468

Garg, N. (2017). Workplace spirituality and employee well-being: An empirical exploration. *Journal of Human Values*, *23*(2), 129–147. doi:10.1177/0971685816689741

Geurts, S., Rutte, C., & Peeters, M. (1999). Antecedents and consequences of work–home interference among medical residents. *Social Science & Medicine*, *48*(9), 1135–1148. doi:10.1016/S0277-9536(98)00425-0 PMID:10220015

Ghadi, M. Y. (2017). The impact of workplace spirituality on voluntary turnover intentions through loneliness in work. *Journal of Economic and Administrative Sciences*, *33*(1), 81–110. doi:10.1108/JEAS-03-2016-0005

Gomez, R., & Fisher, J. W. (2003). Domains of spiritual well-being and development and validation of the Spiritual Well-Being Questionnaire. *Personality and Individual Differences*, *35*(8), 1975–1991. doi:10.1016/S0191-8869(03)00045-X

Groarke, J. M., Berry, E., Graham-Wisener, L., McKenna-Plumley, P. E., McGlinchey, E., & Armour, C. (2020). Loneliness in the UK during the COVID-19 pandemic: Cross-sectional results from the COVID-19 Psychological Wellbeing Study. *PLoS One*, *15*(9), e0239698. doi:10.1371/journal.pone.0239698 PMID:32970764

Heidegger, M. (1954). The question concerning technology. *Technology and values: Essential readings*, *99*, 113.

Hill, P. C., Pargament, K. I., Hood, R. W., McCullough, J. M. E., Swyers, J. P., Larson, D. B., & Zinnbauer, B. J. (2000). Conceptualizing religion and spirituality: Points of commonality, points of departure. *Journal for the Theory of Social Behaviour*, *30*(1), 51–77. doi:10.1111/1468-5914.00119

Hirschfeld, R. R., & Feild, H. S. (2000). Work centrality and work alienation: Distinct aspects of a general commitment to work. *Journal of Organizational Behavior: The International Journal of Industrial. Occupational and Organizational Psychology and Behavior*, *21*(7), 789–800. doi:10.1002/1099-1379(200011)21:7<789::AID-JOB59>3.0.CO;2-W

Holt-Lunstad, J., Smith, T. B., Baker, M., Harris, T., & Stephenson, D. (2015). Loneliness and Social Isolation as Risk Factors for Mortality: A Meta-Analytic Review. *Perspectives on Psychological Science*, *10*(2), 227–237. doi:10.1177/1745691614568352 PMID:25910392

Hwang, T. J., Rabheru, K., Peisah, C., Reichman, W., & Ikeda, M. (2020). Loneliness and Social Isolation during the COVID-19 Pandemic. *International Psychogeriatrics*, 1–15. PMID:32450943

Issa, H., & Jaleel, E. (2020). Social isolation and psychological wellbeing: Lessons from Covid-19. *Management Science Letters*, *11*(2), 609–618.

Joelle, M., & Coelho, A. M. (2019). The impact of spirituality at work on workers' attitudes and individual performance. *International Journal of Human Resource Management*, *30*(7), 1111–1135. doi:10.1080/09585192.2017.1314312

Joensen, L. E., Madsen, K. P., Holm, L., Nielsen, K. A., Rod, M. H., Petersen, A. A., Rod, N. H., & Willaing, I. (2020). Diabetes and COVID-19: Psychosocial consequences of the COVID-19 pandemic in people with diabetes in Denmark—what characterizes people with high levels of COVID-19-related worries? *Diabetic Medicine*, *37*(7), 1146–1154. doi:10.1111/dme.14319 PMID:32392380

Jurkiewicz, C. L., & Giacalone, R. A. (2004). A values framework for measuring the impact of workplace spirituality on organizational performance. *Journal of Business Ethics*, *49*(2), 129–142. doi:10.1023/B:BUSI.0000015843.22195.b9

Kanungo, R. N. (1979). The concepts of alienation and involvement revisited. *Psychological Bulletin Journal*, *86*(1), 119–138. doi:10.1037/0033-2909.86.1.119

Karakas, F. (2010). Spirituality and performance in organizations: A literature review. *Journal of Business Ethics*, *94*(1), 89–106. doi:10.100710551-009-0251-5

Kaushik, M., & Guleria, N. (2020). The Impact of Pandemic COVID-19 in Workplace. *European Journal of Business and Management*, *12*(15), 1–10.

Kirchmeyer, C. (1992). Perceptions of nonwork-to-work spillover: Challenging the common view of conflict-ridden domain relationships. *Basic and Applied Social Psychology*, *13*(2), 231–249. doi:10.120715324834basp1302_7

Kramer, A., & Kramer, K. Z. (2020). The potential impact of the Covid-19 pandemic on occupational status, work from home, and occupational mobility. *Journal of Vocational Behavior*, *119*, 103442. doi:10.1016/j.jvb.2020.103442 PMID:32390661

Laconi, S., Tricard, N., & Chabrol, H. (2015). Differences between specific and generalized problematic Internet uses according to gender, age, time spent online and psychopathological symptoms. *Computers in Human Behavior*, *48*, 236–244. doi:10.1016/j.chb.2015.02.006

Lam, L. W., & Lau, D. C. (2012). Feeling lonely at work: Investigating the consequences of unsatisfactory workplace relationships. *International Journal of Human Resource Management*, *23*(20), 4265–4282. doi:10.1080/09585192.2012.665070

Lazenby, J. M. (2010). On" spirituality,"" religion," and" religions": A concept analysis. *Palliative & Supportive Care*, *8*(4), 469–476. doi:10.1017/S1478951510000374 PMID:20875214

Leiter, M. P., & Durup, M. J. (1996). Work, home, and in-between: A longitudinal study of spillover. *The Journal of Applied Behavioral Science*, *32*(1), 29–47. doi:10.1177/0021886396321002

Lopes Morrison, R. (2005). *Informal relationships in the workplace: Associations with job satisfaction, organisational commitment and turnover intentions* (Doctoral dissertation). Massey University.

Luthans, F., Luthans, K. W., & Luthans, B. C. (2004). Positive psychological capital: Beyond human and social capital. *Business Horizons*, *47*(1), 45–50. doi:10.1016/j.bushor.2003.11.007

Maslow, A. (1954). *A theory of human motivation: The goals of work. The Future of Work*. Prentice-Hall.

Mata, J., Wenz, A., Rettig, T., Reifenscheid, M., Moehring, K., Krieger, U., ... Naumann, E. (2020). *Health behaviors and mental health before and during the COVID-19 pandemic: A longitudinal population-based survey*. Academic Press.

Matias, T., Dominski, F. H., & Marks, D. F. (2020.). Human needs in COVID-19 isolation. *Journal of Health Psychology*, *1*, 12. PMID:32375564

McClelland, D. C. (1987). *Human motivation*. CUP Archive.

Menon, V., Padhy, S. K., & Pattnaik, J. I. (2020). COVID-19 pandemic and suicidality: Durkheim revisited. *The Australian and New Zealand Journal of Psychiatry*. PMID:32900218

Morin, C. M., & Carrier, J. (2020). The acute effects of the COVID-19 pandemic on insomnia and psychological symptoms. *Sleep Medicine*. Advance online publication. doi:10.1016/j.sleep.2020.06.005 PMID:32595107

Mucci, F., Mucci, N., & Diolaiuti, F. (2020). Lockdown and isolation: Psychological aspects of COVID-19 pandemic in the general population. *Clinical Neuropsychiatry: Journal of Treatment Evaluation*, *17*(2), 63–64.

Odekerken-Schröder, G., Mele, C., Russo-Spena, T., Mahr, D., & Ruggiero, A. (2020). Mitigating loneliness with companion robots in the COVID-19 pandemic and beyond: An integrative framework and research agenda. *Journal of Service Management*, *31*(6), 1149–1162. doi:10.1108/JOSM-05-2020-0148

Öge, E., Cetin, M., & Top, S. (2018). The effects of paternalistic leadership on workplace loneliness, work family conflict and work engagement among air traffic controllers in Turkey. *Journal of Air Transport Management*, *66*, 25–35. doi:10.1016/j.jairtraman.2017.10.003

Peng, J., Chen, Y., Xia, Y., & Ran, Y. (2017). Workplace loneliness, leader-member exchange and creativity: The cross-level moderating role of leader compassion. *Personality and Individual Differences, 104*, 510–515. doi:10.1016/j.paid.2016.09.020

Perlman, D., & Peplau, L. A. (1981). Toward a social psychology of loneliness. *Personal Relationships, 3*, 31–56.

Pesut, B., Fowler, M., Taylor, E. J., Reimer-Kirkham, S., & Sawatzky, R. (2008). Conceptualising spirituality and religion for healthcare. *Journal of Clinical Nursing, 17*(21), 2803–2810. doi:10.1111/j.1365-2702.2008.02344.x PMID:18665876

Prasad, D. K., Rao, M., Vaidya, D. R., & Muralidhar, B. (2020). Organizational Climate, Opportunities, Challenges and Psychological Wellbeing of the Remote Working Employees during COVID-19 Pandemic: A General Linear Model Approach with Reference to Information Technology Industry in Hyderabad. *International Journal of Advanced Research in Engineering and Technology, 11*(4).

Rice, R. W., Near, J. P., & Hunt, R. G. (1980). The job-satisfaction/life-satisfaction relationship: A review of empirical research. *Basic and Applied Social Psychology, 1*(1), 37–64. doi:10.120715324834basp0101_4

Rosso, B. D., Dekas, K. H., & Wrzesniewski, A. (2010). On the meaning of work: A theoretical integration and review. *Research in Organizational Behavior, 30*, 91–127. doi:10.1016/j.riob.2010.09.001

Sachdeva, G. (2019). Impact of Spirituality in Management: A Review. In Science and Spirituality for a Sustainable World: Emerging Research and Opportunities (pp. 1-22). IGI Global. doi:10.4018/978-1-5225-9893-0.ch001

Said, R. M., & El-Shafei, D. A. (2020). Occupational stress, job satisfaction, and intent to leave: Nurses working on front lines during COVID-19 pandemic in Zagazig City, Egypt. *Environmental Science and Pollution Research International*, 1–11. PMID:33067794

Shaw, W. S., Main, C. J., Findley, P. A., Collie, A., Kristman, V. L., & Gross, D. P. (2020). Opening the Workplace After COVID-19: What Lessons Can be Learned from Return-to-Work Research? *Journal of Occupational Rehabilitation*, 1. PMID:32562129

Sirgy, M. J., Efraty, D., Siegel, P., & Lee, D. J. (2001). A new measure of quality of work life (QWL) based on need satisfaction and spillover theories. *Social Indicators Research, 55*(3), 241–302. doi:10.1023/A:1010986923468

Sood, S. (2020). Psychological effects of the Coronavirus disease-2019 pandemic. *Research & Humanities in Medical Education, 7*, 23–26.

Tanyi, R. A. (2002). Towards clarification of the meaning of spirituality. *Journal of Advanced Nursing, 39*(5), 500–509. doi:10.1046/j.1365-2648.2002.02315.x PMID:12175360

Tavares, A. I. (2017). Telework and health effects review. *International Journal of Healthcare, 3*(2), 30. doi:10.5430/ijh.v3n2p30

Trzebiński, J., Cabański, M., & Czarnecka, J. Z. (2020). Reaction to the COVID-19 pandemic: The influence of meaning in life, life satisfaction, and assumptions on world orderliness and positivity. *Journal of Loss and Trauma, 25*(6-7), 1–14. doi:10.1080/15325024.2020.1765098

Tull, M. T., Edmonds, K. A., Scamaldo, K., Richmond, J. R., Rose, J. P., & Gratz, K. L. (2020). Psychological Outcomes Associated with Stay-at-Home Orders and the Perceived Impact of COVID-19 on Daily Life. *Psychiatry Research, 289*, 113098. doi:10.1016/j.psychres.2020.113098 PMID:32434092

van Tilburg, T. G., Steinmetz, S., Stolte, E., van der Roest, H., & de Vries, D. H. (2020). Loneliness and mental health during the COVID-19 pandemic: A study among Dutch older adults. *The Journals of Gerontology: Series B.*

Walia, K. (2018). The Relationship Between Employee Wellbeing and Spirituality at Workplace. *IUP Journal of Organizational Behavior, 17*(3).

Weiss, R. S. (1973). *Loneliness: The experience of emotional and social isolation.* MIT Press.

Wiesenfeld, B. M., Raghuram, S., & Garud, R. (2001). Organizational identification among virtual workers: The role of need for affiliation and perceived work-based social support. *Journal of Management, 27*(2), 213–229. doi:10.1177/014920630102700205

Williams, S. D., & Williams, J. (2020). Posttraumatic stress in organizations: Types, antecedents, and consequences. *Business and Society Review, 125*(1), 23–40. doi:10.1111/basr.12192

Wright, S., Burt, C., & Strongman, K. (2006). Loneliness in the workplace: Construct definition and scale development. *New Zealand Journal of Psychology, 35*(2), 59–68.

Yamamoto, T., Uchiumi, C., Suzuki, N., Yoshimoto, J., & Murillo-Rodriguez, E. (2020). The psychological impact of'mild lockdown'in Japan during the COVID-19 pandemic: a nationwide survey under a declared state of emergency. medRxiv.

Zhang, S. X., Liu, J., Jahanshahi, A. A., Nawaser, K., Yousefi, A., Li, J., & Sun, S. (2020). At the height of the storm: Healthcare staff's health conditions and job satisfaction and their associated predictors during the epidemic peak of COVID-19. *Brain, Behavior, and Immunity.*

Zheng, L., Miao, M., & Gan, Y. (2020). Perceived Control Buffers the Effects of the COVID-19 Pandemic on General Health and Life Satisfaction: The Mediating Role of Psychological Distance. *Applied Psychology: Health and Well-Being.*

## KEY TERMS AND DEFINITIONS

**Alienation:** Feelings of meaninglessness and isolation from others and self.

**Distance Working:** Working from home or somewhere outside the traditional workplace.

**Identification:** Feelings of belongingness and inclusion.

**Loneliness:** Lack of sufficient social companion and support.

**Micromanagement:** Managing with high and close supervision, without delegation, trust and transfer of responsibility and authority.

**Posttraumatic Stress Disorder:** Having long-lasting psychological symptoms after a traumatic life experience such as loss of a loved one or a disaster.

**Psychological Capital:** A state where individuals are hopeful, psychologically resilient, optimistic and efficient to cope with work and life demands.

**Social Distancing:** Keeping away from others, social events, and groups of people physically for avoiding the transmission of the virus.

**Spillover:** Transmission of the emotions or attitudes from one life domain to another.

**Spiritual Well-Being:** A state where individuals feel fulfillment, meaning and balance.

# Chapter 12
# Responding to the Challenge of Employee Engagement During Uncertain Times:
## Adaptive Leadership is the Answer

**Mohammad Faraz Naim**
https://orcid.org/0000-0003-3771-7665
*Department of Management, Birla Institute of Technology and Science, Pilani, India*

## ABSTRACT

*This chapter aims to combat the challenge of employee engagement faced by organizations across the globe during this uncertain world. This theoretical study suggests a conceptual model that explores adaptive leadership to evoke employee engagement in this pandemic context. Based on the theoretical lens of social exchange theory (SET), the conceptual model of the study illustrates the role of adaptive leaders in facilitating employee development, formation of social capital, and articulation of organizational vision. This, in turn, boosts employee engagement levels, in particular affective, cognitive, and physical engagement. The rationale of the conceptual model is provided with testable propositions. This chapter extends the human resource management scholarship on how to deal with employee engagement challenge. Simultaneously, it takes aim to expand the adaptive leadership theory research by exploring its possible effect on employee engagement outcomes.*

## INTRODUCTION

Leadership has been extensively studied in organizational scholarship. Scholarly literature has published umpteen studies on leadership for several decades. However, ever since 1980s, the scholarly attention has shifted from behavioral contingency approaches to leadership towards the concept of adaptive leadership (McKechnie et al., 2020). The contemporary business environment has been badly hit by the COVID-19 pandemic and ever since the outbreak of the viral disease; organizations across the globe are reeling with numerous challenges (Wang et al., 2020). The COVID-19 context has further increased the turbulence

DOI: 10.4018/978-1-7998-6948-1.ch012

and uncertainty of the business environment, as different organizations have to shift to virtual mode of operations in no time, and business prospects dwindled due to anxiety and fear in the minds of customers. Importantly, these are the very conditions under which adaptive leadership thrives (Baker, Irwin, & Mathews, 2020). Consequently, it is vital to exercise effective adaptive leadership, in order to respond to current business environment. Nonetheless, the present unprecedented conditions have added to the anxiety of employees and organizations. Numerous studies indicate that a large chunk of employees finding it difficult to stay engaged with their work (Chanana & Sangeeta, 2020). As a result, it poses a grave challenge to design effective employee engagement strategies. Recent studies indicate that globally, organizations are finding it increasingly difficult to bolster employee engagement rates, particularly in contemporary times (Quantum workplace Best Place to Work, 2020).

Along the similar lines, the extant literature has suggested the need for adaptive leadership to achieve organizational performance and competitive advantage (Dunn, 2020). Interestingly, an adaptive leader is heedful to the dynamism of the present business landscape and responds with appropriate strategies. In addition, the present business landscape is forcing adaptive leaders to leverage human capital and design a resilient organization capable of dealing with environmental turbulence and complexities. All this in turn, lead organizations pursue adaptive leadership as a business imperative measure (Yuki & Mahsud, 2010). However, there is still a paucity of academic research, particularly the empirical investigation on adaptive leadership. In this vein, our endeavor to explore a linkage between adaptive leadership and employee attitudinal outcomes (employee engagement) is a valuable addition to the extant body of research. More importantly, the domain of employee engagement has been widely researched during past few decades and following antecedents to employee engagement are identified namely job characteristics, organizational culture, supportive leadership styles, organizational trust, and individual characteristics. Also, the extant literature indicates a linkage between leadership and motivation, job satisfaction, and competitive advantage; still there is considerable gap in literature regarding the role of leadership to nurture employee engagement within organizations.

In this line of thought, the current study explores a potential linkage of adaptive leadership and employee engagement in the present COVID-19 context. In this study, we propose a conceptual model that focuses on adaptive leader's relational behavior and its impact on employee engagement. To this end, adaptive leader's role in supporting organizational learning, communicating the vision, and developing the social capital are linked to affective, cognitive, and physical engagement of employees.

## LITERATURE REVIEW

### Understanding Adaptive Leadership

Broadly, adaptive leadership is conceived as the leadership style focusing on adaptation in a given context and responding to the complexity, ambiguity, and uncertainty in the environment. Specifically, adaptive leadership is conceived as "the practice of mobilizing people to tackle tough challenges and thrive" (Heifetz *et al.*, 2009, p. 14). Adaptive leaders seek to mobilize knowledge quickly, are responsive to contextual needs, and seek to empower their colleagues to act, even when the path is unclear, and the journey might be messy. Due to this, an adaptive organization is able to respond swiftly to rapidly changing opportunities and demands as they occur" (Dunn, 2020, p. 33). An adaptive leader may not know what the perfect course of action is and must do something to acquire information so that the team can adapt his or her actions to correspond more directly with the context they are working within. An effective adaptive leader thrives in the times of uncertainty and disturbance and foresees a ray of opportunity in unfavorable conditions (Grisogono & Radenovic 2011). At the heart of adaptive leadership lies the concept of adaptive management, which incorporates collective ability to identify which interventions – or combinations of interventions – might work best and why, as well as understanding the impacts of these interventions. Adaptive leadership encompasses following key aspects namely, 1) creating larger organizational goals, ii) formulating action plan to achieve organizational goals, and iii) translating larger organizational strategy into operational protocols to design routine activities (Coleman, 2020). Operational adaptability is needed for sensemaking activities especially in present complex situations as in the case of COVID times. Adaptive leadership is considered an amalgamation of absorptive capacity (includes the awareness, learning and practice of acquiring and assimilating new information), adaptive capacity ability to adapt or to change to respond to an unpredictable environment), and managerial wisdom (ability of being aware of intuition, environmental perception and social relations) (Ramalingam, Wild, & Ferrari, 2020).

The most important aspects of adaptive leaders are shared values and shared understanding. It also facilitates the development of a vision that fuel focus and commitment of employees. Heifetz and colleagues (2009) points it out "bold aspirations amid their challenging realities" (p. 2). It helps leaders set priorities and balance short-term and long-term measures, and gives the entire organization a sense of confidence about the future. Adaptive leaders are able to communicate this vision in order to inspire others to build commitment to organization's goals. Then, they empower the members to enact the adaptive vision of the organization. Moreover, they have positive expectations of the performance from their peers, subordinates and themselves.

Adaptive leadership style is centered around Adaptive Leadership Framework, which considers an individual (patient) to be a complex adaptive system, adapting both physically and psychologically to their environment through a process of adaptive work (Thygeson, 2013). Two types of challenges and corresponding work are recognized: technical and adaptive. Technical challenges are "simple or complicated problems that can be identified and specified with considerable accuracy, and are amenable to solution by experts using methods and technologies that do not require major changes to the system itself" (Thygeson, 2013, p. 664). Adaptive challenges, however, are "complex problems that are hard to identify or specify completely, and that require the patient to learn new attitudes, beliefs, and behaviors" (Thygeson, 2013, p. 664). In practice, certain challenges are more troublesome as they can be resolved effectively only through rigorous efforts of the individual itself (the patient) and not by resorting to external consultants or experts. However, a plethora of literature on adaptive leadership is prescriptive in nature and mainly focused on deciphering the characteristics and nature of such a leadership approach. Recently, a research study suggests that current pandemic requires changes at operational and leadership levels. In terms of operational adaptation, adjustments need to make in management practices. From leadership perspective, adaptive approach to leadership is the need of the hour that fosters collective decision-making, transparent work culture and building trust among individuals (Ramalingam, Wild, & Ferrari, 2020). Therefore, there is a definite scope to explore the possible effects of adaptive leadership on individual attitudes such as employee engagement.

## EMPLOYEE ENGAGEMENT IN THE UNCERTAIN TIMES OF COVID-19: EMPLOYEE ENGAGEMENT PRACTICES DURING THE COVID-19

The severe respiratory disease recently appeared in Wuhan (Hubei province), China. Epidemiological examinations have suggested that the epidemic was related to a seafood market in Wuhan, China (Fan et al., 2020). COVID-19 is a pandemic that has already reached 5,934,936 confirmed cases globally, with at least 367,166 deaths as reported by the World Health Organization (WHO) as of May 31, 2020 (Chanana & Sangeeta, 2020). Consequently, most organizations started working online and initiated a work-from-home (WFH) regime. Due to lockdown, most organizations provide the facility to their employees to work from home. But work from home is difficult for employees as they do not feel the organizational climate at home, as lack of concentration due to frequent invasion of family members; work–life conflict arise due to this. Even they do not have proper equipment and tools (computer, mouse, printers, scanners, headphones, webcam, internet connection, and dedicated workspace—a quiet place to work). Most employees feel stressed due to rising cases of COVID-19 in the world. They are not sure about their job security and also about their salary. Due to these problems, employees could not concentrate/focus on their work, so there is a need for employee engagement. The prime responsibility of the organization is to take care of their employees' well-being and engage them properly. Those employees who are engaged well are giving 100% result. Leaders should provide some motivational talk lectures, boost their morale, and provide psychologically safe and open environment so employees can raise their voice if they are having some issues. Leaders can use multimedia for communication. But work-from-home regime is challenging for employees as well as for organizations during this difficult situation.

However, with the rapid changes in the business world owing to global pandemic of COVID-19, organizational leaders must endeavor to innovate and create effective ways to engage the employees in a healthier way during this difficult time. "Employee engagement is a workplace attitude that is ensuing all adherents of an organization to give of their excellence every day, committed toward their organization's goals and values" (Chanana & Sangeeta, 2020, p. 2). In accordance with the pioneering work of Kahn (1990), employee engagement is construed as "the harnessing of organization members' selves to their work roles; in engagement, people employ and express themselves physically, cognitively, and emotionally during role performances." (p. 694). In addition, research demonstrates that higher engagement levels are linked to improved productivity and a healthier bottom line. In good times or bad, worker engagement should be a top priority of organizations (Vickers, 2019).

Resource-based view of the firm asserts that employees are the most critical adaptive resource of an organization that ultimately shapes the competiveness of an organization. However, to stay sustainable organizations not only need to attract talented employees but also need to effectively engage their current workforce. Given the present unprecedented times of, organizations are finding it increasingly difficult to engage their distributed workforce, working indoors away from the workplace. Although, the concept of employee engagement is an extensively researched domain both in scholarly and popular press, still there is a scope to craft commensurate engagement strategy relevant to the present context. As per a recent Gallup sturdy, in the USA alone employee engagement rates have experienced a decline relative to the last one year (Harter, 2020).

## TOWARDS A CONCEPTUAL MODEL

The present study is theoretical in nature and presents a conceptual model illustrating the role of adaptive leaders in evoking employee engagement from the lens of Social Exchange theory (SET). SET argues that employees and management operate as an amalgamation of social exchanges, whereby organization's policies and practices evoke reciprocal responses among employees (Cropanzano, Anthony, Daniels, & Hall, 2017). There is a sense of reciprocity. Specifically, when organizations offer support to employees by practicing adaptive leadership to facilitate developmental opportunities, social capital formation, and link organizational vision and individual goals. All this is facilitated by adaptive leadership. As employees' higher order psycho-social needs are fulfilled, it will translate into positive outcomes of higher engagement (see Figure 1).

### Adaptive Leadership, Employee Development, and Affective Engagement

Adaptive leaders consider the contemporary complex environment not only posing serious challenges, but also opening up window of opportunities in terms of supporting employee development. The aim is to create resilient organizations characterized by high level of flexibility, agility, adaptability, and continuous learning capabilities. One of the effective means is through development of human capital. There is a compelling evidence in the literature that point out organization wide learning initiatives, and a focus on sensemaking activates are quintessential to survive and flourish in this complex and turbulent business landscape (Doyle, 2017).

Adaptive leaders play a key role in this regard, as their adaptive or visionary dimension builds employee commitment towards organizational vision. Contrastingly, creative leadership dimension is focused on developing and managing intangible resources of the firm in particular, human capital as well as reinforcing learning-oriented environment. They inspire employees to focus on their individual development (Yuki & Mahsud, 2010). In this line of thought, nurture an enabling culture for continuous learning, collaboration, opportunities for information sharing and leveraging internal expertise to foster learning and development, and innovation (Coleman, 2020). Besides, they are able to sense the market demands and hence have a holistic approach of development i.e. by focusing on their operational aspects of adaptation; they strive to facilitate organizations to be learning-centric workplaces.

Drawing from the past studies, there is a strong relationship between adaptive leadership and organization leaning (Nicolaides & McCallum, 2013). On the similar lines, adaptive leaders contribute in enhancing the absorptive capacity of organizations by facilitating knowledge sharing and learning at individual and organizational levels (DeRue, 2011; Mumford *et al.*, 2002). This encouragement of organization learning, knowledge creation and sharing create conducive conditions for employees' development as organizational members can share their knowledge, skills, and experiences to relatively inexperienced employees, who quickly grab any opportunity for learning and development. In other words, adaptive leaders facilitate employee development by fostering key learning aspects including knowledge sharing, organization learning, and supportive work environment. This will lead to the fulfillment of cognitive needs of employees and create a perception of a supportive organization which has a concern and focus towards employee development. All in all, it generates a sense of affective or emotional engagement. Thus we propose-

**Proposition 1**- *Adaptive leader's focus on development of employees has a positive influence on employees' affective engagement.*

## Adaptive Leadership, Social Capital Development, and Physical Engagement

The extant literature has revealed the significance of relationships or social ties for leadership effectiveness. Balkundi and Kilduff (2006) conceptualizes leadership as "social capital that collects around certain individuals" (p. 421) and suggest that successful leadership harnesses "social intelligence, or the accurate perception of social relationships in organizations" (p. 7). In board terms, effective leadership must leverage individuals' personal networks, and relationships among organization members for the benefit of the organization. Therefore, the significance of social capital cannot be overstated. In the similar vein, prior literature demonstrates that formation of social capital is an important activity of adaptive leaders (Ramalingam, Wild, & Ferrari, 2020).

Adaptive leaders have to manage demands of multiple stakeholders though the collaborative efforts of the team of executives (McKechnie et al., 2020). In addition to developing human capital, adaptive leaders also build social capital by encouraging members to build relationships and work collaboratively in teams. This enables formation of communities of organizational members or citizens with diverse skills and characterized by common interests, trust, and reciprocity, which facilitate the creation and sharing of knowledge leading to collaboration, collective intelligence, and innovation. Communities in turn, generate internal social capital i.e. value gained through relationships in interconnected or networked assets (Glover, Friedman & Jones, 2002). Importantly, social capital is also considered pivotal to harness an organization's human capital and in turn, fuels sustainable competitiveness (Samad, 2020). Importantly, adaptive leaders create a culture of trust, which is vital for social capital development and effective cooperation and coordination among members to achieve common goals.

Along similar lines, research indicates a positive association of quality relationships and vigor of employees (Jindo et al., 2020). Research suggests that vigor has its roots connected with emotions including moods and affect. Vigor is found to be a key facet of work engagement (Bakker & Demerouti, 2007). Parallely, relational aspects of work such as interpersonal relations, leader member exchange, peer-to-peer bonding act as strong determinants of employee engagement. Therefore, social and relational aspects of work facilitate development of employee vigor. Moreover, through their relational behaviors of collaboration, community development, and open communication, adaptive leaders nurture positive relationships, which in turn, strengthen social capital formation manifested in terms of cordial relationships among employees. This, in turn, breeds a feeling of vigor in employees. In a similar vein, feeling of vigor has been found closely related to physical engagement (May, Gilson & Harter, 2004). Also, cultivating a work environment supportive to developing interpersonal relationships at workplace; engenders a sense of being valued, listened, and respected in the minds and hearts of employees. Therefore, the generation of social capital promotes engagement levels of employees as they desire to develop relationships and social ties to satisfy their social and cognitive needs. In other words, development of social capital by adaptive leaders translates to a greater physical engagement of employees. Thus we propose-

**Proposition 2**- *Adaptive leader's development of social capital has a positive influence on employees' physical engagement.*

## Adaptive Leadership, Vision Articulation, and Cognitive Engagement

"Cognitive engagement means being aware of one's role and its linkage with organizational objectives" (Naim & Lenka, 2017, p.31). The extant scholarly and practitioner research has suggested that leader has a definite role in engaging the employees (Harter, Schmidt & Heyes, 2002). It is envisaged that employees respond positively when their personal objectives are congruent with the organizational mission (Naim & Lenka, 2020). Similarly, their goals must be well-defined and aligned with larger organizational objectives so that they can realize that their performances are contributing to achieve the bottom-line. Adaptive leaders will aptly fill the bill here as they communicate the organizational vision in order to spur employees' commitment to overall objectives. The key facets of adaptive leaders are shared values and a well-defined vision for the future. A well-articulated vision accelerates the pace at which an organization realize its long term objectives and increase organizational sustainability (Glover, Friedman & Jones, 2002). It is essential that top leadership of an organization have a focus towards overall strategy implementation to realize the benefits of adaptive leadership (Coleman, 2020) Along the similar lines, Slatten and Mehmetoglu (2011) reveals' that employee's adaptive attention enhances engagement; wherein adaptive attention denotes the provision of guidance and direction by strategy.

More importantly, they develop fitment between individual goals and overall strategy of the organization, it increases awareness of big picture. Consequently, it evokes a feeling of belongingness and connectedness with the organizational objectives. Moreover, this alignment further provides a direction to aim at. In other words, they help employees visualize the association between what they do and the success of the organization. It results in employees feeling valued and aware of their contributions in achieving larger organizational goals, in turn fulfilling their higher order psychological needs, ultimately translating into a feeling of higher cognitive engagement. Unsurprisingly, the extant employee engagement scholarship corroborates that alignment between employee objectives and organizational objectives engenders a higher feeling of engagement (Slatten & Mehmetoglu, 2011). Thus we propose-

**Proposition 3**- *Adaptive leader's articulation of vision has a positive influence on employees' cognitive engagement.*

*Figure 1. The conceptual model*

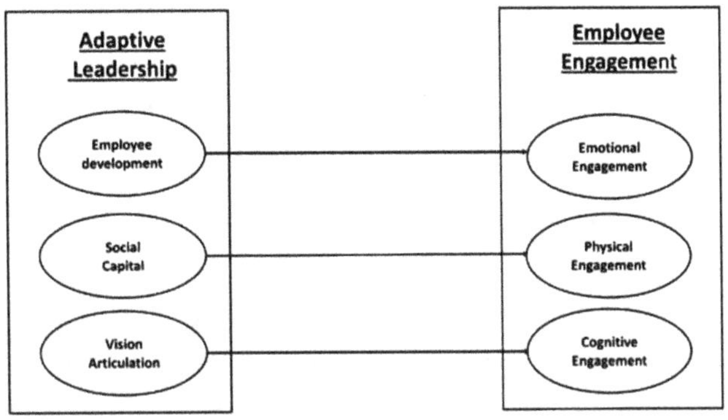


## DISCUSSION AND IMPLICATIONS

The post-COVID-19 era has thrown numerous human resource challenges. Employee engagement is one such challenge faced by organizations globally. Organizations are making efforts to engage their workforce to stay sustainable and gain competitive advantage. To this end, never before has there been much emphasis placed on exploring the linkage of top leadership and engagement. Therefore, a conceptual model to link adaptive leadership and employee engagement is envisaged. The model elucidates the influence of adaptive leaders on nurturing organizational learning, developing social capital, and articulating the vision, in turn enhancing affective, physical, and cognitive engagement of employees. The extant literature on employee engagement asserts the significance of management and leadership as a key driver-in this connection. "If we don't believe in the messenger, we won't believe the message" holds true from the leadership perspective. Leaders with a focus on positive interactions with followers, relationship building, and trust development have been shown to improve engagement levels (Bakker & Schaufeli, 2007). Likewise, transformational leaders are shown to exert a positive impact on shaping positive employee attitudes such as employee satisfaction, and employee engagement (Walumbwa *et al.*, 2005). The present study is corroborated by the extant literature that reveals a need for adaptive leadership as a potential strategy to people management challenges imposed by this pandemic. Recent experience highlights the need for adaptive leadership in national and global responses to the outbreak (Ramalingam, Wild, & Ferrari, 2020).

Adaptive leaders emphasize on the values of cooperation, consideration, agreement, fairness, and social equality. The adaptability culture has adaptive leaders that support values promoting autonomy, individual initiative, responsibility, creativity, risk-taking, learning, and entrepreneurship that allow the organization to interpret and translate signals from the environment into new goals and strategies. They influence others by articulating vision, values, strategy and nurturing quality relationships instead of command and control. In the process, adaptive leaders delegate decision making powers, and provide the necessary resources to perform jobs, and provide a linkage between individual goals and organization's vision. It is this linkage that gives a sense of direction, thereby gaining commitment of employees towards pursuit of organizational vision. The present study has key theoretical and managerial implications. From managerial vantage point, the study will encourage human resource managers to refurbish their employee engagement strategy by exercising adaptive leadership to enhance affective, cognitive, and physical engagement. From theoretical vantage point, this study broadens our understanding on relational aspects of adaptive leadership by providing a thorough review on adaptive leadership and adding to the literature on its positive influence on employee engagement. To the best of our knowledge, so far no academic work examines adaptive leadership in the given context. This has also addressed the call for further academic research on employee engagement (Saks, 2006).

## LIMITATIONS AND FUTURE AVENUES

This study being theoretical lacks empirical investigation, and hence it is the primary limitation of this work. This chapter opens new avenues for future research to further explore adaptive leadership in the given context. Firstly, conduct empirical validation of the proposed conceptual model. Secondly, identify effective moderating conditions to bolster the effect of adaptive leadership. In this regard, investigating the impact of variables such as organizational culture, organizational trust, organizational justice, and perceived organizational support offer a potential line of research for future studies.

## CONCLUSION

In the contemporary world, organizations are innovating with unprecedented ways of operating , given the work from home situation forced by COVID-19 outbreak. There is a sharp decline in employee motivation and employee engagement. As engaged employees are the drivers of sustainable competitive advantage for organizations, therefore organizations must emphasize on practicing adaptive leadership styles to support employee development, develop social capital, and articulate the vision of organizations. It lead organizations to effectively engage their workforce.

## REFERENCES

Baker, E. L., Irwin, R., & Matthews, G. (2020). Thoughts on Adaptive Leadership in a Challenging Time. *Journal of Public Health Management and Practice*, *26*(4), 378–379. doi:10.1097/PHH.0000000000001179 PMID:32433390

Bakker, A. B., & Demerouti, E. (2007). The job demands-resources model: State of the art. *Journal of Managerial Psychology*, *22*(3), 309–328. doi:10.1108/02683940710733115

Balkundi, P., & Kilduff, M. (2005). The ties that lead: A social network approach to leadership. *The Leadership Quarterly*, *16*(6), 941–961. doi:10.1016/j.leaqua.2005.09.004

Chanana, N. & Sangeeta. (2020). Employee engagement practices during COVID-19 lockdown. *Journal of Public Affairs*, 2508. PMID:33041656

Coleman, A. (2020). What are your "odds-of-success"? Reflecting on the role of adaptive leadership in Leicester City's (2015/16) English Football Premier League Title win. *Development and Learning in Organizations*, *35*(1), 1–3. doi:10.1108/DLO-09-2019-0227

Cropanzano, R., Anthony, E. L., Daniels, S. R., & Hall, A. V. (2017). Social exchange theory: A critical review with theoretical remedies. *The Academy of Management Annals*, *11*(1), 479–516. doi:10.5465/annals.2015.0099

DeRue, D. S. (2011). Adaptive leadership theory: Leading and following as a complex adaptive process. *Research in Organizational Behavior*, *31*, 125–150. doi:10.1016/j.riob.2011.09.007

Doyle, A. (2017). Adaptive challenges require adaptive leaders. *Performance Improvement*, *56*(9), 18–26. doi:10.1002/pfi.21735

Glover, J., Friedman, H., & Jones, G. (2002). Adaptive leadership: When change is not enough (part one). *Organization Development Journal*, *20*(2), 15.

Harter, J. (2020). *Historic drop in Employee engagement follows record rise.* Accessed 15 September 2020. https://www.gallup.com/workplace/313313/historic-drop-employee-engagement-follows-record-rise.aspx#:~:text=It%20was%2014%25%20in%20June,June%201%2D14%2C%202020

Heifetz, R., Grashow, A., & Linsky, M. (2009). *The Practice of Adaptive Leadership*. Harvard Business School Publishing.

Jindo, T., Kai, Y., Kitano, N., Tsunoda, K., Nagamatsu, T., & Arao, T. (2020). Relationship of workplace exercise with work engagement and psychological distress in employees: A cross-sectional study from the MYLS study. *Preventive Medicine Reports*, *17*, 101030. doi:10.1016/j.pmedr.2019.101030 PMID:31890476

Kahn, W. A. (1990). Psychological conditions of personal engagement and disengagement at work. *Academy of Management Journal*, *33*(4), 692–724.

Kaushik, M., & Guleria, N. (2020). Employee Relations and Engagement during COVID-19. *Sparkling International Journal of Multidisciplinary Research Studies*, *3*(2), 1–11.

May, D. R., Gilson, R. L., & Harter, L. M. (2004). The psychological conditions fmeaningfulness, safety and availability and the engagement of the human spirit at work. *Journal of Occupational and Organizational Psychology*, *7*(7), 11–37. doi:10.1348/096317904322915892

McKechnie, A. C., Johnson, K. A., Baker, M. J., Docherty, S. L., Leuthner, S. R., & Thoyre, S. (2020). Adaptive leadership in parents caring for their children born with life-threatening conditions. *Journal of Pediatric Nursing*, *53*, 41–51. doi:10.1016/j.pedn.2020.03.018 PMID:32438191

Mumford, M. D., Scott, G. M., Gaddis, B., & Strange, J. M. (2002). Leading creative people: Orchestrating expertise and relationships. *The Leadership Quarterly*, *13*(6), 705–750. doi:10.1016/S1048-9843(02)00158-3

Naim, M. F., & Lenka, U. (2017). Investigating the impact of social media on Gen Y employees' engagement: An Indian perspective. *International Journal of Human Capital and Information Technology Professionals*, *8*(3), 29–48. doi:10.4018/IJHCITP.2017070103

Naim, M. F., & Lenka, U. (2020). Organizational learning and Gen Y employees' affective commitment: The mediating role of competency development and moderating role of strategic leadership. *Journal of Management & Organization*, *26*(5), 815–831. doi:10.1017/jmo.2018.19

Nicolaides, A., & McCallum, D. C. (2013). Inquiry in action for leadership in turbulent times: Exploring the connections between transformative learning and adaptive leadership. *Journal of Transformative Education, 11*(4), 246–260. doi:10.1177/1541344614540333

Quantum Workplace Best Place to Work. (2020). *The Impact of COVID-19 on Employee Engagement A Quantum Workplace Benchmark Report and Analysis.* Accessed September 14, 2020 https://www.quantumworkplace.com/impact-of-covid-19-on-employee-engagement

Rahman, N., Othman, M., Yajid, M., Rahman, S., Yaakob, A., Masri, R., ... Ibrahim, Z. J. M. S. L. (2018). Impact of adaptive leadership on organizational performance, adaptive orientation and operational strategy. *Management Science Letters, 8*(12), 1387–1398. doi:10.5267/j.msl.2018.9.006

Ramalingam, B., Wild, L., & Ferrari, M. (2020). *Adaptive leadership in the coronavirus response.* Academic Press.

Samad, S. (2020). Achieving innovative firm performance through human capital and the effect of social capital. *Management & Marketing. Challenges for the Knowledge Society, 15*(2), 326–344. doi:10.2478/mmcks-2020-0019

Singh, P. (2020). *COVID 19: The evolution of employee engagement.* Accessed September14, 2020 http://bwpeople.businessworld.in/article/COVID-19-The-Evolution-Of-Employee-Engagement/26-04-2020-190293/

Slatten, T., & Mehmetoglu, M. (2011). Antecedents and effects of engaged frontline employees: A study from the hospitality industry. *Managing Service Quality, 21*(1), 88–107. doi:10.1108/09604521111100261

Vickers, M. (2019, January 24). *Boosting worker engagement in tough times.* American Management Association. Retrieved from https://www.amanet.org/articles/boosting-worker-engagement-in-tough-times/

Walumbwa, F. O., Orwa, B., Wang, P., & Lawler, J. J. (2005). Transformational leadership, organizational commitment, and job satisfaction: A comparative study of Kenyan and US financial firms. *Human Resource Development Quarterly, 16*(2), 235–256. doi:10.1002/hrdq.1135

Wang, J., Wang, Z., Liu, X., Yang, X., Zheng, M., & Bai, X. (2020). The impacts of a COVID-19 epidemic focus and general belief in a just world on individual emotions. *Personality and Individual Differences*, 110349. PMID:32843782

Watkins, K. E., & Marsick, V. J. (1993). Sculpting the learning organization: Lessons in the art and science of systemic change. Jossey-Bass Inc.

Yukl, G., & Mahsud, R. (2010). Why flexible and adaptive leadership is essential. *Consulting Psychology Journal, 62*(2), 81–93. doi:10.1037/a0019835

# Chapter 13
# Leadership in the Post-COVID-19 Era:
## New Leaders of the New Normal

**Yeşim Kurt**
https://orcid.org/0000-0002-9827-2471
*Kırklareli University, Turkey*

**Dilek Erdoğan**
https://orcid.org/0000-0002-2079-777X
*Gaziantep University, Turkey*

## ABSTRACT

*The purpose of this study is to explain the relationship between the COVID-19 crisis and leadership and to demonstrate the leadership skills necessary in the post-COVID-19 era. This study is based on literature research. In the study, firstly, the effects of COVID-19 on human life are explained. Then, the relationship between crisis management and leadership is discussed. Later, the features of the new era after COVID-19 and the concept of the digital age are explained. The role of leaders in this new era is emphasized. In the last part of this study, three leadership types that attract attention during the pandemic process are briefly explained. These are ethical, digital, and pandemic leadership. In the last section, the skills and abilities required for leaders who are to succeed after COVID-19 also add value to the research.*

## INTRODUCTION

The COVID-19 pandemic, which emerged in the Wuhan region of China in late 2019 and then spread to the whole world and turned into a COVID-19 global health crisis, plunged the world into unprecedented chaos. This pandemic has plunged health systems into a crisis of unprecedented magnitude (Ahlsson, 2020, p. 1). According to the World Health Organization, on October 6, 2020, the number of COVID-19 confirmed cases worldwide was 36,237,403, while 1,054,868 of them resulted in death (WHO, 2020).

DOI: 10.4018/978-1-7998-6948-1.ch013

This disease, which causes great damage to human health and kills many people, has also destroyed global markets (Altamirano & Collazo, 2020, p. 65).

This global public crisis has also brought many difficulties for leaders who have made intensive efforts to manage the effects of the enormous threats it poses and has led to unprecedented decisions to be made (Nicola, et. al., 2020, p. 123). Many governments have started a huge struggle over how to prepare for the pandemic, how to respond, and how to mitigate its effects (Moon, 2020, p. 1). Countries all over the world have tried to manage this process by imposing various bans and restrictions. For example, schools were closed, face-to-face education was suspended (Husbands, 2020, p. 6). People's work lives, social lives, and travel patterns have been changed (Horná, 2020, p. 2). People have put an end to their social lives by putting physical distances between them and have started not to travel on a regional or global scale. In this process, all businesses, large and small, whose commercial losses gradually increased, began to follow policies that would lead to increased unemployment (Altamirano & Collazo, 2020, p. 72).

All these changes in a micro and macro sense have created an impetus towards a new human age by moving countries, sectors, individuals, in other words, all humanity, away from known social and economic structures. How this age will take shape relates to the decisions of leaders (Dirani, et. al., 2020, p. 380). Crises such as COVID-19 pose multiple challenges for leaders. Leaders must identify problems coming in a rapidly changing situation and understand a dynamic threat with limited information, make critical decisions in response, and coordinate the process. In times of crisis, people turn to their leaders, and leaders turn to the people they influence (Roberts, 2020, p. 232). At such times, communities or employees follow their leaders and are influenced by their decisions. In other words, leaders are put under the spotlight in difficult times such as the COVID-19 crisis due to their positions (Lagowska, et. al., 2020, p. 1). This is because people expect guidance, hope, and accurate information from leaders. In summary, at such times, the spotlights are turned to the leaders. In such cases, it becomes very important to manage the process successfully. For example, in the process of the coronavirus pandemic, the key role played by the leadership during crises is emerging, with some global leaders rising in popularity and others declining rapidly (Lagowska, et. al., 2020, p. 4). During this period, although the virus was a problem found all over the world, world leaders showed significant differences in their reactions. This has significantly different consequences in terms of virus reduction, public health, and economic stability. This is because leaders adopt different approaches (charismatic, ideological, pragmatic (CIP) model) to understand the crisis, and the difference in decision-making and communication methods (Crayne & Medeiros, 2020, p. 1)

In summary, the destruction brought by COVID-19 and the new order it will bring will lead to the reshaping of systems, the emergence of new structures, economic successes, or failures. All of these relate to the decisions taken by the leaders. How leaders respond to the crisis will permanently change the economic, social, and health fundamentals of their communities (Dirani, et. al., 2020, p. 381). These changes point to the new era after COVID-19.

At this stage, the relationship between the COVID-19 crisis and leadership emerges as an issue worth discussing. What will their leadership styles and behavior be like in this new normal full of uncertainty? How do global threats change the way we manage the global workforce? (Caligiuri, et. al, 2020). What should be done about leading people, organizations, or societies in the new era? What are the leadership competencies required during and after the crisis? (Dirani, et. al., 2020, p. 380). What changes are there in the future of leadership? (Husbands, 2020, p. 3). Responding to all this will help prepare leaders for the new age and future (Lagowska, et. al., 2020, 4). For all these reasons, one of the aims of this chapter is to investigate the relationship between the COVID-19 crisis and leaders. Another aim of the chapter is to reveal the leadership skills in the post-COVID-19 period.

In the literature, researches on the relationship between COVID-19 and leadership have started. Coscieme et al. (2020), examining the success of male and female leaders in the pandemic period; found that countries, where women are leaders, have six times fewer deaths from COVID-19 than countries led by men. In another study, the concepts of cooperation and compassion in the relationship between the COVID-19 era and leadership were explored in the United States with names such as President Trump (Forester, & McKibbon, 2020). In another study, the reasons for Jacinda Ardern's success in coronavirus crisis leadership were discussed (Wilson, 2020). Dirani (2020) revealed the relationship between leadership skills and human resources development in this period. Bartsch et al. (2020) investigated leadership in virtual environments caused by the COVID-19 pandemic. The research revealed that in such crises, task and relationship-oriented leadership behavior is required for employees to maintain their work performance in a virtual environment. Fernandez and Shaw (2020) explored leadership best practices to tackle the challenges posed by the COVID-19 pandemic. In the research, the concepts of servant, academic, and allostatic leader are emphasized. Wilson (2020) linked leadership to the COVID-19 crisis with a pandemic leadership model.

This research, on the one hand, contributes to the literature with a holistic approach due to the discussion of the relationship between the COVID-19 pandemic crisis and leadership, on the other hand, to reveal the requirements of being a successful leader in the new period after COVID-19. The research first explains the effects of the COVID-19 pandemic on work life, social life, and health. The following section explains the general relationship between crisis management-leadership-COVID-19. Later in the research, the concepts of the new era and digital age after COVID-19 are included. Finally, the research discusses the types and qualities of leadership that will be required to be successful in this new era.

This chapter of the book is based on a conceptual framework, so it has been structured using literature research.

## EFFECTS OF COVID-19 ON HUMAN LIFE

COVID-19 is a virus that first appeared in Wuhan Province, China in late December 2019, and was identified on January 13, 2020, with research on patients. Symptoms of COVID-19 disease are clinical symptoms such as fever, dry cough, tiredness, muscle or body aches, headache, loss of taste or smell, sore throat, nasal congestion or runny nose, nausea, vomiting, diarrhea. The epidemic was first detected in seafood in this region and those found in the animal market. Afterward, it can be transmitted from person to person, and other cities in Hubei province, especially Wuhan, and other provinces of China, and it then spread to other countries around the world (Duygun, 2020, p. 234; Rahmani & Mirmahaleh, 2020).

Different hypotheses have been put forward about the virus that is the cause of the COVID-19 disease and its formation. While some claim that the virus has a zoonotic nature, it is passed from animals called bats and Pangolin, which are possible hosts, to humans; if some they have beliefs that this virus has been artificially or intentionally produced in a laboratory setting (Menachery, et. al., 2015; Liu et. al., 2020).

No matter how this virus originated, the COVID-19 disease created chaos that started in China and spread all over the world. This chaos has led to events and disasters that have never been encountered before. During this period, various prohibitions or measures were put into practice to minimize economic and moral losses. While individuals tried to take precautions, business or country leaders also resorted to various practices for their following groups. All these practices deeply affected both the social life and business life of people. At the same time, this virus has deeply affected public health. All these effects are described below:

1. *Effects on social life:* The main effect on this issue is on the new order brought about by the physical distance rules. People who want to avoid the risk of virus transmission have started not to travel, to go out and to meet their friends and relatives. The leaders of many countries, on the other hand, carried this to a macro dimension, closing the country's land and air border gates, and preventing the global movement of people. In many countries, there have even been new processes where curfews are imposed, and people can only go out for their food needs. All collective activities have been terminated in many regions. Shopping centers have been closed; weddings, funerals, and artistic events were suspended, and football matches were canceled. In many regions, schools and universities were closed, face-to-face education was suspended, and virtual education was started (Husbands, 2020, p. 6; Horná, 2020, p. 2; Blake-Beard, et. al., 2020). Schools and universities have closed in most countries of the world to limit the spread of the new coronavirus disease (COVID-19). Mandatory closure measures are in place in 192 countries; Learning activities stopped for approximately 1.58 billion students (91.4% of enrolled students), almost all education systems started to use distance education solutions (ILO, 2020a)

In the COVID-19 process, even in cases where people could go out, measures that had never been experienced before were encountered. The most important of these is the necessity of using personal protective equipment (mask, gloves, and disinfectant) (Blake-Beard, et. al., 2020).

All these practices caused people to be locked in their homes and isolated them. People who cannot socialize and see their loved ones have also started to struggle with psychological problems. People who want to meet one of their most basic needs, socialization, have tried to find solutions through virtual interactions. Although lessons are conducted on the digital platform for children who cannot go to school, the fact that children who cannot socialize cannot meet their need for play has led to discussions that it will have bad consequences on their development and psychology (Venkatesh, 2020, p. 3; Voyer, 2020, p. 4).

2. *Effects on business life:* Physical distance rules did not only affect social life, but also business life. The routines of people who cannot socialize, go out and travel have deteriorated, and their expenditures have narrowed. This situation puts the economies of entertainment, shopping, catering, sports activities, and many other services and production enterprises in a difficult situation. Industries such as tourism and transportation have come to a standstill. Most of these businesses, which suffered economic losses, had to make changes in their working conditions. While some businesses stopped production completely, some sought different solutions to this crisis. In this process, some enterprises that were in economic crisis resorted to layoffs, and the number of unemployed increased. In the United States alone, around 881,000 Americans lost their jobs in April 2020 (BLS, 2020). In the same region, it is estimated that 6.5 million jobs will be lost in the tourism sector in 2020 (Statista, 2020). These losses are experienced in different sectors not only in America but all over the world (ILO, 2020b). During this period, people who were worried about getting sick and lonely due to COVID-19, lost their jobs, worsening their psychological situation. Employees who have not yet been fired are struggling with the anxiety of dismissal. Another work-related impact is changing working hours and loss of income. Some employees who were not fired

but were employed for shorter periods or started to be employed from home were sentenced to less wages (Venkatesh, 2020, p. 2).

In the COVID-19 process, besides the layoffs, changes in the way things are done were also observed. Many businesses encourage employees to run their jobs from home to maintain their physical distance and minimize the risk of infection. In this process, it is stated that 50% of the workforce in the USA started to work from home (Venkatesh, 2020, p. 1). Conducting work from home and holding meetings has led individuals and businesses to use technology. In this process, the remote working method and digital working conditions have become popular for all jobs that can be carried out remotely (Caligiuri, et. al., 2020).

3. *Effects on health life:* COVID-19 infected millions of people around the world, causing many people to struggle with the disease and the death of more than 1 million people. The number of people infected and who died from this infection is increasing day by day (Fernandez & Shaw, 2020, p. 2; Saidi, et al., 2020, p. 295).

COVID-19 infects the lungs by infecting the upper and lower respiratory tract of some of the infected people (Rahmani & Mirmahaleh, 2020, p. 1). While some people can overcome this disease very mildly, the effect on others is much more devastating. Many cases need intensive care due to problems such as shortness of breath and pneumonia and subsequently, result in death. It has also been determined that individuals who survived the disease may have permanent body damage (Rahmani & Mirmahaleh, 2020, p. 3). Even in individuals who have not yet caught this disease, health problems arising from staying at home have started to emerge. In addition to the ailments caused by physical inactivity, problems such as psychological problems or alcohol addiction have become widespread (Settersten et. Al., 2020, p. 3).

While COVID-19 has affected the whole world, it has caused much greater problems for some disadvantaged groups. For example, the virus has been much more deadly for people with chronic diseases, immune problems, and advanced age groups. For example, because the population density of Italy consists of people of the advanced age group, the death rates were also higher. (Settersten et.al., 2020, p. 3; Saidi, et.al., 2020, p. 296).

As the burden on hospitals and health systems has increased too much, time and resources devoted to other diseases have been halted; doctors had to stop their operations except in compulsory cases, and most of the healthcare professionals, regardless of the branches, were assigned to the detection and treatment of COVID-19 patients. During this period, many healthcare professionals continued to work at risk by fighting this virus on the front lines (Halawi, et. al., 2020, p. 759-760).

During this period, some of the disadvantaged groups were working remotely, transportation, etc., while many people were close to their homes. Employees in ongoing services. Low-income individuals, neighborhoods, and regions consisting of these individuals are also heavily affected by this disease.

Individuals in underdeveloped countries are also among disadvantaged groups. The health systems of these countries cannot provide enough resources for the detection and treatment of the virus involved. In such countries, people are not provided with safe protection or employment opportunities due to social injustices, so the spread and the mortality rate in these countries is higher (Chiriboga, et.al., 2020, p. 1690; Settersten et.al., 2020, p. 2).

In addition to all these effects, another change that concerns health is the use of new digital methods such as telehealth and remote treatment for certain groups who are not able to go to hospitals, who are afraid to go (Halawi, et.al., 2020, p. 759).

## THE RELATIONSHIP BETWEEN LEADERSHIP AND CRISIS MANAGEMENT

Under this title, first of all, the basic relationship between crisis management and leadership is mentioned briefly. Next, the relationship between the COVID-19 crisis and leadership is discussed.

### Crisis Management and Leadership

Traditionally leadership is defined as the whole of the characteristics related to gathering a certain group of people around certain goals and having the necessary qualifications, skills, and experience to mobilize them to achieve these goals. However, leadership today is not limited to the processes of influencing people and activating the structure. Today, the knowledge, skills, and ability levels of humanity, the way of understanding and perceiving the management, the tendency to see success as a necessity, have removed the leader from being the "person who creates thought" and the watcher from being the "person who does the job" (Erarslan, 2004, p.2).

No matter how it is defined, times of crisis bring many difficulties for leaders (Roberts, 2020, p. 232). In an environment of high uncertainty, rapidly changing conditions, when it is unknown what the future will bring, it is very risky to make the right decisions. Because how leaders react to the crisis can permanently change, improve, or worsen societies' economic, social, and health systems (Dirani, et. al., 2020, p. 381). Leaders look for ways to make critical decisions that can positively affect people's lives. In times of crisis, people look for strong leaders who can guide this process in the right direction (Dolan et. al., 2020). Therefore, leadership is primarily about people.

Leadership, which is associated with inspiring, exciting, persuading, and directing people, acts as a bridge between today and the future due to these characteristics (Blake-Beard, et. al., 2020; Husbands, 2020, p. 6) The right decisions made cause this bridge to be stronger. In other words, the right behavior of leaders ensures that society or its masses survive and reach the future.

For all these reasons, leaders, who play an extremely important role in terms of the sustainability of the systems, depending on certain talents or skills to be successful in times of crisis. In other words, not all leaders can achieve the same success in times of crisis. In these periods, the most effective leaders are those who emerged with the creation of a proactive organizational culture, who are compatible with the organizational culture, and who have the skills to manage the crisis (Bhaduri, 2019, p. 535). Some researchers argue that different leadership abilities are required at different crisis stages to be successful in crisis management (Wooten & James, 2008; Pearson & Mitroff, 1993). At this point, the crisis life cycle emerges as an important issue (Bhaduri, 2019, p. 541). According to this organizational crisis management process is explained through the five-stage life cycle, including signal detection, prevention, damage containment, recovery, and learning. Each of these stages requires different leadership abilities. Pre-crisis, sense-making, and perspective-taking are critical leadership competencies to detect the signals or red flags before the crisis happens and take sufficient processes to minimize the damage at an early stage. In addition to "issue telling, organizational agility, and creativity," competencies critical during the prevention stage. During the crisis and containment stage, "decision making, effective communication, and risk-taking" are the main competencies required. In the recovery stage, leaders are required to "promote organizational resiliency and act with integrity." Finally, the learning stage, a leader's "learning orientation," is critical for successful crisis management (Bhaduri, 2019, p. 538-540).

## COVID-19 Crisis and Leadership

The ongoing COVID-19 crisis has reminded everyone of the critical role leaders to play in dealing with unexpected events that threaten the existence of organizations around the world and moving them into the future (Lagowska, et. al., 2020, p. 1). Although this crisis occurred all over the world, the reactions of leaders to the crisis differed, so different processes were experienced and different results were obtained regarding crisis management (Crayne & Medeiros, 2020, p. 1)

Leadership behavior during the COVID-19 crisis period has also attracted the attention of academics. In this process, it has been started to investigate how leaders manage the COVID-19 process, what are the leadership problems that may arise during the crisis process, what the roles of leaders or the competencies that should be in leaders during and after the crisis (Dolan et. al., 2020). In another study, the masculine leadership and feminine leadership styles for the COVID-19 pandemic period were discussed. Accordingly, in addition to the aggressive, strong, and risk-taking aspects of masculine leadership, emotional, loving, and sensitive aspects of feminine leadership were emphasized. In the research, the necessity of the Androgynous leadership type that combines the two leadership types is emphasized. According to research, leaders need to use both masculine and feminine traits in their leadership styles to achieve success in COVID-19 conditions. In other words, an androgynous leadership style is a success factor (Blake-Beard, et. al., 2020).

In a study investigating the reactions of the political leaders of the country during the COVID-19 process, attention was drawn to the charismatic, ideological, and pragmatic types of leadership. According to research, there is no single better way to lead effective leadership and any path can be followed according to situational conditions (Crayne & Medeiros, 2020, p. 3). Research links pragmatic leadership with rationality, science, and education. The research links the success of Angela Merkel's practices in the pandemic process with pragmatic leadership (Crayne & Medeiros, 2020, p. 7). In the research, Justin Trudeau, with charismatic leadership due to his hopeful and inspiring speeches (Crayne & Medeiros, 2020, p. 4); Jair Bolsonaro, on the other hand, has been associated with ideological leadership only because of his statements prioritizing economic issues (Crayne & Medeiros, 2020, p. 6). Besides, the research suggests that pragmatic leadership is more effective in the success of pandemic management (Crayne & Medeiros, 2020, p. 9).

In addition to all these, it is necessary to emphasize the relationship of health leaders with this process. During this period, health leaders had to deal with the COVID-19 crisis by assuming a more important role than anyone else. They supported this struggle both by guiding decision-makers with their scientific opinions and by directly contributing to the treatment of infected individuals. Healthcare professionals and their leaders sought to manage the crisis with courage, creativity, and endurance. The transparent sharing of the research results or the data collected about the disease during this period served to inform other healthcare professionals and society. Countries' pandemic science committees and health ministers have been the primary say in managing this process (Hunt, 2020, p. 2; Chiriboga, et. al., 2020). The decisions and practices of health leaders to establish partnerships to overcome the pandemic and achieve success in prevention methods such as diagnosis-treatment or vaccination have also been very effective in managing this process (Saidi, et. al., 2020).

## THE NEW NORMAL OF THE POST-COVID-19 ERA: THE DIGITAL AGE

The effects of COVID-19 on social and business life are briefly described in the previous section. Some of these influences have initiated such a radical transformation that there are beliefs that they cannot go back to the past. According to this belief, a process in which a new human age was triggered started (Dirani, et. al., 2020, p. 380). In this period after COVID-19; new normal, digital transformation, digital progress, digital age names have begun to be given (Horná, 2020, p. 2; Buheji & Buheji, 2020, p. 35; Husbands, 2020, p. 6; Caligiuri, et. al., 2020).

The reason why the post-COVID-19 era started to be called by these names is the applications such as remote working, distance education, and increasing use of technology, which were initiated to protect physical distances all over the world. Nowadays, there are opinions that these practices will not change in the post-pandemic period, will create permanent changes and that business life will not return to the old days (Venkatesh, 2020, p. 1). According to this view, the new normal digital age is associated with the world emerging stronger from every crisis, and COVID-19 will make a great transformation and progress compared to before.

The COVID-19 pandemic has forced many workplaces to adapt to major changes in the work environment around the world. Despite the changes and developments experienced in previous years regarding new technologies and digitalization, the sudden changes in the pandemic period required everyone to learn to use technology quickly (Buheji & Buheji, 2020, p. 35-36). The almost overnight transition from face-to-face to online and distance learning has placed significant and unprecedented demands on leaders, their institutions, and staff (Husbands, 2020, p. 2). As these demands arise simultaneously by all individuals and businesses, new solutions and technologies for working from home have been sought. Concepts such as self-learning, e-learning, distance education, and teaching have started to be used by everyone. These new trends have forced organizations and leaders to integrate technology into their businesses (Dirani, et. al., 2020, p. 388).

In this process, leaders started to develop digital strategiesto meet the technological needs of employees and customers (Dirani, et. al., 2020, p. 389). Business meetings and pieces of training have been transformed into virtual conferences; blackboard, zoom, etc. applications have become widely used for virtual studies and gatherings (Slanetz, et. al., 2020, p. 1; Altamirano & Collazo, 2020, p. 68). For all these reasons, in the new digital age, the managers and leaders of the enterprises need to find new opportunities by bringing various technological programs to their businesses and employees. Since digitalization is a tremendous source of change in the business world, leaders must also be able to deal with this digital transformation (Horná, 2020, p. 2). Leaders should invest in digital transformation technologies that are appropriate for their purpose and business. According to the European Commission (2018, p. 7), the agents of digital transformation consist of 9 basic technologies:

- Social Media

Social media has a wide-ranging impact on digital entrepreneurs, such as providing a better insight into customer behavior. Recent trends include social media going company-wide beyond marketing and community-building functions, and a decline in email use as instant messaging becomes an office fixture, allowing for real-time communication and information sharing.

- Mobile services

Mobile devices are technological advances that are transforming traditional businesses. Monitoring the use of mobile services is a prime indicator of how digital technologies influence how businesses work.

- Cloud technologies

The convergence of the cloud is promoting the growth of centrally coordinated applications that can be delivered to any device. Important business data, forms, and other documents can now be accessed from virtually anywhere, and cloud computing is making it easier to do business.

- Internet of Things

Mobile devices e.g. phones and wearable devices are now part of an expanded computing environment including – among others – consumer electronics and connected screens in the workplace. This network of Internet of Things (IoT) will raise management challenges for IT and manufacturing/logistics organizations as they lose control of user endpoint devices.

- Cybersecurity solutions

Cybersecurity has never been more essential, as companies have more digital valuable assets than ever before. The increasingly used hybrid cloud architecture requires a new approach to cybersecurity. The pervasive use of mobile devices by employees means that corporate IT now must manage the security of many more devices.

- Robotics and automated machinery

Robotics shift the labor/capital mix while managing societal expectations. End-user industries are rapidly adopting robots for industrial purposes to improve the quality of products and reduce manufacturing costs.

- Big data and data analytics

Companies are beginning to utilize big data and data analytics to gain business insights. As analytical technologies mature, they will leverage what computers do best, while freeing decision-makers from complex data analysis to deliver "intelligence at the moment".

- 3D printing

3D printing is poised to transform nearly every industry. Recent developments have transformed how products are designed, developed, manufactured, and distributed. Mass production remains the biggest challenge, but it is already used to produce parts faster.

- Artificial intelligence

AI will change the world and be ubiquitous in tomorrow's economy. AI major gains are likely to focus on productivity, efficiency, automation, and costs, enabling consumers and businesses to capitalize on the dig.

## The Role of Leadership in Digital Transformation

Digitalization is described by some as the biggest revolution that has come after the steam, steel, electricity, and petrochemical revolutions. As a result of digitalization that has had such a big impact, technology has begun to be used in all systems, and societies have started to advance the digital transformation process by not adopting the use of technology (Sainger, 2018, p. 1). The COVID-19 crisis played an unexpected and unprecedented rapid trigger in this transformation. Leaders' role is also very important in this transformation. Organizations can't realize this digital transformation without a leader. In this process, leaders should implement practices that will encourage the use of the 9 basic technologies described above. Also, its leaders should set a vision for digital transformation as well as making decisions that will reveal, develop, and lead to digitalization. It should share this vision with all other stakeholders, in other words, it should create an organizational culture compatible with digitalization (Sainger, 2018, p. 2). Leaders must work with different dimensions such as business model, structure, people, processes, technological adaptation, proposals, and engagement to successfully create an organization that can digitally transform. According to Sainger (2018, p. 4), these dimensions are important elements of an organization's value chain and digital transformation would not be possible without them.

## Challenges of Leaders in Digital Transformation

The virtual work environment, which has emerged as a requirement of digital transformation, brings certain challenges for leaders. The main reason for this is that it is more difficult to lead individuals or teams working in virtual environments. For example, the change in working and living conditions of service workers exposed to the COVID-19 pandemic may have brought resistance to change. During this process, employees may feel uncertainty-insecurity-tension. These emotions can create changes in individuals' performance (Bartsch, et. al., 2020). People resist change, and leaders must help people overcome their resistance to change. Since digital transformation is itself a form of change, then the same kind of resistance arises. It is also clear that technology alone is not something that will lead the organization towards its intended goals. Leaders should create a culture where people are empowered by technology to adapt and drive change (Sainger, 2018, p. 4). In this culture, leaders should develop new engagement strategies, taking into account the expectations of virtual teams in the digital era. Leaders should establish their digital transformation vision by evaluating new management strategies for the workforce (Sainger, 2018, p. 5). Virtual workers are not easy to influence - motivate - coordinate and control. Therefore, leaders should focus on strategies that will improve employees' self-management skills. It is recommended to display task-relationship-oriented leadership behaviors to overcome these difficulties. In this process, employees should understand the stress experienced and flexibility should be given to them regarding their mistakes (Bartsch, et. al., 2020).

# LEADERSHIP TYPES, QUALITIES, AND SKILLS AFTER COVID-19

By destroying known systems of the COVID-19 crisis at once; has made individuals, communities, or businesses seek guidance from their leaders (Dirani, et. al., 2020, p. 380). How leaders guide this crisis not only determines the success of the crisis management process but also the future of the systems collapsing due to this crisis and how much adaptation will be made to the major changes that will occur after the crisis. While some leaders can see this process as an opportunity for development and growth and manage it successfully, others fail. This is because, in times of crisis, leadership creates an enormous challenge that requires exceptional physical, technical, social, and emotional skills. For this reason, recommendations for conducting research revealing the relationship between leadership development and crisis are also seen (Lagowska, et. al., 2020, p. 3). Some researchers have also begun to investigate the leadership qualities necessary to be successful during and after the crisis (Dirani, et. al., 2020, p. 381; Horná, 2020, p. 6). In this research, it is aimed to answer this need. In this section, three leadership types supported by research are given briefly for the COVID-19 crisis period. Second, the leadership qualities and skills required for successful leadership in the new period after COVID-19 are explained.

## Pandemic, Ethical and Digital Leadership

Wilson (2020) brought the pandemic leadership concept to the agenda by associating it with the successful management of the pandemic process. During the COVID-19 pandemic period, a model was created by analyzing the New Zealand example practices and the decisions of the New Zealand leader, which were accepted by everyone, and brought it to the literature as pandemic leadership. Wilson (2020, p. 285-289) attributed the distinctive feature and success factor of this model to building trust and providing creative responses.

Also, Wilson (2020, p. 285) explains the basic requirements of pandemic leadership as follows:

- Be led by expertise:
    - Follow the science
    - Use facts & evidence
    - Listen to advice from relevant experts
- Mobilise collective effort:
    - Inform & educate
    - Pull no punches
    - Convey direction, meaning & empathy
    - Unite
    - Address practicalities
    - Avoid defensiveness
    - Solicit feedback
- Enable coping:
    - Enable planning
    - Build relevant knowledge and skills
    - Enable sensemaking
    - Enable kindness
    - Develop creative responses

Ethical leadership is also a type of leadership that is explained by building trust. The uncertainties and sudden changes experienced during the pandemic process have led all individuals to seek explanations they can trust. Ethical leadership also comes into play here. It is about behavior that gives employees confidence in both the COVID-19 pandemic and post-pandemic periods. The feeling that employees can trust their leaders is most evident in this importance, so ethical leadership has become more important than ever to express the honest and transparent practices of leaders towards them (Horná, 2020, p. 2).

Ethical leadership in the digital age after COVID-19 is keeping up with the digital transformation. Leaders' attitudes towards ethics and trust need to be radically changed and developed about the works that are starting to be carried out remotely and the different stakeholder groups that manage this process. Therefore, transparency and ethical management and leadership are seen as much more important in the next period. According to Horná (2020, p. 3), it is also important for leaders to develop trust-based approaches and gain new skills in this new era in which digital systems are used. Leaders of the business world are expected to cope with this change and develop skills that include ethical and moral behaviors to be successful in the digital age. Leaders based on the revitalization of the ethical environment and ethical culture organizations in the post-COVID-19 era will be better prepared to control/explore the digital world using digital technologies (Horná, 2020, p. 2-4; Nicola, et.al., 2020, p. 121).

In the previous sections, it was stated that the most important effect of the COVID-19 pandemic on business life was that it led to a digital age where remote work would prevail. In this period, there is a need for leaders who can adapt to the intensive use of technology, organize remote working people or teams, and lead them. It would not be wrong to call these leaders, who will be the best to integrate with technology, as digital leaders. Because the main characteristic of these leaders is to recognize digital innovations, to adapt to them, and to use digital communication processes successfully.

Digital leaders are expected to have digital speed and knowledge, as well as ethical and trustworthy behaviors. In the digital leadership style, digital applications in the new era after COVID-19 are seen as opportunities, and leaders who adapt to the best practices encountered in digital transformation with theologies are needed. These leaders are expected to take an active role in online environments through coaching or simulations (Horná, 2020, p. 3-6).

These three types of leadership are very important to mitigate the effects of the COVID-19 pandemic on social life, economic life, and the psychological health of employees. During this period, the goal of leaders is to contribute to economic recovery by minimizing these negative effects.

Leaders in both the pandemic period and the post-pandemic period; By leading digital transformation, by developing ethical behaviors, it can contribute to the fast and correct performance of work and motivate employees. For all these reasons, the types of leadership described here are critical to mitigate the effects of pandemics on work, life, and employee psychology, and to effectively lead remote workers with the increased use of technology.

## New Leaders of the New Normal

Until this part of the study, information about the effects of COVID-19 disease on business and social life has been trying to be given, and the relationship of these effects with leadership has been discussed. At the same time, in this study, the new normal and digital age concepts after COVID-19 are also briefly explained and the three leadership types that are thought to be effective in the digital age are briefly emphasized.

The comparison of the leaders of the COVID-19 crisis with the problems that they have not faced so far, and the practices of the leaders to solve these problems and to cope with this crisis led some to success while others made unsuccessful decisions. Experiences in this process have raised the question of what qualities should be in leaders in such a major crisis and post-crisis period. Written to contribute to leadership development for the post-COVID-19 era (Lagowska, et. al., 2020, p. 3), this section explains the basic characteristics, abilities, or behaviors required for new leaders in the new era after COVID-19 to achieve success.

## Increased Digital Skills

With the COVID-19 virus, efforts to run the work from home, which were carried out by the whole world at once, increased the use of digital platforms at once. With this development, while all people are trying to keep up with this digital transformation, digital platforms have begun to be developed rapidly. It is thought that this period, when the works are carried out remotely, will continue to a large extent in the post-COVID-19 period. For this reason, the most basic task for the leaders of the new normal is to be aware of this digital transformation and keep up with the transformation.

In this process, it becomes a necessity for leaders to use digitalization to its advantages. Therefore, leaders must be able to continue digital progress as they develop their digital skills and operate. In other words, leaders must embrace digital transformation more than anyone else and acquire talent to go beyond simple digitalization (Horná, 2020, p. 5-6).

## Increased Communication Skills

During COVID-19, individuals, and businesses also experienced communication difficulties due to changing conditions and physical distances (Altamirano & Collazo, 2020, p. 71). One of the new features that normally should be in leaders is to develop some of their social skills in this new era of physical distances and digital progress. The first of these is the ability to communicate.

Leaders must stay in constant contact with remote groups. Thanks to uninterrupted communication, they should be able to monitor not only their business information but also their mental and emotional states (Dirani, et. al., 2020, p. 384). At the same time, leaders should be able to answer the questions of those who are in constant contact with the influential group, prevent misinformation, inform them constantly and remove uncertainties (Dirani, et. al., 2020, p. 386; Nicola, et. al., 2020, p. 123; Altamirano & Collazo, 2020, p. 70). Therefore, leaders should focus on effective communication techniques in the new era. In this way, a strong bond can be established between people in different places. Leaders' communication techniques should be based on transparency and ethics and should give confidence to their followers (Horná, 2020, p. 5; Nicola, et. al., 2020, p. 123)

## Emotional Intelligence

Emotional intelligence is one of the important characteristics that will contribute to the success of leaders in the new period. In a rapidly developing world, leaders and managers need to practice a certain level of emotional intelligence to cope with the evolving challenges around them (Altamirano & Collazo, 2020, p. 69). Leaders need to show empathy towards influence groups, demonstrate that they are attentive to people's distress, and are taking measures to support followers (Lagowska, et. al., 2020, p. 2).

### Quick Decision Making

One of the most important behaviors to be prepared for new crises and to achieve success in crisis processes in the upcoming period is speed. Leaders need to act swiftly and decisively and implement practices that will alleviate the negative impact of the crisis without wasting time. One of the main things that set leaders apart during the pandemic is their ability to rapidly process information and make decisions (Dirani, et. al., 2020, p. 384). One of the key reasons for New Zealand's success in the COVID-19 crisis is attributed to its leaders' quick decisions and their implementation without delay (Nicola, et. al., 2020, p. 126-127).

### Self-awareness and Listening to Science

During crises, leaders will encounter information from outside their area of expertise. At the same time, leaders do not have time to learn new skills, given the high urgency of critical events. Therefore, to increase the effectiveness of crisis management, they need to reach people with relevant knowledge, rather than act intuitively (Lagowska, et. al., 2020, p. 3). Leaders' ability to do this has to do with their self-awareness. For this reason, in the next period, leaders should be able to distinguish between what they know and what they do not know and take decisions by listening to science in such vital crises that affect all humanity.

According to Wilson (2020, p. 280), there is ample evidence that the behavior or negligence of some political or business leaders contributes to the spread of the virus and results in mass deaths that could be prevented if these leaders followed the advice of scientists.

### Ability to Lead Remote Workers

Remote working conditions that lead to digital transformation force leaders to adapt to this new working order. The belief that the home-working system will continue after COVID-19 (Dirani, et. al., 2020, p. 384), also requires leaders to acquire new skills on this issue.

In this process, leaders should find ways to follow the physical and mental health of employees, find ways to motivate them away and make efforts to gain the knowledge and skills necessary to work remotely. Leaders should be able to guide their remote workers (Dirani, et. al., 2020, p. 388).

In the new era, empowering employees, and reduced constraints are necessary to maintain the productivity and performance of remote teams (Succi, 2020, p. 72). Leaders should seek to support and develop self-employed virtual teams (Nicola, et. al., 2020, p. 121).

Leaders should focus on the unexpected benefits of virtual teams in the new normal remote working conditions (Caligiuri, et. al, 2020). Leaders who want to realize these benefits need to acquire new skills to motivate, manage, and direct the remote workforce.

## SOLUTIONS AND RECOMMENDATIONS

In this chapter of the book, the relationship between leadership and the COVID-19 pandemic that brought the whole world to the brink of an unprecedented crisis is explored. Leaders steer the future by making critical decisions that affect individuals, employees, or societies at the micro and macro level.

Their decisions will affect the success of the crisis process as well as reshape the post-crisis period. This relationship between leaders and crises is discussed in this chapter. The remote working environment and digitalization efforts created by the COVID-19 pandemic have triggered a new era that will continue to be effective during the pandemic problem. This age is called by the authors of the digital age. How leaders will be successful in this new era is also one of the important issues discussed in the research. Accordingly, the secrets of the success of the new normal leaders are hiding in increasing their digital skills and communication skills, dropping science when they need to process the information they do not know, making quick decisions, and developing skills that can lead remote workers. In the research, it is suggested that a new leader who normally wants to achieve success improves their skills regarding these listed behaviors. At the same time, in this period, leaders must set a vision for digital transformation and create an organizational culture that will strengthen this transformation.

## FUTURE RESEARCH DIRECTIONS

In this section, the relationship between the COVID-19 pandemic and leadership is explained based on a literature review. In the research, the roles of leaders in this crisis and post-crisis period were discussed and skills that help to achieve success in leadership were included. However, this unit is limited to literature research. It is suggested that such a critically important subject should be enriched with different research methods and data sources.

The first of these recommendations is to investigate the decision-making methods and experiences of leaders who make critical decisions in the COVID-19 process and how they manage the process. New data that can be collected from the perceptions and experiences of leaders in different sectors through semi-structured interview techniques will contribute to the enlightenment of this process. At the same time, the data that can be collected from the groups influenced by the said leaders will be useful to reveal what employees expect from their leaders in times of crisis and the new normal remote working conditions.

## CONCLUSION

The subject of this research is the COVID-19 pandemic and the leadership relationship that brought all humanity to the brink of an unprecedented crisis. In this study, first, the effects of the pandemic on human life are explained in three parts: social, business, and health life. In the second part, the relationship between this crisis- leadership- COVID-19 is discussed. Following this relationship, the concepts of the new era after COVID-19 and the digital age were brought up for discussion, and the roles of leaders in the digital transformation process and the challenges they could face were discussed. According to this section, the main role of leaders is to determine a vision that will contribute to digital transformation and to create an organizational culture accordingly. The main challenges that may face are resistance to change and leading remote workers. In the last section, the concepts of the pandemic, ethics, and digital leadership, which attracted attention in this period, are briefly explained. One of the important issues covered in the last section is the basic characteristics or skills that should be in the leaders in the new era. Accordingly, the secrets of new normally successful leadership are hidden in increased digital skills, enhanced communication skills, emotional intelligence, rapid decision-making, self-awareness and listening to science, and finally being able to lead remote workers.

## REFERENCES

Ahlsson, A. (2020). Why change? Lessons in leadership from the COVID-19 pandemic. *European Journal of Cardio-Thoracic Surgery*, 1–3. PMID:32688379

Altamirano, M. A., & Collazo, C. E. R. (2020, June). Leading with emotional intelligence: How leaders of a diverse-based urban college in new york successfully respond to the COVID-19 crisis of 2020. *Journal of Education, Innovation, and Communication*, (Special Issue), 65–75.

Bartsch, S., Weber, E., Büttgen, M., & Huber, A. (2020). Leadership matters in crisis-induced digital transformation: How to lead service employees effectively during the COVID-19 pandemic. *Journal of Service Management, 32*(1), 71–85. doi:10.1108/JOSM-05-2020-0160

Bhaduri, R. M. (2019). Leveraging culture and leadership in crisis management. European Journal of Training and Development. *European Journal of Training and Development, 43*(5/6), 554–569. doi:10.1108/EJTD-10-2018-0109

Blake-Beard, S., Shapiro, M., & Ingols, C. (2020). Feminine? Masculine? Androgynous leadership as a necessity in COVID-19. *Gender in Management: An International Journal.*

Buheji, M., & Buheji, A. (2020). Characteristics of 'Problem-Based Learning'in post-COVID-19 workplace. *Human Resource Management Review, 10*(2), 33–39.

Caligiuri, P., De Cieri, H., Minbaeva, D., Verbeke, A., & Zimmermann, A. (2020). International HRM insights for navigating the COVID-19 pandemic: Implications for future research and practice. *Journal of International Business Studies*, 1. PMID:32836500

Chiriboga, D., Garay, J., Buss, P., Madrigal, R. S., & Rispel, L. C. (2020). Health inequity during the COVID-19 pandemic: A cry for ethical global leadership. *Lancet, 395*(10238), 1690–1691. doi:10.1016/S0140-6736(20)31145-4 PMID:32419711

Coscieme, L., Fioramonti, L., Mortensen, L. F., Pickett, K. E., Kubiszewski, I., Lovins, H., & De Vogli, R. (2020). *Women in power: female leadership and public health outcomes during the COVID-19 pandemic.* MedRxiv; doi:10.1101/2020.07.13.20152397

Crayne, M. P., & Medeiros, K. E. (2020). Making sense of crisis: Charismatic, ideological, and pragmatic leadership in response to COVID-19. *American Psychologist.*

Dirani, K. M., Abadi, M., Alizadeh, A., Barhate, B., Garza, R. C., Gunasekara, N., & Majzun, Z. (2020). Leadership competencies and the essential role of human resource development in times of crisis: A response to Covid-19 pandemic. *Human Resource Development International, 23*(4), 380–394. doi:10.1080/13678868.2020.1780078

Dolan, L., Raich, M., Garti, A., & Landau, A. (2020). *"The COVID-19 Crisis" as an opportunity for introspection: A multi-level reflections on values, needs, trust and leadership in the future.* https://www.europeanbusinessreview.com/the-covid-19-crisis-as-an-opportunity-for-introspection/

Duygun, A. (2020). Evaluation of consumers' lifestyles during The COVID-19 pandemic. *Econder Uluslararası Akademik Dergi, 4*(1), 232–247. doi:10.35342/econder.744621

Eraslan, L. (2004). Liderlikte post-modern bir paradigma: Dönüşümcü liderlik. *Journal of Human Sciences*, *1*(1).

European Commission. (2018). *Digital Transformation Scoreboard 2018: EU businesses go digital: Opportunities, outcomes and uptake*. Publications Office of the European Union.

Fernandez, A. A., & Shaw, G. P. (2020). Academic Leadership in a Time of Crisis: The Coronavirus and COVID-19. *The Journal of Leadership Studies*, *14*(1), 39–45. doi:10.1002/jls.21684

Forester, J., & McKibbon, G. (2020). Beyond blame: Leadership, collaboration and compassion in the time of COVID-19. *Socio-Ecological Practice Research*, *2*(3), 205–216. doi:10.100742532-020-00057-0

Halawi, M. J., Wang, D. D., & Hunt, T. R. III. (2020). What's important: weathering the COVID-19 crisis: time for leadership, vigilance, and Unity. *The Journal of Bone and Joint Surgery. American Volume*, *102*(9), 759–760. doi:10.2106/JBJS.20.00419 PMID:32379115

Horná, P. T. (2020). The Post-COVID-19 Challenges in ethical leadership. *Journal of Global Science*.

Hunt, D. (2020). *A publication from the Association of Chiefs and Leaders of General Internal Medicine*. ACLGIM.

Husbands, C. (2020). *Leading, learning and lockdown: first thoughts on lessons for leadership from the coronavirus crisis*. Sheffield Hallam University.

Lagowska, U., Sobral, F., & Furtado, L. M. G. P. (2020). Leadership under crises: A research agenda for the post-COVID-19 era. *BAR - Brazilian Administration Review*, *17*(2), e200062. doi:10.1590/1807-7692bar2020200062

Li, J., Ghosh, R., & Nachmias, S. (2020). A special issue on the impact of the COVID-19 pandemic on work, worker, and workplace!? Implications for HRD research and practices in time of crisis. *Human Resource Development International*, *23*(4), 329–332. doi:10.1080/13678868.2020.1780715

Liu, S. L., Saif, L. J., Weiss, S. R., & Su, L. (2020). No credible evidence supporting claims of the laboratory engineering of SARS-CoV-2. *Emerging Microbes & Infections*, *9*(1), 505–507. doi:10.1080/22221751.2020.1733440 PMID:32102621

Menachery, V. D., Yount, B. L. Jr, Debbink, K., Agnihothram, S., Gralinski, L. E., Plante, J. A., Graham, R. L., Scobey, T., Ge, X.-Y., Donaldson, E. F., Randell, S. H., Lanzavecchia, A., Marasco, W. A., Shi, Z.-L., & Baric, R. S. (2015, December). A SARS-like cluster of circulating bat coronaviruses shows potential for human emergence. *Nature Medicine*, *21*(12), 1508–1514. doi:10.1038/nm.3985 PMID:26552008

Moon, M. J. (2020). Fighting Against COVID-19 with Agility, Transparency, and Participation: Wicked policy problems and new governance challenges. *Public Administration Review*, *80*(4), 651–656. doi:10.1111/puar.13214 PMID:32836434

Nicola, M., Sohrabi, C., Mathew, G., Kerwan, A., Al-Jabir, A., Griffin, M., Agha, M., & Agha, R. (2020). Health policy and leadership models during the COVID-19 pandemic-review article. *International Journal of Surgery*, *81*, 122–129. doi:10.1016/j.ijsu.2020.07.026 PMID:32687873

Pearson, C. M., & Mitroff, I. I. (1993). From crisis prone to crisis prepared: A framework for crisis management. *The Academy of Management Perspectives*, *7*(1), 48–59. doi:10.5465/ame.1993.9409142058

Rahmani, A. M., & Mirmahaleh, S. Y. H. (2020). Coronavirus disease (COVID-19) prevention and treatment methods and effective parameters: A systematic literature review. *Sustainable Cities and Society*, 102568. PMID:33110743

Roberts, R. (2020). COVID-19, Leadership and lessons from physics. *The Australian Journal of Rural Health*, *28*(3), 232–235. doi:10.1111/ajr.12649 PMID:32592229

Saidi, A. M. O., Nur, F. A., Al-Mandhari, A. S., El Rabbat, M., Hafeez, A., & Abubakar, A. (2020). Decisive leadership is a necessity in the COVID-19 response. *Lancet*, *396*(10247), 295–298. doi:10.1016/S0140-6736(20)31493-8 PMID:32628904

Sainger, G. (2018). Leadership in digital age: A study on the role of leader in this era of digital transformation. *International Journal on Leadership*, *6*(1), 1.

Settersten, R. A. Jr, Bernardi, L., Härkönen, J., Antonucci, T. C., Dykstra, P. A., Heckhausen, J., ... Mulder, C. H. (2020). Understanding the effects of Covid-19 through a life course lens. 45. *Advances in Life Course Research*, *45*, 100360. doi:10.1016/j.alcr.2020.100360

Slanetz, P. J., Bedi, H., Kesler, T., & Chetlen, A. (2020). Optimizing journal clubs in the post–coronavirus disease 2019 (COVID-19) era. *Journal of the American College of Radiology*.

Succi, C. (2020). Freedom & vulnerability: How people develop new skills in an unexpected work environment. In Managing a post-Covid19 era. (pp. 69-73). ESCP Research Institute of Management (ERIM).

Venkatesh, V. (2020). Impacts of COVID-19: A research agenda to support people in their fight. *International Journal of Information Management*, *55*, 102197. doi:10.1016/j.ijinfomgt.2020.102197 PMID:32836648

Voyer, B. (2020). What behavioural science can tell us about human behaviour in the wake of pandemic? In Managing a post-Covid19 era. (pp. 1-5). ESCP Research Institute of Management (ERIM).

Wilson, S. (2020). Pandemic leadership: Lessons from New Zealand's approach to COVID-19. *Leadership*, *16*(3), 279–293. doi:10.1177/1742715020929151

Wooten, L. P., & James, E. H. (2008). Linking crisis management and leadership competencies: the role of human resource development. *Advances in Developing Human Resources, 10*(3), 352-379. https://covid19.who.int/ doi:10.1177/1523422308316450

## ADDITIONAL READING

Ansell, C., Sørensen, E., & Torfing, J. (2020). The COVID-19 pandemic as a game changer for public administration and leadership? The need for robust governance responses to turbulent problems. *Public Management Review*, 1–12. doi:10.1080/14719037.2020.1820272

Avolio, B. J. (2010). *Full range leadership development*. Sage Publications.

Daft, R. L. (2014). *The leadership experience*. Cengage Learning.

Day, D. V. (2000). Leadership development: A review in context. *The Leadership Quarterly*, *11*(4), 581–613. doi:10.1016/S1048-9843(00)00061-8

DePree, M. (2011). *Leadership is an art*. Currency.

Kouzes, J. M., & Posner, B. Z. (2006). *The leadership challenge* (Vol. 3). John Wiley & Sons.

Lyden, P. (2020). Temporary emergency guidance to US stroke centers during the COVID-19 pandemic on behalf of the AHA/ASA Stroke Council Leadership. *Stroke*, 10.

Meindl, J. R., Ehrlich, S. B., & Dukerich, J. M. (1985). The romance of leadership. *Administrative Science Quarterly*, *30*(1), 78–102. doi:10.2307/2392813

Vroom, V. H., & Yetton, P. W. (1973). *Leadership and decision-making* (Vol. 110). University of Pittsburgh.

## KEY TERMS AND DEFINITIONS

**Communication:** It is the transfer of feelings, thoughts, and all kinds of information between individuals. It is performed double-sided, verbally and non-verbally, using various tools.

**Decision Making:** It is the individuals' choosing among all their options, sometimes with their feelings, sometimes with their intuition, and sometimes rationally.

**Digitalization:** It is the transfer of existing information sources to computer systems with the help of various technologies. It is the integration of technological equipment into the business life and social life of the individual.

**Emotional Intelligence:** It is the ability of an individual to watch, evaluate, and understand the emotions of himself and those around him. Individuals with high emotional intelligence are successful in managing their emotions and empathizing with others.

**Leader:** It is a person who can attract attention by affecting people both physically and mentally, appealing to their feelings, motivating and uniting them towards a specific goal, and making them do what they want.

**Remote Working:** The way employees perform their duties regarding job requirements and definitions outside of the employer's buildings.

**Self-Awareness:** In short, is the individual's understanding and recognition of himself by being aware of what is happening in his inner world. Individuals with high self-awareness analyze better what they know and what they do not know.

# Chapter 14
# COVID-19 and the Call for Elder Change Leadership

**Stan Amaladas**
https://orcid.org/0000-0002-2066-3261
*Baker College, USA*

## ABSTRACT

*The author argues that post-COVID-19 change leadership is neither a matter of technically improving what change leaders are already doing or refining existing systems and regulation. Within the context of abrupt, sudden, and unexpected change, two questions are raised. First, if it is not a matter of technically improving what change leaders are already doing, or refining existing systems, what more do post-COVID-19 change leaders need to do? Second, what new qualities would change leaders need to embrace (theory) so that they can meaningfully fulfill their change leadership practices in a post-COVID-19 era? Approaching various paradigms of change leadership as stories, the author addresses (1) the seduction of pre-COVID-19 story of change leadership, (2) offers a post-COVID-19 elder change leadership model, (3) offers a post-COVID-19 elder change leadership framework centered around four dimensions: humility, generating meaning amid chaos, compassion and empathy, and affirming hope through story telling.*

## INTRODUCTION

While there is a common understanding that processes of organizational change must be well managed in that they must be planned, organized, directed, and controlled (Gill, 2002, Northouse, 2018), today, organizational managers across the globe find themselves in the middle of an unplanned, uninvited, and deadly 'guest' called COVID-19. This virus knows no boundaries, geographical or otherwise, and in addition to creating chaos, confusion, fear, stress, and anxiety it is indifferent to whom it attacks and kills. At the same time, while we may not have consciously invited this 'guest' into our world, in living or not living the way we have lived, we have created a context that opened the door for this virus to take a centre stage in our lives. While it's destructive force can readily be seen through the number of those infected across the globe (78.2 million, and who have died (1.62 million) - as of December 15, 2020 -

DOI: 10.4018/978-1-7998-6948-1.ch014

COVID-19 has also exposed how fragmented we really are in spite of our technological hyper and inter connectivity. In his most recent Encyclical, *Fratelli Tutti,* Pope Francis (2020) for example, candidly states

*As I was writing this letter, the Covid-19 pandemic unexpectedly erupted, exposing our false securities. Aside from the different ways that various countries responded to the crisis, their inability to work together became quite evident. For all our hyper-connectivity, we witnessed a fragmentation that made it more difficult to resolve problems that affect us all. Anyone who thinks that the only lesson to be learned was the need to improve what we were already doing, or to refine existing systems and regulations, is denying reality. (#7)*

The unexpected eruptions that Pope Francis references is what management and leadership scholars place in the realm of *discontinuous change* (Fish, 1992; Grundy, 1994; Pullen, 1993; Morais et al., 2020; Romanelli and Tushman, 1994; Tushman et al., 1986). Part of our COVID-19 reality is that it has randomly thrown all into an unplanned condition of discontinuity. This pandemic has been variously described as a disaster, catastrophe, and a black swan, and to paraphrase Taleb (2007) - an unpredictable event beyond normal expectations that has severe consequences..

At the same time, Mirvis (2020) makes a case that the coronavirus was predictable. For example, in recent years we have seen outbreaks of corona-type viruses Ebola (2014-2016), HIV/AIDS (1983), H1N1 (2009), MERS (2012), and SARS (2002). He points to a 2015 TED talk, where Microsoft co-founder turned health care expert, Bill Gates, warned that a virus like the 1918 Spanish flu would spread 'very quickly' around the world. Gates went on to say, "We've actually invested very little in a system to stop an epidemic," adding, "We're not ready for the next epidemic" (as cited in Mirvis, 2020, p. 283). As prepared or unprepared as we have been, the significance of COVID-19 is that while it is a "frame-breaking change that disrupts existing cultures, structures, and processes," it is forcing managers and leaders in organizations, as Morais et al (2020) note, to make some "fundamental shifts in order for (any) business to stay competitive and survive" (p. 1).

## Questions

Within this context of the expected or unexpected eruption of COVID-19, changing contexts, societal fragmentations that make it more difficult to resolve problems together, the politicizing of this pandemic especially in the United States of America, and an inability to work together, in spite of the espoused maxim: "we are all in this together," the questions raised in this Chapter are:

- If Post COVID-19 change leaders are not to deny reality, and if it is not a matter of technically improving what we are already doing, or refining existing systems and regulations, what *more* do they need to do?
- What new model of leadership would they need to embrace so that they can meaningfully fulfill their change leadership practices in a Post COVID-19 Era?

## METHODOLOGY/METHOD

In this Chapter, I take a narrative approach to the study of leading change. Simply put, I will orient to the various approaches to leading change as "stories." The use of stories and storytelling has a rich history in organizational studies (Brown et al, 2011; Their, 2018; Yiannis, 2000). To speak of stories rather than 'reality,' means that "truth" in the tradition of logical positivism is not available to narrative theory and research. At the same time, while stories as they are told, are always social constructions, narrative researchers acknowledge that each story bears "a" truth, or as May (1991) says, "a myth around which we pattern our lives" (p. 33) - organizational lives included. However, it is not if these 'myths,' are simply illusions. On the contrary, as May (1993) further states "myths challenge us to confront our destiny, our death, or love, our joy. The myth adds the universal dimension because every adult has to confront his or her fate in love and death" (p. 190).

In an audiotape entitled "Telling Your Story," Sam Keen (1991) remarks that we are inevitably dramatic narrative-creating human beings who cannot <u>not</u> tell stories. He believes that our stories may be mythic, ideological, or biographical, that around each of us is woven a web of family stories, and that every relationship has its own story. This is another way of saying that stories become our experienced reality. In the words of Mair (1998)

*Stories are habitations. We live in and through stories. They conjure worlds. We do not know the world other than as a story world, Stories inform life. They hold us together and keep us apart. We inhabit great stories of our culture. We live through stories. We are lived by...stories... (p. 127)*

To orient to the literature on leading change as 'stories' challenges us to take yet another look at the dominant stories that has come to inform practices of leading change. And if we agree that stories are social constructions, then we would, along with Watzlawick (1984) ask: "What would the world of a person (or organization) be like who managed to accept reality fully and totally as his or her own construction?" (p. 326. Parenthesis, mine). To accept the idea that stories are but social constructions moves us in the direction of being "aware of the ever-present possibility of constructing it differently" (Watzlawick, 1884, p. 327).

## ORGANIZING OF CHAPTER

This Chapter is divided into six sections. Section 1 will address the seduction of Pre-COVID-19 story of change leadership. Section 2 introduces change leadership from the perspective of a post-industrial paradigm/story. Section 3 will build on Lopez's (2019) anthropological, ecological, and sociological narrative of Indigenous cultures across the globe, and propose a new (yet old) Post COVID-19 Elder change leadership model. Lopez's research will serve as my 'single case study.' Rather than concerning myself with generalizing, I will seek to build <u>another</u> understanding of what it means to lead in time of unprecedented change. To paraphrase Stake (2008), this single case study is both "bounded" and "defined by an interest" (p. 443) and "not by the methods of inquiry used" (p. 445). Our interest is exploring stories about change leadership while offering the story and significance of elder as a valid Post COVID-19 change leadership story. Barry Lopez was elected to the American Academy of Arts and Letters in February 2020, and he is a premier anthropologist and paleontologist whose sincere ecological efforts places him in a higher awareness plane for his humanitarian and environmental concerns.

Relying on Lopez's (2019) qualitative research, Section 4 will outline ten critical qualities of Elder change leadership. They will be collected under four critical dimensions: (a) Humility; (b) Generating Meaning Amid Chaos; (c) Compassion and Empathy; and (d) Affirming Hope through Storytelling. Section 5 will offer a Post COVID-19 Elder change leadership learning framework that is grounded within in the context of these four dimensions. Section 6 will close this Chapter by offering 11 recommendations for Post-COVID-19 change leadership

## SECTION 1: THE SEDUCTION OF THE INDUSTRIAL PARADIGM/STORY

Within the context of discontinuous change, part of the problem, as Todnem, Hughes, and Ford (2016), argue is that stories presented for leading through discontinuous change are themselves similar to incremental change in that they are linear and rationalistic. In his review of change management and leadership literature, between January 1, 1978 and December 31, 2014, Hughes (2015), for example discovered the most cited references:

6,638 Citations – *Leading Change* (Kotter, 1996)
4,340 Citations – John Kotter on *Leading Change: Why transformation efforts fail* (Kotter, 1995)
3,539 Citations - Transformational leadership (Bass & Riggio, 2006)

What this suggests is that Kotter's eight steps to leading change appears to have become the orthodoxy for change leadership and management. What is particularly problematic is that while a revised edition of *Leading Change* appeared in 2012, Kotter (2012), in his new preface wrote "the material in this book is not only still relevant now, sixteen years after it was published, but I believe it is more relevant, and for one reason the speed of change continues to increase" (p. vii). So,, while "the title might be *Leading Change...*" Todnem et al (2016) take issue with the contents in his book in that it "does not change..." (p. 11). What this suggests is that while the context for change has changed, the rationalistic and linear thinking about managing, or for that matter, leading change, has not changed. Others argue that part of the problem in the literature on discontinuous change is that while it has focused on technological discontinuities (Smith, 2012), it has excluded a focus on societal change (Birkinshaw et al., 2016), financial and economic crises, or reputational issues confronting organizations (Morais, et al., 2020).

How is it possible that the industrial paradigm/story of managing change continues to be dominated by rationalistic and linear thinking like the one offered by Kotter (1995; 2011) especially when (a) management scholars like Uhl-Bien, Marion, and McKelvey (2007) affirm that it is "hopelessly out of date" (p. 298), and (b) leadership scholars like Rost (1997) say that the "that it increasingly ill serves the needs of a world rapidly being transformed by a massive paradigm shift in societal values" (p. 181)? It is here that we need to attend to the seduction of this industrial story.

Historically, the dominance of the industrial change model originated from a radical change in the world known as the Industrial Revolution. As a 20th century political theorist Arendt (1994) notes, it is "the greatest revolution in the shortest span of time mankind has ever witnessed: in a few decades it changed our whole globe more radically than all the three thousand years of recorded history before it" (p. 316). A similar argument was made by Marx in the 19th century. Recall, for instance, Marx's (1856/1978), reflections on the surprise and horror of industrialization:

*On the one hand, there have started into life, industrial and scientific forces, which no epoch of human history had ever suspected. On the other hand, there exist symptoms of decay, far surpassing the horrors of the latter times of the Roman Empire... No earlier century had even a presentiment that such productive forces slumbered in the lap of social labour. (pp. 577 -578)*

The success of the industrial paradigm, as Marx (1856/1978) noted, is a result of the productive capacity to create "massive and more colossal productive powers than have all preceding generations together" (p. 477). It was indeed the success of a total "subjection of nature's forces to man" (Marx, 1978, p. 577), that moved the industrialized 'man' to "embellish" themselves with, as the sociologist Weber (1958) noted, a "sort of convulsive sense of self-importance" (p. 182). In the face of this reality, Marx (1856/1978) makes a passionate plea: it is time for all to sober up, and "face with sober senses his real conditions of life, and his real relations with his kind" (p. 476).

Marx (1856/1978) and Weber (1958) appear to be suggesting that industrial attempts to control nature or attempts to engage in the excessive consumerism and acquisition of capital, and its resulting human arrogance, are consequences of being totally *addicted* to their own success. For Marx, individuals who are addicted/intoxicated are incapable of facing the real conditions of their lives because they are too busy being intoxicated in their haughtiness that they are in control. According to Bateson (1979), this arrogance of control is itself a pathology of Occidental/Western epistemology. While nature is necessarily a part of who we are, the pathology of the addicted motivates them to behave as if they are separate from nature. For the addicted, it is "them" against nature. This epistemology of separation continues to seduce the addicted to neurotically exert more autocratic control over all interrelated systems.

On the other hand, to face the real conditions of life with sobriety, implies that while the subjection of nature's forces to one's will is always a possibility, it is to choose to do otherwise. Sobriety chooses restraint because it understands that we are in a relationship with nature. But here's the rub. While COVID-19 has triggered and interrupted Pre COVID-19 processes of planned change, it is also part of nature's process, and it has got our attention in ways that appears as a surprise. What this suggests is that while some problems may be anticipated, others, like COVID-19, has emerged out of a unique and unexpected configuration. This further suggests that the vital health of any system or organization needs it occupants to prepare for both the anticipated and the unexpected.

## The Problem With Intentional Planning

Part of the problem with the industrial successes of the 19th century, as a hermeneutic philosopher Gadamer (1981) theorized, is that it has generated "a novel expectation" (Illusion?) in the 20th century, that the mastery of the forces of nature can be transferred into social life, and that the mastery of society (or organizational success) can be brought about by intentional planning (pp. 71-72). In our technological age of planning, for instance, experts are sought to discharge practical, political, organizational, and economic decisions. However, in turning over decision making capacities to experts, and thereby renouncing and surrendering one's own capacity to make decisions, organizational members have created a new problem. What is this new problem?

In her article *Managing Change*, Duck (1998), offers a story of one COO as he explained the creation of a new problem when they turned problem solving in times of chaos and crisis over to experts with an industrial thinking mindset.

*It's like the company is undergoing five medical procedures at the same time. One person is in charge of the root-canal job, someone else is setting the broken foot, another person is working on the displaced shoulder, and still another is getting rid of the gallstone. Each operation is a success, but the patient dies of shock. (Duck, 1998, p. 57)*

The presence of this unwanted visitor called Covid-19, and the chaos that it has created is raising the awareness for change leaders to reconsider their previous understanding of managing change. To act in the same way that the medical doctors or experts behaved in this COO's story, is to court with a fatal disaster. In dealing with the breakdowns/ailments independently from each other, in focusing only on their expertly trained task at hand, and while successfully fixing their particular ailments/problems, these expert technicians created a new organizational problem: their patient (organization) died of shock.

## Creation of a New Setting

This COO's story underscores the notion that the *vital health* of any organization (society) in times of *both* chaos *and* stability requires all stakeholders to intentionally attend to the interaction between the many parts of an organization. The vital health of any organization would require a focus on all moving and stagnant parts and not simply on one part independently of other ailing or healthy parts.

In a curious way, COVID-19 can be interpreted as creating a new setting, namely as re-situating human beings within the context of an ecological reality (Lopez, 2019; Sarason, 1972) of interdependence. The addiction to industrial successes, might make it seem that 'control' and 'mastery over' nature or others, is a 'natural' thing to do. For Sarason (1972), however, "what seems natural is almost a function of [a] culture...that usually renders us incapable of recognizing wherein we are prisoners of [that] culture" (p. xvi). By virtue of their own success, like addicts, Pre Covid-19 change leaders have become imprisoned to their industrial culture. Amid COVID-19 they continue to believe that they are "in control." Our 'new normal' is such that we can no longer behave as if it is 'business as usual.' If we accept this proposition, then we need to proceed by affirming that Post COVID-19 change leaders would need to do different things and not simply do things differently, in a new setting.

## You Cannot Go Into the Same River Twice

The presence of COVID-19 is raising our awareness for a different kind of change leadership discourse. It is a conversation that is especially mindful, as a Greek philosopher, Heraclitus, once noted: "you cannot go into the same river twice" (as cited in Plato, *Cratylus*, 402). Our river (context) has changed, and COVID-19 is changing our Pre-Covid-19 consciousness. In a paradoxical way, the presence of COVID-19 is humbling in that it is in fact arrogantly *telling* change leaders to re-think the conventional industrial paradigm informing their business. It is not accidental then, that leadership writers like Rost (1997) call for a shift towards a Post-Industrial paradigm, or for our purposes, a Post COVID-19 way of thinking and acting, for both leadership development (education), and for change leadership (practice).

At the same time, like many addictions, it is a shift that is mindfully aware of the potential of being disarmed by old categories of thought which may inadvertently contribute to producing the very conditions that Post COVID-19 change leadership hopes to remedy (Sarason, 1972). Like addicts, in other words, there is a real possibility of 'falling off the wagon' and hence, a returning to a state of addiction and back into the seductive lap of industrial success.

## SECTION 2: POST INDUSTRIAL PARADIGM/STORY OF LEADERSHIP

Rost (1997) offers us a definition of post-industrial change leadership that may help change leaders move in a different direction: "*Leadership is an influence relationship among leaders and followers who intend real changes that reflect their mutual purposes*" [Italics in original] (p. 102). With this definition, Rost highlights, four essential elements for post-industrial change leadership. First the influence relationship is based on reciprocity, multi-directionality, and non-coerciveness. Second, change leaders understand that they need others to willingly join in to achieve mutually desired purposes. Both leaders and followers are the people in the relationship. Third, both leaders and followers intend *rea*l changes in that the intended changes are both substantive and transforming. Fourth leaders and followers develop mutual purposes and not goals.

While the "goal concept of leadership has had a long and illustrious history among leadership scholars in the industrial era..." (Rost, 1997, p. 118), Rost chooses to talk about mutual purposes because it offers change leaders an opportunity to think about (a) who they are rather than what they do, (b) the culture of the organization rather than with its effectiveness, and (c) how both leaders and followers integrate into the community or society they serve, rather than with how they get their needs and wants met as individuals or as a group (pp. 118-119). It is in response to thinking about the identity, culture, and community, within a Post COVID-19 organization, that I turn to an Elder Change Leadership Model as proposed by Lopez (2109).

## SECTION 3: ELDER CHANGE LEADERSHIP MODEL

Lopez's (2019) observations of the place of Elders as he "passed through different troubled parts of the world," and in his deliberate attempts to seek "local advice on Indian reservations in the United States, at Banda Aceh in northern Sumatra after the Boxing Day tsunami in 2004, (and) in Western Australia during the heady days of mining ceaselessly for iron (financed by the Chinese)" [Parenthesis in original] (p. 311), offer us a new (yet old) metaphor and model for Post COVID-19 change leadership.

### Deferential Local Cooperation in Times of Disaster

As he passed through troubled parts of the world, and especially in traditional villages, Lopez witnessed a consistent pattern of coping with disaster: "deferential local cooperation" (p. 311). And by deferential, he meant respectful. It is as if the seeds of post-industrial paradigm/story of cooperation, collaboration were already sowed in traditional villages. For Lopez (2019), what this suggests is that in those villages, "for many people in difficult circumstances, the notion of needing help from a centralized authority, especially one living at a remove from the problem and the notion of fully protecting certain types of economic progress, are not much on people's minds" (p. 311). In situations of chaos, he witnessed the "emergence of individuals who embody the culture's sense of competence in positions of authority" (p. 311). These individuals were called 'the elders' who, among other things, were also the community's "wellspring of calmness" (p. 311). In addition, Elders, as evidenced in Lopez's research, (a) have the largest repertoire of stories which may be brought to bear on chaos, (b) encompass concern for all people in the village, (c) are not necessarily the oldest, (d) may not be the designated leader, and (e) are aware that all solutions may generate new problems. If this is who "elders' are (identity), what is their cultural state of being? How do they embody their identity in practice and in their communities?

## SECTION 4: CULTURAL QUALITIES OF ELDERS

Lopez (2019) evidenced ten cultural qualities of Elders. In Table 1, these are collected under four dimensions. While the Elder cultural qualities belong to Lopez, the naming of the four dimensions belong to the author. These cultural qualities are presented in no order of importance.

*Table 1. Elder Cultural Qualities and its Dimensions*

| Elder Cultural Qualities | Dimensions |
|---|---|
| • Are not self-serving or insincere in their promise to be just and respectful.<br>• Do not require reassurance in their commitments to abstractions such as justice and reverence.<br>• Are willing to disappear into the fabric of ordinary life.<br>• They look neither for an audience nor for confirmation.<br>• Are more accessible than other adults. | **Humility** |
| • Feelings about life all around them are more tender, their capacity for empathy greater.<br>• Are more often listeners than speakers. And when they speak, they can talk for a long while without using the word "I". | **Compassion & Empathic Listening** |
| • Have the ability to organize chaos into meaning and who can point recovery in a good direction. | **Generating Meaning Amid Chaos** |
| • Engage in conversations in ways that do not patronize or infantilize.<br>• Confirm the other in their sense of wonder through storytelling. | **Affirming Hope through Storytelling** |

### Not All Doom and Gloom

While a leadership scholar, Burns (2003) calls for transformative change, and the need for change leaders to allow for "new cultures and value systems (to) take the places of the old" (p. 25), Lopez (2019) makes a different argument. Lopez (2109) can be viewed as arguing for the need to return to an old and often forgotten place of Elders as they present themselves in what is considered as "old" cultures. However, what must be noted is that Lopez (2019) does not limit these 'old' cultural qualities as being embodied only in the persons of Elders in traditional villages. For example, in recollecting "bits of conversation" that he had "with people well placed in international business," around the world, he was encouraged to hear that not all of them believed in "a world of successful commercial strategies and conventional success" (p. 418).

*Instead, they appeared to believe in something quite different in affection for certain parts of the broken world, and in the possibility of changing the corporate enterprises they ran, so that they would no long be contributing to the social and environmental wreckage around them. (Lopez, 2019, p. 218)*

These "bits of conversation" and renewed conviction moved Lopez to write:

*An affection for humanity had swelled in me that morning, a hope that we would be all right, find the grace to accommodate each other more completely, invest more deeply in the philosopher's cardinal virtues, the ones that transcend all religions: courage, justice, reverence, compassion. (p. 418)*

Embodied in Lopez's affection for humanity, is his underlying conviction of hope, "that we would be all right" and, that we will "find the grace to accommodate each other more completely." He does not give in to despair in spite of the trouble that he sees occurring around him. Within the field of management and organizational literature, McArthur-Blair and Cockell (2019) note, "organizational despair is that fateful state in which an entire organization or a team within an organization can't lift its head to the horizon..." (Para 1). To add to despair's debilitating effect there is also a resistance to talking about one's fears. As one change leader shared his story with McArthur-Blair and Cockell:

*We don't commonly talk about our fears, and most of us are terrified of despair, of depression, of being immobilized forever by these dark feelings, and so we develop all sorts of defense systems...Sometimes they work, work for years, but ultimately, they go beyond their sell-by date, and it's only then that you can talk to somebody who is immersed in dark feelings who has successfully avoided them for years... One of the things is about recognizing fear and being able to acknowledge and accept people's defense mechanisms against those fears and those black holes of despair. (Para 2)*

To not be immobilized by fear or despair, and to be mobilized by hope, would require change leaders to create a space where all can talk about their fears and to begin again with renewed hope. Post COVID-19 change leaders would serve themselves well by listening to Lopez's retelling a cautionary story of what "a prior of a monastery" shared with him: "The caution...is to understand that justice (or courage, reverence, compassion) without liturgy is barbarism, and liturgy without justice (or any of the other philosopher's cardinal virtues) is sentimentality" [Parenthesis, mine] (p. 118). Lopez (2019) interprets the prior's story to mean that to pursue the philosopher's cardinal virtues

*... outside an ethical framework (the Bible, the Qur'an, the Constitution of the United States) would be intolerable in a society that enshrines its ethics; and to imagine that evil is not a force in the organization of human societies is to remain unenlightened. [Parenthesis in original] (pp. 181-182)*

For purposes of this Chapter, an argument can also be made that the cultural and moral qualities of Elders and their corresponding dimensions., as reflected in Table 1, could also serve as an ethical (liturgical) learning and development framework for Post COVID-19 change leadership.

## SECTION 5 POST COVID-19 CHANGE LEADERSHIP LEARNING AND DEVELOPMENT FRAMEWORK

Figure 1 offers a Post-COVID-19 change leadership learning and development framework aimed at enhancing change leadership qualities in these four critical dimensions (theory). In this section, following a theoretical formulation for each dimension (theory), particular learning questions will be raised for the sake of translating theory into practice (application). It is proposed that the learning conversations be a series of safe small group conversations among 4-5 individuals. The results of those conversations can then be shared with the larger group. While decisions will be made along the way, the primary intent of this Post COVID-19 change leadership learning program is to share and seek to understand their own experiences while in the middle of discontinuous change or being in the midst of an uninvited guest. It must be noted that the cultural qualities of change leadership and its corresponding four dimensions, are interdependent and interconnected. Several change leadership qualities from within each dimension weave and flow organically into other dimensions.

*Figure 1. Post COVID-19 Elder Change Leadership Learning Framework*

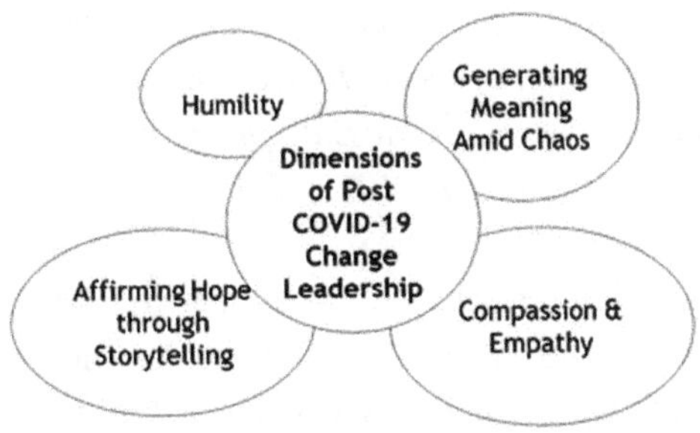


### Dimension #1: Humility

#### Theory

The presence of COVID-19 is teaching us one humbling lesson: we are not in control. While humility is a rich topic in the fields of religion and philosophy, it has not been equally recognized as an important quality in the theory and practice of management (Andragona, 2015). However, today, this quality (virtue) is becoming increasingly seen as a necessary and desirable virtue in management and leadership ethics (Andragona, 2015; Etzioni, 1989; Hilbig, & Zettler, 2009; Nielsen, Marrone, & Slay, 2010; Owens, 2009; Vera & Rodriguez-Lopez, 2004).

As noted earlier in this Chapter, unlike the addiction of arrogance that seduces individuals "to embellish themselves with a convulsive sense of self-importance" (Weber, 1958, p. 182), Ou et al., (2014) describe humility as a "dispositional quality" that reflects "a self-view that something greater than self exists" (p. 37). For Nielsen and Marrone (2018), understanding this quality is "important for organizational scholars because it underlies the choice and capacity to approach one's work (and life) from a larger, interdependent perspective that is productive, relational and sustainable" [Parenthesis in original] (p. 805). The five cultural qualities of Elders collected under the dimension of humility in

Table 1, underscore Gandhi's comment that "service without humility is selfishness and egoism" (as cited in Burgess, 1984, p. 47).

Unlike the arrogance of egoism that seduces some individuals into believing that it is all a "one-man-show," humility in the "here and now," as Schein (2013) describes it, is fundamentally an acknowledgment that change leaders need others to join in to accomplish mutual purposes. This acknowledgment is itself humbling in that change leaders understand that they are interdependent on others to do the right things and to do them in the right way. Humility, in other words, brings a Post COVID-19 (Post Industrial Paradigm) pro-relational perspective, namely that it is increasingly necessary for local co-operation and collaboration with diverse stakeholders within and across organizational boundaries and across organizations.

At the same time, whereas the language and practices of "control" or attempts to control, can be seen as efforts to do more or try harder to manage that which is not in their control, the language of "humility" offers the possibility of acting with restraint. The relationship between humility and restraint, was captured well by the 44th President of the United States, Barack Obama (2009). In his *First Inaugural Address,* he states:

*Recall that earlier generations faced down fascism and communism not just with missiles and tanks, but with the sturdy alliances and enduring convictions. They understood that our power alone cannot protect us, nor does it entitle us to do as we please. Instead, they knew that our power grows through its prudent use; our security emanates from the justness of our cause, the force of our example, the tempering qualities of humility and restraint. (Para 18-19)*

Today, missiles, tanks, and varying destructive implements of force that many countries possess for their own protection or otherwise, cannot save them from the destructive power of COVID-19, let alone save them from feeling entitled to do as they please. COVID-19 is moving all instead, to exercise prudence through the tempering qualities of humility and restraint. It is a prudence that an ancient philosopher, Aristotle, called 'practical wisdom,' or *phronesis*.

In his book *Nicomachean Ethics*, Aristotle defines the practical wisdom of phronetic leadership as an integration of five critical elements. Phronetic leadership (a) entertain remote goals and (b) makes them real through enlightened choices. Their enlightened choices are governed by (c) just deliberation, (d) subordinating self under common ends, and (e) holding fast to binding norms. In essence "practical wisdom (is) a reasoned and true state of the capacity to act with regard to human goods...practical wisdom is a virtue" (Aristotle, 1941, p. 1027). Therein lies the 'liturgy' or ethical framework, for practical wisdom.

For Aristotle, however, practical wisdom is other than the ability to instrumentally decide how to achieve what one thinks is good and then doing what can be done to achieve it. It is other than instrumental rationality because if *techné* is all there is, Gadamer (1981) cautions that we can just as easily fall prey to the seduction of sharp operators and con artists that get what they want by lying, deceiving, brainwashing, or manipulating. In as much as our COVID-19 maxim today is "we are all in this together,' in times of Post COVID-19, prudent humility is calling all to return to the wisdom of our ancient literature, namely, to hold fast to binding in ways that subordinates self under common and mutual purposes. To paraphrase the cautionary story of the prior of the monastery, practical wisdom/*phronesis*, is guided by a 'liturgical rationality.'

## Change Leaders Learning Application

In relation to humility, what questions would a Post-Covid-19 change leadership learning framework need to raise?

### *Organizational Cultural Assessment*

- Is our organizational culture one of telling others what they need to do or is it one that asks questions about what needs to be done?
- What are practices of 'telling' or 'asking' that you see displayed in our organization?
- How are practices of 'telling' or 'asking' aligned or not aligned with our espoused organizational values?
- Is there a higher propensity for answers to organizational challenges to come from managerial executives rather than from others across the organization?
- In what decision-making practices do we demonstrate a higher propensity to be 'exclusive?'
- Is there a higher propensity in our organization to celebrate and reward individual rather than team performances?

Organizational Cultural Change

- What more can we do to develop a more inclusive organizational environment?
- As people can sense self-interest and pretense, what do we need to do to develop trust, be true to ourselves, and to genuinely live our organizational values?
- What more can we do to celebrate the achievement of teams in our organization?

## Dimension #2: Generating Meaning Amid Chaos

### Theory

Elders understand that one critical enduring human need in times of discontinuous change is the need for meaning. This is what a leadership scholar, Burns (20030 hints at when he notes that the "*ultimate test of practical leadership is the realization of intended real change that meets people's enduring needs*" [Italics in original] (p. 461). It is through the organization of chaos into meaning (enduring need) that Elders begin to "point to recovery in a good direction." This understanding is confirmed, for example, by Dutton et al., (2002) in their article *Leading in Times of Trauma*. While conventional managerial rule books rely heavily on strategic and intentional planning to navigate organizations through change, Dutton et al (2002) note, that in times of chaos, "the managerial rule books fail..." because "people are searching for meaning and a reason to hope for the future" (p. 55).

Dutton et al. (2002), as well McKee and Massimilian (2006) suggest that one of the ways through which change leaders can generate meaning amid chaos and discontinuous change is by openly revealing their own humanity. Openly expressing feelings of anxiousness in the face of uncertainty and showing a deep concern for both self and others, "can be very powerful for those who witness it, especially during times of extreme pain" (Dutton et al, 2002, p. 57). To lead well in times of discontinuous change, then, is to give oneself permission to step out from behind the shadows of one's organizational position. It is to appear as a human being among other human beings without fanfare, or the garb and attire of organizational title, rank, or position.

Another way change leaders can generate meaning amid chaos is by returning to the very idea of purpose. Mutual purpose, as Rost (1997) sees it, centers on the larger purpose of who we are, why we do what we do, and "why we exist?" as an organization(society). Perhaps the presence of COVID-19 is making visible the need to communicate the larger mission of an organization and its espoused values to all stakeholders in any organization, in ways that enables all to regain a sense of clarity while in the middle of discontinuous change. More recently, we notice Lencioni (2012) connecting clarity with the health of an organization. In his book *The Advantage*, for example, it is not accidental to see him subtitling his book with *Why Organizational Health Trumps Everything Else in Business.*

## Change Leaders Learning Application

In relation to generating meaning amid chaos, what questions then would a Post-Covid-19 change leadership learning framework need to raise?

- How am I feeling while I am in the middle of this pandemic called COVID-19?
- Within the context of COVID-19, what are some outstanding questions for me as a member within our organization?
- Why do we exist as an organization? What is our larger purpose?
- How can we continue to stay committed to our larger purpose while in the middle of COVID-19 and Post COVID-19?
- What do we need to do to not give in to despair?

## Dimension #3: Compassion and Empathy

## Theory

While McKee and Massimilian (2006) note that compassion is rarely discussed in a business context as it is seen as irrelevant in a world of competition, they also argue that "in a leadership context, compassion is more than relevant, it is integral" (p. 48). Lencioni (2012) would add that it is integral to the vital health of any organization. Elders demonstrate compassion through the art of empathic listening, by taking people's lives seriously and by "treating persons as persons" (Burns, 1978, p. 462) and not as pawns for one's own ends. In understanding and embracing these qualities of compassion (care) and empathic listening [See Table 1), Post COVID-19 change leaders are being encouraged to listen in ways that suspend judgment and by being genuinely interested in understanding others *for its own sake* and not "in order to..." get others to do what they (change leaders) want them to do, or to manipulate others into compliance. Without compassion and empathy, change leaders discover that in times of crisis, the harder they push, the harder others push back, and in so doing, they create yet another organizational monster, resistance - not to change - but to change leaders who press others in ways that are oblivious to its impact on those around them.

Post COVID-19 change leaders are being called to *tune in* to how others are thinking and feeling in times of discontinuous change. Therein lies their capacity for compassion and empathy. To what then do Post COVID-19 empathic change leaders need to attune? Brittle's (2012) acronym of A.T.T.U.N.E. may be useful. Post COVID-19 change leaders attune to:

**A**wareness

They are mindfully aware of where they and others are - mentally, relationally, physically, emotionally, and spiritually. It is both self-awareness and other awareness. They are also aware of the conventional categories they use in managing change.

**T**urning Toward

They create conditions where all can safely and consciously turn toward each other and let their needs be known in their experience of discontinuity. They are not afraid to turn toward the fears and the hopes of all in their organization.

**T**olerance

Insofar as 'we are all in this together,' they understand that tolerance is not about "us" tolerating "them" but rather that it is <u>all</u> about "us." The "them" is part of the "us," and like Elders their "guiding thought is no one left behind" (Lopez, 2019, p. 416).

**U**nderstanding

They understand the difference between understanding and having correct information. Understanding, as Arendt (1994) notes, is the human need "to reconcile ourselves to a world in which such things as (COVID-19) are possible at all" [Parenthesis mine] (p. 108). Post COVID-19 change leaders need to understand that in times of discontinuous change, all are seeking to reconcile themselves to a new reality in ways that tries to be at home in this new reality. They deeply understand that others are not looking for more information. They are instead seeking a new story while in the midst of their new reality.

**N**on-Defensive Responding

Kashdan et al. (2011) suggest that curiosity as well as mindful attention can enhance one's capacity to reduce defensive responses to existential threats. They argue that "because curiosity concerns an embrace of novelty and openness to new experiences, it may operate to counter attempts to avoid or alter difficult thoughts, feelings, or situations" (p. 1227). At the same time, in being mindfully attentive, Elders are also equipped with their capacity to listen rather than take pleasure in hearing their own voices. And, as Lopez (2019) observed, when they speak, they can do so for long periods without using the pronoun "I."

**E**mpathy

Elders embrace the idea that "empathy is the capacity to understand what another person is experiencing from within the other person's frame of reference, i.e., the capacity to place oneself in another's shoes" (Bellet & Maloney, 1991, p. 1831). This quality is so important that authors in a study with the

UK National Health Service placed the personal relationship of empathy at the centre of their Leadership Quality framework (Skinner & Spurgeon, 2005). On the other hand, an American research conducted by Holt and Marques (2012), over a period between 2008-2010, reported that on a scale of 1-10, their research participants (undergraduate and MBA students), consistently listed empathy as the lowest quality that they considered essential or appropriate for leaders in a business setting. Some of the reasons their student participants considered empathy as not being important for leaders included:

- Empathy is perceived as a sign of weakness
- Empathy interferes with rational and ethical decision making
- Empathy is fleeting/situation, while other qualities are stable

Notwithstanding the small sample size for their study, or the fact that participants in this study were students, what is important to raise is that Post COVID-19 change leaders are being challenged to check their own understanding of the place of empathy in leading change and to understand how others in their organizations perceive the place of empathy in organizational life.

### Change Leaders Learning Application

In relation to compassion and empathy, what questions would a Post-Covid-19 change leadership learning need to raise?

- Is empathy and empathic listening critical? Why or why not?
- How are we currently demonstrating care for all in our organization in times of COVID-19?
- What more needs to be done to demonstrate care for all in our Post COVID-19 Era?
- How did you manage to stay healthy through our COVID-19 times?
- What were/are your personal and relational challenges as you lived through COVID-19?
- How are you personally coming to terms with this new reality called Post COVID-19?

## Dimension #4: Affirming Hope Through Story-Telling

Elders engage in conversations that keep the spirit of imagination and wonder - that we often see in children – alive, through storytelling. Elders understand that adults also need a story because, as Isak Dinesen noted, "all sorrows can be borne if you put them into a story or tell a story about them" (as cited in Arendt, 1983, p. 104). And, as Arendt (1983) notes, stories have the capacity to "reveal the meaning of what otherwise would remain an unbearable sequence of sheer happenings" (p. 104). What is the power inherent in storytelling?

In his story book *Crow and Weasel,* Barry Lopez (1998), offers one response by telling a story of two young men as they journeyed toward maturity. Written in the Native American tradition, the characters in his book, Crow and Weasel, are both animals and people at the same time. While staying at Badger's home, they engage in a meaningful conversation.

*Crow: We are very grateful for your hospitality Badger. Each place we go, we learn something, and your wisdom has helped us.*

*Badger: I would ask you to remember only this thing. The stories people tell have a way of taking care of them. If stories come to you, care for them. And learn to give them away where they are needed. Sometimes a person needs a story more than food to stay alive. That is why we put these stories in each other's memories. This is how people care for themselves. One day you will be good storytellers. Never forget these obligations. (p. 30)*

Elders understand that stories people tell have a way of taking care of them. They also understand that receivers of stories are also called to care for the stories they receive because that is a way of taking care of themselves and others. Elders also know that receivers of stories would do an injustice to stories received, by keeping those stories to themselves and not give them away when needed. Amid COVID-19, the leader of the Catholic Church, Pope Francis (2020) told a story which reminds us of our capacity to not give our power away to this disease.

*This recent pandemic has enabled us to recognize and appreciate [the courage of] all those around us, who in the midst of fear, responded by putting their lives on the line... doctors, nurses, pharmacists, storekeepers, supermarket workers, cleaning personnel, caretakers, transport workers, men and women working to provide essential services and public safety, volunteers, priests and religious...They understood that no one is saved alone. (# 54, Parenthesis mine)*

Pope Francis appears to concur with Lopez (2019). Despite our "dark clouds," (Pope Francis, 2020 Para #54) or our "'dark times" (Arendt 1993), it appears as if there is an underlying conviction that has held steady (and which) might never have become visible without the appearance of COVID-19. It is a conviction that

*Even in the darkest of times we have the right to expect some illumination, and that such illumination may well come less from theories and concepts than from the uncertain, flickering, and often weak light that some men and women, in their lives and their works, will kindle under almost all circumstances and shed over the time span that was given them on earth... (Arendt, 1993, p. ix)*

Arendt's (1993) and Pope Francis' (2020) stories are stories of hope. And "hope," for Pope Francis "is bold" in its expectation and aspiration. Hope enables humankind to look "beyond personal convenience... petty securities, and compensations" (#55). Hope enables change leaders to expect lights of illumination in times of darkness or perhaps even be that light of illumination.

As recently as October 7, 2020, Pope Francis shared his 'liturgical story' of what it could mean to lead well in Covid-19 and Post COVID-19 times. He shared with his followers that "We need the spirit of Elijah." The disciple Luke, for example, speaks to the "spirit and power of Elijah" as "turning the hearts of fathers to the children, and the disobedient to the wisdom of the just..." (Luke 1:17). While acknowledging that the prophet Elijah is "one of the most compelling characters in the whole of Sacred Scripture," Pope Francis also emphasized the illuminating light of Elijah as an "example of all people of faith who know...suffering, but do not fail to live up to the ideal for which they were born" (Vatican News, 2020, Para 1 & 4). In the face of the suffering of humanity, and not knowing, perhaps stories like Elijah's, can become a daring and hopeful way for Post COVID-19 change leaders to not only dream the impossible dream, but also to understand and live up to the ideal for which they are born.

It is perhaps appropriate to recall yet another liturgical story, namely the story of King Solomon. His God, Yahweh, appeared in a dream, and invited Solomon to: "Ask what you would like me to give you?" Solomon could have asked for anything – strength, power, money, fame – but he did not. Instead, he asked for the gift of an "understanding heart" (1 Kings, 3:9). Arendt (1993) translates the biblical language of "understanding heart," to the faculty of imagination. Unlike fantasy or wishful thinking, for Arendt, true understanding "trusts that imagination [understanding heart] will (a) catch at least a glimpse of the always frightening light of truth," (b) "enable us to see things in their proper perspective," and that, as Elders do, it will (c) point to recovery in a good direction by enabling us "to take our bearings in the world" (pp. 322-323). It is, she further attests, "the only inner compass we have" (p. 323). It appears as if Arendt is suggesting that to be at home in our world, we must courageously participate and take part in the interminable dialogue with discontinuous change and with the peculiar density which surrounds everything that is real with COVID19.

### Change Leaders Learning Application

In relation to affirming hope though storytelling, what questions would a Post-Covid-19 change leadership learning need to raise?

- What stories are we telling ourselves in times of COVID-19 (Crisis)?
- How are our stories empowering (or disempowering)?
- How are our stories enabling hope to presence or absence itself while in the middle of chaos?
- What stories can we tell of all those in our own organization who, in the midst of fear, responded by putting their lives on the line?
- What stories can we envision for ourselves and in ways that point to recovery in a good direction?

## SECTION 6: RECOMMENDATIONS

In a deliberate way, the proposed *new* Post COVID-19 Elder change leadership model is in fact a return to *old,* forgotten, and often times excluded, dimensions of change leadership. Unlike organizational senior executive titles like CEO, COO, CFO, and/or CAO, "Elders" is not a language of contemporary businesses or organizations. Yet, it is suggested that the social construct of Elders as proposed in this Chapter, is precisely what is needed in our Post COVID-19 Era. As revealed in this Chapter, here are 11 recommendations for Post Covid-19 change leaders.

1. Respect local cooperation. Create conditions that would enable the local cooperation of others to attend to the challenges at hand. Answers do not belong to any one person. The *vital health* of any organization in times of crisis and chaos requires all stakeholders to intentionally attend to higher levels of local cooperation and collaboration.
2. Listen to, rather than tell people what they need to do, with the underlying conviction that the 'answers' lie within the collective.
3. Proceed with the belief that answers to discontinuous change will emerge through the construction of an egalitarian space where all in the community (organization) are granted the right and the responsibility to speak and act together.

4. Focus on the common purpose of your organization rather than on 'me,' 'myself,' and 'I."
5. Subordinate yourselves as individuals and as a collective to the justness of a common purpose that is greater than any individual or collective.
6. Attend to constructing meaning amid discontinuous change. This is not to say that there is only one 'meaning' but rather that multiple meanings can emerge from how others experience discontinuous change. Believe that those multiple meanings can point to recovery in a good direction.
7. Create safe conditions where all are able to A.T.T.U.N.E. to each other, and feel free to talk about their fears without judgment, and not to be immobilized with despair and hopelessness.
8. Build a culture of an 'understanding heart' and trust in the power of imagination. Speak and act from the perspective of imagination and an 'understanding heart.'
9. Temper the possibility of falling off the wagon and being seduced by addictions to success, with practical wisdom, prudence, humility, and restraint.
10. Encourage all to share stories in ways that orient to imagination and the possibility of renewed hope. While the reality of COVID-19 has its own finite realities, stories of hope and imagination offer the possibility of equifinality – limitless possibilities.
11. All stories are social constructions. To orient to the social construction of stories suggests that other possibilities (stories) can be constructed and can possibly point to recovery in a good direction. It also recognizes that imagined possibilities are experimental. Acting on any of those imagined possibilities is to experiment with living.

## CONCLUSION: LIMITATIONS AND FUTURE RESEARCH

The conceptual framework for this chapter is constructed from within the lens of narrative thinking. While this Chapter has its limitations, it offers the possibility of research in new directions, particularly from a narrative perspective. While some might charge that this Chapter is biased, narrative researchers would affirm bias as a necessary feature of thinking. Whereas traditional scientific research would separate the observed from the observer, narrative researchers would ask: "where can we be in the world and not be a part of it?" As a sociologist, C. Wright Mills (1959) wrote in a classic essay, "the most admirable scholars within the scholarly community...would not split their work from their lives. They seem to take both too seriously to allow such dissociation, and they want to use each for the enrichment of the other" (p. 195).

Future studies could concentrate on exploring, possibly through different case studies, how organizational authorities can respond meaningfully to wicked problems of discontinuous change and co-evolve with the evolution of such wicked problems. It is hoped that this Chapter brings another (fresh?) perspective to open up new avenues of inquiry and practice for leading change. Finally, this Chapter hopes to serve as a reminder that the *vital health* of any organization in a Post COVID-19 era is calling change leaders to pay deliberate attention to the 11 recommendations with compassion and care. To ignore them is to open ourselves to the real possibility that their organizations may die of shock.

## REFERENCES

Andragona, A. (2015). Humility in Management. *Journal of Business Ethics*, *132*(1), 63–71. doi:10.100710551-014-2311-8

Arendt, H. (1983). Isak Dinesen. In Men in Dark Times (pp. 95-109). A Harvest Book.

Arendt, H. (1994). Understanding and Politics. In J. Kohn (Ed.), *Essays in Understanding* (pp. 307–327). Schocken Books.

Aristotle. (1941). Nicomachean Ethics. In R. McKeon (Ed.), *The basic works of Aristotle* (pp. 935–1122). Random House.

Bateson, G. (1979). *Mind and nature: A necessary unity*. Bantam Books.

Bateson, G., & Bateson, M. C. (1987). *Angels fear*. Macmillan Publishing Company.

Bateson, M. C. (1989). *Composing a life*. Grove Press.

Bellet, P., & Maloney, M. (1991). The Importance of Empathy as an Interviewing Skill in Medicine. *Journal of the American Medical Association*, *266*(13), 1831–1832. doi:10.1001/jama.1991.03470130111039 PMID:1909761

Bennis, W., & Nanus, B. (1985). *Leaders: The strategies for taking charge*. Harper & Row.

Birkinshaw, J., Zimmermann, A., & Raisch, S. (2016). How Do firms Adapt to Discontinuous Change? *California Management Review*, *58*(4), 36–58. doi:10.1525/cmr.2016.58.4.36

Brittle, Z. (2015). *How to Build Trust in Your Relationship*. https://www.gottman.com/blog/trust/

Brown, J., Denning, S., Groh, K., & Prusak, L. (2011). *Storytelling in organizations: Why storytelling is transforming 21st century organizations and Management*. Routledge.

Burgess, P. H. (1984). *The sayings of Mahatma Gandhi*. Graham Brash.

Burns, J. M. (1978). *Leadership*. Harper & Row.

Burns, J. M. (2003). *Transforming leadership*. Grove Press.

Duck, J. D. (1998). *Managing Change: The Art of Balancing. Harvard Business Review on Change*. Harvard Business School Press.

Dutton, J., Frost, P., Worline, M., Lilius, J., & Kanov, J. (2002). Leading in Times of Trauma. *Harvard Business Review*, (January), 54–61. PMID:12964467

Enochs, J. C. (1981). Up from management. *Phi Delta Kappan*, 175–178.

Etzioni, A. (1989). Humble decision-making. *Harvard Business Review*, *67*, 45–57. PMID:10293838

Fish, J. M. (1992). Discontinuous Change. *Behavior and Social Issues*, *2*(1), 59–70. doi:10.5210/bsi.v2i1.174

Flemons, D. (1991). *Completing distinctions*. Shambala Publications, Inc.

Francis, P. (2020). *Fratelli Tutti*. Retrieved from http://www.vatican.va/content/francesco/en/encyclicals/documents/papa-francesco_20201003_enciclica-fratelli-tutti.html

Gilbert, D. (2006). *Stumbling on happiness*. Knopf.

Gill, R. (2003). Change management – or change leadership? *Journal of Change Management, 3*(4), 307–318. doi:10.1080/714023845

Hilbig, B. E., & Zettler, I. (2009). Pillars of cooperation: Honesty humility, social value orientations, and economic behavior. *Journal of Research in Personality, 43*(3), 516–519. doi:10.1016/j.jrp.2009.01.003

Hitt, M., Keats, B., & DeMarie, S. (1998). Navigating in the new competitive landscape: Building strategic flexibility and competitive advantage in the 21st century. *The Academy of Management Executive, 12*(4), 22–42. doi:10.5465/ame.1998.1333922

Holt, S., & Marques, J. (2012). Empathy in Leadership: Appropriate or Misplaced? An Empirical Study on a Topic That is Asking for Attention. *Journal of Business Ethics, 105*(1), 95–105. doi:10.100710551-011-0951-5

Hughes, M. (2007). *The leadership of organizational change*. Routledge.

Kashdan, T., Afram, A., Brown, K., Birnbeck, M., & Drvoshanov, M. (2012). Curiosity enhances the role mindfulness in reducing defensive responses to existential threat. *Personality and Individual Differences, 50*(8), 1227–1232. doi:10.1016/j.paid.2011.02.015

Keen, S. (1991). *Telling Your Story* [audiotape]. New York: Sound Horizons Audio Video.

Kotter, J. (1996). *Leading change*. Harvard Business Review Press.

Lencioni, P. (2012). *The advantage: Why organizational health trumps everything else in business*. Jossey-Bass.

Lopez, B. (2019). *Horizon*. Random House Canada.

Mair, M. (1988). Psychology as storytelling. *International Journal of Personal Construct Psychology, 1*(2), 125–138. doi:10.1080/10720538808412771

Marx, K. (1978). Speech at the anniversary of the people's power. In R. C. Tucker (Ed.), *The Marx-Engels Reader* (pp. 577–578). W.W. Norton & Company, Inc. (Original work published 1856)

May, R. (1991). *The cry for myth*. Norton.

McArthur-Blair, J., & Cockell, J. (2019). *Helping Organizations Deal with Despair*. Retrieved from https://trainingmag.com/helping-organizations-deal-despair/

McKee, A., & Massimilian, D. (2006). Resonant leadership: A new kind of leadership for the digital age. *The Journal of Business Strategy, 27*(5), 45–49. doi:10.1108/02756660610692707

Mills, C. W. (1995/2000). *The sociological imagination*. Oxford University Press, Inc.

Mirvis, P. (2020). Reflections: US Coronavirus Crisis Management - Learning from Failure January – April 2020. *Journal of Change Management, 20*(4), 283–311. doi:10.1080/14697017.2020.1836721

Morais, F., Kakabadse, A., & Kakabadse, N. (2020). Leading through discontinuous change: A typology of problems and leadership approaches in UK boards. *Long Range Planning*, *53*(2), 1–15. doi:10.1016/j.lrp.2019.02.003

Nielsen, R., & Marrone, J. (2018). Humility: Our Current Understanding of the Construct and its Role in Organizations. *International Journal of Management Reviews*, *20*(4), 802–824. doi:10.1111/ijmr.12160

Nielsen, R., Marrone, J. A., & Slay, H. S. (2010). A new look at humility: Exploring the humility concept and its role in socialized charismatic leadership. *Journal of Leadership & Organizational Studies*, *17*(1), 33–43. doi:10.1177/1548051809350892

Northouse, P. (2019). *Leadership: Theory and practice*. Sage.

Obama, B. (2009). *President Barack Obama's Inaugural Address*. Retrieved from, https://obamawhitehouse.archives.gov/blog/2009/01/21/president-barack-obamas-inaugural-address

Ou, A. Y., Tsui, A. S., Kinicki, A. J., Waldman, D. A., Xiao, Z., & Song, L. J. (2014). Humble chief executive officers' connections to top management team integration and middle managers' responses. *Administrative Science Quarterly*, *59*(1), 34–72. doi:10.1177/0001839213520131

Owens, B. P. (2009). Humility in organizations: Establishing construct, nomological, and predictive validity. In *Academy of Management best papers proceedings*. Academy of Management. doi:10.5465/ambpp.2009.44263542

Plato. (1892/1937). Cratylus. In *Dialogues of Plato* (M. A. Jowett, Trans.; pp. 173–232). Random House.

Pullen, W. (1993). Strategic Shocks: Managing discontinuous change. *International Journal of Public Sector Management*, *6*(1), 30–39. doi:10.1108/09513559310023563

Rost, J. C. (1993). *Leadership for the twenty-first century*. Praeger.

Sarason, S. (1972). *The creation of settings and the future of societies*. Brookline Books, Inc.

Schein, E. (2013). *Humble inquiry: The gentle art of asking instead of telling*. Berrett-Koehler Publishers, Inc.

Skinner, C., & Spurgeon, P. (2005). Valuing empathy and emotional intelligence in health leadership: A study of empathy, leadership behaviour and outcome effectiveness. *Health Services Management*, *18*(1), 1–12. doi:10.1258/0951484053051924 PMID:15807976

Smith, D. (2012). Technological discontinuities, outsiders, and social capital: A case study from Formula 1. *European Journal of Innovation Management*, *15*(3), 332–350. doi:10.1108/14601061211243666

Stake, R. E. (2008). Qualitative Case Studies. In N. K. Denzin & Y. S. Lincoln (Eds.), *Strategies of Qualitative Inquiry*. Sage Publications.

Taleb, N. N. (2007). *The black swan: The impact of the highly improbable* (Vol. 2). Random house.

Their, K. (2018). *Storytelling in organizations. Management for Professionals*. Springer Nature. doi:10.1007/978-3-662-56383-0_1

Todnem, R., Hughes, M., & Ford, J. (2016). Change Leadership: Oxymoron and Myths. *Journal of Change Management, 16*(1), 8–17. doi:10.1080/14697017.2016.1137425

Vatican News. (2020). *Pope Francis: We need the spirit of Elijah.* Retrieved from https://www.ind-catholicnews.com/news/40628

Vera, D., & Rodriguez-Lopez, A. (2004). Strategic virtue: Humility as a source of competitive advantage. *Organizational Dynamics, 33*(4), 393–408. doi:10.1016/j.orgdyn.2004.09.006

Watzlawick, P. (1984). *The invented reality*. Norton.

Weber, M. (1958). *The protestant ethic and the spirit of capitalism.* Charles Scribner's Sons.

WHO. (2020). *Severe Acute Respiratory Syndrome (SARS).* Retrieved from https://www.who.int/health-topics/severe-acute-respiratory-syndrome#tab=tab_1

Yiannis, G. (2000). *Storytelling in organizations: Facts, fictions, and fantasies.* Oxford University Press.

# Chapter 15
# Task Forces as Silver Bullets for Crisis Management:
## A Case Study of an SME During COVID-19

**Laura Schärrer**
*University of Lucerne, Switzerland*

**Reto M. Wegmann**
https://orcid.org/0000-0002-1926-5557
*University of Lucerne, Switzerland*

## ABSTRACT

*In 2020, the corona virus disease 2019 (COVID-19) triggered a global health crisis, disrupting economies, societies, and private companies. Organizations faced urgent challenges, and most of them installed so called "task forces" to respond. Small or medium enterprises (SMEs), which play a major role in most economies, however, often encounter problems of limited resources to do so. The purpose of this chapter is to derive theoretical and practical implications on how such crises can be handled. A literature review identifies the characteristics of successful task forces and then validates them with a case study of a Swiss transport company during COVID-19, which is based on multiple interviews with the CEO between Spring 2020 and in Fall 2020. The findings include that task forces are crucial for SMEs despite their limited resources. A critical success factor is the quality of human resources, which demands careful selection. Concepts used in crisis management can also be applied in day-to-day operations to increase the organization's resilience and also general profitability.*

## INTRODUCTION

In 2020, the severe acute respiratory syndrome coronavirus 2 (SARS-CoV-2) triggered the biggest global health crisis since World War II. The global pandemic outbreak of the respective coronavirus disease 2019 (Covid-19) disrupted economies and organizations, but also changed individual lives. By the end of the first half year of 2020, more than 500,000 people have died and economic losses were

DOI: 10.4018/978-1-7998-6948-1.ch015

expected to be tremendous (Roser *et al.*, 2020). In addition to the threat to public health and wellbeing of millions of people, organizations suddenly faced change management and leadership challenges of unprecedented urgency. Strategic visions, and day-to-day operations had to be adapted to a new reality within a short time.

Public authorities, multinational organizations and small and medium enterprises (SMEs) often installed so called 'task forces' to manage the new situation. Generally speaking, a task force is a temporary organization consisting of individuals within an organization and operating in an ad hoc structure tailored to solve one specific problem (e.g. Lundin and Söderholm, 1995; Burke and Morley, 2016; Einola and Alvesson, 2019). Task forces handle situations by managing information flows and they are generally designed to cover all capacities and competencies needed to support the decision-making of the executive board in regard to this situation.

Although crisis management in general is thoroughly researched (e.g. Billings, Milburn and Lou, 1980; Weick, 1988; Benini, 1999; Boin, Kuipers and Overdijk, 2013; Bundy *et al.*, 2017), and there are even first publications on Covid-19 (e.g. Bailey and Breslin, 2020; Fernandez and Shaw, 2020; He and Harris, 2020; Wegmann and Schärrer, 2020), there is no clear understanding of the morphologies, nor the value of these Covid-19 task forces, let alone the mechanics at play within them. From a theoretical perspective, there are several theoretical concepts that address mechanisms within a newly formed temporary team. Most of these theories have their roots in the modern neoclassical economic literature. For instance, Human Capital theory (Becker, 1962, 1964) emphasizes that people and their capacities influence the performance of the organizations. Specifically, it is specified that human capital gains importance when the talent in question is not readily available in the labor market, which corresponds precisely to Covid-19 task forces (Crook *et al.*, 2011).

From a practical perspective, there is a lack of guidelines on how such task forces should be both composed and led, in order to be successful during Covid-19 and equally as an instrument of organizational resilience for the post-Covid-19 era. Additionally, while for larger organizations, the installation of a task force seems to be easier and more feasible, for small or medium enterprises (SMEs) problems in terms of their limited resources (Sharma, 2020) are far more prevalent. An additional difficulty is that managers are subject to a double pressure as they are already involved in the daily business, on the one hand, and have to get control of their functions in the newly formed Covid-19 task forces, which should handle the pandemic on the other hand.

In literature, there is no clear definition of SMEs (e.g. Omar and Ismail, 2009), but often the size of the enterprises (i.e., fewer than 250 employees) is the unique criterion. Worldwide, there are approximately 400 million SMEs that make up over 95% of firms and create two thirds of the jobs (Shift, 2019). Consequently, these SMEs and their task forces move into focus when it comes to handling the Covid-19 crisis and oncoming crises in organizations.

This chapter aims to examine these task forces in SMEs and to particularly explain which characteristics make them useful instruments to respond to incidents. The aim is to answer to the following research question: *What characteristics of task forces in small and medium-sized organizations lead to effective management of the Covid-19 crisis?*

To answer this question, this chapter starts by summarizing crisis management and change management literature and adds rare but existing research results on the Covid-19 context. From this, it identifies the most relevant theories (e.g., Human Capital and Social Capital theory) and underlying concepts needed to understand the context. Subsequently, a case study of a Swiss transport and logistics company navigating the situation of Covid-19 will shed light onto specific challenges experienced and lessons learned. The Swiss medium-sized company operates mainly in the domestic market and has more than 200 employees. As most of the organizations, the company decided in March 2020 to install a task force of five members to handle the Covid-19 situation.

The head of the organization is interviewed multiple times and answers questions from the beginning of the crisis (Spring 2020) until at the peak of the second 'wave' of the pandemic in Switzerland (Fall 2020), enabling the chapter to identify a learning curve and to see where hindsight differs from forecast, and where experience improved expectations. A particular focus is given to the question of task force manning, task force mission and the difference between handling Covid-19 and handling day-to-day operations in management meetings and other decision-making bodies. The qualitative semi-structured interviews are coded and structured along the methods and concepts identified in the literature. Finally, the comparison between the current theoretical and empirical research literature and the case study, based on an in-depth examination of a Swiss company handling the crisis, provides conclusions and practical implications for organizations, now and in the future. Specifically, this chapter points out the important characteristics of Covid-19 task forces in small and medium-sized organizations with the goal to inform future decisions on change management and leadership.

## THEORETICAL BACKGROUND

The corona pandemic outbreak in spring 2020 massively increased the global academic and practical interest for crisis management. Particularly organizations that usually do not deal with disruptive and unexpected events threatening to harm the organization or its stakeholders (Bundy *et al.*, 2017) were caught off-guard. Other than professional firefighters, humanitarian aid workers, soldiers or hospital staff, small and medium enterprises (SME) of various industries do not usually have to consider how to tackle external shocks in their day-to-day operations.

To cope with this new situation and the fast speed of onset, numerous organizations decided to install specialized Covid-19 task forces in order to handle the crisis. The term *task force*, originally coined to group naval vessels together to achieve a particular military goal (Robinson, 2020), describes cross-functional teams, which are funded in response to a situation and staffed based on the needs of that situation (Hollenbeck, Beersma and Schouten, 2012). Task forces are by nature always temporary organizations, which are in turn defined as "temporally bounded group of [...] actors, formed to complete a task" (Burke and Morley, 2016, p. 1237), which is along the lines of its military legacy and the respective meaning. They are tailored for the action a specific situation calls for, and which would normally dissolve again when a certain goal is achieved or a certain time span has passed.

Having outlined that, task forces are by nature different from *crisis management teams*, which are cross-functional teams, too. However, crisis management teams tend to be pre-defined and pre-trained standby-organizations, activated when a respective situation calls for it (Barton, 1993; Coombs, 1999), while task forces respond and are staffed ad hoc. Crisis management teams, as they are pre-defined, would classically rely on being staffed with the functions 'usually' needed, such as IT, communications or HR, while task forces can take any shape or any composition, depending on the morphology and the needs of the situation that triggered its creation.

Although crisis management in general is thoroughly researched (e.g. Boin, Kuipers and Overdijk, 2013), there is only limited evidence of the intersection between temporary organizations and performance, and thus on how effective (or not) task forces truly are. A recent study, using a grounded theory approach, inducts four categories of performance drivers: human resources, tools and support, processes and methodology, and (uncontrollable) environmental factors (Wegmann, 2020). As this chapter aims to understand factors at least partially under our control, uncontrollable environmental factors will not be considered any further. Therefore, the characteristics of Covid-19 task forces that lead to an effective crisis management can be broken down into three dimensions (see Table 1).

*Table 1. Characteristics of task forces*

| Dimension | Content |
|---|---|
| Human resources | - Individual members' competencies<br>- Available skills on team level<br>- Team composition |
| Tools and support | - Partners<br>- Logistics<br>- Safety and security<br>- Information and communication technology |
| Processes and methodology | - Leadership and management<br>- Information management |

First, the importance of the human resources for an effective Covid-19 task force can be explained by the well-established human capital theory. The human capital theory, set forth by Becker (1962, 1964), points out that individuals and their capacities influence the performance of organizations. Especially in a crisis situation, human capital in the form of the "best and brightest" must be attracted and retained (Crook *et al.*, 2011). At the same time, the theory postulates that individuals' education and, most importantly, a customized training is human capital which influences performance (Becker, 1964). With regard to Covid-19 task forces, this means that, besides individuals and the effectiveness of their collaboration, also a specific crisis management training can lead to a successful functioning of a task force. In most industries and for most SME, this is particularly true because crisis management training is not something that is anyway available. So far, there are only very few empirical studies investigating the human resources in a task force. However, Wegmann and Schärrer (2020), for instance, analyzed the structure of Covid-19 task forces in different countries and showed that individual competencies, team collaboration, and assignment of tasks and roles are decisive factors for the performance of a task force.

Second, various tools and support, being represented as actual physical resources or immaterial instruments such as processes and guidelines, can make a difference. The main tools and support identified as performance drivers in crisis management teams can be grouped into these sub-concepts: a) partners and partner organizations, indicating the degree to which the organization or the firm is embedded in its environment and the freedom of action to ensure external capacities can be gotten ahold of in reasonable time; b) logistics, meaning the capacity to transport, store and maintain the resources necessary to cope with the crisis at hand; c) safety and security, which encompasses all measures aimed at keeping the employees and the organization's other resources free from harm; and d) information and communication technology (ICT), generally all the technological assets and tools in place to enable the organization's information flows and data storage.

Third, processes and methodology matter. These processes and methodologies can generally be grouped into two separate concepts: everything which has to do with how the employees and the organizations are led and managed and everything which has to do with how information gets acquired, analyzed, verified, and disseminated. Quite clearly, as managing the information flows is a key task for leadership persons on every level, these two are not content-wise separate,, but closely linked, as the inform each other and represent preconditions for each other. Particularly when tasks are complex, time-critical, and managed in a more or less de-central and agile way, dissemination the information available quickly and correctly enough to enable de-central decision-making in the first place, is *the* critical antecedent for success (e.g. Lucas Jr and Palley, 1986; De Groot, 1988; Wong, Ormiston and Tetlock, 2011; Wegmann and Newett, 2020).

As these characteristics can inform us to predict under which conditions task forces are successful in general, the actual setting up and the structuring of task forces in SMEs is more difficult. Compared to larger organizations, SMEs are strongly confronted with resources constraints (Hong, Huang and Li, 2012). Additionally, most of crisis management research tend to focus on large organizations or public authorities, and SMEs are not adequately investigated for sound theory and practical implications for management (e.g. Acquier, Gand and Szpirglas, 2008; Herbane, 2010). The following case study aims to contribute to more evidence and practical guidelines on the important characteristics of task forces in smaller organizations.

## CASE STUDY CHOICE AND DATA COLLECTION

This case study's research aims at finding an SME providing services or producing goods in an industry branch only loosely affected by Covid-19. The effects on employees and organizations, and the management of the crisis is to be analyzed, rather than business effects because of crumbling markets or unstable supply chains. For this purpose, Mittelland Transport AG (MLT) serves as an appropriate SME. MLT provides transport and logistics solutions for the construction industry, operating in the Northwestern part of Switzerland. The medium-sized company operates as an independent subsidiary of the Swiss Jura Materials Group that is part of the Irish CRH Group. The key expertise of MLT is distributing a diverse range of superior building materials and products, which are used extensively in construction projects of all sizes. The company employs more than 220 people (220 full-time equivalents), and owns 160 distribution trucks to carry out their solely road-based transportation services.

To serve the research focus, generally accepted case study methods were adopted in terms of level of research, questionnaire development, data collection, and data analysis (Yin, 1994; Chetty, 1996). In this case study, the head of the MLT was invited for his business knowledge, understanding of the entire organization (Perren and Ram, 2004), and the critical role he plays for crisis management in SMEs in general (Runyan, 2006) but also for the tasks force. Thus, the head of MLT was interviewed multiple times, starting with a structured and partly quantitative survey at the onset of the crisis (Spring 2020) and ending with a personal interview on the developments during the second 'wave' of Covid-19 in Switzerland (Fall 2020). The qualitative semi-structured interviews were coded and structured along the theoretically developed characteristics of task forces (see Table 1). As the functioning of task forces in SMEs is more unique, the questions were loosely structured and gave the head of the organization more opportunities to fully express himself and to receive responses for more in-depth information (Alsaawi, 2014). The interviews were recorded, transcribed, and are included in the following section.

## THE CASE OF MITTELAND TRANSPORT AG DURING COVID-19

Similar to most Western European countries, in 13 March 2020, the Swiss Federal Council (Switzerland's political executive body) announced the so-called 'lockdown' with restrictions of far-reaching consequences (e.g. closure of schools, restaurants and bars or temporary restrictions on immigration). Covid-19 struck the Swiss economy hard. The Swiss State Secretariat for Economic affairs estimates the Gross National Product to decrease in 2020 by 3.3% (SECO, 2020), having made continuous downwards adjustments after a comparatively stable start during the first wave. Between March 16 and April 19, the country was in a national state of emergency, which included not only the closing of various institutions but also a prohibition of gatherings of more than five people. However, particularly during the first wave, but with after-effects into Winter 2020/2021, the government swiftly introduced also a fast-track credit access system with a focus on SMEs to bridge liquidity shortfalls, and distributed easy and quick access to more than 76'000 businesses, considerably more than any other country in Europe (WEF, 2020). The speed and unbureaucratic loans were indeed so fast, that Swiss Minister of Finance, Ueli Maurer, announced in March 2020 "You go to your bank. Within half an hour, you will have your loan" (Swissinfo, 2020).

However, even without loans and immediate liquidity problems during the first wave, the economy and the society as a whole were still struck hard. People in their daily jobs feared infections, families organized their childcare new due to the closed schools, and sales were low. Even though some economic activities including the construction business continued and thus, MLT was only indirectly affected, within the following two days, the CEO of the company decided to install a task force. The goal of this task force was to handle the situation by maintaining the daily business and simultaneously ensuring the safety of the employees. The purpose, the structure and the manning of the task force were partly built on existing standards and management processes in place according to what the International Organization for Standardization (ISO) required for the firm's quality management (ISO 9001) certification. The most important aspect required by ISO 9001 for this study's situation is the fact that firms striving for a certification must demonstrate and document risks, and implement measures to respond to disruptive events. In this case, the CEO adapted the existing contingency plans to the specific Covid-19 needs. Only three days after the announced lockdown, the task force was internally communicated and implemented.

The task force of MLT consisted of five people, including the chief of staff. Whereas the CEO of MLT was deployed as the chief of staff of the task force, all other individuals hold a management position within MLT (as Head of Services and Human Resources or Head of a Transport Region). Each of the task force members is responsible for a specific task: Management and risk evaluation (chief of staff), occupational health and safety (task force member 1), business activities (task force member 2), logistics (task force member 3), and IT projects (task force member 4). The task force composition of MLT, including some personal details, is displayed in Figure 1.

*Figure 1. Task force chart of MLT*

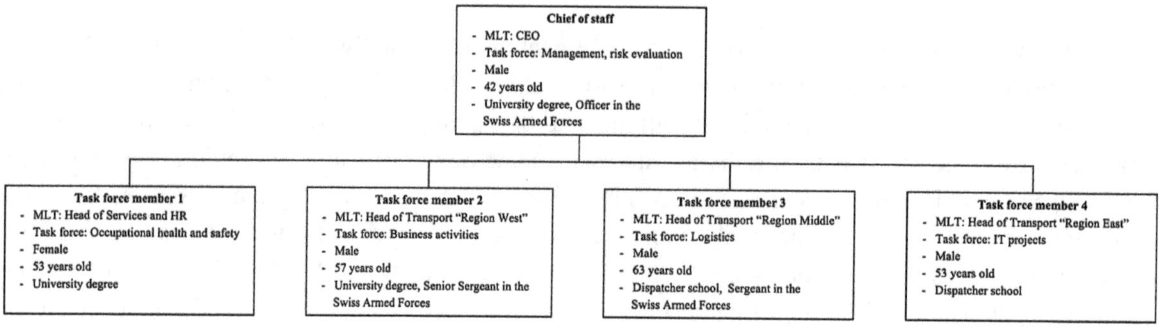


All five members of the task force were simultaneously part of the executive board of MLT. Consequently, all members were subject to multiple sources of pressure. They were highly involved in their daily business – their actual functions, so to speak – and in their temporary function in the newly formed Covid-19 task force. In order to mitigate this double workload, the executive board of MLT decided to temporarily charge other firm managers with more responsibility regarding decision-making processes in the day-to-day business operation. Daily business was delegated down in order to free capacity for the task force members to handle Covid-19. In contrast, the task force did not differ from the already established management structure of the SME, so that it was a well-coordinated team.

The members of the Covid-19 task force of the company did not receive any previous and specific internal crisis management training. However, most of the individuals possessed similar relevant skills that had been acquired in a different context (e.g., previous education or job, or military service in leadership positions in the Swiss military system of conscription-driven active reserves). The firm culture to talk and act in standards and clearly defined wordings helped the executive board to change into this crisis mode in stride.

In contrast to the regular monthly meetings of the executive board, the task force set up an additional weakly Covid-19 meeting (held online) to discuss the relevant issues. Additionally, each of the task force members had to submit a daily status report (clocked at 09:00am) to the chief of staff. These status reports came in the form of 'PALF', a German abbreviation for the items Personnel, Business, Logistics, Leadership. MLT adopted the idea of 'PALF' from the armed forces, where a similar structure is used on various levels to indicate situation reports. 'PALF' is used at MLT for various purposes which meant that these daily situation reports came in standards already well-known to all people involved, both in form and structure but also in content and meaning.

At the end of May 2020, after the Swiss Federal Council had eased some of the national restrictions, MLT returned to their normal business and the task force was dissolved. In summer, the executive board of the company intensively discussed the lessons-learned of their crisis management in spring within the regular executive board meetings. The financial loss was estimated at five percent of the annual turnover. Additionally, depending on the further exogenous developments, the risk of liquidity shortages because of closures of construction sites or general construction project freezes was identified. Besides that, so far, the biggest challenge of the Covid-19 crisis had been averted by the task force in charge of MLT.

However, the crisis led to less visible challenges for the organization. For instance, because of the physical distance to the employees, it was difficult to motivate and encourage them in their daily work. In order to mitigate these negative effects, the CEO of MLT decided to launch an Easter gratification in

April and produced a special Easter bunny wearing a mask made of chocolate. Each of the 200 employees received one bunny. The idea behind this little surprise with a pinch of humor was to express the organizational gratitude to all individuals and to increase the commitment. Additionally, in August, the task force of MLT organized a first physical staff meet-and-greet event after the lockdown.

At the end of October 2020, following the rapid increase in Covid-19 cases and the renewed restrictions made by the authorities in Switzerland, the task force of MLT was reinstated. On the basis of the perceived well-functioning of the task force with its human resources and processes, the task force of MLT was reinstated in exactly the same way as in March 2020.

## CASE ANALYSIS

This case structures its analysis based on the task force characteristics introduced above. The different dimensions – human resources, tools and support and processes and methodology – are used as a handle to break down the MLT narrative into discrete singular items of analysis. Keeping in mind, however, the research question (*What characteristics of task forces in small and medium-sized organizations lead to effective management of the Covid-19 crisis?),* this study will purposefully exclude the dimension 'Tools and Support'. The research question aims at the task force and its endogenous characteristics, thus around the human resources constituting the task forces and the processes used to operationally run it.

Therefore, the analysis will be structured along these two main lines: the people in the task force and the (leadership) processes used to run it (see Table 2).

*Table 2. Characteristics of task forces adopted by case study organization*

| Dimension | Content | MLT |
|---|---|---|
| Human resources | - Individual members' competencies<br>- Available skills on team level<br>- Team composition | •<br>•<br>∅ |
| Processes and methodology | - Leadership and management<br>- Information management | •<br>• |

Key to symbols: • directly applied, ∅ indirectly applied

### Human Resources

One of the most obvious but perhaps most important feature of SMEs is their scarce resources, particularly in terms of management and administrative capacity, which could potentially be freed to handle an unexpected external shock such as Covid-19. Therefore, conventional crisis management wisdoms might partly not apply or need to be adapted to slim versions of how they are actually meant. The 'leaner' such an SME is, meaning the more overhead it has reduced, the less it possesses reserves. If crisis preparedness experts advocate for building crisis management groups or task forces to handle a crisis, it might simply prove impossible to do so if there are only limited management resources available in the first place. MLT coped with this by essentially using the executive board in a double function – as executive board in their original role and as Covid-19 task force ad hoc.

On the other hand, MLT displayed strong and perhaps intuitively adapted principles by running the company much in the way a crisis management team is run also outside of the crisis. In practice, this meant for example that the importance of human resources had been understood a long time before the Coronavirus disrupted the world. In branches such as transportation, a lot of human resource quality is defined by practical understanding of the trade rather than educational degrees. MLT is run by an executive board which features 40% of members without university degrees. However, they understand the employees, the business they are conducting, and they acquired leadership and other generic, non-technical skills in other functions. For example, 3 of the 5 board members also acquired leadership skills in leadership functions of the Swiss Armed Forces.

MLT had understood the importance of the quality of human resources. Accordingly, they had all the preconditions necessary to possess the necessary individual competencies to run the ad hoc task force, but they also had all the skills on team level and a team composition which not only covered skills and competencies, but which was a trained and practiced management team. They run the company in day-to-day operations, and now they managed the same company with the same employees during a crisis. As a consequence, they sensed the need to keep the employees emotionally close early on in the crisis and extended an honest felt duty of care to them. The example of the Easter bunny gratification mentioned above shows that they understood that gratification needs to be personal and emotionally binding rather than material (such as a cash gratification).

## Processes and Methodology

In terms of leadership, the CEO himself assumed a 'Captain at the Helm'-attitude. He was physically, personally and emotionally present and expected the same presence of his middle management. He went ahead as a role model, assuming additional responsibilities in the task force as well, such as taking up the risk assessment and the information management of the task force himself rather than delegating these tasks in order to stay free for management decisions (as conventional crisis management would perhaps propose). He credibly adopted Xenophone's millenia-old adage "do not ask your men to do something that you won't do yourself" (Lowry, 1995, p. 10) in order to ensure that his keep the loyalty of his subordinates while also making sure at the same time that the task force is run in a way that he sees fit.

Apart from these observations, a striking finding can be identified in regard to information management. The CEO was clearly well-prepared to understand both the importance and the difficulty of coordinated and smooth information flows. Not only is he a senior officer in the armed forces with advanced training (reserve officer of the General Staff), but he also pursued and completed a continuing education program dedicated to the very subject. The information management challenge during Covid-19 was perhaps not information acquisition, but rather analysis and dissemination, as well as containing rumors and uncertainties. However, when asked in the interview, he asserted that in terms of information management, he "just followed the situation's necessities" without acknowledging that he, in his multiple roles as CEO, chief of staff, chief risk officer and intelligence officer, also achieved an additional feat. The way that the internal information was managed seems extraordinary for a structure built from the daily operation's management structure. The meeting rhythm was adapted, and in order to have all the information necessary to make appropriate decisions in the meeting, a rhythm and a form to report the status of sub-organizations was swiftly introduced. This form relied on a standard form, 'PALF', which was already known to everyone involved and the only adaptation needed from subordinated personnel was to speed up the reporting rhythm. Another advantage of the MLT task force was that all members were already part of the established management structure. Thus, they were familiar with the general processes and meeting culture, which made the functioning of the team much easier.

Taken together, MLT relied on processes they already knew. No additional structures were built, processes and concepts were taken from day-to-day operations as much as possible. Simplicity was key. And simplicity meant working with the processes already known and the resources already available.

## CONCLUSION AND RECOMMENDATIONS

This article provides findings of a case study from a Swiss SME that installed a task force in order to handle the Covid-19 outbreak in spring 2020. The aim was to examine characteristics of task forces in SMEs that lead to an effective crisis management.

The literature review revealed in particular three important dimensions: human resources, tools and support, and processes and methodology. Each of these dimensions can be divided in several subcategories. For instance, based on human capital theory and other recent empirical evidence on Covid-19 task forces, this article identified that individual members' competencies, available skills on team level, and team composition are critical task force characteristics (i.e. dimension "human resources"). Furthermore, physical resources can make a different in crisis management. According to the theory, mainly partners, logistics, safety and security, and information and communication technology are relevant characteristics (i.e. dimension "tools and support"). Finally, an effective management of a crisis needs holistic processes and methodology, that can be grouped in leadership and management and information management (i.e. dimension "processes and methodology"). Thus, these dimensions with its relevant subchapters provide guidelines how an organization can set up a task force from a theoretical perspective. However, as these results shed some light on the installation and functioning of task forces, the practical implementation is more complex. This applies specifically for SMEs that are often strongly confronted with resources constraints.

The case study of MLT showed an example of a Swiss SME during the Covid-19 crisis from March to November 2020. Several in-depth interviews with the head of the organization and a comprehensive data analysis presented a case of an organization dealing with the crisis. In summary, MLT installed a task force right after the by Swiss Federal Council's announced lockdown. The group of five people (each of them simultaneously holding a management position at MLT), met on a weekly basis to discuss the relevant Covid-19 issues. At the same time, each of the task force member had to submit a daily status report to the chief of staff, using the above-mentioned concept of 'PALF'. Thereby, the task force directly applied the characteristics of individual members' competencies and available skills on team level. Additionally, they included the relevant ideas of leadership and management and information management in their work. Team composition on the dimension human resources was only indirectly applied. Despite the financial losses of the organization, some challenges regarding the motivation of the employees, and the problem of double pressure of the task force members, the task force of MLT has, so far, successfully handled the Covid-19 crisis.

Of course, the mere observation that people are important for performance may not sufficiently the criterion of "non-obviousness" for relevant research (Thomas and Tymon, 1982). However, on the following recommendations, based on the literature and the case study, can be gained:

First, the installation of a task force in order to handle the Covid-19 crisis is crucial for an organization in general, including for an SME. External shocks demand the need to change processes and structures to cope with exogenous factors usually not present. Despite limited resources of SME, the case of MLT showed that a task force is essential to cover specific capacities and competencies and to support the decision-making of the executive board. Resources can be freed when competences are delegated down.

Second, several characteristics of task forces in SMEs lead to an effective management of the Covid-19 crisis. However, one of the most important one is the quality of human resources, which is intensified by the fact that managers in SMEs are subject to a double pressure as they are often highly involved into the daily business and the task force. Consequently, there is a need for a considered team member selection to ensure the necessary individual competencies to run the ad hoc task force are available, but also a team composition with different and complementary skills.

Third, as the task force and all other relevant parties are working under enormous time pressure during the Covid-19 crisis, it is crucial that the team is well prepared for such unexpected situations. The task force was able to fall back on already existing standards and processes to deal with difficult circumstances. For instance, task force members of MLT were all familiar with the concept of PALF, on which the team structured its analyses and decisions. Therefore, crisis management training of the individuals in advance, through specific workshops or former experiences (e.g., military services), is key to handling the Covid-19 crises in SMEs.

Fourth, the case of MLT also shows that strict adherence to terminologies and concept originally developed for high-pressure situation can also be applied in normal operations, and thus do not only prepare the organization for external shocks, but their efficiency is prone to drive profitability in day-to-day operations.

Finally, one of the most important roles in a task force, in SMEs and also in every other organization, is the chief of staff. The case study of MLT showed impressively that a task force leader who is physically, personally and emotionally present and who takes up the risk assessment and the information management of the task force himself rather than delegating these tasks, can serve as role model and lead the whole organization through the crisis. Of course, other situations might have made this approach unfeasible and possible, other CEOs, other companies and other forms of crisis might teach us different answers to the question of what the tasks of a CEO should be. However, in this case, the solution outlined clearly worked.

Besides these more generalizable lessons on how the Covid-19 crisis can be withstood, much depends on the specific situation or on external factors. For instance, this article has presented one single case study of an SME in Switzerland and in the construction industry – an industry branch only loosely affected by Covid-19. Consequently, the results and recommendations need to be put into the appropriate context. The authors particularly advocate further research on determination of the functioning of task forces in SMEs that could provide important guidelines for organization to handle the Covid-19 crisis.

## REFERENCES

Acquier, A., Gand, S., & Szpirglas, M. (2008). From Stakeholder to Stake S holder Management in Crisis Episodes: A Case Study in a Public Transportation Company. *Journal of Contingencies and Crisis Management*, *16*(2), 101–114. doi:10.1111/j.1468-5973.2008.00538.x

Alsaawi, A. (2014). A critical review of qualitative interviews. *European Journal of Business and Social Sciences*, *3*(4).

Bailey, K. & Breslin, D. (2020). The COVID-19 Pandemic: What can we learn from past research in organizations and management. *International Journal of Management Reviews*. . doi:10.1111/ijmr.12237

Barton, L. (1993). *Crisis in Organizations: Managing and Communicating in the Heat of Chaos*. South-Western Publishing Company.

Becker, G. S. (1962). Investment in human capital: A theoretical analysis. *Journal of Political Economy*, *70*(5, Part 2), 9–49. doi:10.1086/258724

Becker, G. S. (1964). *Human Capital*. National Bureau of Economic Research.

Benini, A. A. (1999). Network without centre? A case study of an organizational network responding to an earthquake. *Journal of Contingencies and Crisis Management*, *7*(1), 38–47. doi:10.1111/1468-5973.00097

Billings, R. S., Milburn, T. W., & Lou, M. (1980). A Model of Crisis Perception : A Theoretical and Empirical Analysis. *Administrative Science Quarterly*, *25*(2), 300–316. doi:10.2307/2392456

Boin, A., Kuipers, S., & Overdijk, W. (2013). Leadership in Times of Crisis: A Framework for Assessment. *International Review of Public Administration*, *18*(1), 79–91. doi:10.1080/12294659.2013.10805241

Bundy, J., Pfarrer, M. D., Short, C. E., & Coombs, W. T. (2017). Crises and Crisis Management: Integration, Interpretation, and Research Development. *Journal of Management*, *43*(6), 1661–1692. Advance online publication. doi:10.1177/0149206316680030

Burke, C. M., & Morley, M. J. (2016). On temporary organizations: A review, synthesis and research agenda. *Human Relations*, *69*(6), 1235–1258. doi:10.1177/0018726715610809

Chetty, S. (1996). The case study method for research in small- and medium-sized firms. *International Small Business Journal*, *15*(1), 73–85. doi:10.1177/0266242696151005

Coombs, W. T. (1999). *Ongoing Crisis Communication: Planning, Managing, and Responding*. SAGE Publications.

Crook, T. R., Todd, S. Y., Combs, J. G., Woehr, D. J., & Ketchen, D. J. (2011). Does human capital matter? a meta-analysis of the relationship between human capital and firm performance. *The Journal of Applied Psychology*, *96*(3), 443–456. doi:10.1037/a0022147 PMID:21244126

De Groot, H. (1988). Decentralization decisionsin bureaucracies as a principle-agent problem. *Journal of Public Economics*, *36*(3), 323–337. doi:10.1016/0047-2727(88)90014-X

Einola, K., & Alvesson, M. (2019). The making and unmaking of teams. *Human Relations*, *72*(12), 1891–1919. doi:10.1177/0018726718812130

Fernandez, A. A., & Shaw, G. P. (2020). Academic Leadership in a Time of Crisis: The Coronavirus and Covid-19. *The Journal of Leadership Studies*, *14*(1), 39–45. doi:10.1002/jls.21684

He, H., & Harris, L. C. (2020). The impact of Covid-19 pandemic on corporate responsibility and marketing philosophy. *Journal of Business Research*, *116*, 176–182. doi:10.1016/j.jbusres.2020.05.030 PMID:32457556

Herbane, B. (2010). Small business research: Time for a crisis-based view. *International Small Business Journal, 28*(1), 43–64. doi:10.1177/0266242609350804

Hollenbeck, J. R., Beersma, B., & Schouten, M. E. (2012). Beyond team types and taxonomies: A dimensional scaling conceptualization for team description. *Academy of Management Review, 37*(1), 82–106.

Hong, P., Huang, C., & Li, B. (2012). Crisis management for SMEs: Insights from a multiple-case study. *International Journal of Business Excellence, 5*(5), 535–553. doi:10.1504/IJBEX.2012.048802

Lowry, S. T. (1995). The Ancient Greek Administrative Tradition and Human Capital. *Archives of Economic History, 6*(1).

Lucas, H. C. Jr, & Palley, M. A. (1986). Plant management, the locus of decision making, and the information services department. *Journal of Management Information Systems, 3*(3), 34–48. doi:10.1080/07421222.1986.11517769

Lundin, R. A., & Söderholm, A. (1995). A Theory of the Temporary Organization. *Scandinavian Journal of Management, 11*(4), 437–450. doi:10.1016/0956-5221(95)00036-U

Omar, S. S., & Ismail, M. (2009). The background and challenges faced by the small / medium enterprises. A human resource development perspective. *Journal of Business and Management, 4*(10), 95–102.

Perren, L., & Ram, M. (2004). Case-study method in small business and entrepreneurial research. *International Small Business Journal, 22*(1), 83–101. doi:10.1177/0266242604039482

Robinson, C. D. (2020). The U.S. Navy's task forces: 1-199. *Defense & Security Analysis, 36*(1), 109–110. doi:10.1080/14751798.2020.1712028

Roser, M. (2020) *Coronavirus Pandemic (COVID-19)*. Available at: https://ourworldindata.org/coronavirus

Runyan, R. C. (2006). Small business in the face of crisis: Identifying barriers to recovery from natural disaster. *Journal of Contingencies and Crisis Management, 14*(1), 12–26. doi:10.1111/j.1468-5973.2006.00477.x

SECO. (2020). *Konjunkturprognose*. Konjunkturtendenzen SECO.

SharmaN. (2020) 'COVID-19: Challenges and Opportunities for Small and Medium Enterprises (SMEs)', SSRN 3650473. doi:10.2139srn.3650473

Shift. (2019) *SMEs and the Corporate Responsibility to Respect Human Rights*. Available at: https://globalnaps.org/issue/small-medium-enterprises-smes/

Swissinfo. (2020). *Vorerst keine Ausgangssperre - Milliarden für Wirtschaft, Swiss Perspectives in 10 Languages*. Academic Press.

Thomas, K. W., & Tymon, W. G. Jr. (1982). Necessary Properties of Relevant Research: Lessons from Recent Criticisms of the Organizational Sciences. *Academy of Management Review, 7*(3), 345–352. doi:10.5465/amr.1982.4285308

WEF. (2020). *Switzerland fast-tracks emergency aid for small businesses weathering COVID-19*. World Economic Forum.

Wegmann, R. M. (2020). A grounded theory for the performance of temporary disaster response teams. *Journal of Organizational Effectiveness: People and Performance*, *7*(2), 155–172. doi:10.1108/JOEPP-04-2020-0059

Wegmann, R. M., & Newett, J. L. (2020). When Complexity Costs Lives: Secondary Goals and Compartmentalized Information in the Second World War's Greatest Raid. Historians on Leadership and Strategy, 79–92. doi:10.1007/978-3-030-26090-3_5

Wegmann, R. M., & Schärrer, L. (2020). Outpacing the pandemic? A factorial survey on decision speed of COVID-19 task forces. *Journal of Organizational Effectiveness: People and Performance*, *7*(2), 191–202. doi:10.1108/JOEPP-05-2020-0089

Weick, K. E. (1988). Enacted Sensemaking in Crisis Situations. *Journal of Management Studies*, *25*(4), 305–317. doi:10.1111/j.1467-6486.1988.tb00039.x

Wong, E. M., Ormiston, M. E., & Tetlock, P. E. (2011). The effects of top management team integrative complexity and decentralized decision making on corporate social performance. *Academy of Management Journal*, *54*(6), 1207–1228. doi:10.5465/amj.2008.0762

Yin, R. K. (1994). *Case Study Research: Design and Methods*. Sage.

# Chapter 16
# Leadership as a Change Trigger in Unsettling Conditions:
## The Case of Werenbach Watches

**Vasilios Stouraitis**
*Glasgow Caledonian University, UK*

**Andres J. Arenas F.**
*Universidad Antonio de Nebrija, Spain*

**Kostantinos Tsanis**
*Hult International Business School, USA*

**Jessica Bayón Pérez**
*Universidad Antonio de Nebrija, Spain*

## ABSTRACT

*The case focuses on Werenbach watches, a micro SME based in Switzerland which managed to survive the current crisis of COVID-19 in an innovative way. The focus is on the behavioural aspects of leadership present in the case and which have led to tangible innovations. The innovations examined have led to the ability to source extensively and access funding to create a stronger global presence. The reasons for choosing servant leadership as an example are presented and the moderating links between attitude and implementation are listed and examined. Suggestions for managers and further research are presented. The chapter aims to be a toolkit for micro SMEs' CEOs willing to understand the fundamental behaviours behind access of funds and sources for a small firm.*

DOI: 10.4018/978-1-7998-6948-1.ch016

## INTRODUCTION

Small and medium-sized enterprises (SMEs) in the European Union (EU), consist of firms employing less than 250 employees, and account for 99.8 percent of all firms (European Commission, 2005). However, despite their significance, SMEs are vulnerable to several issues –dependency on debt, and in particular bank loans, for liquidity. Usually, in stable economic conditions, liquidity shortages can be controlled using short-term loans or capital without jeopardising the survival chances of the company. Nevertheless, in times of a crisis such as COVID-19, SMEs' reliance on financing, reliance on sourcing, and the lack of ability to procure other streams of funds in the short-run can turn a liquidity issue into a serious solvency issue. Eventually this issue has transformed into a critical concern for policymakers globally (Gourinchas et al., 2020).

Werenbach watches is a micro SME based in Zurich, Switzerland with 2 partners and a CEO, and a strategy based on mostly word of mouth, which managed to achieve; a very successful online strategy using social networks, funding and a worldwide presence including a succesful crowdfunding, and a succesful pricing strategy in several markets all during the Covid-19 period. Werenbach watches has a varied pricing strategy aiming at varied layers of customer base from high end to mainstream (e.g. 200USD to 600USD). Having interviewed the CEO using semi-structured questions, this case study aims to analyze how servant leadership (particularly providing direction and stewardship) helped the SME grow within the Covid-19 period. Intrinsic case study reseach involves in depth analysis of an individual unit. The following chapter is an intrinsic case study which does not aim to be used for theory building but for a better understanding of the particular case. This can be seen as a deviant case as it is quite unusual due to the extensive final media presence generated from a small firm size (Baskarada, 2013). Although our case is focused on behaviour, the case study collected evidence of the results and of factors encouraging the behaviour rather than perceptions of potential results.As case study research is based on analytical generalisation and is made to theory and not to population, the chapter focuses on servant leadership theory as a foundation of comparison. The reason for its selection is seen below. The findings are also shown below.

The company essentially secured funds and a survival throughout 2020 using an intertwining of innovations led and selected by a proactive attitude towards servant leadership. In essence, all innovations undertaken complement each other and intersect to create the situation the company is in. As in most entrepreneurial decisions, the action taken can be reactive or proactive (Stouraitis et al, 2017). In the case of Werenbach, most of the decisions seem to come from a proactive leadership stance showing a sense of direction (a servant stance) which was coined by Greenleaf (1970). The following sections will examine the three innovations and present a background on the company followed by the three innovations and then recommendations for management. Entrepreneurial action is directly linked to the entrepreneurs' evaluation of the opportunities and surroundings in which the company operates. Therefore, the issue for entrepreneurial action is not just if a rapid change in the business model could be of use. It is more about comprehending the meaning for the company inside and the environment outside, during the process of fixing their plans or business model. As Hoch et al. (2016) mention, leaders can be transformational but also unethical, abusive of followers and act in way that may be contrary to the values and organizational intersts, at times also without realising.

Presenting a background on the innovative product, the case will focus on the leadership actions taken in 2020 and during the covid pandemic (aka themes) to secure funds for the company and internationalize further rather than shrink. In the case of entrepreneurs like Werenbach, the reaction to an economic shock such as the COVID-19 crisis dictates the need for a primary evaluation to comprehend the current situation we are in (Lettieri et al., 2009): is it the in-crisis emergency response situation?; is the company moving towards a recovery post-crisis phase? To what extent is the company preparing for potential unexpected shocks? In the case of Werenbach the latter applies most, as shall be see later. Therefore the case shall focus on three themes or innovations achieved by Werenbach and the role of (servant) leadership in insigating them. The chapter aims to provide a behavioural tool and handbook for other micro SMEs to find inspiration towards a specific style of leadership that can appeal to funders and also to explain how this specific style of "moral" leadership can lead to the following innovations which are per se inter-linked and triggered by it:

1. The succesful pricing strategy for a worldwide presence (Developing international supply chains and outweighing costs)
2. The succesful online strategy via social networks (expanding the social network and sourcing)
3. The succesful international social media presence including interviews (promoting and expanding access to varied funders)

The three concepts are all stemming from a servant leadership stance and intertwine to provide sourcing and financing. This is in essence the link between the three and the final result.

The chapter unfolds as follows; a background on the Company is presented along with the space industry idea to understand the foundations and context. From there, servant leadership is defined and explained as the theoretical framework to be used in the chapter.From there the three innovations are examined in relation to the servant leadership section and definition. From there, the chapter moves on to a discussion and key findings section, a conclusion and recommendations for future research.

## BACKGROUND ON WERENBACH WATCHES

There are several fundamental questions we need to ask when researching the innovation and strategy of Werenbach. For example, what factors underlie new-product success? What have been the difficulties in the setup? Representative of this are the high failure rates of new products and the poor innovation performance in industry even before Covid-19: around 40% of new products are estimated to fail at launch, even after all the development and testing work; out of every 7 to 10 new-product concepts, only one is a commercial success; and only 13% of firms report that their total new product efforts achieve their annual profit objectives (Cooper, 2017b; Cooper, Edgett, & Kleinschmidt, 2004).

As a brief introduction on the company it is important to take a look at how the product began its journey to understand what is being sold now; Werenbach produces watches in extremely small quantities to international customers from the atelier in Zurich; a business model both fragile due to supply but also lucrative due to the exclusivity and rare nature of the product. Specifically, Werenbach sold 36 watches through its own atelier in 2016. Although the watches are put toghether in Patrick's atelier in Zurich, the case is sourced from Hong Kong. To expand the business and grow once the crisis began, Patrick needed resources and funds which were not readily available, more so under Covid-19, and this was threatening the fragile Business model. In an example of both leadership and business intellect, he decided to crowdfund his next series of watches including dials cut from the shell of the space-bound Soyuz rocket through Kickstarter, a crowdsourcing platform focused on creativity. In order to achieve this, he would have to expand the business (and his skills) in terms of social networks and social media. An unknown territory so far for this small Business.

Taking a step back, we can see how the business began; ie.. On the 23rd January, 2013, Andrea Duttweiler, Marco Vannotti and Patrick Hohmann created the company Werenbach in Zürich-Hottingen, Switzerland with the purpose to produce watches from genuine rocket material. In so doing, Werenbach sought to go one step further than other comparable watch brands, who had thus far succeeded solely in incorporating single pieces of historic or unusual material into their watches. At Werenbach, the idea was for the entire casing to be made of legendary rocket material showcasing an innovative drive from the early stage.

The vision of Patrick Hohmann, director and owner of the company "I want to create watches that are more evocative, colourful and inspiring than the rest." The journey started with the Trip to Kazakhstan, Patrick travels to this country to deal with a local rocket scrap metal dealer, Mr Murat. He has an exclusive contract with Roscomos (The Russian space agency comparable with NASA) to collect, recycle and sell the rocket materials that felt back to earth when rockets are launched.They visited the junkyard at the Baikonur Space Center, the largest rocket launch site in the world. Also, collected samples of rocket materials for testing and prototypes.

*Figure 1. An example of a Werenbach watch*
*(Source: Kickstarter.com)*

Both parties agreed to buy the rocket parts, based on the market price of the recycled material. In addition, Werenbach offered to cover all the additional costs that would be incurred by the order and to pay a small quantity surcharge.They agreed on a long-term mutual commitment that consisted of purchasing only specific and selected parts of the Soyuz rocket, including an exclusivity clause, whereby only Patrick could buy recycled rockets material for the production of watches. This clause could be canceled after the 20th shipment.For his part, Mr. Murat promised to decontaminate the recycled material, if he did not do so, he would have to cover the costs and assume all the legal consequences in customs.Both agreed to obtain the export permit, pay a surcharge for small quantities and guarantee the acceptance of goods for the predefined number of shipments.

All this despite the fact that Mr. Murat emphasized that each shipment could differ in prices and materials, since each rocket launch was unique, as well as the quality of the rocket material or the usable material could be different. This meant that the price had not been closed, we mean a fixed and fair price, as it seemed to have already been discussed, when what had been discussed was that the price should be based on a market price for recycled products.

Despite all the inconveniences, Patrick showed a servant leadership stance and agreed and compromised on different aspects to close the deal:

- To pay the surcharge for small quantities If the reference price per ton was close to the recycled material
- To pay more costs when entering customs

Another problem Patrick later encountered was that the production and manufacturing phase of the watches took much longer than expected. The problem lay in the design of the parts, they finally had to be adjusted due to difficulties in obtaining the initially planned mechanism. This is the beginning of Werenbach Watches. The chapter will focus on the change and leadership aspects that allowed the company to endure the economic hardships of the covid-19 pandemic.

## THE SPACE INDUSTRY IDEA

A major part of the Kickstarter and social media marketing was the innovative space industry idea. Patrick found the idea of rocket material especially exciting as astronomy and space exploration hold a special fascination for many, and it seems like humankind is always striving for a connection with space. Werenbach was initially looking for war airplane scrap metal, but neither the Swiss army nor the US Army gave them approval to use this classified material. They argued that an F-16, for example, could not be used with commercial purposes and that they should recycle the materials after the airplanes were put off services. Other watchmakers used meteorites, some used different materials and designs inspired in space related issues, but in this case study Patrick Hohmann, after watching a documentary about tours expeditions to Kazakhstan to see the rockets that felt back to earth after launching, the idea was crystal clear.

After several trips to the area, language barriers and endless negotiations they signed an exclusivity contract that give them access to specific parts of the rockets from the Soyuz expeditions. There is no other manufacturer of watches or any other product in the world that uses space rockets materials as the raw material for their product. This makes the product even more original and its concept too similar to other manufacturers like Apple that are selling a dream, an idea, a concept. In this case study the philosophy of “Space Born” meaning that a person can be part of a piece of history. The history of humans reaching space.

No other country offers the opportunity to entrepreneurs to have access to space rocket materials. China, United States and India are actively involved in the race to have more astronauts in the International Space Station, and even private companies like Elon Musk’s SpaceX are not developing any ideas out their space rocket debris, nonetheless they are now reutilizing their rockets so the materials used to manufacture this watches may soon become more and more difficult to obtain. This provides Werenbach a temporarily monopoly in this business and also a one of a kind product.

*Figure 2. The transition from rocket to watch*
*(Source: Werenbach.ch)*

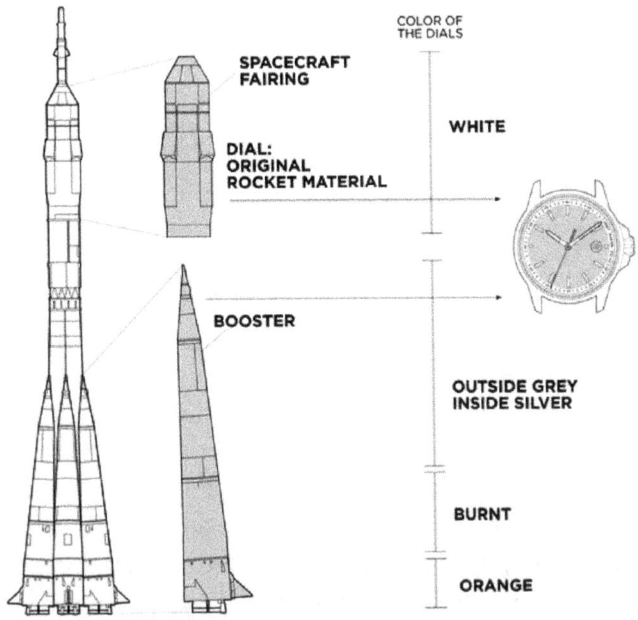


## SERVANT LEADERSHIP IN THE CHANGE PROCESS

Andersen (2012) hypothesises that even though several people are born with inborn qualities and character traits that promote their journey into leadership, the majority of people live in a functional reality where their leadership abilities must be intentionally cultured to achieve their all-out possible leadership output. This leads back to the reactive and proactive discussion on motivations as they can be instigated or led internally (Stouraitis et al., 2017) in firms that focus on leader behaviours and interpersonal dynamics that grow the followers' (network,media and employees') confidence and hence result in positive outcomes, at times beyond task compliance such as going beyond expectations, positive self-development and prosocial behaviours. The innovation created by Patrick and Werenbach was not only founded in the innovative capabilities already inherent in Patrick but also in his leadership skills which propelled the innovations through decisive action. Charismatic and transformational styles of leadership emphasize on stimulating and winning followers as main ways to reach structural goals within unsettling economic conditions (Winston & Fields, 2015). Earlier literature (Davis, Schoorman, & Donaldson, 1997) has highlighted the significance of shifting management theory outside the fundamental engagement ideologies of agency theory—with its supposition of the manager who is opportunistic, and self-serving— to management based on observing individuals as self-actualizing, and dependable with the common good of the company in mind. This concept is similar to the stress in servant leadership theory on the personal development of supporters and the growth of the company.

Table 1 presents several general personality characteristics of leaders.

*Table 1. Personality characteristics of leaders*

| Physical characteristics | Personality | Work-related characteristics |
|---|---|---|
| Energy<br>Physical stamina | Self-confidence<br>Honesty and integrity<br>Optimism<br>Desire to lead<br>Independence | Achievement drive, desire to Excel<br>Conscientiousness in pursuit of goals<br>Persistence against obstacles, tenacity |
| **Intelligence and ability** | **Social characteristics** | **Social background** |
| Intelligence, cognitive ability<br>Knowledge<br>Judgement, decisiveness | Sociability, interpersonal skills<br>Cooperativeness<br>Ability to enlist cooperation<br>Tact, diplomacy | Education<br>Mobility |

(Source: Bass, 1990)

It is evident that several, if not most, match Patrick's characteristics; how this evolves into servant leadership will be examined below. The study focuses on servant leadership as it seems to load with more practical and operational criteria than the other two major theories (ethical and transformational theory)(Hoch et al., 2016). More specifically, servant leadership can be seen as Patrick's tool in this situation and the theoretical underpinning of this case. The word *servant leadership* was generated by Robert Greenleaf (1904-1990) in the work "The Servant as Leader," from 1970:

*"The Servant-Leader is servant first. . . . It begins with the natural feeling that one wants to serve, to serve first. Then conscious choice brings one to aspire to lead. . . . The best test, and difficult to administer is this: Do those served grow as persons? Do they, while being served, become healthier, wiser, freer, more autonomous, and more likely themselves to become servants? And, what is the effect on the least privileged in society? Will they benefit, or at least not further be harmed?" (1977: 7)*

"going beyond one's self-interest" was placed by Greenleaf as a major characteristic of servant leadership. However, the case study emphasizes that servant leadership is not only a way of looking at leadership or an approach; It is directly linked to business success by creating the direct link between attitude and implementation. The following are expanded traits of servant leadership:

*(1) listening, emphasizing the importance of communication; (2) empathy, understanding others; (3) restorative; (4) consciousness; (5) persuading, (6) conceptualization, (7) farsightedness, (8) stewardship, (9) commitment to the growth of people, (10) constructing community (Van Dierendonck, 2010).*

According to a study by Hoch et al. (2016), servant leadership was observed to be directly linked to criteria and results of motivation (ie. practical implications) such as; behavioural measures (Job performance, employee deviance), attitudinal measures (employee engagement, job satisfaction, organizational commitment, affective commitment) and relational perceptions (trust in supervisor or manager, leader-member exchange). Leadership has become progressively more challenging, and multi-layered for companies of all types globally, thus bringing new queries and tests concerning what can be seen as the optimal type of leader (Gandolfi & Stone, 2016). It is significant to note that, regardless of disagreement, the one common feature that can be found through almost all of the current leadership literature is that leadership is crucial to a business in a practical aspect and more so in turbulent times such as these. The explanation for that is that when leadership is unproductive or absent, the result is that the organization is negatively impacted (Gandolfi & Stone, 2016). Leadership let-downs have been well-documented and, sometimes, appear to be the canon which can be witnessed in firm performance and access to funding. (Gandolfi & Stone, 2016).

Servant leadership, as seen in the conceptual model below, is deriving from three elements; Culture, Motivation and Individual characteristics. The case focuses on the individual characterstics of Patrick (mainly), particularly self-determination and cognitive complexity which lead directly to the 3 innovations mentioned above. These are the characteristics that stand out more in terms of the case; being a micro SME made of 3 members, the leadership is most evident in the CEO's actions towards the strategy and less on employee motivation itself as a leadership trait. The effectiveness of efficient leadership in the judgements of stakeholders is linked to the leader and manager being able to inspire, and rank wants, which in turn creates a sense of direction and security for stakeholders. However the end result can sometimes be elusive; the result of effective leadership is not only seen in motivation for employees but it is evidenced in tangible business results which come from a direct action.

*Figure 3. A conceptual model of Servant Leadership*
*(Source: Van Dierendonck, 2010)*

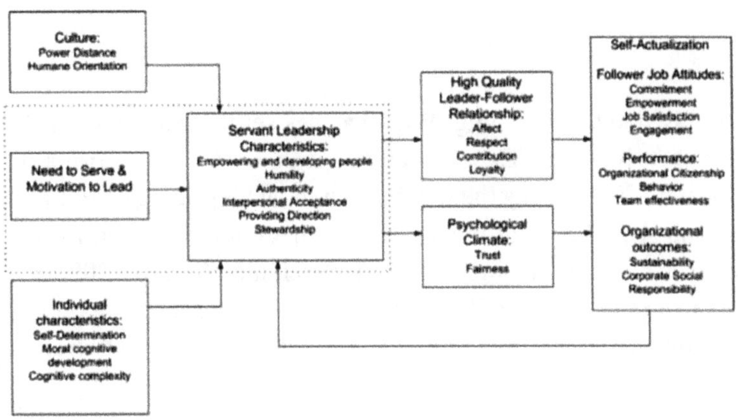


## THE WATCH AS A SUSTAINABLE FASHION BRAND

What is the situation in the company's market? Is it profitable and sustainable? SMEs are now challenged with a fiercly cutthroat market which demands products to be renewed frequently. Sustainability has become harder and harder to obtain – but what is the case of watches? Werenbach's main market – Switzerland – has seen a rise in sales up until Covid-19. That presents an environment with potential but also the requirement for a safety net through international markets. The Swiss watch industry has witnessed amplified rivalry, both in the higher value sector and at entry level, where volumes suffered. Finally, Swiss watch exports were worth 21.7 billion Swiss francs in 2019, an increase of 2.4% compared with 2018.

*Figure 4. Watches by price range*
*(Source: Federation of the Swiss Watch Industry FH, 2020)*

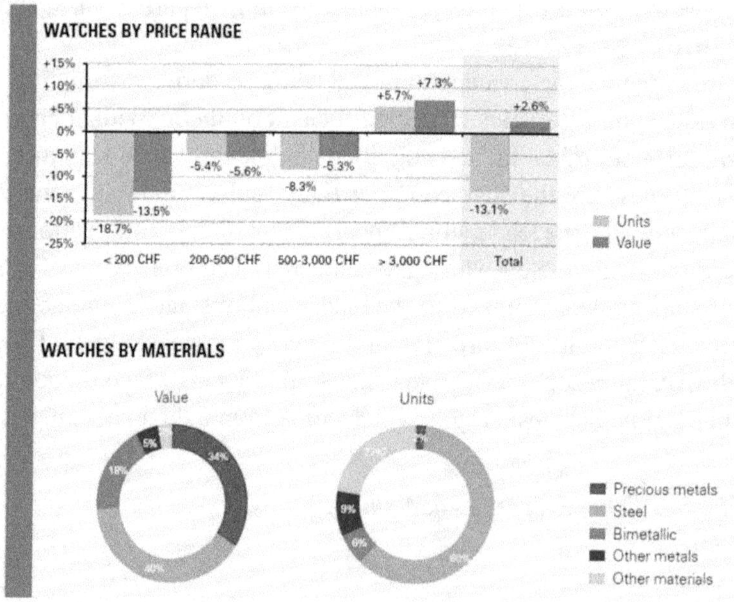


However interestingly due to the timing, Wristwatches set the tendency for 2019, and constituting almost 95% of total exports by worth. Exports passed the 20 billion francs brink (to 20.5 billion), a rise of 2.6% in comparison with 2018 paving the way for Werenbach's pricing strategy opportunity. However, even though Switzerland sent 20.6 million watches to other countries, it still was 3.1 million less than in the previous year. This historically low level, under even the crisis of 2009, is similar to the volume exported during the fall in the early 1980s and was of course expanded upon during the Covid 2020 crisis. So what has Werenbach done to maximise its survival from this situation and become sustainable?

*Figure 5. Main markets*
*(Source: Federation of the Swiss Watch Industry FH, 2020)*

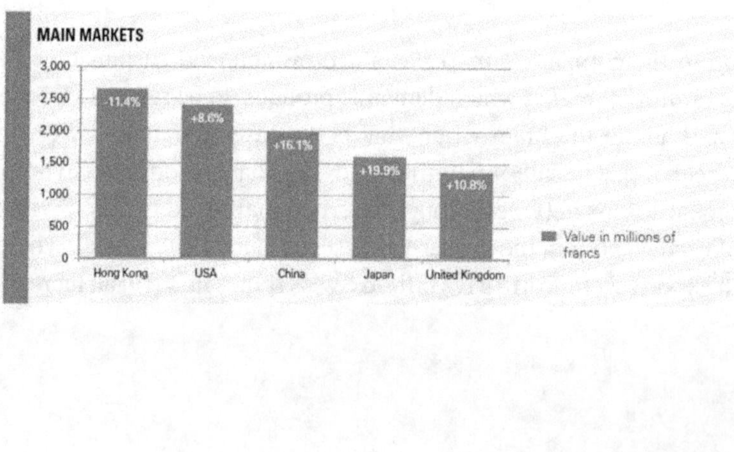

*Figure 6. Innovation strategies for new products and technologies*
*(Source: Reinmoller and Van Baardwijk, 2005)*

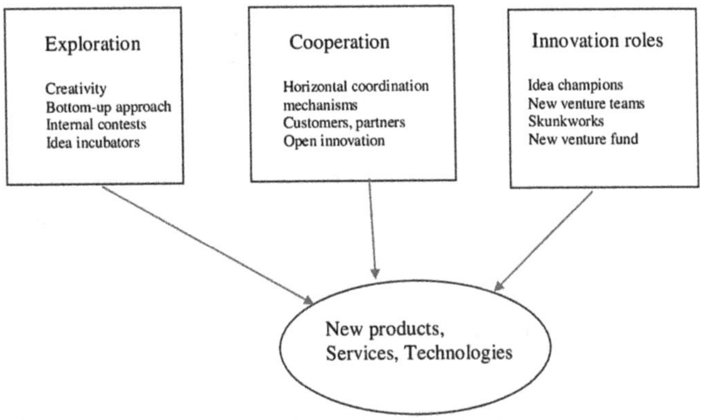


## THE PRICING STRATEGY (DEVELOPING INTERNATIONAL SUPPLY CHAINS AND OUTWEIGHING COSTS)

Werenbach's princing strategy is a result of its product innovation strategy which has been supplemented by its social media strategy and promoted by servant leadership. It can be attributed to self-determination or a will to survive and cognitive complexity; ie forward thinking strategy which led to sourcing and the creation of innovative new products which would have an international appeal. During unsettling times and changing environements, companies must get used to many types of change. As mentioned above, one significant area of innovation is the introduction of novel products and the promotion of said introduction. In this case the "space" watch is the new product introduced by Werenbach and also a new technology. In the case of Werenback the change lies in several aspects of the change process. The innovation strategy adopted and the coordination model for innovation must both be analyzed to get a clearer view of the antecedents of change stemming from leadership.

*Table 2. Entrepreneurial action in a crisis context*

Adjusting entrepreneurial action in a crisis context using insights from planning, frugality, and emotional support research.

| Crisis Phases | Business Planning (organizing activities and resource management) | Frugality (resource management) | Emotional Support (human & social capital management) |
|---|---|---|---|
| Pre-Crisis: •Mitigation •Preparedness | •Adjust the resource base (plan for contingencies), create buffers for unexpected shortfalls. | •Adopt a frugal culture, incentivize resourceful behaviors and focus on the long-term survival of the venture. | •Enable informal support groups that allow for implicit and explicit support exchanges. |
| In-Crisis: | •Adjust the planning mode, reduce formality, but be detailed and increase frequency. | •Focus on resource conservation, identify and prioritize resources that contribute directly to the product/service revenues. | •Encourage emotional openness, making culturally appropriate to share feelings and ask for support. |
| •Response (emergency) | | •Sell-off and divest resources with no contribution to the long-term vision. | |
| Post-Crisis: | •Adjust the planning mode and activity documents, | •Adopt a frugal culture for resource acquisition. Focus on quality goods and services instead of the most cost-effective. | •Organize informal support, e.g., online meetings, to strengthen cohesion and collective identity. |
| •Recovery | •Adopt a minimum documentation unit. | •Time acquisitions to reinforce your negotiation power. | •Sustain emotional openness, make sharing concerns and feelings a regular behavior. |

(Source: Lettieri et al., 2009)

A firm's product innovation strategy has a vital part in determining organizational urgencies and supply chain wide movements (Quinn, 2000) particularly in turbulent times. The strategic arrangement of inter-organizational actions results in innovative products, which are usually characterized as being original and valued. Yet, before marketing, a managerial task organizations face is in evolving supply chains adept in creating innovative products in an effective, effectual, and reliable manner. Figure 3 shows us several innovation strategies for new products and technologies;

Table 2 depicts some strategies available to entrepreneurs during a time of crisis.

It is evident that Patrick and Werenbach have gone through these stages in programming, executing and sustaining their innovative business idea through developing a supply chain to market their product base don servant leadership. During the earlier stages of production, the product life cycle has been condensed due to the increased rivalry on the market and hence a diversified approach is necessary. Firms can only enhance their competitiveness through innovations and supporting their supply chain like Werenbach is correctly doing. Firms are directed to push innovation through technical advantages and found brands and marketing channel strategies (supply chains) so as to allow innovative products to enter into the niche market with less friction and rivalry. Thus, and as is linked to the other 3 innovations, it can also develop into a product innovation model if consumers can partake in the customization design (ie. through social networks and media) through the value chain innovation procedure (Mascarenhas, et al., 2004; Khadke & Gershenson, 2008). Something we see in the Werenbach kickstarter strategy. Furthermore, this approach can deliver an improved level of services including cost decrease in the long run (Martin & Ishii, 2002; Unger & Eppinger, 2011; Cheng & Liu, 2012). Historically, novel products and services would be released into the market only after the project was complete. Nevertheless, in certain products customers play an important role in the final customization. The main issue for enterprises is if they can keep up with customers' follow-up necessities during the process of evolving new technologies and commercialize new technologies as early as conceivable (Kuester et al., 2012). A large element of this is testing the waters through social media and social networks, both for sourcing and for determining the requirements of demand.

Therefore, following from the above, it can be stated that a market focus should succeed through the whole new product plan (Griffin & Hauser, 1996) – For example in each of the supply chain steps;

- Idea generation: It is evident that consumer input in ideas is vital for product development. Market-oriented idea generation actions, such as focus groups, to determine unmet wants or glitches, can lead to vital ideas (Cooper & Dreher, 2010). Ideas can also come from web-based customer inputs (such as open innovation).
- Product design: Often, market research is performed too late – usually just to check the final result. Nonetheless market research can and must be utilized as a supplementary input to the design choices both final and temporary, starting with a user needs-and-wants study (VoC research).
- In advance to pushing ahead with development: The optimal results can be obtained by testing the product concept with the participation of the consumer by offering a depiction of the product – for example, via models, mock-ups, and even virtual prototypes – and thus evaluating the customer's purchase resolve (if any). In the end, and in a situation where funds are scarce, it is much more financially viable to test and learn in advance of development than to advance customer testing once the product is designed (aka the Lean model).

As mentioned above, corporate growth, an international diverse pricing strategy and profitability beyond mere survival be contingent on creating a international business strategy linked to product innovation (Kleinschmidt, de Brentani, & Salome, 2007). It has been evidenced in the literature that firms that take a diverse and international approach to new product development have higher chances of survival than those that focus their R&D spending on their home market (de Brentani & Kleinschmidt, 2004; de Brentani, Kleinschmidt, & Salomo, 2010; Kleinschmidt et al., 2007). International goods that are intended for a global audience or nearest neighbour export markets tend to be the products that perform best. Therefore, the management insinuations of these studies is that the globalization of markets requires a global innovation culture and a global innovation strategy (de Brentani & Kleinschmidt, 2015) as is being followed by Werenbach.

However, the reason we point this out is that this international aspect is often ignored or is controlled late in the development process. The consequence is either a global product (in other words, one form for the whole world) or a "glocal product" (one development work but several product variants to cover the demand in diverse international regions). An international orientation also requires the task of product design and assessing in multiple countries as opposed to only in the national market, and followed by custom-made international launch tactics. It also means being savvy enough to hire a global project team (through social networks) with team members in numerous countries (de Brentani et al., 2010; Kleinschmidt et al., 2007).

Regarding the launch, a quality launch (e.g. a kickstarter or a different type of social media event) is highly linked to the profitability of new products (Di Benedetto, 1999; Montoya-Weiss & Calantone, 1994; Song & Parry, 1996). Quality novel goods don't promote themselves, and the launch should not be seen as a side idea to be left for the latter stages of the scheme. A well-integrated and precisely beset introduction is generally the consequence of a well-tuned social marketing scheme stemming from the leadership decisions of the manager. It is significant to keep in mind that the product launch must be adequately equipped in terms of both employee support and funding; a strong new product many times does not attain its sales targets due to an under-resourced introduction. Overall, those who will achieve the introduction – the sales force, the management, technical support employees – should generally be involved in the development of the market launch plan directly and consequently should be affiliates of the project team as is the case in Werenbach's small team. The reason for this is that it ensures valuable understanding into the design of the introduction, also obtainability of assets – all essentials vital to a fruitful launch (Hultink & Atuahene- Gima, 2000). However, consumer input shouldn't stop at the conclusion of the pre-development market studies; it is a cycle that reinforces itself. Through consumer participation into the process to view sides of the product via a sequence of rapid prototypes-and tests, the developer verifies all assumptions.

## SERVANT LEADERSHIP AND SOCIAL NETWORKS

In the case of Werenbach, social networks have been key as they allowed the company to grow, to strengthen social media and develop an international product and access resources grown from the CEO's servant leadership style. These ranged from international business contacts in the supply stage to media and social media contacts in the promotion and funding stage. It is not coincidence that organizations tend to devote substantial time, energy, and monetary resources in leadership growth (O'Leonard & Krider, 2014). Nevertheless, notwithstanding these efforts, there is a rising worry in the literature that these efforts are not appropriately growing and sustaining the leadership volume essential in today's multifaceted organizations (e.g., Day & Dragoni, 2015).Usually, leadership development actions are aimed to enhance the universal knowledge, networks, skills, and abilities of individual leaders and managers (Day, 2001). These methods are therefore based on old-fashioned conceptualizations of leadership as the behaviours of individuals (e.g.,managers, CEOs) who direct, align, and motivate others in search of communal objectives and the growth of the company (e.g., Carlyle, 1907). Adding to that, the leadership literature has shown that leadership is both a interpersonal and multilevel issue, which involves not only leaders, but also supporters, and social relational processes linking followers of larger collectives and networks which show its tangible results (e.g., Eberly, Johnson, Hernandez, & Avolio, 2013). To understand the value of servant leadership in leading to tangible goals, multilevel interpretations of leadership, which highlight the social processes linking individuals and collectives, point out the importance of growing social networks (i.e., patterns of social relationships; Wasserman & Faust, 1994) as an essential part of leadership improvement. In more detail, the essential approaches for fruitful social networking are seen as being the following: (1) Individuals must develop social competence; (2) Individuals must be able to shape Networks; and (3) Collectives must work toghether to co-create networks (Cullen-Lester et al., 2017).

## SERVANT LEADERSHIP AND THE SUCCESSFUL SOCIAL MEDIA PRESENCE INCLUDING INTERVIEWS

Werenbach's social media success can be attributed to self-determination or a will to survive and cognitive complexity which was mirrored by a strong interpersonal relationshio ability; ie forward thinking and stewardship as a part of the servant leadership model as mentioned above. This complements social networks and allows for pricing. This has led Werenbach to become an opinion leader in its field and through its social media presence, interviews and networks enabling access to media. The role of social media and its number of users has amplified radically since 2000 providing endless opportunities for sourcing and doing business. Since 2015, around 65% of American adults have used social networking sites as a instrument in order to interchange information (Perrin, 2015). By 2015, Instagram and Whatsapp, sister companies of Facebook, had also become important gateways of social networking with around 400 and 900 million active users each (Rao, 2015). In addition, several other sites and applications by small and large online players—Google Plus, LinkedIn, Pinterest, Tumblr, MySpace, Blogger, and Flickr—are being utilized as platforms for various purposes.

Previous readings have shown that several features of opinion leaders in traditional relational communication could still apply to opinion leaders in the digital setting, for example, education, income, and occupational position (Lyons & Henderson, 2005). Regarding personality qualities, studies indicate that opinion leaders tend to be extraverted (Marshall & Gitosudarmo, 1995); exhibitionistic and narcissistic (Baumgarten, 1975); self-confident (Baumgarten, 1975); explorative (Coulter, Feick, & Price, 2002); open to novel thoughts (McElroy, Hendrickson, Townsend, & DeMarie, 2007); and curious, creative, and experimental. We can abbreviate these varied features into the personality behaviours of openness, exhibitionism, and competence in interpersonal relationships supported by self-determination. This ability to sustain interpersonal relationships with consumers, followers and employees allowed the CEO to maintain and expand an international media presence. This was also backed up by the uniqueness of the product.

## DISCUSSION AND KEY FINDINGS

The theoretical framework presented in the case can be seen in Figure 7.

*Figure 7. Theoretical framework (based on the conceptual model of servant leadership)*

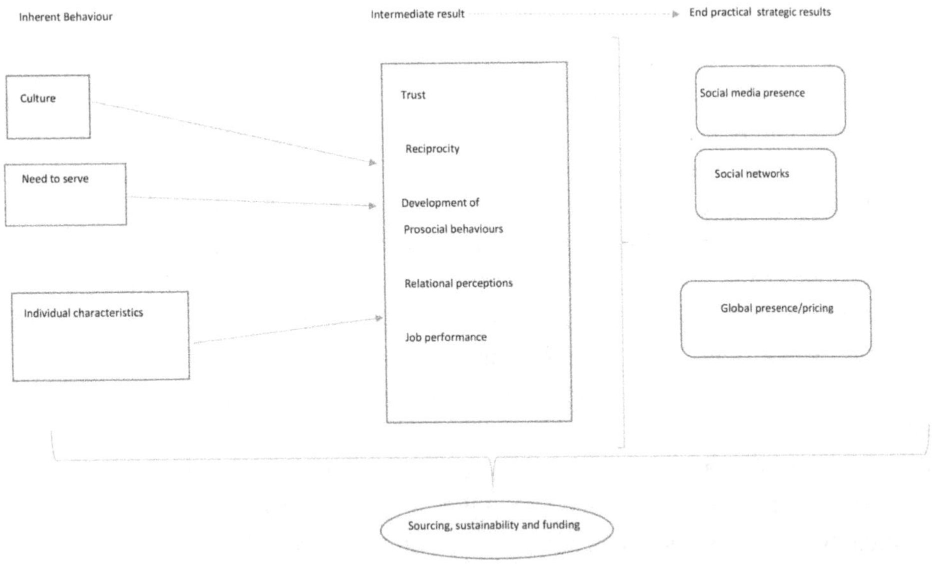


As can be seen in the theoretical framework, and based on the literature mentioned above, the fundamental inherent behaviour of servant leadership created an attitude which led to intermediate moderating tangible and intangible results. From there, we can see the development of practical strategic results as mentioned above.The company navigated Covid-19 and not only found a way to innovate but also to expand and sustain its brand. The succesful combination of servant leadership during turbulent times and creative product innovation led to sustainable advantage that is growing. The Kickstarter program shows innovative thinking and flexibility in times were a shift to the online consumer base and funding base is necessary. The product expanded on the core technology and created a sustainable offering.

As mentioned above, a company's product innovation strategy plays a dynamic part in determining supply chain wide activities especially pricing and sourcing (Quinn, 2000). Profitable products tend to be superior to rival products as far as meeting users' wants is concerned, they tend to present exceptional features not obtainable in standard products, or they tend to solve a problem the consumer has with other products. Furthermore, they present greater worth for money for the consumer, decrease the consumer's total costs, and claim an outstanding price/performance ratio. How has Werenbach achieved this? What are the key findings? It is evident that through servant leadership and in particular self-determination (ie. The will to succeed) and cognitive abilities (the ability to think outside the box) Patrick has managed to innovate and grow in a stagnant period and against the tide. The 3 innovative actions taken have been examined and the theoretical background on them has been presented. The elements in the theoretical framework present a visual representation of the findings and associations that make up this case. The intermediate results must be obtained and can be measured to avoid trying to jump from the inherent behaviour straight to strategic results. These findings can help managers of micro SMEs understand what is their leadership style and how can it be leveraged to bring change potentially through social media or netoworks. It can also help understand were on the framework are the actions of managers having an impact.

## CONCLUSION

The chapter aims to be a behavioural tool and guide for micro SME CEOs aiming to maximise the performance of their SME under situations of stress. The chapter focuses more on the characteristics needed to suceed in creating the fundamental background needed for a small firm to present an innovative, media friendly product. This type of access then will lead to opening new doors in financing and sourcing. The chapter has aimed to present an innovative case study and analyze it by backing it up with theoretical underpinning and mapping the company's innovations to the servant leadership model. The case of Werenbach wataches fits very well with the guidelines and theoretical background. The case is innovative, guided by strong and servant leadership, consumer based marketing and a critical awareness of the obstacles of Covid-19. The leadership style of Werenbach's CEO was examined as being servant and being the conductor of all three innovative elements. The elements of the leadership style were presented as cognitive abilities and self-determination. Based on the above discussion it is evident that the company managed to achieve growth during turbulent times such as Covid-19 by leveraging the abilities of its CEO. Social networks, pricing strategies and social media presence allowed the Brand to grow from a small SME with some minor international presence to wider markets and a crowdsourcing success. More specifically servant leadership allowed for the following final results by passing through the moderating phase:

- Self-determination allowed the CEO to pursue goals and uncover opportunities that would not have shown initially. It also allowed the CEO to understand the position and potential of the company.
- Moral cognitive development allowed the CEO to both provide a strong image on social media but also continue pursuing sourcing even after the initial setbacks.
- Cognitive complexity allowed the CEO to devise a complex product that could trigger the interest of social networks and also allow for a global market.
- Empowering and developing people allowed for the construction (albeit much before 2020) of a gradual social network which grew and helped in hard times.
- Authenticity allowed the CEO to present a product which showed a moral stance and a feeling of uniqueness to the consumer. Something vital for an SME trying to find space in a market.
- Interpersonal acceptance allowed the CEO to confront his partners and sources to expand the firm even under duress.
- Providing direction allowed the CEO to navigate turbulent economic conditions while maintaining a set vision through trust.
- Reciprocity between the leader and employees/followers allowed the CEO to created a significant social media presence. (Cf: Gandolfi, 2018; Hoch et al., 2016)

The resulting effect of this led to:

- A large consumer base and kickstarter funding program led by a social media campaign and presence.
- Opportunities for supply chain expansion, media presence and sourcing led by social networks.
- The chance to provide a global product and hence exploit international markets through pricing by using social networks to establish a presence.

## FUTURE RESEARCH DIRECTIONS AND RECOMMENDATIONS

Aside from a successful launch in terms of product pricing, a strong social media and social network presence is key. Regarding social media, the case has shown that it is evident that the attribute of capability in social relationships and networks also raises the inclination to be an opinion leader in social media and is vital to becoming an opinion leader and potentially altering product development and accessing funding. This significance shows that businesses could profit from proposing venues where opinion leaders can set their interpersonal capability to work for the company, such as proposing online discussion communities and/or even offline face-to-face events in which they can network with opinion seekers in a more direct manner.

It is important to note that opinion leadership propensity is significantly affected by openness and servant leadership. Those managers with a great level of directness are more probable to be trusted on and asked for info in a social media setting. To tempt and trigger opinion leaders, businesses should offer info that could stimulate their inquisitiveness. This type of content can allure the openness attribute in opinion leaders, thus aiding to improve their commitment to the brand and company. Likewise, the characteristics of leaders needed to assimilate building a sustainable company with the barriers of day-to-day operations highlighted the importance of truthfulness, long-term perspective, ethical behaviour, care for people, respectful communication, and managing responsibility outside the organization, all aspects that can be seen in the key servant leadership characteristics and warrant further research especially for SMEs.

Following from the discussion above and theory presented, some practical recommendations are presented below in order to create a sustainable and consistent competitive advantage under Covid-19 for Werenbach. Several of these recommendations can be transposed into any company.

- The web page of a company in an international setting should be in several languages, not only German and English. Main suggestions: Spanish, Italian, Chinese, Portuguese, Arabic, and French
- Werenbach is a unique product, anyone can buy an Omega Watch if they have the resources to pay it, but Werenbach is definitely a unique piece (specially the BTO´s). When you present a unique product you should have a marketing strategy based on the product uniqueness.
- Due to the advancements in the Sustainable Development Goals more emphasis should be placed on the ecological spirit of the product, for example if it uses recycled materials and they do not use batteries.
- Search other sources of raw materials that give the sense of uniqueness and exclusivity.
- Create a female line of products to diversify your market.
- If the product is limited, customers must be made aware that they are purchasing limited production units due to the limited raw materials.

- Keep an eye on global markets, for example, are growing specifically in USA, Hong Kong, China, Japan and UK. So the marketing strategy should aim at emerging markets and developed markets also.
- Make sure your product reminds the consumer why it is of value and unique.
- A good strategy is to promote some Kickstarter buyers to buy the product directly from their webpage. This is an indication that next campaign can be held alone without the Kickstarter costs.

## REFERENCES

Andersen, J. A. (2012, November). Reintroducing the Owner: On Corporate Governance, Goals, Organization and Leadership Theories. In *Proceedings of the 8th European Conference on Management, Leadership and Governance*. Academic Conferences International Limited.

Balocco, R., Cavallo, A., Ghezzi, A., & Berbegal-Mirabent, J. (2019). Lean business models change process in digital entrepreneurship. *Business Process Management Journal, 25*(7), 1520–1542. doi:10.1108/BPMJ-07-2018-0194

Baskarada, S. (2014). Qualitative case study guidelines. *Qualitative Report, 19*(40), 1–25.

Bass, B. M. (1990). From transactional to transformational leadership: Learning to share the vision. *Organizational Dynamics, 18*(3), 19–31. doi:10.1016/0090-2616(90)90061-S

Baumgarten, S. A. (1975). The innovative communicator in the diffusion process. *JMR, Journal of Marketing Research, 12*(1), 12–18. doi:10.1177/002224377501200103

Carlyle, T. (1907). *On heroes, hero-worship, and the heroic in history*. Houghton Mifflin.

Carter, D. R., DeChurch, L. A., Braun, M. T., & Contractor, N. (2015b). Social network approaches to leadership: An integrative conceptual review. *The Journal of Applied Psychology, 100*(3), 597–622. doi:10.1037/a0038922 PMID:25798551

Cheng, J. H., & Liu, S. F. (2017). A study of innovative product marketing strategies for technological SMEs. *Journal of Interdisciplinary Mathematics, 20*(1), 319–337. doi:10.1080/09720502.2016.1258837

Cooper, R. G. (2019). The drivers of success in new-product development. *Industrial Marketing Management, 76*, 36–47. doi:10.1016/j.indmarman.2018.07.005

Cooper, R. G., & Dreher, A. (2010). Voice-of-customer methods. *Marketing Management, 19*(4), 38-43.

Coulter, R. A., Feick, L. F., & Price, L. L. (2002). Changing faces: Cosmetics opinion leadership among women in the new Hungary. *European Journal of Marketing, 36*(11/12), 1287–1308. doi:10.1108/03090560210445182

Day, D. V. (2001). Leadership development: A review in context. *The Leadership Quarterly, 11*(4), 581–613. doi:10.1016/S1048-9843(00)00061-8

Day, D. V., & Dragoni, L. (2015). Leadership development: An outcome-oriented review based on time and levels of analyses. *Annual Review of Organizational Psychology and Organizational Behavior*, *2*(1), 133–156. doi:10.1146/annurev-orgpsych-032414-111328

De Brentani, U., & Kleinschmidt, E. J. (2015). The impact of company resources and capabilities on global new product program performance. *Project Management Journal*, *46*(1), 12–29. doi:10.1002/pmj.21470

De Brentani, U., Kleinschmidt, E. J., & Salomo, S. (2010). Success in global new product development: Impact of strategy and the behavioral environment of the firm. *Journal of Product Innovation Management*, *27*(2), 143–160. doi:10.1111/j.1540-5885.2010.00707.x

De Quinn, J. B. (2000). *Outsourcing innovation: the new engine of growth*. Sloan Management.

Di Benedetto, C. A. (1999). Identifying the key success factors in new product launch. *Journal of Product Innovation Management: An International Publication of The Product Development & Management Association*, *16*(6), 530–544. doi:10.1111/1540-5885.1660530

Dinh, J. E., Lord, R. G., Gardner, W. L., Meuser, J. D., Liden, R. C., & Hu, J. (2014). Leadership theory and research in the new millennium: Current theoretical trends and changing perspectives. *The Leadership Quarterly*, *25*(1), 36–62. doi:10.1016/j.leaqua.2013.11.005

Eberly, M. B., Johnson, M. D., Hernandez, M., & Avolio, B. J. (2013). An integrative processmodel of leadership: Examining loci, mechanisms, and event cycles. *The American Psychologist*, *68*(6), 427–443. doi:10.1037/a0032244 PMID:23528243

Europäische Kommission and Equal Opportunities. Unit E. (2005). The new SME definition: User guide and model declaration. Office for Official Publications of the European Communities.

Facebook Inc. (2015). *Third quarterly earnings 2015 report*. PR Newswire.

Gandolfi, F. (2016). *Fundamentals of leadership development*. Executive Master's in Leadership Presentation.

Gandolfi, F., & Stone, S. (2016). Clarifying leadership: High-impact leaders in a time of leadership crisis. *Revista de Management Comparat International*, *17*(3), 212.

Gandolfi, F., & Stone, S. (2018). Leadership, leadership styles, and servant leadership. *Journal of Management Research*, *18*(4), 261–269.

Giones, F., Brem, A., Pollack, J. M., Michaelis, T. L., Klyver, K., & Brinckmann, J. (2020). Revising entrepreneurial action in response to exogenous shocks: Considering the COVID-19 pandemic. *Journal of Business Venturing Insights*, *14*, e00186. doi:10.1016/j.jbvi.2020.e00186

Gourinchas, P. O., Kalemli-Özcan, Ṣ., Penciakova, V., & Sander, N. (2020). *Covid-19 and SME failures (No. w27877)*. National Bureau of Economic Research.

Griffin, A., & Hauser, J. R. (1996). Integrating R&D and marketing: A review and analysis of the literature. *Journal of Product Innovation Management: An International Publication of the Product Development & Management Association*, *13*(3), 191–215. doi:10.1111/1540-5885.1330191

Hoch, J. E., Bommer, W. H., Dulebohn, J. H., & Wu, D. (2016). Do ethical, authentic, and servant leadership explain variance above and beyond transformational leadership? A meta-analysis. *Journal of Management, 44*(2), 501–529. doi:10.1177/0149206316665461

Hultink, E. J., & Atuahene-Gima, K. (2000). The effect of sales force adoption on new product selling performance. *Journal of Product Innovation Management, 17*(6), 435–450. doi:10.1111/1540-5885.1760435

Jajja, M. S. S., Kannan, V. R., Brah, S. A., & Hassan, S. Z. (2017). Linkages between firm innovation strategy, suppliers, product innovation, and business performance. *International Journal of Operations & Production Management, 37*(8), 1054–1075. doi:10.1108/IJOPM-09-2014-0424

Jurisch, M. C., Rosenberg, Z., & Krcmar, H. (2016). Emergent risks in business process change projects. *Business Process Management Journal, 22*(4), 791–811. doi:10.1108/BPMJ-01-2015-0002

Khadke, K., & Gershenson, J. K. (2008). Technology-driven product platform development. *International Journal of Product Development, 6*(3-4), 353–374. doi:10.1504/IJPD.2008.020400

Kleinschmidt, E. J., De Brentani, U., & Salomo, S. (2007). Performance of global new product development programs: A resource-based view. *Journal of Product Innovation Management, 24*(5), 419–441. doi:10.1111/j.1540-5885.2007.00261.x

Kuester, S., Homburg, C., & Hess, S. C. (2012). Externally directed and internally directed market launch management: The role of organizational factors in influencing new product success. *Journal of Product Innovation Management, 29*, 38–52. doi:10.1111/j.1540-5885.2012.00968.x

Lettieri, E., Masella, C., & Radaelli, G. (2009). Disaster management: Findings from a systematic review. Disaster Prev. Manag. *International Journal (Toronto, Ont.), 18*(2), 117–136. doi:10.1108/09653560910953207

Lyons, B., & Henderson, K. (2005). Opinion leadership in a computer-mediated environment. *Journal of Consumer Behaviour, 4*(5), 319–329. doi:10.1002/cb.22

Marshall, R., & Gitosudarmo, I. (1995). Variation in the characteristics of opinion leaders across cultural borders. *Journal of International Consumer Marketing, 8*(1), 5–22. doi:10.1300/J046v08n01_02

Martin, M. V., & Ishii, K. (2002). Design for variety: Developing standardized and modularized product platform architectures. *Research in Engineering Design, 13*(4), 213–235. doi:10.100700163-002-0020-2

Mascarenhas, O. A., Kesavan, R., & Bernacchi, M. (2004). Customer value-chain involvement for co-creating customer delight. *Journal of Consumer Marketing, 21*(7), 486–496. doi:10.1108/07363760410568707

McElroy, J. C., Hendrickson, A. R., Townsend, A. M., & DeMarie, S. M. (2007). Dispositional factors in internet use: Personality versus cognitive style. *Management Information Systems Quarterly, 31*(4), 809–820. doi:10.2307/25148821

McNally, R. C., Cavusgil, E., & Calantone, R. J. (2010). Product innovativeness dimensions and their relationships with product advantage, product financial performance, and project protocol. *Journal of Product Innovation Management, 27*(7), 991–1006. doi:10.1111/j.1540-5885.2010.00766.x

Melnyk, S. A., Davis, E. W., Spekman, R. E., & Sandor, J. (2010). Outcome-driven supply chains. *MIT Sloan Management Review*, *51*(2), 33.

Modi, S. B., & Mabert, V. A. (2010). Exploring the relationship between efficient supply chain management and firm innovation: An archival search and analysis. *The Journal of Supply Chain Management*, *46*(4), 81–94. doi:10.1111/j.1745-493X.2010.03207.x

Montoya-Weiss, M. M., & Calantone, R. (1994). Determinants of new product performance: A review and meta-analysis. *Journal of Product Innovation Management: An International Publication of the Product Development & Management Association*, *11*(5), 397–417. doi:10.1111/1540-5885.1150397

O'Leonard, K., & Krider, J. (2014, May). *Leadership development factbook® 2014: Benchmarks and trends in U.S. leadership development*. BERSIN by Deloitte.

Perrin, A. (2015). *Social media usage: 2005–2015*. Washington, DC: Pew Research Center. Retrieved from http://www.pewinternet.org/files/2015/10/PI_2015-10-08_Social-Networking-Usage-2005-2015_FINAL.pdf

Rao, L. (2015). WhatsApp hits 900million users. Fortune tech. *Fortune Magazine*. Retrieved from https://fortune.com/2015/09/04/whatsapp-900-million-users/

Reinmoeller, P., & Van Baardwijk, N. (2005). The link between diversity and resilience. *MIT Sloan Management Review*, *46*(4), 61.

Sattayaraksa, T., & Boon-itt, S. (2016). CEO transformational leadership and the new product development process. *Leadership and Organization Development Journal*, *37*(6), 730–749. doi:10.1108/LODJ-10-2014-0197

Song, X. M., & Parry, M. E. (1996). What separates Japanese new product winners from losers. *Journal of Product Innovation Management, 13*(5), 422-439.

Stouraitis, V., Harun, M. H. M., & Kyritsis, M. (2017). Motivators of SME initial export choice and the European Union regional effect in manufacturing. *International Journal of Entrepreneurial Behaviour & Research, 23*(1), 35–55. doi:10.1108/IJEBR-05-2015-0120

*The Swiss and World Watchmaking Industries in 2019*. (2019). Federation of the Swiss Watch Industry FH 2020.

Unger, D., & Eppinger, S. (2011). Improving product development process design: A method for managing information flows, risks, and iterations. *Journal of Engineering Design*, *22*(10), 689–699.

Wasserman, S., & Faust, K. (1994). *Social network analysis. Methods and applications* (Vol. 8). Cambridge University Press.

Winston, B., & Fields, D. (2015). Seeking and measuring the essential behaviors of servant leadership. *Leadership and Organization Development Journal*.

Woods, S. A., & West, M. A. (2010). *The psychology of work and organizations*. South-Western Cengage Learning.

# Chapter 17
# The Banking Sector During COVID-19:
## The Case of Bahrain Islamic Bank

**Yomna Abdulla**
*University of Bahrain, Bahrain*

## ABSTRACT

*In this chapter, the authors explore the banking sector during coronavirus era by using Bahrain Islamic Bank as a case. Overall, the pandemic has speeded several decisions and actions in the digital transformation journey of the banking sector. Prior literature has identified four main strategies, namely retrenchment, preserving, innovating, and exit in response to a crisis. The findings show that the decisions taken by Bahrain Islamic Bank support the preserving and innovating strategies, which are mostly related to the continuation of its operations and preservation of its market share and customers as well as digitalization of their services and reliance on technological solutions to cope with the precautionary measures imposed by the pandemic.*

## 1. INTRODUCTION

During the year 2020, the globe has been invaded with Coronavirus (COVID-19) which was initially thought to be a health crisis, however, later it turned out to much more than that as it affected almost every aspects of our lives. On 11th March 2020, the World Health Organization (WHO) has declared COVID-19 as a pandemic which caused governments worldwide to take robust decisions ranging from schools and universities closures, airports shutdowns, entertainments and public facilities closures, lock downs and other social distancing measures. Some experts argue that the COVID-19 crisis is the most challenging after the World War II. Regarding the Gulf Cooperation Council (GCC), they were affected not only by the pandemic but also with the accompanied decline in oil prices. During the period from January 2020 to April 2020, the price of Brent oil has declined from $68.9 to $25.27. Consequently, the GCC Statistics Centre anticipates that the average growth of GCC countries' GDP in 2020 will be -2.2%. Similarly, the growth of Bahrain's GDP is predicted by International Monetary Fund (IMF) is

DOI: 10.4018/978-1-7998-6948-1.ch017

expected to be -3.2% in 2020. Whereas Bahrain's financial sector it is predicted to have a growth of 3.5% in 2020 which was trigged by the use of digital banking that helped the banks and financial institutions to continue their operations despite of the lockdowns and social distancing measures.

In this chapter, we utilize Bahrain Islamic Bank (BISB) as a case to examine the impact of COVID-19 on the banking sector's strategies. We chose BISB because it is the one of the established banks in Bahrain, operating from 1979. It is also known for their focus on digitalization and corporate social responsibility which are two important elements during COVID-19 era. This was reflected in several awards achieved by BISB such as winner of the prestigious awards for 'Best Corporate Social Responsible Bank 2020, Bahrain' and 'Most Innovative Retail Bank Product 2020 and Most Innovative Islamic Bank Award' for the year 2018 from International Finance Magazine (IFM). Our methodology involves the evaluation of BISB decisions during the period March- August 2020, against the four main responses strategies to a crisis, namely, retrenchment, preserving, innovating and exit. The data relies on publicly available data, including BISB official website and official press announcements. The findings show that BISB has taken persevering and innovating strategies during the pandemic period. These strategies will enhance the growth of sustainable finance which has been given nowadays greater attention and could one of the factors of recovery from pandemic. It can be argued that environmental, social and governance (ESG) issues, being parts of sustainable finance, are vital variables that firms should manage appropriately in the coming period.

We contribute to prior literature in various ways. First, as far we are concern, we are the first to examine the effect of COVID-19 on banking sector in Bahrain using a case study. Second, we add to the existing literature on the impact of COVID-19 on businesses and their strategies (Seetharaman, 2020; Garvey and Carovale, 2020; Verma and Gustafasson, 2020; Kraus et al., 2020).

## 2. LITERATURE REVIEW

The pandemic has altered several aspects in our lives out of which is the strategies of businesses and organizations. However, only a few papers have explored this effect. Seetharaman (2020) argues that COVID-19 has added a new dimension to the business model. This dimension entails the necessity of the product, in other words, he suggests that essential products were not highly affected compared to other products. He also highlights the importance of digitization of the services which help the banking and media sectors to be less affected by the pandemic.

Garvey and Carovale (2020) indicate that firms have changed their decisions related to manufacturing technologies, sourcing, and complexity of products to enhance their supply chain management. In line with that, Ivanov (2020) highlights the change in customer's preferences to online shopping than traditional one which requires a parallel change in suppliers' strategies. In the same context, Lee et al. (2020) argue that COVID-19 has boosted the risk of fragility in supply chains because of the change in demand trends of products and services. Firms need to revise their operations sustainability and resilience, transparency of expenses and costs as well as digitalization of their processes (Verma and Gutafsson, 2020). The pandemic has also adverse effects of employment, therefore, Carnevale and Hatak (2020) suggest that firms need to focus on enhancing the IT skills of their employees. Verma and Gustafasson (2020) indicate that the pandemic has caused firms to develop sustainable business strategies, new operating models to cope with change in demand and customer preferences as well as reforms in trade policies to mitigate the adverse effects of the pandemic.

Using family business data, Kraus et al. (2020) examine the effect of COVID-19 on the operations of family firms in five Western European countries. They find that the sector and firm size are the main important determinants of the chosen crisis management strategy. The results show that family firms have utilize retrenchment, preserving and innovation strategies to cope with the pandemic. Retrenchment involves the reduction of costs and complexity. Preserving includes measures related to continuation of operations. While innovation focus on a firm's strategic renewal which may involve focusing on robust products, opening new products lines and using new technology.

Although, there have been a few papers which explore the effect of COVID-19 on some businesses' strategies, as far we are concern, none of them have considered banks in general and Bahraini banks in specific. In this chapter, we attempt to fill this gap in the literature.

## 3. THEORETICAL FRAMEWORK

Crisis management can be seen from different perspectives because a crisis can be caused by internal or external factors. These perspectives range from stakeholder relationship, strategic responses to crisis and effect of crisis to decision making. There have been several papers which investigate the responses of firms to crises such as 1997 Asian economic crisis, 9/11 terrorist attacks, 1970s oil crisis, global financial crisis 2007-2008. Based on prior literature, Wenzel et al. (2020) have identified four strategic crisis responses to crisis. Table 1 provides an overview of these response. Each of these responses can have positive and negative impacts on the company. We evaluate the decisions of Bahrain Islamic Bank during COVID-19 in relation to these strategies and identify the possible impacts of these decision.

## 4. COVID-19 IN BAHRAIN

Similar to other GCC countries, Bahrain has suffered from two simultaneous crises, one being the COVID-19 and the other is the collapse of oil prices. The growth of Bahrain's GDP is predicted by International Monetary Fund (IMF) is expected to be -3.2% in 2020. Bahrain has been a unique country in the GCC, being the only country that did not impose curfew or lockdowns and this describes that it had the lowest mobility reduction during the pandemic era. However, schools and universities were shut down, restaurants and entertainment places were also closed, shops were closed for a period of 2 weeks, and work from home scheme was encouraged. The highest mobility reduction was in retail and recreation areas due to their closures.

Although most sectors were suffered by these crises, there has been some sectors which were expected to achieve a growth rate in 2020. According to the GCC Statistical center, the most affected sector is hospitality sector which is expected to have a negative growth of 16% in 2020. On the other hand, the best performing sector is the health care sector of about 8% growth rate due to the high investments by GCC government in that sector. The IT sector is also anticipated to have a growth of 5.8% as technology was the first aid solution in continuation of operations in several sectors of the economy.

In respect to the financial sector, it is predicted to have a growth of 3.5% in 2020 which can be caused by the use of digital banking which helped the banks and financial institutions to continue their operations despite of the lockdowns and social distancing measures. This is in line with the findings of the Bahrain Chamber of Commerce and Industry's survey on a sample of 1,180 business owners operating in 10 sectors of the economy (BCCI, 2020). The results show that the financial sector is least sector affected by COVID-19 compared to other sectors and that there has been a high reliance of electronic means of payments. On the other hand, business owners were concerned about their decline of revenues during the period of closures of commercial and industrial shops and their ability to pay the salaries and other expenses. Furthermore, majority of participants in the survey anticipates that the economy will recover during the next 2-3 years.

*Table 1. Overview of responses of crisis management*

| Response | Description | Positive Impact | Negative Impact |
|---|---|---|---|
| Retrenchment | Actions to reduce costs and complexity (Pearce and Robbins, 1993; Benner and Zenger, 2016) | Maintenance of liquidity (Pearce and Robbins, 1994). | Indication of decreased performance (Barker and Duhaime, 1997). |
| Preserving | Actions to continue operations of firms | Frequent strategic changes can cause a reduction in strategic renewal value (Stieglitz et al. 2016) | |
| Innovating | Renewal of strategic of business | Enable new ways and things (Roy et al. 2018). Opportunities for business model innovation | May be limited by low liquidity during crisis. (Wenzel et al. 2020) |
| Exit | Last resort response | Free up resources (Carnahan, 2017). Formation of a new business (Ren et al., 2019) | |

There have been various effects of COVID-19 on societal habits and behavior of Bahrain's population. Alsulaiti (2020) find that there has been a change in habits in Bahraini people as there was an evidence of increase of habits such as hygiene concerns, home-based hobbies, home-made meals and the monitor of the official media channels. Whereas there has been a decrease of habits related to socializing with others, visiting entertainment places, dealing with cash and ordering fast-food.

Since the spread of COVID-19, the government of Kingdom of Bahrain has taken several measures and made tremendous efforts to mitigate the financial consequences of the pandemic on individuals and businesses. On March 17, 2020, they announced BD 4.3 billion (26.9% of Bahrain's annual GDP) economic stimulus package. These measures include the payment of salaries of Bahraini workers employed in the private sector, payment of electricity and water bills for individuals and businesses, exemption of municipal charges for individuals and businesses, deferment of loan installments by six months, exclusion from tourism fees and rent to government owning shops and commercial facilities, increase in liquidity support to small and medium enterprise and support from Tamkeen to affected businesses and occupations such as drivers, driving teachers. Additionally, there has been also BD177 million allocated for health care sector needs and BD 5.5 million to affected families.

## 5. FINANCIAL SECTOR AND DIGITAL TRANSFORMATION

According to the Central bank of Bahrain factsheet, the financial sector is considered on the main sectors in Bahrain's economy as it contributed in 2018 to about 16.5% of the GDP. As of January 2020, there are 376 financial institutions, out of which 94 are banks. The retails banks represent about 33% of total number of banks, whereas the remaining banks are wholesale. The total assets of the financial institutions as of November 2019 is about $205.5 billion. As of 2018, the financial sector employs about 14,148 people.

Prior to COVID-19, the Central Bank of Bahrain has allocated a great importance to the digital transformation of financial sector and therefore, have conducted several initiatives in that aspect. First, they have established a FinTech and Innovation unit which provides a regulatory framework that enhances the development of FinTech and innovation as well as it approves and supervise the participation in regulatory sandbox. Second, they started a regulatory sandbox for startups and FinTech companies to support their banking and financial solutions and the issuance of crowfunding regulations (CBB, 2020).

With the widespread of COVID-19, the World Health Organization (WHO) has advised people to use contactless payment and avoid handling banknotes as much as possible. Most banks have reduced their branches working hours and increased the available services electronically. It was obvious that financial institutions of all sizes have focused on improving their digital engagement levels. In Bahrain, there has been not only increase in the use of e-banking applications. Banks has started several initiatives such as customer-centric chat service on the WhatsApp Business social media platform, instant finance and enhancing their digital applications. Moreover, CBB has increased the volume limit of contactless transactions on POS devices to BD50/- without the need to use a PIN code.

## 6. BAHRAIN ISLAMIC BANK

### 6.1. Overview

Bahrain Islamic Bank (BISB) is considered as the first Islamic bank in Bahrain and the fourth in GCC. It is established in 1979 with the objective to conduct banking activities in accordance to Islamic principles. The success of BISB is attributed to their focus on ongoing innovation, robust corporate governance, risk management, employee advancement and the use of technology. They implement a customer centric strategy and utilize innovation in their operations which enabled them to be a pivotal provider of Islamic Banking in Bahrain.

Table 2 presents the members of the board of directors. The board directors of BISB consists of 9 members, out of which one member is female.

*Table 2. Composition of Board of Directors of BISB*

| Name | Role |
|---|---|
| Dr. Esam Fakhro | Chairman |
| Mr. Khalid AbdulRahman | Vice Chairman |
| Mr. Jean Durand | Vice Chairman |
| Mr. Mohamed Noorudin | Board Member |
| Mr. Khalid Al Jassim | Board Member |
| Mr. Marwan Tabbara | Board Member |
| Mr. Mohamed Al Jalahama | Board Member |
| Mr. Yaser Al Sharifi | Board Member |
| Ms. Dana Buheji | Board Member |

BISB has developed "BISB Brand DNA" which state "Fueled by Bahraini devotion, we craft new ways of simplifying your money matters". The brand describes their promises, values and pillars which enhances their relationship with their customers, partners, and all internal and external stakeholders. One of the important characteristics in the brand is the stress of innovation and continuous development that is seen in the achievements in the digital transformation journey.

*Table 3. Pillars and Values of BISB*

| Pillars | Values |
|---|---|
| Bahrain-ness | Bahraini |
| Banking re-imagined | Innovative |
| Start-up mindset | Simple |
| Social innovations | Bold |

Table 3 summarizes the pillars and values of BISB. There are four pillars of BISB brand, first is the Bahrain-ness that highlight the local values and insights believing that this will make them closer to customers. Second, the banking re-imagined which indicate the importance of use of technology in offering their services. Third, the start-up mindset that directs to BISB innovation labs with its role of creation of new ideas and tools. Finally, the social innovations that entails the social responsibility of BISB in projects that adds positive value to the society.

Similar to the pillars, there are four elements of the brand values which are closely connected to the brand and to the pillars. The first element is Bahraini that indicate the importance of establishing trust, loyalty, and strong relationship with customers. The second pillar is simple which highlight the importance of providing clear and consistent banking experience to customers. The third pillar is innovation that presents the significance of being up-to-date and to cope with external changes. The fourth pillar is bold that specifies BISB's role as a driver for transformational growth.

It is noticed that in all the three, elements, values and brand, promises they emphasize on Bahraini which indicate the importance of the localization aspect to BISB.

To well serve their customers, BISB have several branches around Bahrain. There are 4 financial malls, 4 branches and 1 digital branch. The financial malls are in Budaiya, Arad, Hamad town and Riffa. The branches are situated in Muharraq, Zayed town, diplomatic area, Sitra and Galleria mall. BISB has granted the digital transformation of offering the financial services a grant importance which was translated in the several initiatives such as BISB online, digital branch, interactive teller machine and Kisok.

BISB online has been granted the "Best Online Bank" in 2018 by Global Business outlook. There are services that can be easily done using BISB online such managing credit limits, local and international transfers, account aggregation, Teejroi account opening, online instant cash withdrawal, cardless withdrawal, managing card security, budgeting and savings, sending and receiving money. BISB Kisok is developed internally by BISB innovation lab to provide various services, during the 24 hours a day, such as account opening, issue and replace debit card, prepaid card issuance, document printing and update customer information. The digital branch has the advantage of providing services 24 hours a day, unlike other branches, it is not limited by working hours. The interactive teller machine is available in two branches. It enables customers to cash deposits and withdrawal with larger amounts compared to traditional automatic teller machine. It also allows cheque deposit, cheque cashing and cheque book printing.

## 6.2. Data Analysis

We use publicly available data during the period March- August 2020, to examine the strategies taken by BISB during the pandemic period. The data sources include BISB official website and official press announcements. The main advantage of public data is their accessibility and reliability which will enhance the accuracy of the analysis.

Like most businesses, BISB had taken various strategies to mitigate the effects of COVID-19 and cope with its consequences. These strategies can be divided into three types: first is the strategies towards its customers, second is the strategies towards the society and third is the strategies towards its employees.

### 6.2.1 Strategies Towards Its Customers

BISB has recognized the impacts of COVID-19 on the everyday life of their customers and therefore it has taken several steps to provide an ongoing support and help to them. BISB Digital is a great tool to provide banking on the go and replaces the need of visiting bank branches and so encourage the take at home scheme. Through the mobile application, customers can open an account, settle credit card payments, top up finance and update their customer details. Furthermore, BISB has announced their readiness to offer advisory services to their retail and corporate as an initiative of financial support.

According to BISB website (BISB, 2020a), for retail customers, in line with Bahraini's government initiative, they were granted a six months deferral of their installments starting from March 2020, without any fees. This deferral applies to current and new customers applying for new personal and auto financing loans. Moreover, with respect to credit cardholders, there will be no minimum monthly payments required starting from March 2020. The direct debit service has also been suspended for a period of 6 months effective from March 2020. BISB has also given the option to customer if they prefer not to utilize these grace periods, they can pay any amount due through the bank various payment channels.

In respect to corporate customers, with any new drawdown and existing facilities a grace period of 6 months will be allowed. The bank also offers consultation service to analyze and evaluate the liquidity position as well as suggest possible solutions for any mismatch of cashflows that could have occurred due to the pandemic. BISB also offers cash collection services at an acceptable rate. Similar to retail customers, BISB Corporate Digital enables corporate customers to carry out several of their banking services remotely.

During the pandemic period and the wave of digital financial transformation, BISB has warn their customers from increase numbers of scams, therefore, they should not provide their private banking information via an email or a message that claims that it is required by the bank.

### 6.2.2. Strategies Towards the Society

BISB has been always keen to support and give back to the society. Their corporate social responsibility has been a vital part of their corporate strategy. Consequently, during the hard period of the pandemic, the bank ought to provide gratitude and appreciation to the healthcare staff who have been working very hard to mitigate the spread of the virus. On 23rd March 2020, BISB have announced its donation of BD 50,000 to the medical team (BISB, 2020 b). BISB has also contributed by BD 250,000 to the national campaign 'Feena Khair' (There is Good in Us) which intends to raise funds to combat the adverse effect of the pandemic. Furthermore, the bank has allocated BD 30,000 as prizes for its medical staff customers.

### 6.2.3 Strategies Towards Its Employees

BISB has considered the safety and health of its employee a top priority and therefore have initiated a work from home scheme which benefited 88% of the employees. In any given time, about 60% of the employees were able to work remotely (BISB, 2020 c).

On the other hand, there has been several measures to protect employees who worked in BISB's branches. These measures include BISB's buildings and facilities were prepared to adhere of the precautionary measures of social distancing by limiting the number of customers waiting in branches, shortening the working hours of branches, leaving the required distance as well as using protection shields between customers and staff and all staff were required to wear masks and gloves.

It was essential to maintain the mental wellbeing of employees and especially during the COVID-19, in this context, BISB has been a pioneer in providing virtual training programs, virtual coffee rooms and motivational online sessions for their employees to boost their morale and spirits. Online inductions have also been provided to new employees that have recently joined the bank.

## 6.3. Discussion of Findings

Overall, the decisions taken by BISB can be related to preserving strategy where the bank was keen to continue its operations and preserves its market share and customers. For instance, the continuation of the opening of the branches and the reliance of its mobile application to run most of their service is believed to be a part of the preserving strategy. The contribution to the medical team and Bahraini's society was also considered as a way to retain its position as a leading local bank. Wenzel et al. (2020) indicate that preserving strategy fits best as a medium-term response to a crisis. Furthermore, there has been several decisions taken by BISB that supports the innovating strategy which are mostly related to digitalizing their services and relying on technological solutions to cope with the precautionary measures imposed to fight the pandemic. The adoption of work from home scheme along with the use of pioneering techniques to maintain the teamwork spirit and the mental wellbeing of employees can be counted to also one of the elements innovating strategy. There is no evidence of retrenchment or exit strategies. The use of innovating response will have several positive impacts on BISB as it will enable the use of new models and ways of services (Roy et al. 2018). Wenzel et al. (2020) argue that innovating response is unavoidable strategy to the company's survival in the long run.

It can be noticed that BISB has employed medium to long-term responses to the pandemic which are relevant decisions as it is not clear yet when the pandemic will be over. These forward-looking strategies is expected to have a positive impact on the bank sustainability and at the same time immunize it against the adverse effects of COVID-19.

The pandemic has taught a lesson to businesses to be able to adapt quickly and adjust to changing environment. Additionally, they need to have a hybrid setup consisting of both traditional and digital tools. Another important takeaway of COVID-19 is the emphasis on continuous exploitation and implementation of new technology.

## 7. CONCLUSION

We examine the effects of COVID-19 on the strategies of Bahrain's banking sector using Bahrain Islamic Bank as a case study. The pandemic has been associated with a decline in oil prices which made it more challenging for oil exporters companies such as the GCC. The financial sector is one of the main sectors in Bahrain's economy, in line with other businesses in other sectors, banks have taken several actions to cope with COVID-19. We utilize publicly available data, including BISB official website and official press announcements, to examine the strategies taken by BISB during the pandemic period. The decisions and initiatives announced by BISB have been evaluated against the four main responses strategies to a crisis, namely, retrenchment, preserving, innovating and exit. The findings show that BISB has taken persevering and innovating strategies during the pandemic period. These strategies are expected to have a positive impact on BISB survival as they allow the exploitation of new technology as well as the utilization of the current slack resources. However, as we are still in the COVID-19 era, we are unable to examine the aftermath of the crisis to have a more comprehensive analysis to companies' responses, especially in the long run.

Finally, it would be interesting for future research to examine the effects of COVID-19 on some of the adversely affected sectors such as travel, hospitality, and tourism in the GCC.

## REFERENCES

Alsulaiti, M. (2020). *Impact of the novel coronavirus (COVID-19) on societal habits and behaviours*. Retrieved from https://www.derasat.org.bh/survey-impact-of-the-novel-cornavirus-covid-19-on-societal-habits-and-behaviors/

Barker, V. L. III, & Duhaime, I. M. (1997). Strategic change in the turnaround process: Theory and empirical evidence. *Strategic Management Journal*, *18*(1), 13–38. doi:10.1002/(SICI)1097-0266(199701)18:1<13::AID-SMJ843>3.0.CO;2-X

BCCI. (2020). *The Economic Impact of Coronavirus*. Retrieved from https://bahrainchamber.bh/ar/node/69239

Benner, M. J., & Zenger, T. (2016). The lemons problem in markets for strategy. *Strategy Science, 1*(2), 71–89. doi:10.1287tsc.2015.0010

BISB. (2020a). *Coronavirus (COVID-19) Help & Support.* Retrieved from https://www.bisb.com/en/covid-19

BISB. (2020b). *COVID-19.* Retrieved from https://www.bisb.com/en/node/1183

BISB. (2020c). *BisB Implements Additional Health & Safety Measures During COVID-19.* Retrieved from https://www.bisb.com/en/bisb-implements-additional-health-safety-measures-during-covid-19

Carnahan, S. (2017). Blocked but not tackled: Who founds new firms when rivals dissolve? *Strategic Management Journal, 38*(11), 2189–2212. doi:10.1002mj.2653

Carnevale, J. B., & Hatak, I. (2020). Employee adjustment and well-being in the era of COVID-19: Implications for human resource management. *Journal of Business Research, 117*, 183–187. doi:10.1016/j.jbusres.2020.05.037 PMID:32501303

CBB. (2020). *FinTech and Innovation.* Retrieved from https://www.cbb.gov.bh/fintech/

Garvey, M. D., & Carnovale, S. (2020). The rippled newsvendor: A new inventory framework for modelling supply chain risk severity in the presence of risk propagation. *International Journal of Production Economics, 228*, 107752. doi:10.1016/j.ijpe.2020.107752 PMID:32292241

Ivanov, D. (2020). Predicting the impacts of epidemic outbreaks on global supply chains: A simulation-based analysis on the coronavirus outbreak (COVID-19/SARS-CoV-2) case. *Transportation Research Part E, Logistics and Transportation Review, 136*, 101922. doi:10.1016/j.tre.2020.101922 PMID:32288597

Kraus, S., Clauss, T., Breier, M., Gast, J., Zardini, A., & Tiberius, V. (2020). The economics of COVID-19: Initial empirical evidence on how family firms in five European countries cope with the corona crisis. *International Journal of Entrepreneurial Behaviour & Research, 26*(5), 1067–1092. doi:10.1108/IJEBR-04-2020-0214

Lee, S. J., Venkataraman, S., Heim, G. R., Roth, A. V., & Chilingerian, J. (2020). Impact of the value-based purchasing program on hospital operations outcomes: An econometric analysis. *Journal of Operations Management, 66*(1–2), 151–175. doi:10.1002/joom.1057

Pearce, J. A. II, & Robbins, K. (1993). Toward improved theory and research on business turnaround. *Journal of Management, 19*(3), 613–636. doi:10.1177/014920639301900306

Pearce, J. A., & Robbins, K. (1994). Retrenchment remains the foundation of business turnaround. *Strategic Management Journal, 15*(5), 417–417. doi:10.1002mj.4250150507

Ren, C. R., Hu, Y., & Cui, T. H. (2019). Responses to rival exit: Product variety, market expansion, and preexisting market structure. *Strategic Management Journal, 40*(2), 253–276. doi:10.1002mj.2970

Roy, R., Lampert, C. M., & Stoyneva, I. (2018). When dinosaurs fly: The role of firm capabilities in the „avianization— of incumbents during disruptive technological change. *Strategic Entrepreneurship Journal, 12*(2), 261–284. doi:10.1002ej.1278

Seetharaman, P. (2020). Business models shifts: Impact of Covid-19. *International Journal of Information Management*, *54*, 102173. doi:10.1016/j.ijinfomgt.2020.102173 PMID:32834338

Stieglitz, N., Knudsen, T., & Becker, M. C. (2016). Adaptation and inertia in dynamic environments. *Strategic Management Journal*, *37*(9), 1854–1864. doi:10.1002mj.2433

Verma, S., & Gustafsson, A. (2020). Investigating the emerging COVID-19 research trends in the field of business and management: A bibliometric analysis approach. *Journal of Business Research*, *118*, 253–261. doi:10.1016/j.jbusres.2020.06.057 PMID:32834211

Wenzel, M., Stanske, S., & Lieberman, M. B. (2020). Strategic responses to crisis. *Strategic Management Journal*, *41*, V7–V18.

# Chapter 18
# The Role of Leadership and Related Work Factors Caused by COVID-19:
## The Impact on Employee Effectiveness

**Adel Ismail Al-Alawi**
https://orcid.org/0000-0003-0775-4406
*University of Bahrain, Bahrain*

**Arpita Anshu Mehrotra**
*Royal University for Women, Bahrain*

**Samah Sabri Ali**
*University of Bahrain, Bahrain*

**Fatima Ali Al-Ammar**
*University of Bahrain, Bahrain*

## ABSTRACT

*This chapter aims to analyze the role of leadership and related work factors caused by COVID-19, the impact on employee effectiveness, and workforce performance in the workplace. Several studies have examined the effect of such crises in different sectors and countries that shed an interesting comparison and distinction. Still, there is limited research published on the workplace's impact due to COVID-19 concerning employee productivity. However, most studies highlight different independent variables on employees and the organization's work effectiveness. A limited number of systemic research studies have led to various studies conducted based on new theoretical frameworks. The literature on change management's effectiveness during such a pandemic is not widely available. Future research should cover various factors such as motivation, remuneration, global environment, employee stress, health and safety, and HRM policies. Moreover, demographic variables should be taken into account as studies have briefly found that some age groups are affected differently than others.*

DOI: 10.4018/978-1-7998-6948-1.ch018

## INTRODUCTION

The Novel Coronavirus outbreak in 2019 (COVID-19) has caught the world by surprise as it continues to spread and successfully disrupt everyday lives. In March 2020, the virus was officially considered a pandemic by the World Health Organization (Singh & Singh, 2020). The virus has caused the need for social distancing measures to prevent the rapid spread of infection, and as a result, a social and economic impact has been created. These preventative measures have caused many groups to experience severe states of stress.

A key role in implementing proactive approaches stems from intuitive organizations that can determine processes to achieve organizational recovery in the time of crises (Bowers et al., 2017). As the working trait changes with each generation, it has become necessary for managers to change their leadership style in accordance (Wolor et al., 2020). However, proactive approaches entail new policies and processes that could lead to disorientation without significant change management.

During a crisis, leadership means to lead under pressure due to the uncertainties caused by unforeseen events (Brandebo, 2020). Despite the obvious measures that could be implemented by understanding acceptable practices, sometimes there is the reluctance to deal with difficult situations and therefore lead to uncertainties with employees (Al-Alawi et al., 2019). Poor leadership achieves the contrary to what it aims. For this reason, proactive leadership that enables right decision is essential to ensure that the organization takes a holistic approach towards implementing policies for unforeseen situations.

According to Singh & Singh (2020), several groups of people have been forced to work from home, avoid social gatherings, and avoid travel. The stressful states have led to a sense of fear as well as mental disorders. Well-being has been identified as a significant part of human life that has been affected by this ordeal in various areas.

In work, the challenges faced have come from substantial changes in work process arrangements and conditions. Additionally, to the previous point, these have brought about new challenges psychologically both in the scope of health and well-being of employed workers. This affects all workers – frontline, remote-workers, or those who have been unfortunately made unemployed (Papandrea&Azzi, 2020).

In general, stressors can decrease organizational performance and employees' overall performance, leading to reduced work quality and high staff turnover (Al-Alaw & Al-Alawi, 2014; Pandey, 2020). This has become a significant issue for many organizations worldwide. As a result, itis paramount to understand the influences of such stresses and the impact of the critical work factors, practices, and policies that can overcome this (Al-Alawi & Al-Alawi, 2014).

Studies lack amplitude of factors that can bring substance to research, such as geographical exposure, sample size, and data collection. This causes a missed opportunity in performing longitudinal analysis for a study in pandemic scenarios and its correlation to leadership and work effectiveness (Sembiring et al., 2020). While pandemic situations cause panic and therefore lead to decreased performance, there is a lack of literature on the possibility of mitigation from workplace practices.

Evidence of studies that have analyzed the effect of such crises in different sectors and countries shed interesting comparisons and distinctions (Refer to Tables 1 to 4).

In a study conducted on employees of McKinsey & Company, addressing the basic needs of employees during COVID-19, it has been found that the top three experience factors are organizational stability, compensation and benefits, and trust in leadership. While these do shed light on this study's direction, it appears that need fulfillment can be accomplished by establishing motivation elements (Emmett et al., 2020).

Studies that determine the effectiveness of implementing electronic forms of training and leadership and accomplishing work-life balance related to work motivation are needed to explore further. A study by Wolor et al. (2020) has been calling attention to the factors that keep employees motivated amid challenging times, specifically during the outbreak of the COVID-19 pandemic. In another study conducted by Sembiring et al. (2020)primary concern was to analyze the factors that affect the banking employee's performance and investigate the remuneration effect on employee motivation during the outbreak of COVID-19. It has been seen that the banking sector in Indonesia found that the impact of remuneration on employees' performances had major influence.

A similar study in the agricultural research sector, in Hyderabad, India, looked at the implications occurring out of the pandemic alongside job stressors that could impact the effectiveness of employees' work. This study further breaks down the three elements by understanding the different factors contributing to them (Prasad & Vaidya, 2020).

There is limited research published on the workplace's impact due to COVID-19 concerning Employee Productivity. However, most studies highlight different independent variables on Employees and the Organization's Work Effectiveness. It should be noted that these variables impact various sectors and job roles differently. The application of Flexible Work Arrangements (FWA), such as working from home and reduced working hours, do pose several limitations in different industries. In contrast, other factors such as motivation and remuneration could be enforced instead of potentially leading to the same desired impact.

The Chapter covers the role that leadership plays in an organization, the effects of work-life balance on work motivation, the impact of remuneration and motivation on performance, implementing practices in flexible work arrangements (FWA), effect of crisis parameters, occupational stress, and remote working on employee performance, managerial decisions in response to COVID-19, leadership effectiveness & managerial implications overall analysis of literature, conclusions, and finally recommendation for future research

## THE ROLE THAT LEADERSHIP PLAYS IN AN ORGANIZATION

While it is difficult to define precisely, leadership within the management framework is understood as "implementation of those task-oriented duties that facilitate, support, and direct the timely and efficient maintenance of operations". Leadership today demands that a multitude of characteristics from thinking outside the box, the ability to capture historical information to prepare for educated next step actions within timeframes (Klingborg et al., 2006).

Navigating a crisis in the management context entails an organization's awareness of the disaster's potential impact. Depending on their team, it could either lead to a devastating outcome or a purposeful and controlled situation. The organization's response will determine the timeline of recovery and its performance (Bowers et al., 2017). Organizational performance very well stems from an employee's effectiveness. Similarly, Fener &Cevik (2015) refer to a person's key characteristics that make them a leader, where they have highlighted "intuition" as one of the critical elements necessary for leadership.

As for COVID-19, the type of leadership demanded stems from the ability to manage an ongoing crisis in order to mitigate the negative impacts throughout and even after. It is suggested that change management during such a scenario embodies a collective of personal traits, innate leadership styles, and a combination of technical, human, and technical skills (Brandebo, 2020).

According to Bowers et al. (2017), certain principles of effective leadership during crisis scenarios consider the organizational culture, leadership traits, and proactive approach to implementing processes that prepare organizations for a serious situation. In managing work effectiveness, the common trend adopted globally is the adaptation of remote working, which could also be encompassed under the new concept of e-leadership. Although remote working could be considered under its umbrella, e-leadership is a term that has been implemented specifically to adopt the millennial generation into the working environment. Organizations have found that every generation has a different trait. With the millennial generation, the focus has been on "freedom, flexibility, dialogue, open communication, and the use of technology" (Wolor et al., 2020).

Kia et al. (2019) has discussed employee performance due to ethical leadership by bridging an employee's sense of belonging with the organization. In this context, an organization can improve effectiveness through employee performance by "empowering subordinates and encouraging them to internalize ethical values," reflecting the organization's intention and direction of implementing new processes. Literature is mostly available on organizational change rather than managing change during pandemics, such as COVID-19 (Bartsch et al., 2020).

These factors of including employees in the process add value to an organization's overall ability to navigate unfamiliar situations. It is believed that decision-making in crisis-induced cases is not only central to one leader but to a collective of individuals from different backgrounds, experiences, and skills. While these add to the suitability of finding a favorable solution, a seamless information network is required (Schraagen& van de Ven, 2008).

Managing a crisis is an organization's ability to coordinate its overall units throughout a crisis promptly (UIC, 2017). Organizations that are determined to navigate the arena of unpredictable scenarios such as COVID-19 require strong leaders that would be able to lead them into a transformational change. Leadership should influence the factors, such as current emotional state and adaptability that should be considered while implementing a new process, affecting the individual or team performance accordingly (Bartsch et al., 2020).

## EFFECTS OF WORK-LIFE BALANCE ON WORK MOTIVATION

In order to survive financially, companies that try to curb the effects of a crisis continue their operations by adopting a remote working approach or arranging employees' shifts along with safety support. Although companies try to adopt proactive approaches, they may have overlooked integration areas that predict the necessary preparations required for the transition. Thus, employees experience challenges to balance between life demands and work pressures during the outbreak of COVID-19.

There is a necessity to examine the consequences of work-life on employee motivation in stressful and dangerous conditions. Work motivation is mainly related to the tendency, individual characteristics, and external factors on the behaviors that allow employees to perform and attain organizational objectives through their accomplishments (Pancasila et al., 2020, Al-Alawi et al., 2021).

According to Woloret al. (2020), there is strong evidence that states there is a direct impact on employees' motivation to maintain a work-life balance. The researcher has set practical implications for companies during the COVID-19 pandemic by implementing strategic actions related to life balance and improving employee motivation and performance. For instance, companies adopted "working from home" protocols and guidelines and implemented flexible working hours. Therefore, that may raise questions about whether these approaches will provide real solutions to the problem and ensure employee productivity and engagement.

Alternatively, in implementing such policies, it is imperative to be aware of its implications. While working from home may provide the comfort of safety, it could result in isolation, which is psychological due to loneliness. Organizations should find the suitability of such a solution for the employees in their industries (Banerjee & Rai, 2020). Interestingly, those studies that have suggested remote working also highlight communication parameters as an integral part of mitigating the impact of COVID-19 (Prasad & Vaidya, 2020).

With this regard, Mas-Machuca et al. (2016) stated that motivation stems from maintaining a work-life balance. Still, there is a strong correlation between an employee's pride in being related to the organization and satisfaction with their job.

Wolor et al. (2020) found significant evidence that work motivation directly affects employee performance. Understanding and satisfying employee's needs will lead to motivate employees to work well. According to Orel (2019), flexibility at work can improve employees' social lives and create further career opportunities. Moreover, control over work and family roles can improve performance, which leads to job satisfaction (Aryeeet al., 2005; Al-Alawi et al., 2021).

## IMPACT OF REMUNERATION AND MOTIVATION ON PERFORMANCE

Motivating employees is not an easy task, especially in challenging circumstances such as the COVID-19 pandemic. In the banking sector, bank services must remain competitive despite unstable and uncertain situations. Sembiring et al. (2020) pointed out that "Banking performance is considered to be disrupted by the impact of the spread of the coronavirus (COVID-19)". Thus, financial institutions should seek the best methods to motivate the employees, make them enthusiastic toward work, and have a high commitment level.

One of the powerful, proven methods to improve the employee's performance is to design an appropriate rewards system that motivates the employee to work well. Hameed &Waheed (2011) indicate that employees are the key elements of the organization. As a result, the success or failure of any organization depends on the employee's performance. However, the levels of dedication, adjustment, and production may vary and differ depending on changing conditions.

Employees are required to have high performance, although it might be difficult in the pandemic. The primary purpose of Sembiring et al. (2020) research is to examine the effects of remuneration and motivation on banking employees' performance directly or indirectly. These findings reinforce an exciting study by Dharma (2018), which found evidence that work motivation significantly impacts employee's performance and organizational citizenship behavior. These findings, consistent with the other research, state that proper motivation and remuneration have a strong and direct impact on employee performance (Oren et al., 2013).

In order to promote employee performance and job satisfaction, companies implement efficient remuneration management systems (Al-Alawi, Al-Azri& Mohammad, 2016). A study conducted by Ibrar and Khan (2015) indicated that remuneration rewards lead to outstanding performance and increase employees' ability to achieve their goals.

## IMPLEMENTING PRACTICES IN FLEXIBLE WORK ARRANGEMENTS (FWA)

Occupational stress occurs due to various factors in the employee's work life. Occupational stress is commonly understood as a process in which different sources in a work environment, referred to as stressors, can lead to various ailments such as psychological, behavioral, or physiological. These stressors lead to the manifestations of stress, known as a strain, leading to complications in long-term health (Landsbergis et al., 2017; Al-Alawi & Al-Alawi, 2014).

According to Keshavarz&Mohammadi (2011), their study of job stressors on performance found various factors relevant to this topic: "excessive workload, unsatisfactory working conditions, and interpersonal relations." These stressors could both negatively or positively affect employees' physical health and, in turn, affect their performance, commitment, and overall satisfaction with the job.

In the particular study by Sedaju et al. (2020), they have created a unique methodology of first identifying through qualitative surveys the measures that have impacted work effectiveness during the crisis of COVID-19 in the manufacturing sector in Indonesia. They have found that three measures were adopted that have caused some kind of impact.

Work policies revolving around improving work-life balance resulted in 43.9 percent of positive responses, whereas work motivation resulted in 52 percent positive responses. Another significant remark is that these results varied between the departments of production and departments of support. The work output of the production team relied heavily on an important factor of being present physically in the office or campus of work.

This was a study to determine whether any means of Flexible Working Arrangements (FWA) would be beneficial to employees during the crisis (Sedaju et al., 2020). Nonetheless, 52.9 percent of all respondents were happy with the new policies that were introduced regarding FWA.

## EFFECT OF CRISIS PARAMETERS, OCCUPATIONAL STRESS, AND REMOTE WORKING ON EMPLOYEE PERFORMANCE

It has been found that both Occupational Stress and the parameters resulting from COVID-19 have a significant impact on employee's performance. According to Hamouche (2020), it is found that the major organizational factors that impact well-being are occupational role, safety, and teleworking. Occupational role refers to the nature of work that the employee is involved in, whether their physical presence is required or not. Safety and health are the collaborative management obligation and workforce to carry out the assigned duties. Furthermore, the organization is responsible for non-compliance to protection and health regulation and legislation. Finally, teleworking is another term used to describe remote working, which appears to be the most effective and favored method. Although remote working, or working from home, has been seen as a potential solution to the current situation, it does impose implications such as social isolation and professional-personal ambiguity (Hamouche, 2020).

In the study conducted by Prasad & Vaidya (2020), they have found several impacts (parameters) that have stemmed from COVID-19, such as Workplace isolation, Lack of Peer advice, Lack of communication, Family distractions, and Role Overload. This in-depth study considers the role factors of employees and the challenges they face during this crisis. These result in occupational stress (stressors) in Role Ambiguity, Role Conflict, Social Support, Career, and Job-Control.

To combat these challenges, the companies have adopted flexible working such as remote working concerning the specific stressors to avoid the harmful decline in employee productivity. They have found a significant impact on the implementation, and another notable point to mention is that particular age groups of 20-30 experience more stress than other groups (Prasad & Vaidya, 2020).

According to Belzunegui-Eraso&Erro-Garcés (2020), to understand the implications and adoption of remote working, various factors, such as job nature, technology, individual personality, organizational structure, and social implications, determine remote working effectiveness. While it is the preferred method to combat the current crisis and to ensure employee safety, yet some job roles are not significantly apt when performed from home. Some companies have adopted a combination of remote working and on-premise working; however, the right formulae is not yet realized.

## MANAGERIAL DECISIONS IN RESPONSE TO COVID-19

During crises, the right leader will make an educated decision that considers a thoughtful approach that is strategic, tactical, and operative at an organizational level. Regardless of the type of crisis and supported by other literature, a leader must be "timely, rational, implemental, protected, compatible and ductile (Subošić et al., 2008)".

In order to mitigate the crisis, managers are to evaluate priorities in the context of preventing injuries, minimizing damage to surroundings, protecting the organization's image, and returning to operational normalcy (UIC, 2017). While keeping these points in mind, managers are encouraged to look into methods that could accelerate smart-working growth while looking at internet-based solutions that have already thrived in other organizations (Amini et al., 2020).

Confronting a crisis is not expected to be easily solved by an individual in leadership by sharing knowledge and skill, but rather the approach is taken to assess the situation. While unfamiliar crises leave the managers making unusual decisions, most of it begins in the situation's assessment phase. It later collects information from professionals to enable them to make informed choices (Bakker et al., 2018).

As with the example of the Waldo Canyon wildfire in Colorado, which is considered a natural crisis, the government shared information on navigating the scenario for individuals to protect themselves rather than the mundane situational updates. Following this example, managers are encouraged to study the impacts of crises on employees by collaborating with professionals to understand the right measures to implement (Bakker et al., 2018).

## LEADERSHIP EFFECTIVENESS AND MANAGERIAL IMPLICATIONS

While leadership theories and traits, bundled with a set of skills and knowledge, support finding the right leader in navigating the organization through crises, the role in today's time continually changes (Klingborg et al., 2006).

To examine the leadership effectiveness on employee's performance during COVID-19 pandemic, Bartsch et al. (2020) have investigated the leadership behavior of a sample of 206 employees who experienced digital transformation at the workplace offers some insights about new normal leadership. The research results show that leadership significantly affects the employees' job performance in unexpected work circumstances, particularly in crisis times. However, Bartsch et al. (2020) have found that work-related tension has no significant impact on employees' performance.

In the new standard, organizations that aim to lead in uncertain times effectively may vary in their ways or methods of tackling the challenges and changes in the work environment. Among the limited studies that examined the leadership implication during the COVID-19 pandemic, Francisco and Nuqui (2020) pointed out that organizations need to stay healthy and adjust to the uncertain situations at work.

Moreover, managers are encouraged to help their employees adapt to unexpected work situations and understand how the virtual transition practices affect the future of organizations' values and culture. These new practices could attract and retain employees differently from traditional approaches (Carnevale&Hatak, 2020). Accordingly, a better re-balancing between virtual work activities and traditional techniques would ensure that organizations stay responsive and supportive in leading their workforce.

## OVERALL ANALYSIS OF LITERATURE

Table-1 to Table-4 illustrates the overall literature analysis related to the COVID-19 pandemic in various sectors and countries worldwide. Table-1 demonstrates the effectiveness of e-Training, e-Leadership, and Work-Life Balance on Employee Performance during COVID-19. The study's variables employed in the theoretical framework are not entirely consistent or closely connected. Moreover, there are no practical guidelines for keeping the employees highly motivated toward the COVID-19 virus outbreak.

In Table-2, Sembiring et al. (2020) have adopted a straightforward theoretical framework that consists of only three variables. In order to avoid oversimplifying, an elaborated framework might be implemented, paying attention to different elements and mediating variables. The researchers should clarify the ideal motivation and rewarding strategies that can be executed during challenging situations, such as involving employees in decision making, related to the remuneration management systems.

Table-3 illustrates the categorization that makes the flow of understanding easier. There is a minimal literature review that may shake the credibility of the methods used. Regardless of category, information flow can be understood and brings to mind some understanding of the study. The paper sheds light on FWA's critical interpretations: better FWA policies should consider various departments' different nature within the same industry. The nature of work is quite different as some roles demand on-premise availability. However, future studies could expand on FWA and isolated-type practice for those who require to attend work physically (e.g., strict groups of independent shifts to avoid cross-mixing, the limited number of people per shift, the combination of WFA and work attendance, etc.). This paper has set the way to consider looking into this direction.

Table-4 shows occupational stress and employee performance during the COVID-19 crisis. The structure of the study is confusing and could be better laid out. Although the work is not refined, yet the direction adopted by the survey became the cornerstone for future studies. A glimpse into the impact of stress factors and COVID-19 parameters has shown that there could be a way to cope with the current scenario. Indeed, specific studies into various industries should be taken for future research in order to tackle various aspects such as maintaining employee health, performance, and organizational continuity.

*Table 1. Employee Performance During COVID-19*

| | |
|---|---|
| Author Name/s | Wolor et al. (2020) |
| Purpose | The paper aims to explore and measure certain variables' effectiveness on employee performance in the workplace during the COVID-19 pandemic. That includes e-leadership, e-training, work motivation, and work-life balance. |
| Research Methodology | The research adopts two approaches, which are online questionnaires and the "Structural Equation Modeling (SEM)" method. The data set consists of 200 employees at one of the Indonesian Honda motorcycle dealers. Random sampling technique: This study's sampling technique is the "side probability method with proportional." |
| Research Questions/ Hypotheses | The research hypotheses addressed in this paper are:<br>1. "How does e-training influences employee performance.<br>2. How does e-leadership influences employee performance<br>3. How does work-life balance affect employee performance<br>4. How does work-life balance affect work motivation<br>5. How does work Motivation influences employee performance." |
| Independent Variables | E-leadership, E-training, and work-life balance. |
| Dependent Variables | Work motivation and employee performance. |
| Key Finding | Considering 200 employees, the results show that E-leadership, work-life balance, and e-training positively affect motivating employees and enhancing their performance. Moreover, the study indicates the importance of e-leadership, work-life balance, and providing e-training to keep employees motivated and maintain high task performance during difficult conditions caused by COVID-19. |
| Research Gap and Limitation / Future Research | The research has limitations such as geographical exposure, sample size, and data collection, and thus results may lack the opportunity to be generalized. The authors didn't specify any research limitations, although it's important to address what can be learned from the study for future perspectives. It would be better if future research highlights the theoretical and managerial applications by providing valuable recommendations to companies. Moreover, research can explore the beneficial methods that increase the employee's performance. |

## CONCLUSION AND RECOMMENDATION FOR FUTURE RESEARCH

The global impact of COVID -19 can be contemplated as an exclusive phenomenon at the economic and social level. The precautionary measures of social distancing have brought the entire world to a standstill with future operational strategies ill-defined. In spite of these predicaments, the modern advancement in technology and intellect paves way swiftly and positively in comparison to past decades.

This study was carried out in October 2020. The impact of COVID-19 occurred in late 2019. A limited number of systemic research studies have led to various studies conducted and based on new theoretical frameworks. The Chapter recommends using flexible working in particularly the manufacturing industry, alongside variables such as age groups and nature of departments, suggesting little research on pandemic impact by industry. Furthermore, there is a lack of studies, both theoretical and managerial, that could help improve employee performance in companies.

Additionally, the literature on change management's effectiveness during such a pandemic is not widely available. There is a need to uncover the relationship between both organizational support or leadership towards its employee bodies through HR practices, through both quantitative and qualitative approaches.

The approach to understanding various impacts of the crisis on people's lives' different realms have been inconsistent. For example, most studies only focus on the effects of remote working to find instant solutions to the current scenario and in achieving or improving work-life balance. However, policies may not benefit from this, as the focus should be, to study various factors such as motivation and remuneration that could also contribute to work effectiveness.

*Table 2. Banking Employee Performance During Pandemic COVID-19*

| Author Name/s | Sembiring et al. (2020). |
|---|---|
| Purpose | The paper aims to explore and measure how effective it is to implement specific measures during COVID-19 that may impact employees' performances by implementing electronic platforms of training and leadership and initiating work-life balances and motivation in the banking sector. |
| Research Methodology | The approach was through quantitative methods that utilized SPSS 20 to analyze the data collected from a chosen sample of employees from the Surabaya city's banking sector. |
| Research Questions/ Hypotheses | The research investigation focused on the following:<br>1. Do remuneration and motivation have a simultaneous influence on the performance of banking employees?<br>2. Remuneration dominates as a significant influencer on the employees' performances from the banking sector. |
| Independent Variables | Remuneration.<br>Motivation. |
| Dependent Variables | Employee Performance. |
| Key Finding | The work's main findings highlighted a simultaneous impact on employees' performance when both remuneration and work motivation are implemented. Additionally, it appears that those who work in the banking sector have improvements in their work performance during COVID-19 when remuneration is used to stimulate them. As a result, it is considered the dominant influencer. |
| Research Gap and Limitation / Future Research | Collecting and analyzing the data should be evaluated. The sample size is limited to a specific city; thus, it lacks the longitudinal analysis opportunity. Future research cab covers the relationship between organizational support and employee motivation, engagement, and task performance. Moreover, there is a need to implement quantitative and qualitative approaches to identify appropriate motivating methods. |

In addition to the given Research Gap and Limitation / Future Research in Table-1 to Table-4, it is recommended that prospective research study specific industries,' human resource policies and the possible modification to these policies aligned to cope with the restrictions imposed as a result of similar crises. Studies have concluded that variables such as career development, training, and remote working may contribute positively to such situations. Leadership theories should be taken into account alongside change management as a tool for adapting to crises. The investigation of leadership traits, coupled with skills and connection to crisis scenarios, would unfurl a new ambit of study widely non-existent. It would help determine the protocols established in identifying the right leader during recruitment in crisis-centric roles.

A study on a company with an established risk mitigation department and its role in revising current company policies may also help shed light on its adaptation to the new global environment, which is also part of a significant change management implementation. Demographic variables should also be taken into account as some studies have briefly found that some age groups are affected differently from others. The HR policies have become increasingly complex, and it is imperative more than ever to take into account such variables when conducting future studies.

*Table 3. Flexible Work Arrangement in Manufacturing during the COVID-19 crisis*

| | |
|---|---|
| Author Name/s | Sedaju, Haryono, &Anisahwati, (2020). |
| Purpose | The aim is to identify and measure how far an impact can occur by applying FWA (Flexible Work Arrangements) specifically in Indonesia's manufacturing industry during the COVID-19 crisis, with an understanding of the outcomes produced on employee productivity. |
| Research Methodology | The limited literature review is utilized; however, it is probably due to the methodology's nature. The study will be based on discovering the "outputs" of FWA, which is only realized after the initial survey. The approach was to understand the FWA factors adopted in the organization due to the COVID-19 situation with their impact on Work Effectiveness.<br>The authors mostly utilized a qualitative approach through open questionnaires, interviews, and observations, whereby 1,460 respondents completed them with opinions.<br>The data analyzed went through four stages:<br>1. "Collecting categories,<br>2. Direct interpretations,<br>3. Researchers formed patterns and looked for correspondences between two or more categories, and<br>4. Researchers developed naturalistic generalizations through data analysis." |
| Research Questions/ Hypotheses | The questions asked:<br>1. "How the effectiveness of the implementation of flexible work arrangements during Pandemic COVID-19 in the manufacturing company P.T. INKA Madiun?<br>2. What are outputs generated from the home program's work as a modification of the flexible work arrangement?<br>3. How to implement an ideal flexible work arrangement to support productivity in the manufacturing company P.T. INKA Madiun?" |
| Independent Variables | FWA as a result of COVID-19. |
| Dependent Variables | Work Effectiveness. |
| Key Finding | Although not a key finding, it may be essential to note that 11.2% of the 1,460 respondents were female, and the rest were male. It appears that 52.9% of respondents were happy with WFH during the crisis. The initial survey identified the factors through 6 keywords that affected FWH categorized under two personal and organization themes.<br>**Independent Variable: FWA**<br>Themes and Factors realized as a result of FWA:<br>1. Personal Factors<br>• Personal Hard Competency (mastery of software applications)<br>• Personal Soft Competency (work relationships, processes, and interactions)<br>• Personal environment (homework and childcare)<br>• Personal Facilities (resources such as laptop and internet to complete work)<br>2. Organization Factors<br>• Organization Leaders (providing instruction, direction, mentoring, etc.)<br>• Organization System (distribution of work, reporting, access to data, etc.)<br>The Outputs realized as a result of these adopted measures:<br>1. Work-Life Balance (43.9% positivity of respondents)<br>2. Psychological Well-being (the positive indication of respondents)<br>3. Work Motivation (52% positivity of respondents)<br>Remarks:<br>Three types of work are identified – production, engineering, and support departments. It appears that the production team perceived WFH as an opportunity to rest at home but was eager to return to work due to the nature of their work that requires them to be on-premise.<br>**Impact on the Dependent Variable: Work Effectiveness**<br>39.7% reported productivity; however, as previously mentioned, the production department did not benefit from this policy in terms of work optimization. Supporting departments and engineering departments had some benefits, although some not optimal.<br>**Key Take-Aways**<br>The dynamics that are realized as a result of COVID-19, particularly in the manufacturing industry, highlight the difference in work benefits between the three departments.<br>The two themes realized above are what influence Work Effectiveness. For the production team, the main obstacle is Facilities. The obstacles are equipment (laptop, internet, etc.) and software applications for the support and engineering department. |
| Research Gap and Limitation / Future Research | Future research is recommended for industrial practice to understand the optimal use of FWA for manufacturing industries, implement health and safety measures amidst the pandemic, and consider the different departments and age groups. |

*Table 4. COVID-19 and employee performance in Hyderabad Metro.*

| Author Name/s | Prasad & Vaidya (2020). |
|---|---|
| Purpose | The goal is to study the effects of parameters and occupational stress factors resulting from COVID-19 on employees' performance in India's agricultural research sector. |
| Research Methodology | The research introduces literature review on the variables that will be analyzed in the study: Occupational Stress, Performance, COVID-19 Pandemic, and COVID-19 Parameters (Workplace isolation, Lack of Communication, Family distractions, and Role overload).<br>The theoretical framework created is based on a model proposed by Prasad et al. (2020) on occupational stress and Remote working performance.<br>A questionnaire with a systematic mix of statements to avoid bias was used to assess 400 respondents (estimated using the Cochran formula). The survey consisted of a five-point Likert-type scale to include 5 COVID-19 parameters and 6 Independent occupational stress factors. These were covered over 20 statements after utilizing the model of (Taxonomy of Higher-Order Performance Dimensions). Campbell proposed this model, and it was later analyzed through Cronbach alpha reliability statistic, multiple regression analysis, and ANOVA test results. |
| Research Questions/ Hypotheses | The Research objectives are summarized as:<br>• To study the effect of parameters and occupational stressors caused by COVID-19 in remote-working, applicable roles and the impact on their work performance.<br>• To study if any differences in gender and age may influence employees' performance in the agriculture research sector. |
| Independent Variables | COVID-19 Parameters<br>• A lack of communication<br>• Workplace isolation<br>• Lack of Peer advise<br>• Distractions from Family<br>• Overload from job Role<br>Occupational Stresses<br>• Ambiguity from Job Role<br>• Conflict from Job Role<br>• Social Support<br>• Career<br>• Job-Control |
| Dependent Variables | Performance<br>• Task Competence<br>• Employee Motivation<br>• Commitment<br>• Non-job assignments<br>• Integrity<br>• Co-workers |
| Key Finding | It has been found that both Occupational Stress and the parameters resulting from COVID-19 have a significant impact on Employee performance.<br>However, the other hypothesis that can focus on is the performance difference between gender and age groups. The study found no difference in impact experienced by gender. However, different age groups, specifically the group 20-30 years of age, experience more stress than the other groups. |
| Research Gap and Limitation / Future Research | It is recommended that various stress factors be studied in response to the COVID-19 situation, as some factors may be overlooked. An understanding of these factors could help significantly with the health sector and sanitation workers.<br>Future research is suggested to look at strategies within the HR development function of employees in pandemics: career development, training, remote working, and understanding methods for modifying current organizational policies to cope with the recent events. |

## REFERENCES


Al-Alawi, A., Abdulmohsen, M., Al-Malki, F., & Mehrotra, A. (2019). Investigating the barriers to change management in public sector educational institutions. *International Journal of Educational Management, 33*(1), 112–148. doi:10.1108/IJEM-03-2018-0115

Al-Alawi, A. I., & Al-Alawi, E. I. (2014). Measuring Occupational Stress among Management Information Systems Workers and Users in the Financial Services Sector: The Case of Bahraini Bankers. *International Journal of Scientific and Research Publications, 4*(8), 1–25.

Al-Alawi, A. I., Al-Azri, A. S., & Mohammad, H. N. (2016). Investigating the factors affecting job satisfaction and turnover: Case of Sultan Qaboos University. *Journal of Human Resources Management Research, 2016*, c1–c15. doi:10.5171/2016.301731

Al-Alawi, A. I., Al-Saffar, E., Almohammedsaleh, Z., Alotaibi, H., & Al-Alawi, E. I. (2021). study of work-family conflict, family-work conflict and work-life balance on Saudi female teachers' performance in public education sector with job satisfaction as a moderate. *Journal of International Women's Studies, 22*(1).

Amini, S., Koolivand, A., & Nazari, J. (2020). Managerial challenges and solutions for COVID-19 outbreak: New insights for global primary healthcare system. *Ethics, Medicine, and Public Health, 15*, 100567. doi:10.1016/j.jemep.2020.100567 PMID:32837998

Aryee, S., Tan, H. H., & Srinivas, E. S. (2005). Rhythms of Life: Antecedents and Outcomes of Work-Family Balance in Employed Parents. *The Journal of Applied Psychology, 90*(1), 132–146. doi:10.1037/0021-9010.90.1.132 PMID:15641894

Bakker, M., Kerstholt, J., van Bommel, M., & Giebels, E. (2018). Decision-making during a crisis: The interplay of narratives and statistical information before and after crisis communication. *Journal of Risk Research, 22*(11), 1409–1424. doi:10.1080/13669877.2018.1473464

Banerjee, D., & Rai, M. (2020). Social isolation in Covid-19: The impact of loneliness. *The International Journal of Social Psychiatry, 66*(6), 525–527. doi:10.1177/0020764020922269 PMID:32349580

Bartsch, S., Weber, E., Büttgen, M., & Huber, A. (2020). Leadership matters in crisis-induced digital transformation: How to lead service employees effectively during the COVID-19 pandemic. *Journal of Service Management, 32*(1), 71–85. Advance online publication. doi:10.1108/JOSM-05-2020-0160

Belzunegui-Eraso, A., & Erro-Garcés, A. (2020). Teleworking in the Context of the COVID-19 Crisis. *Sustainability, 12*(3662), 3662. Advance online publication. doi:10.3390u12093662

Bowers, M., Hall, J., & Srinivasan, M. (2017). Organizational culture and leadership style: The missing combination for selecting the right leader for effective crisis management. *Business Horizons, 60*(4), 551–563. doi:10.1016/j.bushor.2017.04.001

Brandebo, M. F. (2020). Destructive leadership in crisis management. *Leadership and Organization Development Journal, 41*(4), 567–580. doi:10.1108/LODJ-02-2019-0089

Carnevale, J. B., & Hatak, I. (2020). Employee adjustment and well-being in the era of COVID-19: Implications for human resource management. *Journal of Business Research, 116*, 183–187. doi:10.1016/j.jbusres.2020.05.037 PMID:32501303

Dharma, Y. (2018). The Effect of Work Motivation on the Employee Performance with Organization Citizenship Behavior as Intervening Variable at Bank Aceh Syariah. In *Proceedings of MICoMS 2017*. Emerald Publishing Limited. 10.1108/978-1-78756-793-1-00065

Emmett, J., Schrah, G., Schrimper, M., & Wood, A. (2020). *COVID-19 and the employee experience: How leaders can seize the moment*. Academic Press.

Fener, T., & Cevik, T. (2015). Leadership in Crisis Management: Separation of Leadership and Executive Concepts. *Procedia Economics and Finance, 26*, 695–701. doi:10.1016/S2212-5671(15)00817-5

Francisco, C., & Nuqui, A. (2020). *Emergence of a situational leadership during COVID-19 pandemic called New Normal Leadership. International Journal of Academic Multidisciplinary Research.*

Hameed, A., & Waheed, A. (2011). Employee Development and Its Effect on Employee Performance a Conceptual Framework. *International Journal of Business and Social Science, 2*, 224–229.

Hamouche, S. (2020). COVID-19 and employees' mental health: Stressors, moderators, and agenda for organizational actions. *Emerald Open Research, 2*(15), 15. Advance online publication. doi:10.35241/emeraldopenres.13550.1

Ibrar, M., & Khan, O. (2015). The Impact of Reward on Employee Performance (A Case Study of Malakand Private School). *International Letters of Social and Humanistic Sciences, 52*, 95–103. . doi:10.18052/www.scipress.com/ILSHS.52.95

Keshavarz, M., &Mohammadi, R. (2011). Occupational stress and Organizational performance, Case study: Iran. *Procedia - Social AndBehavioral Sciences, 30*, 390-394. doi:10.1016/j.sbspro.2011.10.077

Kia, N., Halvorsen, B., & Bartram, T. (2019). Ethical leadership and employee in-role performance. *Personnel Review, 48*(7), 1716–1733. doi:10.1108/PR-12-2018-0514

Klingborg, D., Moore, D., & Varea-Hammond, S. (2006). What Is Leadership? *Journal of Veterinary Medical Education, 33*(2), 280–283. doi:10.3138/jvme.33.2.280 PMID:16849311

Landsbergis, P., Dobson, M., LaMontagne, A., Choi, B., Schnall, P., & Baker, D. (2017). *Occupational and Environmental Health*. Oxford Scholarship Online. doi:10.1093/oso/9780190662677.001.0001

Mas-Machuca, M., Berbegal-Mirabent, J., & Alegre, I. (2016). Work-life balance and its relationship with organizational pride and job satisfaction. *Journal of Managerial Psychology, 31*(2), 586–602. doi:10.1108/JMP-09-2014-0272

Ongori, H., & Agolla, J. (2008). Occupational Stress in Organizations and Its Effects on Organizational Performance. *Journal of Management Research, 8*(3), 123–133. Retrieved October 29, 2020, from http://www.indianjournals.com/ijor.aspx?target=ijor:jmr&volume=8&issue=3&article=001

Orel, M. (2019). Supporting work-life balance with the use of coworking spaces. *Equality, Diversity and Inclusion, 39*(5), 549–565. doi:10.1108/EDI-01-2019-0038

Oren, L., Tziner, A., Nahshon, Y., & Sharoni, G. (2013). Relations between OCBs, organizational justice, work motivation and self-efficacy. *Amfiteatru Economic Journal, 15*(34), 505-517. http://hdl.handle.net/10419/168796

Pancasila, I., Haryono, S., & Sulistyo, B. A. (2020). Effects of work motivation and leadership toward work satisfaction and employee performance: Evidence from Indonesia. *The Journal of Asian Finance, Economics, and Business*, *7*(6), 387–397. doi:10.13106/jafeb.2020.vol7.no6.387

Pandey, D. (2020). Work Stress And Employee Performance: An Assessment Of Impact Of Work Stress. *International Research Journal of Human Resource And Social Sciences, 7*(5).

Papandrea, D., & Azzi, M. (2020). *Managing work-related psychosocial risks during the COVID-19 pandemic*. International Labour Organization.

Prasad, K., & Vaidya, R. (2020). Association among COVID-19 parameters, occupational stress and employee performance: An empirical study with reference to Agricultural Research Sector in Hyderabad Metro. *Sustainable Humanosphere*, *16*(2), 235–253. https://www.researchgate.net/publication/341211360

Schraagen, J., & van de Ven, J. (2008). Improving Decision Making in Crisis Response through Critical Thinking Support. *Journal of Cognitive Engineering and Decision Making*, *2*(4), 311–327. doi:10.1518/155534308X377801

Sedaju, A., Haryono, S., & Anisahwati, N. (2020). Flexible Work Arrangement in Manufacturing during the COVID-19 Pandemic: An Evidence-Based Study of Indonesian Employees. *International Journal Of Advanced Science And Technology*, *29*(6), 3914-3924. https://www.researchgate.net/publication/341700500

Sembiring, M. J., Fatihudin, D., Mochklas, M., & Holisin, I. (2020). Banking Employee Performance During Pandemic COVID-19: Remuneration and Motivation. *Journal of Xi'an University of Architecture & Technology*, *12*, 64–71.

Singh, J., & Singh, J. (2020). COVID-19 and Its Impact on Society. *Electronic Research Journal Of Social Sciences And Humanities, 2*(1).

Subošić, D., Milošević, G., & Kekić, D. (2008). *Decision Making During The Crisis Situations.* Academic Press.

UIC. (2017). *Recommendations for Crisis Management.* 6 UIC Additional Global Security Programme.

Wolor, C. W., Solikhah, S., Fidhyallah, N. F., & Lestari, D. P. (2020). Effectiveness of E-Training, E-Leadership, and Work-Life Balance on Employee Performance during COVID-19. *The Journal of Asian Finance Economics and Business*, *7*(10), 443–450.

# Chapter 19
# Impact of COVID-19 on an Educational Institution of India:
## Perceptions of Teachers Towards Online Classes

**Elizabeth Madathilathu Samuel**
*Royal University for Women, Bahrain*

## ABSTRACT

*The year 2020 has made a mark in the history of mankind. India, too, was affected by the pandemic. To ensure a curb on the spread of the disease, India adopted a sequence emergency mechanism. It announced the closure of all educational institutions along with all the other establishments as a part of strict social distancing measures. The traditional mode of teaching and learning transitioned into online teaching. Online learning and virtual classrooms became the 'new normal'. The analysis was carried out using the data collected through structured questionnaire from 35 teachers in Kottayam District, Kerala a southern state of India. Data collected was analyzed using descriptive statistics. It is evident from the study that the teachers lack in the use of various teaching methods for motivating and encouraging students. Further on, since the teachers were caught off guard, they had not received any formal or professional training to conduct online classes or use the advanced modes of technology.*

## 1. INTRODUCTION

Every big and small sector of the world is affected by the widespread of COVID 19 and India too is not spared of its effects. The whole country is still reeling under the after effects of this pandemic. It is estimated that the impact of COVID 19 on the Indian economy during 2020 may reach early 8 trillion Indian rupees (Keelery, 2020) and the Indian quarterly GDP was estimated to a decline of over 7% in the second quarter of financial year 2021. Almost all the sectors are affected due to this pandemic. In India, the primary influenced instance of Covid-19 was distinguished on 30 January 2020 in the province of Kerala and the influenced had a travel history from Wuhan, China (Wikipedia). In India, the first CO-

DOI: 10.4018/978-1-7998-6948-1.ch019

VID death was announced on March 12, 2020 and the country witnessed a Janta Curfew for a one day, on March 22, 2020. India was a witness to yet another 14 hours Janta Curfew on March 24 to minimize the spread of Corona virus pandemic and evaluate the nation's capacity to battle the infection. At that point, the first period of lockdown was declared by the Prime Minister of India on March 25, 2020 for 21 days. Based on a close monitoring of the situation, the Indian Government broadened the lockdown period in various stages. The lockdown 5.0 was announced on April 30, a robust measure to ensure social distancing across the nation with an aim to combat the disease. Through the different phases of lockdown ranging from 'lockdown 1.0 to lockdown 5.0', it was the educational sector that was caught unaware. The switch from regular structure to online mode was abrupt and without any prior groundwork. Thus, the pandemic Covid-19 had a significant impact on the education sector. According to (UNESCO, 2020) around 320 million children are affected in India alone. As indicated by a study report of the Ministry of Human Resource Development (MHRD), Government of India, led on advanced education it was seen that there are 993 universities, 39931 Colleges and 10725 independent organizations recorded on their portal (Kumar, 2020).

As a solution to impose social distancing, the government of India has announced the closure of educational institutions. On March 21, 2020, the MHRD (Ministry of Human Resource Development) shared various free digital e learning platforms for continuing learning. For secondary education, they came up with Diksha portal, e pathshala, National Repository of open Educational resources (NROER). Diksha portal and e-pathshala are e-learning apps by NCERT for classes 1 to 12 in multiple languages (English, Hindi and Urudu). NROER portal provides resources for students and teachers in multiple languages as well as books and videos including a host of STEM based games. For Higher education, Swayam which is a national online education platform for undergraduate and postgraduate students in all Majors including engineering, humanities and management courses.

While e-PG Pathshala is concentrated on various postgraduate courses, Swayam Prabha has 32 DTH TV channels transmitting educational programs catering to the wide range of courses in higher education, which is resourceful for students. The students can access e-books, online courses and study materials.

Apart from these apps other online arrangements like Zoom, Google classroom, Google meet MS team etc. are available to students so that they may capitalize on it and continue their learning during this pandemic situation.

Since many years the Indian educational system had been thinking of adopting online studies in their curriculum. The pandemic created an emergency situation wherein the online platform got embraced and the prevailing situation has accelerated adoption of digital technology. This helped everyone to improve their professional skills. According to (Pravat, 2020) online learning is the best solution and it is a fact that technology based education is more transparent with all respect. Due to COVID 19 the shift has happened from the traditional sage on stage learning methodology to educational technology model where teachers and students were exposed to new innovative educational methodologies. It is further noticeable that many of the educational institution of India are technology enabled institutions; therefore it was easy for-these institutions to adapt technology.

Even though majority of Indian educational institution are equipped with technology, online teaching is relatively a new concept. Due to the outbreak of COVID 19, it became mandatory for the teachers to use online platform, for delivering courses and hence they started to conduct various assessments through online mode. Teachers face many new challenges like lack of technical infrastructure; technical support and many institutions use open source platforms, which raise questions on the quality and confidentiality of assessments.

The success of online teaching truly depends on the involvement of teachers in an effective way and building a sense of community in online courses. The successful online instructor develops the skills necessary for facilitating interaction and communication in online environment (Pietro, 2008). In order to reap the benefit of online classes we need to analyze the perception of teachers on the effectiveness of online courses over traditional classroom learning.

## 1.1 Objectives of the Study

The main objective of this study is to analyze the perception of teachers about online classes. This research tries to explain whether the teachers are confident about conducting online classes based on teaching practice, efficacy, training and development.

# 2. LITERATURE REVIEW

The educational system of India is in peril due to the COVID 19 pandemic. All the educational institutions of India were forced to adopt asynchronous learning methods. This is actually a challenge for a developing country like India. Shifting from the sage on the stage learning to online components, demanded teachers to veer their teaching methods.

The COVID-19 pandemic has affected the whole education world. Almost all the Universities and schools are remained closed (Murphy, 2020). Accordingly, the rise of online education is happening in the education system (Bozkurt et al., 2020). Though online learning helps to teach or learn in the pandemic period, implementation of a planned and structured online learning system is essential to have a successful online learning system. According to (Lockyer& Bennett, 2004) due to the advancement of digital technology and continuous recommendations by students, many of the educational institutions implement online classes along with normal class. Online studies are considered as a modern tool for handling learning process (Agustina, 2017). In a study by (Meyen et al 2002) suggest that the demand for online classes will increase in educational as well as in the corporate field. Many college has started implementing online classes without proper planning (Abhinandan, 2018).

Lately, numerous researchers have examined the issues identified with online teaching. Teachers are reviewing their perceptions towards the new culture of learning and teaching. This leads to challenges in teacher beliefs, judgments, interpretations, assumptions, and expectations (Coppola, Hiltz, & Rotter, 2002; Lee & Tsai, 2010). According to (Kreber2006) noted online teaching is different from traditional classroom teaching; however, teachers who do not receive professional development have a habit of carrying traditional educational practices to the online environments. Numerous researches have tended to the difficulties faced by teachers in online instructing and learning. It was found that the teachers have mixed opinion about online classes. Many teachers suggested that they can handle online classes efficiently if they get proper training programme (Billings, 2008). According to,(Arora and Srinivasan 2020) in their study they have mentioned that absence of individual touch and difficulties in connectivity are the major difficulties in online learning. In addition, (Kaup et al. 2020) expressed difficulties identified with innovation, preparing and understudy commitment in continuing scholastics during the COVID-19 pandemic, because teachers are not having adequate foundation.

Many researchers addressed the problems related to online teaching and learning during this pandemic but sarcastically only very few researches addressed the problems faced by teachers related to online teaching and learning. It was found that many teachers are not well equipped with configured laptops, internet and microphones to efficiently impart education. In a study conducted by (Verma et al, 2020) identified that many educational institutions in India did not have trained teachers who can work remotely through online platform and grapple to accept the transition. (Baralt et al. 2016) recommend that internet learning might be less viable than class room learning and (Tang 2019) contends that face to face learning is more effective.

There are numerous studies that clarify the limitations of online classes. Some state that the online classes are convenient, less costly and simple to get to, so these variables made contrasts between on-line learning and eye to eye learning. In some studies it was found that students who are successful in traditional classrooms are not equally as successful in an online class.

For effectual surveillance of online classes, there needs to be appropriate training and skills for teachers and students. Based on the all these reviews, it is noted that there is an urgent need to research on how teachers perceive online classes. Therefore a survey was conducted to collect the opinion of teachers from Kottayam District of Kerala.

## 3. RESEARCH METHODOLOGY

The main aim and objective of this study is to investigate the perception of teachers towards online classes. The researcher used both primary and secondary data collection methods. The respondents of this study consisted of teachers from 4 different colleges of Kottayam district, Kerala, a southern state of India. The respondents for this study were selected using purposeful sampling who has online teaching experience, across different disciplines. Participants were full-time and adjunct faculty members who are engaged in the development and teaching of online courses at universities. The researcher used a convenient sampling technique of selecting the samples. Primary data collection was done through structured questionnaire (Appendix A). The questionnaire consisted of three sections, Section A describes the demographic profile of respondents and Section B describes the various tools used for online studies and in Section C the researcher uses a Five-point Likert Scale to collect the opinion of teachers, about the online classes and to analyze the teaching practices, efficacy, training and development. The questionnaire was sent to 35 teachers who are working in various disciplines like arts, science, commerce and humanities. The data was collected via email and WhatsApp. Secondary data was collected from various magazines, newspaper, websites and journals. The collected data was analyzed using excel. Secondary data was used for reviewing the concept and supporting the findings.

## 4. DATA ANALYSIS AND INTERPRETATION

The primary data collected was analyzed using various statistical methods.

### 4.1 Section A: A Demographic Profile of the Respondents

The demographics details of teachers were collected to know their gender, age, teaching experience and experience in teaching online classes. The following table 1 explains the demographic background of the respondents.

*Table 1.*

| Demographic profile of teachers | | |
|---|---|---|
| **Gender** | **No** | **Frequency** |
| Male | 12 | 34% |
| Female | 23 | 66% |
| **Age** | | |
| Below 29 | 5 | 14% |
| 30 -49 | 27 | 77% |
| 50 & above | 3 | 9% |
| **Teaching Experience** | | |
| 0 - 5 yrs | 3 | 9% |
| 6 - 10 yrs | 14 | 40% |
| 11- 15 yrs | 15 | 42% |
| 16 - 20 yrs | 3 | 9% |
| **Conducting Online class** | | |
| Yes | 34 | 97% |
| No | 1 | 3% |
| **Online teaching experience** | | |
| year 1 | 32 | 91% |
| 1 - 2 year | 2 | 6% |
| 3 - 5 year | 1 | 3% |

The table 1 shows that the major respondents are females. Out of 35 samples 23 (66%) of them are female teachers. Majority of the respondents are under the age of 30 -49. It is noticeable that 97% of the teachers are conducting online class and 91% of the total samples are having online teaching experience for a period of less than 1 year. The study reveals that these teachers started online classes only after the COVID 19 outbreak.

## 4.2 Section B: Tools Used for Online Class

A lot of online tools are available in the digital field. In order to get better understanding of the type of tools used for online teaching, the researcher asked the participants to mention the tools they used for online teaching.

*Figure 1.*

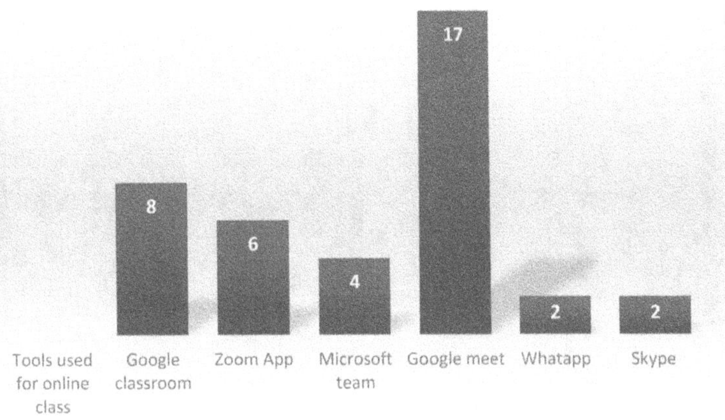


Among the many popular online tools available in India, Google Meet (N =17) is the most used and preferred tool for conducting online classes. Secondly, the most popular app was Google classroom (N = 8), Thirdly, Zoom app (N= 6) and finally Microsoft Team (N = 4). Even though, Skype and WhatsApp are the most important and popular online tools for communication, but for online teaching methods these were the least used tools. Surprisingly the interesting fact is that the majority of teachers prefer using WhatsApp for social networking to cater to the demands of online classes.

## 4.3 Section C: A Teacher's Perception Towards Online Class

Teachers are the pillars of every educational institution. A teacher should be a role model; they should teach the students through experience, commitment and inspire the students to strive towards accomplishing their goals. In order to encourage and motivate students, teachers require unique skills and different learning styles. In this online "new normal" situation the different tactics and techniques adopted by teachers need to be ascertained. Therefore, the researcher felt that it is essential to survey teacher's perception towards online classes that related to their teaching practices, efficacy of teaching and training programs attended. A five point Likert scale was used to collect the opinion of teachers. The Likert scale indicates with '1' being strongly disagree and '5' with strongly agree.

With reference to figure 2 and table 2, the 9 questions pertain to the teaching practices adopted by teachers during online classes. From the results of descriptive statistics, it appeared that teachers agree with the teaching practices with a maximum mean score of 4.4, which states that the teachers are responding to students in a timely manner and the minimum score of 3.42 which shows that the teachers are not using various methods of teaching techniques according to the needs of the students. The mean score of all the nine questions range from 3.41 – 4.4, which represents that, all teachers agree with the teaching practices they adopt in the class. For the statistics (table: 3) the teachers strongly believe that they have strong confidence in the effectiveness of online class with a mean score of 5, at the same time Table no: 4 shows that the teachers have received less professional training or they have received no training to conduct the online classes. Teachers rated an average mean score of 2.3 for training and development in organizing the online classes.

*Figure 2. Teaching Practice*

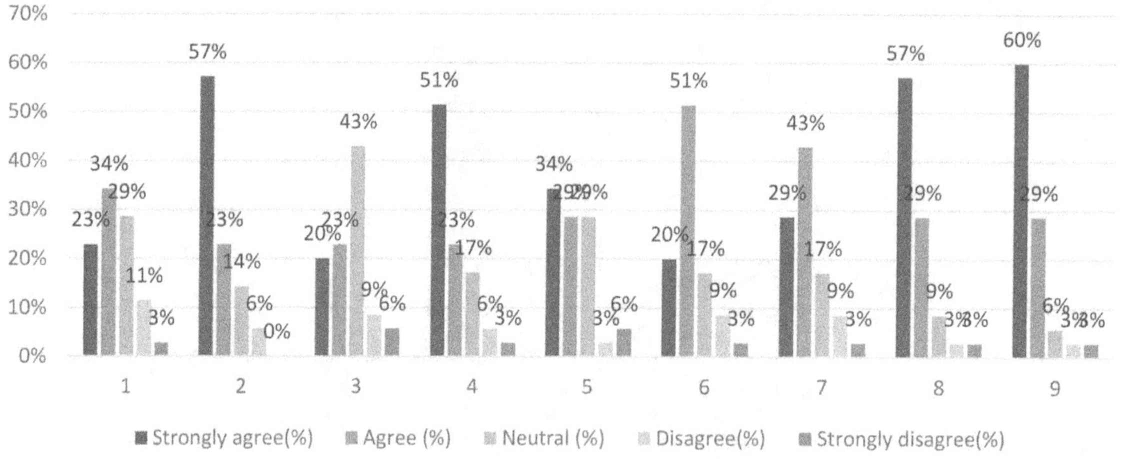


*Table 2. Teaching Practice*

| Questions | Strongly Agree | Agree | Neutral | Disagree | Strongly Disagree | Total | Mean | SD |
|---|---|---|---|---|---|---|---|---|
| 1 | 8 | 12 | 10 | 4 | 1 | 35 | 3.628571 | 3.260149 |
| 2 | 20 | 8 | 5 | 2 | 0 | 35 | 4.314286 | 3.891382 |
| 3 | 7 | 8 | 15 | 3 | 2 | 35 | 3.428571 | 3.079889 |
| 4 | 18 | 8 | 6 | 2 | 1 | 35 | 4.142857 | 3.764496 |
| 5 | 12 | 10 | 10 | 1 | 2 | 35 | 3.828571 | 3.47234 |
| 6 | 7 | 18 | 6 | 3 | 1 | 35 | 3.771429 | 3.372155 |
| 7 | 10 | 15 | 6 | 3 | 1 | 35 | 3.857143 | 3.47234 |
| 8 | 20 | 10 | 3 | 1 | 1 | 35 | 4.342857 | 3.927922 |
| 9 | 21 | 10 | 2 | 1 | 1 | 35 | 4.4 | 3.978514 |

*Table 3. Efficacy*

| Questions | Strongly Agree | Agree | Neutral | Disagree | Strongly Disagree | Total | Mean | SD |
|---|---|---|---|---|---|---|---|---|
| 1 | 20 | 10 | 5 | 0 | 0 | 35 | 5 | 3.891382 |
| 2 | 18 | 12 | 3 | 2 | 0 | 35 | 5.114286 | 3.772078 |
| 3 | 12 | 15 | 5 | 2 | 1 | 35 | 4.657143 | 3.509172 |
| 4 | 10 | 15 | 7 | 3 | 0 | 35 | 4.4 | 3.426785 |
| 5 | 20 | 10 | 4 | 1 | 0 | 35 | 5.085714 | 3.861902 |

*Table 4. Training and development*

| Questions | Excellent | Above Average | Average | Below Average | None | Total | Mean | SD |
|---|---|---|---|---|---|---|---|---|
| 1 | 0 | 2 | 5 | 25 | 3 | 35 | 2.171429 | 1.723783 |
| 2 | 0 | 2 | 10 | 20 | 3 | 35 | 2.314286 | 1.882248 |
| 3 | 0 | 2 | 10 | 20 | 3 | 35 | 2.314286 | 1.882248 |

While considering the overall opinion, the researcher identified that the teachers have a varied opinion about the online classes. In a country like India the online classes serve as a blessing in disguise. The main concern of teachers is the barriers they face in using different learning methods or styles. In spite of the fact that majority of the respondents are using the online platform to conduct classes, sadly they lack in proper training and expertise while using this online platform.

## 5. CONCLUSION AND RECOMMENDATION

The abrupt move to online instructing on account of COVID 19 pandemic was a force coercive. It has brought positive and negative impact on the teaching methodology. To an extent the traditional training method has changed to self-learning mode. One of the main advantages of online teaching is the availability of resources, any time the students can use the resources so the coverage is more. Teachers are optimistic about the online studies. Yet, there is a room for improvement.

As the above investigation clarifies that teachers across different education institutions have positive discernment towards online classes during Covid 19 pandemic. It is evident from the study that the teachers lack in the use of various teaching methods for motivating and encouraging students. The teachers are not well trained, almost all the educational institutions are using common online platform for conducting classes. So, it is essential that in order to increase the effectiveness of online studies the institutions has to provide excellent training and support to teachers regarding the usage of techniques and technology in online classes. In the traditional method the students are "spoon fed" but the "new normal" necessitates a learner centered environment. In order to attain the expected outcomes, the teachers require unique skills to motivate and direct students. The result of the study can help the top management of educational institutions to improve their actions. The educational institutions have to provide training to teachers in order to achieve the desired goal. Every form of technology comes with its boon and bane, it is the way we determine how or how much it can influence us. It is the same 'can' for online teaching as well, if used properly it 'can 'be a blessing.

The results of the study were examined and interpreted, based on the perspective of teachers and concluded with a view of future research. This study will be beneficial for academic researchers from different countries with a different set of students and framework.

### Limitation of the Study

In order to reap the benefits of online classes, teachers, students and parents need to work hand in hand. In this study, the researcher considered only the teacher's perception towards online classes, at the same time the sample size was limited to one district. Further study is therefore essential and it is vital to consider the perception of students and parents towards online classes.

## REFERENCES


Abhinandan. (2018). Information literacy among lectures in colleges: a study on Mangalore University college, *IOSR Journal of Business and Management*, *20*(1), 23-29.

Agustina, E., & Cahyono, B. Y. (2017). Perceptions of Indonesian teachers and students on the use of quipper school as an online platform for extended EFL learning. *Journal of Language Teaching and Research*, *8*(4), 794. doi:10.17507/jltr.0804.20

Allen, I. E., & Seaman, J. (2014). *Grade change: Tracking online education in the United States*. Retrieved http://www.onlinelearningsurvey.com/reports/gradechange.pdf

Allen, I. E., & Seaman, J. (2015). *Grade level: Tracking online education in the United States*. Retrieved from http://www.onlinelearningsurvey.com/reports/gradelevel.pdf

Arora, A. (2017). *Online Education Market in India 2016–2020*. Franchise India Education. Available at: https://www.franchiseindia.com/education/Online-education-Market-in-india-2016-2020.9263

Arora, A. K., & Srinivasan, R. (2020). Impact of pandemic COVID-19 on the teaching-learning process: A study of higher education teachers. *Prabandhan. Indian Journal of Management*, *13*(4), 43–56. doi:10.17010/pijom/2020/v13i4/151825

Bennett, S., & Lockyer, L. (2004). Becoming and online teacher: Adapting to a changed environment for teaching and learning in higher education. *Educational Media International*, *41*(3), 231–248. doi:10.1080/09523980410001680842

Billings, D. M., & Kowalski, K. (2008). Developing your career as a nurse educator the professional portfolio. *Journal of Continuing Education in Nursing*, *39*(12), 532–533. doi:10.3928/00220124-20081201-09 PMID:19110727

Coppola, N., Hiltz, S., & Rotter, N. (2002). Becoming a virtual professor: Pedagogical roles and asynchronous learning networks. *Journal of Management Information Systems*, *18*(4), 169–189. doi:10.1080/07421222.2002.11045703

DiPietro, M., Ferdig, R. E., Black, E. W., & Preston, M. (2008). Best practices in teaching K-12 online: Lessons learned from Michigan virtual school teachers. *Journal of Interactive Online Learning*, *7*(1), 10–35.

Kaup, S., Jain, R., Shivalli, S., Pandey, S., & Kaup, S. (2020). Sustaining academics during COVID-19 pandemic: The role of remote teaching-learning. *Indian Journal of Ophthalmology*, *68*(6), 1220. doi:10.4103/ijo.IJO_1241_20 PMID:32461490

Keelery, S. (2020). *India – estimated economic impact of COVID-19 by sector 2020 | Statista*. Statista. Available at: www.statista.com/statistics/1107798/india-estimated-economic-impact-of-coronavirus-by-sector/

Kumar. (2020). *Impact of COVID-19 on Higher Education*. Retrieved on Dec 5, 2020 from https://www.highereducationdigest.com/impact-of-covid-19-on-higher-education

Lin, C., & Zheng, B. (2015). Teaching practices and teacher perceptions in online world language courses. *Journal of Online Learning Research, 1*(3), 275–304.

Lloyd, S. A., Byrne, M. M., & McCoy, T. S. (2012). Faculty-perceived barriers of online education. *Journal of Online Learning and Teaching, 8*(1).

Meyen, E. L., Gauch, J. M., Hinton, H. S., & Tee, M. Y. (2002). Elearning a programmatic research construct for the future. *Journal of Special Education Technology, 17*(3), 37–46. doi:10.1177/016264340201700303

MHRD. (2020a). *Students to continue their learning by making full use of the available digital e-Learning platforms – Shri Ramesh Pokhriyal 'Nishank'*. Available at: https://pib.gov.in/PressReleasePage.aspx?PRID=1607521

MHRD. (2020c). National education policy 2020. *Information Bureau*, 33-49. Available at: https://static.pib.gov.in/WriteReadData/userfiles/NEP_Final_English_0.pdf

Murphy, M. P. A. (2020). COVID-19 and emergency eLearning: Consequences of the securitization of higher education for post-pandemic pedagogy. *Contemporary Security Policy, 41*(3), 492–505.

Notice, M. H. R. D. (2020). *COVID-19 Stay Safe: Digital Initiatives*. https://www.mohfw.gov.in/pdf/Covid19.pdf

Online, M. H. R. D. (n.d.). *Online Learning Resources of MHRD*. Retrieved on Dec 5, 2020 from https://mhrd.gov.in/sites/upload_files/mhrd/files/upload_document/Write_up_online_learning_resources.pdf

Pravat, K. (2020a). Challenges and Opportunities created by Covid-19 for ODL: A case study of IGNOU. *International Journal for Innovative Research in Multidisciplinary Field, 6*(5), 217–222.

Pravat, K. (2020b). Impact of Pandemic COVID-19 on Education in India. *International Journal for Innovative Research in Multidisciplinary Field, 31*(46), 142–149.

Pravat, K. (2020c). Online learning during lock down period for Covid-19 in India. *International Journal of Multidisciplinary Educational Research, 5*(8), 82–92.

Sharma, A. K. (2020). COVID-19: creating a paradigm shift in India's education system. *Economic Times Blog*. Available at: https://economictimes.indiatimes.com/blogs/et-commentary/covid-19-creating-a-paradigm-shift-in-indias-education-system/

UNESCO. (2020). *COVID-19 Educational Disruption and Response*. UNESCO. Available at: https://en.unesco.org/covid19/educationresponse

Verma, G. (2020). Science teacher education in the times of the COVID-19 pandemic. *Journal of Science Teacher Education, 10*(8), 2–7.

## APPENDIX 1

### Questionnaire

Perception of Teachers Towards Online Class

Section A: Demographic Profile

1. Gender : Male ☐ Female ☐
2. Age : below 29 ☐ 30 -49 ☐ 50 and above ☐
3. Teaching experience: 0 -5 years ☐ 6 – 10 years ☐ 11 -15 years ☐ 16 – 20 years ☐
4. Conducting Online class : Yes ☐ No ☐
5. Online teaching experience in years: 1 year ☐ 1 – 2 year ☐ 3 -5 year ☐

Section B: Please Tick the Appropriate Tool Used for Online Class

6. Tools used for online class:

Google Class Room ☐
Zoom App ☐
Microsoft Teams ☐
Web chat ☐
Google meet ☐
Whatsapp ☐
Skype ☐

*Section C*

*Thank you*

*Table 5. Teaching Practice*

| | Description | Strongly Agree | Agree | Neutral | Disagree | Strongly Disagree |
|---|---|---|---|---|---|---|
| Q1. | I use different methods to grasp the attention of students | | | | | |
| Q2. | I try to support my students | | | | | |
| Q3. | I use different teaching methods based on student needs | | | | | |
| Q4. | I encourage students to participate promptly | | | | | |
| Q5. | I use different medias and visuals for motivating students | | | | | |
| Q6. | I communicate with my students regularly to engage them | | | | | |
| Q7. | I make sure that my students feel connected to me as same as in class | | | | | |
| Q8. | I communicate clearly and patiently with my students | | | | | |
| Q9. | I respond to students in a timely manner | | | | | |

*Table 6. Efficacy*

| | Description | Strongly Agree | Agree | Neutral | Disagree | Strongly Disagree |
|---|---|---|---|---|---|---|
| Q1. | I am confident that I can teach successfully | | | | | |
| Q2. | I am confident that I can work with my students | | | | | |
| Q3. | I can develop creative and innovative teaching methods | | | | | |
| Q4. | I am confident that I can motivate students to do their work | | | | | |
| Q5. | I am confident that I can guide them properly to attain their goals | | | | | |

*Table 7. Training and Development*

| | Description | Excellent | Above Average | Average | Below Average | None |
|---|---|---|---|---|---|---|
| Q1. | Professional development based on technological skills | | | | | |
| Q2. | Professional development related to online classroom management | | | | | |
| Q3. | Professional development on different teaching and learning styles | | | | | |

# Compilation of References


(2020, May 27). *Coronavirus-Pandemie: medizinische Versorgung und patientennahe Forschung in einem adaptiven gesundheitssystem: 4. Ad-hoc Stellungnahme.* Leopoldina - Nationale Akademie der Wissenschaften. https://www.leopoldina.org/uploads/tx_leopublication/2020_05_27_Stellungnahme_Corona_Gesundheitssystem.pdf

Abdul Karim, M., & Wadoo, O. (2020). In the Arabian Gulf region - Implications beyond the Covid-19 pandemic. *Asian Journal of Psychiatry*, *54*, 102397. Advance online publication. doi:10.1016/j.ajp.2020.102397 PMID:33271697

Abhinandan. (2018). Information literacy among lectures in colleges: a study on Mangalore University college, *IOSR Journal of Business and Management*, *20*(1), 23-29.

Achtziger, A., & Gollwitzer, R. M. (2008). Motivation and volition in the course of action. In J. Heckhausen & H. Heckhausen (Eds.), *Motivation and action* (2nd ed., pp. 272–295). Cambridge University Press. doi:10.1017/CBO9780511499821.012

Acquier, A., Gand, S., & Szpirglas, M. (2008). From Stakeholder to Stake S holder Management in Crisis Episodes: A Case Study in a Public Transportation Company. *Journal of Contingencies and Crisis Management*, *16*(2), 101–114. doi:10.1111/j.1468-5973.2008.00538.x

ADB. (2020). *COVID-19 Economic Impact Could Reach $8.8 Trillion Globally.* New ADB Report.

Adeccogroup. (2020). *Comparing Government economic responses to COVID-19: Short-time work and size of stimulus package matter most.* Retrieved October 5, 2020, from https://press.adeccogroup.com/news/comparing-government-economic-responses-to-covid-19-short-time-work-and-size-of-stimulus-package-matter-most-3cb2-2cb12.html

afp/aerzteblatt.de. (2020, October 7). *Bundesregierung will internationale Zusammenarbeit in Gesundheitsfragen stärken* [Press release]. https://www.aerzteblatt.de/nachrichten/117189/Bundesregierung-will-internationale-Zusammenarbeit-in-Gesundheitsfragen-staerken

Agustina, E., & Cahyono, B. Y. (2017). Perceptions of Indonesian teachers and students on the use of quipper school as an online platform for extended EFL learning. *Journal of Language Teaching and Research*, *8*(4), 794. doi:10.17507/jltr.0804.20

Ahlsson, A. (2020). *Why change? Lessons in leadership from the COVID-19 pandemic*. Academic Press.

Ahlsson, A. (2020). Why change? Lessons in leadership from the COVID-19 pandemic. *European Journal of Cardio-Thoracic Surgery*, 1–3. PMID:32688379

Ahmad, N. (2018). Attitudes Towards Family Formation Among Young Adults in Brunei Darussalam. *Pakistan Journal of Women's Studies*, *25*(1).

Ajzen, I. (1991). The theory of planned behavior. *Organizational Behavior and Human Decision Processes*, *50*(2), 179–211. doi:10.1016/0749-5978(91)90020-T

Akat, M., & Karataş, K. (2020). Psychological Effects of COVID-19 Pandemic on Society and Its Reflections on Education. *Electronic Turkish Studies, 15*(4).

Akila, A., & Priyadarshini, R. G. (2018). The impact of workplace friendships on organizational commitment and intention to leave. *IOP Conference Series. Materials Science and Engineering, 390*(1), 012064. doi:10.1088/1757-899X/390/1/012064

Akkermans, J., Richardson, J., & Kraimer, M. (2020). The Covid-19 crisis as a career shock: Implications for careers and vocational behavior. *Journal of Vocational Behavior, 119*(June), 103434. Advance online publication. doi:10.1016/j.jvb.2020.103434 PMID:32390655

Al A'ali, E. A., & Al-Sarraf, A. R. (2016). Ethical Consumerism: Contextual Issues of Ethical Decision-Making processes: An Exploratory Study. In Ethical and Social Perspectives on Global Business interaction in Emerging Markets (pp.133-149). IGI Global.

Al-A'Ali, E. (2020). *The role of Auditing Firms in promoting Ethical Consumerism: Ethical programs for business companies in Ethical Consumerism and comparative studies Across Different Cultures.* IGI Global. doi:10.4018/978-1-7998-0272-3.ch004

Al-Alawi, A. I., & Al-Alawi, E. I. (2014). Measuring Occupational Stress among Management Information Systems Workers and Users in the Financial Services Sector: The Case of Bahraini Bankers. *International Journal of Scientific and Research Publications, 4*(8), 1–25.

Al-Alawi, A. I., Al-Azri, A. S., & Mohammad, H. N. (2016). Investigating the factors affecting job satisfaction and turnover: Case of Sultan Qaboos University. *Journal of Human Resources Management Research, 2016*, c1–c15. doi:10.5171/2016.301731

Al-Alawi, A. I., Al-Marzooqi, N. Y., & Mohammed, Y. F. (2007). Organizational culture and knowledge sharing: Critical success factors. *Journal of Knowledge Management, 2*(11), 22–42. doi:10.1108/13673270710738898

Al-Alawi, A. I., Al-Saffar, E., Almohammedsaleh, Z., Alotaibi, H., & Al-Alawi, E. I. (2021). study of work-family conflict, family-work conflict and work-life balance on Saudi female teachers' performance in public education sector with job satisfaction as a moderate. *Journal of International Women's Studies, 22*(1).

Al-Alawi, A., Abdulmohsen, M., Al-Malki, F., & Mehrotra, A. (2019). Investigating the barriers to change management in public sector educational institutions. *International Journal of Educational Management, 33*(1), 112–148. doi:10.1108/IJEM-03-2018-0115

AlAteeq, D., AlDaoud, A., AlHadi, A., AlKhalaf, H., & Milev, R. (2018). The experience and impacts of stigma in Saudi people with mood disorder. *Annals of General Psychiatry, 17*(1), 51. doi:10.118612991-018-0221-3 PMID:30498517

Al-Hanawi, M.K., Mwale, M.L., & Alsharqi, O. (2020). *Psychological Distress Among Health Workers and the General Public During the COVID-19 Pandemic in Saudi Arabia.* Dove Press. DOI doi:10.2147/RMHP.S264037.volume2020:13

Ali, K. K., Ramly, Z., & Chai, L. T. (2014). *Business Ethics.* Oxford Fajar Sdn.

AlKnawy, B. (2018). Leadership in times of crisis. *BMJ Leader, 3*(1), 1–5. doi:10.1136/leader-2018-000100

Allen, I. E., & Seaman, J. (2014). *Grade change: Tracking online education in the United States.* Retrieved http://www.onlinelearningsurvey.com/reports/gradechange.pdf

Allen, I. E., & Seaman, J. (2015). *Grade level: Tracking online education in the United States.* Retrieved from http://www.onlinelearningsurvey.com/reports/gradelevel.pdf

Allen, T. D., Cho, E., & Meier, L. L. (2014). Work–family boundary dynamics. *Annual Review of Organizational Psychology and Organizational Behavior, 1*(1), 99–121. doi:10.1146/annurev-orgpsych-031413-091330

Alrubaiee, L., & Al-Nazer, N. (2010). Investigate the impact of relationship marketing orientation on customer loyalty: The customer's perspective. *International Journal of Marketing Studies, 2*(1), 155–174. doi:10.5539/ijms.v2n1p155

Alsaawi, A. (2014). A critical review of qualitative interviews. *European Journal of Business and Social Sciences, 3*(4).

AlSaffar, G. (2020). *Ethical Programs for Patients in Bahrain in Ethical Consumerism and Comparative studies Across Cultures*. IGI Global.

Alsalman, A., Mubarak, H., Aljabal, M., Abdulnabi, M., Ishaq, A., Yusuf, A., . . . Jahrami, H. (2020). *The Psychological Impact of COVID-19 Pandemic on the Population of Bahrain.* Available at SSRN: https://ssrn.com/abstract=3660648

Alsulaiti, M. (2020). *Impact of the novel coronavirus (COVID-19) on societal habits and behaviours.* Retrieved from https://www.derasat.org.bh/survey-impact-of-the-novel-cornavirus-covid-19-on-societal-habits-and-behaviors/

Altamirano, M. A., & Collazo, C. E. R. (2020, June). Leading with emotional intelligence: How leaders of a diverse-based urban college in new york successfully respond to the COVID-19 crisis of 2020. *Journal of Education, Innovation, and Communication*, (Special Issue), 65–75.

Al-Youbi, A. O., Al-Hayani, A., Rizwan, A., & Choudhry, H. (2020). Implications of COVID-19 on the Labor Market of Saudi Arabia: The Role of Universities for a Sustainable Workforce. *Sustainability, 12*(17), 7090. doi:10.3390u12177090

Amanat, F., & Krammer, F. (2020). Sars-CoV-2 Vaccines: Status Report. *Immunity, 52*(4), 583–589. https://doi.org/10.1016/j.immuni.2020.03.007

Amante, A. (2020). Help Us Like You Were Helped After War, Italy's Virus Hit Cities Tell Germany. *Reuters*. Retrieved from https://www.reuters.com/article us-health-coronavirus-italy-germany/help-us-like-you-were-helped-after-war-italys-virus-hit-cities-tell-german-idUSKBNZ1I1HT

Amini, S., Koolivand, A., & Nazari, J. (2020). Managerial challenges and solutions for COVID-19 outbreak: New insights for global primary healthcare system. *Ethics, Medicine, and Public Health, 15*, 100567. doi:10.1016/j.jemep.2020.100567 PMID:32837998

Anand, P., & Mishra, S. K. (2019). Linking core self-evaluation and emotional exhaustion with workplace loneliness: Does high LMX make the consequence worse? *International Journal of Human Resource Management*, 1–26. doi:10.1080/09585192.2019.1570308

Andersen, J. A. (2012, November). Reintroducing the Owner: On Corporate Governance, Goals, Organization and Leadership Theories. In *Proceedings of the 8th European Conference on Management, Leadership and Governance.* Academic Conferences International Limited.

Andragona, A. (2015). Humility in Management. *Journal of Business Ethics, 132*(1), 63–71. doi:10.100710551-014-2311-8

Anshari, M., Almunawar, M. N., Shahrill, M., Wicaksono, D. K., & Huda, M. (2017). Smartphones usage in the classrooms: Learning aid or interference? *Education and Information Technologies, 22*(6), 3063–3079. doi:10.100710639-017-9572-7

Anshari, M., & Lim, S. A. (2017). E-government with big data enabled through smartphone for public services: Possibilities and challenges. *International Journal of Public Administration, 40*(13), 1143–1158. doi:10.1080/01900692.2016.1242619

Antonakis, J., & Atwater, L. (2002). Leader distance: A review and a proposed theory. *The Leadership Quarterly, 13*(6), 673–704. doi:10.1016/S1048-9843(02)00155-8

Antonakis, J., Bastardoz, N., Jacquart, P., & Shamir, B. (2016). Charisma: An ill-defined and ill-measured gift. *Annual Review of Organizational Psychology and Organizational Behavior, 3*(1), 293–319. doi:10.1146/annurev-orgpsych-041015-062305

Antonakis, J., & Day, D. V. (2017). Leadership: Past, present, and future. In J. Antonakis & D. Day (Eds.), *The nature of leadership* (3rd ed., pp. 56–81). SAGE Publications.

Arbinger Institute. (2010). *Leadership and self-deception* (2nd ed.). San Francisco: Berrett-Koehler.

Arendt, H. (1983). Isak Dinesen. In Men in Dark Times (pp. 95-109). A Harvest Book.

Arendt, H. (1994). Understanding and Politics. In J. Kohn (Ed.), *Essays in Understanding* (pp. 307–327). Schocken Books.

Aristotle. (1941). Nicomachean Ethics. In R. McKeon (Ed.), *The basic works of Aristotle* (pp. 935–1122). Random House.

Arndt, M. (2020). *Ärzteschaft und Pflege „dürfen" jetzt länger arbeiten.* https://ku-gesundheitsmanagement.de/2020/06/12/aerzteschaft-und-pflege-duerfen-jetzt-laenger-arbeiten/

Arnold, N. (2020). *Wissenschaftliche Politikberatung zur gesundheitlichen Bewältigung der Corona-Pandemie. Analysen & Argumente* (Vol. 394). Konrad-Adenauer-Stiftung.

Arora, A. (2017). *Online Education Market in India 2016–2020.* Franchise India Education. Available at: https://www.franchiseindia.com/education/Online-education-Market-in-india-2016-2020.9263

Arora, A. K., & Srinivasan, R. (2020). Impact of pandemic COVID-19 on the teaching-learning process: A study of higher education teachers. *Prabandhan. Indian Journal of Management, 13*(4), 43–56. doi:10.17010/pijom/2020/v13i4/151825

Aryee, S., Tan, H. H., & Srinivas, E. S. (2005). Rhythms of Life: Antecedents and Outcomes of Work-Family Balance in Employed Parents. *The Journal of Applied Psychology, 90*(1), 132–146. doi:10.1037/0021-9010.90.1.132 PMID:15641894

Ashmos, D. P., & Duchon, D. (2000). Spirituality at work: A conceptualization and measure. *Journal of Management Inquiry, 9*(2), 134–144. doi:10.1177/105649260092008

Augurzky, B., & Schmidt, C. M. (2020). *Nach Corona: Jetzt stabile Krankenhausstrukturenschaffen* (RWI Positionen No. 79). https://www.econstor.eu/bitstream/10419/225077/1/1735634603.pdf

Avey, J. B., Luthans, F., & Jensen, S. M. (2009). Psychological capital: A positive resource for combating employee stress and turnover. *Human Resource Management, 48*(5), 677–693. doi:10.1002/hrm.20294

Avolio, B. J., Gardner, W. L., Walumbwa, F. O., Luthans, F., & May, D. R. (2004). Unlocking the mask: A look at the process by which authentic leaders impact follower attitudes and behaviors. *The Leadership Quarterly, 15*(6), 801–823. doi:10.1016/j.leaqua.2004.09.003

Azizaha, Y. N., Rijalb, M. K., Rumainurc, U. N. R., Pranajayae, S. A., Ngiuf, Z., Mufidg, A., ... Maui, D. H. (2020). Transformational or Transactional Leadership Style: Which Affects Work Satisfaction and Performance of Islamic University Lecturers During COVID-19 Pandemic. *Systematic Reviews in Pharmacy, 11*(7), 577–588.

Bailey, K. & Breslin, D. (2020). The COVID-19 Pandemic: What can we learn from past research in organizations and management. *International Journal of Management Reviews.* . doi:10.1111/ijmr.12237

Baker, E. L., Irwin, R., & Matthews, G. (2020). Thoughts on Adaptive Leadership in a Challenging Time. *Journal of Public Health Management and Practice, 26*(4), 378–379. doi:10.1097/PHH.0000000000001179 PMID:32433390

Baker, M. G., Wilson, N., & Anglemyer, A. (2020). Successful elimination of Covid-19 transmission in New Zealand. *The New England Journal of Medicine, 383*(8), e56. doi:10.1056/NEJMc2025203 PMID:32767891

Bakker, A. B., & Demerouti, E. (2007). The job demands-resources model: State of the art. *Journal of Managerial Psychology*, *22*(3), 309–328. doi:10.1108/02683940710733115

Bakker, M., Kerstholt, J., van Bommel, M., & Giebels, E. (2018). Decision-making during a crisis: The interplay of narratives and statistical information before and after crisis communication. *Journal of Risk Research*, *22*(11), 1409–1424. doi:10.1080/13669877.2018.1473464

Balkundi, P., & Kilduff, M. (2005). The ties that lead: A social network approach to leadership. *The Leadership Quarterly*, *16*(6), 941–961. doi:10.1016/j.leaqua.2005.09.004

Balocco, R., Cavallo, A., Ghezzi, A., & Berbegal-Mirabent, J. (2019). Lean business models change process in digital entrepreneurship. *Business Process Management Journal*, *25*(7), 1520–1542. doi:10.1108/BPMJ-07-2018-0194

Banai, M., Reisel, W. D., & Probst, T. M. (2004). A managerial and personal control model: Predictions of work alienation and organizational commitment in Hungary. *Journal of International Management*, *10*(3), 375–392. doi:10.1016/j.intman.2004.05.002

Bandura, A. (1977). Self-efficacy: Toward a unifying theory of behavioral change. *Psychological Review*, *84*(2), 191–215. doi:10.1037/0033-295X.84.2.191 PMID:847061

Bandura, A. (1986). *Social foundations of thought and action: A social cognitive theory*. Prentice-Hall.

Banerjee, D., & Rai, M. (2020). Social isolation in Covid-19: The impact of loneliness. *The International Journal of Social Psychiatry*, *66*(6), 525–527. doi:10.1177/0020764020922269 PMID:32349580

Barker, V. L. III, & Duhaime, I. M. (1997). Strategic change in the turnaround process: Theory and empirical evidence. *Strategic Management Journal*, *18*(1), 13–38. doi:10.1002/(SICI)1097-0266(199701)18:1<13::AID-SMJ843>3.0.CO;2-X

Bar-On, R. (1997). EQ-i Bar-On emotional quotient inventory: A measure of emotional intelligence. Toronto: Technical Manual, Multi Health Systems.

Barr, J., Hwang, E. S., & Shortell, C. K. (2020). *Surgeons, plague, and leadership: A historical mantle to carry forward*. Academic Press.

Barrow, J. C. (1977). The variables of leadership: A review and conceptual framework. *Academy of Management Review*, *2*(2), 233–251. doi:10.5465/amr.1977.4409046

Bartik, A. W., Bertrand, M., Cullen, Z., Glaeser, E. L., Luca, M., & Stanton, C. (2020). The impact of COVID-19 on small business outcomes and expectations. *Proceedings of the National Academy of Sciences of the United States of America*, *117*(30), 17656–17666. doi:10.1073/pnas.2006991117 PMID:32651281

Bartone, P. T. (1995). A short hardiness scale *American Psychological Society Annual Convention*, New York, NY.

Bartone, P. T., Kelly, D. R., & Matthews, M. D. (2013). Psychological Hardiness Predicts Adaptability in Military Leaders: A prospective study. *International Journal of Selection and Assessment*, *21*(2), 200–210. doi:10.1111/ijsa.12029

Barton, L. (1993). *Crisis in Organizations: Managing and Communicating in the Heat of Chaos*. South-Western Publishing Company.

Bartsch, S., Weber, E., Büttgen, M., & Huber, A. (2020). Leadership matters in crisis-induced digital transformation: How to lead service employees effectively during the COVID-19 pandemic. *Journal of Service Management*, *32*(1), 71–85. Advance online publication. doi:10.1108/JOSM-05-2020-0160

Basir, K. H. (2021). COVID-19 and Islamic Social Finance. Unlocking Islamic Social Finance to Assist Micro Small Medium Enterprises (Msmes). In *Brunei Darussalam*. Routledge.

Baskarada, S. (2014). Qualitative case study guidelines. *Qualitative Report, 19*(40), 1–25.

Bass, B. M. (1990). From transactional to transformational leadership: Learning to share the vision. *Organizational Dynamics, 18*(3), 19–31. doi:10.1016/0090-2616(90)90061-S

Bateson, G. (1979). *Mind and nature: A necessary unity*. Bantam Books.

Bateson, G., & Bateson, M. C. (1987). *Angels fear*. Macmillan Publishing Company.

Bateson, M. C. (1989). *Composing a life*. Grove Press.

Baumgarten, S. A. (1975). The innovative communicator in the diffusion process. *JMR, Journal of Marketing Research, 12*(1), 12–18. doi:10.1177/002224377501200103

Baum, H. (2005). Transparent leadership. *Leader to Leader, 2005*(37), 41–47. doi:10.1002/ltl.139

BCCI. (2020). *The Economic Impact of Coronavirus*. Retrieved from https://bahrainchamber.bh/ar/node/69239

Becker, G. S. (1962). Investment in human capital: A theoretical analysis. *Journal of Political Economy, 70*(5, Part 2), 9–49. doi:10.1086/258724

Becker, G. S. (1964). *Human Capital*. National Bureau of Economic Research.

Beer, M., & Nohria, N. (2000). Cracking the code of change. *Harvard Business Review, 78*(3), 133–141. PMID:11183975

Begerow, A., Michaelis, U., & Gaidys, U. (2020). Wahrnehmungen von Pflegenden im Bereich der Intensivpflege während der COVID-19-Pandemie. *Pflege, 33*(4), 229–236. https://doi.org/10.1024/1012-5302/a000744

Behrendt, P., Matz, S., & Göritz, A. S. (2017). An integrative model of leadership behavior. *The Leadership Quarterly, 28*(1), 229–244. doi:10.1016/j.leaqua.2016.08.002

Bein, B., Bachmann, M., Huggett, S., & Wegermann, P. (2020). SARS-CoV-2/COVID-19: Empfehlungen zu Diagnostik und Therapie [SARS CoV-2/COVID-19: Evidence-Based Recommendation on Diagnosis and Therapy]. *Anästhesiologie, Intensivmedizin, Notfallmedizin, Schmerztherapie, 55*(4), 257–265. https://doi.org/10.1055/a-1146-8674

Bellet, P., & Maloney, M. (1991). The Importance of Empathy as an Interviewing Skill in Medicine. *Journal of the American Medical Association, 266*(13), 1831–1832. doi:10.1001/jama.1991.03470130111039 PMID:1909761

Belzunegui-Eraso, A., & Erro-Garcés, A. (2020). Teleworking in the Context of the COVID-19 Crisis. *Sustainability, 12*(3662), 3662. Advance online publication. doi:10.3390u12093662

Benefiel, M., Fry, L. W., & Geigle, D. (2014). Spirituality and religion in the workplace: History, theory, and research. *Psychology of Religion and Spirituality, 6*(3), 175–187. doi:10.1037/a0036597

Benini, A. A. (1999). Network without centre? A case study of an organizational network responding to an earthquake. *Journal of Contingencies and Crisis Management, 7*(1), 38–47. doi:10.1111/1468-5973.00097

Benner, M. J., & Zenger, T. (2016). The lemons problem in markets for strategy. *Strategy Science, 1*(2), 71–89. doi:10.1287tsc.2015.0010

Bennett, N., & Lemoine, G. J. (2014). What a difference a word makes: Understanding threats to performance in a VUCA world. *Business Horizons, 57*(3), 311–317. doi:10.1016/j.bushor.2014.01.001

Bennett, S., & Lockyer, L. (2004). Becoming and online teacher: Adapting to a changed environment for teaching and learning in higher education. *Educational Media International, 41*(3), 231–248. doi:10.1080/09523980410001680842

Bennis, W. (2007). The challenges of leadership in the modern world: Introduction to the special issue. *The American Psychologist, 62*(1), 2–5. doi:10.1037/0003-066X.62.1.2 PMID:17209674

Bennis, W., & Nanus, B. (1985). *Leaders: The strategies for taking charge*. Harper & Row.

Berg-Weger, M., & Morley, J. E. (2020). Loneliness and Social Isolation in Older Adults During the Covid-19 Pandemic: Implications for Gerontological Social Work. *The Journal of Nutrition, Health & Aging, 24*(5), 1–3. doi:10.100712603-020-1366-8 PMID:32346678

Berliner Bildungscampus für Gesundheitsberufe gGmbH. (2020, March 29). *CORONA -Schulungskonzepte für die pflege in der krisensituation*. Berlin. https://www.bildungscampus-berlin.de/fileadmin/content/news/downloads/Schulungskonzept_Corona_BBG.pdf

Berlit, P. (2020). S1-Leitlinie: Neurologische Manifestationen bei COVID-19. *DGNeurologie, 3*(6), 495–519. doi:10.100742451-020-00254-x

Berman, E. M., West, J. P., & Richter, M. N. Jr. (2002). Workplace relations: Friendship patterns and consequences (according to managers). *Public Administration Review, 62*(2), 217–230. doi:10.1111/0033-3352.00172

Bernardez, M., & Mead, M. (2009). The power of entrepreneurial ecosystems: Extracting boom from bust. *PII Review, 2*(2), 12–45.

Bhaduri, R. M. (2019). Leveraging culture and leadership in crisis management. European Journal of Training and Development. *European Journal of Training and Development, 43*(5/6), 554–569. doi:10.1108/EJTD-10-2018-0109

Bhargava, S., Sarkar, R., & Kroumpouzos, G. (2020). Mental distress in dermatologists during COVID-19 pandemic: Assessment and risk factors in a global, cross-sectional study. *Dermatologic Therapy, e14161*(6). doi:10.1111/dth.14161 PMID:32770716

Bhaskaran, M. (2010). Economic diversification in Brunei Darussalam. *CSPS Strategy and Policy Journal, 1*(1), 1–12.

Bhave, D. P., Teo, L. H., & Dalal, R. S. (2020). Privacy at work: A review and a research agenda for a contested terrain. *Journal of Management, 46*(1), 127–164. doi:10.1177/0149206319878254

BIBD. (2020). *Easing the Nation's Support of the Covid-19 Relief Fund*. http://www.bibd.com.bn/assets/pdf/media-centre/media-releases/2020/PR018_BIBD_QUICKPAY_COVID_19.pdf

Biermann, K., & Gutensohn, D. (2020, April 1). Ärzte und Pfleger warnen vor Zwangsarbeit. *ZEIT ONLINE GmbH*. https://www.zeit.de/arbeit/2020-04/corona-krise-aerzte-pflegekraefte-arbeit-verpflichtung-armin-laschet

Billings, D. M., & Kowalski, K. (2008). Developing your career as a nurse educator the professional portfolio. *Journal of Continuing Education in Nursing, 39*(12), 532–533. doi:10.3928/00220124-20081201-09 PMID:19110727

Billings, R. S., Milburn, T. W., & Lou, M. (1980). A Model of Crisis Perception : A Theoretical and Empirical Analysis. *Administrative Science Quarterly, 25*(2), 300–316. doi:10.2307/2392456

Birkenshaw, J., Zimmermann, A., & Raisch, S. (2016). How do firms adapt to discontinuous change? Bridging the dynamic capabilities and ambidexterity perspectives. University of California, Berkeley.

Birkinshaw, J., Zimmermann, A., & Raisch, S. (2016). How Do firms Adapt to Discontinuous Change? *California Management Review, 58*(4), 36–58. doi:10.1525/cmr.2016.58.4.36

BISB. (2020a). *Coronavirus (COVID-19) Help & Support*. Retrieved from https://www.bisb.com/en/covid-19

BISB. (2020b). *COVID-19*. Retrieved from https://www.bisb.com/en/node/1183

BISB. (2020c). *BisB Implements Additional Health & Safety Measures During COVID-19.* Retrieved from https://www.bisb.com/en/bisb-implements-additional-health-safety-measures-during-covid-19

Biz Brunei. (2020). *Live tracking, tiered delivery rates see GoMamam reach 200 daily orders.* https://www.bizbrunei.com/2020/04/live-tracking-tiered-delivery-rates-see-gomamam-reach-200-daily-orders/

Blake-Beard, S., Shapiro, M., & Ingols, C. (2020). Feminine? Masculine? Androgynous leadership as a necessity in COVID-19. *Gender in Management: An International Journal.*

Bleckwenn, M. (2020). Behandlung von Patienten in Corona-Ambulanzen: COVID-19-Pandemie [Treatment of patients in a corona ambulance]. *MMW Fortschritte der Medizin, 162*(9), 54–56. https://doi.org/10.1007/s15006-020-0479-7

Bodenheimer, M., & Leidenberger, J. (2020). COVID-19 as a window of opportunity for sustainability transitions? Narratives and communication strategies beyond the pandemic. *Sustainability: Science, Practice and Policy, 16*(1), 61–66. doi:10.1080/15487733.2020.1766318

Boes, A., Kämpf, T., Lühr, T., & Ziegler, A. (2018). Is agility an opportunity for a new attempt towards a democratic company? *Berliner Journal fur Soziologie*, *28*(1–2), 181–208. doi:10.100711609-018-0367-5

Bohm, D. (1992). *Thought as a system.* Routledge.

Boin, A., Kuipers, S., & Overdijk, W. (2013). Leadership in times of crisis: A framework for assessment. *International Review of Public Administration, 18*(1), 79–91. doi:10.1080/12294659.2013.10805241

Bolden, R. (2020). *Leadership, complexity and change: Learning from the Covid-19 pandemic.* Research, Business and Innovation.

Bolman, L., & Deal, T. (2013). Reframing organizations: Artistry, choice, and leadership (5th ed.). Hoboken, NJ: John Wiley & Sons.

Bolton, A. (2020). *H-E-B continues to evolve procedures during COVID-19 emergency.* Retrieved November 4, 2020, from http://a.msn.com/05/en-us/BB11ZzaZ?ocid=se

Bonk, M., Döring, O., & Ulrichs, T. (2020). Global Health Think Tanks – Think Tanks im Bereich der Globalen Gesundheit. In D. Matusiewicz (Ed.), FOM-Edition. Think tanks im gesundheitswesen: Deutsche denkfabriken und ihre (pp. 307–324). Gabler. https://doi.org/10.1007/978-3-658-29728-2_25

Borneo Bulletin. (2011). *Monetary authority to ensure nation's stability.* Author.

Borneo Bulletin. (2020a). *Solidarity strong in fighting COVID-19.* https://borneobulletin.com.bn/2020/04/solidarity-strong-in-fighting-covid-19/

Borneo Bulletin. (2020b). *DCCA warns against hiking medical mask, hand sanitiser prices.* https://borneobulletin.com.bn/2020/02/dcca-warns-hiking-medical-mask-hand-sanitiser-prices

Borneo Bulletin. (2020c). *Preparedness, cooperation are key.* https://borneobulletin.com.bn/2020/09/preparedness-cooperation-are-key/

Borneo Bulletin. (2020d). *Stiff penalty for Infectious Disease Act violations.* https://borneobulletin.com.bn/2020/06/stiff-penalty-for-infectious-disease-act-violations/

Borneo Bulletin. (2020e). *Gym owner in the soup for breaking MoH rules.* https://borneobulletin.com.bn/2020/04/gym-owner-in-the-soup-for-breaking-moh-rules-2/

Borneo Bulletin. (2020f). *Youth charged for posting video breaching peace.* https://borneobulletin.com.bn/2020/03/youth-charged-for-posting-video-breaching-peace/

Borneo Bulletin. (2020g). *'Operasi Merati' At Business Premises.* https://www.brudirect.com/news.php?id=106329

Borneo Bulletin. (2020h). *'Party-goers' to learn fate on Saturday.* https://borneobulletin.com.bn/2020/06/party-goers-to-learn-fate-on-saturday-2/

Borneo Bulletin. (2020i). *BruHealth app to get new features.* https://www.mofe.gov.bn/Lists/News/NewDispForm.aspx?ID=164

Borneo Bulletin. (2020j). *UNN working with ministries to facilitate online learning.* https://borneobulletin.com.bn/2020/03/unn-working-with-ministries-to-facilitate-online-learning/

Borneo Bulletin. (2020k). *Tutors go online with classes.* https://borneobulletin.com.bn/2020/04/tutors-go-online-with-classes/

Borneo Bulletin. (2020l). *Brunei Info Department the most active Instagram government account in the world.* https://borneobulletin.com.bn/ig-posts-info-dept-is-top-of-the-world/

Borneo Bulletin. (2020m). *COVID-19 Brunei: Youth volunteers heed nation's call.* https://borneobulletin.com.bn/2020/04/youth-volunteers-heed-nations-call/

Borneo Bulletin. (2020n). *JIS teachers produce 100 face shields for frontliners.* https://borneobulletin.com.bn/2020/04/jis-teachers-produce-100-face-shields-for-frontliners/

Borneo Bulletin. (2021). *15 new imported cases found.* Accessed https://borneobulletin.com.bn/2021/01/15-new-imported-cases-found-2/

Bouckenooghe, D. (2010). Positioning change recipients' attitudes toward change in the organizational change literature. *The Journal of Applied Behavioral Science*, *46*(4), 500–531. doi:10.1177/0021886310367944

Bouziri, H., Smith, D. R., Descatha, A., Dab, W., & Jean, K. (2020). Working from home in the time of covid-19: How to best preserve occupational health? *Occupational and Environmental Medicine*, *77*(7), 509–510. doi:10.1136/oemed-2020-106599 PMID:32354748

Bowers, M. R., Hall, J. R., & Srinivasan, M. M. (2017). Organizational culture and leadership style: The missing combination for selecting the right leader for effective crisis management. *Business Horizons*, *60*(4), 551–563. doi:10.1016/j.bushor.2017.04.001

Brandebo, M. F. (2020). Destructive leadership in crisis management. *Leadership and Organization Development Journal*, *41*(4), 567–580. doi:10.1108/LODJ-02-2019-0089

Brandi, C., Dzebo, A., & Janetschek, H. (2017). *The Case for Connecting the Implementation of the Paris Climate Agreement and the 2030 Agenda for Sustainable Development.* Briefing Paper 21/2017.

Brewer, J. A., Worhunsky, P. D., Gray, J. R., Tang, Y. Y., & Weber, J., & kober, H. (2011). Meditation experience is associated with differences in default mode network activity and connectivity. *Proceedings of the National Academy of Sciences*, *108*(50), 20254-20259. 10.1073/pnas.1112029108

Breyton, R., & Naber, I. (2020, November 3). Berliner Polizeipräsidentin: „Auf Corona-Demos auch Menschen, die mit Messern bewaffnet sind". *WELT.* https://www.welt.de/politik/deutschland/plus219211512/Berliner-Polizeipraesidentin-Auf-Corona-Demos-auch-Menschen-die-mit-Messern-bewaffnet-sind.html?cid=onsite.onsitesearch#Comments

Bridges, W. (2009). *Managing transitions: Making the most of change.* Addison Wesley.

Brittle, Z. (2015). *How to Build Trust in Your Relationship*. https://www.gottman.com/blog/trust/

Brown, J., Denning, S., Groh, K., & Prusak, L. (2011). *Storytelling in organizations: Why storytelling is transforming 21st century organizations and Management*. Routledge.

Brown, K. W., Ryan, R. M., Loverich, T. M., Biegel, G. M., & West, A. M. (2011). Out of the armchair and into the streets: Measuring mindfulness advances knowledge and improves interventions: Reply to Grossman. *Psychological Assessment, 23*(4), 1041–1046. doi:10.1037/a0025781

Brozovic, D. (2018). Strategic flexibility: A review of the literature. *International Journal of Management Reviews, 20*(1), 3–31. doi:10.1111/ijmr.12111

Bruch, H., & Ghoshal, S. (2003). Unleashing organizational energy. *MIT Sloan Management Review, 45*(1), 45–52.

Brunei Year Book. (2015). *Brunei Year Book*. Brunei Press Sdn Bhd.

Brzezinski, A., Kecht, V., Van Dijcke, D., & Wright, A. L. (2020). *Belief in science influences physical distancing in response to covid-19 lockdown policies*. University of Chicago, Becker Friedman Institute for Economics Working Paper, (2020-56).

BSP. (n.d.). *Overview of our Business*. https://www.bsp.com.bn/main/about-bsp/overview-of-our-business

Buchanan, R. W., & Gillies, C. S. (1990). Value managed relationships: The key to customer retention and profitability. *European Management Journal, 8*(4), 523–526. doi:10.1016/0263-2373(90)90115-M

Buheji, M., & Buheji, A. (2020). Characteristics of 'Problem-Based Learning'in post-COVID-19 workplace. *Human Resource Management Review, 10*(2), 33–39.

Bundy, J., Pfarrer, M. D., & Coombs, W. T. (2017). Crises and Crisis Management: Integration, Interpretation, and Research Development. *Journal of Management, 43*(6), 1661–1692. doi:10.1177/0149206316680030

Burgess, P. H. (1984). *The sayings of Mahatma Gandhi*. Graham Brash.

Burke, C. M., & Morley, M. J. (2016). On temporary organizations: A review, synthesis and research agenda. *Human Relations, 69*(6), 1235–1258. doi:10.1177/0018726715610809

Burke, C. S., Stagl, K. C., Klein, C., Goodwin, G. F., Salas, E., & Halpin, S. M. (2006). What type of leadership behaviors are functional in teams? A meta-analysis. *The Leadership Quarterly, 17*(3), 288–307. doi:10.1016/j.leaqua.2006.02.007

Burkle, F. M. Jr. (2010). Do Pandemic Preparedness Planning Systems Ignore Critical Community and Local-Level Operational Challenges? *Disaster Medicine and Public Health Preparedness, 4*(1), 24–29. doi:10.1097/DMP.0b013e3181cb4193 PMID:20389192

Burns, J. M. (1978). *Leadership*. Harper & Row.

Burns, J. M. (2003). *Transforming leadership*. Grove Press.

Burrell, D. N., Abdul-Malik, O., Rahim, E., Huff, A., & Finklea, K. (2010). An analysis of the application of situational leadership in the post 9/11 evolving public health managerial environments. *Leadership Journal, 5*(1), 49-59.

Burrell, D. N. (2020). Understanding the Talent Management Intricacies of Remote Cybersecurity Teams in Covid-19 Induced Telework Organizational Ecosystems. *Land Forces Academy Review, 25*(3), 232–244. doi:10.2478/raft-2020-0028

Byrd, M. Y. (2020). *A New Normal: The Changed Landscape of Human Resource Development in the Wake of COVID-19*. Academic Press.

Cahn, B. R., Delorme, A., & Polich, J. (2012). Event-related delta, theta, alpha and gamma correlates to auditory oddball processing during Vipassana meditation. *Social Cognitive and Affective Neuroscience*, *8*(1), 100–111. doi:10.1093can/nss060 PMID:22648958

Cairney, P. (2020). The UK government's COVID-19 policy: Assessing evidence-informed policy analysis in real time. *British Politics*, 1–27.

Caldwell, S. D. (2013). Are Change Readiness Strategies Overrated? A Commentary on Boundary Conditions. *Journal of Change Management*, *13*(1), 19–35. doi:10.1080/14697017.2013.768428

Caligiuri, P., De Cieri, H., Minbaeva, D., Verbeke, A., & Zimmermann, A. (2020). International HRM insights for navigating the COVID-19 pandemic: Implications for future research and practice. *Journal of International Business Studies*, 1. PMID:32836500

Campbell, K. A. (2015). Can effective risk management signal virtue-based leadership? *Journal of Business Ethics*, *129*(1), 115–130. doi:10.100710551-014-2129-4

Carlyle, T. (1907). *On heroes, hero-worship, and the heroic in history*. Houghton Mifflin.

Carmeli, A., Reiter-Palmon, R., & Ziv, E. (2010). Inclusive leadership and employee involvement in creative tasks in the workplace: The mediating role of psychological safety. *Creativity Research Journal*, *22*(3), 250–260. doi:10.1080/10400419.2010.504654

Carnahan, S. (2017). Blocked but not tackled: Who founds new firms when rivals dissolve? *Strategic Management Journal*, *38*(11), 2189–2212. doi:10.1002mj.2653

Carnevale, J. B., & Hatak, I. (2020). Employee adjustment and well-being in the era of COVID-19: Implications for human resource management. *Journal of Business Research*, *117*, 183–187. doi:10.1016/j.jbusres.2020.05.037 PMID:32501303

Carter, D. R., DeChurch, L. A., Braun, M. T., & Contractor, N. (2015b). Social network approaches to leadership: An integrative conceptual review. *The Journal of Applied Psychology*, *100*(3), 597–622. doi:10.1037/a0038922 PMID:25798551

Cavanaugh, J. C. (2006). Effectively managing major disasters. *The Psychologist Manager Journal*, *9*(1), 3–11. doi:10.120715503461tpmj0901_2

CBB. (2020). *FinTech and Innovation*. Retrieved from https://www.cbb.gov.bh/fintech/

Celik, A., Akgemci, T., & Akyazi, T. E. (2016). A comparison between the styles of transformational leaders and authentic leaders in crisis management. *International Journal of Academic Research in Business & Social Sciences*, *6*(2), 183–196. doi:10.6007/IJARBSS/v6-i2/2023

Cener, P. (2007). *Crisis management*. Academic Press.

Çetin, M. (2019). Effects of Religious Participation on Social Inclusion and Existential Well-Being Levels of Muslim Refugees and Immigrants in Turkey. *The International Journal for the Psychology of Religion*, *29*(2), 64–76. doi:10.1080/10508619.2019.1580092

Champoux, J. E. (1978). Perceptions of work and nonwork: A reexamination of the compensatory and spillover models. *Sociology of Work and Occupations*, *5*(4), 402–422. doi:10.1177/073088847800500402

Chanana, N. & Sangeeta. (2020). Employee engagement practices during COVID-19 lockdown. *Journal of Public Affairs*, 2508. PMID:33041656

Chan, J. K. L., & King, V. T. (2019). Covid-19 and Tourism in Southeast Asia. *Network (Bristol, England)*.

Charbonnier-Voirin, A., & Roussel, P. (2012). Adaptive Performance: A New Scale to Measure Individual Performance in Organizations. *Canadian Journal of Administrative Sciences-Revue Canadienne Des Sciences De L Administration, 29*(3), 280-293. doi:10.1002/cjas.232

Charbonnier-Voirin, A., El Akremi, A., & Vandenberghe, C. (2010). A multilevel model of transformational leadership and adaptive performance and the moderating role of climate for innovation. *Group & Organization Management, 35*(6), 699–726. doi:10.1177/1059601110390833

Charoensukmongkol, P., & Phungsoonthorn, T. (2020). The effectiveness of supervisor support in lessening perceived uncertainties and emotional exhaustion of university employees during the COVID-19 crisis: The constraining role of organizational intransigence. *The Journal of General Psychology*, 1–20. PMID:32691689

Chaw, L., Koh, W. C., Jamaludin, S. A., Naing, L., Alikhan, M. F., & Wong, J. (2020). Analysis of SARS-CoV-2 transmission in different settings, Brunei. *Emerging Infectious Diseases, 26*(11), 2598–2606. doi:10.3201/eid2611.202263 PMID:33035448

Chawla, V., & Guda, S. (2010). Individual spirituality at work and its relationship with job satisfaction, propensity to leave and job commitment: An exploratory study among sales professionals. *Journal of Human Values, 16*(2), 157–167. doi:10.1177/097168581001600203

Chen, C. F., & Kao, Y. L. (2012). Investigating the antecedents and consequences of burnout and isolation among flight attendants. *Tourism Management, 33*(4), 868–874. doi:10.1016/j.tourman.2011.09.008

Chen, G., Thomas, B., & Wallace, J. C. (2005). A multilevel examination of the relationships among training outcomes, mediating regulatory processes, and adaptive performance. *The Journal of Applied Psychology, 90*(5), 827–841. doi:10.1037/0021-9010.90.5.827 PMID:16162057

Cheng, J. H., & Liu, S. F. (2017). A study of innovative product marketing strategies for technological SMEs. *Journal of Interdisciplinary Mathematics, 20*(1), 319–337. doi:10.1080/09720502.2016.1258837

Cheong, D. (2019). *The Fourth Industrial Revolution, Job Futures and Policy Implications for Reducing Youth Unemployment in Brunei Darussalam.* CSPS.

Chetty, S. (1996). The case study method for research in small- and medium-sized firms. *International Small Business Journal, 15*(1), 73–85. doi:10.1177/0266242696151005

Cheung, J. C. S. (2017). Rentier welfare states in hydrocarbon-based economies: Brunei Darussalam and Islamic Republic of Iran in comparative context. *Journal of Asian Public Policy, 10*(3), 287–301. doi:10.1080/17516234.2015.1130468

Chhaya, N. (2020). *Here Are The Top Five Leadership Challenges During The Coronavirus Pandemic.* Retrieved November 1, 2020, from https://www.forbes.com/sites/niharchhaya/2020/03/23/here-are-the-top-five-leadership-challenges-during-the-coronavirus-pandemic/

Chiaburu, D. S., Lorinkova, N. M., & Van Dyne, L. (2013). Employees' Social Context and Change-Oriented Citizenship: A Meta-Analysis of Leader, Coworker, and Organizational Influences. *Group & Organization Management, 38*(3), 291–333. doi:10.1177/1059601113476736

Chiriboga, D., Garay, J., Buss, P., Madrigal, R. S., & Rispel, L. C. (2020). Health inequity during the COVID-19 pandemic: A cry for ethical global leadership. *Lancet, 395*(10238), 1690–1691. doi:10.1016/S0140-6736(20)31145-4 PMID:32419711

Christensen, T., & Lægreid, P. (2007). The whole-of-government approach to public sector reform. *Public Administration Review, 67*(6), 1059–1066. doi:10.1111/j.1540-6210.2007.00797.x

Clift, K., & Court, A. (2020). *COVID-19: How companies are responding to the coronavirus crisis?* Retrieved October 1, 2020, from https://www.weforum.org/agenda/2020/03/how-are-companies-responding-to-the-coronavirus-crisis-d15bed6137/

Coelho, P. S., & Henseler, J. (2012). Creating customer loyalty through service customization. *European Journal of Marketing*, *46*(3–4), 331–356. doi:10.1108/03090561211202503

Coleman, A. (2020). What are your "odds-of-success"? Reflecting on the role of adaptive leadership in Leicester City's (2015/16) English Football Premier League Title win. *Development and Learning in Organizations*, *35*(1), 1–3. doi:10.1108/DLO-09-2019-0227

Cooley, D., Pedersen, S., & Mainsbridge, C. (2014). Assessment of the impact of a workplace intervention to reduce prolonged occupational sitting time. *Qualitative Health Research*, *24*(1), 90–101. doi:10.1177/1049732313513503 PMID:24231074

Coombs, W. T. (1999). *Ongoing Crisis Communication: Planning, Managing, and Responding*. SAGE Publications.

Cooper, R. G., & Dreher, A. (2010). Voice-of-customer methods. *Marketing Management, 19*(4), 38-43.

Cooper, R. G. (2019). The drivers of success in new-product development. *Industrial Marketing Management*, *76*, 36–47. doi:10.1016/j.indmarman.2018.07.005

Coppola, N., Hiltz, S., & Rotter, N. (2002). Becoming a virtual professor: Pedagogical roles and asynchronous learning networks. *Journal of Management Information Systems*, *18*(4), 169–189. doi:10.1080/07421222.2002.11045703

Corlett, R. T., Primack, R. B., Devictor, V., Maas, B., Goswami, V. R., Bates, A. E., ... Pakeman, R. J. (2020). Impacts of the coronavirus pandemic on biodiversity conservation. *Biological Conservation*, *246*, 108571. Advance online publication. doi:10.1016/j.biocon.2020.108571 PMID:32292203

Cortez, R. M., & Johnston, W. J. (2020). The Coronavirus crisis in B2B settings: Crisis uniqueness and managerial implications based on social exchange theory. *Industrial Marketing Management*, *88*, 125–135. doi:10.1016/j.indmarman.2020.05.004

Corvellec, H., Böhm, S., Stowell, A., & Valenzuela, F. (2020). Introduction to the special issue on the contested realities of the circular economy. *Culture and Organization*, *26*(2), 97–102. doi:10.1080/14759551.2020.1717733

Coscieme, L., Fioramonti, L., Mortensen, L. F., Pickett, K. E., Kubiszewski, I., Lovins, H., & De Vogli, R. (2020). *Women in power: female leadership and public health outcomes during the COVID-19 pandemic*. MedRxiv; doi:10.1101/2020.07.13.20152397

Coulter, R. A., Feick, L. F., & Price, L. L. (2002). Changing faces: Cosmetics opinion leadership among women in the new Hungary. *European Journal of Marketing*, *36*(11/12), 1287–1308. doi:10.1108/03090560210445182

Council for Industry and Higher Education. (2011). *Global graduates into global leaders*. http://www.cihe.co.uk/category/knowledge/publications/

Cousin, G. (2005). Case study research. *Journal of Geography in Higher Education*, *29*(3), 421–427. doi:10.1080/03098260500290967

Crane, A., & Matten, D. (2016). *Business ethics: Managing corporate citizenship and sustainability in the age of globalization*. Oxford, UK: University Press.

Crayne, M. P., & Medeiros, K. E. (2020). Making sense of crisis: Charismatic, ideological, and pragmatic leadership in response to COVID-19. *American Psychologist*.

Crook, T. R., Todd, S. Y., Combs, J. G., Woehr, D. J., & Ketchen, D. J. (2011). Does human capital matter? a meta-analysis of the relationship between human capital and firm performance. *The Journal of Applied Psychology*, *96*(3), 443–456. doi:10.1037/a0022147 PMID:21244126

Cropanzano, R., Anthony, E. L., Daniels, S. R., & Hall, A. V. (2017). Social exchange theory: A critical review with theoretical remedies. *The Academy of Management Annals*, *11*(1), 479–516. doi:10.5465/annals.2015.0099

Crouter, A. C. (1984). Spillover from family to work: The neglected side of the work-family interface. *Human Relations*, *37*(6), 425–441. doi:10.1177/001872678403700601

CSPS. (2020a). *Brunei Economic Update, July 2020*. CSPS.

CSPS. (2020b). *Brunei Economic Update, October 2020*. CSPS.

Cui, J., Li, F., & Shi, Z. L. (2019). *Origin and evolution of pathogenic coronaviruses*. doi:10.103841579-018-0118-9

Cullen, W., Gulati, G., & Kelly, B. D. (2020). Mental health in the Covid-19 pandemic. *QJM: An International Journal of Medicine*, *113*(5), 311–312. doi:10.1093/qjmed/hcaa110 PMID:32227218

CumEx Haltet die Steuerdiebe. (2020, September 7). Retrieved from https://www.finanzwende.de/themen/cumex/?L=0

Dan, B. (1999). Spirituality at work: An overview. *Journal of Organizational Change Management*, *12*(4), 328–332. doi:10.1108/09534819910282162

Dane, E. (2011). Paying attention to mindfulness and its effects on task performance in the workplace. *Journal of Management*, *37*(4), 997–1018. doi:10.1177/0149206310367948

Dansereau, F. Jr, Graen, G., & Haga, W. J. (1975). A vertical dyad linkage approach to leadership within formal organizations: A longitudinal investigation of the role making process. *Organizational Behavior and Human Performance, Vol*, *13*(1), 46–78. doi:10.1016/0030-5073(75)90005-7

Day, D. V. (2001). Leadership development: A review in context. *The Leadership Quarterly*, *11*(4), 581–613. doi:10.1016/S1048-9843(00)00061-8

Day, D. V., & Dragoni, L. (2015). Leadership development: An outcome-oriented review based on time and levels of analyses. *Annual Review of Organizational Psychology and Organizational Behavior*, *2*(1), 133–156. doi:10.1146/annurev-orgpsych-032414-111328

Dayton, B. W., & Bernhardsdottir, A. (2015). *Crisis management*. International Encyclopedia of Peace.

De Brentani, U., & Kleinschmidt, E. J. (2015). The impact of company resources and capabilities on global new product program performance. *Project Management Journal*, *46*(1), 12–29. doi:10.1002/pmj.21470

De Brentani, U., Kleinschmidt, E. J., & Salomo, S. (2010). Success in global new product development: Impact of strategy and the behavioral environment of the firm. *Journal of Product Innovation Management*, *27*(2), 143–160. doi:10.1111/j.1540-5885.2010.00707.x

De Groot, H. (1988). Decentralization decisionsin bureaucracies as a principle-agent problem. *Journal of Public Economics*, *36*(3), 323–337. doi:10.1016/0047-2727(88)90014-X

De Quinn, J. B. (2000). *Outsourcing innovation: the new engine of growth*. Sloan Management.

De Vienne, M. S. (2015). Brunei: From the age of commerce to the 21st century. NUS Press.

Demerouti, E., Bakker, A. B., Nachreiner, F., & Schaufeli, W. B. (2001). The job demands-resources model of burnout. *The Journal of Applied Psychology*, *86*(3), 499–512. doi:10.1037/0021-9010.86.3.499 PMID:11419809

Dennis, R. S., Kinzler-Norheim, L., & Bocarnea, M. (2010). Servant leadership theory. In *Servant leadership* (pp. 169–179). Palgrave Macmillan. doi:10.1057/9780230299184_14

Dente, S. M. R., & Hashimoto, S. (2020). COVID-19: A pandemic with positive and negative outcomes on resource and waste flows and stocks. *Resources, Conservation & Recycling Journal*, (161), 104979. doi:10.1016/j.resconrec.2020.104979

Dent, E. B., & Goldberg, S. G. (1999). Challenging "resistance to change". *The Journal of Applied Behavioral Science*, *35*(1), 25–41. doi:10.1177/0021886399351003

DEPD. (2020). *Labor Force Survey 2019*. http://www.deps.gov.bn/DEPD%20Documents%20Library/DOS/Labour%20force%20survey_KTK/2019/KTK_2019.pdf

DePietro, A. (2020). *Here's a look at the impact of coronavirus (COVID-19) on colleges and universities in the U.S.* Retrieved from https://www.forbes.com/sites/andrewdepietro/ 2020/04/30/impact-coronavirus-covid-19-colleges-universities/#44fea1bf61a6

DeRue, D. S. (2011). Adaptive leadership theory: Leading and following as a complex adaptive process. *Research in Organizational Behavior*, *31*, 125–150. doi:10.1016/j.riob.2011.09.007

DeRue, D. S., Nahrgang, J. D., Wellman, N. E. D., & Humphrey, S. E. (2011). Trait and behavioral theories of leadership: An integration and meta-analytic test of their relative validity. *Personnel Psychology*, *64*(1), 7–52. doi:10.1111/j.1744-6570.2010.01201.x

Desbordes, G., Negi, L. T., Pace, T. W., Wallace, B. A., Raison, C. L., & Schwartz, E. L. (2012). Effects of mindful-attention and compassion meditation training on amygdala response to emotional stimuli in an ordinary, non-meditative state. *Frontiers in Human Neuroscience*, *6*, 292. doi:10.3389/fnhum.2012.00292 PMID:23125828

DGIIN. (2020, May 25). *Intensivpflege als tragende Säule bei der Pandemie-Bewältigung Arbeitsbedingungen in der Intensivpflege prekärer denn je – DGIIN veröffentlicht Stellungnahme* [Press release]. https://dgiin.de/allgemeines/pressemitteilungen/pm-leser/intensivpflege-als-tragende-saeule-bei-der-pandemie-bewaeltigung-arbeitsbedingungen-in-der-intensivpflege-prekaerer-denn-je.html

Dharma, Y. (2018). The Effect of Work Motivation on the Employee Performance with Organization Citizenship Behavior as Intervening Variable at Bank Aceh Syariah. In *Proceedings of MICoMS 2017*. Emerald Publishing Limited. 10.1108/978-1-78756-793-1-00065

Di Benedetto, C. A. (1999). Identifying the key success factors in new product launch. *Journal of Product Innovation Management: An International Publication of The Product Development & Management Association*, *16*(6), 530–544. doi:10.1111/1540-5885.1660530

Diab-Bahman, R., & Al-Enzi, A. (2020). The impact of COVID-19 pandemic on conventional work settings. *The International Journal of Sociology and Social Policy*, *40*(9/10), 909–927. doi:10.1108/IJSSP-07-2020-0262

Dinges, S. (2020). Corona und die Alten – um wen sorgen wir uns wirklich? In W. Kröll, J. Platzer, H.-W. Ruckenbauer, & W. Schaupp (Eds.), *Die Corona-Pandemie* (pp. 69–84). Nomos Verlagsgesellschaft mbH & Co. KG. doi:10.5771/9783748910589-69

Dinh, J. E., Lord, R. G., Gardner, W. L., Meuser, J. D., Liden, R. C., & Hu, J. (2014). Leadership theory and research in the new millennium: Current theoretical trends and changing perspectives. *The Leadership Quarterly*, *25*(1), 36–62. doi:10.1016/j.leaqua.2013.11.005

DiPietro, M., Ferdig, R. E., Black, E. W., & Preston, M. (2008). Best practices in teaching K-12 online: Lessons learned from Michigan virtual school teachers. *Journal of Interactive Online Learning*, *7*(1), 10–35.

Dirani, K. M., Abadi, M., Alizadeh, A., Barhate, B., Garza, R. C., Gunasekara, N., Ibrahim, G., & Majzun, Z. (2020). Leadership competencies and the essential role of human resource development in times of crisis: A response to Covid-19 pandemic. *Human Resource Development International*, *23*(4), 380–394. doi:10.1080/13678868.2020.1780078

DIVI. (2020a). *DIVI Intensivregister*. https://www.intensivregister.de/#/index

DIVI. (2020b). *Handlungsempfehlungen der DIVI zu COVID-19*. https://www.divi.de/register/aktuelle-informationen

Dixon, D. P., & Weeks, M. R. (2017). Leading in Extremis Situations: how can leaders improve? In Leadership in Extreme Situations. doi:10.1007/978-3-319-55059-6_14

Dodt, C., & Schneider, N. (2020). Notfallmedizinische und intensivmedizinische Aspekte von COVID-19-Infektionen [Emergency and intensive care medicine aspects of COVID-19 infections]. *Der Radiologe*, *60*(10), 899–907. https://doi.org/10.1007/s00117-020-00742-x

Doe, F., & Puplampu, B. B. (2019). Coercive management behaviour causes scale: Validation and reliability. *The International Journal of Organizational Analysis*, *27*(3), 729–744. doi:10.1108/IJOA-08-2018-1508

Dolan, L., Raich, M., Garti, A., & Landau, A. (2020). *"The COVID-19 Crisis" as an opportunity for introspection: A multi-level reflections on values, needs, trust and leadership in the future.* https://www.europeanbusinessreview.com/the-covid-19-crisis-as-an-opportunity-for-introspection/

Donthu, N., & Gustafsson, A. (2020). Effects of COVID-19 on business and research. *Journal of Business Research*, *117*, 284–289. doi:10.1016/j.jbusres.2020.06.008 PMID:32536736

Dorn, F., Fuest, C., Gstrein, D., Peichl, A., & Stöckli, M. (2020, October 12). *Corona-Infektionen und die Dunkelziffer: Vergleichen wir Äpfel mit Birnen?* ifo Institut – Leibniz-Institut für Wirtschaftsforschung an der Universität München e.V. https://www.nordthueringen.de/_daten/mm_objekte/2020/10/607552_1012_97493801.pdf

Doshi, P. (2011). The elusive definition of pandemic influenza. *Bulletin of the World Health Organization*, *89*(7), 532–538. doi:10.2471/BLT.11.086173 PMID:21734768

Doyle, B. (2019). *The Whole-of-Nation and Whole-of-Government Approaches in Action*. Academic Press.

Doyle, A. (2017). Adaptive challenges require adaptive leaders. *Performance Improvement*, *56*(9), 18–26. doi:10.1002/pfi.21735

Drabek, T. E., & McEntire, D. A. (2003). Emergent phenomena and the sociology of disaster: Lessons, trends and opportunities from the research literature. *Disaster Prevention and Management*, *12*(2), 97–112. doi:10.1108/09653560310474214

Duck, J. D. (1998). *Managing Change: The Art of Balancing. Harvard Business Review on Change*. Harvard Business School Press.

Dunleavy, P., Margetts, H., Bastow, S., & Tinkler, J. (2006). New public management is dead—Long live digital-era governance. *Journal of Public Administration: Research and Theory*, *16*(3), 467–494. doi:10.1093/jopart/mui057

Dutton, J., Frost, P., Worline, M., Lilius, J., & Kanov, J. (2002). Leading in Times of Trauma. *Harvard Business Review*, (January), 54–61. PMID:12964467

Duygun, A. (2020). Evaluation of consumers' lifestyles during The COVID-19 pandemic. *Econder Uluslararası Akademik Dergi*, *4*(1), 232–247. doi:10.35342/econder.744621

Dyer, O. (2020). Trump claims public health warnings on covid-19 are a conspiracy against him. *BMJ, 368*, m941.

Eberly, M. B., Johnson, M. D., Hernandez, M., & Avolio, B. J. (2013). An integrative processmodel of leadership: Examining loci, mechanisms, and event cycles. *The American Psychologist*, *68*(6), 427–443. doi:10.1037/a0032244 PMID:23528243

Eckerd, A., & Heidelberg, R. L. (2020). Administering Public Participation. *American Review of Public Administration*, *50*(2), 133–147. doi:10.1177/0275074019871368

Einola, K., & Alvesson, M. (2019). The making and unmaking of teams. *Human Relations*, *72*(12), 1891–1919. doi:10.1177/0018726718812130

Eldor, L., & Harpaz, I. (2016). A process model of employee engagement: The learning climate and its relationship with extra-role performance behaviors. *Journal of Organizational Behavior*, *37*(2), 213–235. doi:10.1002/job.2037

Ellemers, N., De Gilder, D., & Haslam, S. A. (2004). Motivating individuals and groups at work: A social identity perspective on leadership and group performance. *Academy of Management Review*, *29*(3), 459–478. doi:10.5465/amr.2004.13670967

Emmett, J., Schrah, G., Schrimper, M., & Wood, A. (2020). *COVID-19 and the employee experience: How leaders can seize the moment*. Academic Press.

Enochs, J. C. (1981). Up from management. *Phi Delta Kappan*, 175–178.

Eraslan, L. (2004). Liderlikte post-modern bir paradigma: Dönüşümcü liderlik. *Journal of Human Sciences*, *1*(1).

Etzioni, A. (1989). Humble decision-making. *Harvard Business Review*, *67*, 45–57. PMID:10293838

Eufinger, A. (2020). Die COVID-19-Pandemie: Arbeitsrecht im Krankenhaus in bewegten Zeiten. *Medizinrecht: MedR*, 1–8. doi:10.100700350-020-5559-2

Europäische Kommission and Equal Opportunities. Unit E. (2005). The new SME definition: User guide and model declaration. Office for Official Publications of the European Communities.

European Commission. (2018). *Circular economy: Implementation of the Circular Economy Action Plan*. https://ec.europa.eu/environment/circular-economy/index_en.htm

European Commission. (2018). *Digital Transformation Scoreboard 2018: EU businesses go digital: Opportunities, outcomes and uptake*. Publications Office of the European Union.

Facebook Inc. (2015). *Third quarterly earnings 2015 report*. PR Newswire.

Facebook. (2020a). *Hua Ho Job Ad for 300 Positions*. https://www.facebook.com/HuaHoSymbOFFICIAL/photos/pb.123990884417648.-2207520000./1813899762093410/?type=3&theater

Facebook. (2020b). *MOH COVID-19 Awareness Video*. https://www.facebook.com/692035914258111/videos/203051744287275

Farnia, F., & Nafukho, F. M. (2016). Emotional intelligence research within human resource development scholarship. *European Journal of Training and Development*, *40*(2), 90–110. doi:10.1108/EJTD-11-2014-0073

Farooq, A., Laato, S., & Islam, A. N. (2020). Impact of online information on self-isolation intention during the COVID-19 pandemic: Cross-sectional study. *Journal of Medical Internet Research*, *22*(5), e19128. doi:10.2196/19128 PMID:32330115

Fathi, K. (2020). Die multi-resiliente Gesellschaft: Orientierungspunkte für die Corona-Krise und darüber hinaus. *Forschungsjournal Soziale Bewegungen*, *33*(1), 22–36. https://doi.org/10.1515/fjsb-2020-0004

Felber, C. (2019). *Change everything: Creating an economy for the common good*. Zed Books.

Fener, T., & Cevik, T. (2015). Leadership in crisis management: Separation of leadership executive concepts. *Procedia Economics and Finance*, *26*, 695–701. doi:10.1016/S2212-5671(15)00817-5

Feng, Z., & Savani, K. (2020). Covid-19 created a gender gap in perceived work productivity and job satisfaction: Implications for dual-career parents working from home. *Gender in Management*, *35*(7/8), 719–736. doi:10.1108/GM-07-2020-0202

Fernandez, A. A., & Shaw, G. P. (2020). Academic Leadership in a Time of Crisis: The Coronavirus and COVID-19. *The Journal of Leadership Studies*, *14*(1), 39–45. doi:10.1002/jls.21684

Ferrell, O. C., Fraedrich, J., & Ferrell, L. (2015). *Business ethics: Ethical decision making and cases*. Cengage Learning.

Fineberg, H. V. (2014). Pandemic preparedness and response—Lessons from the H1N1 influenza of 2009. *The New England Journal of Medicine*, *370*(14), 1335–1342. doi:10.1056/NEJMra1208802 PMID:24693893

Fishbein, M., & Ajzen, I. (1975). *Belief, attitude, intention and behavior: An introduction to theory and research*. Addison–Wesley.

Fish, J. M. (1992). Discontinuous Change. *Behavior and Social Issues*, *2*(1), 59–70. doi:10.5210/bsi.v2i1.174

Fleishman, E. A. (1953). The description of supervisory behavior. *The Journal of Applied Psychology*, *37*(1), 1–6. doi:10.1037/h0056314 PMID:6038475

Flemons, D. (1991). *Completing distinctions*. Shambala Publications, Inc.

Foerster, M., Henneke, A., Chetty-Mhlanga, S., & Röösli, M. (2019). Impact of adolescents' screen time and nocturnal mobile phone-related awakenings on sleep and general health symptoms: A prospective cohort study. *International Journal of Environmental Research and Public Health*, *16*(3), 518. doi:10.3390/ijerph16030518 PMID:30759792

Forester, J., & McKibbon, G. (2020). Beyond blame: Leadership, collaboration and compassion in the time of COVID-19. *Socio-Ecological Practice Research*, *2*(3), 205–216. doi:10.100742532-020-00057-0

Fowler, M., & Highsmith, J. (2001). The agile manifesto. *Software Development*, *9*(8), 28–35.

Francis, P. (2020). *Fratelli Tutti*. Retrieved from http://www.vatican.va/content/francesco/en/encyclicals/documents/papa-francesco_20201003_enciclica-fratelli-tutti.html

Francisco, C., & Nuqui, A. (2020). *Emergence of a situational leadership during COVID-19 pandemic called New Normal Leadership*. Academic Press.

Francisco, C., & Nuqui, A. (2020). *Emergence of a situational leadership during COVID-19 pandemic called New Normal Leadership. International Journal of Academic Multidisciplinary Research.*

Franzkowiak, P. (2015). *Gesundheitswissenschaften / Public Health*. https://www.leitbegriffe.bzga.de/alphabetisches-verzeichnis/gesundheitswissenschaften-public-health/ https://doi.org/10.17623/BZGA:224-I061-1.0

Galea, S., Merchant, R. M., & Lurie, N. (2020). The mental health consequences of COVID-19 and physical distancing: The need for prevention and early intervention. *JAMA Internal Medicine*, *180*(6), 817–818. doi:10.1001/jamainternmed.2020.1562 PMID:32275292

Gallagher, M. W. (2012). Self-Efficacy. In V. S. Ramachandran (Ed.), *Encyclopedia of Human Behavior* (2nd ed., pp. 314–320). Academic Press., doi:10.1016/B978-0-12-375000-6.00312-8

Gandolfi, F. (2016). *Fundamentals of leadership development*. Executive Master's in Leadership Presentation.

Gandolfi, F., & Stone, S. (2016). Clarifying leadership: High-impact leaders in a time of leadership crisis. *Revista de Management Comparat International*, *17*(3), 212.

Gandolfi, F., & Stone, S. (2018). Leadership, leadership styles, and servant leadership. *Journal of Management Research*, *18*(4), 261–269.

Gao, G., & Sai, L. (2020). Towards a 'virtual'world: Social isolation and struggles during the COVID-19 pandemic as single women living alone. *Gender, Work and Organization*, *27*(5), 754–762. doi:10.1111/gwao.12468

Gardner, W. L., Avolio, B. J., Luthans, F., May, D. R., & Walumbwa, F. (2005). "Can you see the real me?" A self-based model of authentic leader and follower development. *The Leadership Quarterly*, *16*(3), 343–372. doi:10.1016/j.leaqua.2005.03.003

Garg, N. (2017). Workplace spirituality and employee well-being: An empirical exploration. *Journal of Human Values*, *23*(2), 129–147. doi:10.1177/0971685816689741

Gartner. (2020, Apr. 14). Gartner HR survey reveals 41% of employees likely to work remotely at least some of the time post coronavirus pandemic. *News Release*.

Garvey, M. D., & Carnovale, S. (2020). The rippled newsvendor: A new inventory framework for modelling supply chain risk severity in the presence of risk propagation. *International Journal of Production Economics*, *228*, 107752. doi:10.1016/j.ijpe.2020.107752 PMID:32292241

George, B. (2003). *Authentic leadership: Rediscovering the secrets to creating lasting value*. John Wiley & Sons.

Gergs, H. J. (2019). Agilität und Organisationsentwicklung – Ziemlich beste Freunde? *Gruppe. Interaktion. Organisation Zeitschrift für Angewandte Organisationspsychologie*, *50*(2), 101–110.

German Hospital Association. (2020a, September 17). *DKG zum Welttag der Patientensicherheit: Ohne engagierte kompetente Mitarbeiterinnen und Mitarbeiter ist Versorgung nicht möglich* [Press release]. https://www.dkgev.de/dkg/presse/details/ohne-engagierte-kompetente-mitarbeiterinnen-und-mitarbeiter-ist-versorgung-nicht-moeglich/

German Hospital Association. (2020b, October 15). *DKG zu steigenden Infektionszahlen: Krankenhäuser blicken mit Sorge auf die steigende Zahl an Neuinfektionen* [Press release]. https://www.dkgev.de/dkg/presse/details/krankenhaeuser-blicken-mit-sorge-auf-die-steigende-zahl-an-neuinfektionen/

Geurts, S., Rutte, C., & Peeters, M. (1999). Antecedents and consequences of work–home interference among medical residents. *Social Science & Medicine*, *48*(9), 1135–1148. doi:10.1016/S0277-9536(98)00425-0 PMID:10220015

Ghadi, M. Y. (2017). The impact of workplace spirituality on voluntary turnover intentions through loneliness in work. *Journal of Economic and Administrative Sciences*, *33*(1), 81–110. doi:10.1108/JEAS-03-2016-0005

Ghitulescu, B. E. (2013). Making Change Happen: The Impact of Work Context on Adaptive and Proactive Behaviors. *The Journal of Applied Behavioral Science*, *49*(2), 206–245. doi:10.1177/0021886312469254

Gigauri, I. (2020b). Influence of Covid-19 Crisis on Human Resource Management and Companies' Response: The Expert Study. *International Journal of Management Science and Business Administration*, 15-24. doi:10.18775/ijmsba.1849-5664-5419.2014.66.1002

Gigauri, I. (2020a). Effects of covid-19 on human resource management from the perspective of digitalization and work-life-balance. *International Journal of Innovative Technologies in Economy*, *4*(31). Advance online publication. doi:10.31435/rsglobal_ijite/30092020/7148

Gilbert, D. (2006). *Stumbling on happiness*. Knopf.

Gill, R. (2003). Change management – or change leadership? *Journal of Change Management*, *3*(4), 307–318. doi:10.1080/714023845

Giones, F., Brem, A., Pollack, J. M., Michaelis, T. L., Klyver, K., & Brinckmann, J. (2020). Revising entrepreneurial action in response to exogenous shocks: Considering the COVID-19 pandemic. *Journal of Business Venturing Insights*, *14*, e00186. doi:10.1016/j.jbvi.2020.e00186

Girboveanu, S., & Pavel, S. (2010). How to manage a public relations crisis. *Annals of University of Craiova — Economic Sciences Series, 3*(38). Available at http://feaa.ucv.ro/ annals/v3_2010/0038v3-038.pdf

Glöckl, R., Buhr-Schinner, H., Koczulla, A. R., Schipmann, R., Schultz, K., Spielmanns, M., Stenzel, N., & Dewey, S. (2020). Recommendations from the German Respiratory Society for Pulmonary Rehabilitation in Patients with COVID-19. *Pneumologie (Stuttgart, Germany)*, *74*(8). https://doi.org/10.1055/a-1193-9315

Glover, J., Friedman, H., & Jones, G. (2002). Adaptive leadership: When change is not enough (part one). *Organization Development Journal*, *20*(2), 15.

Goldman, Benjamin, & Dixon. (2020). Mental Health Policy in the Era of COVID-19. *Psychiatry On Line*. doi:10.1176/appi.ps.202000219

Goldratt, E. (1999). *Theory of constraints*. North River Press.

Goleman, D. (1998). *Working with emotional intelligence*. Bantam Books.

Gomersall, C. D., Loo, S., Joynt, G. M., & Taylor, B. L. (2007). Pandemic preparedness. *Current Opinion in Critical Care*, *13*(6), 742–747. doi:10.1097/MCC.0b013e3282f1bafd PMID:17975401

Gomez, R., & Fisher, J. W. (2003). Domains of spiritual well-being and development and validation of the Spiritual Well-Being Questionnaire. *Personality and Individual Differences*, *35*(8), 1975–1991. doi:10.1016/S0191-8869(03)00045-X

Good, D. (2014). Predicting real-time adaptive performance in a dynamic decision-making context. *Journal of Management & Organization*, *20*(6), 715–732. doi:10.1017/jmo.2014.54

Good, D. J., Lyddy, C. J., Glomb, T. M., Bono, J. E., Brown, K. W., Duffy, M. K., & Lazar, S. W. (2016). Contemplating mindfulness at work: An integrative review. *Journal of Management*, *42*(1), 114–142. doi:10.1177/0149206315617003

Gostautaite, B., & Buciuniene, I. (2015). The role of work characteristics in enhancing older employees' performance: Evidence from a post-Soviet country. *International Journal of Human Resource Management*, *26*(6), 757–782. doi:10.1080/09585192.2014.949820

Gottfried, R. S. (2010). *Black death*. Simon and Schuster.

Gourinchas, P. O., Kalemli-Özcan, Ş., Penciakova, V., & Sander, N. (2020). *Covid-19 and SME failures (No. w27877)*. National Bureau of Economic Research.

Gräuler, V. (2020). *Organisation einer strukturierten Personalführung im Pandemiefall: Crashkurs Covid-19*. WWU Münster; UKM Trainingszentrum. https://www.divi.de/joomlatools-files/docman-files/publikationen/covid-19-dokumente/Organisation%20Personalnachf%C3%BChrung_final.pdf

Grewal, R., & Tansuhaj, P. (2001). Building organizational capabilities for managing economic crisis: The role of market orientation and strategic flexibility. *Journal of Marketing*, *65*(2), 67–80. doi:10.1509/jmkg.65.2.67.18259

Griffin, A., & Hauser, J. R. (1996). Integrating R&D and marketing: A review and analysis of the literature. *Journal of Product Innovation Management: An International Publication of the Product Development & Management Association*, *13*(3), 191–215. doi:10.1111/1540-5885.1330191

Griffin, B., & Hesketh, B. (2003). Adaptable behaviours for successful work and career adjustment. *Australian Journal of Psychology*, *55*(2), 65–73. doi:10.1080/00049530412331312914

Griffin, B., & Hesketh, B. (2005). Are Conscientious Workers Adaptable? *Australian Journal of Management*, *30*(2), 245–259. doi:10.1177/031289620503000204

Griffin, M. A., Neal, A., & Parker, S. K. (2007). A new model of work role performance: Positive behavior in uncertain and interdependent contexts. *Academy of Management Journal*, *50*(2), 327–347. doi:10.5465/amj.2007.24634438

Griffin, M. A., Parker, S. K., & Mason, C. M. (2010). Leader Vision and the Development of Adaptive and Proactive Performance: A Longitudinal Study. *The Journal of Applied Psychology*, *95*(1), 174–182. doi:10.1037/a0017263 PMID:20085414

Groarke, J. M., Berry, E., Graham-Wisener, L., McKenna-Plumley, P. E., McGlinchey, E., & Armour, C. (2020). Loneliness in the UK during the COVID-19 pandemic: Cross-sectional results from the COVID-19 Psychological Wellbeing Study. *PLoS One*, *15*(9), e0239698. doi:10.1371/journal.pone.0239698 PMID:32970764

Gruber, J., & Trickett, E. J. (1987). Can we empower others? The paradox of empowerment in the governing of an alternative public school. *American Journal of Community Psychology*, *15*(3), 353–371. doi:10.1007/BF00922703

Gruzd, A., & Mai, P. (2020). Going viral: How a single tweet spawned a COVID-19 conspiracy theory on Twitter. *Big Data & Society*, *7*(2). doi:10.1177/2053951720938405

Gutteres, A. (2020). *Climate Change and COVID-19: UN urges nations to 'recover better'*. UN Department of Global Communications. Retrieved August 22, 2020, from https://www.un.org/en/un-coronavirus-communications-team/un-urges-countries-'build-back-better'

Haddon, A., Loughlin, C., & McNally, C. (2015). Leadership in a time of financial crisis: What do we want from our leaders? *Leadership and Organization Development Journal*, *36*(5), 612–637. doi:10.1108/LODJ-12-2013-0166

Hahnen, D., Reichartz, P., Heßling, C., & Markus, S. (2020). Schulentwicklung in Zeiten der Pandemie: Wie eine Berufsfachschule für den Rettungsdienst die Krise als Chance zur Weiterentwicklung nutzt. *Pflegewissenschaft, Sonderausgabe: Die Corona-Pandemie,* (April), 165–169.

Ha, K. M. (2019). Learning or Ignoring Lessons from Natural Disasters. *Journal of Professional Issues in Engineering Education and Practice*, *145*(4), 02519001. doi:10.1061/(ASCE)EI.1943-5541.0000428

Halawi, M. J., Wang, D. D., & Hunt, T. R. III. (2020). What's important: weathering the COVID-19 crisis: time for leadership, vigilance, and Unity. *The Journal of Bone and Joint Surgery. American Volume*, *102*(9), 759–760. doi:10.2106/JBJS.20.00419 PMID:32379115

Halek, M., Reuther, S., & Schmidt, J. (2020). Herausforderungen für die pflegerische Versorgung in der stationären Altenhilfe. *MMW Fortschr Med, 162*(9), 51–53.

Halpin, A. W., & Winer, B. J. (1957). A factorial study of the leader behavior descriptions. In R. M. Stogdill & A. E. Coons (Eds.), Leader behavior: Its description and measurement (pp. 39–51). Columbus, OH: Bureau of Business Research, Ohio State University.

Hamdan, M., & Hoon, C. Y. (2019). Brunei Darussalam: Making strides with a renewed focus on the future. *Southeast Asian Affairs*, *2019*(1), 84–102.

Hameed, A., & Waheed, A. (2011). Employee Development and Its Effect on Employee Performance a Conceptual Framework. *International Journal of Business and Social Science*, *2*, 224–229.

Hamouche, S. (2020). COVID-19 and employees' mental health: Stressors, moderators and agenda for organizational actions. *Emerald Open Research*, *2*, 15. doi:10.35241/emeraldopenres.13550.1

Hamrefors, S. (2010). Communicative leadership. *Journal of Communication Management (London)*, *14*(2), 141–152. doi:10.1108/13632541011034592

Hans Böckler Foundation. (2020). *Arbeitsbedingungen in der Pflege*. https://www.boeckler.de/de/auf-einen-blick-17945-zahlen-und-studien-zum-pflegenotstand-und-wege-hinaus-17962.htm

Han, T. Y., & Williams, K. J. (2008). Multilevel Investigation of Adaptive Performance Individual- and Team-Level Relationships. *Group & Organization Management*, *33*(6), 657–684. doi:10.1177/1059601108326799

Harris, A., & Jones, M. (2020). *COVID 19: School leadership in disruptive times*. Academic Press.

Harter, J. (2020). *Historic drop in Employee engagement follows record rise*. Accessed 15 September 2020. https://www.gallup.com/workplace/313313/historic-drop-employee-engagement-follows-record-rise.aspx#:~:text=It%20was%20 14%25%20in%20June,June%201%2D14%2C%202020

Hartley, K., & Vu, M. K. (2020). Fighting fake news in the COVID-19 era: Policy insights from an equilibrium model. *Policy Sciences*, *53*(4), 735–758. doi:10.100711077-020-09405-z PMID:32921821

Hasan, A., & Rjoub, H. (2017). The role of effective leadership styles in crisis. *International Journal of Economics, Commerce and Management, 5*(4), 107-121.

Hashim, A. A. H. (2010). Challenges in achieving wawasan 2035 goals: Economic diversification in perspective. *CSPS Strategy and Policy Journal*, *1*(1), 29–54.

Haslbeck, K., Schwarz, K., Hohlfeld, J. M., Seume, J. R., & Koch, W. (2010). Submicron droplet formation in the human lung. *Journal of Aerosol Science*, *41*(5), 429–438. https://doi.org/10.1016/j.jaerosci.2010.02.010

Hassan, S., & Jiang, Z. N. (2019). Facilitating learning to improve performance of law enforcement workgroups: The role of inclusive leadership behavior. *International Public Management Journal*, *25*, 1–25. Advance online publication. doi:10.1080/10967494.2019.1680465

Hasseler, M., & Hartleb, B. (n.d.). Stationäre Langzeitpflege unter Covid-19 Bedingungen –: ein reflektiert-kritischer Blick auf die derzeitige Situation und zukünftige Entwicklungen. Pflege in Zeiten der Pandemie.

Hasseler, M., Krebs, S., & Lietz, A. L. (2020). Vertrauens- und kompetenzbasiertes Delegationsmodell in Zeiten von Corona. *Pflegewissenschaft (Sonderausgabe: Die Corona-Pandemie),* 109-111.

Hasseler, M., Lietz, A. L., & Krebs, S. (2020). Delegation im Krisenfall: Entscheidungen erleichtern. *Pflege Zeitschrift*, 6.

Haun, M. W., Hoffmann, M., Tönnies, J., Dinger, U., Hartmann, M., & Friederich, H.-C. (2020). Videokonsultationen durch Psychotherapeuten in Zeiten der COVID-19-Pandemie: Wirksamkeit, Gestaltung des Settings und erste Erfahrungen aus einer Machbarkeitsstudie sowie mit dem Routineangebot im Krankenhaus [Realtime video consultations by psychotherapists in times of the COVID-19 pandemic]. *Psychotherapeut*, 1–6. doi:10.100700278-020-00438-6

Hauschildt, K., & Konradt, U. (2012). Self-leadership and team members' work role performance. *Journal of Managerial Psychology*, *27*(5-6), 497–517. doi:10.1108/02683941211235409

Hayashi, C., & Soo, A. (2012). Adaptive leadership in times of crisis. *Prism*, *4*(1), 78–86.

Heckhausen, H., & Gollwitzer, P. (1987). Thought contents and cognitive functioning in motivational versus volitional states of mind. *Motivation and Emotion*, *11*(2), 101–120. doi:10.1007/BF00992338

He, H., & Harris, L. (2020). The Impact of Covid-19 Pandemic on Corporate Social Responsibility and Marketing Philosophy. *Journal of Business Research, 116*, 176–182. Advance online publication. doi:10.1016/j.jbusres.2020.05.030 PMID:32457556

Heidegger, M. (1954). The question concerning technology. *Technology and values: Essential readings, 99*, 113.

Heifetz, R. A., Grashow, A., & Linsky, M. (2009). *The practice of adaptive leadership: Tools and tactics for changing your organization and the world.* Harvard Business Press.

Heifetz, R. A., & Heifetz, R. (1994). *Leadership without easy answers.* Harvard University Press.

Heifetz, R., Grashow, A., & Linsky, M. (2009). *The Practice of Adaptive Leadership.* Harvard Business School Publishing.

Henricks, M. D., Young, M., & Kehoe, E. J. (2020). Attitudes toward Change and Transformational Leadership: A Longitudinal Study. *Journal of Change Management, 20*(3), 1–18. doi:10.1080/14697017.2020.1758529

Henry, A. (2008). *Understanding Strategic Management.* Oxford University Press.

Herbane, B. (2010). Small business research: Time for a crisis-based view. *International Small Business Journal, 28*(1), 43–64. doi:10.1177/0266242609350804

Herbane, B. (2013). Exploring crisis management in UK small-and medium-sized enterprises. *Journal of Contingencies and Crisis Management, 21*(2), 82–95. doi:10.1111/1468-5973.12006

Hermes, C., & Ochmann, T. (2020). Nursing Division on the current intensive care situation in Germany: Working group of the Nursing Division of the German Society of Medical Intensive Care and Emergency Medicine (DGIIN). *Medizinische Klinik, Intensivmedizin und Notfallmedizin, 115*(6). https://doi.org/10.1007/s00063-020-00705-z

Hertel, G., Geister, S., & Konradt, U. (2005). Managing virtual teams: A review of current empirical research. *Human Resource Management Review, 15*(1), 69–95. doi:10.1016/j.hrmr.2005.01.002

Hidayat, S. E. (2020). *Islamic Economy in ASEAN Countries During the Covid-19 Era.* Academic Press.

Hilbig, B. E., & Zettler, I. (2009). Pillars of cooperation: Honesty humility, social value orientations, and economic behavior. *Journal of Research in Personality, 43*(3), 516–519. doi:10.1016/j.jrp.2009.01.003

Hill, P. C., Pargament, K. I., Hood, R. W., McCullough, J. M. E., Swyers, J. P., Larson, D. B., & Zinnbauer, B. J. (2000). Conceptualizing religion and spirituality: Points of commonality, points of departure. *Journal for the Theory of Social Behaviour, 30*(1), 51–77. doi:10.1111/1468-5914.00119

Hirschfeld, R. R., & Feild, H. S. (2000). Work centrality and work alienation: Distinct aspects of a general commitment to work. *Journal of Organizational Behavior: The International Journal of Industrial. Occupational and Organizational Psychology and Behavior, 21*(7), 789–800. doi:10.1002/1099-1379(200011)21:7<789::AID-JOB59>3.0.CO;2-W

Hitt, M., Keats, B., & DeMarie, S. (1998). Navigating in the new competitive landscape: Building strategic flexibility and competitive advantage in the 21st century. *The Academy of Management Executive, 12*(4), 22–42. doi:10.5465/ame.1998.1333922

HKEx. (2020). *News Centre.* Retrieved November 14, 2020, from https://www.hkex.com.hk/News/News-Centre?sc_lang=en

Hoch, J. E., Bommer, W. H., Dulebohn, J. H., & Wu, D. (2016). Do ethical, authentic, and servant leadership explain variance above and beyond transformational leadership? A meta-analysis. *Journal of Management, 44*(2), 501–529. doi:10.1177/0149206316665461

Hoe, S. L. (2007). Is interpersonal trust a necessary condition for organisational learning? *Journal of Organisational Transformation & Social Change*, *4*(2), 149–156. doi:10.1386/jots.4.2.149_1

Hogan, R., & Hogan, J. (2007). *Hogan Personality Inventory Manual* (3rd ed.). Hogan Assessment Systems.

Hollaus, S. (2020). *Pflege-Berufsaussteiger kommen in der Corona-Krise zurück – und nun? - Marktforschung*. https://newsroom.psyma.com/de/themen/pflegemarktforschung/pflege-berufsaussteiger-kommen-in-der-corona-krise-zurueck-und-nun/

Hollenbeck, J. R., Beersma, B., & Schouten, M. E. (2012). Beyond team types and taxonomies: A dimensional scaling conceptualization for team description. *Academy of Management Review*, *37*(1), 82–106.

Holt-Lunstad, J., Smith, T. B., Baker, M., Harris, T., & Stephenson, D. (2015). Loneliness and Social Isolation as Risk Factors for Mortality: A Meta-Analytic Review. *Perspectives on Psychological Science*, *10*(2), 227–237. doi:10.1177/1745691614568352 PMID:25910392

Holt, S., & Marques, J. (2012). Empathy in Leadership: Appropriate or Misplaced? An Empirical Study on a Topic That is Asking for Attention. *Journal of Business Ethics*, *105*(1), 95–105. doi:10.100710551-011-0951-5

Hong, P., Huang, C., & Li, B. (2012). Crisis management for SMEs: Insights from a multiple-case study. *International Journal of Business Excellence*, *5*(5), 535–553. doi:10.1504/IJBEX.2012.048802

Horná, P. T. (2020). The Post-COVID-19 Challenges in ethical leadership. *Journal of Global Science*.

House, R. (1971). A Path Goal Theory of Leader Effectiveness. *Administrative Science Quarterly*, *16*(3), 321–339. doi:10.2307/2391905

Houser, D., Levy, D. M., Padgitt, K., Peart, S. J., & Xiao, E. (2014). Raising the price of talk: An experimental analysis of transparent leadership. *Journal of Economic Behavior & Organization*, *105*, 208–218. doi:10.1016/j.jebo.2014.05.003

Hower, K. I., Pförtner, T.-K., & Pfaff, H. (2020). *Pflegerische Versorgung in Zeiten von Corona -Drohender Systemkollaps oder normaler Wahnsinn? Wissenschaftliche Studie zu Herausforderungen und Belastungen aus der Sichtweise von Leitungskräften*. https://kups.ub.uni-koeln.de/11201/1/Pflegerische%20Versorgung%20in%20Zeiten%20von%20Corona_Ergebnisbericht.pdf

Hsu, E. B., Li, Y., Bayram, J. D., Levinson, D., Yang, S., & Monahan, C. (2013). State of virtual reality based disaster preparedness and response training. *PLoS Currents*, •••, 5. doi:10.1371/currents.dis.1ea2b2e71237d5337fa53982a38b2aff PMID:23653102

Huang, J. L., Ryan, A. M., Zabel, K. L., & Palmer, A. (2014). Personality and Adaptive Performance at Work: A Meta-Analytic Investigation. *The Journal of Applied Psychology*, *99*(1), 162–179. doi:10.1037/a0034285 PMID:24016205

Hughes, M. (2007). *The leadership of organizational change*. Routledge.

Hultink, E. J., & Atuahene-Gima, K. (2000). The effect of sales force adoption on new product selling performance. *Journal of Product Innovation Management*, *17*(6), 435–450. doi:10.1111/1540-5885.1760435

Hunt, D. (2020). *A publication from the Association of Chiefs and Leaders of General Internal Medicine*. ACLGIM.

Hunt, J. G. J., Osborn, R. N., & Boal, K. B. (2009). The architecture of managerial leadership: Stimulation and channeling of organizational emergence. *The Leadership Quarterly*, *20*(4), 503–516. doi:10.1016/j.leaqua.2009.04.010

Husbands, C. (2020). *Leading, learning and lockdown: first thoughts on lessons for leadership from the coronavirus crisis*. Sheffield Hallam University.

Hwang, T. J., Rabheru, K., Peisah, C., Reichman, W., & Ikeda, M. (2020). Loneliness and Social Isolation during the COVID-19 Pandemic. *International Psychogeriatrics*, 1–15. PMID:32450943

Ibrar, M., & Khan, O. (2015). The Impact of Reward on Employee Performance (A Case Study of Malakand Private School). *International Letters of Social and Humanistic Sciences*, *52*, 95–103. . doi:10.18052/www.scipress.com/ILSHS.52.95

ifo Institut. (2020a). *Corona-Krise: Anzahl der Kurzarbeiter in Deutschland nach Sektoren im Juli 2020* [Press release]. https://www.ifo.de/node/57307

ifo Institut. (2020b). *Sonderfragen im 2. Quartal 2020: Homeoffice und Digitalisierung unter Corona*. https://www.ifo.de/personalleiterbefragung/202008-q2

Ingham, A. G., Levinger, G., Graves, J., & Peckham, V. (1974). The Ringelmann effect: Studies of group size and group performance. *Journal of Experimental Social Psychology*, *10*(4), 371–384. doi:10.1016/0022-1031(74)90033-X

Issa, H., & Jaleel, E. (2020). Social isolation and psychological wellbeing: Lessons from Covid-19. *Management Science Letters*, *11*(2), 609–618.

Ivanov, D. (2020). Predicting the impacts of epidemic outbreaks on global supply chains: A simulation-based analysis on the coronavirus outbreak (COVID-19/SARS-CoV-2) case. *Transportation Research Part E, Logistics and Transportation Review*, *136*, 101922. doi:10.1016/j.tre.2020.101922 PMID:32288597

Jäckel, A. (2018). *Gesundes Vertrauen in Organisationen*. Springer Fachmedien Wiesbaden. doi:10.1007/978-3-658-19253-2

Jacobs, K., Kuhlmey, A., Greß, S., Klauber, J., & Schwinger, A. (2020). *Pflege-Report 2019*. Springer Berlin Heidelberg. doi:10.1007/978-3-662-58935-9

Jajja, M. S. S., Kannan, V. R., Brah, S. A., & Hassan, S. Z. (2017). Linkages between firm innovation strategy, suppliers, product innovation, and business performance. *International Journal of Operations & Production Management*, *37*(8), 1054–1075. doi:10.1108/IJOPM-09-2014-0424

James, E. H., & Wooten, L. P. (2010). *Leading under pressure: From surviving to thriving before, during, and after a crisis*. Routledge Academic.

James, E. H., Wooten, L. P., & Dushek, K. (2011). Crisis management: Informing a new leadership research agenda. *The Academy of Management Annals*, *5*(1), 455–493. doi:10.5465/19416520.2011.589594

Janssens, U., Schlitt, A., Hein, A., Salzberger, B., Grill, E., Kaduszkiewicz, H., Platz, T., Rossaint, R., Böttiger, B. W., Dietz, A., Borucki, K., Fickenscher, H., Al-Nawas, B., Marini, A., Kersten, A., & Stemmer, R. (2020). *SARS-CoV-2 Infektion bei Mitarbeiterinnen und Mitarbeitern im Gesundheitswesen – Bedeutung der RT-PCR Testung*. https://www.awmf.org/uploads/tx_szleitlinien/040-015l_S1_SARS-CoV-2-Infektion-im-Gesundheitswesen%E2%80%93RT-PCR_2020-09_2.pdf

Jindo, T., Kai, Y., Kitano, N., Tsunoda, K., Nagamatsu, T., & Arao, T. (2020). Relationship of workplace exercise with work engagement and psychological distress in employees: A cross-sectional study from the MYLS study. *Preventive Medicine Reports*, *17*, 101030. doi:10.1016/j.pmedr.2019.101030 PMID:31890476

Ji, Y., Qian, H., Ye, J., & Zheng, X. (2018). The impact of ambient humidity on the evaporation and dispersion of exhaled breathing droplets: A numerical investigation. *Journal of Aerosol Science*, *115*, 164–172. https://doi.org/10.1016/j.jaerosci.2017.10.009

Joelle, M., & Coelho, A. M. (2019). The impact of spirituality at work on workers' attitudes and individual performance. *International Journal of Human Resource Management*, *30*(7), 1111–1135. doi:10.1080/09585192.2017.1314312

Joensen, L. E., Madsen, K. P., Holm, L., Nielsen, K. A., Rod, M. H., Petersen, A. A., Rod, N. H., & Willaing, I. (2020). Diabetes and COVID-19: Psychosocial consequences of the COVID-19 pandemic in people with diabetes in Denmark—what characterizes people with high levels of COVID-19-related worries? *Diabetic Medicine*, *37*(7), 1146–1154. doi:10.1111/dme.14319 PMID:32392380

Johansson, C., Miller, V. D., & Hamrin, S. (2014). Conceptualizing Communicative Leadership. *Corporate Communications*, *2*(2), 147–165. doi:10.1108/CCIJ-02-2013-0007

Jurisch, M. C., Rosenberg, Z., & Krcmar, H. (2016). Emergent risks in business process change projects. *Business Process Management Journal*, *22*(4), 791–811. doi:10.1108/BPMJ-01-2015-0002

Jurkiewicz, C. L., & Giacalone, R. A. (2004). A values framework for measuring the impact of workplace spirituality on organizational performance. *Journal of Business Ethics*, *49*(2), 129–142. doi:10.1023/B:BUSI.0000015843.22195.b9

Kahn, W. A. (1990). Psychological conditions of personal engagement and disengagement at work. *Academy of Management Journal*, *33*(4), 692–724.

Kanten, P., Kanten, S., & Gurlek, M. (2015). The effects of organizational structures and learning organization on job embeddedness and individual adaptive performance. In A. I. Iacob (Ed.), *2nd Global Conference on Business, Economics, Management and Tourism* (Vol. 23, pp. 1358-1366). 10.1016/S2212-5671(15)00523-7

Kant, N. (2020). Climate Strategy Proactivity (CSP) and its Theoretical Underpinnings. In W. L. Filho, A. M. Azul, L. Brandli, A. L. Salvia, & T. Wall (Eds.), *Industry, Innovation and Infrastructure, Encyclopedia of the UN Sustainable Development Goals (Living Reference). Switzerland AG: Springer Nature.*

Kant, N., & Anjali, K. (2020). Climate Strategy Proactivity (CSP): A Stakeholders-Centric Concept. In W. L. Filho, A. M. Azul, L. Brandli, A. L. Salvia, & T. Wall (Eds.), *Partnerships for the Goals, Encyclopedia of the UN Sustainable Development Goals (Living Reference). Switzerland AG: Springer Nature.* doi:10.1007/978-3-319-71067-9_121-1

Kanungo, R. N. (1979). The concepts of alienation and involvement revisited. *Psychological Bulletin Journal*, *86*(1), 119–138. doi:10.1037/0033-2909.86.1.119

Kapucu, N., & Van Wart, M. (2008). Making Matters Worse: An Anatomy of Leadership Failures in Managing Catastrophic Events. *Administration & Society*, *40*(7), 711–740. doi:10.1177/0095399708323143

Karakas, F. (2010). Spirituality and performance in organizations: A literature review. *Journal of Business Ethics*, *94*(1), 89–106. doi:10.100710551-009-0251-5

Karau, S. J., & Williams, K. D. (1993). Social loafing: A meta-analytic review and theoretical integration. *Journal of Personality and Social Psychology*, *65*(4), 681–706. doi:10.1037/0022-3514.65.4.681

Karunathilake, K. (2020). Positive and negative impacts of COVID - 19, an analysis with special reference to challenges on the supply chain in South Asian countries. *Journal of Social and Economic Development*. Advance online publication. doi:10.100740847-020-00107-z

Kashdan, T., Afram, A., Brown, K., Birnbeck, M., & Drvoshanov, M. (2012). Curiosity enhances the role mindfulness in reducing defensive responses to existential threat. *Personality and Individual Differences*, *50*(8), 1227–1232. doi:10.1016/j.paid.2011.02.015

Katz, J. H., & Miller, F. A. (2013). *Opening doors to teamwork and collaboration: 4 keys that change everything*. Berrett-Koehler Publishers.

Kauffeld, S. (2019). Einführung in die Arbeits-, Organisations- und Personalpsychologie. In S. Kauffeld (Ed.), *Arbeits-, Organisations- und Personalpsychologie für Bachelor* (2nd ed., pp. 1–20). Springer. doi:10.1007/978-3-662-56013-6_1

Kauffeld, S., & Maier, G. W. (2020). Schöne digitale Arbeitswelt: Chancen, Risiken und Herausforderungen. *Gr Interakt Org, 51*(3), 255–258. doi:10.100711612-020-00532-y

Kaufman, R. (2010). From myths to creating a new future: A crisis is a terrible thing to waste. *Performance Improvement, 49*(2), 37–44. doi:10.1002/pfi.20125

Kaup, S., Jain, R., Shivalli, S., Pandey, S., & Kaup, S. (2020). Sustaining academics during COVID-19 pandemic: The role of remote teaching-learning. *Indian Journal of Ophthalmology, 68*(6), 1220. doi:10.4103/ijo.IJO_1241_20 PMID:32461490

Kaushik, M., & Guleria, N. (2020). Employee Relations and Engagement during COVID-19. *Sparkling International Journal of Multidisciplinary Research Studies, 3*(2), 1–11.

Kaushik, M., & Guleria, N. (2020). The Impact of Pandemic COVID-19 in Workplace. *European Journal of Business and Management, 12*(15), 1–10.

Keast, R. (2011). Joined-up governance in Australia: How the past can inform the future. *International Journal of Public Administration, 34*(4), 221–231. doi:10.1080/01900692.2010.549799

Kedia, S., Sinha, R., Pandey, R., Bhattacharjya, S., Syiemlieh, J. D., Chaudhury, S., . . . Bajpai, N. (2020). Greening Post COVID-19 Economic Recovery in India: A Case for Green Fiscal Stimulus. Academic Press.

Keelery, S. (2020). *India – estimated economic impact of COVID-19 by sector 2020 | Statista*. Statista. Available at: www.statista.com/statistics/1107798/india-estimated-economic-impact-of-coronavirus-by-sector/

Keen, S. (1991). *Telling Your Story* [audiotape]. New York: Sound Horizons Audio Video.

Kelly, S., & MacDonald, P. (2019). A look at leadership styles and workplace solidarity communication. *International Journal of Business Communication, 56*(3), 432–448. doi:10.1177/2329488416664176

Kemp, S. (2019). *Global Digital Report 2019-We Are Social*. We Are Social.

Keshavarz, M., &Mohammadi, R. (2011). Occupational stress and Organizational performance, Case study: Iran. *Procedia - Social AndBehavioral Sciences, 30*, 390-394. doi:10.1016/j.sbspro.2011.10.077

Kettl, D. F. (2016). *Politics of the administrative process*. Cq Press.

Khadke, K., & Gershenson, J. K. (2008). Technology-driven product platform development. *International Journal of Product Development, 6*(3-4), 353–374. doi:10.1504/IJPD.2008.020400

Kia, N., Halvorsen, B., & Bartram, T. (2019). Ethical leadership and employee in-role performance. *Personnel Review, 48*(7), 1716–1733. doi:10.1108/PR-12-2018-0514

Kienast, V. (2020). Zweifel & Angst. *Procare: das forbildungsmagazin fur pflegeberufe, 25*(4), 1. doi:10.100700735-020-1183-7

Kim, E., Beckman, S. L., & Agogino, A. (2018). Design roadmapping in an uncertain world: Implementing a customer-experience-focused strategy. *California Management Review, 61*(1), 43–70. doi:10.1177/0008125618796489

King, N. (2012). *Doing template analysis. Qualitative organizational research: Core*. Academic Press.

Kirchmeyer, C. (1992). Perceptions of nonwork-to-work spillover: Challenging the common view of conflict-ridden domain relationships. *Basic and Applied Social Psychology, 13*(2), 231–249. doi:10.120715324834basp1302_7

Kleinschmidt, E. J., De Brentani, U., & Salomo, S. (2007). Performance of global new product development programs: A resource-based view. *Journal of Product Innovation Management, 24*(5), 419–441. doi:10.1111/j.1540-5885.2007.00261.x

Klingborg, D., Moore, D., & Varea-Hammond, S. (2006). What Is Leadership? *Journal of Veterinary Medical Education*, *33*(2), 280–283. doi:10.3138/jvme.33.2.280 PMID:16849311

Klös, H.-P. (2020). *Nach dem Corona-Schock: Digitalisierungspotenziale für Deutschland* (IW-Policy Paper 14/2020). https://www.econstor.eu/handle/10419/219033

Kluge, S., Janssens, U., Welte, T., Weber-Carstens, S., Marx, G., & Karagiannidis, C. (2020b). Empfehlungen zur intensivmedizinischen Therapie von Patienten mit COVID-19 [Recommendations for critically ill patients with COVID-19]. *Medizinische Klinik, Intensivmedizin und Notfallmedizin.* Advance online publication. doi:10.100700063-020-00674-3

Kluge, S., Janssens, U., Welte, T., Weber-Carstens, S., Marx, G., & Karagiannidis, C. (2020a). Empfehlungen zur intensivmedizinischen Therapie von Patienten mit COVID-19 [Recommendations for critically ill patients with COVID-19]. *Medizinische Klinik, Intensivmedizin und Notfallmedizin*, *115*(3), 175–177. https://doi.org/10.1007/s00063-020-00674-3

Kniffin, K. M., Narayanan, J., Anseel, F., Antonakis, J., Ashford, S. J., Bakker, A. B., ... Creary, S. J. (2020). *COVID-19 and the workplace: Implications, issues, and insights for future research and action*. Academic Press.

Koh, W. C., Naing, L., & Wong, J. (2020). Estimating the impact of physical distancing measures in containing COVID-19: An empirical analysis. *International Journal of Infectious Diseases*, *100*, 42–49. doi:10.1016/j.ijid.2020.08.026 PMID:32800859

Kolditz, T. A., & Brazil, D. M. (2005). Authentic Leadership in In Extremis Settings: A Concept for Extraordinary Leaders in Exceptional Situations. In Monographs in Leadership and Management. Authentic Leadership Theory and Practice: Origins, Effects and Development. Elsevier.

Kolditz, T. A. (2005). The in Extremis Leader. In *Leader to leader* (pp. 6–18). John Wiley.

Kortmann, B., & Schulze, G. G. (2020). *Jenseits von Corona: Unsere Welt nach der Pandemie - Perspektiven aus der Wissenschaft. X-Texte zu Kultur und Gesellschaft*. Transcipt Verlag.

Kotter, J. P. (2015). *Leading change: Wie Sie Ihr Unternehmen in acht Schritten erfolgreich verändern* (W. Seidenschwarz, Trans.). Vahlen.

Kotter, J. P. (1995). Leading Change: Why Tranformation Efforts Fail. *Harvard Business Review*, *73*(2), 59–67.

Kotter, J. P. (1996). *Leading change*. Harvard Business School Press.

Kouzes, O., & Posner, B. (1995). *The leadership challenge*. Jossey-Bass.

Kozasa, E. H., Sato, J. R., Lacerda, S. S., Barreiros, M. A., Radvany, J., Russell, T. A., & Amaro, E. Jr. (2012). Meditation training increases brain efficiency in an attention task. *NeuroImage*, *59*(1), 745–749. doi:10.1016/j.neuroimage.2011.06.088 PMID:21763432

Kramer, S. J., & Amabile, T. M. (2011). The Progress Principle: Using Small Wins to Ignite Joy, Engagement, and Creativity at Work. Harvard Business School Press Books.

Kramer, A., & Kramer, K. Z. (2020). The potential impact of the Covid-19 pandemic on occupational status, work from home, and occupational mobility. *Journal of Vocational Behavior*, *119*, 103442. doi:10.1016/j.jvb.2020.103442 PMID:32390661

Kraus, S., Clauss, T., Breier, M., Gast, J., Zardini, A., & Tiberius, V. (2020). The economics of COVID-19: Initial empirical evidence on how family firms in five European countries cope with the corona crisis. *International Journal of Entrepreneurial Behaviour & Research*, *26*(5), 1067–1092. doi:10.1108/IJEBR-04-2020-0214

Kropp, C. (2020). *Pandemien, globaler Umweltwandel und ‚smarte' Risikopolitik: Chancen für Wandel?* Advance online publication. doi:10.17879/SUN-2020-2943

Kuester, S., Homburg, C., & Hess, S. C. (2012). Externally directed and internally directed market launch management: The role of organizational factors in influencing new product success. *Journal of Product Innovation Management, 29*, 38–52. doi:10.1111/j.1540-5885.2012.00968.x

Kumar. (2020). *Impact of COVID-19 on Higher Education.* Retrieved on Dec 5, 2020 from https://www.highereducationdigest.com/impact-of-covid-19-on-higher-education

Laconi, S., Tricard, N., & Chabrol, H. (2015). Differences between specific and generalized problematic Internet uses according to gender, age, time spent online and psychopathological symptoms. *Computers in Human Behavior, 48*, 236–244. doi:10.1016/j.chb.2015.02.006

Lagowska, U., Sobral, F., & Furtado, L. M. G. P. (2020). Leadership under crises: A research agenda for the post-COVID-19 era. *BAR - Brazilian Administration Review, 17*(2), e200062. doi:10.1590/1807-7692bar2020200062

Laloux, F. (2014). *Reinventing organizations: A guide to creating organizations inspired by the next stage in human consciousness.* Nelson Parker.

Lambrecht, O., & Baars, C. (2020, October 14). Corona-Pandemie: Mehr Covid-19-Patienten in Kliniken. *Tagesschau. De.* https://www.tagesschau.de/inland/corona-kliniken-107.html

Lam, L. W., & Lau, D. C. (2012). Feeling lonely at work: Investigating the consequences of unsatisfactory workplace relationships. *International Journal of Human Resource Management, 23*(20), 4265–4282. doi:10.1080/09585192.2012.665070

Landsbergis, P., Dobson, M., LaMontagne, A., Choi, B., Schnall, P., & Baker, D. (2017). *Occupational and Environmental Health.* Oxford Scholarship Online. doi:10.1093/oso/9780190662677.001.0001

Lane, J. E. (2000). *New public management.* Taylor & Francis US.

Lant, T. K., & Mezias, S. J. (1990). Managing discontinuous change: A simulation study of organizational learning and entrepreneurship. *Strategic Management Journal*, 147–179.

Laub, J. A. (1999). *Assessing the servant organization: Development of the servant organizational leadership assessment (SOLA) instrument* (Doctoral Dissertation). Florida Atlantic University.

Lazenby, J. M. (2010). On" spirituality,"" religion," and" religions": A concept analysis. *Palliative & Supportive Care, 8*(4), 469–476. doi:10.1017/S1478951510000374 PMID:20875214

Lee, S. J., Venkataraman, S., Heim, G. R., Roth, A. V., & Chilingerian, J. (2020). Impact of the value-based purchasing program on hospital operations outcomes: An econometric analysis. *Journal of Operations Management, 66*(1–2), 151–175. doi:10.1002/joom.1057

Leiter, M. P., & Durup, M. J. (1996). Work, home, and in-between: A longitudinal study of spillover. *The Journal of Applied Behavioral Science, 32*(1), 29–47. doi:10.1177/0021886396321002

Lencioni, P. (2012). *The advantage: Why organizational health trumps everything else in business.* Jossey-Bass.

LePine, J. A., Colquitt, J. A., & Erez, A. (2000). Adaptability to changing task contexts: Effects of general cognitive ability conscientiousness, and openness to experience. *Personnel Psychology, 53*(3), 563–593. doi:10.1111/j.1744-6570.2000.tb00214.x

Lerbinger, O. (2012). *The crisis manager: Facing disasters, conflicts, and failures.* Routledge. doi:10.4324/9780203222133

Lesch, W., & Schütt, A. (2017). *Gesundheitsforschung kommunizieren, Stakeholder Engagement gestalten*. Medizinisch Wissenschaftliche Verlagsgesellschaft. doi:10.32745/9783954663637

Lettieri, E., Masella, C., & Radaelli, G. (2009). Disaster management: Findings from a systematic review. Disaster Prev. Manag. *International Journal (Toronto, Ont.)*, *18*(2), 117–136. doi:10.1108/09653560910953207

Lichtenstein, B. B., & Plowman, D. A. (2009). The leadership of emergence: A complex systems leadership theory of emergence at successive organizational levels. *The Leadership Quarterly*, *20*(4), 617–630. doi:10.1016/j.leaqua.2009.04.006

Li, J., Ghosh, R., & Nachmias, S. (2020). A special issue on the impact of the COVID-19 pandemic on work, worker, and workplace!? Implications for HRD research and practices in time of crisis. *Human Resource Development International*, *23*(4), 329–332. doi:10.1080/13678868.2020.1780715

Likert, R. (1961). *New patterns of management*. McGraw-Hill.

Lin, C., & Zheng, B. (2015). Teaching practices and teacher perceptions in online world language courses. *Journal of Online Learning Research*, *1*(3), 275–304.

Liu, L., Li, Y., Nielsen, P. V., Wei, J., & Jensen, R. L. (2017). Short-range airborne transmission of expiratory droplets between two people. *Indoor Air*, *27*(2). https://doi.org/10.1111/ina.12314

Liu, S. L., Saif, L. J., Weiss, S. R., & Su, L. (2020). No credible evidence supporting claims of the laboratory engineering of SARS-CoV-2. *Emerging Microbes & Infections*, *9*(1), 505–507. doi:10.1080/22221751.2020.1733440 PMID:32102621

Lloyd, S. A., Byrne, M. M., & McCoy, T. S. (2012). Faculty-perceived barriers of online education. *Journal of Online Learning and Teaching*, *8*(1).

Lockwood, N. R. (2005). Crisis management in today's business environment: HR's strategic role. *HR Magazine*, *50*(12), 1-10.

Long, B. (2020b). Mindfulness and Use of Self Better Together. *Organization Development Review*, *52*(1).

Long, B. (2019). *Mindfulness and Leadership: The Lived Experience of Long-term Mindfulness Practitioners*. Proquest Dissertations.

Long, B. (2020a). The Universe's Doorway: Long-Term Mindfulness as a Way to Leadership. In D. Satinder (Ed.), *The Routledge Companion to Mindfulness at Work*. Routledge.

Lopes Morrison, R. (2005). *Informal relationships in the workplace: Associations with job satisfaction, organisational commitment and turnover intentions* (Doctoral dissertation). Massey University.

Lopez, B. (2019). *Horizon*. Random House Canada.

Lowry, S. T. (1995). The Ancient Greek Administrative Tradition and Human Capital. *Archives of Economic History*, *6*(1).

Lucas, H. C. Jr, & Palley, M. A. (1986). Plant management, the locus of decision making, and the information services department. *Journal of Management Information Systems*, *3*(3), 34–48. doi:10.1080/07421222.1986.11517769

Lundin, R. A., & Söderholm, A. (1995). A Theory of the Temporary Organization. *Scandinavian Journal of Management*, *11*(4), 437–450. doi:10.1016/0956-5221(95)00036-U

Luthans, F., Luthans, K. W., & Luthans, B. C. (2004). Positive psychological capital: Beyond human and social capital. *Business Horizons*, *47*(1), 45–50. doi:10.1016/j.bushor.2003.11.007

Lutz, A., Slagter, H. A., Dunne, J. D., & Davidson, R. J. (2008). Attention regulation and monitoring in meditation. *Trends in Cognitive Sciences*, *12*(4), 163–169. doi:10.1016/j.tics.2008.01.005 PMID:18329323

Lvina, E. (2015). The Role of Cross-Cultural Communication Competence: Effective Transformational Leadership Across Cultures. *Jurnal Ilmiah Peuradeun*, *3*(1), 1–18.

Lykins, E. L., & Baer, R. A. (2009). Psychological functioning in a sample of long-term practitioners of mindfulness meditation. *Journal of Cognitive Psychotherapy*, *23*(3), 226–241. doi:10.1891/0889-8391.23.3.226

Lyons, B., & Henderson, K. (2005). Opinion leadership in a computer-mediated environment. *Journal of Consumer Behaviour*, *4*(5), 319–329. doi:10.1002/cb.22

MacDonald, P., Kelly, S., & Christen, S. (2014). A path model of workplace solidarity, satisfaction, burnout, and motivation. *International Journal of Business Communication*, *52*, 1–19. doi:10.1177/2329488414525467

Madhav, N., Oppenheim, B., Gallivan, M., Mulembakani, P., Rubin, E., & Wolfe, N. (2017). *Pandemics: risks, impacts, and mitigation*. Academic Press.

-Maher Negm, H. (2020). Could COVID-19 improve psychiatric awareness at the heart of the Middle East?- A personal reflection on Bahrain' response. *Irish Journal of Psychological Medicine*, 1-8. doi:10.1017/IOMC.2020.74

Mair, M. (1988). Psychology as storytelling. *International Journal of Personal Construct Psychology*, *1*(2), 125–138. doi:10.1080/10720538808412771

Mak, H.-Y., & Shen, Z.-J. (2012). Risk diversification and risk pooling in supply chain design. *IIE Transactions*, *44*(8), 603–621. doi:10.1080/0740817X.2011.635178

Malecki, K., Keating, J. A., & Safdar, N. (2020). Crisis communication and public perception of COVID-19 risk in the era of social media. *Clinical Infectious Diseases*, ciaa758. doi:10.1093/cid/ciaa758 PMID:32544242

Malhotra, Y. (1997). Knowledge management in inquiring organizations. *Proceedings of 3rd Americas Conference on Information Systems, August*, 293-295.

Mariner, W. K., Annas, G. J., & Parmet, W. E. (2009). Pandemic preparedness: A return to the rule of law. *Drexel L. Rev.*, *1*, 341.

Marinoni, G., Van't Land, H., & Jensen, T. (2020). *The impact of Covid-19 on higher education around the world.* IAU Global Survey Report.

Marshall, R., & Gitosudarmo, I. (1995). Variation in the characteristics of opinion leaders across cultural borders. *Journal of International Consumer Marketing*, *8*(1), 5–22. doi:10.1300/J046v08n01_02

Martin, M. V., & Ishii, K. (2002). Design for variety: Developing standardized and modularized product platform architectures. *Research in Engineering Design*, *13*(4), 213–235. doi:10.100700163-002-0020-2

Marx, K. (1978). Speech at the anniversary of the people's power. In R. C. Tucker (Ed.), *The Marx-Engels Reader* (pp. 577–578). W.W. Norton & Company, Inc. (Original work published 1856)

Mascarenhas, O. A., Kesavan, R., & Bernacchi, M. (2004). Customer value-chain involvement for co-creating customer delight. *Journal of Consumer Marketing*, *21*(7), 486–496. doi:10.1108/07363760410568707

Maslow, A. (1954). *A theory of human motivation: The goals of work. The Future of Work.* Prentice-Hall.

Mas-Machuca, M., Berbegal-Mirabent, J., & Alegre, I. (2016). Work-life balance and its relationship with organizational pride and job satisfaction. *Journal of Managerial Psychology*, *31*(2), 586–602. doi:10.1108/JMP-09-2014-0272

Mata, J., Wenz, A., Rettig, T., Reifenscheid, M., Moehring, K., Krieger, U., ... Naumann, E. (2020). *Health behaviors and mental health before and during the COVID-19 pandemic: A longitudinal population-based survey*. Academic Press.

Matias, T., Dominski, F. H., & Marks, D. F. (2020.). Human needs in COVID-19 isolation. *Journal of Health Psychology, 1*, 12. PMID:32375564

Mat, N. F. C., Edinur, H. A., Razab, M. K. A. A., & Safuan, S. (2020). A single mass gathering resulted in massive transmission of COVID-19 infections in Malaysia with further international spread. *Journal of Travel Medicine*. PMID:32307549

May, D. R., Gilson, R. L., & Harter, L. M. (2004). The psychological conditions fmeaningfulness, safety and availability and the engagement of the human spirit at work. *Journal of Occupational and Organizational Psychology, 7*(7), 11–37. doi:10.1348/096317904322915892

May, R. (1991). *The cry for myth*. Norton.

Mazzucato, M., & Kattel, R. (2020). COVID-19 and Public-sector Capacity. *Oxford Review of Economic Policy, 36*(Supplement_1), S256–S269. doi:10.1093/oxrep/graa031

McArthur-Blair, J., & Cockell, J. (2019). *Helping Organizations Deal with Despair*. Retrieved from https://trainingmag.com/helping-organizations-deal-despair/

McClelland, D. C. (1987). *Human motivation*. CUP Archive.

McConnell, A., & Drennan, L. (2006). Mission Impossible? Planning and Preparing for Crisis. *Journal of Contingencies and Crisis Management, 14*(2), 59–70. doi:10.1111/j.1468-5973.2006.00482.x

McDaniel, R. R. Jr. (1997). Strategic leadership: A view from quantum and chaos theories. *Health Care Management Review, 22*(1), 21–37. doi:10.1097/00004010-199724000-00003 PMID:9058085

McElroy, J. C., Hendrickson, A. R., Townsend, A. M., & DeMarie, S. M. (2007). Dispositional factors in internet use: Personality versus cognitive style. *Management Information Systems Quarterly, 31*(4), 809–820. doi:10.2307/25148821

McKechnie, A. C., Johnson, K. A., Baker, M. J., Docherty, S. L., Leuthner, S. R., & Thoyre, S. (2020). Adaptive leadership in parents caring for their children born with life-threatening conditions. *Journal of Pediatric Nursing, 53*, 41–51. doi:10.1016/j.pedn.2020.03.018 PMID:32438191

McKee, A., & Massimilian, D. (2006). Resonant leadership: A new kind of leadership for the digital age. *The Journal of Business Strategy, 27*(5), 45–49. doi:10.1108/02756660610692707

McMenamin, J. P. (2009). Pandemic Influenza: Is There a Corporate Duty to Prepare. *Food and Drug Law Journal, 64*, 69. PMID:19998573

McNally, R. C., Cavusgil, E., & Calantone, R. J. (2010). Product innovativeness dimensions and their relationships with product advantage, product financial performance, and project protocol. *Journal of Product Innovation Management, 27*(7), 991–1006. doi:10.1111/j.1540-5885.2010.00766.x

Melnyk, S. A., Davis, E. W., Spekman, R. E., & Sandor, J. (2010). Outcome-driven supply chains. *MIT Sloan Management Review, 51*(2), 33.

Menachery, V. D., Yount, B. L. Jr, Debbink, K., Agnihothram, S., Gralinski, L. E., Plante, J. A., Graham, R. L., Scobey, T., Ge, X.-Y., Donaldson, E. F., Randell, S. H., Lanzavecchia, A., Marasco, W. A., Shi, Z.-L., & Baric, R. S. (2015, December). A SARS-like cluster of circulating bat coronaviruses shows potential for human emergence. *Nature Medicine, 21*(12), 1508–1514. doi:10.1038/nm.3985 PMID:26552008

Men, L. R. (2014a). Why leadership matters to internal communication: Linking transformational leadership, symmetrical communication, and employee outcomes. *Journal of Public Relations Research, 26*(3), 256–279. doi:10.1080/1062726X.2014.908719

Men, L. R. (2014b). Strategic internal communication: Transformational leadership, communication channels, and employee satisfaction. *Management Communication Quarterly*, *28*(2), 264–284. doi:10.1177/0893318914524536

Menon, V., Padhy, S. K., & Pattnaik, J. I. (2020). COVID-19 pandemic and suicidality: Durkheim revisited. *The Australian and New Zealand Journal of Psychiatry*. PMID:32900218

Meyen, E. L., Gauch, J. M., Hinton, H. S., & Tee, M. Y. (2002). Elearning a programmatic research construct for the future. *Journal of Special Education Technology*, *17*(3), 37–46. doi:10.1177/016264340201700303

MHRD. (2020a). *Students to continue their learning by making full use of the available digital e-Learning platforms – Shri Ramesh Pokhriyal 'Nishank'*. Available at: https://pib.gov.in/PressReleasePage.aspx?PRID=1607521

MHRD. (2020c). National education policy 2020. *Information Bureau*, 33-49. Available at: https://static.pib.gov.in/WriteReadData/userfiles/NEP_Final_English_0.pdf

Michel, A., By, R. T., & Burnes, B. (2013). The limitations of dispositional resistance in relation to organizational change. *Management Decision*, *51*(4), 761–780. doi:10.1108/00251741311326554

Miller, F. A., & Katz, J. H. (2013). 4 Keys to Accelerating Collaboration. *Core Practices*, *46*(1), 6.

Miller, R. (2018). *Transforming the future: anticipation in the 21st century*. Taylor & Francis.

Millich, N. (2020, April 6). *Wie das Coronavirus die Pflege beeinflusst*. https://www.bibliomed-pflege.de/news/40233-wie-das-coronavirus-die-pflege-beeinflusst

Mills, C. W. (1995/2000). *The sociological imagination*. Oxford University Press, Inc.

Mirvis, P. (2020). Reflections: US Coronavirus Crisis Management - Learning from Failure January – April 2020. *Journal of Change Management*, *20*(4), 283–311. doi:10.1080/14697017.2020.1836721

Misumi, J., & Peterson, M. (1985). The Performance-Maintenance (PM) Theory of Leadership: Review of a Japanese Research Program. *Administrative Science Quarterly*, *30*(2), 198–223. doi:10.2307/2393105

Modi, S. B., & Mabert, V. A. (2010). Exploring the relationship between efficient supply chain management and firm innovation: An archival search and analysis. *The Journal of Supply Chain Management*, *46*(4), 81–94. doi:10.1111/j.1745-493X.2010.03207.x

MOFE. (2020). *Measures Undertaken by the Government in Addressing the Impact of Covid-19 in Brunei Darussalam*. https://www.mofe.gov.bn/Shared%20Documents/MEASURES%20UNDERTAKEN%20BY%20THE%20GOVERNMENT%20IN%20HANDLING%20THE%20IMPACT%20OF%20COVID-19%20%20issued%2027.04.2020%20v7.pdf

MoH. (2020a). *PR: Health Information Regarding Severe Pneumonia Cases in Wuhan, China*. http://www.moh.gov.bn/Shared%20Documents/2019%20ncov/FINAL%20Wuhan_Pneumonia_6-1-2020_PR.pdf

MoH. (2020b). *PR: 24th January 2020*. http://www.moh.gov.bn/Shared%20Documents/2019%20ncov/FINAL%20Press%20Release%20(eng)%20-%20SOP%20MOH%20terhadap%20Influenza%20dan%20Mesej%20Tular%20mengenai%20Influenza%2024%20Jan%202020.pdf

MoH. (2020c). *PR: Detection of the First Case of Covid-19 Infection in Brunei Darussalam*. Accessed http://www.moh.gov.bn/Shared%20Documents/2019%20ncov/press%20releases/FINAL%20Press%20Release%20(eng)%20-%20First%20Case%20COVID-19%20in%20Brunei%20Darussalam%20(2).pdf

MoH. (2020d). *PR: Travel Restrictions During COPVID-19 Pandemic Brunei Darussalam*. http://www.moh.gov.bn/Shared%20Documents/2019%20ncov/Travel_English%20version.pdf

MoH. (2020e). *PR: 9th November 2020*. http://www.moh.gov.bn/Shared%20Documents/2019%20ncov/press%20releases/Press%20Release%20on%20the%20current%20situation%20of%20COVID-19%20in%20Brunei%20Darussalam%20(09.11.2020).pdf

Mohamad, S. M. (n.d.). *Creative Production of 'COVID-19 Social Distancing' Narratives on Social Media*. Tijdschrift voor economische en sociale geografie.

Monitor, I. L. O. (2020). *COVID-19 and the world of work. Updated estimates and analysis*. Author.

Montoya-Weiss, M. M., & Calantone, R. (1994). Determinants of new product performance: A review and meta-analysis. *Journal of Product Innovation Management: An International Publication of the Product Development & Management Association, 11*(5), 397–417. doi:10.1111/1540-5885.1150397

Moon, M. J. (2020). Fighting Against COVID-19 with Agility, Transparency, and Participation: Wicked policy problems and new governance challenges. *Public Administration Review, 80*(4), 651–656. doi:10.1111/puar.13214 PMID:32836434

Moore, M. (2018). *Leadership under fire: A Phenomenological Study of Senior Administrator's Perceived Leadership Identity and Crisis Response at Higher Education Institutions in the United States*. Fisher Digital Publications.

Morais, F., Kakabadse, A., & Kakabadse, N. (2020). Leading through discontinuous change: A typology of problems and leadership approaches in UK boards. *Long Range Planning, 53*(2), 1–15. doi:10.1016/j.lrp.2019.02.003

Moreno, C., Wykes, T., Galderisi, S., Nordentoft, M., Crossley, N., Jones, N., Cannon, M., Correll, C. U., Byrne, L., Carr, S., Chen, E. Y. H., Gorwood, P., Johnson, S., Kärkkäinen, H., Krystal, J. H., Lee, J., Lieberman, J., López-Jaramillo, C., Männikkö, M., ... Arango, C. (2020, September 1). How mental health care should change as a consequence of the COVID-19 pandemic, THE. *The Lancet. Psychiatry, 7*(9), 813–824. doi:10.1016/S2215-0366(20)30307-2 PMID:32682460

Morgan, S. J., Pullon, S. R., Macdonald, L. M., McKinlay, E. M., & Gray, B. V. (2017). Case study observational research: A framework for conducting case study research where observation data are the focus. *Qualitative Health Research, 27*(7), 1060–1068. doi:10.1177/1049732316649160 PMID:27217290

Morgeson, F. P., & Humphrey, S. E. (2006). The Work Design Questionnaire (WDQ): Developing and validating a comprehensive measure for assessing job design and the nature of work. *The Journal of Applied Psychology, 91*(6), 1321–1339. doi:10.1037/0021-9010.91.6.1321 PMID:17100487

Morin, C. M., & Carrier, J. (2020). The acute effects of the COVID-19 pandemic on insomnia and psychological symptoms. *Sleep Medicine*. Advance online publication. doi:10.1016/j.sleep.2020.06.005 PMID:32595107

Mucci, F., Mucci, N., & Diolaiuti, F. (2020). Lockdown and isolation: Psychological aspects of COVID-19 pandemic in the general population. *Clinical Neuropsychiatry: Journal of Treatment Evaluation, 17*(2), 63–64.

Mueller-Hanson, R. A., & Pulakos, E. D. (2018). *Transforming performance management to drive performance: An evidence-based roadmap*. Routledge. doi:10.4324/9781315168128

Mulfinger, N., Lampl, J., Dinkel, A., Weidner, K., Beutel, M. E., Jarczok, M. N., Hildenbrand, G., Kruse, J., Seifried-Dübon, T., Junne, F., Beschoner, P., & Gündel, H. (2020). Psychische Belastungen durch Epidemien bei Beschäftigten im Gesundheitswesen und Implikationen für die Bewältigung der Corona-Krise: Eine Literaturübersicht [Psychological stress caused by epidemics among health care workers and implications for coping with the corona crisis: a literature review]. *Zeitschrift für Psychosomatische Medizin und Psychotherapie, 66*(3), 220–242. https://doi.org/10.13109/zptm.2020.66.3.220

Mumford, M. D., Scott, G. M., Gaddis, B., & Strange, J. M. (2002). Leading creative people: Orchestrating expertise and relationships. *The Leadership Quarterly, 13*(6), 705–750. doi:10.1016/S1048-9843(02)00158-3

Münch, U. (2020). Wenn dem Bundesstaat die Stunde der Exekutive schlägt: der deutsche (Exekutiv-)Föderalismus in Zeiten der Coronakrise. In *Jahrbuch des Föderalismus 2020* (pp. 207–226). Nomos Verlagsgesellschaft mbH & Co. KG. doi:10.5771/9783748910817-207

Münch, U., Müller, H., Deffner, T., von, S. A., Kern, M., Kiepke-Ziemes, S., & Radbruch, L. (2020). Recommendations for the support of suffering, severely ill, dying or grieving persons in the corona pandemic from a palliative care perspective: Recommendations of the German Society for Palliative Medicine (DGP), the German Interdisciplinary Association for Intensive and Emergency Medicine (DIVI), the Federal Association for Grief Counseling (BVT), the Working Group for Psycho-oncology in the German Cancer Society, the German Association for Social Work in the Healthcare System (DVSG) and the German Association for Systemic Therapy, Counseling and Family Therapy (DGSF). *Schmerz (Berlin, Germany), 34*(4). doi:10.100700482-020-00483-9

Murphy, M. P. A. (2020). COVID-19 and emergency eLearning: Consequences of the securitization of higher education for post-pandemic pedagogy. *Contemporary Security Policy, 41*(3), 492–505.

Murray, C. J., & Lopez, A. D. (1996). Evidence-based health policy—Lessons from the Global Burden of Disease Study. *Science, 274*(5288), 740–743. doi:10.1126cience.274.5288.740 PMID:8966556

Musa, S. F. P. D., & Idris, D. S. R. P. H. (2020). Addressing Issues of Unemployment in Brunei: The Mismatch Between Employers Expectations and Employees Aspirations. *International Journal of Asian Business and Information Management, 11*(2), 88–101. doi:10.4018/IJABIM.2020040106

Nadler, D. A., & Shaw, R. B. (1995). Change leadership: Core competency for the twenty-first century. In Discontinuous change: Leading organizational transformation. San Francisco: Jossey-Bass.

Nadler, D. A., & Tushman, M. L. (1995). Types of organizational change: From incremental improvement to discontinuous transformation. In Discontinuous change: Leading organizational transformation. San Francisco: Jossey-Bass.

Nadler, D. A., & Tushman, M. L. (1990). Beyond the charismatic leader: Leadership and organizational change. *California Management Review, 32*(2), 77–97. doi:10.2307/41166606

Naim, M. F., & Lenka, U. (2017). Investigating the impact of social media on Gen Y employees' engagement: An Indian perspective. *International Journal of Human Capital and Information Technology Professionals, 8*(3), 29–48. doi:10.4018/IJHCITP.2017070103

Naim, M. F., & Lenka, U. (2020). Organizational learning and Gen Y employees' affective commitment: The mediating role of competency development and moderating role of strategic leadership. *Journal of Management & Organization, 26*(5), 815–831. doi:10.1017/jmo.2018.19

Nandy, M., Lodh, S., & Tang, A. (2020). Lessons from COVID-19 and a resilience model for higher education. *Industry and Higher Education.*

Naqvi, H. A. (n.d.). Mental health in the aftermath of COVID-19: A new normal. *Journal of Pakistan Medical Association, 70*(Sppl 3). doi:10.5455/JPMA.30

National Health Regulatory Authority. (2017). *Annual report of 2017*. Retrieved from www.nhra.bh

Nätti, S., Rahkolin, S., & Saraniemi, S. (2014). Crisis communication in key account relationships. *Corporate Communications, 19*(3), 234–246. doi:10.1108/CCIJ-08-2012-0056

Nayak, S. R., Kant, N., & Anjali, K. (2020). *Strategy of Using ICT in ODL to Disseminate Higher Education in Tribal Communities: A Case of MP. Asian Association of Open Universities Journal.*

Neal, A. F., & Hesketh, B. (1999). Technology and performance. In D. Ilgen & D. Pulakos (Eds.), *The Changing Nature of performance: Implications for Staffing, Motivation and Development* (pp. 21–55). Jossey-Bass.

Ngcamu, B. S. (2019). Digitalizing South African Universities: Exploring Benefits, Barriers and Risks. In Digital Leadership-A New Leadership Style for the 21st Century. IntechOpen.

Ngwenya, N., Helfand, R., McNamara, A., Cooper, M., Espinosa, P. A. O. L. A., Flenley, D., Steiner, N., Awoyemi, S., Dicke, I., Musasa, M., & Sandbrook, C. (2020). A call for collective crisis leadership. *Oryx, 54*(4), 431–432. doi:10.1017/S0030605320000496

Nichols, C., Chatterjee-Hayden, S., & Trendler, C. (2020). Four Behaviors That Help Leaders Manage Crisis. *Harvard Business Review.* Retrieved from https://hbr.org/2020/04/4_behaviorsthat_help_leaders_manage_crisis

Nicolaides, A., & McCallum, D. C. (2013). Inquiry in action for leadership in turbulent times: Exploring the connections between transformative learning and adaptive leadership. *Journal of Transformative Education, 11*(4), 246–260. doi:10.1177/1541344614540333

Nicola, M., Sohrabi, C., Mathew, G., Kerwan, A., Al-Jabir, A., Griffin, M., Agha, M., & Agha, R. (2020). Health policy and leadership models during the COVID-19 pandemic-review article. *International Journal of Surgery, 81*, 122–129. doi:10.1016/j.ijsu.2020.07.026 PMID:32687873

Nielsen, R., & Marrone, J. (2018). Humility: Our Current Understanding of the Construct and its Role in Organizations. *International Journal of Management Reviews, 20*(4), 802–824. doi:10.1111/ijmr.12160

Nielsen, R., Marrone, J. A., & Slay, H. S. (2010). A new look at humility: Exploring the humility concept and its role in socialized charismatic leadership. *Journal of Leadership & Organizational Studies, 17*(1), 33–43. doi:10.1177/1548051809350892

Nijkrake, J., Gosselt, J. F., & Gutteling, J. M. (2015). Competing frames and tone in corporate communication versus media coverage during a crisis. *Public Relations Review, 41*(1), 80–88. doi:10.1016/j.pubrev.2014.10.010

Northouse, P. (2019). *Leadership: Theory and practice.* Sage.

Northouse, P. G. (2016). *Leadership: Theory and Practice* (7th ed.). Sage Publications.

Notice, M. H. R. D. (2020). *COVID-19 Stay Safe: Digital Initiatives.* https://www.mohfw.gov.in/pdf/Covid19.pdf

NST. (2020). *How Sri Petaling tabligh became Southeast Asia's Covid-19 hotspot.* https://www.nst.com.my/news/nation/2020/03/575560/how-sri-petaling-tabligh-became-southeast-asias-covid-19-hotspot

O'Reilly, C. A. III, & Tushman, M. L. (2008). Ambidexterity as a dynamic capability: Resolving the innovator's dilemma. *Research in Organizational Behavior, 28*, 185–206. doi:10.1016/j.riob.2008.06.002

Obama, B. (2009). *President Barack Obama's Inaugural Address.* Retrieved from, https://obamawhitehouse.archives.gov/blog/2009/01/21/president-barack-obamas-inaugural-address

Odekerken-Schröder, G., Mele, C., Russo-Spena, T., Mahr, D., & Ruggiero, A. (2020). Mitigating loneliness with companion robots in the COVID-19 pandemic and beyond: An integrative framework and research agenda. *Journal of Service Management, 31*(6), 1149–1162. doi:10.1108/JOSM-05-2020-0148

OECD. (2019). *Government at a Glance Southeast Asia 2019 Country Fact Sheet. Brunei Darussalam.* https://www.oecd.org/gov/gov-at-a-glance-sea-country-factsheet-brunei-darussalam.pdf

Öge, E., Cetin, M., & Top, S. (2018). The effects of paternalistic leadership on workplace loneliness, work family conflict and work engagement among air traffic controllers in Turkey. *Journal of Air Transport Management, 66*, 25–35. doi:10.1016/j.jairtraman.2017.10.003

O'Leonard, K., & Krider, J. (2014, May). *Leadership development factbook® 2014: Benchmarks and trends in U.S. leadership development.* BERSIN by Deloitte.

Omar, A. M. (2020a). Digital Era Governance and Social Media: The Case of Information Department Brunei. In Employing Recent Technologies for Improved Digital Governance (pp. 19-35). IGI Global.

Omar, A. M. (2020b). The Whole-of-Nation Approach: The Case of Brunei Darussalam, Wawasan 2035, and the 4th Industrial Revolution. In Handbook of Research on Global Challenges for Improving Public Services and Government Operations (pp. 291-309). IGI Global.

Omar, S. S., & Ismail, M. (2009). The background and challenges faced by the small / medium enterprises. A human resource development perspective. *Journal of Business and Management*, *4*(10), 95–102.

OMW-Netzwerk. (2020, October 20). https://omw.hdz-nrw.de/omw-netzwerk.html

Ongori, H., & Agolla, J. (2008). Occupational Stress in Organizations and Its Effects on Organizational Performance. *Journal of Management Research*, *8*(3), 123–133. Retrieved October 29, 2020, from http://www.indianjournals.com/ijor.aspx?target=ijor:jmr&volume=8&issue=3&article=001

Online, M. H. R. D. (n.d.). *Online Learning Resources of MHRD*. Retrieved on Dec 5, 2020 from https://mhrd.gov.in/sites/upload_files/mhrd/files/upload_document/Write_up_online_learning_resources.pdf

Online-Portal für professionell Pflegende. (2020, October 29). *Arbeiten trotz Corona-Infektion - DBfK lehnt RKI-Empfehlung grundsätzlich ab.* https://www.bibliomed-pflege.de/news/dbfk-lehnt-rki-empfehlung-grundsaetzlich-ab

Onyx, J., & Leonard, R. J. (2011). Complex systems leadership in emergent community projects. *Community Development Journal: An International Forum*, *46*(4), 493–510. doi:10.1093/cdj/bsq041

Oreg, S. (2003). Resistance to change: Developing an individual differences measure. *The Journal of Applied Psychology*, *88*(4), 680–693. doi:10.1037/0021-9010.88.4.680 PMID:12940408

Orel, M. (2019). Supporting work-life balance with the use of coworking spaces. *Equality, Diversity and Inclusion*, *39*(5), 549–565. doi:10.1108/EDI-01-2019-0038

Oren, L., Tziner, A., Nahshon, Y., & Sharoni, G. (2013). Relations between OCBs, organizational justice, work motivation and self-efficacy. *Amfiteatru Economic Journal, 15*(34), 505-517. http://hdl.handle.net/10419/168796

Osborn, R. N., Hunt, J. G., & Jauch, L. R. (2002). Toward a contextual theory of leadership. *The Leadership Quarterly Yearly Review of Leadership*, *13*(6), 797–837. doi:10.1016/S1048-9843(02)00154-6

Ou, A. Y., Tsui, A. S., Kinicki, A. J., Waldman, D. A., Xiao, Z., & Song, L. J. (2014). Humble chief executive officers' connections to top management team integration and middle managers' responses. *Administrative Science Quarterly*, *59*(1), 34–72. doi:10.1177/0001839213520131

Owens, B. P. (2009). Humility in organizations: Establishing construct, nomological, and predictive validity. In *Academy of Management best papers proceedings*. Academy of Management. doi:10.5465/ambpp.2009.44263542

Pancasila, I., Haryono, S., & Sulistyo, B. A. (2020). Effects of work motivation and leadership toward work satisfaction and employee performance: Evidence from Indonesia. *The Journal of Asian Finance, Economics, and Business*, *7*(6), 387–397. doi:10.13106/jafeb.2020.vol7.no6.387

Pandey, D. (2020). Work Stress And Employee Performance: An Assessment Of Impact Of Work Stress. *International Research Journal of Human Resource And Social Sciences, 7*(5).

Pang, L. L. (2020). Leadership and Crisis Communication During Covid-19: The Case of Brunei Darussalam. *Indonesian Association of Public Administration (IAPA) Virtual Conference 2020.*

Pantelimon, F. V., Georgescu, T. M., & Posedaru, B. Ş. (2020). The impact of mobile e-commerce on GDP: A comparative analysis between Romania and Germany and how COVID-19 influences the e-commerce activity worldwide. *Informações Econômicas, 24*(2), 27–41. doi:10.24818/issn14531305/24.2.2020.03

Papandrea, D., & Azzi, M. (2020). *Managing work-related psychosocial risks during the COVID-19 pandemic.* International Labour Organization.

Parker, D. W., Holesgrove, M., & Pathak, R. (2015). Improving productivity with self-organised teams and agile leadership. *International Journal of Productivity and Performance Management.*

Park, S., & Park, S. (2019). Employee Adaptive Performance and Its Antecedents: Review and Synthesis. *Human Resource Development Review, 18*(3), 294–324. doi:10.1177/1534484319836315

Parris, D. L., & Peachey, J. W. (2013). A systematic literature review of servant leadership theory in organizational contexts. *Journal of Business Ethics, 113*(3), 377–393. doi:10.100710551-012-1322-6

Parson, K., Allen, M. P., Alvarado-Little, W., & Rudd, R. (2017). *Health literacy insights for health crises. NAM Perspectives.* Discussion Paper, National Academy of Medicine. doi:10.31478/201707f

Pearce, J. A. II, & Robbins, K. (1993). Toward improved theory and research on business turnaround. *Journal of Management, 19*(3), 613–636. doi:10.1177/014920639301900306

Pearce, J. A., & Robbins, K. (1994). Retrenchment remains the foundation of business turnaround. *Strategic Management Journal, 15*(5), 417–417. doi:10.1002mj.4250150507

Pearson, C. M., & Mitroff, I. I. (1993). From crisis prone to crisis prepared: A framework for crisis management. *The Academy of Management Perspectives, 7*(1), 48–59. doi:10.5465/ame.1993.9409142058

Peng, J., Chen, Y., Xia, Y., & Ran, Y. (2017). Workplace loneliness, leader-member exchange and creativity: The cross-level moderating role of leader compassion. *Personality and Individual Differences, 104*, 510–515. doi:10.1016/j.paid.2016.09.020

Perlman, D., & Peplau, L. A. (1981). Toward a social psychology of loneliness. *Personal Relationships, 3*, 31–56.

Perren, L., & Ram, M. (2004). Case-study method in small business and entrepreneurial research. *International Small Business Journal, 22*(1), 83–101. doi:10.1177/0266242604039482

Perrin, A. (2015). *Social media usage: 2005–2015.* Washington, DC: Pew Research Center. Retrieved from http://www.pewinternet.org/files/2015/10/PI_2015-10-08_Social- Networking-Usage-2005-2015_FINAL.pdf

Pesut, B., Fowler, M., Taylor, E. J., Reimer-Kirkham, S., & Sawatzky, R. (2008). Conceptualising spirituality and religion for healthcare. *Journal of Clinical Nursing, 17*(21), 2803–2810. doi:10.1111/j.1365-2702.2008.02344.x PMID:18665876

Pfeifer, M., Ewig, S., Voshaar, T., Randerath, W., Bauer, T., Geiseler, J., Dellweg, D., Westhoff, M., Windisch, W., Schönhofer, B., Kluge, S., & Lepper, P. M. (2020). Positionspapier zur praktischen Umsetzung der apparativen Differenzialtherapie der akuten respiratorischen Insuffizienz bei COVID-19 [Position Paper for the State of the Art Application of Respiratory Support in Patients with COVID-19 - German Respiratory Society]. *Pneumologie (Stuttgart, Germany), 74*(6), 337–357. https://doi.org/10.1055/a-1157-9976

Pfenninger, E. G., & Kaisers, U. X. (2020). Bevorratung persönlicher Schutzausrüstung in Kliniken zur Vorbereitung auf eine Pandemie [Provisioning of personal protective equipment in hospitals in preparation for a pandemic]. *Der Anaesthesist.* Advance online publication. doi:10.100700101-020-00843-1

Phillips, J. S., & Lord, R. G. (1986). Notes on the practical and theoretical consequences of implicit leadership theories for the future of leadership measurement. *Journal of Management, 12*(1), 31–41. doi:10.1177/014920638601200104

Pike, A., Rodríguez-Pose, A., Tomaney, J., Torrisi, G., & Tselios, V. (2012). In search of the 'economic dividend' of devolution: Spatial disparities, spatial economic policy, and decentralisation in the UK. *Environment and Planning. C, Government & Policy, 30*(1), 10–28. doi:10.1068/c10214r

Plato. (1892/1937). Cratylus. In *Dialogues of Plato* (M. A. Jowett, Trans.; pp. 173–232). Random House.

Podsakoff, P. M., & Organ, D. W. (1986). Self-reports in organizational research: Problems and prospects. *Journal of Management, 12*(4), 531–544. doi:10.1177/014920638601200408

Prasad, K. D., & Kant, N. (2020, Nov.). Achieving SDGs & NDCs. *Yojana, A Development Monthly*, 70–76.

Prasad, D. K., Rao, M., Vaidya, D. R., & Muralidhar, B. (2020). Organizational Climate, Opportunities, Challenges and Psychological Wellbeing of the Remote Working Employees during COVID-19 Pandemic: A General Linear Model Approach with Reference to Information Technology Industry in Hyderabad. *International Journal of Advanced Research in Engineering and Technology, 11*(4).

Prasad, K., & Vaidya, R. (2020). Association among COVID-19 parameters, occupational stress and employee performance: An empirical study with reference to Agricultural Research Sector in Hyderabad Metro. *Sustainable Humanosphere, 16*(2), 235–253. https://www.researchgate.net/publication/341211360

Pravat, K. (2020a). Challenges and Opportunities created by Covid-19 for ODL: A case study of IGNOU. *International Journal for Innovative Research in Multidisciplinary Field, 6*(5), 217–222.

Pravat, K. (2020b). Impact of Pandemic COVID-19 on Education in India. *International Journal for Innovative Research in Multidisciplinary Field, 31*(46), 142–149.

Pravat, K. (2020c). Online learning during lock down period for Covid-19 in India. *International Journal of Multidisciplinary Educational Research, 5*(8), 82–92.

Pulakos, E. D., Arad, S., Donovan, M. A., & Plamondon, K. E. (2000). Adaptability in the workplace: Development of a taxonomy of adaptive performance. *The Journal of Applied Psychology, 85*(4), 612–624. doi:10.1037/0021-9010.85.4.612 PMID:10948805

Pulakos, E. D., Kantrowitz, T., & Schneider, B. (2019). What leads to organizational agility: It's not what you think. *Consulting Psychology Journal, 71*(4), 305–320. doi:10.1037/cpb0000150

Pulakos, E. D., Schmitt, N., Dorsey, D. W., Arad, S., Borman, W. C., & Hedge, J. W. (2002). Predicting adaptive performance: Further tests of a model of adaptability. *Human Performance, 15*(4), 299–323. doi:10.1207/S15327043HUP1504_01

Pullen, W. (1993). Strategic Shocks: Managing discontinuous change. *International Journal of Public Sector Management, 6*(1), 30–39. doi:10.1108/09513559310023563

Purnamasari, D. I., Heriyanto, H., & Oliver, S. S. (2020). *Similarity factors affecting the use of online applications for business process reengineering (BPR) acceleration in micro, small and medium enterprises (MSMEs) as a consequence of Covid-19 pandemic.* Academic Press.

Quantum Workplace Best Place to Work. (2020). *The Impact of COVID-19 on Employee Engagement A Quantum Workplace Benchmark Report and Analysis.* Accessed September 14, 2020 https://www.quantumworkplace.com/impact-of-covid-19-on-employee-engagement

Rabes, C., Bläuer, C., Büche, V., Gisler Ries, I., Knüppel Lauener, S., Kuehl, R., Osthoff, M., Pfeiffer, M., Probst, S., Todorov, V., & Panfil, E.-M. (2020). Zwischen Traum und Trauma - Aufbau und Betrieb einer Kohortenstation für Patient_innen mit COVID-19 in einem Akutspital. *Pflege, 33*(4), 247–255. https://doi.org/10.1024/1012-5302/a000746

Rafferty, A. E., Jimmieson, N. L., & Armenakis, A. A. (2012). Change Readiness. *Journal of Management, 39*(1), 110–135. doi:10.1177/0149206312457417

Rahman, H. A., Aziz, A. A., Ibrahim, M. A., Suhaili, N. A., Daud, A. Z., & Naing, L. (2019). Development and validation of Islamic Governance Examination tool in healthcare settings. *International Journal of Health Governance.*

Rahmani, A. M., & Mirmahaleh, S. Y. H. (2020). Coronavirus disease (COVID-19) prevention and treatment methods and effective parameters: A systematic literature review. *Sustainable Cities and Society*, 102568. PMID:33110743

Rahman, N., Othman, M., Yajid, M., Rahman, S., Yaakob, A., Masri, R., ... Ibrahim, Z. J. M. S. L. (2018). Impact of adaptive leadership on organizational performance, adaptive orientation and operational strategy. *Management Science Letters, 8*(12), 1387–1398. doi:10.5267/j.msl.2018.9.006

Rajkumar, R. V. (2020). COVID-19 and mental health: A review of the existing literature. *Asian Journal of Psychiatry, 52.* DOI:.2020.102066 doi:10.1016/j.ajp

Ramalingam, B., Wild, L., & Ferrari, M. (2020). *Adaptive leadership in the coronavirus response.* Academic Press.

Rangachari, P., & Woods, L, J. (2020). Preserving organizational resilience, patient safety, and staff retention during COVID-19 requires a holistic consideration of the psychological safety of healthcare workers. *International Journal of Environmental Research and Public Health, 17*(12), 4267. doi:10.3390/ijerph17124267 PMID:32549273

Rao, L. (2015). WhatsApp hits 900million users. Fortune tech. *Fortune Magazine.* Retrieved from https://fortune.com/2015/09/04/whatsapp-900-million-users/

Rasheed, Z. (2020). COVID-19 Pandemic is Testing Worlds Leaders. Who's Stepping Up? *Aljazeera.* Retrieved from https://aljazeera.com/news/2020/04/covid-10-pandemic-is-testing-leaders-whos-stepping-up-200402201221844

Rasmussen, C. E. (2011). *The autonomous animal: Self-governance and the modern subject.* U of Minnesota Press. doi:10.5749/minnesota/9780816669561.001.0001

Reb, J., Narayanan, J., & Chaturvedi, S. (2014). Leading mindfully: Two studies on the influence of supervisor trait mindfulness on employee well-being and performance. *Mindfulness, 5*(1), 36–45. doi:10.100712671-012-0144-z

Reddit. (2020). *Circulated Via whatsapp SKH Sg. Hanching grand opening. Where are the MOH guidelines & social distancing measures?* https://www.reddit.com/r/Brunei/comments/jq9yt7/circulated_via_whatsapp_skh_sg_hanching_grand/

Regener, H., Cranshaw, A., & Hofmann, K. (2020). Corona-Pandemie:Wie hat sich die rettungsdienstliche Bildung verändert? *Rettungsdienst, 43*(6), 534–539. https://backend.paraplegie.ch/sites/default/files/2020-07/distance_learning_waehrend_corona._rettungsdienst_sk_06_2020.pdf

Reinhard, M. A., Burkhardt, G., Grosse-Wentrup, F., Eser-Valerie, D., Mumm, F. H. A., & Barniko, B.-O. (2020). Psychosoziale Unterstützung während der COVID-19-Pandemie: interdisziplinäres Versorgungskonzept an einem Universitätsklinikum. *Der Nervenarzt*, 1–7. doi:10.100700115-020-01014-8

Reinmoeller, P., & Van Baardwijk, N. (2005). The link between diversity and resilience. *MIT Sloan Management Review*, *46*(4), 61.

Ren, C. R., Hu, Y., & Cui, T. H. (2019). Responses to rival exit: Product variety, market expansion, and preexisting market structure. *Strategic Management Journal*, *40*(2), 253–276. doi:10.1002mj.2970

Reynolds, B., & Quinn, S. C. (2008). Effective communication during an influenza pandemic: The value of using a crisis and emergency risk communication framework. *Health Promotion Practice*, *9*(4, suppl), 13S–17S. doi:10.1177/1524839908325267 PMID:18936255

Rice, R. W., Near, J. P., & Hunt, R. G. (1980). The job-satisfaction/life-satisfaction relationship: A review of empirical research. *Basic and Applied Social Psychology*, *1*(1), 37–64. doi:10.120715324834basp0101_4

RKI. (2020, November 13). *Täglicher Lagebericht des RKI zur Coronavirus-Krankheit-2019 (Covid-19)*. https://www.rki.de/DE/Content/InfAZ/N/Neuartiges_Coronavirus/Situationsberichte/Nov_2020/2020-11-13-de.pdf?__blob=publicationFile

Robert-Koch-Institut. (2020a). *Epidemiologischer Steckbrief zu SARS-CoV-2 und COVID-19*. https://www.rki.de/DE/Content/InfAZ/N/Neuartiges_Coronavirus/Steckbrief.html

Robert-Koch-Institut. (2020b, May 13). *Optionen zur getrennten Versorgung von COVID-19-Fällen, Verdachtsfällen und anderen Patienten im stationären Bereich* [Press release]. https://www.rki.de/DE/Content/InfAZ/N/Neuartiges_Coronavirus/Getrennte_Patientenversorg_stationaer.html

Robertson, B. J. (2015). *Holacracy: The new management system for a rapidly changing world*. Henry Holt and Company.

Roberts, R. (2020). COVID-19, Leadership and lessons from physics. *The Australian Journal of Rural Health*, *28*(3), 232–235. doi:10.1111/ajr.12649 PMID:32592229

Robinson, C. D. (2020). The U.S. Navy's task forces: 1-199. *Defense & Security Analysis*, *36*(1), 109–110. doi:10.1080/14751798.2020.1712028

Rocco, T. S., & Shuck, B. (2019). Death and dying: Grief, compassion and workplace responses. *New Horizons in Adult Education and Human Resource Development*, *32*(1), 1–4. doi:10.1002/nha3.20268

Rochlin, G. I., La Porte, T. R., & Roberts, K. H. (1987). The self-designing high-reliability organization: Aircraft carrier flight operations at sea. *Naval War College Review*, *40*(4), 76–92.

Roigk, P., & Becker, C. (2020). Umsetzung einer Empfehlung des Robert-Koch-Institutes im Kontext der Corona-Pandemie in die Strukturen und Prozesse eines Krankenhauses - Ein Praxisbericht. *Pflegewissenschaft*, 47–48.

Romme, A. G. L. (1995). The sociocratic model of organizing. *Journal of Strategic Change*, *4*(4), 209–215. doi:10.1002/jsc.4240040404

Roser, M. (2020) *Coronavirus Pandemic (COVID-19)*. Available at: https://ourworldindata.org/coronavirus

Rosso, B. D., Dekas, K. H., & Wrzesniewski, A. (2010). On the meaning of work: A theoretical integration and review. *Research in Organizational Behavior*, *30*, 91–127. doi:10.1016/j.riob.2010.09.001

Rost, J. C. (1993). *Leadership for the twenty-first century*. Praeger.

Roth, R. (2020). *Demokratie und Bürgerbeteiligung in Zeiten von COVID-19* (Opuscula, 141). https://nbn-resolving.org/urn:nbn:de:0168-ssoar-68889-1

Roux-Dufort, C., & Lalonde, C. (2013). Editorial: Exploring the theoretical foundations of crisis management. *Journal of Contingencies and Crisis Management*, *21*(1), 1–3. doi:10.1111/1468-5973.12014

Roy, R., Lampert, C. M., & Stoyneva, I. (2018). When dinosaurs fly: The role of firm capabilities in the „avianiza-tion— of incumbents during disruptive technological change. *Strategic Entrepreneurship Journal, 12*(2), 261–284. doi:10.1002ej.1278

Rumelt, R. (1982). Diversification Strategy and Profitability. *Strategic Management Journal, 3*(4), 359–369. doi:10.1002mj.4250030407

Runyan, R. C. (2006). Small business in the face of crisis: Identifying barriers to recovery from natural disaster. *Journal of Contingencies and Crisis Management, 14*(1), 12–26. doi:10.1111/j.1468-5973.2006.00477.x

RussellReynolds. (2020). *Leadership through Uncertainty 10 Enduring lessons for turbulent times*. Retrieved November 5, 2020, from www.russellreynolds.com/insights/thought-leadership/leadership-through-uncertainty

RWI - Leibniz-Institut für Wirtschaftsforschung e. V. (2020, March 25). *Unstatistik - Corona-Pandemie: Statistische Konzepte und ihre Grenzen* [Press release]. https://www.rwi-essen.de/unstatistik/101/

Sachdeva, G. (2019). Impact of Spirituality in Management: A Review. In Science and Spirituality for a Sustainable World: Emerging Research and Opportunities (pp. 1-22). IGI Global. doi:10.4018/978-1-5225-9893-0.ch001

Sahin, F., & Gurbuz, S. (2014). Cultural intelligence as a predictor of individuals' adaptive performance: A study in a multicultural environment. *International Area Studies Review, 17*(4), 394–413. doi:10.1177/2233865914550727

Sahu, P. (2020). Closure of universities due to coronavirus disease 2019 (COVID-19): Impact on education and mental health of students and academic staff. *Cureus, 12*(4), e7541. doi:10.7759/cureus.7541 PMID:32377489

Saidi, A. M. O., Nur, F. A., Al-Mandhari, A. S., El Rabbat, M., Hafeez, A., & Abubakar, A. (2020). Decisive leader-ship is a necessity in the COVID-19 response. *Lancet, 396*(10247), 295–298. doi:10.1016/S0140-6736(20)31493-8 PMID:32628904

Said, R. M., & El-Shafei, D. A. (2020). Occupational stress, job satisfaction, and intent to leave: Nurses working on front lines during COVID-19 pandemic in Zagazig City, Egypt. *Environmental Science and Pollution Research International*, 1–11. PMID:33067794

Sainger, G. (2018). Leadership in digital age: A study on the role of leader in this era of digital transformation. *International Journal on Leadership, 6*(1), 1.

Saksvik, I. B., & Hetland, H. (2009). Exploring dispositional resistance to change. *Journal of Leadership & Organizational Studies, 16*(2), 175–183. doi:10.1177/1548051809335357

Salo, A., Tähtinen, J., & Ulkuniemi, P. (2009). Twists and turns of triadic business relationship recovery. *Industrial Marketing Management, 38*(6), 618–632. doi:10.1016/j.indmarman.2009.05.009

Salomo, S., Steinhoff, F., & Trommsdorff, V. (2003). Customer orientation in innovation projects and new product development success-the moderating effect of product innovativeness. *International Journal of Technology Management, 26*(5–6), 442–463. doi:10.1504/IJTM.2003.003417

Salvatico, R. (2006). Enabling transparent leadership: A small business manager's perspective. *Journal of Management Development, 25*(10), 1018–1020. doi:10.1108/02621710610708658

Samad, S. (2020). Achieving innovative firm performance through human capital and the effect of social capital. *Management & Marketing. Challenges for the Knowledge Society, 15*(2), 326–344. doi:10.2478/mmcks-2020-0019

Sanchez, R. (1997). Preparing for an uncertain future: Managing organizations for strategic flexibility. *International Studies of Management & Organization, 27*(2), 71–94. doi:10.1080/00208825.1997.11656708

Sarason, S. (1972). *The creation of settings and the future of societies*. Brookline Books, Inc.

Sattayaraksa, T., & Boon-itt, S. (2016). CEO transformational leadership and the new product development process. *Leadership and Organization Development Journal, 37*(6), 730–749. doi:10.1108/LODJ-10-2014-0197

Schäfer, C. (2020). Wenn nicht jetzt, wann dann? *Dialyse Aktuell, 24*(4), 145. doi:10.1055/a-1076-4335

Scharmer, C. O. (2009). *Theory U: Learning from the future as it emerges*. Berrett-Koehler Publishers Schneider, B. (1987). The people make the place. *Personnel Psychology, 40*, 437–453.

Schein, E. (2013). *Humble inquiry: The gentle art of asking instead of telling*. Berrett-Koehler Publishers, Inc.

Schmidt, F. L., & Hunter, J. E. (1998). The Validity and Utility of Selection Methods in Personnel Psychology: Practical and Theoretical Implications of 85 Years of Research Findings. *Psychological Bulletin, 124*(2), 262–274. doi:10.1037/0033-2909.124.2.262

Schmitz, C., Zwahlen, M., & Berchtold, P. (2020). Management und Medizin post-Corona. *Bulletin Des Médecins Suisses*. Advance online publication. doi:10.4414/bms.2020.19137

Schnitzbauer, A. A., Kempf, V. A. J., Hack, D., Ciesek, S., Meier, S., Vehreschild, M. J. G. T., Wicker, S., Kippke, U., Graf, J., & Marzi, I. (2020). SARS-CoV-2/COVID-19: Systematischer Review zu Anforderungen an die persönliche Schutzausrüstung bei primärem Patientenkontakt und Strukturierung des Operationsbereiches [SARS-CoV-2/COVID-19: systematic review of requirements for personal protective equipment in primary patient contact and organization of the operating area]. *Der Chirurg; Zeitschrift fur alle Gebiete der operativen Medizen, 91*(7), 576–585. doi:10.100700104-020-01229-0

Schraagen, J., & van de Ven, J. (2008). Improving Decision Making in Crisis Response through Critical Thinking Support. *Journal of Cognitive Engineering and Decision Making, 2*(4), 311–327. doi:10.1518/155534308X377801

Schraub, E. M., Stegmaier, R., & Sonntag, K. (2011). The Effect of Change On Adaptive Performance: Does Expressive Suppression Moderate the Indirect Effect of Strain? *Journal of Change Management, 11*(1), 21–44. doi:10.1080/14697017.2010.514002

Schumacher, C. (2006). Trust: A source of success in strategic alliances? *Schmalenbach Business Review, 58*(3), 259–278. doi:10.1007/BF03396734

Schwab, K., & Malleret, T. (2020). *Covid-19: The Great Reset*. Forum Publishing. World Economic Forum.

Schwella, E. (2020). *Post-COVID academic pointers: On social innovation, engaged scholarship, and learning leadership*. School of Social Innovation, Hugenote College.

SECO. (2020). *Konjunkturprognose*. Konjunkturtendenzen SECO.

Sedaju, A., Haryono, S., & Anisahwati, N. (2020). Flexible Work Arrangement in Manufacturing during the COVID-19 Pandemic: An Evidence-Based Study of Indonesian Employees. *International Journal Of Advanced Science And Technology, 29*(6), 3914-3924. https://www.researchgate.net/publication/341700500

Seetharaman, P. (2020). Business models shifts: Impact of Covid-19. *International Journal of Information Management, 54*, 102173. doi:10.1016/j.ijinfomgt.2020.102173 PMID:32834338

Seifert, A., Batsis, J. A., & Smith, A. C. (2020). Telemedicine in Long-Term Care Facilities During and Beyond COVID-19: Challenges Caused by the Digital Divide. *Frontiers in Public Health, 8*, 690. doi:10.3389/fpubh.2020.601595 PMID:33194999

Sembiring, M. J., Fatihudin, D., Mochklas, M., & Holisin, I. (2020). Banking Employee Performance During Pandemic COVID-19: Remuneration and Motivation. *Journal of Xi'an University of Architecture & Technology, 12*, 64–71.

Settersten, R. A. Jr, Bernardi, L., Härkönen, J., Antonucci, T. C., Dykstra, P. A., Heckhausen, J., ... Mulder, C. H. (2020). Understanding the effects of Covid-19 through a life course lens. 45. *Advances in Life Course Research, 45*, 100360. doi:10.1016/j.alcr.2020.100360

Shadraconis, S. (2013). Organizational Leadership in Times of Uncertainty: Is Transformational Leadership the Answer? *LUX: A Journal of Transdisciplinary Writing and Research from Claremont Graduate University, 2*(1), 28.

Sharma, A. K. (2020). COVID-19: creating a paradigm shift in India's education system. *Economic Times Blog*. Available at: https://economictimes.indiatimes.com/blogs/et-commentary/covid-19-creating-a-paradigm-shift-in-indias-education-system/

SharmaN. (2020) 'COVID-19: Challenges and Opportunities for Small and Medium Enterprises (SMEs)', SSRN 3650473. doi:10.2139srn.3650473

Shaw, W. S., Main, C. J., Findley, P. A., Collie, A., Kristman, V. L., & Gross, D. P. (2020). Opening the Workplace After COVID-19: What Lessons Can be Learned from Return-to-Work Research? *Journal of Occupational Rehabilitation*, 1. PMID:32562129

Shear, M. D., Goodnough, A., Kaplan, S., Fink, S., Thomas, K., & Weiland, N. (2020, March 29). The lost month: How the failure to test blinded the U.S. to covid-19. *New York Times*. https://www.nytimes.com/2020/03/28/us/testing-coronavirus-pandemic.html

Shereen, M. A., Khan, S., Kazmi, A., Bashir, N., & Siddique, R. (2020). COVID-19 infection: Origin, transmission, and characteristics of human coronaviruses. *Journal of Advanced Research, 24*, 91–98. doi:10.1016/j.jare.2020.03.005 PMID:32257431

Sherehiy, B., & Karwowski, W. (2014). The relationship between work organization and workforce agility in small manufacturing enterprises. *International Journal of Industrial Ergonomics, 44*(3), 466–473. doi:10.1016/j.ergon.2014.01.002

Shift. (2019) *SMEs and the Corporate Responsibility to Respect Human Rights*. Available at: https://globalnaps.org/issue/small-medium-enterprises-smes/

Shingler-Nace, A. (2020). COVID-19 when leadership calls. *Nurse Leader, 18*(3), 202–203.

Shrivastava, P. (1995). Industrial/ environmental crises and corporate social responsibility. *Journal of Socio-Economics, 24*(1), 211–227. doi:10.1016/1053-5357(95)90036-5

Shufutinsky, A. (2019). Tribalism and Clone Theory in New Leaders and the Resulting Degradation of Organizational Culture. *Psychology and Behavioral Science International Journal, 10*(2).

Shufutinsky, A., Sibel, J.R., Beach, A. A., Saraceno, A. J. (2020b). OD for Robots? Industry 4.0, Emerging Technologies, and the Implications on Organizational Talent Acquisition and Development Practices. *Organization Development Journal, 38*(3).

Shufutinsky, A., DePorres, D., Long, B., & Sibel, J. (2020). Shock Leadership Development for the Modern Era of Pandemic Management and Preparedness. *International Journal of Organizational Innovation, 13*(1), 1–23.

Shufutinsky, A., Sibel, J. R., Long, B., & Kravitz, C. (2020c). *Comparison of Leadership in Large Enterprises During the Whole System Shock of the 2019-2020 Coronavirus Pandemic*. Unpublished Research.

Shufutinsky, A., Sibel, J., Murray Hayden, P., Shufutinsky, D., & Cox, R. (2018). Holoportation: The Disruptive Technology that Will Change the Practice of Conflict Analysis and Resolution. *OD Practitioner, 50*(3).

Sieber, C. (2020). COVID-19 aus Sicht der Geriatrie [COVID-19: a geriatric point-of-view]. *Deutsche medizinische Wochenschrift, 145*(15), 1039–1043. doi:10.1055/a-1164-4261

Silies, K., Schley, A., Sill, J., Fleischer, S., Müller, M., & Balzer, K. (2020). Die COVID-19-Pandemie im akutstationären Setting aus Sicht von Führungspersonen und Hygienefachkräften in der Pflege. *Pflege, 33*(5), 289–298. https://doi.org/10.1024/1012-5302/a000756

Simhofer, D. (2020). Arbeiten am Limit. *Psychopraxis. Neuropraxis, 23*(3), 107–109. doi:10.100700739-020-00645-5

Singh, J., & Singh, J. (2020). COVID-19 and Its Impact on Society. *Electronic Research Journal Of Social Sciences And Humanities, 2*(1).

Singh, P. (2020). *COVID 19: The evolution of employee engagement.* Accessed September14, 2020 http://bwpeople.businessworld.in/article/COVID-19-The-Evolution-Of-Employee-Engagement/26-04-2020-190293/

Sirgy, M. J., Efraty, D., Siegel, P., & Lee, D. J. (2001). A new measure of quality of work life (QWL) based on need satisfaction and spillover theories. *Social Indicators Research, 55*(3), 241–302. doi:10.1023/A:1010986923468

Skinner, C., & Spurgeon, P. (2005). Valuing empathy and emotional intelligence in health leadership: A study of empathy, leadership behaviour and outcome effectiveness. *Health Services Management, 18*(1), 1–12. doi:10.1258/0951484053051924 PMID:15807976

Skolnik, R. L. (2008). *Essentials of global health.* Jones & Bartlett Publishers.

Slanetz, P. J., Bedi, H., Kesler, T., & Chetlen, A. (2020). Optimizing journal clubs in the post–coronavirus disease 2019 (COVID-19) era. *Journal of the American College of Radiology.*

Slatten, T., & Mehmetoglu, M. (2011). Antecedents and effects of engaged frontline employees: A study from the hospitality industry. *Managing Service Quality, 21*(1), 88–107. doi:10.1108/09604521111100261

Smallwood, J., & Schooler, J. W. (2015). The science of mind wandering: Empirically navigating the stream of consciousness. *Annual Review of Psychology, 66*(1), 487–518. doi:10.1146/annurev-psych-010814-015331 PMID:25293689

Smith, D. (2012). Technological discontinuities, outsiders, and social capital: A case study from Formula 1. *European Journal of Innovation Management, 15*(3), 332–350. doi:10.1108/14601061211243666

Song, X. M., & Parry, M. E. (1996). What separates Japanese new product winners from losers. *Journal of Product Innovation Management, 13*(5), 422-439.

Sood, S. (2020). Psychological effects of the Coronavirus disease-2019 pandemic. *Research & Humanities in Medical Education, 7*, 23–26.

Stake, R. E. (2005). *Qualitative case studies.* Academic Press.

Stake, R. E. (2008). Qualitative Case Studies. In N. K. Denzin & Y. S. Lincoln (Eds.), *Strategies of Qualitative Inquiry.* Sage Publications.

Stanwick, P. S., & Stanwick, S. D. (2009). *Understanding Business Ethics.* Pearson Education, Inc.

Steil, J. J., & Maier, G. W. (2017). Robots in the digitalized workplace. In G. Hertel, D. Stone, R. Johnson, & J. Passmore (Eds.), *Wiley Blackwell handbook of the psychology of the Internet at work* (pp. 403–422). Wiley–Blackwell. doi:10.1002/9781119256151.ch18

Stemmer, R., Sirsch, E., Büker, C., Holle, B., & Köpke, S. (2020). COVID-19 und die Rolle der Pflege(wissenschaft). *Pflegewissenschaft, Sonderausgabe: Die Corona-Pandemie,* (April), 116–117.

Stewart, G. L., & Nandkeolyar, A. K. (2006). Adaptation and intraindividual variation in sales outcomes: Exploring the interactive effects of personality and environmental opportunity. *Personnel Psychology*, *59*(2), 307–332. doi:10.1111/j.1744-6570.2006.00016.x

Stieglitz, N. T., Knudsen, T., & Becker, M. C. (2016). Adaptation and inertia in dynamic environments. *Strategic Management Journal*, *37*(9), 1854–1864. doi:10.1002mj.2433

Stoker, J. I., Garretsen, H., & Soudis, D. (2019). Tightening the leash after a threat: A multi-level event study on leadership behavior following the financial crisis. *The Leadership Quarterly*, *30*(2), 199–214. doi:10.1016/j.leaqua.2018.08.004

Stouraitis, V., Harun, M. H. M., & Kyritsis, M. (2017). Motivators of SME initial export choice and the European Union regional effect in manufacturing. *International Journal of Entrepreneurial Behaviour & Research*, *23*(1), 35–55. doi:10.1108/IJEBR-05-2015-0120

Stringham, S. (2012). *Strategic leadership and strategic management: Leading and managing change on the edge of chaos*. iUniverse.

Stroop, J. R. (1935). Studies of interference in serial verbal reactions. *Journal of Experimental Psychology*, *18*(6), 643–662. doi:10.1037/h0054651

Subošić, D., Milošević, G., & Kekić, D. (2008). *Decision Making During The Crisis Situations.* Academic Press.

Succi, C. (2020). Freedom & vulnerability: How people develop new skills in an unexpected work environment. In Managing a post-Covid19 era. (pp. 69-73). ESCP Research Institute of Management (ERIM).

Suprapti, S., Asbari, M., Cahyono, Y., & Mufid, A. (2020). Leadership Style, Organizational Culture And Innovative Behavior On Public Health Center Performance During Pandemic COVID-19. *Journal of Industrial Engineering & Management Research*, *1*(2), 76–88. doi:10.7777/jiemar.v1i2

Sutton, S. A. (1999). The panda syndrome II: Innovation, discontinuous change and LIS education. *Journal of Education for Library and Information Science*, *40*(4), 247–262. doi:10.2307/40324096

Swissinfo. (2020). *Vorerst keine Ausgangssperre - Milliarden für Wirtschaft, Swiss Perspectives in 10 Languages.* Academic Press.

tagesschau. (2020, May 6). Bund überlässt Ländern die Verantwortung bei Corona-Lockerungen. *Tagesschau.De*. https://www.tagesschau.de/inland/merkel-ministerpraesidenten-lockerungen-107.html

tagesschau.de. (2020). *Corona-Gästelisten: Lokale wollen nicht selbst kontrollieren.* tagesschau.de. https://www.tagesschau.de/inland/kontrollen-restaurants-corona-101.html

Taleb, N. N. (2007). *The black swan: The impact of the highly improbable* (Vol. 2). Random house.

Talevi, D., Socci, V., Carai, M., Carnaghi, G., Faleri, S., Trebbi, E., Di Bernardo, A., Capelli, F., & Pacitti, F. (2020). Mental health outcomes of the CoViD-19 pandemic. *Rivista di Psichiatria*, *55*(3), 137–144. https://doi.org/10.1708/3382.33569

Talib, N. S. (2002). A resilient monarchy: The Sultanate of Brunei and regime legitimacy in an era of democratic nation-states. *New Zealand Journal of Asian Studies*, *4*(2), 134–147.

Tang, Y., Ma, Y., Wang, J., Fan, Y., Feng, S., Lu, Q., & Posner, M. I. (2007). Short-term meditation training improves attention and self-regulation. *Proceedings of the National Academy of Sciences of the United States of America*, *104*(43), 17152–17156. doi:10.1073/pnas.0707678104 PMID:17940025

Tanyi, R. A. (2002). Towards clarification of the meaning of spirituality. *Journal of Advanced Nursing*, *39*(5), 500–509. doi:10.1046/j.1365-2648.2002.02315.x PMID:12175360

Tavares, A. I. (2017). Telework and health effects review. *International Journal of Healthcare*, *3*(2), 30. doi:10.5430/ijh.v3n2p30

Taylor, V. A., Grant, J., Daneault, V., Scavone, G., Breton, E., Roffe-Vidal, S., & Beauregard, M. (2011). Impact of mindfulness on the neural responses to emotional pictures in experienced and beginner meditators. *NeuroImage*, *57*(4), 1524–1533. doi:10.1016/j.neuroimage.2011.06.001 PMID:21679770

The ASEAN Post. (2020). *Brunei's Response To COVID-19*. https://theaseanpost.com/article/bruneis-response-covid-19

The Bruneian. (2020a) *Health Minister Officiates New Virology Laboratory*. Author.

The Bruneian. (2020b). *Government Introduces Premises Scan App*. https://www.thebruneian.news/government-introduces-premisescan-app/

The Scoop. (2020a). *Gov't releases first digital economy masterplan*. https://thescoop.co/2020/06/05/govt-releases-first-digital-economy-masterplan/

The Scoop. (2020b). *COVID-19 live updates: March archive*. https://thescoop.co/2020/03/13/covid-19-live-updates/

The Scoop. (2020c). *New isolation centre building set to more than double number of beds*. https://thescoop.co/2020/04/24/new-isolation-centre-building-set-to-more-than-double-number-of-beds/

The Scoop. (2020d). *Aman Hills partygoers jailed for flouting COVID-19 restrictions*. https://thescoop.co/2020/06/14/aman-hills-party-goers-jailed-for-flouting-covid-19-restrictions/

The Scoop. (2020e). *COVID-19 live updates: June archive*. https://thescoop.co/2020/06/01/covid-19-live-updates-4/

The Scoop. (2020f). *HM announces special $400 monthly allowance for healthcare workers*. https://thescoop.co/2020/04/14/hm-announces-special-400-monthly-allowance-for-healthcare-workers/

The Scoop. (2020g). *COVID-19 live updates: June archive*. https://thescoop.co/2020/06/01/covid-19-live-updates-4/

The Star. (2020a). *Sultan: Brunei to expand virus testing capacity with new virology lab*. Author.

The Star. (2020b). *Brunei Cabinet donates BN$100,000 to fight Covid-19*. https://www.thestar.com.my/news/regional/2020/04/23/brunei-cabinet-donates-bn100000-to-fight-covid-19

*The Swiss and World Watchmaking Industries in 2019*. (2019). Federation of the Swiss Watch Industry FH 2020.

Their, K. (2018). *Storytelling in organizations. Management for Professionals*. Springer Nature. doi:10.1007/978-3-662-56383-0_1

Theodoridis, C., & Priporas, C. V. (2013). Strategic decision-making during uncertainty: Implications for SMEs. In D. Vrontis & A. Thrassou (Eds.), *Innovative business practices: Prevailing a turbulent era* (pp. 87–111). Scholars Publishing.

Thomas, K. W., & Tymon, W. G. Jr. (1982). Necessary Properties of Relevant Research: Lessons from Recent Criticisms of the Organizational Sciences. *Academy of Management Review*, *7*(3), 345–352. doi:10.5465/amr.1982.4285308

Thorndike, E. L. (1920). A constant error in psychological ratings. *The Journal of Applied Psychology*, *4*(1), 25–29. doi:10.1037/h0071663

Todnem, R., Hughes, M., & Ford, J. (2016). Change Leadership: Oxymoron and Myths. *Journal of Change Management*, *16*(1), 8–17. doi:10.1080/14697017.2016.1137425

Treiblmaier, H. (2018). Optimal levels of (de)centralization for resilient supply chains. *International Journal of Logistics Management, 29*(1), 435–455. doi:10.1108/IJLM-01-2017-0013

Treverton, G. F., & Jahn, M. (2020). COVID-19: We Had The Warning But We Lacked The Leadership. *The Hill.* Retrieved from https://www.thehill.com/opinion/

Triggs, A., & Kharas, H. (2020). *The Triple Economic Shock of COVID-19 and Priorities for an Emergency G-20 Leaders Meeting*. Brookings Institution.

Trilla, A., Trilla, G., & Daer, C. (2008). The 1918 "Spanish flu" in Spain. *Clinical Infectious Diseases, 47*(5), 668–673. doi:10.1086/590567 PMID:18652556

Trzebiński, J., Cabański, M., & Czarnecka, J. Z. (2020). Reaction to the COVID-19 pandemic: The influence of meaning in life, life satisfaction, and assumptions on world orderliness and positivity. *Journal of Loss and Trauma, 25*(6-7), 1–14. doi:10.1080/15325024.2020.1765098

Tull, M. T., Edmonds, K. A., Scamaldo, K., Richmond, J. R., Rose, J. P., & Gratz, K. L. (2020). Psychological Outcomes Associated with Stay-at-Home Orders and the Perceived Impact of COVID-19 on Daily Life. *Psychiatry Research, 289*, 113098. doi:10.1016/j.psychres.2020.113098 PMID:32434092

Tyssen, A. K., Wald, A., & Heidenreich, S. (2014). Leadership in the Context of Temporary Organizations: A Study on the Effects of Transactional and Transformational Leadership on Followers' Commitment in Projects. *Journal of Leadership & Organizational Studies, 21*(4), 376–393. doi:10.1177/1548051813502086

Uhl-Bien, M., Marion, R., & McKelvey, B. (2007). Complexity leadership theory: Shifting leadership from the industrial age to the knowledge era. *The Leadership Quarterly, 18*(4), 298–318.

UIC. (2017). *Recommendations for Crisis Management.* 6 UIC Additional Global Security Programme.

UN ECLAC. (2020). The 2030 Agenda for Sustainable Development in the new global and regional context: Scenarios and projections in the current crisis. Author.

UNESCO. (2020). *COVID-19 Educational Disruption and Response*. UNESCO. Available at: https://en.unesco.org/covid19/educationresponse

Unger, D., & Eppinger, S. (2011). Improving product development process design: A method for managing information flows, risks, and iterations. *Journal of Engineering Design, 22*(10), 689–699.

Universität Heidelberg. (2020, December 21). *Angst vor Corona und Impfskepsis: Nr. 115/2020* [Press release]. https://www.uni-heidelberg.de/de/newsroom/angst-vor-corona-und-impfskepsis

UNSD. (2019). *The Sustainable Development Goals Report 2019*. UNSD.

van Dorp, L., Acman, M., Richard, D., Shaw, L. P., Ford, C. E., Ormond, L., ... Ortiz, A. T. (2020). Emergence of genomic diversity and recurrent mutations in SARS-CoV-2. *Infection, Genetics and Evolution, 83*, 104351. doi:10.1016/j.meegid.2020.104351 PMID:32387564

van Knippenberg, D., & Sitkin, S. B. (2013). A critical assessment of charismatic–transformational leadership research: Back to the drawing board? *The Academy of Management Annals, 7*(1), 1–60. doi:10.5465/19416520.2013.759433

van Tilburg, T. G., Steinmetz, S., Stolte, E., van der Roest, H., & de Vries, D. H. (2020). Loneliness and mental health during the COVID-19 pandemic: A study among Dutch older adults. *The Journals of Gerontology: Series B.*

Van Wart, M., & Kapucu, N. (2011). Crisis management competencies: The case of emergency managers in the USA. *Public Management Review, 13*(4), 489–511.

Vatican News. (2020). *Pope Francis: We need the spirit of Elijah.* Retrieved from https://www.indcatholicnews.com/news/40628

Vaziri, H., Casper, W. J., Wayne, J. H., & Matthews, R. A. (2020). Changes to the work-family interface during the COVID-19 pandemic: Examining predictors and implications using latent transition analysis. *The Journal of Applied Psychology, 105*(10), 1073–1087. Advance online publication. doi:10.1037/apl0000819 PMID:32866024

Venkatesh, V. (2020). Impacts of COVID-19: A research agenda to support people in their fight. *International Journal of Information Management, 55*, 102197. doi:10.1016/j.ijinfomgt.2020.102197 PMID:32836648

Vera, D., & Rodriguez-Lopez, A. (2004). Strategic virtue: Humility as a source of competitive advantage. *Organizational Dynamics, 33*(4), 393–408. doi:10.1016/j.orgdyn.2004.09.006

Verbeke, A. (2020). Will the COVID-19 pandemic really change the governance of global value chains? *British Journal of Management, 31*(3), 444–446. doi:10.1111/1467-8551.12422

Verma, B. (2020). *Agile leadership for higher education: Post COVID-19 response.* Mediawire.

Verma, G. (2020). Science teacher education in the times of the COVID-19 pandemic. *Journal of Science Teacher Education, 10*(8), 2–7.

Verma, S., & Gustafsson, A. (2020). Investigating the emerging COVID-19 research trends in the field of business and management: A bibliometric analysis approach. *Journal of Business Research, 118*, 253–261. doi:10.1016/j.jbusres.2020.06.057 PMID:32834211

Vickers, M. (2019, January 24). *Boosting worker engagement in tough times.* American Management Association. Retrieved from https://www.amanet.org/articles/boosting-worker-engagement-in-tough-times/

Vieta, E., Pe'rez, V., & Arango, C. (2020). Psychiatry in the aftermath of COVID-19. *Journal of Psychiatry and Mental Health, 13*(2). Advance online publication. doi:10.1026/j.rpsm.2020.04.004

Vindegaard, N., & Benros, M. E. (2020). COVID-19 pandemic and mental health consequences: Systematic review of the current evidence. *Brain, Behavior, and Immunity, 89.* doi:10.1016/j.bbi.2020.05.048

vom Lehn, B. (2020, October 15). *Erstmals arbeiten Pflegekräfte mit Corona-Infektion*. pflege-online.de. https://www.pflegen-online.de/erstmals-arbeiten-pflegekraefte-mit-corona-infektion

Voyer, B. (2020). What behavioural science can tell us about human behaviour in the wake of pandemic? In Managing a post-Covid19 era. (pp. 1-5). ESCP Research Institute of Management (ERIM).

Wadin, J. L., & Ode, K. A. (2019). Business Models for Sustainability-Change in Dynamic Environments. *Journal of Business Models, 7*(1), 13–38.

Walia, K. (2018). The Relationship Between Employee Wellbeing and Spirituality at Workplace. *IUP Journal of Organizational Behavior, 17*(3).

Walker, S. (2020). Covid-19 Was a Leadership Test. It Came Back Negative. *Wall Street Journal.* Retrieved from https://www.wsj.com/article/great-leaders-are-killjoys-nags-or-neurotics-until-theres-a-pandemic-11584144175

Walumbwa, F. O., Orwa, B., Wang, P., & Lawler, J. J. (2005). Transformational leadership, organizational commitment, and job satisfaction: A comparative study of Kenyan and US financial firms. *Human Resource Development Quarterly, 16*(2), 235–256. doi:10.1002/hrdq.1135

Wang, J. (2008). Developing Organizational Learning Capacity in Crisis Management. *Advances in Developing Human Resources, 10*, 425–445.

Wang, J., Wang, Z., Liu, X., Yang, X., Zheng, M., & Bai, X. (2020). The impacts of a COVID-19 epidemic focus and general belief in a just world on individual emotions. *Personality and Individual Differences*, 110349. PMID:32843782

Warner, R. (1962). *The Peloponnesian War*. Cassell.

Wasserman, S., & Faust, K. (1994). *Social network analysis. Methods and applications* (Vol. 8). Cambridge University Press.

Watkins, K. E., & Marsick, V. J. (1993). Sculpting the learning organization: Lessons in the art and science of systemic change. Jossey-Bass Inc.

Watzka, K. (2018). *Fachkräftemangel in der Pflege: Kritische Situationsbewertung und Skizzierung einer Handlungsalternative*. Jena contributions to economic research: Jahrgang 2018, Heft 2. Ernst-Abbe-Hochschule Fachbereich Betriebswirtschaft. http://hdl.handle.net/10419/181866

Watzlawick, P. (1984). *The invented reality*. Norton.

WBCSD. (n.d.). *Moving beyond the "turbulent teens."* Author.

WCED. (1987). *Our Common Future*. World Commission on Environment and Development. doi:10.1080/07488008808408783

Weber, M. (2015). Bureaucracy. In Working in America (pp. 29-34). Routledge.

Weber, M. (1958). *The protestant ethic and the spirit of capitalism*. Charles Scribner's Sons.

WEF. (2020). *Switzerland fast-tracks emergency aid for small businesses weathering COVID-19*. World Economic Forum.

WEF. (2020). The Global Risks Report 2020. Geneva, Switzerland: WEF.

Wegmann, R. M., & Newett, J. L. (2020). When Complexity Costs Lives: Secondary Goals and Compartmentalized Information in the Second World War's Greatest Raid. Historians on Leadership and Strategy, 79–92. doi:10.1007/978-3-030-26090-3_5

Wegmann, R. M. (2020). A grounded theory for the performance of temporary disaster response teams. *Journal of Organizational Effectiveness: People and Performance*, *7*(2), 155–172. doi:10.1108/JOEPP-04-2020-0059

Wegmann, R. M., & Schärrer, L. (2020). Outpacing the pandemic? A factorial survey on decision speed of COVID-19 task forces. *Journal of Organizational Effectiveness: People and Performance*, *7*(2), 191–202. doi:10.1108/JOEPP-05-2020-0089

Weick, k. & Obstfeld, D., 2005. Organization and the process of sensemaking. *Organ Sci, 16*(4), 409-421.

Weick, K. E. (1988). Enacted Sensemaking in Crisis Situations. *Journal of Management Studies*, *25*(4), 305–317. doi:10.1111/j.1467-6486.1988.tb00039.x

Weick, K. E., & Quinn, R. E. (1999). Organizational change and development. *Annual Review of Psychology*, *50*(1), 361–386. doi:10.1146/annurev.psych.50.1.361 PMID:15012461

Weiss, R. S. (1973). *Loneliness: The experience of emotional and social isolation*. MIT Press.

Wennmann, D. O., Dlugos, C. P., Hofschröer, A., Hennies, M., Kühn, J., Hafezi, W., Kampmeier, S., Mellmann, A., Triphaus, S., Sackarnd, J., Tepasse, P., Keller, M., van Aken, H., Pavenstädt, H., & Kümpers, P. (2020). Umgang mit COVID-19 in der Notaufnahme: Erfahrungsbericht der interdisziplinären Notaufnahme des Universitätsklinikums Münster [Handling of COVID-19 in the emergency department: Field report of the emergency ward of the University Hospital Münster]. *Medizinische Klinik, Intensivmedizin und Notfallmedizin*, *115*(5), 380–387. https://doi.org/10.1007/s00063-020-00693-0

Wenzel, M., Stanske, S., & Lieberman, M. B. (2020). Strategic responses to crisis. *Strategic Management Journal, 41*, V7–V18.

Whatsneue.online. (2020). *9 To 5: What's Neue With Rano Adidas*. https://www.whatsneue.online/2020/05/25/9-to-5-rano-adidas/

Whiteside, S. (2020). *How major companies are responding to COVID-19*. Retrieved October 25, 2020, from https://www.warc.com/newsandopinion/opinion/how-major-companies-are-responding-to-covid-19/3473

WHO. (2012). *Resolution adopted by the General Assembly*. https://www.who.int/nmh/events/un_ncd_summit2011/political_declaration_en.pdf

WHO. (2020). *Coronavirus disease (COVID-19)*. Retrieved October20, 2020, from https://www.who.int/emergencies/diseases/novel-coronavirus-2019

WHO. (2020). *Live from Geneva on the new #coronavirus outbreak*. WHO.

WHO. (2020). *Severe Acute Respiratory Syndrome (SARS)*. Retrieved from https://www.who.int/health-topics/severe-acute-respiratory-syndrome#tab=tab_1

WHO. (n.d.). *Coronavirus Disease (COVID-19) Dashboard*. https://covid19.who.int/

Wiesenfeld, B. M., Raghuram, S., & Garud, R. (2001). Organizational identification among virtual workers: The role of need for affiliation and perceived work-based social support. *Journal of Management, 27*(2), 213–229. doi:10.1177/014920630102700205

Wilasang, C., Sararat, C., Jitsuk, N. C., Yolai, N., Thammawijaya, P., Auewarakul, P., & Modchang, C. (2020). Reduction in effective reproduction number of COVID-19 is higher in countries employing active case detection with prompt isolation. *Journal of Travel Medicine, 27*(5), taaa095. doi:10.1093/jtm/taaa095 PMID:32519743

Williams, S. D., & Williams, J. (2020). Posttraumatic stress in organizations: Types, antecedents, and consequences. *Business and Society Review, 125*(1), 23–40. doi:10.1111/basr.12192

Williams, T. A., Gruber, D. A., Sutcliffe, K. M., Shepherd, D. A., & Zhao, E. Y. (2017). Organizational response to adversity: Fusing crisis management and resilience research streams. *The Academy of Management Annals, 11*(2), 733–769.

Wilmot, M. P., & Ones, D. S. (2019). A century of research on conscientiousness at work. *Proceedings of the National Academy of Sciences of the United States of America, 116*(46), 23004–23010. doi:10.1073/pnas.1908430116 PMID:31666330

Wilson, W. (1886). *The study of public administration*. Academic Press.

Wilson, S. (2020). Pandemic leadership: Lessons from New Zealand's approach to COVID-19. *Leadership, 16*(3), 279–293. doi:10.1177/1742715020929151

Winston, B., & Fields, D. (2015). Seeking and measuring the essential behaviors of servant leadership. *Leadership and Organization Development Journal*.

Wirth, L. M., & Hülsken-Giesler, M. (2020). Wenn nicht jetzt, wann dann? *Pflegewissenschaft, Sonderausgabe: Die Corona-Pandemie,* (April), 118–120.

Wirtz, D. C., & Stöckle, U. (2020). Künftige Versorgungsstrukturen in Deutschland: Gibt es Lehren aus der Corona-Pandemie? *Zeitschrift fur Orthopadie und Unfallchirurgie, 158*(2), 163–164. https://doi.org/10.1055/a-0876-4652

Wolf, J., & Molzberger, K. (2021). Das Krankenhaus als anpassungsfähiges Netzwerkarrangement? In C. Stegbauer & I. Clemens (Eds.), Corona-netzwerke - Gesellschaft im zeichen des virus (pp. 139–150). VS Verlag fur Sozialwisse., https://doi.org/10.1007/978-3-658-31394-4_14.

Wolff, T., Minkler, M., Wolfe, S. M., Berkowitz, B., Bowen, L., Butterfoss, F. D., & … . (2016). Collaborating for equity and justice: Moving beyond collective impact. *The Nonprofit Quarterly*, *24*, 42–52.

Wolf-Ostermann, K., Rothgang, H., Domhoff, D., Friedrich, A.-C., Heinze, F., Preuß, B., Schmidt, A., Seibert, K., & Stolle, C. (2020). *Zur Situation der Langzeitpflege in Deutschland während der Corona-Pandemie. Ergebnisse einer Online-Befragung in Einrichtungen der (teil)stationären und ambulanten Langzeitpflege.* doi:10.26092/ELIB/116

Wolor, C. W., Solikhah, S., Fidhyallah, N. F., & Lestari, D. P. (2020). Effectiveness of E-Training, E-Leadership, and Work-Life Balance on Employee Performance during COVID-19. *The Journal of Asian Finance Economics and Business*, *7*(10), 443–450.

Wong, E. M., Ormiston, M. E., & Tetlock, P. E. (2011). The effects of top management team integrative complexity and decentralized decision making on corporate social performance. *Academy of Management Journal*, *54*(6), 1207–1228. doi:10.5465/amj.2008.0762

Wong, J., Abdul Aziz, A. B., Chaw, L., Mahamud, A., Griffith, M. M., Ying-Ru, L. O., & Naing, L. (2020b). High proportion of asymptomatic and presymptomatic COVID-19 infections in travelers and returning residents to Brunei. *Journal of Travel Medicine*.

Wong, J., Chaw, L., Koh, W. C., Alikhan, M. F., Jamaludin, S. A., Poh, W. W. P., & Naing, L. (2020c). Epidemiological investigation of the first 135 COVID-19 cases in Brunei: Implications for surveillance, control, and travel restrictions. *The American Journal of Tropical Medicine and Hygiene*, *103*(4), 1608–1613. doi:10.4269/ajtmh.20-0771 PMID:32815514

Wong, J., Koh, W. C., Alikhan, M. F., Aziz, A. B. A., & Naing, L. (2020a). Responding to COVID-19 in Brunei Darussalam: Lessons for small countries. *Journal of Global Health*, *10*(1), 010363. doi:10.7189/jogh.10.010363 PMID:32566154

Woods, S. A., & West, M. A. (2010). *The psychology of work and organizations.* South-Western Cengage Learning.

Wooten, L. P., & James, E. H. (2008). Linking crisis management and leadership competencies: the role of human resource development. *Advances in Developing Human Resources, 10*(3), 352-379. https://covid19.who.int/ doi:10.1177/1523422308316450

World Health Organization. (2006). Mental health in the Eastern Mediterranean Region. Reaching the unreached. *WHO Regional Publications. Eastern Mediterranean Series*, 29.

Worley, C. G. (1996). *Integrated strategic change: How OD builds competitive advantage.* Ft Press.

Wright, S., Burt, C., & Strongman, K. (2006). Loneliness in the workplace: Construct definition and scale development. *New Zealand Journal of Psychology*, *35*(2), 59–68.

Yamamoto, T., Uchiumi, C., Suzuki, N., Yoshimoto, J., & Murillo-Rodriguez, E. (2020). The psychological impact of' mild lockdown' in Japan during the COVID-19 pandemic: a nationwide survey under a declared state of emergency. medRxiv.

Yang, K. (2020). Unprecedented Challenges, Familiar Paradoxes: COVID-19 and Governance in a New Normal State of Risks. *Public Administration Review*, *80*(4), 657–664. doi:10.1111/puar.13248 PMID:32836451

Yawson, R. (2020). Strategic flexibility analysis of HRD research and practice post COVID-19 pandemic. *Human Resource Development International*, *23*(4), 406–417. doi:10.1080/13678868.2020.1779169

Yawson, R. M., & Greiman, B. C. (2017). Strategic flexibility analysis of agrifood nanotechnology skill needs identification. *Technological Forecasting and Social Change*, *118*(C), 184–194. doi:10.1016/j.techfore.2017.02.019

Yiannis, G. (2000). *Storytelling in organizations: Facts, fictions, and fantasies*. Oxford University Press.

Yin, R. K. (1994). *Case Study Research: Design and Methods*. Sage.

Yin, R. K. (2017). *Case study research and applications: Design and methods*. Sage publications.

Yukl, G. (2012). Effective leadership behavior: What we know and what questions need more attention. *The Academy of Management Perspectives*, *26*(4), 66–85. doi:10.5465/amp.2012.0088

Yukl, G. (2013). *Leadership in organizations* (8th ed.). Upper Saddle River.

Yukl, G., & Mahsud, R. (2010). Why flexible and adaptive leadership is essential. *Consulting Psychology Journal*, *62*(2), 81–93. doi:10.1037/a0019835

Zaini, K. H. (2020). *Cities and Pandemics: a look into urban preparedness in COVID19 era*. University Putera Malaysia.

Zakeri, B., Barreto, L., Boza-kiss, B., Echeverri, L. G., Fritz, S., Ghoneim, R., … Srivastava, L. (2020). Bouncing Forward Sustainably : Pathways to a post-COVID World. *Sustainable Energy, 43*(June), 1–13.

Zarocostas, J. (2020). How to fight an infodemic. *Lancet*, *395*(10225), 676. doi:10.1016/S0140-6736(20)30461-X PMID:32113495

Zeeh, J., Memm, K., Heppner, H.-J., & Kwetkat, A. (2020). Beatmung geriatrischer Patienten— Ein ethisches Dilemma? Corona-Pandemie 2020. *MMW Fortschritte der Medizin*, *162*(9), 40–45. https://doi.org/10.1007/s15006-020-0475-y

Zhang, S. X., Liu, J., Jahanshahi, A. A., Nawaser, K., Yousefi, A., Li, J., & Sun, S. (2020). At the height of the storm: Healthcare staff's health conditions and job satisfaction and their associated predictors during the epidemic peak of COVID-19. *Brain, Behavior, and Immunity*.

Zhang, J., Zhang, Y., Song, Y. H., & Gong, Z. X. (2016). The different relations of extrinsic, introjected, identified regulation and intrinsic motivation on employees' performance Empirical studies following self-determination theory. *Management Decision*, *54*(10), 2393–2412. doi:10.1108/MD-01-2016-0007

Zhang, S. S., Zhou, M. J., Zhang, J. X., & Chen, S. (2012). The nonlinear effects of conscientiousness on overall job performance and performance dimensions in the Chinese context. *Asian Journal of Social Psychology*, *15*(4), 231–237. doi:10.1111/j.1467-839X.2012.01375.x

Zhang, Z., Jia, M., & Gu, L. (2012). Transformational leadership in crisis situations: Evidence from the People's Republic of China. *International Journal of Human Resource Management*, *23*(19), 4085–4109.

Zheng, L., Miao, M., & Gan, Y. (2020). Perceived Control Buffers the Effects of the COVID-19 Pandemic on General Health and Life Satisfaction: The Mediating Role of Psychological Distance. *Applied Psychology: Health and Well-Being*.

# About the Contributors

**Ebtihaj Al Aali** is an Associate professor. She worked for thirty years at the University of Bahrain. She holds a PhD in industrial psychology and industrial sociology from University of Lancaster in U.K. She published extensively in different areas. Her research interest varies from women in management, Business ethics, Organizational Behavioral, research methodology and Chang management. She published two books with IGI.

**Meryem Masmoudi** is Assistant Professor of Management at the University of Bahrain, College of Business Administration. She holds a PhD in Management from University of Tunis (2013). She has been involved in teaching and research in the areas of management, organizational change and development and management science. Meryem has published research papers in top international refereed journals (ANOR, JORS, ITOR, INFOR). She is a member of the International Society on Multiple Criteria Decision Making and the Tunisian Decision Aid Society.

* * *

**Adel Al-Alawi** is an Associate Professor of Management and Information Systems at the University of Bahrain, College of Business, earned his BS and MBA in Business and Information Systems (USA), a PhD in MIS from University of Leeds, UK. Dr Al-Alawi was the founder of Business Information Systems Dep (BIS) and a Chairperson of BIS department at the College of Business in UOB and also one of the founders of College of Information Technology, and Head of BIS Department, where he served UOB for more than 25 years. His research have been published in several Scopus indexed journals such as Journal of Knowledge Management, Journal of Computer Science, Information Technology Journal, Research Journal of Business Management, Research Journal of Business Management, Journal of International Women's Studies, International Journal of Business Information Systems. His main interest in research is in management and information systems (refer to https://www.researchgate.net/profile/Adel_Al-Alawi). Adel is also one of the founders and the President of ISACA, Bahrain Chapter. Adel is considered as an MIS Authority in the Kingdom of Bahrain.

**Fatima Ali Al-Ammar** holds a BSc. in Mass Communication – Marketing Management from the University of Bahrain. She is a candidate for a Master of Science in Human Resources Management (HRM) at the University of Bahrain. Fatima carries many years of experience in Administration and Coordinating conferences and seminars in the Bahraini private sector. She is also involved in Training and Development with projects that focus on soft business skills, training implementation, Labor Law, and Real Estate Regulator Laws awareness.

**Samah Ali** holds a B.A. in Journalism from the American University in Cairo (AUC), Egypt, and is currently an MBA candidate at the University of Bahrain. She is a MEPI TL alumni, a program sponsored by the U.S. Department of State that fosters a culture of professional leadership and nurtures the spirit of civic engagement. Samah carries many years of experience in Human Resources and Management in primarily Bahraini hospitality group that owns several high operating restaurant outlets on the island. Prior to her role, she was previously engaged in vocational consultancy, Intelaaq, which empowers Bahraini undergraduate students across universities in delivering carefully crafted business solutions in partnership with local companies. She is a holder of the U.K.'s CIPD Levels 3 and 5, Data Analysis for Management from the London School of Economics, and Competency-Based Management from HRSG.

**Stan Amaladas** is currently an Associate Professor with Baker College, Centre for Graduate Studies. Stan completed his Ph.D. in Applied Management and Decision Sciences from Walden University with a research focus on leadership and change in the public sector. His dissertation was awarded the Walden University's Harold L. Hodgkinson Award. The Hodgkinson award is awarded annually to a graduate whose dissertation meets the highest university standards. His qualitative tradition of inquiry includes narrative inquiry, phenomenology, and hermeneutics. The study and analysis of narratives/stories and story-telling is close to his heart and soul. He has published two books on leadership, co-edited a book of Peace Leadership, and written numerous articles on the topic of Leadership.

**Asma Ayari** is a Ph.D. holder in Management from IAE University de Lille _ France Assistant Professor at the University of Bahrain teaching management, organizational behavior, and HRM MSc and MBA Thesis supervisor and reviewer.

**Timothy Colin Bednall** is a Senior Lecturer in Management at Swinburne University of Technology. He previously worked at the Australian School of Business at the University of New South Wales. Dr Bednall is a registered psychologist, with an area of practice endorsement in organisational psychology. He is the former national Chair of the APS College of Organisational Psychologists (2015-2018). Dr Bednall's broad research area is employee learning, expertise, and innovation.

**Peter Behrendt** founded the Freiburg Institut in 2012 and in 2018 the Coachingzentrum Freiburg. As part of his doctorate at the Freiburg Institut, the industrial and organizational psychologist researched successful behavior in leadership, coaching, consulting and innovation. Dr. Behrendt has several years of experience as an organizational consultant and human resources manager. In 2006, he received the "Muwit Award" for the conception of an outstanding human resources program, followed by two "Great Place to Work Awards" in 2010 and 2011 for his work in the Stryker Navigation department in Freiburg. His innovative contributions to the scientific field of coaching were recognized by the Deutscher Bundesverband Coaching e.V. (German Coaching Association) with a nomination for the German Coaching Award as one of the three best coaching concepts in both 2012 and 2014. Dr. Peter Behrendt holds training certificates in coaching, mediation, video-based consulting and organizational development. He was named Top Coach of the Year 2016 by Xing and Focus Network. Since 2016 he has been founder and board member of the Allianz für werte-orientierte Demokratie (AllWeDo e.V., Alliance for Value-Oriented Democracy) in the course of which he was awarded at the German competition "Aktiv für Demokratie und Toleranz" ("Active for Democracy and Tolerance") 2018 and 2019 for the innovative advancement and strengthening of democracy.

**Darrell Norman Burrell** is post-graduate student and a 2017 graduate of the National Coalition Building Institute's (NCBI) Leadership Diversity Institute. He is a Certified Diversity Professional. He is a Certified Diversity Professional (CDP) and an alum of the prestigious Presidential Management Fellows Program. Dr Burrell has a doctoral degree with majors in Education and Executive Leadership Coaching from A.T. Still University. He also holds an Education Specialist (EdS) degree in Higher Education Administration from the George Washington University, Masters degrees in Human Resource Development and Organizational Management from National Louis University, and Master of Arts in Sales and Marketing Management from Prescott College. He has extensive years of university teaching experience at several universities.

**Mehmet Çetin** was born in 1985. Has masters and PhD in Organizational Behavior. Worked as management consultant and academician.

**Dilek Erdoğan** received her bachelor's, master's and doctoral degrees from Anadolu University Aviation Management Department. She is currently working at Gaziantep University, Faculty of Aeronautics and Astronautics. She conducts research on aviation and management.

**Amanina Halim** completed her MSc in Gerontology from King's College London and her BSc Healthcare Science (Audiology) at Aston University. Her research interest is in Public Health and Public Policy.

**Martina Hasseler** is a habilitated rehabilitation scientist. Her focus as a university professor is on innovative teaching combining theory, research, and practice as well as applied research. In particular, she is interested in findings for high-quality health and nursing care. Furthermore, she would like to contribute research to an improvement of the framework conditions of health and care as well as the inter-professional and inter-setting cooperation and qualification of health and care professions.

**Matthew David Henricks** completed his undergraduate studies at Macquarie University in 1999, his Master of Psychology (Organisational) at the University of New South Wales in 2007, and his PhD at the University of New South Wales in 2020. He has been practicing as the Principal Psychologist at Henricks Consulting Pty Ltd since 2007 and is the Founder and Non-Executive Director of both Helping Hands Program Pty Ltd and Water Works Program Pty Ltd. He is also a Visiting Research Fellow at the University of New South Wales where his research interests include Adaptive Performance and Employee Attitudes Toward Change. Matthew is a Registered Psychologist and Endorsed Organisational Psychologist (AHPRA).

**Alexander Holicki** studied psychology at the Albert-Ludwigs University of Freiburg and graduated with a Bachelor's degree in 2019. He then completed a six-month internship in the field of human resources development and is now studying the Master's degree in "Cognitive Psychology, Learning and Working" at the Albert-Ludwigs University of Freiburg. He is currently undergoing a study-accompanying trainee program at the Freiburg Institut and is writing his master's thesis within the project "Future-Viable Organizations" under the supervision of Dr. Peter Behrendt.

**Nikhil Kant** is pursuing PhD in Management from SOMS, IGNOU, New Delhi and is currently working as Assistant Registrar in IGNOU. He has varied experience of 08 years in leading Public sector

Banks and 10 years in Administration & Finance in IGNOU. He has completed MBA, JAIIB, CAIIB, PGDFA, PGDDE and is UGC-NET qualified. Additionally, He is professionally trained in Soft Skills & Applications of IT tools such as Blockchain etc. and attends training workshops as resource person on invitation. He has several publications in International Journals and participation in Conferences/Seminars.

**Stephanie Krebs**, M.Sc., is research assistant and lecturer at the Ostfalia University of Applied Sciences. Based on her studies in biology, German language and literature as well as business administration and further education in training and human resources development, her research focuses on an interdisciplinary and systemic understanding of health care systems. After working in various projects in commerce, she was involved in different research projects, including the development of an algorithm for targeted personnel deployment, the development of quality indicators and the idea of implementing a delegation model in home care.

**Yeşim Kurt** received her bachelor's, master's and doctoral degrees from Anadolu University Aviation Management Department. She is currently working at Kırlareli University, Lüleburgaz Faculty of Aeronautics and Astronautics. She conducts research on aviation and management.

**Anna Larina Lietz**, M.Sc., is a nursing scientist. After her studies in Nursing Science and Evidence-based Health Care, she did research in the field of digitalization and nursing internal delegation.

**Bena Long,** PhD, MSM specializes in bringing mindfulness into leadership development programming and organization-wide implementation that is culturally aligned in each level - individual, group, intergroup and/or total organizational systems. She provides integration of mindfulness, meditation, and embodied leadership that is both long-term practitioner-based and scientifically informed. For more than 20 years this was done through applying mindfulness methodology seamlessly into the goals and contexts most relevant for the organization. Providing a wide range of options from organizational consulting, keynotes, workshops, retreats and executive coaching, her program development has been at the forefront of bringing mindfulness and mindful cultural competency into business education through MBA, executive education, and corporate training. Dr. Bena enjoys partnerships with some of the most inspiring leaders motivated to be the best people they can be and uplifting those around them.

**Veronika Matzner** is a psychologist and works as a trainer, coach, and consultant at Freiburg Institute. Advanced training in systemic solution-oriented consulting, facilitation and consensus-building, conflict mediation as well as environmental and experiential education enable her to take a comprehensive look at systems and interactions in cooperation. She accompanies organizations in the fast-moving world of work to systematically develop a corporate culture so that focus and orientation on the one hand and a high level of personal responsibility on the other hand are guaranteed.

**Arpita Anshu Mehrotra** earned her Bachelor's and Master's degrees in Commerce (India) and holds a Ph.D. in Commerce from India. She is an Assistant Professor of Accounting, Finance, and Management at the Royal University For Women (RUW), Kingdom of Bahrain. Dr. Arpita is Acting Dean and the Head of the Banking & Finance Department at the College of Business & Financial Sciences, RUW. She is also the RUW Alumnae Committee chairperson and the Teaching and Learning committee's co-chairperson at RUW. In her 15 years of experience, she has also served as the Director of Marketing and Academics in Mumbai School of Business, India. Dr. Arpita has been a leading academician with in-depth teaching experience in Financial Management, Accounting, and Marketing both at the undergraduate and postgraduate levels. Further, she led a team that organized a national level seminar on “The Emerging Economies and their rising Global Influence” in India. The seminar witnessed the participation of professors, corporate dignitaries, and university level students. Dr. Arpita has also presented several research papers in Banking & Finance in International Conferences; wherein two received the “best paper” award.

**Mohammad Naim** is a competent professional with 5 years of rich and diverse experience in Academics & Consulting. 4 years full-time research in Human Resource Management on the topic “Gen Y Talent Management”. Published research articles in reputed peer-reviewed journals of international repute from Emerald, Springer, Inderscience, and IGI publishers. Presented research articles in numerous International conferences held in India as well as overseas. Received ‘Young Researcher Award’ for the paper titled ‘Mentoring as a driver of Gen Y employees’ engagement: Toward a conceptual model ‘ at 14th HUSOC Conference held in Dubai in February 2016.

**Abdul Malik Omar** is a PhD Candidate in Public Policy studying at the University of Brunei Darussalam. He completed his MSc in Local Economic Development at LSE and BSc in International Enterprise & Business Development at the University of Essex. His research interest is in digital technology, governance, and public policy.

**Jessica Bayon Perez** is a Doctor in Social Sciences with a specialty in Direction and People Management. Awarded with the Gold Medal for Work Merit by the European Association for Economics and Competitiveness. Professional career focused on Human Resources in the Social Health field. Best academic record of the Degree in Labor Relations and Human Resources with a mention in business consulting. This empowers him to apply for the national award for academic career by the Ministry of Education, Culture and Sports. Author of E-books in the business area: Strategic Business Management, Business Culture and Strategic and Economic Management of Airports. Trajectory in different Universities in the Legal and Human Resources field. Speaker of International Conferences, interviewed in the media. Postdoctoral stay at the University of Hamk (Finland) and at the Universidad del Istmo (Panama). Thesis Director: The Strategic Management of Human Talent as Potential for Competitive Advantage in the Maritime and Airport Organizations of Panama. University of the Isthmus. Researcher with more than seven indexed International publications. Member of the Spanish Association of Labor Law and Social Security. Member of the advisory committee of the Ethos Indexed Magazine. Member of the Doctoral Thesis defense jury at the University of the Isthmus of Panama. More than 700 hours of teaching at the undergraduate and graduate level.

**Elisabeth Samuel** earned her doctorate and two master degrees from, India. Her doctorate thesis was in the area of business management and his master thesis was on Finance and Accounting. She is also a Fellow member of Higher Education Academy, UK. She has extensive experience (over 18 years) as accounting, finance and management educator. Dr. Elizabeth has also served as an Assistant Professor at a leading higher education institution in Bahrain, teaching Bachelor and Master level courses in Business and Management. Over the past Years, Dr. Elizabeth has been working as a Academic Instructor, researcher and Advisor. She has been teaching both the undergraduate and graduate students in various curriculum. She was a committee member of Quality Assurance for Academic Standards at her previous university and at RUW . She has also conducted a one day workshop on "In house training programmes for the faculties of business Dr. Elizabeth also presented research papers in national and international conferences in different parts of the world and has published articles in referred journals.

**Sohayla Khidir Sanosi** holds a B.Sc. in Management Information System (MIS) from Yanbu University College, Kingdom of Saudi Arabia (KSA). She studied her M.Sc. in Human Resource Management at the University of Bahrain in the Kingdom of Bahrain. Sohayla Carries many years of experience in Management in an International School. She has a strong passion for literacy coupled with exceptional knowledge of handling functions to ensure an environment conducive to learning & growth—the track record of organizing administrative support systems to enable operations. Sohayla received the Awards of recognition and honor of outstanding contributions in Admin Excellence from the Ministry of Education. Sohayla was representative of KSA at the World Youth Forum 2018. Sohayla is also one of the founders and board members in volunteering teams, and she is a very active member of several volunteering campaigns.

**Laura Schärrer** studied Business Administration at the University of Zurich and researches at the Center for Human Resource Management at the University of Lucerne. Her research interests include New Work, project-based organizations, and change management, with a strong focus on empirical research methodologies.

**Anton Shufutinsky**, PhD, DHSc, MSPH, is a scholar-practitioner and thought leader in organization development, leadership, management, occupational health and safety, environmental health, and public health. He is currently faculty of organization development & change and leadership at Cabrini University's Department of Leadership, Organization Development, and Change. His research foci are in organizational design, leadership development, sociotechnical systems, research methods, crisis leadership, emergency management, safety culture, and public health leadership.

**James R. Sibel**, PhD, MA, is CFO of Accu-Trade, an internet technology company specializing in applications for the automotive industry powering online valuation software throughout the US and Canada. He has over 40 years corporate experience in various elected, appointed, and advanced leadership positions holding numerous licenses and certifications throughout the Mid-Atlantic region of the US. In various capacities, Dr. Sibel is an author, speaker, and lecturer, presenting throughout the US and Europe at professional conferences and seminars on Corporate Social Responsibility, Team Building, Leadership, and the power of True Storytelling.

**Vasilios Stouraitis** is a lecturer in International Business and Management at Glasgow Caledonian University in the UK and visiting lecturer in several institutions abroad including Italy and Panama. Specializing in small and medium-sized enterprises and with a background in International Business and Economics, he holds a PhD from Henley Business School/University of Reading, an Msc in Development studies from University College London and an MBA and Bsc from the University of Kent. He has worked on development issues (agribusiness and governance) for the United Nations (Food and Agriculture Organization and the International Fund for Agricultural Development) and European Commission (DG Enterprise and Industry) and is also a published author in international business strategy and entrepreneurship. Regarding academic work, he has taught in several institutions (Edinburgh Business School at Athens, The American University of Rome, Link Campus Rome, Swiss School of Management Rome) and supervised several BA/BSc and MA/MSc theses on International Business topics and Food Economics. He has published in journals such as the International Journal of Entrepreneurial Behavior and Research, Journal of Small Business and Enterprise Development and in United Nations working paper series. His academic interests include SMEs, entrepreneurship, internationalization, exporting and agri-business smallholders. He speaks Italian, Greek, French, English and Spanish. Regarding research, he collects data and publishes in academic journals regularly with many collaborations and pending projects including books. He is a member of the Africa Children and Bread-Action NGOs based in Rome and Athens, a board member of the GCU UHatch incubator and start-up advisor.

**Konstantinos Tsanis** has spent the last 12 years working in Digital Transformation and FinTech projects in the Middle East, Africa and Asia. Prior to joining IFC he was based in Lagos, Nigeria, where he worked as Chief Innovation and Data Officer for WEMA Bank. Before that, he worked in Bloomberg, developing new markets and new products, and Thomson Reuters, working in their VC investments arm within MEA. He also worked for Bayzat, the highest funded insurtech in the MENA region and as a strategy consultant with Kaiser Associates, and as University lecturer at the Universities of Edinburgh, Glasgow and City, in London. In overall, he has worked in digital project execution with more than 400 Financial Institutions across 70 countries. During his professional life, he has gained different recognitions and awards for his achievements (Innovative Bank of the year, Finnovator of the Year, work output became an HBR case study etc). He gained his PhD from the University of Edinburgh (Stephen Cooke scholar), and his research focused in Strategic Decision Making and Financial Performance in Rapidly Changing Environments. He is also a Chartered FCSI, he is adjunct professor at the Universities of Hult and Edinburgh in ''Digital Transformation and FinTech'', and he is a resident fellow on ''scaling business in Africa'' at the University of Edinburgh Business School. He is also a frequent conference keynote speaker and author of multiple publications (book chapters, journals, articles) in Digital Finance topics.

**Reto Wegmann** studied Computer Science at Zurich's University of Applied Sciences, Military Affairs at the Military Academy at ETH Zurich and International Relations at Freie Universität Berlin. His professional experience includes project and line management positions in IT and a decade as senior leader in Switzerland's Department of Defense. He works for the University of Lucerne, where he researches leadership challenges in complex or hazardous situations under time pressure. He developed and now runs a post-degree master's program for leaders in public administration and business.

# Index

## A

adaptive leadership 142-143, 146, 151, 155, 188-190, 192-198
adaptive performance 71-88
adaptivity 71, 77-78, 80-83
agile strategies 90, 96
alienation 169-171, 173-174, 177-180, 183, 186

## B

Bahrain 24-27, 29-33, 125, 160-161, 163-165, 274-278, 280, 282, 285, 300
banking sector 274-275, 282, 287, 289
best practice 118-119
Brunei 35-37, 40-55

## C

change 1, 3-4, 7, 9-15, 19, 25, 33, 39, 47, 54, 56-57, 59-64, 68-69, 71-74, 76, 78-79, 81-82, 85-88, 90-97, 99-103, 105-106, 110-117, 119-121, 123-126, 129-131, 133, 136-146, 150-160, 162, 165, 169-171, 174, 178-181, 190, 197-198, 200, 204, 206, 208, 210, 213-214, 218-239, 241-242, 246, 249, 254-255, 258-259, 263, 268, 270, 272, 275, 277, 282-283, 285-288, 293-294, 297, 308
change leadership 157, 218-221, 223-224, 226-227, 229-230, 232, 234, 237, 239
change management interventions 90-92, 95, 97, 99, 102
Change Readiness 71-72, 85, 87
climate change 56-57, 59-63, 68-69
Climate Strategy Proactivity (CSP) 56, 64, 68
communication 6, 8-10, 14-16, 36, 39, 41, 52-53, 67, 95-97, 109, 113-114, 116, 122-123, 130, 143-144, 148, 155-158, 161-163, 165-167, 171-172, 174, 176-177, 180, 191, 193, 200, 204, 206, 210-211, 213-214, 217, 243, 249, 251, 260, 266, 269, 288-290, 297, 302, 305
corporate cultures 13
COVID-19 1-14, 16-22, 24-25, 28-58, 62-73, 77, 83, 90, 92-97, 99-107, 110, 112-120, 123, 125-143, 145-148, 151-153, 157-163, 165-172, 174, 178, 180-186, 188-189, 191, 196-206, 208-224, 226-228, 230-235, 240-256, 258, 261, 267-269, 271, 274-278, 280-302, 308-309
crisis leadership 104, 136, 151-152, 201
crisis management 3, 13, 39, 100, 102, 125, 128, 130, 143, 147, 153-156, 158-160, 162-163, 167-168, 199, 204-205, 209, 212, 214, 216, 237, 240-244, 246-252, 276-277, 297-299
crisis-viability 106, 110, 114, 119

## D

decision making 33, 143, 162, 167, 195, 204, 212, 217, 222, 232, 252-253, 276, 292, 299
decision speed 240, 253
decision-making 2, 6, 13, 33, 39, 73, 76, 78, 83, 86, 92-93, 99, 115, 123, 137, 140, 142-144, 147-150, 190, 200, 213, 217, 229, 236, 240-242, 244, 246, 250, 288, 297
delegation 1, 7, 18, 186
development 1, 6-8, 12-15, 36-37, 40, 47, 53, 56-64, 66, 68-70, 72, 80, 86-88, 90-95, 98-99, 101-105, 107, 110, 115, 119-121, 123, 126-127, 130-131, 136, 141-142, 144, 147-152, 154-158, 168, 182, 186, 188, 190, 192-193, 195-199, 201-202, 209, 211, 214-217, 223, 226-227, 244, 251-252, 256, 259, 264-273, 278-279, 294, 297-298, 301-303, 305, 307, 311
digital age 199, 201, 206, 210, 213, 216, 237
digital leadership 91, 209-210, 213
digitalization 116, 131, 133, 135, 169, 174, 180, 206, 208, 211, 213, 217, 274-275
discontinuous change 136-139, 141, 145-146, 150-153, 156-157, 159, 218-219, 221, 227, 229-231,

234-236, 238
distance working 169, 171, 173-174, 176-177, 179, 186
dynamic capabilities 36, 48, 153, 254

## E

emerging markets 33, 270, 274
emotional intelligence 94, 103-104, 177, 211, 213-214, 217, 238
employee development 188, 192, 196, 298
employee engagement 82, 86, 91, 95, 130, 188-198, 260
employee selection 71, 73-77, 88
Ethical leadership 210, 215, 288, 298
evaluation 15, 25, 77, 98, 108, 139, 143, 184, 214, 245, 255-256, 275

## F

Flexible Work 287, 290, 295, 299
future-viability 106-107, 110-112, 114-115, 118-119, 124

## G

GCC 274, 276, 278, 282
Goal Congruence 76, 88
governance 35-36, 38-40, 48, 51, 53-55, 57, 67, 100, 215, 217, 270, 275, 278
government responses 35, 127
Gregory Bateson 218
grounded theory 90, 92, 242, 253
guiding coalition 1, 3, 5-6

## H

Health Care Worker (hcw) 1
health services 24, 26, 28-29, 31, 238
Human Resource Management 86, 126, 128, 132, 135, 159, 180, 183-184, 188, 214, 240, 283, 298
human resources 6-7, 15, 29, 90-91, 93, 95, 100, 125, 134, 138, 168, 201, 216, 240, 243, 245, 247-250, 285, 297
HUMAN RESOURCES DEPARTMENTS 90, 95
Human Resources Management 125, 134, 297

## I

identification 105, 172, 174-175, 177-178, 186
innovation 66, 68, 82, 85, 97, 103, 105, 116, 123, 138, 158-159, 192-193, 214, 238, 254, 256, 259, 263-265, 267, 271-273, 276, 278-280, 283, 302

## J

Job Resources 73, 78, 88

## L

leader 48, 71-73, 80, 83, 85-86, 101, 103, 106, 109-110, 116, 119, 121, 130-131, 136, 139, 142-143, 145-147, 152-154, 157, 162, 165-168, 175, 185, 189-190, 193-194, 201, 204-205, 208-209, 213, 216-217, 225-226, 233, 250, 259-261, 266, 268-269, 287-288, 291, 294, 297
leader behaviour 71, 73, 80, 83
leadership 1-4, 6-7, 36, 53, 59, 66, 72, 75-76, 80-81, 85-87, 90-95, 97-109, 111-113, 115, 117, 119-125, 129-131, 133-163, 165-168, 170, 175, 177-178, 181, 184, 188-190, 192-201, 204-205, 208-221, 223-230, 232, 234, 236-242, 244, 246-249, 251, 253-256, 258-261, 263-273, 285-288, 291-294, 297-299
LEADERSHIP CHANGE 125, 129
leadership development 90-92, 94-95, 98-99, 101-102, 136, 141, 147-148, 150, 152, 158, 199, 209, 211, 217, 223, 266, 270-271, 273
leadership skills 93, 98, 101, 149, 199, 201, 248, 259
literature 20, 25, 28, 31-32, 34, 38, 40, 57, 71, 73-74, 85, 90, 92, 99, 103, 108-109, 117, 131, 140, 143, 148, 154, 157, 163, 180, 183, 188-190, 192-193, 195-196, 199, 201, 209, 213, 216, 220-221, 226, 228, 240-242, 249, 259-260, 265-267, 271, 274-276, 285-288, 291-293, 302
loneliness 169-176, 178-186, 289, 297

## M

management 1-4, 13-15, 21, 33, 35-36, 38-40, 42, 45, 47, 51-54, 56-58, 71-73, 77, 85-88, 90-92, 94-97, 99-100, 102-105, 113, 120-126, 128-135, 137, 140, 142-143, 147, 152-163, 167-170, 174, 176, 180-186, 188, 190, 192, 195-199, 204-205, 207-210, 212, 214, 216-217, 219, 221, 226-227, 236-255, 259, 265, 270-278, 282-287, 289-290, 292-294, 297-299, 301, 307-308
MANAGEMENT CHANGE 125, 130
Mary Catherine Bateson 218
micromanagement 177-178, 180, 186

## N

narrative thinking 218, 235
Nationally Determined Contributions (NDC) 56-57,

61, 69

## O

Online platform perception online tools 300
organizational climate 89, 171, 174, 185, 191
organizational culture 89, 134-135, 141, 153, 158, 189, 196, 204, 208, 213, 229, 288, 297
Organizational Innovation 158

## P

pandemic leadership 136, 141, 199, 201, 209, 216
Pandemic Management 35-36, 39-40, 42, 45, 47, 158, 205
performance 26, 71-88, 90-91, 93-95, 97-105, 116, 121-122, 128-131, 135, 141, 143, 145-146, 150, 153-154, 158, 160, 166, 170, 172-173, 177-178, 181, 183, 189-190, 197-198, 201, 208, 210, 212, 241-243, 249, 251, 253, 256, 260-261, 267-268, 271-273, 285-294, 296-299
performance management 71, 73, 77, 91, 100, 102, 104-105, 122
policies 12, 36-39, 41-43, 47, 50, 57, 66, 73, 82, 89, 91, 94, 96, 101-102, 126-128, 170, 174-175, 179, 192, 200, 275, 285-286, 289-290, 292-294
post-COVID-19 era 48, 93, 99, 102, 106-107, 110-111, 113, 119, 124, 169, 178, 180, 195, 199, 206, 210-211, 215, 218, 241
Posttraumatic Stress Disorder 177, 186
productivity 67, 93-97, 99, 102, 104-105, 174, 177, 182, 191, 208, 212, 285, 287, 289, 291
Psychiatry 24, 27, 29, 31-34, 184, 186, 297
psychological capital 177, 180, 184, 186
Public Policy 35-36, 39, 47, 50

## Q

qualitative research 25, 47, 92, 160, 163-164, 221

## R

remote working 43, 97, 100-101, 128, 130, 174, 185, 203, 206, 210, 212-213, 217, 287-291, 293-294

## S

self-awareness 142-143, 212-213, 217, 231
Shock Leadership 136-137, 146-148, 150-152, 158
SME 240, 242-244, 246-247, 249-250, 254-255, 261, 268, 271, 273
social capital 184, 188-189, 192-193, 195-196, 198, 238, 241
social distancing 29-30, 39, 41-43, 46, 52-53, 127, 169-170, 176, 179, 187, 274-276, 281, 286, 293, 300-301
spillover 169-170, 178, 181, 183-185, 187
spiritual well-being 169-171, 178, 180, 182, 187
stakeholders for health systems 24-25, 27
Strategic Management 33, 105, 123, 156, 159, 274, 282-284
success factor 113-119, 124, 205, 209, 240
success factors 26, 106-107, 110-112, 117-120, 134, 271
sustainability 16, 33, 56-57, 59-60, 62-67, 97, 114, 127, 134, 152, 194, 204, 261, 274-275, 282, 297
Sustainable Development Goals (SDG) 56-57, 60, 70
systemically relevant 1

## T

targeted communication 9, 15
The Great Reset 35-36, 53
training 2, 7-8, 10, 13, 31, 46, 65, 71, 73, 75-77, 80-81, 85, 93-95, 102, 104, 119, 126, 128-130, 132, 148-152, 154-156, 159, 177, 179, 206, 214, 243, 246, 248, 250, 281, 287, 294, 300, 302-303, 305, 307, 311

## U

uncertainty 4, 9, 24, 44, 58, 71-72, 88, 97, 106, 112-113, 119, 123, 135, 137, 139, 145, 158, 161, 176, 189-190, 200, 204, 229
Unsettling Markets 254

## V

vision 3, 7-8, 58, 61, 65-66, 73, 79-82, 86, 94, 131, 144, 161-162, 188-190, 192, 194-196, 208, 213, 257, 268, 270
VUCA 136-137, 140-142, 144, 147, 150-151, 153

## W

Whole-of-Nation 35-41, 44-48, 51, 53
work design 71, 73, 78, 83, 87, 89
work motivation 287-290, 298-299
work-life balance 12, 131, 174, 285, 287-290, 292-293, 297-299

Ensure Quality Research is Introduced to the Academic Community

# Become an Evaluator for IGI Global Authored Book Projects

**The overall success of an authored book project is dependent on quality and timely manuscript evaluations.**

**Applications and Inquiries may be sent to:**
development@igi-global.com

Applicants must have a doctorate (or equivalent degree) as well as publishing, research, and reviewing experience. Authored Book Evaluators are appointed for one-year terms and are expected to complete at least three evaluations per term. Upon successful completion of this term, evaluators can be considered for an additional term.

If you have a colleague that may be interested in this opportunity, we encourage you to share this information with them.

www.ingramcontent.com/pod-product-compliance
Lightning Source LLC
LaVergne TN
LVHW060408300926
849162LV00006B/1372